Contributions to Economics

More information about this series at http://www.springer.com/series/1262

Nezameddin Faghih • Ali Hussein Samadi
Editors

Dynamics of Institutional Change in Emerging Market Economies

Theories, Concepts and Mechanisms

Springer

Editors
Nezameddin Faghih
Cambridge, MA, USA

Ali Hussein Samadi
Department of Economics
Shiraz University
Shiraz, Iran

ISSN 1431-1933 ISSN 2197-7178 (electronic)
Contributions to Economics
ISBN 978-3-030-61341-9 ISBN 978-3-030-61342-6 (eBook)
https://doi.org/10.1007/978-3-030-61342-6

This Springer imprint is published by the registered company Springer Nature Switzerland AG
The registered company address is: Gewerbestrasse 11, 6330 Cham, Switzerland

Photo by author

This book is dedicated to the loving memory of Mohyeddin Faghih Estahbani (1929–2018), an economist, a physicist, a thinker, and cherished philanthropist, who deeply believed that institutional change and development, as a shared journey of humanity throughout history, provide the key to understanding dynamics of historical change, evolution and performance of a society, and the differential performance of economies over time.

Acknowledgements

The editors would like to express their sincere gratitude to Lorraine Klimowich for her great efforts in the publication process of this book and to all chapter authors, as without their generous contributions, completing this volume would not have been possible. They would also like to wholeheartedly thank those who have devoted their time, efforts, support, and generosity throughout the chapter review process: Fransiskus Lara Aba, Sebastian Aparicio, Samaneh Bahrololoum, Adeleke O. Banwo, Eric Bindah, Nguyen Quang Binh, Ebrahim Bonyadi, Nguyen Phuc Canh, Tanya Chavdarova, Mario Coccia, Onyeje Doki, Elvisa Drishti, Amir Forouharfar, Blesilda P. Badoc-Gonzales, Jahangir Jahangiri, Ermira Hoxha Kalaj, Kirti - Kirti, Vineet Kumar, Mindaugas Laužikas, Ma. Belinda S. Mandigma, Meylinda Maria, Aistė Miliūtė, Hassan Mohebbi, Cuong Nguyen, Lê Đức Nhã, Nazak Nobari, Julio Nogues, Aluisius Hery Pratono, Kuni Raffer, Daniela Rosim, Leyla Sarfaraz, Lida Sarreshtehdari, Abolfazl Shahabadi, Nomita Sharma, Jackson Tan, Sử Đình Thành, Pham Tien Thanh, David Urbano, and Đặng Thị Bạch Vân.

Contents

Contributors

Masoumeh Alipourian Department of Economics, Shiraz University, Shiraz, Iran

Adeleke O. Banwo Consulate General of the Federal Republic of Nigeria, Shanghai, China

Overseas Education College, Jiangsu University, Zhenjiang, Jiangsu Province, China

Nguyen Quang Binh University of Economics Ho Chi Minh City, Ho Chi Minh City, Vietnam

Nguyen Phuc Canh School of Banking, University of Economics Ho Chi Minh City, Ho Chi Minh City, Vietnam

Nezameddin Faghih UNESCO, Cambridge, MA, USA

Amir Forouharfar Department of Public Administration, University of Sistan and Baluchestan, Zahedan, Iran

Salman Gharakhani Faculty of Administrative Sciences and Economics, Department of Economics, University of Isfahan, Isfahan, Iran

Kirti Chanakya National Law University, Patna, India

Ametepe Paul Kojo Faculty of Business Administration, University of Lagos, Lagos, Nigeria

Vineet Kumar St. Xavier's College of Management and Technology, Patna, India

Mitra Mousavand Faculty of Administrative Sciences and Economics, Department of Economics, University of Isfahan, Isfahan, Iran

Nazak Nobari Administrative and Recruitment Organization, Tehran, Iran

Uchechi Onokala Department of Business Administration, University of Lagos, Lagos, Nigeria

Sakine Owjimehr Department of Economics, Shiraz University, Shiraz, Iran

Mohsen Renani Faculty of Administrative Sciences and Economics, Department of Economics, University of Isfahan, Isfahan, Iran

Ali Hussein Samadi Department of Economics, Shiraz University, Shiraz, Iran

Mahshid Sazegar Fars Engineering Association, Shiraz, Iran

Su Dinh Thanh School of Public Finance, University of Economics Ho Chi Minh City, Ho Chi Minh City, Vietnam

Dang Thi Bach Van School of Public Finance, University of Economics Ho Chi Minh City, Ho Chi Minh City, Vietnam

Farzaneh Yarahmadi Oman Tourism College, Muscat, Oman

List of Figures

Does Economic Globalization Have a Similar Effect on Governance for all Countries in the World?

Fig. 1 Selected countries Source: Personal elaboration of authors Note: Group A: 47 countries (including Andorra, Antigua and Barbuda, Australia, Austria, Bahamas, Bahrain, Barbados, Belgium, Brunei, Canada, Cyprus, Czech Republic, Denmark, Estonia, Finland, France, Germany, Greece, Hong Kong, Iceland, Ireland, Israel, Italy, Japan, Kuwait, Luxembourg, Liechtenstein, Macao, Malta, Netherlands, New Zealand, Norway, Oman, Portugal, Puerto Rico, Qatar, Singapore, Slovakia, Slovenia, South Korea, Spain, Sweden, Switzerland, Trinidad and Tobago, United Arab Emirates, United Kingdom, United States) Group B: 1 country (Saudi Arabia) Group C: 101 countries (including Afghanistan, Albania, Algeria, Angola, Azerbaijan, Argentina, Armenia, Belarus, Benin, Bosnia and Herzegovina, Bolivia, Burkina Faso, Burma (Myanmar), Burundi, Cambodia, Cameroon, Central African Republic, Chad, China, Colombia, Comoros, Cuba, Congo Dem. Rep., Dominican Rep., Djibouti, Ecuador, Egypt, El Salvador, Equatorial Guinea, Ethiopia, Fiji, Gabon, Gambia, Georgia, Guatemala, Guinea, Guinea-Bissau, Guyana, Haiti, India, Indonesia, Iran, Iraq, Jordan, Ivory Coast, Kazakhstan, Kenya, Kyrgyzstan, Liberia, Laos, Libya, Lebanon, Lesotho, Madagascar, Malawi, Mali, Macedonia, Maldives, Mauritania, Mozambique, Mexico, Moldova, Mongolia, Morocco, Nepal, Nicaragua, Niger, Nigeria, Pakistan, Palestine, Papua New Guinea, Paraguay, Peru, Philippines, Russia, Rwanda, Senegal, Sierra Leone, Serbia, Sao Tome and Principe, Sri Lanka, Sudan, Switzerland, Tanzania, Tajikistan, Thailand, Togo, Tunisia, Turkey, Turkmenistan, Uganda, Ukraine, Uzbekistan, Vietnam, Yemen, Zambia, Zimbabwe) Group D: 34 countries (including Belize, Bhutan, Botswana, Brazil, Bulgaria, Chile, Costa Rica, Croatia, Dominica, Ghana, Grenada, Hungary, Jamaica, Kiribati, Lithuania, Latvia, Malaysia, Mauritius, Micronesia, Namibia, Panama, Poland, Romania, Saint Lucia, Saint Vincent and the Grenadines, Samoa, Seychelles, South Africa, Suriname, Tonga, Tuvalu, Uruguay, Vanuatu) 222

Public Administration Reforms in the Emerging Markets' Era

De Jure and De Facto Power of Oil and Institutional Change in Modern Iran: A Critical Historicism Analysis (1900–1979)

Examining Institutional Barriers to Transition from a Natural State in Iran During 1941–1979

Does Energy Security Affect Institutional Quality? Empirical Evidence from Emerging Economies

List of Tables

Dynamics of Institutional Change Within the Group of Twenty (G20) and the European Union, and an Assessment of Brexit Impact: A Taxonomic Study

Institutions and Institutional Change: Concepts and Theories

Measuring Institutional Quality: A Review

Institutional Change: Evidence from Some Emerging Market Economies

Does Economic Globalization Have a Similar Effect on Governance for all Countries in the World?

Public Administration Reforms in the Emerging Markets' Era

De Jure and De Facto Power of Oil and Institutional Change in Modern Iran: A Critical Historicism Analysis (1900–1979)

Does Energy Security Affect Institutional Quality? Empirical Evidence from Emerging Economies

An Introduction to Dynamics of Institutional Change in Emerging Markets: Theories, Concepts, and Mechanisms

Nezameddin Faghih and Ali H. Samadi

Every moment the world is renewed,
and we are unaware of its being renewed whilst it remains.
Life is ever arriving anew, like the stream,
though in the body it has the semblance of continuity.
From its swiftness it appears continuous,
like the spark which you whirl rapidly with your hand.
If you whirl a firebrand with dexterity,
it appears to the sight as a very long fire.
Rumi (1207–1273).

we know a lot about institutions and their economic performance,
but we do not know how institutions change.
Douglas C. North (1990).

Institutions and institutional development appear to be a shared journey of humanity throughout history; the conceptual antecedents go back to Plato (1955), Adam Smith (1776), Immanuel Kant (1795) and Friedrich Hegel (1807). Nevertheless, in parallel to Douglass North's description of the concept of institution, especially in contemporary era of globalization, dynamics of institutional change are analogous to the dynamics of change in rules of the games, consisting of changes in formal written rules as well as changes in typically unwritten codes of conduct that underlie and supplement changes in formal rules, i.e., changes in the humanly devised constraints that shape the dynamics of human interaction. Nevertheless, it is essential to include various types of institutions, formal and informal, and their mutual interactions and convolutions.

Institutions and institutional development lead to a number of questions, for instance, what an institution is; how to measure institutional quality; whether institutions change or not; what institutional change would mean and envelope, e.g., improvements, decays, creation of new institutions, and/or elimination of the old ones; if institutions change, whether these changes progress slowly or rapidly; what

N. Faghih (✉)
UNESCO Chair Professor Emeritus, Cambridge, MA, USA

A. H. Samadi
Department of Economics, Shiraz University, Shiraz, Iran

N. Faghih, A. H. Samadi (eds.), *Dynamics of Institutional Change in Emerging Market Economies*, Contributions to Economics,
https://doi.org/10.1007/978-3-030-61342-6_1

mechanisms can bring about institutional changes; etc. In the past years, many economists and socioeconomists have attempted to answer these questions and continue to explore issues that are crucial to understanding institutional change and development. Nonetheless, some fundamental questions still remain open and unresolved.

Furthermore, the evolution of emerging markets can be considered as a source for the development of international business theories and practices. Emerging markets engender the main growth opportunities in the evolving global economy and economic order. The potentials of the emerging markets have already created a change in multinational corporations. As established markets face saturation, multinational corporations turn progressively to emerging markets as main sources and opportunities for further future growth (Arnold and Quelch 1998; London and Hart 2004; Fleury et al. 2018; Faghih 2019). Thus, emerging markets demand new alignment of laws, regulations, and rules of games and impact the dynamics of institutional change.

This book seeks to bridge an important research gap by questioning the types of institutions (legal-economic, social, and political) and institutional change, and to study endogenous and exogenous dynamics of institutional change, and capture its development over time and path dependence, to trace and understand the different evolutionary paths of societies. The objective of this edited volume is to explore concepts, theories, and mechanisms of institutional change. Further, the role of energy, and particularly oil, in some emerging market economies, is also studied. Moreover, institutions and institutional changes, institutional change theories, the causes of institutional change, institutional change behavioral frameworks, institutional quality and its measurement indicators, and mechanism of institutional change are defined and identified. The importance of oil revenues in the process of institutional change, institutional barriers to transition from a natural state, and energy security and institutional quality are also recognized and described as important factors that influence sustainable development.

It is hoped that this book, corresponding with the era of emerging markets development, is appealing to a wide range of global audience and can serve as a useful reference work in education and research. It is also hoped that the book can provide innovative and productive discussions and satisfy the scholarly and intellectual interests, regarding institutional change, and a broad range of its interrelationships and interactions with functioning and development of markets and economies. A number of academics, researchers, and scholars, engaged in education and research in the area of institutions and institutional change, have contributed chapters addressing and discussing the most recent issues in this field. The book contains 14 chapters, including this introductory chapter, and is divided into three parts.

Part I consists of five chapters devoted to concepts, theories, and dynamism of institutional change. It begins by presenting a quantitative framework and computational methods for assessing institutional development. In undertaking this work, some data on institutions, which correspond to the European Union and the Group of Twenty (G20) economies, are analyzed by numerical taxonomy. Thereupon, this study focuses on major advanced and emerging economies, which have joined forces to achieve their goals through targeted planning; aligning their laws, regulations, and rules of games; and conducting harmonious dynamics of institutional change. In particular, the institutional indicators, including institutions, political environment, regulatory environment, and business environment, are used, and the analysis employs six sets of preliminary data, that is, these four indicators plus population and GDP per capita. Then the analysis is performed in three groups of economies, namely, the G20 economies, the European Union economies including the United Kingdom, and the European Union economies excluding the United Kingdom. In other words, before the occurrence of Brexit, it is attempted to explore some hypothetical impacts of Brexit on the dynamics of institutional change within the European Union. Moreover, a method of ranking economies with respect to institutional development is provided and a numerical technique is devised for reference and benchmarking purposes in evaluation and ranking of institutional attributes.

Another chapter examines institutional change contexts and dynamics using different theories and perspectives. Institutions are prevalent in every society, designed to protect the common interest of all stakeholders, serve as restraints on government and economic agents, and provide a framework to model behaviors and decisions. Nevertheless, institutional changes have diverse effects on the formal and informal sectors of the economy. The framework and institutional mechanism are shaped by diverse factors such as culture, context, public policies, and human behavior. Evidence from the literature review confirms that institutions experience gradual or disruptive changes depending on the competing interests of stakeholders in all contexts. Besides, understanding this construct is complex depending on the perspectives. The findings from this study reiterate the importance of using different perspectives to understand the interplay of endogenous and exogenous factors and human behavior motivations in institutional change studies.

However, the failure of some countries to achieve sustainable growth is rooted in the history and poor performance of their social, economic, and political institutions. According to North (1990), institutional change has defined the course of human societies' evolution throughout history and is the key to understanding historical changes. Therefore, the process of development has been closely tied with the process of institutional change and the willingness to break connection with the paths already trodden. What is an institution? What are the different types of institutions? What does institutional change mean? In addition, what are the theories of institutional change? A chapter is devoted to address such important questions.

Nonetheless, human interactions are the key to development and are ubiquitous, and due to this feature, they need structuring and give rise to the foundation of institutions. Institutions foster consistency and institutions, i.e., rules of the game, and shape human interactions. Institutions shape individual and collective actions in economic, social, and political dimensions. It is noteworthy that apart from political and sociological approach, institution and institutional change theories have gained much popularity in economics and empirical research. Thus, a chapter gives a theoretical perspective and review framework for comprehending the foundation of institution and causes of institutional change and analysis of significant theories of institutional change in the context of economics. The chapter is a doctrinal study and primarily proposes the basic idea behind the formation of institution, which will lead the readers of varying disciplines to fathom the realm of institution. Then, the chapter conveys the causes of institutional change like functionality, technological efficiency, diffusion, conflict, and power struggle and finally focuses on the design-based, evolutionary, and equilibrium theories.

Moreover, to empirically assess the role of institutions and institutional quality in economic performance, it is necessary to select the proxy variable(s) for institutional quality. Although several indicators have been suggested in the literature, individuals and international organizations are still attempting to introduce indicators that reflect the actual institutional quality of various countries. As institutions have different dimensions, several indicators have been suggested in the literature to measure the quality of institutions. However, there is no consensus among experts on which index should be used. Each scholar has used a different proxy variable, depending on data access limitations, to measure institutional quality. However, the key question is whether any indicator can be used as a proxy variable to determine institutional quality. The main purpose of this chapter is to answer this important question. To this end, most of the existing indicators are described descriptively and some important points regarding the use of each indicator are made. In addition, some indicators, including the rule of law and property rights as two measures of the quality of legal-economic institutions, are described in more detail. Nonetheless, the literature review shows that not all indicators have a common characteristic. In fact, different indicators are proposed for each specific institution, providing indications of caution when interpreting the results of empirical studies.

Part II contains five chapters focusing on mechanisms of institutional change. The difference in the economic, social, and political functioning of institutions is believed to be one of the main reasons accounting for the differences in the level of economic development between countries. Different institutions can provide the necessary conditions for the orientation and allocation of existing community resources to promoting innovative and productive activities. The attraction of human and social capital, on the one hand, and foreign and domestic physical capital, on the other hand, can bring prosperity to countries. The first chapter, in this part, provides an overview of institutional changes in some emerging market economies, the factors contributing to the successful interaction with and exploitation of various institutions in some countries to achieve sustainable growth and development, and the causes of failure in some countries to achieve this goal. The overall conclusion of this chapter is that East Asian and Southeast Asian countries have been able to experience significant economic progress by implementing economic, cultural, and political institutional changes. Other emerging market economies, however, have failed to implement the same changes because of the diminished institutional quality in these countries and the unwillingness of their governments to introduce radical changes.

Recently, it is argued that social media can not only be considered an institution but also a harbinger of institutional change as it has brought a sustained change in the behavior of the members of a society. It is a vital tool for social interactions over the past two decades. The dominance of the social media as an institution can be felt as it has sufficed to metamorphose the process of consumer buying behavior. The second chapter of this part gives the institutions and institutional change a new dimension in the emerging markets with the integrated marketing communication perspective. The aim of this chapter is to bring forth the impact of social media in building a "brand." If taken in the perspective of institution and institutional change, social media has drastically affected the way consumers explore, research, and share information about the brands. This chapter is a theoretical perspective along with review of literature about impact of social media on branding giving. The chapter focuses on the various aspects like types of social media tools used by the marketers, most dominant brands, and their social media branding strategies and also paves the way for future research in the related fields of study.

Additionally, institutional change is influenced by the economic, social, political, and overall processes of globalization, leading to the deterioration or improvement of the institutions (Samadi 2019). Hence, a chapter is devoted to investigating the impact of economic globalization on governance quality. This is an issue that has been one of the open theoretical and empirical questions in the literature of institutional economics and has always attracted a lot of attention from the scholars. Some scholars have consistently examined the impact of globalization on the quality of governance. However, the question is – how a country's economic and institutional structures can affect the impacts of globalization on the quality of governance? The chapter is an attempt to answer this question using data from 182 countries during 2002–2016. The technique of principal component analysis is employed for combining six sub-indices (dimensions) of governance to compose the overall governance index. Then, the countries are divided into four categories based on the global average of the overall governance and per capita income. The system-generalized method of moments (SYS-GMM) estimation procedure is also used to estimate the model. The results show that the overall globalization and trade openness have a positive effect on the quality of overall governance in countries with higher levels of income and governance than the global average, and a negative effect in countries with lower quality of overall governance and per capita income than the global average. The study indicates that the level of quality of governance of a country is a determining factor in how much a country benefits from globalization.

The next chapter, in this part, presents an original framework for the public administration reform and introduces the main characteristics of the public administration model to increase the efficiency of the emerging markets. This is an important issue due to the difficulty of the governments in dealing with the ambiguous mechanisms behind institutional change and public administration reform. The approach is based on institutional theories and institution-based views, which are considered as the adequate theories of administrative systems and markets by emphasizing the role of emerging markets through the development path. Many emerging market economies are compared based on various longitudinal and cross-sectional variables. This chapter has two main contributions: the first one is the relationship between public administration variables and the economic performance of nations. Results suggest that administration characteristics have a positive impact on country competitiveness and its business situation but no direct impact on the country's economic growth. Economic growth is the result of the administrative system function. It is the result of the country's improved competitiveness and the country's market governance model under globalization pressures. The second contribution corresponds to a variety of strategies under the comprehensive public administration reform model for solving the problem of government effectiveness and the country's growth. This chapter shows that public administration is a significant driver of socioeconomic and political development, and thus, it increasingly helps rebuild and rearrange the public administration continuously, to develop the country's capacity, recognize the new national and international opportunities, enter the markets, and encourage all governance actors to offer products and services efficiently and equitably. The chapter proposes new insights into public administration reform mechanisms by considering their relationship to the success of the emerging markets.

The last chapter of this part concerns an important emerging issue. In the next few decades, the future of higher education may change drastically as its systems are becoming incompatible with the increasing pace of technological advancement brought by the Industrial Revolution 4.0. Recent years have witnessed a rapid pace of new technological transition which played a crucial role in the previous industrial revolutions. This rapid technological transition affects almost every field of the emerging markets in economy, environment, culture, and education. The Fourth Industrial Revolution (4IR) considered as the global technological transformation and revolution is based on diverse modern technologies. In the context of the Fourth Industrial Revolution, education must be prepared to change with this technological transition. The main objective of the study, reported in this chapter, is to explore the emergence of Higher Education 4.0 (HE 4.0) and review new trends, techniques, and teaching methods practiced in few Asian emerging markets in adopting HE 4.0. The study also provides a summary of the industrial revolution and educational evolution from 1.0 to 4.0 and addresses the significance of this transition. The findings of this study reveal that higher education needs to invest in this transition, emphasizing the applicable changes to the education system.

Part III includes three chapters studying the issues related to the role of energy in institutional building and its potential synergies with institutional development. Institutions are organic entities with metamorphosis and evolutionary growth. The first chapter of this part of the book considers the significance of Iranian oil in modern Iranian institutional change process from its early days in the 1900s to the 1970s, while the state had the most petro-rentier budget. Thus, the ever-increasing evolutionary power of oil in forming modern Iranian institutions and its 79-year-old dynamism – embedded and analyzed critically in the Iranian and global historical contexts from the Constitutional Revolution to the 1979/Islamic Revolution – is discussed to shed light on its stupendous catalyzing and transforming features that led to Iran's urbanization, semi-industrialization, new sociopolitical class generation, state-nation conflicts, and revolution.

Moreover, the development theorists and thinkers have proposed various ideas about the lack of convergence of the development path in different societies. In this regard, as one of the new institutionalists, North discussed the transition from limited access order (natural state) to open access order with an emphasis on the issue of violence. This chapter of the book – inspired by the idea of violence and social orders, relates economic performance to the evolution of social orders and examines institutional barriers to transition from the natural state of Iran during 1941–1979. The results of this study indicate that during this era, synergies between extractive political and economic institutions created a vicious cycle. Competition and struggles in this era for gaining benefits were merely in the hands of a certain group; thus, the political demands and aspirations were highly suppressed to protect their interests. Disturbances in this cycle were in order to achieve economic rents under the control of other groups. Under such circumstances, the long-term balance between political and economic institutions was not made possible which led Iran to experience an era of basic limited access order and then to move toward a fragile limited access order and eventually the chaos instead of moving toward an open access order.

Furthermore, in light of an increasingly complex and uncertain environment, energy security and institutional quality are recognized as important factors that influence sustainable development. Emerging economies that seek to address the problems of high energy need/consumption for development and with relatively poor institutional quality have become a topic of interest in current research. This last chapter of the book is the first work to contribute to institutional quality literature by examining the impact of energy security, measured along eight different dimensions, on institutional quality in 43 emerging economies for the period 2002–2017. Panel data analysis is conducted using the panel-corrected standard error (PCSE) and feasible generalized least square (FGLS) techniques to deal with autocorrelation and heteroskedasticity and to check for robustness. The autoregressive distributed lag (ARDL) model and pooled mean group estimator were also employed to check the long-run effects. The results show that (*i*) six of the eight energy security indicators (i.e., energy gap, energy supply capability, energy structure, energy inefficiency, and energy developability in terms of consumption and CO_2 emissions) negatively affect institutional quality, whereas energy developability in terms of the CO_2 emissions per unit of energy consumption and energy acceptability (renewable energy consumption) has significant positive impacts; (*ii*) most of these energy security indicators have insignificantly positive effects on institutional quality in the short run, while seven of the eight energy security indicators have significantly negative effects on institutional quality in the long run. The effects of the energy security indicators on institutional quality were found to be consistent with the six institutional dimensions. Interestingly, these findings imply that emerging economies should increasingly use renewable energy to enhance institutional quality for long-run benefits.

References

Arnold, D. J., & Quelch, J. A. (1998). New strategies in emerging markets, *Sloan Management Review, 40.1* (Fall 1998), p7+.

Faghih, N. (2019). An introduction to: Globalization and development – Economic and socio-cultural perspectives from emerging markets. In N. Faghih (Ed.), *Globalization and development – Economic and socio-cultural perspectives from emerging markets. Contributions to economics*. Cham: Springer.

Fleury, A., Fleury, M. T., & Oliveira, L. (2018), *The evolution of studies on emerging market multinationals: What is new?* In Paper presented at the 6th Copenhagen Conference on: 'Emerging Multinationals': Outward Investment from Emerging Economies, Copenhagen, Denmark, 11–12 October 2018.

Hegel, G. W. F. (1807). *Phenomenology of spirit* (A. V. Miller, Trans.). Oxford: Oxford University Press.

Kant, I. (1795). *Perpetual peace and other essays on politics, history and morals* (HPC classics series). Indianapolis: Hackett Publishing.

London, T., & Hart, S. L. (2004). Reinventing strategies for emerging markets: Beyond the transnational model. *Journal of International Business Studies, 35*, 350–370.

North, D. C. (1990). *Institutions, institutional change and economic performance*. Cambridge, MA: Cambridge University Press.

Plato. (1955). *Republic* (H. D. P. Lee, Trans.). Harmondsworth: Penguin.

Rumi. (1207–1273). *The Mathnawí of Jalaluddín Rumi, Translation and Commentary, Nicholson, Reynold A, Volume I, 1926*. London: Messrs Luzac & Co. LTD. Page 74.

Samadi, A. H. (2019). Institutional quality and globalization in developing countries. In N. Faghih (Ed.), *Globalization and development – Economic and socio-cultural perspectives from emerging markets, contributions to economics*. Cham: Springer.

Smith, A. (1776). *The wealth of nations*. New York: Random House.

Part I
Concepts, Theories, and *Dynamism of Institutional Change*

Dynamics of Institutional Change Within the Group of Twenty (G20) and the European Union, and an Assessment of Brexit Impact: A Taxonomic Study

Nezameddin Faghih and Mahshid Sazegar

1 Introduction

Institutions, as the rules of the game or the humanly devised constraints in societies, shape human interactions and structure incentives in human exchange, whether economic, social, or political. Dynamics of institutional change construct the evolvement route of societies through time and provide the key to understanding dynamics of historical change. Institutions and dynamics of institutional change influence the performance and the differential performance of economies over time (North 1990). Institutions are cognitive processes, normative principles, and regulative activities and structures that provide meaning and stability to social behavior (Scott 1995).

The abovementioned definitions and characterizations contend that institutions establish the rules of the game, formal (such as constitutions, laws, and regulations) and informal (such as norms of behavior, conventions, and codes of conduct), that structure the social, economic, and political relationships in a society, which are generally imposed by the members of the affiliated group (North 1990; Scott 1995). The transaction and transformation costs of production, and consequently, the profitability of engaging in an enterprise or business activities in an economy, are also determined by social, economic, and political institutions, as well as technology (Chan 2008; Khanna and Rivkin 2001; North 1990; Williamson 1985).

Innovation is considered as one of the most crucial drivers of growth and prosperity, and institutions are recognized as the main generators of innovation (Solow 1957; Mokyr 1992; Aghion and Howitt 1992; Grossman and Helpman 1990). Nevertheless, some features of societies impact the ability of economic systems to

N. Faghih
UNESCO Chair Professor Emeritus, Cambridge, MA, USA

M. Sazegar (✉)
Fars Engineering Association, Shiraz, Iran

N. Faghih, A. H. Samadi (eds.), *Dynamics of Institutional Change in Emerging Market Economies*, Contributions to Economics,
https://doi.org/10.1007/978-3-030-61342-6_2

develop new ideas by adapting and translating the innovative efforts. Institutions, both formal and informal, can promote cooperative behaviors that can ultimately lead to the development of societies. Empirical examinations indicate that differences in innovative performance of countries are due to diversity in institutions (Sattar and Mahmood 2011; Tebaldi 2013; Khan et al. 2017).

Both formal and informal institutions can significantly affect innovation performance of economies, and formal institutions have more influence in developed economies, while informal institutions are more effective in developing economies. Contrary to institutions of developed economies, in developing economies institutions are found more supplementary to each other, and formal institutions would be enhanced by informal institutions for improvement of innovative performance in these economies. Moreover, innovation is encouraged by collective work and sharing of knowledge; hence, less developed economies can foster and accelerate innovation activities in collaboration with organizations, establishments, industries, and institutions of developed economies (Khan et al. 2017).

Studies show that long-run economic growth is intrinsically associated with institutions and that an economy with institutional barriers restricting, retarding, or preventing the input of new inventions and technologies will encounter low levels or low growth rates in output and also a relatively small allocation of human capital in research and development. Only sustainable human capital growth generates a growth effect in output, and the long-run output growth is driven by the innovation growth rate, which is ultimately determined by the institutional growth rate. In the short run, institutional arrangements should change at the rate required to follow the path of technological change in order to avoid a slowdown in the innovation rate and thereupon in the output growth rate (Tebaldi and Elmslie 2008).

Furthermore, empirical studies on the links between institutions and innovation show that institutional arrangements can positively contribute to illustrate a considerable amount of cross-country variations in innovations. Specifically, it is evidenced that control of corruption, property rights protection, market-friendly policies, and a more adequate and efficient judiciary system can advance and boost the rate of innovation and patent production in an economy. Additionally, the equality between the growth rate of output per capita (in the steady state) and the rate of technological innovation provides an evidence of a growth effect through innovation and ultimately shows that institutions have an income growth effect by the virtue of institutional quality affecting the rate of innovation in an economy as the engine of economic growth. Nonetheless, institutional quality impacts innovations significantly for the economies both in the technological frontier and far from it. Thus, this idea is refuted that, independently from the quality of institutions, the economies far from the technological frontier do not have innovations as much as the others. It also emphasizes that geography, per se, does not adequately analyze innovation variations across countries. In other words, geography can affect innovation, but more adequately through institutions. More importantly, empirical evidence supports theoretical arguments that in the long-run, sustainable growth and accumulation of human capital is a key factor in shaping institutions (Solow 1956;

Romer 1990; Jones 1995; Aghion and Howitt 1992; Grossman and Helpman 2001; Tebaldi and Elmslie 2008; Lipset 1960).

Nevertheless, in an economy, truly innovative outcomes are bound to the populace capabilities (Arnold and Wade 2015: 670). The "populace" capabilities are linked to capacities in research and development (R&D). If a nation does not have enough scientific skills, educational level, and funding for R&D, there is no innovation-promoting populace. In the absence of a large enough contribution of "native" researchers, an economy's choices are to bring in foreign researchers. However, this latter option removes any possibility of becoming the "first adopter," thereby reducing economic benefits (Nambisan and Sawhney 2007).

However, every economy has its own social, economic, and political institutions that impact national economic growth (Williamson 1985; North 1990; Barro 1991; Olson 1996; Knack and Keefer 1997; La Porta et al. 1997; Hall and Jones 1999; Krueger and Lindahl 2001; Chan 2008). This research focuses on the European Union and the Group of Twenty (G20) economies, as major advanced and emerging economies that have joined forces to achieve their goals through targeted planning; aligning their laws, regulations, and rules of games; and conducting harmonious dynamics of institutional change.

The Global Innovation Index (GII) presents detailed metrics relevant to the innovation performance of many economies worldwide and, thus, provides appropriately applicable data for innovation-oriented economies regarding their innovation strategies. Its extensive indicators offer a broad and comprehensive perspective on innovation, factoring in infrastructure, education, business sophistication, and political environment (GII - The Global Innovation Index 2017; The Global Innovation Index 2018).

This chapter uses data on institutional variables collected from the Global Innovation Index (GII) which is widely used in innovation-related studies, and researchers have used all components of GII, or a few components, or even used a single component depending on the objectives of their studies. The secondary data, extracted from the GII and analyzed by numerical taxonomy, relate to the European Union and the Group of Twenty (G20) economies.

Thus, this chapter presents a quantitative framework and computational methods for assessing institutional development through taxonomic study. It defines the institutional development degree as the extent to which the economic, social, and political institutions in an economy are developed and are favorable to innovation. In particular, the institutional indicators, including institutions, political environment, regulatory environment, and business environment, reported by the Global Innovation Index (GII), are used in the numerical taxonomic approach. Subsequently, the analysis focuses on six sets of preliminary data, that is, the aforementioned four indicators plus population and GDP per capita. It should be noted that institutions impact the rate of innovation, and thus, the institutions impact the growth rate of GDP per capita (Tebaldi and Elmslie 2008).

Moreover, this chapter ranks the economies under study with respect to institutional development and devises a numerical technique for reference and benchmarking purposes in evaluation and ranking of institutional attributes.

Furthermore, the taxonomic analysis is performed in three groups of economies, namely, the G20 economies, the European Union economies including the United Kingdom, and the European Union economies excluding the United Kingdom. In other words, before the occurrence of Brexit, this chapter explores some hypothetical impacts of Brexit on the dynamics of institutional change within the European Union.

The following sections and subsections describe the methodology and the computational procedures of taxonomic analysis, comprising of seven steps, namely, formation of data matrices by using population, GDP per capita, and GII values; forming the standard matrices (containing elements converted to dimensionless values so that they can be compared with each other); computation of compound distance matrices (symmetric matrices with zero diagonal elements and each non-diagonal element showing the "distance" between two economies); assignment of the shortest distances (the lowest value in each matrix row is marked as the shortest distance for the interrelated economies to indicate the closest proximity between them in the year of consideration); depiction of optimal charts (through iterative processes, homogenous groups of comparable economies are obtained, and the shortest distances can be available to depict optimal charts by connecting economies with most commonalities); and finally, ranking of economies in terms of institutional development and measurement of the "institutional development degrees" (fi) for each member within the economic groups (Le Quesne 1969; Phillips 1983; Faghih and Sazegar 2019).

2 Methodology

This chapter presents a quantitative framework and computational methods for assessing institutional development through taxonomic study, using the Global Innovation Index (GII) data on institutions in the years 2010–2018. GII is authored by Cornell University, the European Institute of Business Administration (INSEAD: **Ins**titut **E**uropéen d'**Ad**ministration des Affaires), and the World Intellectual Property Organization (WIPO) and provides detailed metrics relevant to the innovation performance of many economies worldwide. Its extensive indicators offer a broad and comprehensive perspective of innovation, including infrastructure, education, business sophistication, and political environment. The GII report is published annually and its 2018 report,[1] for instance, included 129 economies, representing 91.8% of the world's population and 96.8% of the world's GDP.

GII considers the significant role of innovation in being an engine of well-being and economic growth and recognizes the need for a broad perspective and deep insight of innovation being applicable to emerging markets, with the containment and inclusion of a span of indicators and elements that go beyond the ordinary and traditional scales and measures of innovation (Cornell University et al. 2013).

[1] https://www.globalinnovationindex.org/gii-2018-report

The measurement of GII is based upon two sub-indices, measuring the innovation system inputs and outputs. The innovation input sub-index is a measure of the innovation system inputs, and the innovation output sub-index is a measure of the innovation system outputs. Each element is constructed around some key pillars. There are five input pillars assigned to capture those elements that enable innovation activities within the national economies:

1. Institutions
2. Research and human capital
3. Infrastructure
4. Market sophistication
5. Business sophistication

There are also two output pillars assigned in order to cover innovation outputs and exhibit their actual evidence:

6. Knowledge and technology outputs
7. Creative outputs

The GII uses hard data, instead of qualitative assessments, from more than 30 sources, which spans a wide range of innovation drivers and effects and is a simple statistical average of the scores in the five input and two output sub-indices. Each pillar covers up to five indicators, and their scores are determined by the weighted averaging (Cornell University et al. 2013). Figure 1 illustrates a summary of the GII.

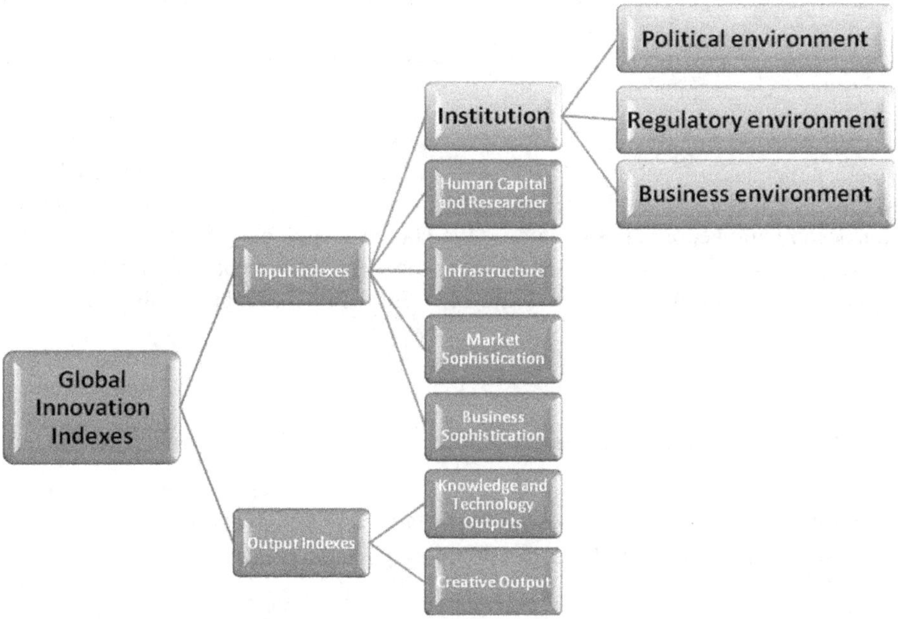

Fig. 1 An illustrative summary of the GII. (Authors' own figure)

This chapter focuses on major advanced and emerging economies, namely, the European Union and the Group of Twenty (G20) economies that have joined forces to achieve their goals through targeted planning; aligning their laws, regulations, and rules of games; and conducting harmonious dynamics of institutional change. Thus, the data for the economies under study are extracted from GII that provides detailed innovation performance metrics and appropriately applicable data for innovation-oriented economies regarding their innovation strategies.[2] In particular, the institutional indicators, including institutions, political environment, regulatory environment, and business environment, reported by GII, are used in the numerical taxonomic approach. Subsequently, the analysis focuses on six sets of preliminary data, that is, the aforementioned four indicators plus population and GDP per capita. Using the "institutions" sub-index, along with its components (political, regulatory, and business environment), leads to differentials reflected in the "standard matrices," signifying the influences of institutional factors of an economy within the taxonomic homogenization processes. For instance, the institution sub-indicators appearing with negative signs in the standard matrices detect the components responsible for the "institutions" index abatement.

As already noted, and observed in Fig. 1, "institution" is an input sub-index of GII that includes three indicators:

- Institutions:
  - Political environment (covering political stability, government effectiveness, and press freedom)
  - Regulatory environment (covering regulatory quality, rule of law, cost of redundancy dismissal)
  - Business environment (covering ease of starting a business, ease of resolving insolvency, ease of paying taxes)

Moreover, the taxonomic analysis is performed in three groups of economies, namely, the G20 economies (consisting of 20 economies), the European Union economies including the United Kingdom (consisting of 28 economies), and the European Union economies excluding the United Kingdom (consisting of 27 economies). This is in order to explore some hypothetical impacts of Brexit on the dynamics of institutional change within the European Union before the occurrence of Brexit.[3]

3 Computational Procedure

The following subsections describe the seven steps of taxonomic computational analysis (Le Quesne 1969; Phillips 1983; Faghih and Sazegar 2019).

[2] https://www.globalinnovationindex.org/about-gii

[3] https://en.wikipedia.org/wiki/Brexit

3.1 Step 1: Formation of Data Matrix

Consider:

$$X_{oj} = \left(\sum_{n}^{i=1} X_{ij} \right) / n \tag{1}$$

In the first step of the computational analysis, primary tables of data matrixes are formed, which contain six indices taken from GII. These tables consist of rows and columns, including economies and the corresponding six indicators. At the bottom of each table, the average of the values in every column is calculated and placed for each year. Matrix is formed with "*n*" members (1, 2, 3… *n*) to represent the variables demonstrated with "*m*" (as an indicator of each study). In Eq. (1), "*i*" refers to rows and "*j*" to columns. Thus, the data matrices for the European Union (in two cases, including and excluding the United Kingdom) and the G20 economies were formed by using the GII data (the corresponding index and sub-indices for institutions), from 2010 to 2018, as shown in Tables 1, 2, 3, 4, 5, 6, 7, 8, 9, 10, 11, 12, 13, 14, 15, 16, 17, 18, 19, 20, 21, 22, 23, 24, 25, 26, and 27), in the Appendix.

It should be noted that all indicators (the scores of the index and sub-indices) were normalized. In the tables that follow, the institutions index and its related sub-indices were extracted from the innovation input for each year and placed in columns. Additionally, population, GDP, and institutions with the three sub-indices of institutions, consisting of political environment, regulatory environment, and business environment, comprise the (GII) Innovation Input Index to be located in the row of the matrix for each country, respectively.

It is noted that the European Union (EU) is also a member of G20 (with 28 economies including the United Kingdom). Thus, the European Union population was calculated as the summation of the population of the member economies, and all other indicators for the European Union were also computed as an average of the corresponding indicators for the European Union members within the time span of 2010–2018. Consequently, the data matrices for the European Union (including the United Kingdom) are demonstrated in Tables 1, 2, 3, 4, 5, 6, 7, and 8 (in the Appendix).

Subsequently, within the same time span (2010–2018), Tables 10, 11, 12, 13, 14, 15, 16, 17, and 18 (in the Appendix) show the data matrices for the European Union, excluding the United Kingdom, and Tables 19, 20, 21, 22, 23, 24, 25, 26, and 27 (in the Appendix) exhibit the data matrices for economies of the Group of Twenty (G20).

3.2 Step 2: Forming the Standard Matrix

Since the selected indices and indicators do not usually have the same dimensions, e.g., population and GDP, they cannot be compared. Thus, such data are converted to dimensionless values, so that they can be compared with each other. This is the

Table 1 GII data matrix (Xij) for the European Union economies in 2010

THE EUROPEAN UNION WITH THE UNITED KINGDOM						
2010 reported in 2011	Population (mn)	GDP (per capita)	Institutions	Political environment	Regulatory environment	Business environment
Austria	8.4	38363.1	85.7	94.1	88.4	74.5
Belgium	10.7	36,249	84.8	86.8	86.1	81.6
Bulgaria	7.5	13332.7	74.5	67.2	68.7	87.6
Croatia	4.4	19805.4	73.6	73.1	59.5	88.1
Cyprus	0.9	30223.4	83.5	77.3	83.2	89.9
Czech Republic	10.7	25,232	82.6	84.1	85.4	78.2
Denmark	5.5	36761.7	94.2	94.2	96.7	91.8
Estonia	1.3	19451.4	80.8	83.2	75.3	84.1
Finland	5.3	34719.7	89.2	98.3	85.5	83.7
France	62.6	33655.5	77.9	80.5	74.3	78.8
Germany	82.1	36267.4	83.5	88.1	81.1	81.2
Greece	11.2	29663.4	67.8	63.5	63.8	76.1
Hungary	10	19764.3	79.3	77.9	77.8	82.1
Ireland	4.6	41278.2	91.2	90.1	93.2	90.3
Italy	60.1	31908.6	71.1	72.3	67.5	73.6
Latvia	2.2	15412.8	76.4	74	70.4	85
Lithuania	3.3	16747.1	78	80.5	70.9	82.7
Luxembourg	0.5	83758.8	88.3	96.1	79.1	89.8
Netherlands	16.7	40714.7	87.5	92.4	84.1	85.8
Poland	38	19058.7	76.4	80.6	74.1	74.5
Portugal	10.7	24569.4	80.4	82.2	73.7	85.3
Romania	21.2	14,278	69.8	64.2	60.7	84.5
Slovakia	5.4	22356.3	79.6	81.1	76.1	81.5
Slovenia	2	27004.4	80.4	82.5	69	89.7
Spain	45.3	32544.8	68.9	67.6	73.7	65.5
Sweden	9.3	37904.6	87.3	95.6	86.1	80.1
United Kingdom	61.9	36495.8	86.4	79.8	92.7	86.6
Sum.	501.8	817521.2	2179.1	2207.3	2097.1	2232.6
Ave.	18.585	30278.563	80.707	81.752	77.670	82.689

Source: Authors' work based on GII data

Table 2 GII data matrix (Xij) for the European Union economies in 2011

THE EUROPEAN UNION WITH THE UNITED KINGDOM						
2011 reported in 2012	Population (mn)	GDP (per capita)	Institutions	Political environment	Regulatory environment	Business environment
Austria	8.4	41805.1	82.3	93.6	96.4	56.8
Belgium	11	37677.4	86.2	87.3	92.4	78.8
Bulgaria	7.5	13562.9	67.2	63.1	78.2	60.4
Croatia	4.4	18338.5	69.2	71.5	72.6	63.5
Cyprus	0.8	29100.3	86.3	83.6	91.5	83.9
Czech Republic	10.5	25933.8	68.2	84.3	75.5	44.8
Denmark	5.5	37741.9	95.3	94.9	99.4	91.6
Estonia	1.3	20182.1	79.9	84.3	86.8	68.5
Finland	5.4	36723.3	92.8	99.5	97.5	81.5
France	63.2	35048.8	82.7	82.6	89.7	76
Germany	81.4	37935.5	76.7	87.3	82.2	60.4
Greece	11.2	27624.3	60.7	64.7	71.7	45.8
Hungary	10	19647.1	72.3	76.1	81.4	59.4
Ireland	4.6	39507.9	93	86.9	97	95.2
Italy	60.6	30165.5	70.2	70.4	82.8	57.5
Latvia	2.2	15448.1	72.8	73.1	84.8	60.6
Lithuania	3.3	18769.5	70	77.3	69.7	63
Luxembourg	0.5	84829.3	83.8	94.6	84.1	72.6
Malta	0.4	25782.7	84.4	81.4	87.4	N/A
Netherlands	16.7	42330.7	88.7	91.2	97.6	77.4
Poland	38.1	20136.9	68.1	80.9	83.5	40
Portugal	10.7	23204.5	70.6	79.9	61.4	70.7
Romania	21.4	12357.9	62.1	64.2	79.1	43.1
Slovakia	5.4	23384.1	69.8	82.2	70.5	56.8
Slovenia	2	29179.1	78	80.1	83	70.9
Spain	46.1	30622.2	68.5	71.5	81.1	53
Sweden	9.4	40613.4	88.6	94.1	92.3	79.6
United Kingdom	62.6	35974.4	90.4	83	97.7	90.6
Sum.	504.6	853627.2	2178.8	2283.6	2367.3	1802.4
Ave.	18.021	30486.686	77.814	81.557	84.546	66.756

Source: Authors' work based on GII data

Table 3 GII data matrix (Xij) for the European Union economies in 2012

THE EUROPEAN UNION WITH THE UNITED KINGDOM						
2012 reported in 2013	Population (mn)	GDP (per capita)	Institutions	Political environment	Regulatory environment	Business environment
Austria	8.8	42477.5	88.5	89.9	95.6	80
Belgium	11.4	38089.4	88.2	86.3	92.1	86.3
Bulgaria	7.7	14234.6	68	61.2	77.2	65.5
Croatia	4.6	18098.8	69.1	68.8	71.9	66.7
Cyprus	1.2	26908.3	84.1	82	89.3	81
Czech Republic	11	27164.8	76.1	83.2	76.9	68.1
Denmark	5.8	37738.1	95.3	94.7	99.7	91.6
Estonia	1.4	21226.6	78.2	80.9	86.3	67.3
Finland	5.7	36458.5	95.3	97.9	96.8	91.2
France	67	35519.6	79	78.4	87.6	70.9
Germany	86.3	39058.8	82.5	85.8	81.3	80.3
Greece	12	25061.5	67.8	62.5	73.5	67.3
Hungary	10.4	19,754	73.5	72	80.8	67.6
Ireland	4.7	41739.4	91.9	86	96.9	93
Italy	64.7	30116.2	73.6	68.3	81.9	70.7
Latvia	2.3	18140.1	77.2	69.2	84.1	78.3
Lithuania	3.4	20088.6	71.4	73.4	68.9	72
Luxembourg	0.5	80679.1	83.5	92.7	84.8	73.1
Malta	0.4	26126.2	79	79.2	91.8	66.1
Netherlands	17.4	42321.6	92.8	91.5	97.9	88.9
Poland	39.7	20976.1	74.4	78.9	74.6	69.7
Portugal	11.2	22991.2	72.9	77.2	59.3	82.1
Romania	22.1	12838.4	66.3	59.5	79.2	60.1
Slovakia	5.6	24283.6	77.4	79.5	81.7	71
Slovenia	2.1	28647.7	78.4	77.3	82.1	75.8
Spain	49.2	30412.1	77.4	71.8	80	80.3
Sweden	10	41749.6	89.9	93.3	92.8	83.6
United Kingdom	65.8	36727.8	88.4	79.7	95.7	89.9
Sum.	532.4	859628.2	2240.1	2221.1	2360.7	2138.4
Ave.	19.014	30701.007	80.004	79.325	84.311	76.371

Source: Authors' work based on GII data

Table 4 GII data matrix (Xij) for the European Union economies in 2013

THE EUROPEAN UNION WITH THE UNITED KINGDOM						
2013 reported in 2014	Population (mn)	GDP (per capita)	Institutions	Political environment	Regulatory environment	Business environment
Austria	8.5	42596.6	88.8	90.4	96.4	79.5
Belgium	11.1	37880.5	87.9	86	91.4	86.2
Bulgaria	7.3	14499.1	68.5	63.2	76.5	65.7
Croatia	4.3	18190.9	69.8	70.9	71	67.4
Cyprus	1.1	25265.4	83.5	81.7	88.5	80.3
Czech Republic	10.5	27200.1	76.2	82.1	75.4	71
Denmark	5.6	37900.5	93.6	91.4	98.2	91.3
Estonia	1.3	23,144	78.6	79.2	85.8	70.7
Finland	5.4	35616.6	95.3	97.7	96.9	91.2
France	65.7	35,784	78.6	78	87	70.7
Germany	81.9	24,012	82.7	85.8	81.5	81
Greece	11.3	24,012	66.6	60.2	71.8	67.7
Hungary	9.9	20065.1	72.3	71.1	78.8	67
Ireland	4.6	39547.4	90.4	86.4	91.7	92.8
Italy	60.9	30289.4	73.2	67.9	81.1	70.7
Latvia	2	19119.5	76.8	72.1	83.9	74.2
Lithuania	3	22747.2	73.4	76.2	69.9	74
Luxembourg	0.5	78669.8	82.9	92.3	83.7	72.8
Malta	0.4	27840.2	79.2	80.6	91.6	65.5
Netherlands	16.8	41710.7	93.3	92.3	97.2	90.4
Poland	38.5	21214.3	74.7	78.8	74.4	71.1
Portugal	10.5	23068.4	77.3	78.6	71.1	82.2
Romania	21.3	13395.9	65.9	58.9	77.4	61.2
Slovakia	5.4	24605.3	74.5	80.5	72.9	70.1
Slovenia	2.1	27899.8	78.7	78.6	81.8	75.8
Spain	46.2	29851.1	74.8	71.8	77.7	75
Sweden	9.5	41188.4	89.7	92.5	93	83.7
United Kingdom	61.2	37306.6	88.6	80.2	95.7	90
Sum.	506.8	844620.8	2235.8	2225.4	2342.3	2139.2
Ave.	18.100	30165.029	79.850	79.479	83.654	76.400

Source: Authors' work based on GII data

Table 5 GII data matrix (Xij) for the European Union economies in 2014

THE EUROPEAN UNION WITH THE UNITED KINGDOM						
2014 reported in 2015	Population (mn)	GDP (per capita)	Institutions	Political environment	Regulatory environment	Business environment
Austria	8.5	43,796	88.7	90.5	95.9	79.5
Belgium	11.1	38826.5	83.3	85.6	80.2	84.2
Bulgaria	7.2	15031.3	69.7	57	75.8	76.3
Croatia	4.3	18354.7	71.8	69.7	71.5	74.1
Cyprus	1.2	24170.5	79.8	77.4	86.6	75.5
Czech Republic	10.7	28086.5	76.4	77.6	75.6	75.9
Denmark	5.6	38916.8	93.1	91.1	98.3	90
Estonia	1.3	23213.4	80.8	75	86.3	81
Finland	5.4	36122.1	95.8	98.9	96.9	91.8
France	64.6	36537.5	81.7	77.9	87	80.4
Germany	82.7	41248.1	83.2	84.8	81.5	83.4
Greece	11.1	24574.1	68.2	56.4	73.1	75
Hungary	9.9	20817.4	73.4	71.1	78.1	71
Ireland	4.7	40586.5	87.2	83.4	89.5	88.7
Italy	61.1	30,803	73.8	65.2	81.4	74.9
Latvia	2	20204.4	77.7	71.8	80.7	80.6
Lithuania	3	23978.1	73.6	75.3	70.2	75.3
Luxembourg	0.5	79,977	83.5	91.1	83.9	75.6
Malta	0.4	28,741	80.6	82.1	91.2	68.6
Netherlands	16.8	42585.9	91.9	90.5	97	88.2
Poland	38.2	22201.1	75.3	74.1	75.4	76.3
Portugal	10.6	23,671	80.6	78.5	77.1	86.1
Romania	21.6	13,932	69.7	53.7	78.5	76.9
Slovakia	5.5	25524.7	75.1	76.9	72.2	76.2
Slovenia	2.1	28372.8	79.5	77	81.7	79.7
Spain	47.1	30637.4	75.2	68.4	77.4	79.7
Sweden	9.6	42624.1	90	92.3	93.1	84.7
United Kingdom	63.5	41158.9	87.3	78.6	95.4	87.9
Sum.	510.3	884692.8	2246.9	2171.9	2331.5	2237.5
Ave.	18.225	31596.171	80.246	77.568	83.268	79.911

Source: Authors' work based on GII data

Table 6 GII data matrix (Xij) for the European Union economies in 2015

THE EUROPEAN UNION WITH THE UNITED KINGDOM						
2015 reported in 2016	Population (mn)	GDP (per capita)	Institutions	Political environment	Regulatory environment	Business environment
Austria	8.5	47249.9	87.6	88.8	94.4	79.6
Belgium	11.3	43,585	80.5	79.3	78.1	84.1
Bulgaria	7.1	19097.3	67.8	53.2	75.4	74.7
Croatia	4.2	21581.4	70.9	68.1	70.4	74.4
Cyprus	1.2	32785.5	81.6	75.3	86.3	83.3
Czech Republic	10.5	31549.5	76.1	77.2	74.3	76.7
Denmark	5.7	45709.4	91.6	87.8	96.6	90.3
Estonia	1.3	28591.8	81.2	74.9	87	81.6
Finland	5.5	41,120	94.3	94.9	95.9	92.1
France	64.4	41180.7	80.4	74.9	85	81.2
Germany	80.7	46893.2	84.1	86.6	81.6	84.1
Greece	11	26448.7	67.1	56.7	69.4	75.1
Hungary	9.9	26,222	71.3	67.1	75.4	71.4
Ireland	4.7	55532.9	88.1	86.4	88.8	89.2
Italy	59.8	35708.3	72.8	62.4	79.2	76.8
Latvia	2	24712.2	77.7	71.4	80.7	81.1
Lithuania	2.9	28359.1	73.3	74.5	69.7	75.7
Luxembourg	0.6	98987.2	82.1	91.2	81.5	73.5
Malta	0.4	35825.6	78.7	79.1	87.3	69.7
Netherlands	16.9	49165.8	91	89.4	95.7	87.9
Poland	38.6	26455.3	75.3	73.2	74	78.7
Portugal	10.3	27834.8	79.1	74.8	75.9	86.5
Romania	19.5	20786.9	69	51.9	77.6	77.5
Slovakia	5.4	29720.1	75	75.7	70.8	78.5
Slovenia	2.1	31007.4	80.8	74.8	80.5	87.2
Spain	46.1	34819.5	75.3	70.9	74.3	80.5
Sweden	9.8	47922.2	88.3	89.2	90.2	85.6
United Kingdom	64.7	41158.9	87.6	78.9	94.7	89.3
Sum.	505.1	1040010.6	2228.6	2128.6	2290.7	2266.3
Ave.	18.039	37143.236	79.593	76.021	81.811	80.939

Source: Authors' work based on GII data

Table 7 GII data matrix for the European Union economies in 2016

THE EUROPEAN UNION WITH THE UNITED KINGDOM						
2016 report in 2017	Population (mn)	GDP (per capita)	Institutions	Political environment	Regulatory environment	Business environment
Austria	8.6	47249.9	87.1	86.3	93	82
Belgium	11.4	43,585	80.5	78.8	77.4	85.4
Bulgaria	7.1	19097.3	67.1	56	72.4	73
Croatia	4.2	21581.4	69.3	66.5	67.1	74.3
Cyprus	1.2	32785.5	81	72.9	84.6	85.7
Czech Republic	10.5	31549.5	77.6	78.1	73.4	81.3
Denmark	5.7	45709.4	91.4	87.6	96.4	90.3
Estonia	1.3	28591.8	81.1	74.5	85.8	82.9
Finland	5.5	41,120	92.2	89	95.1	92.4
France	64.7	41180.7	80.7	74.8	84.2	82.9
Germany	80.7	46893.2	83.5	84	80.6	85.9
Greece	10.9	26448.7	65.2	53.4	66.9	75.2
Hungary	9.8	26,222	70.7	68.2	72.9	71
Ireland	4.7	55532.9	87.6	84	88.8	90.1
Italy	59.8	35708.3	71.9	63	76.9	75.9
Latvia	2	24712.2	77.8	72.8	78.1	82.6
Lithuania	2.9	28359.1	74.1	76.9	69.4	75.9
Luxembourg	0.6	98987.2	82.6	92.2	81.2	74.3
Malta	0.4	35825.6	77.6	76.5	86.3	70.1
Netherlands	17	49165.8	88.2	87.9	88.1	88.7
Poland	38.6	26455.3	75.6	73.9	71.9	81.1
Portugal	10.3	27834.8	80.8	79.4	75.8	87.3
Romania	19.4	20786.9	69	54.9	75.3	76.8
Slovakia	5.4	29720.1	74.5	75.4	68.3	79.9
Slovenia	2.1	31007.4	80.9	76.7	78.7	87.3
Spain	46.1	34819.5	75.9	71.6	72.7	83.3
Sweden	9.9	47922.2	88.3	88	90.5	86.5
United Kingdom	65.1	41158.9	88.4	82.1	94.1	89.1
Sum.	505.9	1040010.6	2220.6	2125.4	2245.9	2291.2
Ave.	18.068	37143.236	79.307	75.907	80.211	81.829

Source: Authors' work based on GII data

Table 8 GII data matrix (Xij) for the European Union economies in 2017

THE EUROPEAN UNION WITH THE UNITED KINGDOM						
2017 report in 2018	Population (mn)	GDP (per capita)	Institutions	Political environment	Regulatory environment	Business environment
Austria	8.7	49868.7	85.6	83	93.4	80.3
Belgium	11.4	46553.1	82.2	77.3	81.3	87.9
Bulgaria	7.1	21686.6	45	53	35	52
Croatia	4.2	24423.5	69.2	64.9	71.9	70.8
Cyprus	1.2	37,023	80.3	72.3	83.7	84.8
Czech Rcpublic	10.6	35512.4	78.5	76.8	76.5	82.1
Denmark	5.7	49,883	91.1	89.4	95.1	88.7
Estonia	1.3	31749.5	81.2	75.5	87.7	80.4
Finland	5.5	44332.6	92.8	89.7	95.9	93
France	65	43760.8	81.2	74.4	85.6	83.6
Germany	82.1	50425.2	85.9	86.4	84.3	86.9
Greece	11.2	27,737	65.4	54.1	68.3	73.9
Hungary	9.7	29473.7	70.4	64.7	75.3	71.2
Ireland	4.8	75538.4	85.7	80.8	88.9	87.5
Italy	59.4	38140.3	74.9	63	78.4	83.2
Latvia	1.9	27644.1	76.5	71.2	81.6	76.6
Lithuania	2.9	32298.9	73.6	75.8	73.7	71.2
Luxembourg	0.6	106373.8	80.7	90.5	84.4	67.1
Malta	0.4	41944.8	74.6	75.7	86.8	61.5
Netherlands	17	53634.6	90	89	91.7	89.3
Poland	38.2	29521.3	74	67.1	74.6	80.2
Portugal	10.3	30416.5	81.2	79.7	78.3	85.5
Romania	19.7	24508.4	67.8	50.9	77.8	74.7
Slovakia	5.4	33025.5	74	71.2	74.3	76.5
Slovenia	2.1	34407.1	82.3	77.9	81.5	87.6
Spain	46.4	38,286	78.2	73.9	78	82.7
Sweden	9.9	51474.8	89.6	88.8	93	87.1
United Kingdom	66.2	44117.7	87.4	81.2	93.4	87.4
Sum.	508.9	1153761.3	2199.3	2098.2	2270.4	2233.7
Ave.	18.175	41205.761	78.546	74.936	81.086	79.775

Source: Authors' work based on GII data

Table 9 GII data matrix (Xij) for the European Union economies in 2018

THE EUROPEAN UNION WITH THE UNITED KINGDOM						
2018 report in 2019	Population (mn)	GDP (per capita)	Institutions	Political environment	Regulatory environment	Business environment
Austria	8.8	52137.4	86	83.9	93.7	80.3
Belgium	11.5	48244.7	82	77	80.4	88.5
Bulgaria	7	23155.6	68.3	58.1	75.5	71.5
Croatia	4.2	2622 1.4	69.3	66.7	71.7	69.4
Cyprus	1.2	39973.2	80.3	72.8	84.8	83.3
Czech Republic	10.6	37,371	78.6	75.6	78.4	81.8
Denmark	5.8	52120.5	91.7	91.1	95.3	88.8
Estonia	1.3	34095.8	81.7	78.3	87.8	78.9
Finland	5.5	46429.5	93.6	92.2	96.1	92.6
France	65.2	45775.1	83.2	80.4	85.5	83.7
Germany	82.3	52558.7	86.4	88.1	84.4	86.9
Greece	11.1	29,123	67.2	59.5	68.2	73.9
Hungary	9.7	31902.7	71.6	67.4	75.8	71.5
Ireland	4.8	78784.8	85.5	81.7	87.3	87.5
Italy	59.3	2398.2	75.3	63.7	79	83.4
Latvia	1.9	29901.3	77.2	72.5	82.2	76.9
Lithuania	2.9	34825.8	76	75.5	82.6	70
Luxembourg	0.6	106704.9	80.7	90.4	84.5	67.1
Malta	0.4	45605.9	75.2	75.9	88.2	61.5
Netherlands	17.1	56383.2	90.9	91.4	91.9	89.3
Poland	38.1	31938.7	73.6	68.2	72.9	79.7
Portugal	10.3	32006.4	81.8	81.2	78.8	85.5
Romania	19.6	26446.7	67.1	51.6	77.9	71.9
Slovakia	5.4	35129.8	73.1	71.6	73.2	74.5
Slovenia	2.1	36745.9	82.3	78	80.7	88.3
Spain	46.4	40138.8	78.1	73.5	77.9	83
Sweden	10	52984.1	90.1	91.1	92	87.1
United Kingdom	66.6	45704.6	87.1	80.2	93.7	87.4
Sum.	509.7	1174807.7	2233.9	2137.6	2320.4	2244.2
Ave.	18.204	41957.418	79.782	76.343	82.871	80.150

Source: Authors' work based on GII data

Table 10 GII's data matrix for the European Union without the United Kingdom in 2010

THE EUROPEAN UNION WITHOUT THE UNITED KINGDOM						
2010 reported in 2011	Population (mn)	GDP (per capita)	Institutions	Political environment	Regulatory environment	Business environment
Austria	8.4	38363.1	85.7	94.1	88.4	74.5
Belgium	10.7	36,249	84.8	86.8	86.1	81.6
Bulgaria	7.5	13332.7	74.5	67.2	68.7	87.6
Croatia	4.4	19805.4	73.6	73.1	59.5	88.1
Cyprus	0.9	30223.4	83.5	77.3	83.2	89.9
Czech Republic	10.7	25,232	82.6	84.1	85.4	78.2
Denmark	5.5	36761.7	94.2	94.2	96.7	91.8
Estonia	1.3	19451.4	80.8	83.2	75.3	84.1
Finland	5.3	34719.7	89.2	98.3	85.5	83.7
France	62.6	33655.5	77.9	80.5	74.3	78.8
Germany	82.1	36267.4	83.5	88.1	81.1	81.2
Greece	11.2	29663.4	67.8	63.5	63.8	76.1
Hungary	10	19764.3	79.3	77.9	77.8	82.1
Ireland	4.6	41278.2	91.2	90.1	93.2	90.3
Italy	60.1	31908.6	71.1	72.3	67.5	73.6
Latvia	2.2	15412.8	76.4	74	70.4	85
Lithuania	3.3	16747.1	78	80.5	70.9	82.7
Luxembourg	0.5	83758.8	88.3	96.1	79.1	89.8
Netherlands	16.7	40714.7	87.5	92.4	84.1	85.8
Poland	38	19058.7	76.4	80.6	74.1	74.5
Portugal	10.7	24569.4	80.4	82.2	73.7	85.3
Romania	21.2	14,278	69.8	64.2	60.7	84.5
Slovakia	5.4	22356.3	79.6	81.1	76.1	81.5
Slovenia	2	27004.4	80.4	82.5	69	89.7
Spain	45.3	32544.8	68.9	67.6	73.7	65.5
Sweden	9.3	37904.6	87.3	95.6	86.1	80.1
Sum.	439.9	781025.4	2092.7	2127.5	2004.4	2146
Ave.	16.919	30039.438	80.488	81.827	77.092	82.538

Source: Authors' work based on GII data

Table 11 GII's data matrix (Xij) for the European Union without the United Kingdom in 2011

THE EUROPEAN UNION WITHOUT THE UNITED KINGDOM						
2011 reported in 2012	Population (mn)	GDP (per capita)	Institutions	Political environment	Regulatory environment	Business environment
Austria	8.4	41805.1	82.3	93.6	96.4	56.8
Belgium	11	37677.4	86.2	87.3	92.4	78.8
Bulgaria	7.5	13562.9	67.2	63.1	78.2	60.4
Croatia	4.4	18338.5	69.2	71.5	72.6	63.5
Cyprus	0.8	29100.3	86.3	83.6	91.5	83.9
Czech Republic	10.5	25933.8	68.2	84.3	75.5	44.8
Denmark	5.5	37741.9	95.3	94.9	99.4	91.6
Estonia	1.3	20182.1	79.9	84.3	86.8	68.5
Finland	5.4	36723.3	92.8	99.5	97.5	81.5
France	63.2	35048.8	82.7	82.6	89.7	76
Germany	81.4	37935.5	76.7	87.3	82.2	60.4
Greece	11.2	27624.3	60.7	64.7	71.7	45.8
Hungary	10	19647.1	72.3	76.1	81.4	59.4
Ireland	4.6	39507.9	93	86.9	97	95.2
Italy	60.6	30165.5	70.2	70.4	82.8	57.5
Latvia	2.2	15448.1	72.8	73.1	84.8	60.6
Lithuania	3.3	18769.5	70	77.3	69.7	63
Luxembourg	0.5	84829.3	83.8	94.6	84.1	72.6
Malta	0.4	25782.7	84.4	81.4	87.4	n/a
Netherlands	16.7	42330.7	88.7	91.2	97.6	77.4
Poland	38.1	20136.9	68.1	80.9	83.5	40
Portugal	10.7	23204.5	70.6	79.9	61.4	70.7
Romania	21.4	12357.9	62.1	64.2	79.1	43.1
Slovakia	5.4	23384.1	69.8	82.2	70.5	56.8
Slovenia	2	29179.1	78	80.1	83	70.9
Spain	46.1	30622.2	68.5	71.5	81.1	53
Sweden	9.4	40613.4	88.6	94.1	92.3	79.6
Sum.	442	817652.8	2088.4	2200.6	2269.6	1711.8
Ave.	16.370	30283.437	77.348	81.504	84.059	65.838

Source: Authors' work based on GII data

Table 12 GII's data matrix (Xij) for the European Union without the United Kingdom in 2012

THE EUROPEAN UNION WITHOUT THE UNITED KINGDOM						
2012 reported in 2013	Population (mn)	GDP (per capita)	Institutions	Political environment	Regulatory environment	Business environment
Austria	8.8	42477.5	88.5	89.9	95.6	80
Belgium	11.4	38089.4	88.2	86.3	92.1	86.3
Bulgaria	7.7	14234.6	68	61.2	77.2	65.5
Croatia	4.6	18098.8	69.1	68.8	71.9	66.7
Cyprus	1.2	26908.3	84.1	82	89.3	81
Czech Republic	11	27164.8	76.1	83.2	76.9	68.1
Denmark	5.8	37738.1	95.3	94.7	99.7	91.6
Estonia	1.4	21226.6	78.2	80.9	86.3	67.3
Finland	5.7	36458.5	95.3	97.9	96.8	91.2
France	67	35519.6	79	78.4	87.6	70.9
Germany	86.3	39058.8	82.5	85.8	81.3	80.3
Greece	12	25061.5	67.8	62.5	73.5	67.3
Hungary	10.4	19,754	73.5	72	80.8	67.6
Ireland	4.7	41739.4	91.9	86	96.9	93
Italy	64.7	30116.2	73.6	68.3	81.9	70.7
Latvia	2.3	18140.1	77.2	69.2	84.1	78.3
Lithuania	3.4	20088.6	71.4	73.4	68.9	72
Luxembourg	0.5	80679.1	83.5	92.7	84.8	73.1
Malta	0.4	26126.2	79	79.2	91.8	66.1
Netherlands	17.4	42321.6	92.8	91.5	97.9	88.9
Poland	39.7	20976.1	74.4	78.9	74.6	69.7
Portugal	11.2	22991.2	72.9	77.2	59.3	82.1
Romania	22.1	12838.4	66.3	59.5	79.2	60.1
Slovakia	5.6	24283.6	77.4	79.5	81.7	71
Slovenia	2.1	28647.7	78.4	77.3	82.1	75.8
Spain	49.2	30412.1	77.4	71.8	80	80.3
Sweden	10	41749.6	89.9	93.3	92.8	83.6
Sum.	466.6	822900.4	2151.7	2141.4	2265	2048.5
Ave.	17.281	30477.793	79.693	79.311	83.889	75.870

Source: Authors' work based on GII data

Table 13 GII's data matrix (Xij) for the European Union without the United Kingdom in 2013

THE EUROPEAN UNION WITHOUT THE UNITED KINGDOM						
2013 reported in 2014	Population (mn)	GDP (per capita)	Institutions	Political environment	Regulatory environment	Business environment
Austria	8.5	42596.6	88.8	90.4	96.4	79.5
Belgium	11.1	37880.5	87.9	86	91.4	86.2
Bulgaria	7.3	14499.1	68.5	63.2	76.5	65.7
Croatia	4.3	18190.9	69.8	70.9	71	67.4
Cyprus	1.1	25265.4	83.5	81.7	88.5	80.3
Czech Republic	10.5	27200.1	76.2	82.1	75.4	71
Denmark	5.6	37900.5	93.6	91.4	98.2	91.3
Estonia	1.3	23,144	78.6	79.2	85.8	70.7
Finland	5.4	35616.6	95.3	97.7	96.9	91.2
France	65.7	35,784	78.6	78	87	70.7
Germany	81.9	24,012	82.7	85.8	81.5	81
Greece	11.3	24,012	66.6	60.2	71.8	67.7
Hungary	9.9	20065.1	72.3	71.1	78.8	67
Ireland	4.6	39547.4	90.4	86.4	91.7	92.8
Italy	60.9	30289.4	73.2	67.9	81.1	70.7
Latvia	2	19119.5	76.8	72.1	83.9	74.2
Lithuania	3	22747.2	73.4	76.2	69.9	74
Luxembourg	0.5	78669.8	82.9	92.3	83.7	72.8
Malta	0.4	27840.2	79.2	80.6	91.6	65.5
Netherlands	16.8	41710.7	93.3	92.3	97.2	90.4
Poland	38.5	21214.3	74.7	78.8	74.4	71.1
Potugal	10.5	23068.4	77.3	78.6	71.1	82.2
Romania	21.3	13395.9	65.9	58.9	77.4	61.2
Slovakia	5.4	24605.3	74.5	80.5	72.9	70.1
Slovenia	2.1	27899.8	78.7	78.6	81.8	75.8
Spain	46.2	29851.1	74.8	71.8	77.7	75
Sweden	9.5	41188.4	89.7	92.5	93	83.7
Sum.	445.6	807314.2	2147.2	2145.2	2246.6	2049.2
Ave.	16.504	29900.526	79.526	79.452	83.207	75.896

Source: Authors' work based on GII data

Table 14 GII's data matrix (Xij) for the European Union without the United Kingdom in 2014

THE EUROPEAN UNION WITHOUT THE UNITED KINGDOM						
2014 reported in 2015	Population (mn)	GDP (per capita)	Institutions	Political environment	Regulatory environment	Business environment
Austria	8.5	43,796	88.7	90.5	95.9	79.5
Belgium	11.1	38826.5	83.3	85.6	80.2	84.2
Bulgaria	7.2	15031.3	69.7	57	75.8	76.3
Croatia	4.3	18354.7	71.8	69.7	71.5	74.1
Cyprus	1.2	24170.5	79.8	77.4	86.6	75.5
Czech Republic	10.7	28086.5	76.4	77.6	75.6	75.9
Denmark	5.6	38916.8	93.1	91.1	98.3	90
Estonia	1.3	23213.4	80.8	75	86.3	81
Finland	5.4	36122.1	95.8	98.9	96.9	91.8
France	64.6	36537.5	81.7	77.9	87	80.4
Germany	82.7	41248.1	83.2	84.8	81.5	83.4
Greece	11.1	24574.1	68.2	56.4	73.1	75
Hungary	9.9	20817.4	73.4	71.1	78.1	71
Ireland	4.7	40586.5	87.2	83.4	89.5	88.7
Italy	61.1	30,803	73.8	65.2	81.4	74.9
Latvia	2	20204.4	77.7	71.8	80.7	80.6
Lithuania	3	23978.1	73.6	75.3	70.2	75.3
Luxembourg	0.5	79,977	83.5	91.1	83.9	75.6
Malta	0.4	28,741	80.6	82.1	91.2	68.6
Netherlands	16.8	42585.9	91.9	90.5	97	88.2
Poland	38.2	22201.1	75.3	74.1	75.4	76.3
Portugal	10.6	23,671	80.6	78.5	77.1	86.1
Romania	21.6	13,932	69.7	53.7	78.5	76.9
Slovakia	5.5	25524.7	75.1	76.9	72.2	76.2
Slovenia	2.1	28372.8	79.5	77	81.7	79.7
Spain	47.1	30637.4	75.2	68.4	77.4	79.7
Sweden	9.6	42624.1	90	92.3	93.1	84.7
Sum.	446.8	843533.9	2159.6	2093.3	2236.1	2149.6
Ave.	16.548	31241.996	79.985	77.530	82.819	79.615

Source: Authors' work based on GII data

Table 15 GII's data matrix (Xij) for the European Union without the United Kingdom in 2015

THE EUROPEAN UNION WITHOUT THE UNITED KINGDOM						
2015 reported in 2016	Population (mn)	GDP (per capita)	Institutions	Political environment	Regulatory environment	Business environment
Austria	8.5	47249.9	87.6	88.8	94.4	79.6
Belgium	11.3	43,585	80.5	79.3	78.1	84.1
Bulgaria	7.1	19097.3	67.8	53.2	75.4	74.7
Croatia	4.2	21581.4	70.9	68.1	70.4	74.4
Cyprus	1.2	32785.5	81.6	75.3	86.3	83.3
Czech Republic	10.5	31549.5	76.1	77.2	74.3	76.7
Denmark	5.7	45709.4	91.6	87.8	96.6	90.3
Estonia	1.3	28591.8	81.2	74.9	87	81.6
Finland	5.5	41,120	94.3	94.9	95.9	92.1
France	64.4	41180.7	80.4	74.9	85	81.2
Germany	80.7	46893.2	84.1	86.6	81.6	84.1
Greece	11	26448.7	67.1	56.7	69.4	75.1
Hungary	9.9	26,222	71.3	67.1	75.4	71.4
Ireland	4.7	55532.9	88.1	86.4	88.8	89.2
Italy	59.8	35708.3	72.8	62.4	79.2	76.8
Latvia	2	24712.2	77.7	71.4	80.7	81.1
Lithuania	2.9	28359.1	73.3	74.5	69.7	75.7
Luxembourg	0.6	98987.2	82.1	91.2	81.5	73.5
Malta	0.4	35825.6	78.7	79.1	87.3	69.7
Netherlands	16.9	49165.8	91	89.4	95.7	87.9
Poland	38.6	26455.3	75.3	73.2	74	78.7
Portugal	10.3	27834.8	79.1	74.8	75.9	86.5
Romania	19.5	20786.9	69	51.9	77.6	77.5
Slovakia	5.4	29720.1	75	75.7	70.8	78.5
Slovenia	2.1	31007.4	80.8	74.8	80.5	87.2
Spain	46.1	34819.5	75.3	70.9	74.3	80.5
Sweden	9.8	47922.2	88.3	89.2	90.2	85.6
Sum.	440.4	998851.7	2141	2049.7	2196	2177
Ave.	16.311	36994.507	79.296	75.915	81.333	80.630

Source: Authors' work based on GII data

Table 16 GII's data matrix (Xij) for the European Union without the United Kingdom in 2016

THE EUROPEAN UNION WITHOUT THE UNITED KINGDOM						
2016 report in 2017	Population (mn)	GDP (per capita)	Institutions	Political environment	Regulatory environment	Business environment
Austria	8.6	47249.9	87.1	86.3	93	82
Belgium	11.4	43,585	80.5	78.8	77.4	85.4
Bulgaria	7.1	19097.3	67.1	56	72.4	73
Croatia	4.2	21581.4	69.3	66.5	67.1	74.3
Cyprus	1.2	32785.5	81	72.9	84.6	85.7
Czech Republic	10.5	31549.5	77.6	78.1	73.4	81.3
Denmark	5.7	45709.4	91.4	87.6	96.4	90.3
Estonia	1.3	28591.8	81.1	74.5	85.8	82.9
Finland	5.5	41,120	92.2	89	95.1	92.4
France	64.7	41180.7	80.7	74.8	84.2	82.9
Germany	80.7	46893.2	83.5	84	80.6	85.9
Greece	10.9	26448.7	65.2	53.4	66.9	75.2
Hungary	9.8	26,222	70.7	68.2	72.9	71
Ireland	4.7	55532.9	87.6	84	88.8	90.1
Italy	59.8	35708.3	71.9	63	76.9	75.9
Latvia	2	24712.2	77.8	72.8	78.1	82.6
Lithuania	2.9	28359.1	74.1	76.9	69.4	75.9
Luxembourg	0.6	98987.2	82.6	92.2	81.2	74.3
Malta	0.4	35825.6	77.6	76.5	86.3	70.1
Netherlands	17	49165.8	88.2	87.9	88.1	88.7
Poland	38.6	26455.3	75.6	73.9	71.9	81.1
Portugal	10.3	27834.8	80.8	79.4	75.8	87.3
Romania	19.4	20786.9	69	54.9	75.3	76.8
Slovakia	5.4	29720.1	74.5	75.4	68.3	79.9
Slovenia	2.1	31007.4	80.9	76.7	78.7	87.3
Spain	46.1	34819.5	75.9	71.6	72.7	83.3
Sweden	9.9	47922.2	88.3	88	90.5	86.5
Sum.	440.8	998851.7	2132.2	2043.3	2151.8	2202.1
Ave.	16.326	72239.019	154.715	148.159	155.948	160.081

Source: Authors' work based on GII data

Table 17 GII's data matrix (Xij) for the European Union without the United Kingdom in 2017

THE EUROPEAN UNION WITHOUT THE UNITED KINGDOM						
2017 report in 2018	Population (mn)	GDP (per capita)	Institutions	Political environment	Regulatory environment	Business environment
Austria	8.7	49868.7	85.6	83	93.4	80.3
Belgium	11.4	46553.1	82.2	77.3	81.3	87.9
Bulgaria	7.1	21686.6	45	53	35	52
Croatia	4.2	24423.5	69.2	64.9	71.9	70.8
Cyprus	1.2	37,023	80.3	72.3	83.7	84.8
Czech Republic	10.6	35512.4	78.5	76.8	76.5	82.1
Denmark	5.7	49,883	91.1	89.4	95.1	88.7
Estonia	1.3	31749.5	81.2	75.5	87.7	80.4
Finland	5.5	44332.6	92.8	89.7	95.9	93
France	65	43760.8	81.2	74.4	85.6	83.6
Germany	82.1	50425.2	85.9	86.4	84.3	86.9
Greece	11.2	27,737	65.4	54.1	68.3	73.9
Hungary	9.7	29473.7	70.4	64.7	75.3	71.2
Ireland	4.8	75538.4	85.7	80.8	88.9	87.5
Italy	59.4	38140.3	74.9	63	78.4	83.2
Latvia	1.9	27644.1	76.5	71.2	81.6	76.6
Lithuania	2.9	32298.9	73.6	75.8	73.7	71.2
Luxembourg	0.6	106373.8	80.7	90.5	84.4	67.1
Malta	0.4	41944.8	74.6	75.7	86.8	61.5
Netherlands	17	53634.6	90	89	91.7	89.3
Poland	38.2	29521.3	74	67.1	74.6	80.2
Portugal	10.3	30416.5	81.2	79.7	78.3	85.5
Romania	19.7	24508.4	67.8	50.9	77.8	74.7
Slovakia	5.4	33025.5	74	71.2	74.3	76.5
Slovenia	2.1	34407.1	82.3	77.9	81.5	87.6
Spain	46.4	38,286	78.2	73.9	78	82.7
Sweden	9.9	51474.8	89.6	88.8	93	87.1
Sum.	442.7	1109643.6	2111.9	2017	2177	2146.3
Ave.	16.396	41097.911	78.219	74.704	80.630	79.493

Source: Authors' work based on GII data

Table 18 GII's data matrix (Xij) for the European Union without the United Kingdom in 2018

THE EUROPEAN UNION WITHOUT THE UNITED KINGDOM						
2018 report in 2019	Population (mn)	GDP (per capita)	Institutions	Political environment	Regulatory environment	Business environment
Austria	8.8	52137.4	86	83.9	93.7	80.3
Belgium	11.5	48244.7	82	77	80.4	88.5
Bulgaria	7	23155.6	68.3	58.1	75.5	71.5
Croatia	4.2	26221.4	69.3	66.7	71.7	69.4
Cyprus	1.2	39973.2	80.3	72.8	84.8	83.3
Czech Republic	10.6	37,371	78.6	75.6	78.4	81.8
Denmark	5.8	52120.5	91.7	91.1	95.3	88.8
Estonia	1.3	34095.8	81.7	78.3	87.8	78.9
Finland	5.5	46429.5	93.6	92.2	96.1	92.6
France	65.2	45775.1	83.2	80.4	85.5	83.7
Germany	82.3	52558.7	86.4	88.1	84.4	86.9
Greece	11.1	29,123	67.2	59.5	68.2	73.9
Hungary	9.7	31902.7	71.6	67.4	75.8	71.5
Ireland	4.8	78784.8	85.5	81.7	87.3	87.5
Italy	59.3	2398.2	75.3	63.7	79	83.4
Latvia	1.9	29901.3	77.2	72.5	82.2	76.9
Lithuania	2.9	34825.8	76	75.5	82.6	70
Luxembourg	0.6	106704.9	80.7	90.4	84.5	67.1
Malta	0.4	45605.9	75.2	75.9	88.2	61.5
Netherlands	17.1	56383.2	90.9	91.4	91.9	89.3
Poland	38.1	31938.7	73.6	68.2	72.9	79.7
Portugal	10.3	32006.4	81.8	81.2	78.8	85.5
Romania	19.6	26446.7	67.1	51.6	77.9	71.9
Slovakia	5.4	35129.8	73.1	71.6	73.2	74.5
Slovenia	2.1	36745.9	82.3	78	80.7	88.3
Spain	46.4	40138.8	78.1	73.5	77.9	83
Sweden	10	52984.1	90.1	91.1	92	87.1
Sum.	443.1	1129103.1	2146.8	2057.4	2226.7	2156.8
Ave.	16.411	41818.633	79.511	76.200	82.470	79.881

Source: Authors' work based on GII data

Table 19 GII's data matrix (Xij) for the G20 economies in 2010

THE G20 COUNTRIES						
2010 reported in 2011 (Xij)	Population (mn)	GDP (per capita)	Institutions	Political environment	Regulatory environment	Business environment
Argentina	40.7	14538.3	51.1	55.2	43.2	55
Australia	21.5	39230.7	91	88.7	97.8	86.5
Brazil	195.4	10412.1	54.1	64.8	52.9	44.7
Canada	33.9	37945.6	93.3	91.5	96.3	92
China	1354.1	6828	51.7	32.8	53.5	68.8
France	62.6	33655.5	77.9	80.5	74.3	78.8
Germany	82.1	36267.4	83.5	88.1	81.1	81.2
India	1214.5	3270.1	52.3	42.2	56.6	58.2
Indonesia	232.5	4198.8	53.4	44.3	45.8	70.1
Italy	60.1	31908.6	71.1	72.3	67.5	73.6
Japan	127	32452.8	83.8	89.2	84.4	77.8
Mexico	110.6	14335.1	58.6	44.1	51.3	80.4
Russia	140.4	18962.6	51.8	37.9	40.3	77.3
Suadi Arabia	26.2	23395.4	67.5	39.8	67.4	95.2
South Africa	50.5	10277.8	71	66.4	61.8	84.6
Rep. of Korea	48.5	27168.5	77.4	73.9	73.3	85.2
Turkey	75.7	13,885	62.1	43.5	60.5	82.1
United Kingdom	61.9	36495.8	86.4	79.8	92.7	86.6
United States	317.6	45989.2	86.5	80.3	93.7	85.5
European Union	501.800	30278.563	80.707	81.752	77.670	82.689
SUM	4757.60	471495.86	1405.21	1297.05	1372.07	1546.29
Ave. (Xoj)	237.88	23574.79	70.26	64.85	68.60	77.31

Source: Authors' work based on GII data

Table 20 GII's data matrix (Xij) for the G20 economies in 2011

THE G20 COUNTRIES						
2011 reported in 2012 (Xij)	Population (mn)	GDP (per capita)	Institutions	Political environment	Regulatory environment	Business environment
Argentina	40.9	17376.1	44.9	61.4	44.6	78.8
Australia	22.5	40836.4	90	88.1	93.5	88.4
Brazil	194.9	11845.8	50.4	59.6	71	20.6
Canada	34.4	40457.6	95	91.7	95.5	97.8
China	1348.1	8394.1	39.1	30.8	51.9	34.7
France	63.2	35048.8	82.7	82.6	89.7	76
Germany	81.4	37935.5	76.7	87.3	82.2	60.4
India	1206.9	3703.5	38.4	42.8	64.3	8.1
Indonesia	240.5	4668.1	25.4	42.4	19	14.8
Italy	60.6	30165.5	70.2	70.4	82.8	57.5
Japan	127.9	34362.1	79	86	89.8	61.1
Mexico	109.7	15121.4	55.9	45.2	59.1	63.5
Russia	142.4	16687.4	49.1	41.1	57.9	48.4
Suadi Arabia	28.2	24056.7	63.8	45.2	65.5	80.8
South Africa	50.6	10977.1	69.7	66.6	76.7	65.9
South Korea	49	31753.5	73.8	74.9	68	78.6
Turkey	72.2	14615.5	50	45.8	56.4	47.7
United Kingdom	62.6	35974.4	90.4	83	97.7	90.6
United States	312.9	48147.2	85.1	78.5	94.4	82.5
European Union	504.600	30486.686	77.814	81.557	84.546	66.756
SUM	4753.500	492613.386	1307.414	1304.957	1444.546	1222.956
Ave. (Xoj)	237.675	24630.669	65.371	65.248	72.227	61.148

Source: Authors' work based on GII data

Table 21 GII's data matrix (Xij) for the G20 economies in 2012

THE G20 COUNTRIES						
2012 reported in 2013 (Xij)	Population (mn)	GDP (per capita)	Institutions	Political environment	Regulatory environment	Business environment
Argentina	42.2	18205.1	50.7	59.8	43.2	49.1
Australia	23.8	42354.2	89.4	86.1	94.5	87.5
Brazil	201.5	12038.5	53.8	56.9	67.9	36.6
Canada	36.1	41506.9	93.3	89.3	95	95.4
China	1374	9146.4	48.3	39.2	50.3	55.5
France	67	35519.6	79	78.4	87.6	70.9
Germany	86.3	39058.8	82.5	85.8	81.3	80.3
India	1267.6	3851.3	51.9	44.4	63.6	47.7
Indonesia	246.8	4957.6	37.2	45.6	17.7	48.5
Italy	64.7	30116.2	73.6	68.3	81.9	70.7
Japan	135.2	36179.4	83.5	80	88.6	81.9
Mexico	117.8	15300.3	61.8	50.3	59.2	75.8
Russia	147	17697.5	56	42.9	57.2	68
Suadi Arabia	28.9	25722.4	58.4	42.8	63.2	69.3
South Africa	51.1	11302.2	70.1	63.5	76.4	70.4
Republic of Korea	49.7	32,431	76	73.2	67.7	87.2
Turkey	75.2	15028.6	55.8	48.8	55.6	63.1
United Kingdom	65.8	36727.8	88.4	79.7	95.7	89.9
United States	327.9	49802.1	86	79.3	94.6	84.2
European Union	532.400	30701.007	80.004	79.325	84.311	76.371
SUM	4941.000	507646.907	1375.704	1293.625	1425.511	1408.371
Ave. (Xoj)	247.050	25382.345	68.785	64.681	71.276	70.419

Source: Authors' work based on GII data

Table 22 GII's data matrix (Xij) for the G20 economies in 2013

THE G20 COUNTRIES						
2013 reported in 2014 (Xij)	Population (mn)	GDP (per capita)	Institutions	Political environment	Regulatory environment	Business environment
Argentina	41.1	18749.3	49.1	58.8	40.2	48.5
Australia	22.7	43073.1	88.9	86.3	93.7	86.9
Brazil	198.7	12220.9	53.9	57.4	66.2	38.2
Canada	34.9	43471.7	92.7	89.1	94.9	94.1
China	1350.7	9844	48.3	40.1	49.3	55.5
France	65.7	35,784	78.6	78	87	70.7
Germany	81.9	40006.7	82.7	85.8	81.5	81
India	1236.7	4077.1	50.8	43.3	62.2	47
Indonesia	246.9	5214.1	38.1	47.9	17.9	48.5
Italy	60.9	30289.4	73.2	67.9	81.1	70.7
Japan	127.6	36899.4	84.1	80.5	90.2	81.7
Mexico	120.8	15562.6	61.8	51.1	59	75.2
Russia	143.5	17884.5	56.4	43.9	56.5	68.9
Saudi Arabia	28.3	31244.7	60	46.4	64.6	69.1
South Africa	51.2	11259.1	69.9	63.5	75.5	70.8
Republic of Korea	50	33189.1	75.8	72.7	66.8	87.8
Turkey	74	15352.6	54.9	47.2	54.9	62.7
United Kingdom	61.2	37306.6	88.6	80.2	95.7	90
United States	313.9	53,101	86.2	81.4	93.2	84
European Union	506.800	30165.029	79.850	79.479	83.654	76.400
SUM	4817.500	524694.929	1373.850	1300.979	1414.054	1407.700
Ave. (Xoj)	240.875	26234.746	68.693	65.049	70.703	70.385

Source: Authors' work based on GII data

Table 23 GII's data matrix (Xij) for the G20 economies in 2014

THE G20 COUNTRIES						
2014 reported in 2015 (Xij)	Population (mn)	GDP (per capita)	Institutions	Political environment	Regulatory environment	Business environment
Argentina	41.8	18917.3	48	49.6	40.3	54.2
Australia	23.6	44345.9	89.3	87.3	93.8	86
Brazil	202	12525.7	55.8	48.3	66.1	53.1
Canada	35.5	44655.7	92.7	89.5	94.9	93.7
China	1393.8	10694.7	54	45.6	49.6	66.7
France	64.6	36537.5	81.7	77.9	87	80.4
Germany	82.7	41248.1	83.2	84.8	81.5	83.4
India	1267.4	4306.9	50	35.5	62.4	52.2
Indonesia	252.8	5499	39.8	43.4	19.6	56.4
Italy	61.1	30,803	73.8	65.2	81.4	74.9
Japan	127	38052.7	86.5	86.5	90.6	82.4
Mexico	123.8	16111.5	61.5	47.8	59.2	77.5
Russia	142.5	18407.8	56.6	38.6	56.9	74.2
Suadi Arabia	29.4	32340.1	60.4	48.5	64.8	67.9
South Africa	53.1	11542.9	71.6	57.9	76.1	80.9
South Korea	49.5	34795.4	76.1	70.9	67.4	90.2
Turkey	75.8	15767.3	55.8	43	55.7	68.9
United Kingdom	63.5	38710.5	87.3	78.6	95.4	87.9
United States	322.6	54979.9	86.8	80.6	92.4	87.4
European Union	510.300	31596.171	80.246	77.568	83.268	79.911
SUM	4922.800	541838.071	1391.146	1257.068	1418.368	1498.211
Ave. (Xoj)	246.140	27091.904	69.557	62.853	70.918	74.911

Source: Authors' work based on GII data

Table 24 GII's data matrix (Xij) for the G20 economies in 2015

THE G20 COUNTRIES						
2015 reported in 2016 (Xij)	Population (mn)	GDP (per capita)	Institutions	Political environment	Regulatory environment	Business environment
Argentina	43.4	22553.6	47.2	49.4	38.5	53.7
Australia	24	47389.1	88.8	86.5	92.9	86.8
Brazil	207.8	15614.5	55.3	48.6	64.6	52.6
Canada	35.9	45552.6	91.7	90	94.1	90.6
China	1376	14107.4	55.2	49.9	50	65.8
France	64.4	41180.7	80.4	74.9	85	81.2
Germany	80.7	46893.2	84.1	86.6	81.6	84.1
India	1311.1	6161.6	50.7	36.2	61.9	54.1
Indonesia	257.6	11125.9	41.6	46.2	20.9	57.7
Italy	59.8	35708.3	72.8	62.4	79.2	76.8
Japan	126.6	38054.2	87.1	88.9	90	82.4
Mexico	127	17534.4	60.5	44.1	59	78.5
Russia	14.5	25410.9	57.9	39.4	56.8	77.4
saudi Arabia	31.5	53624.4	57.9	51.1	63.3	59.3
South Africa	54.5	13165.2	69.1	54.6	74.6	78.1
South Korea	50.3	36,511	75.4	69.6	66.7	89.7
Turkey	78.7	20437.8	54.6	43.1	54.2	66.6
United Kingdom	64.7	41158.9	87.6	78.9	94.7	89.3
United States	321.8	55805.2	85.7	78.9	90.9	87.4
European Union	505.100	37143.236	79.593	76.021	81.811	80.939
SUM	4835.400	625132.136	1383.193	1255.321	1400.711	1493.039
Ave. (Xoj)	241.770	31256.607	69.160	62.766	70.036	74.652

Source: Authors' work based on GII data

Table 25 GII's data matrix (Xij) for the G20 economies in 2016

THE G20 COUNTRIES						
2016 reported in 2017 (Xij)	Population (mn)	GDP (per capita)	Institutions	Political environment	Regulatory environment	Business environment
Argentina	43.8	22553.6	46.4	51.1	36.3	51.7
Australia	24.3	47389.1	87.4	83.9	91.2	86.9
Brazil	209.6	15614.5	51.8	46	60.2	49.1
Canada	36.3	45552.6	91	90.7	92.7	89.5
China	1382.3	14107.4	54.8	51.6	47	65.8
France	64.7	41180.7	80.7	74.8	84.2	82.9
Germany	80.7	46893.2	83.5	84	80.6	85.9
India	1326.8	6161.6	51.4	43.1	59.8	51.2
Indonesia	260.6	11125.9	41.2	42.9	16.7	64
Italy	59.8	35708.3	71.9	63	76.9	75.9
Japan	126.3	38054.2	87.4	87.9	89	85.5
Mexico	128.6	17534.4	58.5	45.1	55.6	74.9
Russia	143.4	25410.9	56.1	37.9	52.5	77.7
Suadi Arabia	32.2	53624.4	52.4	49.1	56.9	51.4
South Africa	55	13165.2	66.3	54.3	71.4	73.2
South Korea	50.5	36,511	74.5	67.4	65.5	90.5
Turkey	79.6	20437.8	50.6	40.5	50.5	60.9
United Kingdom	65.1	41158.9	88.4	82.1	94.1	89.1
United States	324.1	55805.2	86.2	80.3	90.4	88.1
European Union	505.900	37143.236	79.307	75.907	80.211	81.829
SUM	4999.600	625132.136	1359.807	1251.607	1351.711	1476.029
Ave.(Xoj)	249.980	31256.607	67.990	62.580	67.586	73.801

Source: Authors' work based on GII data

Table 26 GII's data matrix (Xij) for the G20 economies in 2017

THE G20 COUNTRIES						
2017 reported in 2018 (Xij)	Population (mn)	GDP (per capita)	Institutions	Political environment	Regulatory environment	Business environment
Argentina	44.3	20875.8	54.7	56.3	49.6	58.2
Australia	24.5	50333.7	88.7	85.3	93.1	87.6
Brazil	209.3	15602.5	55.3	45.3	64.4	56.3
Canada	36.6	48265.2	91.7	91	94.2	89.9
China	1409.5	16660.3	59.4	53.6	54	70.6
France	65	43760.8	81.2	74.4	85.6	83.6
Germany	82.1	50425.2	85.9	86.4	84.3	86.9
India	1339.2	7182.8	55.9	46	63.6	58.1
Indonesia	264	12377.5	50.9	49	30.9	72.8
Italy	59.4	38140.3	74.9	63	78.4	83.2
Japan	127.5	42831.5	89.8	89.8	90.6	88.9
Mexico	129.2	19902.8	62.3	48.2	59.7	79.1
Russia	144	27834.1	57.8	41.2	56.7	75.4
Suadi Arabia	32.9	54777.4	51.9	51.9	63.7	40
South Africa	56.7	13544.6	65.6	55.1	72.8	68.8
Republic of Korea	51	39433.8	78.5	70.7	72.2	92.6
Turkey	80.7	26892.9	51	37	55.6	60.4
United Kingdom	66.2	44117.7	87.4	81.2	93.4	87.4
United States	324.5	59501.1	87.7	78.9	93	91.2
European Union	508.900	41205.761	78.546	74.936	81.086	79.775
SUM	5055.500	673665.761	1409.146	1279.236	1436.886	1510.775
Ave.(Xoj)	252.775	33683.288	70.457	63.962	71.844	75.539

Source: Authors' work based on GII data

Table 27 GII's data matrix (Xij) for the G20 economies in 2018

THE G20 COUNTRIES						
2018 reported in 2019 (Xij)	Population (mn)	GDP (per capita)	Institutions	Political environment	Regulatory environment	Business environment
Argentina	44.7	20537.1	56.7	57	51.5	61.6
Australia	24.8	52373.5	88.8	85.7	93.1	87.7
Brazil	210.9	16154.3	58.9	48.6	63.8	64.4
Canada	37	49651.2	92.3	92	95.1	89.8
China	1415	18109.8	64.1	63	54.6	74.7
France	65.2	45775.1	83.2	80.4	85.5	83.7
Germany	82.3	52558.7	86.4	88.1	84.4	86.9
India	1354.1	7873.7	59.5	53	64.5	60.9
Indonesia	266.8	13229.5	53.2	53.9	31.1	74.6
Italy	59.3	39,637	75.3	63.7	79	83.4
Japan	127.2	44227.2	89.9	88.2	91.7	89.8
Mexico	13.8	20601.7	62.8	51.1	59	78.4
Russia	144	29266.9	60.9	50.2	56.5	75.8
Suadi Arabia	33.6	55943.9	51.3	53.2	60.7	40
South Africa	57.4	13675.3	65.9	57.2	72.6	67.9
Republic of Korea	51.2	41350.6	79.7	77.2	72.4	89.4
Turkey	81.9	27956.1	57.4	53.8	54.1	64.5
United Kingdom	66.6	45704.6	87.1	80.2	93.7	87.4
United States	326.8	62605.6	89.7	84.2	93.9	91.1
European Union	509.700	41957.418	79.782	76.343	82.871	80.150
SUM	4972.300	699189.218	1442.882	1357.043	1440.071	1532.150
Ave.(Xoj)	248.615	34959.461	72.144	67.852	72.004	76.608

Source: Authors' work based on GII data

process of data matrix standardization. Consequently, standard matrices are formed which contain dimensionless elements Z_{ij}:

$$S_j = \sqrt{\sum_{i=1}^{n} \left(X_{ij} - \overline{X_j} \right)^2 / n} \tag{2}$$

$$Z_{ij} = \left(X_{ij} - X_{oj} \right) / \tag{3}$$

"X_{ij}" is a data matrix; "X_{oj}" is an average matrix, as in Eq. (1); and "S_j" is a standard deviation for the "j" indicators derived from the GII data report in the years 2010 to 2018. So, in this data analysis, "i" denotes the European Union and G20 economies from 2010 to 2018. The corresponding standard matrices were computed. Moreover, for the standard matrices, the average and standard deviation of the data (in each group and year) were calculated to have an average of zero and a standard deviation of unity in the *Z* matrices (due to elimination of discrepancies between the indicators' units and generation of scale-free indices). Thus, the "*Z*" matrices could be desirably controlled to contain the required elements; these variables can be affected by core changes that are effective in the rule of institutions (Bruce 2012).

3.3 Step 3: Computation of Compound Distance Matrices

The compound distances, D_{ab}, i.e., the distances between any two economies "a" and "b," for the European Union and G20 economies, are calculated by:

$$D_{\mathrm{ab}} = \sqrt{\sum_{n}^{i=1} \left(Z_{aj} - Z_{bj} \right)^2} \tag{4}$$

It is noted that:

$$D_{\mathrm{aa}} = 0, \qquad D_{\mathrm{bb}} = 0, \qquad D_{\mathrm{ab}} = D_{\mathrm{ba}}$$

It is also noted that the *compound distance matrices* "*D*" are symmetric, with zero diagonal elements, and each element D_{ab} shows the "distance" between two economies (a, b).

At this stage, the compound distance matrices "*D*" were computed for the European Union (once with and then without the United Kingdom) and for the G20 economies. Tables 28 through 54 (in the Appendix) show the results. Each element D_{ab} of matrix *D* represents a distance value between two economies (a, b). Then the smallest value in each row can represent the shortest distance between two economies, i.e., the economies corresponding to the intersecting row and column.

3.4 Step 4: Assignment of the Shortest Distances

At this stage of taxonomic analysis, the elements of the zero diagonal matrices "*D*" represent the distances between interrelated economies in rows and columns. That is, in "*D*" matrices, each element shows the distances between the economies corresponding to the intersecting rows and columns. Thus, the lowest value in each row is marked as the shortest distance for the related economy (to another) in the year of consideration. Thereby, the shortest distance between two economies "a" and "b" can indicate the closest proximity between them (economy "b" is termed a "model" for economy "a," and economy "a" is labeled a "shade").

As will be explained in the following steps, in this research, the shortest distances between the economies under study are computed for the years 2010–2018.

Additionally, the European Union is considered once with and then without the United Kingdom. It should also be pointed out that in 2010, no data was reported by the GII for Malta; hence the European Union was considered with 27 members (including the United Kingdom) and 26 members (excluding the United Kingdom).

3.5 Step 5: Depiction of Optimal Chart

In this step, the shortest distances can be available to depict an optimal chart by connecting the economies with shortest distances between them, namely, having most commonalities. For this purpose, an optimal chart depiction would consist of drawing a vector towards the "model" economy with the vector length equal to the shortest distance between them.

For marking out the homogeneous economies, basically the upper and lower limit distances $d(+)$ and $d(-)$ are computed from Eqs. (5) and (6), where d and S_d are the mean standard deviation of the shortest distances:

$$d(+) = d + 2S_d \tag{5}$$

$$d(-) = d - 2S_d \tag{6}$$

With respect to the central limit theorem that 95.45% of the population lies within a band around the mean, in a Gaussian (normal) distribution with a width of four standard deviations, that is, $-2S_d$ to $+2S_d$ (Le Quesne 1969; Phillips 1983; Faghih and Sazegar 2019).

The values of $d(+)$ and $d(-)$ were computed for the European Union economies, once with and then without the United Kingdom, and G20 economies in the period 2010–2018 from Eqs. (5) and (6). It was examined that the shortest distances between the economies should not be out of upper $d(+)$ and lower $d(-)$ bounds; that is, if an economy under study was found out of the latter range, it had to be eliminated and then the procedure was iterated for the other economies until the remaining economies were settled within the aforementioned range. The purpose of this iterative procedure is to obtain a homogenous group of economies that can be compared with each other.

If computation of compound distance matrices does not lead to homogenous matrices in the initial stage, then they can be obtained by the elimination and reiteration procedure. Tables 28, 29, 30, 31, 32, 33, 34, 35, and 36 (in the Appendix) show the compound distance matrices "*D*" for the European Union (including the United Kingdom) during the years 2010–2018.

Moreover, Tables 37, 38, 39, 40, 41, 42, 43, 44, and 45 (in the Appendix) also show the corresponding results for the European Union, excluding the United Kingdom, during the years 2010–2018.

Furthermore, Tables 46, 47, 48, 49, 50, 51, 52, 53, and 54 (in the Appendix) exhibit the corresponding results for the Group of Twenty (G20) in the years 2010–2018.

Table 28 Compound distance matrix for the European Union economies in 2010 ("D" matrix)

2010	Austria	Belgium	Bulgaria	Croatia	Cyprus	Czech Republic	Denmark	Estonia	Finland	France	Germany	Hungary	Irland	Italy	Latvia	Lithuania	Netherlands	Poland	Portugal	Romania	Slovakia	Slovenia	Spain	United Kingdom	shortest distance
Austria		1.484	5.413	5.255	3.384	2.056	3.252	3.333	1.756	3.471	3.484	3.409	2.835	4.621	4.541	3.866	1.986	3.604	3.228	6.034	3.056	3.793	4.835	3.465	1.484
Belgium	1.484		4.3047289	4.204	1.952	1.443	2.625	2.394	1.553	2.874	3.075	2.447	2.023	4.157	3.531	3.014	1.194	3.194	2.119	5.058	2.159	2.610	4.675	2.556	1.194
Bulgaria	5.413	4.304729		1.392	3.065	3.537	5.896	2.380	5.215	3.967	5.208	2.073	5.494	3.909	1.007	1.872	4.977	3.077	2.417	1.391	2.409	2.546	4.631	4.878	1.007
Croatia	5.255	4.204	1.392		3.170	3.708	5.900	2.386	4.976	3.786	5.082	2.381	5.417	3.731	1.406	1.864	4.689	3.194	2.217	1.628	2.428	1.994	4.679	5.077	1.392
Cyprus	3.384	1.952	3.065	3.170		2.204	3.022	1.920	2.824	3.465	3.985	1.981	2.497	4.483	2.559	2.490	2.388	3.560	1.630	4.114	1.954	1.693	5.191	2.949	1.630
Czech Republic	2.056	1.443	3.537	3.708	2.204		3.558	1.642	2.392	2.783	3.369	1.475	3.194	3.731	2.695	2.116	2.488	2.152	1.727	4.294	1.305	2.597	4.089	3.061	1.305
Denmark	3.252	2.625	5.896	5.900	3.022	3.558		4.029	1.994	4.969	4.399	4.347	0.944	6.538	5.237	4.818	2.050	5.425	3.896	6.947	4.171	3.986	7.211	3.284	0.944
Estonia	3.333	2.394	2.380	2.386	1.920	1.642	4.029		2.970	3.220	4.046	0.857	3.712	3.951	1.438	0.802	3.050	2.337	0.759	3.314	0.648	1.417	4.648	3.818	0.648
Finland	1.756	1.553	5.215	4.976	2.824	2.392	1.994	2.970		3.887	3.620	3.382	1.826	5.333	4.355	3.690	1.166	4.095	2.862	6.059	3.022	3.129	5.969	3.353	1.166
France	3.471	2.874	3.967	3.786	3.465	2.783	4.969	3.220	3.887		1.711	2.824	4.425	1.807	3.548	3.237	3.290	2.088	2.684	3.973	2.791	3.292	3.075	2.661	1.711
Germany	3.484	3.075	5.208	5.082	3.985	3.369	4.399	4.046	3.620	1.711		3.836	4.041	3.407	4.735	4.317	3.033	3.309	3.549	5.438	3.779	4.089	4.525	2.014	1.711
Hungary	3.409	2.447	2.073	2.381	1.981	1.475	4.347	0.857	3.382	2.824	3.836		3.958	3.388	1.250	0.918	3.297	1.846	1.012	2.917	0.549	1.863	3.989	3.544	0.549
Irland	2.835	2.023	5.494	5.417	2.497	3.194	0.944	3.712	1.826	4.425	4.041	3.958		5.919	4.850	4.465	1.446	5.036	3.460	6.464	3.751	3.523	6.569	2.913	0.944
Italy	4.621	4.157	3.909	3.731	4.483	3.731	6.538	3.951	5.333	1.807	3.407	3.388	5.919		3.712	3.619	4.804	2.248	3.538	3.358	3.427	4.098	1.726	4.235	1.726
Latvia	4.541	3.531	1.007	1.406	2.559	2.695	5.237	1.438	4.355	3.548	4.735	1.250	4.850	3.712		0.888	4.242	2.480	1.609	1.995	1.490	1.916	4.396	4.501	0.888
Lithuania	3.866	3.014	1.872	1.864	2.490	2.116	4.818	0.802	3.690	3.237	4.317	0.918	4.465	3.619	0.888		3.717	2.050	1.150	2.638	0.896	1.702	4.310	4.277	0.802
Netherlands	1.986	1.194	4.977	4.689	2.388	2.488	2.050	3.050	1.166	3.290	3.033	3.297	1.446	4.804	4.242	3.717		4.013	2.671	5.731	2.983	2.850	5.565	2.609	1.166
Poland	3.604	3.194	3.077	3.194	3.560	2.152	5.425	2.337	4.095	2.088	3.309	1.846	5.036	2.248	2.480	2.050	4.013		2.298	3.160	1.911	3.171	2.860	3.865	1.846
Portugal	3.228	2.119	2.417	2.217	1.630	1.727	3.896	0.759	2.862	2.684	3.549	1.012	3.460	3.538	1.609	1.150	2.671	2.298		3.214	0.771	0.984	4.415	3.366	0.771
Romania	6.034	5.058	1.391	1.628	4.114	4.294	6.947	3.314	6.059	3.973	5.438	2.917	6.464	3.358	1.995	2.638	5.731	3.160	3.214		3.180	3.362	4.122	5.486	1.391
Slovakia	3.056	2.159	2.409	2.428	1.954	1.305	4.171	0.648	3.022	2.791	3.779	0.549	3.751	3.427	1.490	0.896	2.983	1.911	0.771	3.180		1.638	4.035	3.610	0.549
Slovenia	3.793	2.610	2.546	1.994	1.693	2.597	3.986	1.417	3.129	3.292	4.089	1.863	3.523	4.098	1.916	1.702	2.850	3.171	0.984	3.362	1.638		5.084	3.842	0.984
Spain	4.835	4.675	4.631	4.679	5.191	4.089	7.211	4.648	5.969	3.075	4.525	3.989	6.569	1.726	4.396	4.310	5.565	2.860	4.415	4.122	4.035	5.084		5.083	1.726
United Kingdom	3.465	2.556	4.878	5.077	2.949	3.061	3.284	3.818	3.353	2.661	2.014	3.544	2.913	4.235	4.501	4.277	2.609	3.865	3.366	5.486	3.610	3.842	5.083		2.014

Source: Authors' work based on GII data

Table 29 Compound distance matrix for the European Union economies in 2011 ("D" matrix)

2011	Austria	Belgium	Bulgaria	Croatia	Cyprus	Czech Republic	Denmark	Estonia	Finland	France	Germany	Greece	Hungary	Irland	Italy	Latvia	Lithuania	Netherlands	Poland	Portugal	Romania	Slovakia	Slovenia	Spain	Sweden	United Kingdom	shortest distance
Austria		5.243708	3.644928	4.963649	3.535568	3.0184094	2.920	2.968	2.004	3.124	3.691	3.097	4.663	3.302	3.192	4.119	4.346	2.531	3.248	4.539	4.207	4.899	2.746	2.947	3.110	3.377	2.004
Belgium	5.243708		3.495	4.392566	2.601	3.104	2.134	2.452	0.919	2.722	3.502	3.322	4.321	2.187	2.947	3.694	3.797	2.067	3.556	3.973	4.255	4.563	2.254	2.885	2.435	2.556	0.919
Bulgaria	3.644928	3.495		1.005	2.809	3.340	4.525	4.520	4.292	5.884	4.905	3.315	0.999	4.339	4.648	1.090	1.577	4.140	4.192	2.791	2.213	1.432	2.774	3.300	3.604	5.866	0.999
Croatia	4.963649	4.392566	1.005		4.041	2.619	4.086	3.851	3.790	5.238	4.457	2.402	1.458	3.978	4.123	1.270	0.493	3.793	3.710	1.667	2.000	1.274	1.986	2.800	3.290	5.361	0.493
Cyprus	3.535568	2.601	2.809	4.041		3.923	2.244	2.095	1.230	3.359	4.081	3.388	3.901	2.171	3.340	3.081	3.288	2.481	3.656	3.677	3.938	4.223	2.039	3.159	2.554	3.103	1.230
Czech Republic	3.018409	3.104	3.340	2.619	3.923		4.128	3.570	3.660	4.581	3.854	0.996	2.547	4.335	3.514	2.348	2.016	3.638	2.690	2.257	1.676	2.403	1.968	2.099	3.521	5.050	0.996
Denmark	2.920	2.134	4.525	4.086	2.244	4.128		3.529	2.016	2.946	4.615	4.690	5.778	3.039	3.870	4.996	5.159	3.333	4.518	5.287	5.560	6.086	3.684	4.344	3.784	2.590	2.016
Estonia	2.968	2.452	4.520	3.851	2.095	3.570	3.529		2.627	3.791	4.062	2.349	2.937	3.144	3.210	1.902	2.207	3.038	2.744	2.840	2.443	3.297	1.476	2.588	2.994	3.895	1.476
Finland	2.004	0.919	4.292	3.790	1.230	3.660	2.016	2.627		2.864	4.397	4.159	5.616	3.323	3.557	4.810	4.938	3.347	3.958	5.019	5.131	5.897	3.424	4.004	3.857	2.659	0.919
France	3.124	2.722	5.884	5.238	3.359	4.581	2.946	3.791	2.864		2.317	3.679	4.281	3.228	1.874	4.005	4.065	2.691	3.325	4.115	4.096	4.586	3.116	2.029	3.052	1.832	1.832
Germany	3.691	3.502	4.905	4.457	4.081	3.854	4.615	4.062	4.397	2.317		3.633	4.662	4.498	2.050	4.634	4.451	3.644	3.276	4.230	4.115	4.772	3.757	1.957	3.990	2.994	1.957
Greece	3.097	3.322	3.315	2.402	3.388	0.996	4.690	2.349	4.159	3.679	3.633		2.130	4.631	4.711	2.405	2.145	4.013	4.352	2.718	2.646	0.919	2.891	3.008	3.500	6.192	0.919
Hungary	4.663	4.321	0.999	1.458	3.901	2.547	5.778	2.937	5.616	4.281	4.662	2.130		5.008	3.421	0.917	1.258	3.195	2.888	2.241	1.510	1.990	1.506	2.138	2.918	4.628	0.917
Irland	3.302	2.187	4.339	3.978	2.171	4.335	3.039	3.144	3.323	3.228	4.498	4.631	5.008		4.352	4.655	4.795	2.828	4.051	3.797	2.897	2.527	2.631	2.334	2.693	4.125	2.171
Italy	3.192	2.947	4.648	4.123	3.340	3.514	3.870	3.210	3.557	1.874	2.050	4.711	3.421	4.352		3.238	3.116	3.129	3.406	3.429	2.948	2.977	2.973	1.465	3.054	4.105	1.465
Latvia	4.119	3.694	1.090	1.270	3.081	2.348	4.996	1.902	4.810	4.005	4.634	2.405	0.917	4.655	3.238		2.853	3.470	3.265	2.738	1.739	2.193	1.928	2.751	3.150	4.975	0.917
Lithuania	4.346	3.797	1.577	0.493	3.288	2.016	5.159	2.207	4.938	4.065	4.451	2.145	1.258	4.795	3.116	2.853		4.416	3.472	1.201	1.945	1.710	1.881	2.749	3.503	5.257	0.493
Netherlands	2.531	2.067	4.140	3.793	2.481	3.638	3.333	3.038	3.347	2.691	3.644	4.013	3.195	2.828	3.129	3.470	4.416		4.386	4.761	4.877	5.332	3.021	3.316	2.949	2.309	2.067
Poland	3.248	3.556	4.192	3.710	3.656	2.690	4.518	2.744	3.958	3.325	3.276	4.352	2.888	4.051	3.406	3.265	3.472	4.386		3.344	1.244	2.904	2.772	1.787	3.889	4.834	1.244
Portugal	4.539	3.973	2.791	1.667	3.677	2.257	5.287	2.840	5.019	4.115	4.230	2.718	2.241	3.797	3.429	2.738	1.201	4.761	3.344		3.600	2.260	2.272	2.952	3.745	5.194	1.201
Romania	4.207	4.255	2.213	2.000	3.938	1.676	5.560	2.443	5.131	4.096	4.115	2.646	1.510	2.897	2.948	1.739	1.945	4.877	1.244	3.600		2.728	3.424	3.290	4.271	6.307	1.244
Slovakia	4.899	4.563	1.432	1.274	4.223	2.403	6.086	3.297	5.897	4.586	4.772	0.919	1.990	2.527	2.977	2.193	1.710	5.332	2.904	2.260	2.728		3.818	2.373	3.421	5.033	0.919
Slovenia	2.746	2.254	2.774	1.986	2.039	1.968	3.684	1.476	3.424	3.116	3.757	2.891	1.506	2.631	2.973	1.928	1.881	3.021	2.772	2.272	3.424	3.818		3.059	2.126	3.817	1.476
Spain	2.947	2.885	3.300	2.800	3.159	2.099	4.344	2.588	4.004	2.029	1.957	3.008	2.138	2.334	1.465	2.751	2.749	3.316	1.787	2.952	3.290	2.373	3.059		3.110	4.394	1.465
Sweden	3.110	2.435	3.604	3.290	2.554	3.521	3.784	2.994	3.857	3.052	3.990	3.500	2.918	2.693	3.054	3.150	3.503	2.949	3.889	3.745	4.271	3.421	2.126	3.110		3.553	2.126
United Kingdom	3.377	2.556	5.866	5.361	3.103	5.050	2.590	3.895	2.659	1.832	2.994	6.192	4.628	4.125	4.105	4.975	5.257	2.309	4.834	5.194	6.307	5.033	3.817	4.394	3.553		1.832

Source: Authors' work based on GII data

Table 30 Compound distance matrix for the European Union economies in 2012 ("D" matrix)

2012	Austria	Belgium	Bulgaria	Croatia	Cyprus	Czech Republic	Denmark	Estonia	Finland	Greece	Hungary	Irland	Italy	Latvia	Lithuania	Malta	Netherlands	Portugal	Romania	Slovakia	Slovenia	Spain	Sweden	shortest distance
Austria		0.964	5.244	4.802	2.084	3.167	1.648	3.206	1.731	4.686	3.945	1.492	5.024	3.730	4.434	2.809	1.224	4.656	5.691	3.037	2.660	3.962	0.596	0.596
Belgium	0.964		4.928	4.504	1.647	3.028	1.496	3.103	1.564	4.402	3.680	1.114	4.741	3.241	4.063	2.866	1.126	4.106	5.427	2.807	2.347	3.480	0.847	0.847
Bulgaria	5.244	4.928		1.013	3.622	2.677	6.159	2.502	6.148	1.293	1.400	5.791	4.333	2.041	1.750	2.881	5.965	3.100	1.167	2.402	2.760	3.915	5.471	1.013
Croatia	4.802	4.504	1.013		3.228	1.960	5.757	2.110	5.693	1.105	1.131	5.410	4.375	1.933	0.836	2.609	5.574	2.324	1.879	1.853	2.228	3.772	4.973	0.836
Cyprus	2.084	1.647	3.622	3.228		2.128	2.593	1.724	2.572	3.405	2.430	2.391	4.763	1.812	2.844	1.702	2.670	3.320	4.289	1.558	1.194	3.558	2.170	1.194
Czech Republic	3.167	3.028	2.677	1.960	2.128		4.265	1.337	4.151	2.183	1.410	4.063	3.902	2.164	1.658	1.712	3.993	2.403	3.138	0.826	1.287	3.079	3.294	0.826
Denmark	1.648	1.496	6.159	5.757	2.593	4.265		4.101	0.438	5.789	4.905	1.048	5.982	4.318	5.297	3.853	1.061	5.314	6.685	3.987	3.594	4.758	1.344	0.438
Estonia	3.206	3.103	2.502	2.110	1.724	1.337	4.101		4.038	2.556	1.280	3.995	4.547	1.644	2.060	0.795	4.061	3.215	3.088	0.754	1.319	3.757	3.425	0.754
Finland	1.731	1.564	6.148	5.693	2.572	4.151	0.438	4.038		5.783	4.869	1.324	6.008	4.321	5.197	3.857	1.235	5.160	6.684	3.916	3.561	4.767	1.322	0.438
Greece	4.686	4.402	1.293	1.105	3.405	2.183	5.789	2.556	5.783		1.432	5.295	3.760	2.208	1.506	2.796	5.437	2.570	1.798	2.154	2.320	3.260	4.913	1.105
Hungary	3.945	3.680	1.400	1.131	2.430	1.410	4.905	1.280	4.869	1.432		4.624	3.821	1.386	1.365	1.715	4.692	2.668	1.956	1.078	1.597	3.163	4.155	1.078
Irland	1.492	1.114	5.791	5.410	2.391	4.063	1.048	3.995	1.324	5.295	4.624		5.662	3.972	4.955	3.694	1.090	4.939	6.359	3.761	3.215	4.379	1.331	1.048
Italy	5.024	4.741	4.333	4.375	4.763	3.902	5.982	4.547	6.008	3.760	3.821	5.662		4.454	4.450	4.593	5.199	4.509	3.777	4.144	4.322	1.548	5.156	1.548
Latvia	3.730	3.241	2.041	1.933	1.812	2.164	4.318	1.644	4.321	2.208	1.386	3.972	4.454		1.809	1.975	4.292	2.736	2.867	1.439	1.423	3.439	3.879	1.386
Lithuania	4.434	4.063	1.750	0.836	2.844	1.658	5.297	2.060	5.197	1.506	1.365	4.955	4.450	1.809		2.627	5.147	1.591	2.601	1.607	1.858	3.604	4.522	0.836
Malta	2.809	2.866	2.881	2.609	1.702	1.712	3.853	0.795	3.857	2.796	1.715	3.694	4.593	1.975	2.627		3.762	3.753	3.391	1.198	1.436	3.853	3.147	0.795
Netherlands	1.224	1.126	5.965	5.574	2.670	3.993	1.061	4.061	1.235	5.437	4.692	1.090	5.199	4.292	5.147	3.762		5.111	6.369	3.838	3.445	4.047	0.968	0.968
Portugal	4.656	4.106	3.100	2.324	3.320	2.403	5.314	3.215	5.160	2.570	2.668	4.939	4.509	2.736	1.591	3.753	5.111		3.762	2.574	2.559	3.423	4.565	1.591
Romania	5.691	5.427	1.167	1.879	4.289	3.138	6.685	3.088	6.684	1.798	1.956	6.359	3.777	2.867	2.601	3.391	6.369	3.762		3.025	3.482	3.780	5.945	1.167
Slovakia	3.037	2.807	2.402	1.853	1.558	0.826	3.987	0.754	3.916	2.154	1.078	3.761	4.144	1.439	1.607	1.198	3.838	2.574	3.025		0.769	3.221	3.202	0.754
Slovenia	2.660	2.347	2.760	2.228	1.194	1.287	3.594	1.319	3.561	2.320	1.597	3.215	4.322	1.423	1.858	1.436	3.445	2.559	3.482	0.769		3.228	2.822	0.769
Spain	3.962	3.480	3.915	3.772	3.558	3.079	4.758	3.757	4.767	3.260	3.163	4.379	1.548	3.439	3.604	3.853	4.047	3.423	3.780	3.221	3.228		4.001	1.548
Sweden	0.596	0.847	5.471	4.973	2.170	3.294	1.344	3.425	1.322	4.913	4.155	1.331	5.156	3.879	4.522	3.147	0.968	4.565	5.945	3.202	2.822	4.001		0.596

Source: Authors' work based on GII data

Table 31 Compound distance matrix for the European Union economies in 2013 ("D" matrix)

2013	Austria	Belgium	Bulgaria	Croatia	Cyprus	Czech Republic	Denmark	Estonia	Finland	France	Germany	Greece	Hungary	Irland	Italy	Latvia	Lithuania	Malta	Netherlands	Poland	Portugal	Romania	Slovakia	Slovenia	Spain	Sweden	shortest distance
Austria		5.119	4.319	5.627	3.762	3.295	2.257	2.856	2.283	3.275	4.689	3.851	5.414	3.219	3.457	4.336	4.484	3.379	1.991	3.937	4.187	4.938	5.487	3.135	3.563	2.593	1.991
Belgium	5.119		3.984	5.083	3.161	2.854	1.748	2.733	1.590	3.432	4.081	3.486	4.938	2.532	3.233	3.755	3.829	3.327	1.511	3.572	3.370	4.603	4.944	2.634	3.025	2.185	1.511
Bulgaria	4.319	3.984		1.048	2.612	3.062	5.133	4.427	4.873	6.134	4.463	3.121	0.826	4.679	4.738	1.578	2.049	2.736	5.328	4.529	2.814	2.056	1.464	2.797	3.396	4.343	0.826
Croatia	5.627	5.083	1.048		4.667	2.343	4.866	3.941	4.638	5.670	4.292	2.287	1.478	4.470	4.319	1.704	1.255	2.658	5.049	3.927	2.044	1.824	1.554	2.220	2.936	4.148	1.255
Cyprus	3.762	3.161	2.612	4.667		3.720	2.397	1.933	2.081	4.014	3.847	2.419	3.569	2.820	3.255	2.174	2.534	2.179	2.615	3.031	2.278	3.104	3.752	1.439	2.602	2.492	1.439
Czech Republic	3.295	2.854	3.062	2.343	3.720		3.875	2.629	3.474	4.092	3.579	1.087	2.701	3.602	2.984	2.071	1.384	2.070	3.716	2.715	1.485	2.086	2.696	1.008	1.804	3.119	1.008
Denmark	2.257	1.748	5.133	4.866	2.397	3.875		3.753	2.193	3.874	4.973	4.518	6.080	3.354	4.075	4.775	4.970	4.316	2.151	4.282	4.461	5.591	6.145	3.765	4.210	3.194	1.748
Estonia	2.856	2.733	4.427	3.941	1.933	2.629	3.753		3.051	4.294	3.901	1.850	2.610	3.419	3.308	1.468	1.951	1.243	3.453	3.061	2.173	2.054	2.937	1.050	2.430	2.880	1.933
Finland	2.283	1.590	4.873	4.638	2.081	3.474	2.193	3.051		4.210	5.132	4.518	6.405	3.917	4.112	5.065	5.159	4.602	2.735	4.113	4.598	5.651	6.491	3.980	4.411	3.771	1.590
France	3.275	3.432	6.134	5.670	4.014	4.092	3.874	4.294	4.210		2.225	3.460	4.039	3.943	1.897	3.764	3.843	3.294	3.433	3.415	3.698	3.678	4.226	3.213	1.610	3.197	1.610
Germany	4.689	4.081	4.463	4.292	3.847	3.579	4.973	3.901	5.132	2.225		4.214	4.906	4.768	1.917	4.353	4.215	4.539	4.232	2.819	3.668	3.927	5.111	3.892	2.133	4.447	1.917
Greece	3.851	3.486	3.121	2.287	2.419	1.087	4.518	1.850	4.518	3.460	4.214		1.409	4.247	4.687	2.019	1.909	2.933	5.046	4.751	2.678	2.797	0.436	2.751	3.113	3.908	0.436
Hungary	5.414	4.938	0.826	1.478	3.569	2.701	6.080	2.610	6.405	4.039	4.906	1.409		5.847	3.770	1.112	1.446	1.834	4.408	3.612	2.116	1.512	1.730	1.751	2.470	3.524	0.826
Irland	3.219	2.532	4.679	4.470	2.820	3.602	3.354	3.419	3.917	3.943	4.768	4.247	5.847		4.943	4.331	4.362	4.074	3.662	4.865	2.931	2.844	2.977	2.718	2.045	2.527	2.045
Italy	3.457	3.233	4.738	4.319	3.255	2.984	4.075	3.308	4.112	1.897	1.917	4.687	3.770	4.943		4.103	3.142	3.188	4.024	3.822	3.197	3.171	3.055	3.053	1.561	3.360	1.561
Latvia	4.336	3.755	1.578	1.704	2.174	2.071	4.775	1.468	5.065	3.764	4.353	2.019	1.112	4.331	4.103		3.558	1.762	3.742	3.483	1.927	2.085	2.370	1.406	2.586	3.037	1.112
Lithuania	4.484	3.829	2.049	1.255	2.534	1.384	4.970	1.951	5.159	3.843	4.215	1.909	1.446	4.362	3.142	3.558		3.701	4.325	3.362	1.041	2.232	2.058	1.536	2.417	3.586	1.041
Malta	3.379	3.327	2.736	2.658	2.179	2.070	4.316	1.243	4.602	3.294	4.539	2.933	1.834	4.074	3.188	1.762	3.701		4.247	3.451	3.089	2.582	3.478	1.686	2.831	2.827	1.243
Netherlands	1.991	1.511	5.328	5.049	2.615	3.716	2.151	3.453	2.735	3.433	4.232	5.046	4.408	3.662	4.024	3.742	4.325	4.247		4.587	4.579	5.707	6.243	3.899	4.052	3.173	1.511
Poland	3.937	3.572	4.529	3.927	3.031	2.715	4.282	3.061	4.113	3.415	2.819	4.751	3.612	4.865	3.822	3.483	3.362	3.451	4.587		1.891	1.713	2.769	2.096	1.316	3.764	1.316
Portugal	4.187	3.370	2.814	2.044	2.278	1.485	4.461	2.173	4.598	3.698	3.668	2.678	2.116	2.931	3.197	1.927	1.041	3.089	4.579	1.891		3.573	2.795	1.596	2.131	3.334	1.041
Romania	4.938	4.603	2.056	1.824	3.104	2.086	5.591	2.054	5.651	3.678	3.927	2.797	1.512	2.844	3.171	2.085	2.232	2.582	5.707	1.713	3.573		2.779	3.540	3.722	4.843	1.512
Slovakia	5.487	4.944	1.464	1.554	3.752	2.696	6.145	2.937	6.491	4.226	5.111	0.436	1.730	2.977	3.055	2.370	2.058	3.478	6.243	2.769	2.795	2.779		4.602	2.180	3.464	0.436
Slovenia	3.135	2.634	2.797	2.220	1.439	1.008	3.765	1.050	3.980	3.213	3.892	2.751	1.751	2.718	3.053	1.406	1.536	1.686	3.899	2.096	1.596	3.540	4.602		3.016	2.373	1.008
Spain	3.563	3.025	3.396	2.936	2.602	1.804	4.210	2.430	4.411	1.610	2.133	3.113	2.470	2.045	1.561	2.586	2.417	2.831	4.052	1.316	2.131	3.722	2.180	3.016		3.488	1.316
Sweden	2.593	2.185	4.343	4.148	2.492	3.119	3.194	2.880	3.771	3.197	4.447	3.908	3.524	2.527	3.360	3.037	3.586	2.827	3.173	3.764	3.334	4.843	3.464	2.373	3.488		2.185

Source: Authors' work based on GII data

Table 32 Compound distance matrix for the European Union economies in 2014 ("D" matrix)

2014	Austria	Belgium	Bulgaria	Croatia	Cyprus	Czech Republic	Denmark	Estonia	France	Germany	Greece	Hungary	Irland	Italy	Latvia	Lithuania	Malta	Netherlands	Poland	Portugal	Romania	Slovakia	Slovenia	Spain	shortest distance
Austria		2.598	6.657	5.913	3.547	4.224	2.285	3.634	3.427	4.051	6.450	5.257	2.207	5.153	4.544	5.258	3.353	1.828	5.011	4.239	6.832	4.790	3.460	4.768	1.828
Belgium	2.598		5.185	4.313	2.897	2.623	3.179	2.587	2.811	3.195	4.907	4.132	1.708	4.108	3.062	3.495	3.698	2.863	3.456	2.184	5.460	3.025	2.004	3.158	1.708
Bulgaria	6.657	5.185		1.696	3.382	3.047	7.363	3.354	5.093	6.251	1.314	2.144	6.029	3.399	2.460	2.561	4.548	7.257	2.689	3.722	0.842	2.788	3.391	3.145	0.842
Croatia	5.913	4.313	1.696		2.672	1.828	6.841	2.933	4.645	5.629	1.835	1.184	5.504	3.306	2.039	1.035	3.720	6.694	1.873	3.095	2.336	1.390	2.622	2.850	1.035
Cyprus	3.547	2.897	3.382	2.672		1.704	4.575	1.129	3.364	4.635	3.545	1.990	3.601	3.325	1.545	2.429	1.683	4.462	2.386	2.478	3.675	2.096	1.180	2.927	1.129
Czech Republic	4.224	2.623	3.047	1.828	1.704		5.319	2.048	3.266	4.187	2.791	1.624	3.965	2.806	1.708	1.091	2.712	5.073	1.491	2.190	3.467	0.647	1.273	2.104	0.647
Denmark	2.285	3.179	7.363	6.841	4.575	5.319		4.101	4.278	4.639	7.392	6.439	1.777	6.251	5.036	6.245	5.018	0.809	5.913	4.295	7.476	5.771	4.254	5.585	0.809
Estonia	3.634	2.587	3.354	2.933	1.129	2.048	4.101		3.288	4.488	3.636	2.623	3.033	3.502	1.045	2.696	2.729	4.084	2.542	1.689	3.585	2.338	0.981	2.800	0.981
France	3.427	2.811	5.093	4.645	3.364	3.266	4.278	3.288		1.596	4.800	4.116	3.348	2.434	3.674	4.218	3.866	3.726	2.987	3.373	4.963	3.811	3.061	2.251	1.596
Germany'	4.051	3.195	6.251	5.629	4.635	4.187	4.639	4.488	1.596		5.871	5.286	3.821	3.545	4.797	5.050	5.109	4.015	3.909	4.047	6.156	4.649	4.124	3.188	1.596
Greece	6.450	4.907	1.314	1.835	3.545	2.791	7.392	3.636	4.800	5.871		2.176	5.893	2.924	2.837	2.364	4.510	7.170	2.641	3.898	1.679	2.593	3.354	2.719	1.314
Hungary	5.257	4.132	2.144	1.184	1.990	1.624	6.439	2.623	4.116	5.286	2.176		5.233	2.818	2.064	1.520	2.712	6.240	1.736	3.303	2.562	1.598	2.356	2.706	1.184
Irland	2.207	1.708	6.029	5.504	3.601	3.965	1.777	3.033	3.348	3.821	5.893	5.233		5.006	3.810	4.852	4.349	1.607	4.664	3.007	6.197	4.389	2.935	4.171	1.607
Italy	5.153	4.108	3.399	3.306	3.325	2.806	6.251	3.502	2.434	3.545	2.924	2.818	5.006		3.290	3.305	3.920	5.811	1.997	3.792	3.159	3.143	3.227	1.318	1.318
Latvia	4.544	3.062	2.460	2.039	1.545	1.708	5.036	1.045	3.674	4.797	2.837	2.064	3.810	3.290		1.969	3.198	4.998	2.016	1.586	2.794	1.738	1.237	2.499	1.045
Lithuania	5.258	3.495	2.561	1.035	2.429	1.091	6.245	2.696	4.218	5.050	2.364	1.520	4.852	3.305	1.969		3.448	6.059	1.760	2.613	3.154	0.494	2.089	2.620	0.494
Malta	3.353	3.698	4.548	3.720	1.683	2.712	5.018	2.729	3.866	5.109	4.510	2.712	4.349	3.920	3.198	3.448		4.801	3.433	4.011	4.819	3.171	2.592	3.953	1.683
Netherlands	1.828	2.863	7.257	6.694	4.462	5.073	0.809	4.084	3.726	4.015	7.170	6.240	1.607	5.811	4.998	6.059	4.801		5.639	4.260	7.348	5.573	4.108	5.209	0.809
Poland	5.011	3.456	2.689	1.873	2.386	1.491	5.913	2.542	2.987	3.909	2.641	1.736	4.664	1.997	2.016	1.760	3.433	5.639		2.495	2.813	1.599	2.208	1.486	1.486
Portugal	4.239	2.184	3.722	3.095	2.478	2.190	4.295	1.689	3.373	4.047	3.898	3.303	3.007	3.792	1.586	2.613	4.011	4.260	2.495		3.987	2.259	1.581	2.645	1.581
Romania	6.832	5.460	0.842	2.336	3.675	3.467	7.476	3.585	4.963	6.156	1.679	2.562	6.197	3.159	2.794	3.154	4.819	7.348	2.813	3.987		3.312	3.729	3.088	0.842
Slovakia	4.790	3.025	2.788	1.390	2.096	0.647	5.771	2.338	3.811	4.649	2.593	1.598	4.389	3.143	1.738	0.494	3.171	5.573	1.599	2.259	3.312		1.657	2.384	0.494
Slovenia	3.460	2.004	3.391	2.622	1.180	1.273	4.254	0.981	3.061	4.124	3.354	2.356	2.935	3.227	1.237	2.089	2.592	4.108	2.208	1.581	3.729	1.657		2.409	0.981
Spain	4.768	3.158	3.145	2.850	2.927	2.104	5.585	2.800	2.251	3.188	2.719	2.706	4.171	1.318	2.499	2.620	3.953	5.209	1.486	2.645	3.088	2.384	2.409		1.318

Source: Authors' work based on GII data

Table 33 Compound distance matrix for the European Union economies in 2015 ("D" matrix)

2015	Austria	Bulgaria	Croatia	Cyprus	Czech Republic	Denmark	Estonia	Finland	Greece	Hungary	Irland	Latvia	Lithuania	Netherlands	Poland	Portugal	Romania	Slovakia	Slovenia	Spain	Sweden	shortest distance
Austria		5.307	4.643	2.352	3.231	1.955	2.569	2.471	5.135	4.260	1.987	3.357	3.996	1.687	4.498	3.418	5.167	3.651	3.007	4.683	1.145	1.145
Bulgaria	5.307		1.498	3.505	2.668	6.091	3.231	6.524	1.079	1.588	5.988	2.462	2.294	6.134	3.547	3.235	1.242	2.531	3.557	4.289	5.513	1.079
Croatia	4.643	1.498		2.960	1.625	5.545	2.702	5.875	1.347	1.016	5.356	1.874	0.953	5.582	3.253	2.603	2.180	1.359	2.972	4.113	4.824	0.953
Cyprus	2.352	3.505	2.960		2.042	2.681	0.515	3.096	3.511	2.961	2.787	1.222	2.497	3.002	3.776	1.597	3.526	2.099	0.948	4.280	2.293	0.515
Czech Republic	3.231	2.668	1.625	2.042		4.244	1.947	4.593	2.241	1.501	3.973	1.537	0.999	4.118	2.571	1.795	2.737	0.714	2.165	3.263	3.360	0.714
Denmark	1.955	6.091	5.545	2.681	4.244		3.038	0.893	5.990	5.414	1.374	3.852	4.930	1.137	5.258	3.517	5.843	4.446	2.928	5.358	1.225	0.893
Estonia	2.569	3.231	2.702	0.515	1.947	3.038		3.395	3.349	2.699	3.251	0.950	2.352	3.330	3.688	1.693	3.311	2.026	1.225	4.299	2.659	0.515
Finland	2.471	6.524	5.875	3.096	4.593	0.893	3.395		6.446	5.830	1.995	4.172	5.256	1.598	5.535	3.755	6.290	4.762	3.227	5.702	1.741	0.893
Greece	5.135	1.079	1.347	3.511	2.241	5.990	3.349	6.446		1.389	5.677	2.566	1.880	5.923	3.101	3.015	1.435	2.097	3.463	3.730	5.261	1.079
Hungary	4.260	1.588	1.016	2.961	1.501	5.414	2.699	5.830	1.389		5.216	2.103	1.354	5.304	2.919	2.871	1.999	1.674	3.210	3.701	4.610	1.016
Irland	1.987	5.988	5.356	2.787	3.973	1.374	3.251	1.995	5.677	5.216		3.910	4.615	1.532	5.170	3.472	5.784	4.140	2.933	5.143	1.109	1.109
Latvia	3.357	2.462	1.874	1.222	1.537	3.852	0.950	4.172	2.566	2.103	3.910		1.673	4.081	3.347	1.374	2.655	1.391	1.316	4.076	3.381	0.950
Lithuania	3.996	2.294	0.953	2.497	0.999	4.930	2.352	5.256	1.880	1.354	4.615	1.673		4.955	3.234	2.211	2.766	0.609	2.503	3.992	4.123	0.609
Netherlands	1.687	6.134	5.582	3.002	4.118	1.137	3.330	1.598	5.923	5.304	1.532	4.081	4.955		4.735	3.627	5.737	4.464	3.286	4.685	1.015	1.015
Poland	4.498	3.547	3.253	3.776	2.571	5.258	3.688	5.535	3.101	2.919	5.170	3.347	3.234	4.735		2.884	2.713	2.967	3.695	1.116	4.458	1.116
Portugal	3.418	3.235	2.603	1.597	1.795	3.517	1.693	3.755	3.015	2.871	3.472	1.374	2.211	3.627	2.884		3.019	1.645	0.961	3.439	3.028	0.961
Romania	5.167	1.242	2.180	3.526	2.737	5.843	3.311	6.290	1.435	1.999	5.784	2.655	2.766	5.737	2.713	3.019		2.776	3.515	3.332	5.277	1.242
Slovakia	3.651	2.531	1.359	2.099	0.714	4.446	2.026	4.762	2.097	1.674	4.140	1.391	0.609	4.464	2.967	1.645	2.776		1.999	3.675	3.654	0.609
Slovenia	3.007	3.557	2.972	0.948	2.165	2.928	1.225	3.227	3.463	3.210	2.933	1.316	2.503	3.286	3.695	0.961	3.515	1.999		4.182	2.611	0.948
Spain	4.683	4.289	4.113	4.280	3.263	5.358	4.299	5.702	3.730	3.701	5.143	4.076	3.992	4.685	1.116	3.439	3.332	3.675	4.182		4.551	1.116
Sweden	1.145	5.513	4.824	2.293	3.360	1.225	2.659	1.741	5.261	4.610	1.109	3.381	4.123	1.015	4.458	3.028	5.277	3.654	2.611	4.551		1.015

Source: Authors' work based on GII data

Table 34 Compound distance matrix for the European Union economies in 2016 ("D" matrix)

2016	Austria	Bulgaria	Croatia	Cyprus	Czech Republic	Denmark	Estonia	Finland	Greece	Hungary	Irland	Latvia	Lithuania	Netherlands	Poland	Portugal	Romania	Slovakia	Slovenia	Spain	Sweden	shortest distance
Austria		5.422	4.930	2.416	2.964	1.562	2.492	1.992	5.536	4.409	1.688	3.282	3.806	1.463	4.435	2.970	5.110	3.693	2.720	4.585	0.836	0.836
Bulgaria	5.422		1.252	3.729	3.116	6.334	3.480	6.394	1.107	1.490	6.148	2.797	2.461	5.953	3.754	3.821	1.328	2.630	3.823	4.533	5.769	1.107
Croatia	4.930	1.252		3.299	2.322	5.850	3.054	5.880	1.558	1.090	5.608	2.218	1.392	5.401	3.473	3.135	1.988	1.639	3.192	4.337	5.214	1.090
Cyprus	2.416	3.729	3.299		1.750	2.758	0.653	2.767	3.891	3.228	2.761	1.240	2.526	2.789	3.753	1.485	3.517	2.209	0.794	4.222	2.475	0.653
Czech Republic	2.964	3.116	2.322	1.750		3.764	1.689	3.778	3.125	2.208	3.539	1.249	1.320	3.151	2.571	1.173	2.900	0.894	1.434	3.234	3.056	0.894
Denmark	1.562	6.334	5.850	2.758	3.764		3.001	0.610	6.441	5.531	1.391	3.835	4.767	1.454	5.171	3.266	5.936	4.501	2.965	5.255	1.063	0.610
Estonia	2.492	3.480	3.054	0.653	1.689	3.001		3.001	3.809	2.916	3.179	1.009	2.289	3.068	3.683	1.586	3.351	2.131	1.100	4.284	2.695	0.653
Finland	1.992	6.394	5.880	2.767	3.778	0.610	3.001		6.528	5.643	1.778	3.781	4.813	1.686	5.159	3.114	5.984	4.511	2.870	5.299	1.432	0.610
Greece	5.536	1.107	1.558	3.891	3.125	6.441	3.809	6.528		1.839	6.043	3.087	2.628	5.885	3.569	3.874	1.408	2.599	3.912	4.160	5.802	1.107
Hungary	4.409	1.490	1.090	3.228	2.208	5.531	2.916	5.643	1.839		5.316	2.351	1.446	5.018	3.153	3.204	1.911	1.846	3.279	3.955	4.816	1.090
Irland	1.688	6.148	5.608	2.761	3.539	1.391	3.179	1.778	6.043	5.316		3.836	4.508	1.329	5.071	3.267	5.786	4.176	2.899	5.017	1.146	1.146
Latvia	3.282	2.797	2.218	1.240	1.249	3.835	1.009	3.781	3.087	2.351	3.836		1.613	3.668	3.314	1.356	2.769	1.360	1.136	4.055	3.417	1.009
Lithuania	3.806	2.461	1.392	2.526	1.320	4.767	2.289	4.813	2.628	1.446	4.508	1.613		4.296	3.292	2.295	2.810	0.740	2.322	4.098	4.065	0.740
Netherlands	1.463	5.953	5.401	2.789	3.151	1.454	3.068	1.686	5.885	5.018	1.329	3.668	4.296		4.177	2.831	5.418	3.957	2.816	4.104	0.777	0.777
Poland	4.435	3.754	3.473	3.753	2.571	5.171	3.683	5.159	3.569	3.153	5.071	3.314	3.292	4.177		2.857	2.790	2.976	3.552	1.140	4.460	1.140
Portugal	2.970	3.821	3.135	1.485	1.173	3.266	1.586	3.114	3.874	3.204	3.267	1.356	2.295	2.831	2.857		3.445	1.775	0.882	3.446	2.811	0.882
Romania	5.110	1.327	1.988	3.517	2.900	5.936	3.351	5.984	1.408	1.911	5.786	2.769	2.810	5.418	2.790	3.445		2.722	3.619	3.458	5.376	1.327
Slovakia	3.693	2.630	1.639	2.209	0.894	4.501	2.131	4.511	2.599	1.846	4.176	1.360	0.740	3.957	2.976	1.775	2.722		1.872	3.711	3.818	0.740
Slovenia	2.720	3.823	3.192	0.794	1.434	2.965	1.100	2.870	3.912	3.279	2.899	1.136	2.322	2.816	3.552	0.882	3.619	1.872		4.075	2.616	0.794
Spain	4.585	4.533	4.337	4.222	3.234	5.255	4.284	5.299	4.160	3.955	5.017	4.055	4.098	4.104	1.140	3.446	3.458	3.711	4.075		4.532	1.140
Sweden	0.836	5.769	5.214	2.475	3.056	1.063	2.695	1.432	5.802	4.816	1.146	3.417	4.065	0.777	4.460	2.811	5.376	3.818	2.616	4.532		0.777

Source: Authors' work based on GII data

Table 35 Compound distance matrix for the European Union economies in 2017 ("D" matrix)

2017	Austria	Belgium	Croatia	Cyprus	Czech Republic	Denmark	Estonia	Finland	France	Germany	Greece	Hungary	Italy	Latvia	Lithuania	Netherlands	Poland	Portugal	Romania	Slovakia	Slovenia	Spain	Sweden	United Kingdom	shortest distance
Austria		2.118	5.064	2.396	2.910	1.674	2.355	2.447	2.876	3.455	5.688	4.449	3.975	3.399	3.908	1.763	4.132	3.077	5.312	3.667	2.665	3.136	1.352	2.747	1.352
Belgium	2.118		4.420	1.393	1.728	2.460	2.243	2.767	2.442	3.175	4.714	3.916	2.909	2.964	3.474	2.198	3.042	1.893	4.589	2.828	1.407	2.059	2.176	2.877	1.393
Croatia	5.064	4.420		3.458	2.844	6.251	3.267	6.521	4.657	6.113	1.425	0.763	3.587	1.958	1.513	6.252	2.275	3.369	1.801	1.621	3.824	3.452	5.989	5.864	0.763
Cyprus	2.396	1.393	3.458		1.203	3.064	1.099	3.232	2.792	4.020	3.895	3.001	2.786	1.776	2.748	3.114	2.431	1.301	3.579	2.033	0.855	2.077	2.888	3.362	0.855
Czech Republic	2.910	1.728	2.844	1.203		3.685	1.598	3.912	2.749	3.881	3.387	2.465	2.519	1.567	1.961	3.595	1.780	0.938	3.381	1.290	1.260	1.566	3.421	3.631	0.938
Denmark	1.674	2.460	6.251	3.064	3.685		3.211	0.958	3.545	3.561	6.839	5.720	4.818	4.443	5.123	0.783	5.045	3.484	6.463	4.754	2.933	3.923	0.492	2.784	0.492
Estonia	2.355	2.243	3.267	1.099	1.598	3.211		3.383	3.032	4.296	4.031	2.829	3.185	1.321	2.520	3.426	2.602	1.553	3.542	2.101	1.453	2.428	3.076	3.463	1.099
Finland	2.447	2.767	6.521	3.232	3.912	0.958	3.383		3.840	3.839	7.098	6.051	5.034	4.649	5.505	1.441	5.212	3.490	6.663	5.058	2.930	4.169	1.372	2.919	0.958
France	2.876	2.442	4.657	2.792	2.749	3.545	3.032	3.840		1.765	4.874	4.058	1.792	3.485	3.950	3.168	2.723	2.936	4.423	3.460	2.964	1.443	3.229	1.572	1.443
Germany	3.455	3.175	6.113	4.020	3.881	3.561	4.296	3.839	1.765		6.394	5.559	3.314	4.920	5.184	2.982	4.177	3.920	6.107	4.803	3.919	2.767	3.256	1.599	1.765
Greece	5.688	4.714	1.425	3.895	3.387	6.839	4.031	7.098	4.874	6.394		1.586	3.405	2.850	2.581	6.744	2.424	3.972	1.384	2.286	4.329	3.694	6.558	6.238	1.384
Hungary	4.449	3.916	0.763	3.001	2.465	5.720	2.829	6.051	4.058	5.559	1.586		3.077	1.611	1.250	5.697	1.946	3.100	1.675	1.247	3.478	2.950	5.436	5.284	0.763
Italy	3.975	2.909	3.587	2.786	2.519	4.818	3.185	5.034	1.792	3.314	3.405	3.077		3.013	3.406	4.508	1.528	2.899	3.030	2.733	3.100	1.271	4.516	3.238	1.271
Latvia	3.399	2.964	1.958	1.776	1.567	4.443	1.321	4.649	3.485	4.920	2.850	1.611	3.013		1.538	4.556	1.930	1.871	2.496	1.159	2.167	2.476	4.245	4.341	1.159
Lithuania	3.908	3.474	1.513	2.748	1.961	5.123	2.520	5.505	3.950	5.184	2.581	1.250	3.406	1.538		5.101	2.252	2.628	2.874	0.973	3.055	2.800	4.822	5.033	0.973
Netherlands	1.763	2.198	6.252	3.114	3.595	0.783	3.426	1.441	3.168	2.982	6.744	5.697	4.508	4.556	5.101		4.885	3.490	6.444	4.700	2.985	3.629	0.548	2.483	0.548
Poland	4.132	3.042	2.275	2.431	1.780	5.045	2.602	5.212	2.723	4.177	2.424	1.946	1.528	1.930	2.252	4.885		2.174	2.237	1.592	2.657	1.470	4.772	4.008	1.470
Portugal	3.077	1.893	3.369	1.301	0.938	3.484	1.553	3.490	2.936	3.920	3.972	3.100	2.899	1.871	2.628	3.490	2.174		3.821	2.017	0.802	1.927	3.323	3.494	0.802
Romania	5.312	4.589	1.801	3.579	3.381	6.463	3.542	6.663	4.423	6.107	1.384	1.675	3.030	2.496	2.874	6.444	2.237	3.821		2.469	4.106	3.484	6.230	5.662	1.384
Slovakia	3.667	2.828	1.621	2.033	1.290	4.754	2.101	5.058	3.460	4.803	2.286	1.247	2.733	1.159	0.973	4.700	1.592	2.017	2.469		2.386	2.204	4.471	4.582	0.973
Slovenia	2.665	1.407	3.824	0.855	1.260	2.933	1.453	2.930	2.964	3.919	4.329	3.478	3.100	2.167	3.055	2.985	2.657	0.802	4.106	2.386		2.206	2.810	3.340	0.802
Spain	3.136	2.059	3.452	2.077	1.566	3.923	2.428	4.169	1.443	2.767	3.694	2.950	1.271	2.476	2.800	3.629	1.470	1.927	3.484	2.204	2.206		3.603	2.735	1.271
Sweden	1.352	2.176	5.989	2.888	3.421	0.492	3.076	1.372	3.229	3.256	6.558	5.436	4.516	4.245	4.822	0.548	4.772	3.323	6.230	4.471	2.810	3.603		2.612	0.492
United Kingdom	2.747	2.877	5.864	3.362	3.631	2.784	3.463	2.919	1.572	1.599	6.238	5.284	3.238	4.341	5.033	2.483	4.008	3.494	5.662	4.582	3.340	2.735	2.612		1.572

Source: Authors' work based on GII data

Table 36 Compound distance matrix for the European Union economies in 2018 ("D" matrix)

2018	Austria	Belgium	Bulgaria	Croatia	Cyprus	Czech Republic	Denmark	Estonia	Finland	France	Germany	Greece	Hungary	Latvia	Lithuania	Netherlands	Poland	Portugal	Romania	Slovakia	Slovenia	Spain	Sweden	United Kingdom	shortest distance
Austria		2.256	5.199	4.970	2.189	2.768	1.596	2.191	2.271	2.852	3.589	5.299	4.120	3.195	3.120	1.718	4.208	2.974	5.286	3.827	2.685	3.228	1.323	2.843	1.323
Belgium	2.256		4.410	4.206	1.420	1.574	2.663	2.272	2.943	2.580	3.406	4.130	3.435	2.684	3.140	2.460	2.930	1.798	4.521	2.894	1.269	2.036	2.299	3.051	1.269
Bulgaria	5.199	4.410		1.055	3.416	3.000	6.340	3.389	6.534	4.981	6.311	1.194	1.338	2.238	2.454	6.420	2.360	3.582	0.958	1.955	3.879	3.553	6.041	5.746	0.958
Croatia	4.970	4.206	1.055		3.335	2.728	6.121	3.228	6.368	4.840	6.087	1.154	0.926	2.100	2.034	6.160	2.261	3.322	1.820	1.372	3.715	3.414	5.767	5.735	0.926
Cyprus	2.189	1.420	3.416	3.335		1.031	3.022	1.104	3.251	2.989	4.168	3.477	2.554	1.487	2.097	3.141	2.605	1.479	3.596	2.215	1.099	2.189	2.767	3.387	1.031
Czech Republic	2.768	1.574	3.000	2.728	1.031		3.596	1.447	3.809	2.820	3.990	2.851	2.007	1.263	1.860	3.573	1.803	1.022	3.282	1.510	1.174	1.623	3.237	3.546	1.022
Denmark	1.596	2.663	6.340	6.121	3.022	3.596		3.094	0.854	3.395	3.718	6.390	5.324	4.190	4.398	0.803	5.118	3.386	6.484	4.921	2.995	4.008	0.564	3.011	0.564
Estonia	2.191	2.272	3.389	3.228	1.104	1.447	3.094		3.272	3.161	4.367	3.703	2.521	1.186	1.639	3.356	2.866	1.574	3.701	2.339	1.649	2.580	2.878	3.500	1.104
Finland	2.271	2.943	6.534	6.368	3.251	3.809	0.854	3.272		3.652	3.957	6.628	5.615	4.362	4.745	1.401	5.297	3.389	6.711	5.217	3.017	4.233	1.269	3.137	0.854
France	2.852	2.580	4.981	4.840	2.989	2.820	3.395	3.161	3.652		1.410	4.848	4.040	3.568	3.724	3.006	3.032	2.948	4.846	3.829	3.072	1.676	3.026	1.270	1.270
Germany	3.589	3.406	6.311	6.087	4.168	3.990	3.718	4.367	3.957	1.410		6.061	5.318	4.870	4.971	3.133	4.214	3.985	6.184	5.021	4.069	2.858	3.365	1.714	1.410
Greece	5.299	4.130	1.194	1.154	3.477	2.851	6.390	3.703	6.628	4.848	6.061		1.416	2.576	2.768	6.344	1.972	3.515	1.537	1.653	3.789	3.260	6.025	5.779	1.154
Hungary	4.120	3.435	1.338	0.926	2.554	2.007	5.324	2.521	5.615	4.040	5.318	1.416		1.472	1.367	5.339	1.776	2.757	1.771	0.798	3.077	2.677	4.964	4.906	0.798
Latvia	3.195	2.684	2.238	2.100	1.487	1.263	4.190	1.186	4.362	3.568	4.870	2.576	1.472		1.164	4.354	2.121	1.709	2.666	1.420	1.982	2.458	3.921	4.161	1.164
Lithuania	3.120	3.140	2.454	2.034	2.097	1.860	4.398	1.639	4.745	3.724	4.971	2.768	1.367	1.164		4.515	2.551	2.497	2.847	1.456	2.782	2.814	4.068	4.424	1.164
Netherlands	1.718	2.460	6.420	6.160	3.141	3.573	0.803	3.356	1.401	3.006	3.133	6.344	5.339	4.354	4.515		4.968	3.439	6.516	4.894	3.071	3.742	0.578	2.728	0.578
Poland	4.208	2.930	2.360	2.261	2.605	1.803	5.118	2.866	5.297	3.032	4.214	1.972	1.776	2.121	2.551	4.968		2.313	2.406	1.686	2.711	1.437	4.733	4.004	1.437
Portugal	2.974	1.798	3.582	3.322	1.479	1.022	3.386	1.574	3.389	2.948	3.985	3.515	2.757	1.709	2.497	3.439	2.313		3.960	2.284	0.829	2.031	3.097	3.499	0.829
Romania	5.286	4.521	0.958	1.820	3.596	3.282	6.484	3.701	6.711	4.846	6.184	1.537	1.771	2.666	2.847	6.516	2.406	3.960		2.418	4.173	3.494	6.188	5.574	0.958
Slovakia	3.827	2.894	1.955	1.372	2.215	1.510	4.921	2.339	5.217	3.829	5.021	1.653	0.798	1.420	1.456	4.894	1.686	2.284	2.418		2.578	2.410	4.533	4.742	0.798
Slovenia	2.685	1.269	3.879	3.715	1.099	1.174	2.995	1.649	3.017	3.072	4.069	3.789	3.077	1.982	2.782	3.071	2.711	0.829	4.173	2.578		2.256	2.750	3.470	0.829
Spain	3.228	2.036	3.553	3.414	2.189	1.623	4.008	2.580	4.233	1.676	2.858	3.260	2.677	2.458	2.814	3.742	1.437	2.031	3.494	2.410	2.256		3.604	2.692	1.437
Sweden	1.323	2.299	6.041	5.767	2.767	3.237	0.564	2.878	1.269	3.026	3.365	6.025	4.964	3.921	4.068	0.578	4.733	3.097	6.188	4.533	2.750	3.604		2.830	0.564
United Kingdom	2.843	3.051	5.746	5.735	3.387	3.546	3.011	3.500	3.137	1.270	1.714	5.779	4.906	4.161	4.424	2.728	4.004	3.499	5.574	4.742	3.470	2.692	2.830		1.270

Source: Authors' work based on GII data

Table 37 Compound distance matrix for the European Union economies without the United Kingdom in 2010 ("D" matrix)

2010	Austria	Belgium	Bulgaria	Croatia	Cyprus	Czech Republic	Denmark	Estonia	Finland	France	Germany	Hungary	Irland	Italy	Latvia	Lithuania	Netherlands	Poland	Portugal	Romania	Slovakia	Slovenia	Spain	Sweden	shortest distance
Austria		1.527	5.567	5.475	3.482	2.103	3.404	3.462	1.829	3.716	3.839	3.503	2.962	4.855	4.688	4.015	2.084	3.762	3.357	6.227	3.158	3.972	4.989	1.044	1.527
Belgium	1.527		4.438	4.407	2.013	1.491	2.739	2.501	1.561	3.128	3.427	2.525	2.116	4.405	3.662	3.148	1.231	3.358	2.222	5.239	2.248	2.760	4.865	1.127	1.127
Bulgaria	5.567	4.438		1.455	3.186	3.659	6.093	2.413	5.315	4.203	5.516	2.137	5.681	4.161	1.023	1.888	5.100	3.218	2.453	1.480	2.462	2.583	4.873	5.319	1.023
Croatia	5.475	4.407	1.455		3.361	3.913	6.173	2.496	5.141	4.076	5.455	2.530	5.673	4.009	1.496	1.950	4.871	3.397	2.320	1.686	2.556	2.060	4.945	5.150	1.455
Cyprus	3.482	2.013	3.186	3.361		2.295	3.102	1.996	2.837	3.768	4.358	2.072	2.566	4.797	2.678	2.608	2.434	3.771	1.717	4.307	2.042	1.798	5.462	2.932	1.717
Czech Republic	2.103	1.491	3.659	3.913	2.295		3.700	1.742	2.432	3.040	3.708	1.532	3.322	3.979	2.816	2.239	2.567	2.305	1.831	4.464	1.383	2.755	4.265	2.142	1.383
Denmark	3.404	2.739	6.093	6.173	3.102	3.700		4.210	2.098	5.277	4.778	4.508	0.973	6.870	5.439	5.033	2.171	5.684	4.078	7.210	4.348	4.196	7.504	2.593	0.973
Estonia	3.462	2.501	2.413	2.496	1.996	1.742	4.210		3.045	3.505	4.425	0.887	3.876	4.217	1.462	0.838	3.162	2.515	0.804	3.415	0.674	1.485	4.866	3.128	0.674
Finland	1.829	1.561	5.315	5.141	2.837	2.432	2.098	3.045		4.120	3.973	3.437	1.891	5.566	4.453	3.796	1.208	4.254	2.934	6.213	3.085	3.237	6.156	0.865	1.208
France	3.716	3.128	4.203	4.076	3.768	3.040	5.277	3.505	4.120		1.799	3.068	4.727	1.866	3.822	3.512	3.494	2.206	2.929	4.161	3.061	3.585	3.184	3.684	1.799
Germany	3.839	3.427	5.516	5.455	4.358	3.708	4.778	4.425	3.973	1.799		4.155	4.423	3.537	5.087	4.683	3.345	3.512	3.886	5.705	4.135	4.480	4.697	3.646	1.799
Hungary	3.503	2.525	2.137	2.530	2.072	1.532	4.508	0.887	3.437	3.068	4.155		4.107	3.631	1.316	0.977	3.382	1.984	1.047	3.037	0.566	1.955	4.183	3.341	0.566
Irland	2.962	2.116	5.681	5.673	2.566	3.322	0.973	3.876	1.891	4.727	4.423	4.107		6.240	5.039	4.663	1.540	5.282	3.625	6.713	3.911	3.714	6.848	2.162	0.973
Italy	4.855	4.405	4.161	4.009	4.797	3.979	6.870	4.217	5.566	1.866	3.537	3.631	6.240		3.986	3.874	5.019	2.349	3.765	3.548	3.678	4.369	1.820	5.053	1.820
Latvia	4.688	3.662	1.023	1.496	2.678	2.816	5.439	1.462	4.453	3.822	5.087	1.316	5.039	3.986		0.893	4.370	2.650	1.651	2.087	1.536	1.964	4.634	4.457	0.893
Lithuania	4.015	3.148	1.888	1.950	2.608	2.239	5.033	0.838	3.796	3.512	4.683	0.977	4.663	3.874	0.893		3.852	2.221	1.200	2.709	0.942	1.769	4.521	3.798	0.838
Netherlands	2.084	1.231	5.100	4.871	2.434	2.567	2.171	3.162	1.208	3.494	3.345	3.382	1.540	5.019	4.370	3.852		4.170	2.762	5.895	3.079	2.980	5.750	1.171	1.208
Poland	3.762	3.358	3.218	3.397	3.771	2.305	5.684	2.515	4.254	2.206	3.512	1.984	5.282	2.349	2.650	2.221	4.170		2.442	3.271	2.068	3.368	2.937	3.919	1.984
Portugal	3.357	2.222	2.453	2.320	1.717	1.831	4.078	0.804	2.934	2.929	3.886	1.047	3.625	3.765	1.651	1.200	2.762	2.442		3.298	0.811	1.046	4.610	2.945	0.804
Romania	6.227	5.239	1.480	1.686	4.307	4.464	7.210	3.415	6.213	4.161	5.705	3.037	6.713	3.548	2.087	2.709	5.895	3.271	3.298		3.287	3.450	4.330	6.091	1.480
Slovakia	3.158	2.248	2.462	2.556	2.042	1.383	4.348	0.674	3.085	3.061	4.135	0.566	3.911	3.678	1.536	0.942	3.079	2.068	0.811	3.287		1.723	4.229	2.979	0.566
Slovenia	3.972	2.760	2.583	2.060	1.798	2.755	4.196	1.485	3.237	3.585	4.480	1.955	3.714	4.369	1.964	1.769	2.980	3.368	1.046	3.450	1.723		5.330	3.393	1.046
Spain	4.989	4.865	4.873	4.945	5.462	4.265	7.504	4.866	6.156	3.184	4.697	4.183	6.848	1.820	4.634	4.521	5.750	2.937	4.610	4.330	4.229	5.330		5.505	1.820
Sweden	1.044	1.127	5.319	5.150	2.932	2.142	2.593	3.128	0.865	3.684	3.646	3.341	2.162	5.053	4.457	3.798	1.171	3.919	2.945	6.091	2.979	3.393	5.505		0.865

Source: Authors' work based on GII data

Table 38 Compound distance matrix for the European Union economies without the United Kingdom in 2011 ("D" matrix)

2011	Austria	Belgium	Bulgaria	Croatia	Cyprus	Czech Republic	Denmark	Estonia	Finland	France	Germany	Greece	Hungary	Irland	Italy	Latvia	Lithuania	Netherlands	Poland	Portugal	Romania	Slovakia	Slovenia	Spain	Sweden	shortest distance
Austria		1.795	4.978	4.385	2.630	3.308	2.782	2.845	2.166	3.221	3.785	4.752	3.501	2.945	4.047	3.865	4.232	1.624	3.755	4.539	5.253	3.696	2.605	3.737	1.744	1.624
Belgium	1.795		4.501	3.880	1.164	3.648	1.667	2.255	1.543	2.518	3.754	4.753	3.173	1.441	3.815	3.466	3.790	0.909	4.098	3.930	5.196	3.543	1.850	3.664	0.808	0.808
Bulgaria	4.978	4.501		1.195	3.926	2.785	5.881	2.830	5.718	4.571	5.077	2.054	1.610	5.463	3.180	1.381	1.819	5.289	2.841	2.742	1.457	2.386	2.808	2.768	5.199	1.195
Croatia	4.385	3.880	1.195		3.382	2.053	5.292	2.256	5.060	4.174	4.610	1.951	1.124	4.918	3.095	1.341	0.671	4.708	2.680	1.620	2.118	1.327	2.072	2.589	4.489	0.671
Cyprus	2.630	1.164	3.926	3.382		3.663	1.997	1.640	2.049	3.026	4.390	4.631	2.767	1.664	4.016	2.863	3.347	1.954	4.130	3.630	4.844	3.331	1.534	3.838	1.735	1.163
Czech Republic	3.308	3.648	2.785	2.053	3.663		5.136	2.426	4.604	3.956	3.846	2.189	1.640	5.015	2.985	2.237	1.776	4.231	1.698	2.345	2.678	1.064	2.282	2.303	4.037	1.064
Denmark	2.782	1.667	5.881	5.292	1.997	5.136		3.367	0.902	3.530	4.891	6.372	4.593	0.940	5.299	4.757	5.165	1.443	5.526	5.257	6.662	4.980	3.308	5.247	1.333	0.903
Estonia	2.845	2.255	2.830	2.256	1.640	2.426	3.367		3.049	3.344	4.247	3.655	1.463	3.255	3.515	1.558	2.149	3.010	2.890	2.806	3.560	2.133	1.157	3.169	2.770	1.464
Finland	2.166	1.543	5.718	5.060	2.049	4.604	0.902	3.049		3.454	4.576	6.077	4.287	1.627	5.095	4.514	4.858	1.270	5.040	4.987	6.364	4.560	3.084	4.973	0.992	0.903
France	3.221	2.518	4.571	4.174	3.026	3.956	3.530	3.344	3.454		1.763	4.715	3.510	3.328	2.353	3.962	4.179	2.645	3.552	4.151	4.881	3.977	3.038	2.726	2.896	1.763
Germany	3.785	3.754	5.077	4.610	4.390	3.846	4.891	4.247	4.576	1.763		4.669	4.033	4.814	2.258	4.645	4.512	3.807	3.292	4.353	4.957	4.116	3.922	2.617	3.974	1.763
Greece	4.752	4.753	2.054	1.951	4.631	2.189	6.372	3.655	6.077	4.715	4.669		2.301	5.954	2.899	2.624	2.242	5.420	2.657	2.763	1.883	2.220	3.161	2.220	5.350	1.883
Hungary	3.501	3.173	1.610	1.124	2.767	1.640	4.593	1.463	4.287	3.510	4.033	2.301		4.327	2.675	0.745	1.268	3.923	1.979	2.223	2.179	1.373	1.531	2.177	3.788	0.745
Irland	2.945	1.441	5.463	4.918	1.664	5.015	0.940	3.255	1.627	3.328	4.814	5.954	4.327		4.955	4.478	4.871	1.510	4.706	3.098	3.468	2.656	1.908	2.632	3.909	0.940
Italy	4.047	3.815	3.180	3.095	4.016	2.985	5.299	3.515	5.095	2.353	2.258	2.899	2.675	4.955		3.164	3.295	4.233	2.213	3.496	3.025	3.162	3.125	0.785	4.405	0.784
Latvia	3.865	3.466	1.381	1.341	2.863	2.237	4.757	1.558	4.514	3.962	4.645	2.624	0.745	4.478	3.164		1.646	4.227	2.424	2.713	2.159	1.959	1.877	2.722	4.115	0.745
Lithuania	4.232	3.790	1.819	0.671	3.347	1.776	5.165	2.149	4.858	4.179	4.512	2.242	1.268	4.871	3.295	1.646		4.608	2.677	1.179	2.523	0.835	2.017	2.772	4.307	0.671
Netherlands	1.624	0.909	5.289	4.708	1.954	4.231	1.443	3.010	1.270	2.645	3.807	5.420	3.923	1.510	4.233	4.227	4.608		4.553	4.730	5.862	4.279	2.697	4.148	0.735	0.735
Poland	3.755	4.098	2.841	2.680	4.130	1.698	5.526	2.890	5.040	3.552	3.292	2.657	1.979	4.706	2.213	2.424	2.677	4.553		3.333	2.199	2.338	3.037	1.789	4.573	1.697
Portugal	4.539	3.930	2.742	1.620	3.630	2.345	5.257	2.806	4.987	4.151	4.353	2.763	2.223	3.098	3.496	2.713	1.179	4.730	3.333		3.416	1.364	2.411	3.075	4.348	1.179
Romania	5.253	5.196	1.457	2.118	4.844	2.678	6.662	3.560	6.364	4.881	4.957	1.883	2.179	3.468	3.025	2.159	2.523	5.862	2.199	3.416		2.756	3.622	2.582	5.847	1.457
Slovakia	3.696	3.543	2.386	1.327	3.331	1.064	4.980	2.133	4.560	3.977	4.116	2.220	1.373	2.656	3.162	1.959	0.835	4.279	2.338	1.364	2.756		1.911	2.559	3.975	0.835
Slovenia	2.605	1.850	2.808	2.072	1.534	2.282	3.308	1.157	3.084	3.038	3.922	3.161	1.531	1.908	3.125	1.877	2.017	2.697	3.037	2.411	3.622	1.911		2.720	2.464	1.158
Spain	3.737	3.664	2.768	2.589	3.838	2.303	5.247	3.169	4.973	2.726	2.617	2.220	2.177	2.632	0.785	2.722	2.772	4.148	1.789	3.075	2.582	2.559	2.720		4.254	0.784
Sweden	1.744	0.808	5.199	4.489	1.735	4.037	1.333	2.770	0.992	2.896	3.974	5.350	3.788	3.909	4.405	4.115	4.307	0.735	4.573	4.348	5.847	3.975	2.464	4.254		0.735

Source: Authors' work based on GII data

Table 39 Compound distance matrix for the European Union economies without the United Kingdom in 2012 ("D" matrix)

2012	Austria	Belgium	Bulgaria	Croatia	Cyprus	Czech Republic	Denmark	Estonia	Finland	France	Germany	Greece	Hungary	Irland	Italy	Latvia	Lithuania	Malta	Netherlands	Poland	Portugal	Romania	Slovakia	Slovenia	Spain	Sweden	Shortest distance
Austria		0.987	5.425	4.964	2.086	3.272	1.709	3.264	1.794	3.351	3.797	4.879	4.070	1.541	4.285	3.819	4.576	2.860	1.191	4.144	4.821	5.848	3.122	2.728	3.503	0.619	0.619
Belgium	0.987		5.106	4.658	1.595	3.144	1.538	3.154	1.612	3.285	3.582	4.595	3.809	1.100	4.029	3.303	4.189	2.912	1.125	3.832	4.259	5.601	2.887	2.386	3.004	0.879	0.879
Bulgaria	5.425	5.106		1.042	3.760	2.778	6.412	2.597	6.408	4.269	5.553	1.288	1.454	6.000	3.279	2.112	1.809	2.971	6.166	2.527	3.221	0.937	2.501	2.843	3.386	5.671	0.936
Croatia	4.964	4.658	1.042		3.361	2.009	5.996	2.200	5.936	4.018	5.147	1.065	1.137	5.610	3.190	2.013	0.870	2.705	5.743	2.003	2.394	1.715	1.932	2.304	3.092	5.148	0.869
Cyprus	2.086	1.595	3.760	3.361		2.156	2.683	1.791	2.670	3.304	4.062	3.520	2.485	2.450	3.605	1.882	2.962	1.775	2.610	2.899	3.416	4.327	1.607	1.247	2.661	2.175	1.247
Czech Republic	3.272	3.144	2.778	2.009	2.156		4.437	1.281	4.323	2.911	3.895	2.296	1.462	4.205	2.864	2.198	1.672	1.688	4.132	1.532	2.501	3.209	0.807	1.255	2.465	3.415	0.808
Denmark	1.709	1.538	6.412	5.996	2.683	4.437		4.252	0.456	4.477	4.523	6.044	5.100	1.092	5.385	4.482	5.513	4.005	0.904	5.122	5.524	6.906	4.150	3.747	4.387	1.379	0.456
Estonia	3.264	3.154	2.597	2.200	1.791	1.281	4.252		4.194	3.311	4.519	2.617	1.251	4.122	3.286	1.718	2.146	0.814	4.105	2.129	3.304	3.030	0.747	1.357	2.939	3.497	0.747
Finland	1.794	1.612	6.408	5.936	2.670	4.323	0.456	4.194		4.505	4.480	6.044	5.069	1.382	5.418	4.495	5.416	4.016	1.113	5.020	5.369	6.912	4.083	3.719	4.401	1.354	0.456
France	3.351	3.285	4.269	4.018	3.304	2.911	4.477	3.311	4.505		1.740	3.674	3.252	4.176	1.445	3.651	3.913	3.166	3.806	2.462	4.266	4.231	3.026	3.042	1.742	3.558	1.446
Germany	3.797	3.582	5.553	5.147	4.062	3.895	4.523	4.519	4.480	1.740		4.878	4.520	4.299	2.648	4.692	4.808	4.505	3.836	3.361	4.579	5.607	4.110	4.008	2.411	3.745	1.740
Greece	4.879	4.595	1.288	1.065	3.520	2.296	6.044	2.617	6.044	3.674	4.878		1.489	5.504	2.698	2.238	1.501	2.859	5.663	2.225	2.684	1.757	2.236	2.371	2.746	5.125	1.065
Hungary	4.070	3.809	1.454	1.137	2.485	1.462	5.100	1.251	5.069	3.252	4.520	1.489		4.778	2.685	1.377	1.369	1.698	4.847	1.608	2.775	1.939	1.092	1.585	2.530	4.300	1.092
Irland	1.541	1.100	6.000	5.610	2.450	4.205	1.092	4.122	1.382	4.176	4.299	5.504	4.778		4.939	4.092	5.134	3.822	0.910	4.887	5.110	6.529	3.892	3.334	3.880	1.361	0.910
Italy	4.285	4.029	3.279	3.190	3.605	2.864	5.385	3.286	5.418	1.445	2.648	2.698	2.685	4.939		3.181	3.242	3.305	4.789	1.969	3.704	3.162	2.917	2.989	1.383	4.501	1.383
Latvia	3.819	3.303	2.112	2.013	1.882	2.198	4.482	1.718	4.495	3.651	4.692	2.238	1.377	4.092	3.181		1.884	2.046	4.359	2.369	2.805	2.796	1.484	1.454	2.516	3.980	1.378
Lithuania	4.576	4.189	1.809	0.870	2.962	1.672	5.513	2.146	5.416	3.913	4.808	1.501	1.369	5.134	3.242	1.884		2.726	5.285	1.830	1.601	2.515	1.669	1.921	2.815	4.671	0.869
Malta	2.860	2.912	2.971	2.705	1.775	1.688	4.005	0.814	4.016	3.166	4.505	2.859	1.698	3.822	3.305	2.046	2.726		3.793	2.606	3.861	3.329	1.214	1.490	3.033	3.217	0.814
Netherlands	1.191	1.125	6.166	5.743	2.610	4.132	0.904	4.105	1.113	3.806	3.836	5.663	4.847	0.910	4.789	4.359	5.285	3.793		4.762	5.293	6.604	3.923	3.484	3.854	0.927	0.905
Poland	4.144	3.832	2.527	2.003	2.899	1.532	5.122	2.129	5.020	2.462	3.361	2.225	1.608	4.887	1.969	2.369	1.830	2.606	4.762		2.434	2.694	1.740	2.166	1.873	4.238	1.532
Portugal	4.821	4.259	3.221	2.394	3.416	2.501	5.524	3.304	5.369	4.266	4.579	2.684	2.775	5.110	3.704	2.805	1.601	3.861	5.293	2.434		3.872	2.662	2.614	2.912	4.734	1.601
Romania	5.848	5.601	0.937	1.715	4.327	3.209	6.906	3.030	6.912	4.231	5.607	1.757	1.939	6.529	3.162	2.796	2.515	3.329	6.604	2.694	3.872		3.025	3.449	3.630	6.132	1.714
Slovakia	3.122	2.887	2.501	1.932	1.607	0.807	4.150	0.747	4.083	3.026	4.110	2.236	1.092	3.892	2.917	1.484	1.669	1.214	3.923	1.740	2.662	3.025		0.769	2.394	3.300	0.747
Slovenia	2.728	2.386	2.843	2.304	1.247	1.255	3.747	1.357	3.719	3.042	4.008	2.371	1.585	3.334	2.989	1.454	1.921	1.490	3.484	2.166	2.614	3.449	0.769		2.208	2.899	0.769
Spain	3.503	3.004	3.386	3.092	2.661	2.465	4.387	2.939	4.401	1.742	2.411	2.746	2.530	3.880	1.383	2.516	2.815	3.033	3.854	1.873	2.912	3.630	2.394	2.208		3.597	1.383
Sweden	0.619	0.879	5.671	5.148	2.175	3.415	1.379	3.497	1.354	3.558	3.745	5.125	4.300	1.361	4.501	3.980	4.671	3.217	0.927	4.238	4.734	6.132	3.300	2.899	3.597		0.619

Source: Authors' work based on GII data

Table 40 Compound distance matrix for the European Union economies without the United Kingdom in 2013 ("D" matrix)

2013	Austria	Belgium	Bulgaria	Croatia	Cyprus	Czech Republic	Denmark	Estonia	Finland	Greece	Hungary	Irland	Italy	Latvia	Lithuania	Malta	Netherlands	Poland	Portugal	Romania	Slovakia	Slovenia	Spain	Sweden	Shortest distance
Austria		1.165	5.491	5.074	2.482	3.450	1.537	3.192	1.852	5.350	4.419	1.663	5.116	3.867	4.353	2.833	1.435	4.537	3.961	6.083	3.931	2.900	4.335	0.655	0.695
Belgium	1.165		5.008	4.583	1.889	3.034	1.299	2.868	1.705	4.850	3.991	0.915	4.702	3.322	3.765	2.885	1.308	4.001	3.145	5.645	3.496	2.391	3.782	0.846	0.898
Bulgaria	5.491	5.008		1.096	3.497	2.614	6.059	2.507	6.295	1.319	1.152	5.619	4.175	1.893	2.070	3.110	6.246	2.877	2.823	1.193	2.271	2.789	3.514	5.563	1.163
Croatia	5.074	4.583	1.096		3.134	1.846	5.668	2.165	5.840	1.391	0.984	5.174	4.244	1.774	1.127	2.880	5.842	2.575	2.109	2.035	1.370	2.259	3.366	5.076	1.163
Cyprus	2.482	1.889	3.497	3.134		2.037	2.655	1.277	2.844	3.716	2.580	2.382	4.635	1.640	2.482	1.759	3.040	3.306	2.135	4.320	2.279	1.118	3.618	2.404	1.186
Czech Republic	3.450	3.034	2.614	1.846	2.037		4.168	1.414	4.291	2.504	1.546	3.717	3.749	1.771	1.191	1.991	4.225	2.044	1.445	3.305	0.594	1.127	2.676	3.404	0.630
Denmark	1.537	1.299	6.059	5.668	2.655	4.168		3.783	0.716	6.036	5.076	0.963	5.820	4.246	4.847	3.723	0.892	5.127	4.190	6.741	4.590	3.447	4.969	1.196	0.759
Estonia	3.192	2.868	2.507	2.165	1.277	1.414	3.783		3.954	2.862	1.531	3.510	4.316	0.970	1.863	1.018	4.054	2.827	2.113	3.332	1.498	0.900	3.379	3.271	0.955
Finland	1.852	1.705	6.295	5.840	2.844	4.291	0.716	3.954		6.345	5.289	1.450	6.102	4.473	4.994	3.930	1.199	5.239	4.315	6.998	4.704	3.670	5.230	1.422	0.759
Greece	5.350	4.850	1.319	1.391	3.716	2.504	6.036	2.862	6.345		1.537	5.448	3.728	2.373	1.984	3.373	6.108	2.806	2.708	1.696	2.247	2.778	3.032	5.418	1.399
Hungary	4.419	3.991	1.152	0.984	2.580	1.546	5.076	1.531	5.289	1.537		4.667	3.677	1.221	1.440	2.151	5.215	2.188	2.110	1.897	1.343	1.797	2.852	4.489	1.043
Irland	1.663	0.915	5.619	5.174	2.382	3.717	0.963	3.510	1.450	5.448	4.667		5.464	3.871	4.282	3.590	1.264	4.760	3.591	6.336	4.116	2.977	4.518	1.236	0.971
Italy	5.116	4.702	4.175	4.244	4.635	3.749	5.820	4.316	6.102	3.728	3.677	5.464		4.238	4.261	4.499	5.410	2.255	4.032	3.702	4.086	4.187	1.231	5.162	1.305
Latvia	3.867	3.322	1.893	1.774	1.640	1.771	4.246	0.970	4.473	2.373	1.221	3.871	4.238		1.653	1.846	4.544	2.778	1.894	2.810	1.672	1.260	3.302	3.890	1.029
Lithuania	4.353	3.765	2.070	1.127	2.482	1.191	4.847	1.863	4.994	1.984	1.440	4.282	4.261	1.653		2.693	5.021	2.480	1.156	2.992	0.744	1.563	3.169	4.255	0.789
Malta	2.833	2.885	3.110	2.880	1.759	1.991	3.723	1.018	3.930	3.373	2.151	3.590	4.499	1.846	2.693		3.949	3.348	3.001	3.771	2.188	1.558	3.719	3.103	1.080
Netherlands	1.435	1.308	6.246	5.842	3.040	4.225	0.892	4.054	1.199	6.108	5.215	1.264	5.410	4.544	5.021	3.949		4.958	4.321	6.813	4.718	3.669	4.645	1.076	0.946
Poland	4.537	4.001	2.877	2.575	3.306	2.044	5.127	2.827	5.239	2.806	2.188	4.760	2.255	2.778	2.480	3.348	4.958		2.299	2.881	2.275	2.775	1.437	4.458	1.524
Portugal	3.961	3.145	2.823	2.109	2.135	1.445	4.190	2.113	4.315	2.708	2.110	3.591	4.032	1.894	1.156	3.001	4.321	2.299		3.609	1.444	1.569	2.835	3.724	1.226
Romania	6.083	5.645	1.193	2.035	4.320	3.305	6.741	3.332	6.998	1.696	1.897	6.336	3.702	2.810	2.992	3.771	6.813	2.881	3.609		3.086	3.637	3.382	6.196	1.265
Slovakia	3.931	3.496	2.271	1.370	2.279	0.594	4.590	1.498	4.704	2.247	1.343	4.116	4.086	1.672	0.744	2.188	4.718	2.275	1.444	3.086		1.326	3.031	3.884	0.630
Slovenia	2.900	2.391	2.789	2.259	1.118	1.127	3.447	0.900	3.670	2.778	1.797	2.977	4.187	1.260	1.563	1.558	3.669	2.775	1.569	3.637	1.326		3.113	2.880	0.955
Spain	4.335	3.782	3.514	3.366	3.618	2.676	4.969	3.379	5.230	3.032	2.852	4.518	1.231	3.302	3.169	3.719	4.645	1.437	2.835	3.382	3.031	3.113		4.299	1.305
Sweden	0.655	0.846	5.563	5.076	2.404	3.404	1.196	3.271	1.422	5.418	4.489	1.236	5.162	3.890	4.255	3.103	1.076	4.458	3.724	6.196	3.884	2.880	4.299		0.695

Source: Authors' work based on GII data

Table 41 Compound distance matrix for the European Union economies without the United Kingdom in 2014 ("D" matrix)

2014	Austria	Belgium	Bulgaria	Croatia	Cyprus	Czech Republic	Denmark	Estonia	Finland	France	Germany	Greece	Hungary	Irland	Italy	Latvia	Lithuania	Malta	Netherlands	Poland	Portugal	Romania	Slovakia	Slovenia	Spain	Sweden	Shortest distance
Austria		2.275	5.669	5.116	3.085	3.662	2.004	3.152	2.596	3.249	3.970	5.446	4.538	1.922	4.552	3.933	4.568	2.932	1.614	4.406	3.711	5.803	4.163	2.993	4.170	0.994	0.994
Belgium	2.275		4.397	3.734	2.553	2.276	2.766	2.269	3.171	2.766	3.291	4.104	3.580	1.502	3.692	2.660	3.041	3.266	2.495	3.073	1.924	4.619	2.633	1.746	2.803	1.927	1.502
Bulgaria	5.669	4.397		1.398	2.832	2.541	6.266	2.826	6.752	4.601	5.670	1.177	1.792	5.166	3.252	2.054	2.127	3.853	6.194	2.368	3.121	0.807	2.310	2.852	2.898	5.792	0.807
Croatia	5.116	3.734	1.398		2.314	1.584	5.905	2.550	6.299	4.320	5.259	1.524	1.050	4.790	3.216	1.778	0.886	3.227	5.799	1.823	2.678	1.990	1.188	2.276	2.717	5.250	0.886
Cyprus	3.085	2.553	2.832	2.314		1.517	3.958	0.986	4.425	3.334	4.521	2.966	1.726	3.162	3.210	1.340	2.128	1.471	3.892	2.269	2.192	3.097	1.843	1.044	2.772	3.354	0.986
Czech Republic	3.662	2.276	2.541	1.584	1.517		4.604	1.809	5.022	3.148	4.054	2.267	1.406	3.465	2.697	1.507	0.972	2.391	4.400	1.465	1.919	2.898	0.583	1.133	2.009	3.792	0.583
Denmark	2.004	2.766	6.266	5.905	3.958	4.604		3.526	0.922	3.953	4.454	6.265	5.556	1.513	5.496	4.331	5.408	4.371	0.762	5.174	3.727	6.349	4.999	3.662	4.871	1.267	0.762
Estonia	3.152	2.269	2.826	2.550	0.986	1.809	3.526		3.986	3.274	4.399	3.069	2.290	2.658	3.362	0.905	2.358	2.385	3.548	2.395	1.499	3.037	2.050	0.866	2.677	3.154	0.866
Finland	2.596	3.171	6.752	6.299	4.425	5.022	0.922	3.986		4.440	4.766	6.820	6.010	2.144	6.053	4.746	5.779	4.857	1.426	5.559	4.007	6.858	5.374	4.130	5.377	1.797	0.921
France	3.249	2.766	4.601	4.320	3.334	3.148	3.953	3.274	4.440		1.444	4.292	3.838	3.259	2.053	3.567	3.989	3.730	3.407	2.704	3.249	4.369	3.638	3.083	1.972	3.284	1.444
Germany	3.970	3.291	5.670	5.259	4.521	4.054	4.454	4.399	4.766	1.444		5.285	4.933	3.840	3.036	4.624	4.815	4.911	3.845	3.580	3.964	5.459	4.475	4.101	2.839	3.797	1.444
Greece	5.446	4.104	1.177	1.524	2.966	2.267	6.265	3.069	6.820	4.292	5.285		1.804	5.012	2.807	2.390	1.922	3.799	6.080	2.278	3.260	1.512	2.100	2.793	2.478	5.622	1.177
Hungary	4.538	3.580	1.792	1.050	1.726	1.406	5.556	2.290	6.010	3.838	4.933	1.804		4.559	2.762	1.815	1.341	2.344	5.397	1.664	2.871	2.152	1.392	2.056	2.545	4.836	1.050
Irland	1.922	1.502	5.166	4.790	3.162	3.465	1.513	2.658	2.144	3.259	3.840	5.012	4.559		4.511	3.323	4.235	3.823	1.402	4.152	2.656	5.304	3.834	2.562	3.728	1.243	1.243
Italy	4.552	3.692	3.252	3.216	3.210	2.697	5.496	3.362	6.053	2.053	3.036	2.807	2.762	4.511		3.212	3.201	3.665	5.063	1.813	3.495	2.913	3.033	3.122	1.198	4.774	1.198
Latvia	3.933	2.660	2.054	1.778	1.340	1.507	4.331	0.905	4.746	3.567	4.624	2.390	1.815	3.323	3.212		1.723	2.786	4.330	1.969	1.379	2.365	1.520	1.079	2.452	3.913	0.905
Lithuania	4.568	3.041	2.127	0.886	2.128	0.972	5.408	2.358	5.779	3.989	4.815	1.922	1.341	4.235	3.201	1.723		3.017	5.268	1.761	2.282	2.669	0.430	1.826	2.522	4.659	0.430
Malta	2.932	3.266	3.853	3.227	1.471	2.391	4.371	2.385	4.857	3.730	4.911	3.799	2.344	3.823	3.665	2.786	3.017		4.208	3.135	3.537	4.091	2.783	2.271	3.603	3.575	1.471
Netherlands	1.614	2.495	6.194	5.799	3.892	4.400	0.762	3.548	1.426	3.407	3.845	6.080	5.397	1.402	5.063	4.330	5.268	4.208		4.914	3.716	6.243	4.845	3.564	4.503	0.881	0.762
Poland	4.406	3.073	2.368	1.823	2.269	1.465	5.174	2.395	5.559	2.704	3.580	2.278	1.664	4.152	1.813	1.969	1.761	3.135	4.914		2.272	2.354	1.607	2.120	1.316	4.483	1.316
Portugal	3.711	1.924	3.121	2.678	2.192	1.919	3.727	1.499	4.007	3.249	3.964	3.260	2.871	2.656	3.495	1.379	2.282	3.537	3.716	2.272		3.337	1.975	1.408	2.443	3.372	1.379
Romania	5.803	4.619	0.806	1.990	3.097	2.898	6.349	3.037	6.858	4.369	5.459	1.512	2.152	5.304	2.913	2.365	2.669	4.091	6.243	2.354	3.337		2.780	3.157	2.730	5.925	1.512
Slovakia	4.163	2.633	2.310	1.188	1.843	0.583	4.999	2.050	5.374	3.638	4.475	2.100	1.392	3.834	3.033	1.520	0.430	2.783	4.845	1.607	1.975	2.780		1.453	2.297	4.239	0.430
Slovenia	2.993	1.746	2.852	2.276	1.044	1.133	3.662	0.866	4.130	3.083	4.101	2.793	2.056	2.562	3.122	1.079	1.826	2.271	3.564	2.120	1.408	3.157	1.453		2.343	3.026	0.866
Spain	4.170	2.803	2.898	2.717	2.772	2.009	4.871	2.677	5.377	1.972	2.839	2.478	2.545	3.728	1.198	2.452	2.522	3.603	4.503	1.316	2.443	2.730	2.297	2.343		4.191	1.198
Sweden	0.994	1.927	5.792	5.250	3.354	3.792	1.267	3.154	1.797	3.284	3.797	5.622	4.836	1.243	4.774	3.913	4.659	3.575	0.881	4.483	3.372	5.925	4.239	3.026	4.191		0.881

Source: Authors' work based on GII data

Table 42 Compound distance matrix for the European Union economies without the United Kingdom in 2015 ("D" matrix)

2015	Austria	Bulgaria	Croatia	Cyprus	Czech Republic	Denmark	Estonia	Finland	Greece	Hungary	Irland	Latvia	Lithuania	Netherlands	Poland	Portugal	Romania	Slovakia	Slovenia	Spain	Sweden	Shortest distance
Austria		5.307	4.643	2.352	3.231	1.955	2.569	2.471	5.135	4.260	1.987	3.357	3.996	1.687	4.498	3.418	5.167	3.651	3.007	4.683	1.145	1.145
Bulgaria	5.307		1.498	3.505	2.668	6.091	3.231	6.524	1.079	1.588	5.988	2.462	2.294	6.134	3.547	3.235	1.242	2.531	3.557	4.289	5.513	1.079
Croatia	4.643	1.498		2.960	1.625	5.545	2.702	5.875	1.347	1.016	5.356	1.874	0.953	5.582	3.253	2.603	2.180	1.359	2.972	4.113	4.824	0.953
Cyprus	2.352	3.505	2.960		2.042	2.681	0.515	3.096	3.511	2.961	2.787	1.222	2.497	3.002	3.776	1.597	3.526	2.099	0.948	4.280	2.293	0.515
Czech Republic	3.231	2.668	1.625	2.042		4.244	1.947	4.593	2.241	1.501	3.973	1.537	0.999	4.118	2.571	1.795	2.737	0.714	2.165	3.263	3.360	0.714
Denmark	1.955	6.091	5.545	2.681	4.244		3.038	0.893	5.990	5.414	1.374	3.852	4.930	1.137	5.258	3.517	5.843	4.446	2.928	5.358	1.225	0.893
Estonia	2.569	3.231	2.702	0.515	1.947	3.038		3.395	3.349	2.699	3.251	0.950	2.352	3.330	3.688	1.693	3.311	2.026	1.225	4.299	2.659	0.515
Finland	2.471	6.524	5.875	3.096	4.593	0.893	3.395		6.446	5.830	1.995	4.172	5.256	1.598	5.535	3.755	6.290	4.762	3.227	5.702	1.741	0.893
Greece	5.135	1.079	1.347	3.511	2.241	5.990	3.349	6.446		1.389	5.677	2.566	1.880	5.923	3.101	3.015	1.435	2.097	3.463	3.730	5.261	1.079
Hungary	4.260	1.588	1.016	2.961	1.501	5.414	2.699	5.830	1.389		5.216	2.103	1.354	5.304	2.919	2.871	1.999	1.674	3.210	3.701	4.610	1.016
Irland	1.987	5.988	5.356	2.787	3.973	1.374	3.251	1.995	5.677	5.216		3.910	4.615	1.532	5.170	3.472	5.784	4.140	2.933	5.143	1.109	1.109
Latvia	3.357	2.462	1.874	1.222	1.537	3.852	0.950	4.172	2.566	2.103	3.910		1.673	4.081	3.347	1.374	2.655	1.391	1.316	4.076	3.381	0.950
Lithuania	3.996	2.294	0.953	2.497	0.999	4.930	2.352	5.256	1.880	1.354	4.615	1.673		4.955	3.234	2.211	2.766	0.609	2.503	3.992	4.123	0.609
Netherlands	1.687	6.134	5.582	3.002	4.118	1.137	3.330	1.598	5.923	5.304	1.532	4.081	4.955		4.735	3.627	5.737	4.464	3.286	4.685	1.015	1.015
Poland	4.498	3.547	3.253	3.776	2.571	5.258	3.688	5.535	3.101	2.919	5.170	3.347	3.234	4.735		2.884	2.713	2.967	3.695	1.116	4.458	1.116
Portugal	3.418	3.235	2.603	1.597	1.795	3.517	1.693	3.755	3.015	2.871	3.472	1.374	2.211	3.627	2.884		3.019	1.645	0.961	3.439	3.028	0.961
Romania	5.167	1.242	2.180	3.526	2.737	5.843	3.311	6.290	1.435	1.999	5.784	2.655	2.766	5.737	2.713	3.019		2.776	3.515	3.332	5.277	1.242
Slovakia	3.651	2.531	1.359	2.099	0.714	4.446	2.026	4.762	2.097	1.674	4.140	1.391	0.609	4.464	2.967	1.645	2.776		1.999	3.675	3.654	0.609
Slovenia	3.007	3.557	2.972	0.948	2.165	2.928	1.225	3.227	3.463	3.210	2.933	1.316	2.503	3.286	3.695	0.961	3.515	1.999		4.182	2.611	0.948
Spain	4.683	4.289	4.113	4.280	3.263	5.358	4.299	5.702	3.730	3.701	5.143	4.076	3.992	4.685	1.116	3.439	3.332	3.675	4.182		4.551	1.116
Sweden	1.145	5.513	4.824	2.293	3.360	1.225	2.659	1.741	5.261	4.610	1.109	3.381	4.123	1.015	4.458	3.028	5.277	3.654	2.611	4.551		1.015

Source: Authors' work based on GII data

Table 43 Compound distance matrix for the European Union economies without the United Kingdom in 2016 ("D" matrix)

2016	Austria	Belgium	Bulgaria	Croatia	Cyprus	Czech Republic	Denmark	Estonia	Finland	Greece	Hungary	Irland	Latvia	Lithuania	Malta	Netherlands	Poland	Portugal	Romania	Slovakia	Slovenia	Spain	Sweden	Shortest distance
Austria		2.174	5.582	5.071	2.483	3.059	1.520	2.565	1.940	5.726	4.503	1.655	3.382	3.909	2.915	1.443	4.569	3.038	5.281	3.813	2.782	4.728	0.811	0.811
Belgium	2.174		4.316	3.654	1.730	1.493	2.843	2.070	2.958	4.167	3.363	2.250	2.233	2.591	2.942	2.017	3.237	1.621	3.952	2.173	1.566	3.445	2.048	1.493
Bulgaria	5.582	4.316		1.299	3.770	3.187	6.462	3.551	6.506	1.129	1.540	6.250	2.834	2.550	3.433	6.073	3.839	3.852	1.344	2.691	3.850	4.620	5.908	1.129
Croatia	5.071	3.654	1.299		3.328	2.359	5.961	3.111	5.972	1.618	1.102	5.691	2.231	1.441	3.035	5.500	3.548	3.134	2.048	1.656	3.191	4.421	5.331	1.102
Cyprus	2.483	1.730	3.770	3.328		1.784	2.841	0.646	2.838	3.978	3.194	2.824	1.260	2.530	2.571	2.870	3.849	1.528	3.592	2.252	0.815	4.339	2.557	0.646
Czech Republic	3.059	1.493	3.187	2.359	1.784		3.847	1.741	3.843	3.229	2.184	3.597	1.283	1.315	2.491	3.216	2.643	1.145	2.997	0.920	1.426	3.322	3.138	0.920
Denmark	1.520	2.843	6.462	5.961	2.841	3.847		3.062	0.612	6.608	5.582	1.432	3.929	4.838	4.156	1.494	5.301	3.364	6.085	4.606	3.059	5.405	1.070	0.612
Estonia	2.565	2.070	3.551	3.111	0.646	1.741	3.062		3.043	3.923	2.914	3.229	1.042	2.322	2.219	3.136	3.787	1.611	3.450	2.195	1.098	4.405	2.767	0.646
Finland	1.940	2.958	6.506	5.972	2.838	3.843	0.612	3.043		6.682	5.673	1.821	3.860	4.862	4.386	1.719	5.277	3.203	6.120	4.599	2.954	5.440	1.425	0.612
Greece	5.726	4.167	1.129	1.618	3.978	3.229	6.608	3.923	6.682		1.893	6.178	3.171	2.738	3.862	6.039	3.673	3.950	1.448	2.690	3.984	4.262	5.974	1.129
Hungary	4.503	3.363	1.540	1.102	3.194	2.184	5.582	2.914	5.673	1.893		5.341	2.308	1.462	2.309	5.056	3.179	3.139	1.942	1.816	3.218	3.989	4.877	1.102
Irland	1.655	2.250	6.250	5.691	2.824	3.597	1.432	3.229	1.821	6.178	5.341		3.912	4.552	4.065	1.362	5.183	3.346	5.912	4.252	2.971	5.147	1.154	1.154
Latvia	3.382	2.233	2.834	2.231	1.260	1.283	3.929	1.042	3.860	3.171	2.308	3.912		1.608	2.480	3.758	3.404	1.368	2.845	1.392	1.130	4.166	3.515	1.042
Lithuania	3.909	2.591	2.550	1.441	2.530	1.315	4.838	2.322	4.862	2.738	1.462	4.552	1.608		2.258	4.354	3.367	2.251	2.913	0.716	2.280	4.185	4.141	0.716
Malta	2.915	2.942	3.433	3.035	2.571	2.491	4.156	2.219	4.386	3.862	2.309	4.065	2.480	2.258		4.007	4.299	3.240	3.703	2.659	2.934	4.897	3.537	2.219
Netherlands	1.443	2.017	6.073	5.500	2.870	3.216	1.494	3.136	1.719	6.039	5.056	1.362	3.758	4.354	4.007		4.278	2.910	5.556	4.046	2.899	4.223	0.787	0.787
Poland	4.569	3.237	3.839	3.548	3.849	2.643	5.301	3.787	5.277	3.673	3.179	5.183	3.404	3.367	4.299	4.278		2.913	2.876	3.058	3.631	1.160	4.585	1.160
Portugal	3.038	1.621	3.852	3.134	1.528	1.145	3.364	1.611	3.203	3.950	3.139	3.346	1.368	2.251	3.240	2.910	2.913		3.511	1.772	0.908	3.536	2.893	0.908
Romania	5.281	3.952	1.344	2.048	3.592	2.997	6.085	3.450	6.120	1.448	1.942	5.912	2.845	2.913	3.703	5.556	2.876	3.511		2.814	3.686	3.541	5.533	1.344
Slovakia	3.813	2.173	2.691	1.656	2.252	0.920	4.606	2.195	4.599	2.690	1.816	4.252	1.392	0.716	2.659	4.046	3.058	1.772	2.814		1.875	3.808	3.923	0.716
Slovenia	2.782	1.566	3.850	3.191	0.815	1.426	3.059	1.098	2.954	3.984	3.218	2.971	1.130	2.280	2.934	2.899	3.631	0.908	3.686	1.875		4.183	2.697	0.815
Spain	4.728	3.445	4.620	4.421	4.339	3.322	5.405	4.405	5.440	4.262	3.989	5.147	4.166	4.185	4.897	4.223	1.160	3.536	3.541	3.808	4.183		4.672	1.160
Sweden	0.811	2.048	5.908	5.331	2.557	3.138	1.070	2.767	1.425	5.974	4.877	1.154	3.515	4.141	3.537	0.787	4.585	2.893	5.533	3.923	2.697	4.672		0.787

Source: Authors' work based on GII data

Table 44 Compound distance matrix for the European Union economies without the United Kingdom in 2017 ("D" matrix)

2017	Austria	Belgium	Croatia	Cyprus	Czech Republic	Denmark	Estonia	Finland	France	Greece	Hungary	Italy	Latvia	Lithuania	Netherlands	Poland	Portugal	Romania	Slovakia	Slovenia	Spain	Sweden	Shortest distance
Austria		2.117	5.085	2.420	2.928	1.664	2.394	2.433	3.487	5.698	4.460	4.355	3.432	3.926	1.775	4.277	3.102	5.336	3.684	2.689	3.411	1.342	1.342
Belgium	2.117		4.428	1.448	1.737	2.469	2.283	2.773	3.079	4.711	3.908	3.358	2.993	3.477	2.209	3.194	1.918	4.598	2.835	1.463	2.398	2.178	1.448
Croatia	5.085	4.428		3.453	2.846	6.254	3.265	6.509	5.126	1.441	0.794	4.073	1.957	1.516	6.275	2.560	3.357	1.874	1.623	3.808	3.753	5.999	0.794
Cyprus	2.420	1.448	3.453		1.247	3.072	1.099	3.229	3.578	3.904	3.002	3.450	1.775	2.733	3.172	2.757	1.344	3.630	2.033	0.853	2.611	2.912	0.853
Czech Republic	2.928	1.737	2.846	1.247		3.698	1.636	3.913	3.349	3.376	2.451	3.040	1.598	1.965	3.615	2.025	0.939	3.386	1.296	1.289	2.006	3.434	0.939
Denmark	1.664	2.469	6.254	3.072	3.698		3.225	0.959	4.105	6.839	5.716	5.169	4.453	5.120	0.881	5.180	3.509	6.479	4.756	2.951	4.176	0.513	0.513
Estonia	2.394	2.283	3.265	1.099	1.636	3.225		3.379	3.770	4.041	2.836	3.779	1.321	2.516	3.486	2.906	1.583	3.591	2.108	1.446	2.900	3.107	1.099
Finland	2.433	2.773	6.509	3.229	3.913	0.959	3.379		4.360	7.086	6.034	5.366	4.643	5.489	1.505	5.333	3.502	6.666	5.047	2.936	4.402	1.381	0.959
France	3.487	3.079	5.126	3.578	3.349	4.105	3.770	4.360		5.227	4.494	1.803	4.134	4.506	3.585	2.893	3.514	4.702	4.043	3.695	1.588	3.760	1.588
Greece	5.698	4.711	1.441	3.904	3.376	6.839	4.041	7.086	5.227		1.584	3.799	2.864	2.588	6.748	2.594	3.954	1.420	2.290	4.324	3.888	6.559	1.420
Hungary	4.460	3.908	0.794	3.002	2.451	5.716	2.836	6.034	4.494	1.584		3.528	1.629	1.268	5.701	2.177	3.078	1.706	1.250	3.466	3.209	5.435	0.794
Italy	4.355	3.358	4.073	3.450	3.040	5.169	3.779	5.366	1.803	3.799	3.528		3.625	3.929	4.746	1.705	3.368	3.335	3.320	3.687	1.345	4.836	1.345
Latvia	3.432	2.993	1.957	1.775	1.598	4.453	1.321	4.643	4.134	2.864	1.629	3.625		1.538	4.601	2.310	1.882	2.563	1.173	2.155	2.929	4.269	1.173
Lithuania	3.926	3.477	1.516	2.733	1.965	5.120	2.516	5.489	4.506	2.588	1.268	3.929	1.538		5.124	2.560	2.620	2.924	0.968	3.033	3.179	4.829	0.968
Netherlands	1.775	2.209	6.275	3.172	3.615	0.881	3.486	1.505	3.585	6.748	5.701	4.746	4.601	5.124		4.954	3.526	6.447	4.723	3.052	3.779	0.601	0.601
Poland	4.277	3.194	2.560	2.757	2.025	5.180	2.906	5.333	2.893	2.594	2.177	1.705	2.310	2.560	4.954		2.376	2.321	1.962	2.937	1.505	4.886	1.505
Portugal	3.102	1.918	3.357	1.344	0.939	3.509	1.583	3.502	3.514	3.954	3.078	3.368	1.882	2.620	3.526	2.376		3.815	2.012	0.854	2.308	3.349	0.854
Romania	5.336	4.598	1.874	3.630	3.386	6.479	3.591	6.666	4.702	1.420	1.706	3.335	2.563	2.924	6.447	2.321	3.815		2.515	4.135	3.604	6.241	1.420
Slovakia	3.684	2.835	1.623	2.033	1.296	4.756	2.108	5.047	4.043	2.290	1.250	3.320	1.173	0.968	4.723	1.962	2.012	2.515		2.374	2.628	4.480	0.968
Slovenia	2.689	1.463	3.808	0.853	1.289	2.951	1.446	2.936	3.695	4.324	3.466	3.687	2.155	3.033	3.052	2.937	0.854	4.135	2.374		2.695	2.842	0.853
Spain	3.411	2.398	3.753	2.611	2.006	4.176	2.900	4.402	1.588	3.888	3.209	1.345	2.929	3.179	3.779	1.505	2.308	3.604	2.628	2.695		3.828	1.345
Sweden	1.342	2.178	5.999	2.912	3.434	0.513	3.107	1.381	3.760	6.559	5.435	4.836	4.269	4.829	0.601	4.886	3.349	6.241	4.480	2.842	3.828		0.513

Source: Authors' work based on GII data

Table 45 Compound distance matrix for the European Union economies without the United Kingdom in 2018 ("D" matrix)

2018	Austria	Belgium	Bulgaria	Croatia	Cyprus	Czech Republic	Denmark	Estonia	Finland	France	Germany	Greece	Hungary	Latvia	Lithuania	Netherlands	Poland	Portugal	Romania	Slovakia	Slovenia	Spain	Sweden	Shortest distance
Austria		2.281	5.182	4.980	2.190	2.788	1.589	2.181	2.261	3.055	3.861	5.314	4.125	3.188	3.120	1.716	4.263	2.986	5.259	3.853	2.698	3.325	1.316	1.315
Belgium	2.281		4.378	4.191	1.430	1.564	2.684	2.277	2.963	2.778	3.661	4.117	3.418	2.671	3.131	2.465	2.964	1.779	4.483	2.889	1.269	2.138	2.306	1.269
Bulgaria	5.182	4.378		1.050	3.403	2.974	6.315	3.382	6.514	5.080	6.436	1.210	1.321	2.228	2.436	6.385	2.422	3.553	0.982	1.932	3.855	3.609	6.007	0.982
Croatia	4.980	4.191	1.050		3.342	2.723	6.122	3.248	6.372	4.975	6.248	1.157	0.935	2.115	2.046	6.151	2.348	3.313	1.832	1.362	3.708	3.499	5.759	0.935
Cyprus	2.190	1.430	3.403	3.342		1.060	3.012	1.098	3.244	3.225	4.434	3.497	2.562	1.478	2.091	3.132	2.714	1.485	3.589	2.236	1.098	2.361	2.752	1.060
Czech Republic	2.788	1.564	2.974	2.723	1.060		3.608	1.479	3.824	3.009	4.208	2.845	1.998	1.270	1.865	3.569	1.877	1.012	3.251	1.516	1.184	1.760	3.237	1.012
Denmark	1.589	2.684	6.315	6.122	3.012	3.608		3.078	0.848	3.583	4.005	6.396	5.320	4.176	4.390	0.834	5.164	3.399	6.451	4.936	3.004	4.093	0.577	0.577
Estonia	2.181	2.277	3.382	3.248	1.098	1.479	3.078		3.261	3.384	4.621	3.730	2.538	1.189	1.641	3.343	2.974	1.601	3.693	2.371	1.658	2.731	2.859	1.098
Finland	2.261	2.963	6.514	6.372	3.244	3.824	0.848	3.261		3.829	4.230	6.637	5.615	4.353	4.739	1.414	5.347	3.409	6.683	5.234	3.032	4.317	1.271	0.848
France	3.055	2.778	5.080	4.975	3.225	3.009	3.583	3.384	3.829		1.437	4.957	4.170	3.757	3.903	3.137	3.079	3.127	4.889	4.002	3.300	1.720	3.202	1.437
Germany	3.861	3.661	6.436	6.248	4.434	4.208	4.005	4.621	4.230	1.437		6.193	5.475	5.086	5.182	3.377	4.281	4.205	6.251	5.223	4.339	2.926	3.643	1.437
Greece	5.314	4.117	1.210	1.157	3.497	2.845	6.396	3.730	6.637	4.957	6.193		1.424	2.600	2.785	6.335	2.034	3.502	1.562	1.645	3.788	3.324	6.019	1.156
Hungary	4.125	3.418	1.321	0.935	2.562	1.998	5.320	2.538	5.615	4.170	5.475	1.424		1.485	1.378	5.324	1.857	2.742	1.758	0.800	3.070	2.759	4.951	0.799
Latvia	3.188	2.671	2.228	2.115	1.478	1.270	4.176	1.189	4.353	3.757	5.086	2.600	1.485		1.158	4.336	2.244	1.709	2.662	1.441	1.973	2.598	3.900	1.158
Lithuania	3.120	3.131	2.436	2.046	2.091	1.865	4.390	1.641	4.739	3.903	5.182	2.785	1.378	1.158		4.503	2.646	2.495	2.832	1.478	2.775	2.933	4.053	1.378
Netherlands	1.716	2.465	6.385	6.151	3.132	3.569	0.834	3.343	1.414	3.137	3.377	6.335	5.324	4.336	4.503		4.978	3.435	6.467	4.898	3.076	3.780	0.590	0.591
Poland	4.263	2.964	2.422	2.348	2.714	1.877	5.164	2.974	5.347	3.079	4.281	2.034	1.857	2.244	2.646	4.978		2.366	2.415	1.796	2.797	1.443	4.762	1.444
Portugal	2.986	1.779	3.553	3.313	1.485	1.012	3.399	1.601	3.409	3.127	4.205	3.502	2.742	1.709	2.495	3.435	2.366		3.923	2.281	0.840	2.136	3.096	0.840
Romania	5.259	4.483	0.982	1.832	3.589	3.251	6.451	3.693	6.683	4.889	6.251	1.562	1.758	2.662	2.832	6.467	2.415	3.923		2.406	4.152	3.501	6.145	0.982
Slovakia	3.853	2.889	1.932	1.362	2.236	1.516	4.936	2.371	5.234	4.002	5.223	1.645	0.800	1.441	1.478	4.898	1.796	2.281	2.406		2.579	2.534	4.538	0.799
Slovenia	2.698	1.269	3.855	3.708	1.098	1.184	3.004	1.658	3.032	3.300	4.339	3.788	3.070	1.973	2.775	3.076	2.797	0.840	4.152	2.579		2.408	2.750	0.840
Spain	3.325	2.138	3.609	3.499	2.361	1.760	4.093	2.731	4.317	1.720	2.926	3.324	2.759	2.598	2.933	3.780	1.443	2.136	3.501	2.534	2.408		3.671	1.444
Sweden	1.316	2.306	6.007	5.759	2.752	3.237	0.577	2.859	1.271	3.202	3.643	6.019	4.951	3.900	4.053	0.590	4.762	3.096	6.145	4.538	2.750	3.671		0.577

Source: Authors' work based on GII data

Table 46 Compound distance matrix for G20 economies in 2010 ("D" matrix)

2010	Argentina	Australia	Brazil	Canada	China	France	Germany	India	Indonesia	Italy	Japan	Mexico	Russia	Suadi Arabia	South Africa	Rep. of Korea	Turkey	United Kingdom	United States	European Union	Shortest distance
Argentina=1		5.488	1.247	5.754	4.000	3.753	4.442	3.471	1.669	2.941	4.340	2.254	2.065	3.856	3.031	3.746	2.592	4.974	5.328	4.099	1.247
Australia=2	5.488		5.581	0.513	6.571	1.822	1.188	6.463	5.471	2.626	1.295	4.582	5.243	3.699	3.528	2.059	4.204	0.665	1.125	2.299	0.513
Brazil=3	1.247	5.581		5.889	4.060	3.987	4.583	3.250	2.395	3.269	4.370	3.123	3.139	4.602	3.503	4.101	3.324	5.141	5.453	4.154	1.247
Canada=4	5.754	0.513	5.889		6.724	2.056	1.420	6.665	5.635	2.891	1.571	4.711	5.396	3.740	3.578	2.163	4.333	0.910	1.355	2.370	0.513
China=5	4.000	6.571	4.060	6.724		5.280	5.775	1.105	3.147	4.776	5.635	3.640	3.592	4.611	4.378	5.063	3.812	6.006	5.988	4.502	1.105
France=6	3.753	1.822	3.987	2.056	5.280		0.724	5.115	3.849	0.857	0.852	3.025	3.591	2.706	2.195	0.804	2.786	1.364	1.803	1.509	0.724
Germany=7	4.442	1.188	4.583	1.420	5.775	0.724		5.621	4.522	1.566	0.468	3.696	4.292	3.178	2.714	1.228	3.418	0.913	1.346	1.595	0.468
India=8	3.471	6.463	3.250	6.665	1.105	5.115	5.621		2.908	4.567	5.416	3.648	3.653	4.843	4.263	4.983	3.817	5.933	5.977	4.405	1.105
Indonesia=9	1.669	5.471	2.395	5.635	3.147	3.849	4.522	2.908		3.164	4.430	1.291	1.400	3.034	2.321	3.516	1.659	4.874	5.303	3.760	1.291
Italy=10	2.941	2.626	3.269	2.891	4.776	0.857	1.566	4.567	3.164		1.595	2.414	2.879	2.508	1.969	1.153	2.267	2.121	2.469	1.857	0.857
Japan=11	4.340	1.295	4.370	1.571	5.635	0.852	0.468	5.416	4.430	1.595		3.705	4.339	3.313	2.663	1.326	3.411	1.057	1.516	1.432	0.468
Mexico=12	2.254	4.582	3.123	4.711	3.640	3.025	3.696	3.648	1.291	2.414	3.705		0.949	1.801	1.610	2.582	0.595	3.952	4.401	3.128	0.949
Russia=13	2.065	5.243	3.139	5.396	3.592	3.591	4.292	3.653	1.400	2.879	4.339	0.949		2.413	2.481	3.277	1.486	4.617	4.946	3.814	0.949
Suadi Arabia=14	3.856	3.699	4.602	3.740	4.611	2.706	3.178	4.843	3.034	2.508	3.313	1.801	2.413		1.941	2.072	1.425	3.058	3.532	2.891	1.430
South Africa=15	3.031	3.528	3.503	3.578	4.378	2.195	2.714	4.263	2.321	1.969	2.663	1.610	2.481	1.941		1.586	1.359	2.975	3.637	2.099	1.359
Rep. of Korea=16	3.746	2.059	4.101	2.163	5.063	0.804	1.228	4.983	3.516	1.153	1.326	2.582	3.277	2.072	1.586		2.268	1.486	2.128	1.388	0.804
Turkey=17	2.592	4.204	3.324	4.333	3.812	2.786	3.418	3.817	1.659	2.267	3.411	0.595	1.486	1.425	1.359	2.268		3.566	4.077	2.862	0.595
United Kingdom=18	4.974	0.665	5.141	0.910	6.006	1.364	0.913	5.933	4.874	2.121	1.057	3.952	4.617	3.058	2.975	1.486	3.566		1.025	1.869	0.665
United States=19	5.328	1.125	5.453	1.355	5.988	1.803	1.346	5.977	5.303	2.469	1.516	4.401	4.946	3.532	3.637	2.128	4.077	1.025		1.869	1.025
European Union=20	4.099	2.299	4.154	2.370	4.502	1.509	1.595	4.405	3.760	1.857	1.432	3.128	3.814	2.891	2.099	1.388	2.862	1.869	2.115		1.388

Source: Authors' work based on GII data

Table 47 Compound distance matrix for G20 economies in 2011 ("D" matrix)

2011	Argentina	Australia	Brazil	Canada	China	France	Germany	India	Italy	Japan	Mexico	Russia	Suadi Arabia	South Africa	Rep. of Korea	Turkey	United Kingdom	United States	European Union	Shortest distance
Argentina=1		4.622	3.088	4.962	4.387	3.957	3.724	4.780	3.130	3.970	1.562	1.926	1.963	2.568	2.567	1.783	4.610	4.697	3.694	1.562
Australia=2	4.622		4.835	0.548	6.976	0.907	1.617	6.949	2.257	1.482	4.336	4.816	3.499	3.202	2.131	4.784	0.557	1.157	2.027	0.548
Brazil=3	3.088	4.835		5.300	3.747	3.929	3.491	3.068	2.629	3.497	2.193	1.802	3.037	2.338	3.378	1.702	4.733	4.748	3.366	1.702
Canada=4	4.962	0.548	5.300		7.342	1.389	2.120	7.353	2.754	1.966	4.726	5.251	3.856	3.542	2.514	5.215	0.726	1.472	2.388	0.548
China=5	4.387	6.976	3.747	7.342		6.205	5.926	1.616	5.186	5.940	3.798	3.445	4.600	4.774	5.416	3.635	6.821	6.476	5.115	1.616
France=6	3.957	0.907	3.929	1.389	6.205		0.952	6.110	1.376	0.726	3.553	3.991	2.851	2.395	1.524	3.952	0.919	1.323	1.363	0.726
Germany=7	3.724	1.617	3.491	2.120	5.926	0.952		5.741	1.154	0.584	3.419	3.717	2.929	2.469	1.452	3.658	1.823	1.724	1.347	0.584
India=8	4.780	6.949	3.068	7.353	1.616	6.110	5.741		5.001	5.697	4.031	3.564	4.950	4.629	5.546	3.680	6.791	6.521	5.023	1.616
Italy=9	3.130	2.257	2.629	2.754	5.186	1.376	1.154	5.001		1.134	2.471	2.750	2.080	1.621	1.342	2.718	2.209	2.252	1.452	1.134
Japan=10	3.970	1.482	3.497	1.966	5.940	0.726	0.584	5.697	1.133		3.513	3.833	3.024	2.347	1.712	3.785	1.538	1.630	1.153	0.584
Mexico=11	1.562	4.336	2.193	4.726	3.798	3.553	3.419	4.031	2.471	3.513		0.808	1.212	1.797	2.447	0.789	4.205	4.296	3.216	0.789
Russia=12	1.926	4.816	1.802	5.251	3.445	3.991	3.717	3.564	2.750	3.833	0.808		1.836	2.320	2.956	0.368	4.713	4.670	3.566	0.368
Suadi Arabia=13	1.963	3.499	3.037	3.856	4.600	2.851	2.929	4.950	2.080	3.024	1.213	1.836		1.836	1.787	1.888	3.368	3.464	2.823	1.213
South Africa=14	2.568	3.202	2.338	3.542	4.774	2.395	2.469	4.629	1.622	2.347	1.797	2.320	1.836		1.884	2.180	2.983	3.470	2.220	1.622
Rep. of Korea=15	2.567	2.131	3.378	2.514	5.416	1.524	1.452	5.546	1.341	1.712	2.447	2.956	1.787	1.884		2.888	2.204	2.313	1.727	1.341
Turkey=16	1.783	4.784	1.701	5.215	3.635	3.952	3.658	3.680	2.718	3.785	0.789	0.368	1.888	2.180	2.888		4.691	4.717	3.564	0.368
United Kingdom=17	4.610	0.558	4.733	0.726	6.821	0.919	1.823	6.791	2.209	1.538	4.205	4.713	3.368	2.983	2.204	4.691		1.299	1.957	0.558
United States=18	4.697	1.157	4.748	1.472	6.476	1.323	1.724	6.521	2.252	1.630	4.296	4.670	3.464	3.470	2.313	4.717	1.299		1.804	1.157
European Union=19	3.694	2.027	3.366	2.388	5.115	1.363	1.347	5.023	1.452	1.153	3.216	3.566	2.823	2.220	1.727	3.564	1.957	1.804		1.153

Source: Authors' work based on GII data

Table 48 Compound distance matrix for G20 economies in 2012 ("D" matrix)

2012	Argentina	Australia	Canada	China	France	Germany	India	Italy	Japan	Mexico	Russia	Suadi Arabia	South Africa	Rep. of Korea	Turkey	United Kingdom	United States	European Union	Shortest distance
Argentina=1		5.565	6.071	3.690	4.080	4.539	3.616	3.415	4.702	2.448	1.989	2.327	2.947	3.919	1.514	5.445	5.511	4.266	1.514
Australia=2	5.565		0.687	6.840	1.662	1.114	6.634	2.323	0.954	4.227	4.774	4.268	3.503	2.150	4.860	0.625	1.095	2.029	0.625
Canada=3	6.071	0.687		7.234	2.289	1.621	7.066	2.878	1.477	4.588	5.204	4.732	3.905	2.428	5.313	0.869	1.509	2.435	0.687
China=4	3.690	6.840	7.234		5.586	6.001	1.176	4.939	5.923	3.758	3.367	3.911	4.371	5.374	3.445	6.554	6.409	4.934	1.176
France=5	4.080	1.662	2.289	5.586		0.989	5.279	0.889	0.913	3.116	3.502	3.033	2.274	1.774	3.493	1.654	1.759	1.314	0.889
Germany=6	4.539	1.114	1.621	6.001	0.989		5.829	1.570	0.628	3.428	3.940	3.493	2.794	1.404	3.968	1.267	1.414	1.406	0.628
India=7	3.616	6.634	7.066	1.176	5.279	5.829		4.667	5.705	3.783	3.418	3.933	4.007	5.382	3.385	6.344	6.265	4.695	1.176
Italy=8	3.415	2.323	2.878	4.939	0.889	1.570	4.667		1.441	2.270	2.635	2.183	1.549	1.559	2.652	2.134	2.359	1.485	0.889
Japan=9	4.702	0.954	1.477	5.923	0.913	0.628	5.705	1.441		3.361	3.890	3.434	2.627	1.515	3.965	0.833	1.246	1.216	0.628
Mexico=10	2.448	4.227	4.588	3.758	3.116	3.428	3.783	2.270	3.361		0.868	1.123	1.515	2.368	1.077	3.888	4.260	3.052	0.868
Russia=11	1.989	4.774	5.204	3.367	3.502	3.940	3.418	2.635	3.890	0.868		0.804	2.023	2.999	0.587	4.476	4.680	3.519	0.587
Suadi Arabia=12	2.327	4.268	4.732	3.911	3.033	3.493	3.933	2.183	3.434	1.123	0.804		2.013	2.624	1.138	4.000	4.145	3.244	0.804
South Africa=13	2.947	3.503	3.905	4.371	2.274	2.794	4.007	1.549	2.627	1.515	2.023	2.013		2.258	1.917	3.154	3.721	2.349	1.515
Rep. of Korea=14	3.919	2.150	2.428	5.374	1.774	1.404	5.382	1.559	1.515	2.368	2.999	2.624	2.258		3.116	1.963	2.363	1.833	1.404
Turkey=15	1.514	4.860	5.313	3.445	3.493	3.968	3.385	2.652	3.965	1.077	0.587	1.138	1.917	3.116		4.597	4.832	3.581	0.587
United Kingdom=16	5.445	0.624	0.869	6.554	1.654	1.267	6.344	2.134	0.833	3.888	4.476	4.000	3.154	1.963	4.597		1.300	1.855	0.624
United States=17	5.511	1.095	1.509	6.409	1.759	1.414	6.265	2.359	1.246	4.260	4.680	4.145	3.721	2.363	4.832	1.300		1.839	1.095
European Union=18	4.266	2.029	2.435	4.934	1.314	1.406	4.695	1.485	1.216	3.052	3.519	3.244	2.349	1.833	3.581	1.855	1.839		1.216

Source: Authors' work based on GII data

Table 49 Compound distance matrix for G20 economies in 2013 ("D" matrix)

2013	Argentina	Australia	Brazil	Canada	China	France	Germany	India	Italy	Japan	Mexico	Russia	Suadi Arabia	South Africa	Rep. of Korea	Turkey	United Kingdom	United States	European Union	Shortest distance
Argentina=1		5.483	1.849	5.944	3.764	4.121	4.596	3.712	3.446	4.799	2.336	1.981	2.445	3.005	3.800	1.544	5.418	5.553	4.281	1.545
Australia=2	5.483		1.342	2.407	1.915	2.004	2.117	1.902	1.833	2.163	1.509	1.390	1.544	1.711	1.925	1.227	2.298	2.326	2.043	1.227
Brazil=3	1.849	1.342		5.731	3.584	3.706	4.473	3.005	3.078	4.462	2.594	2.319	2.649	2.537	4.054	1.909	5.092	5.295	3.849	1.342
Canada=4	5.944	2.407	5.731		7.084	2.079	1.406	6.926	2.730	1.290	4.501	5.036	4.301	3.777	2.429	5.242	0.813	1.387	2.335	0.813
China=5	3.764	1.915	3.584	7.084		5.552	5.994	1.121	4.921	5.946	3.744	3.437	4.136	4.404	5.276	3.496	6.485	6.416	4.866	1.121
France=6	4.121	2.004	3.706	2.079	5.552		0.988	5.267	0.896	0.873	3.026	3.425	2.686	2.219	1.712	3.517	1.547	1.818	1.313	0.873
Germany=7	4.596	2.117	4.473	1.406	5.994	0.988		5.843	1.609	0.675	3.425	3.909	3.193	2.783	1.448	4.052	1.183	1.407	1.444	0.674
India=8	3.712	1.902	3.005	6.926	1.121	5.267	5.843		4.656	5.726	3.699	3.424	4.100	4.043	5.282	3.392	6.278	6.305	4.648	1.121
Italy=9	3.446	1.833	3.078	2.730	4.921	0.896	1.609	4.656		1.494	2.170	2.551	1.874	1.495	1.477	2.664	2.077	2.463	1.499	0.896
Japan=10	4.799	2.163	4.462	1.290	5.946	0.873	0.675	5.726	1.494		3.416	3.907	3.202	2.638	1.670	4.080	0.732	1.330	1.270	0.674
Mexico=11	2.336	1.509	2.594	4.501	3.744	3.026	3.425	3.699	2.170	3.416		0.745	1.338	1.438	2.300	1.017	3.854	4.325	2.979	0.745
Russia=12	1.981	1.390	2.319	5.036	3.437	3.425	3.909	3.424	2.551	3.907	0.745		1.182	1.967	2.845	0.545	4.384	4.707	3.442	0.546
Suadi Arabia=13	2.445	1.544	2.649	4.301	4.136	2.686	3.193	4.100	1.874	3.202	1.338	1.182		2.045	2.297	1.431	3.683	3.846	2.998	1.181
South Africa=14	3.005	1.711	2.537	3.777	4.404	2.219	2.783	4.043	1.495	2.638	1.438	1.967	2.045		2.161	1.980	3.076	3.800	2.278	1.439
Rep. of Korea=15	3.800	1.925	4.054	2.429	5.276	1.712	1.448	5.282	1.477	1.670	2.300	2.845	2.297	2.161		3.072	2.019	2.453	1.827	1.448
Turkey=16	1.544	1.227	1.909	5.242	3.496	3.517	4.052	3.392	2.664	4.080	1.017	0.545	1.431	1.980	3.072		4.597	4.933	3.607	1.018
United Kingdom=17	5.418	2.298	5.092	0.813	6.485	1.547	1.183	6.278	2.077	0.732	3.854	4.384	3.683	3.076	2.019	4.597		1.426	1.829	0.732
United States=18	5.553	2.326	5.295	1.387	6.416	1.818	1.407	6.305	2.463	1.330	4.325	4.707	3.846	3.800	2.453	4.933	1.426		1.986	1.387
European Union=19	4.281	2.043	3.849	2.335	4.866	1.313	1.444	4.648	1.499	1.270	2.979	3.442	2.998	2.278	1.827	3.607	1.829	1.986		1.270

Source: Authors' work based on GII data

Table 50 Compound distance matrix for G20 economies in 2014 ("D" matrix)

2014	Argentina	Australia	Brazil	Canada	China	France	Germany	India	Indonesia	Italy	Japan	Mexico	Russia	Suadi Arabia	South Africa	Rep. of Korea	Turkey	United Kingdom	United States	European Union	Shortest distance
Argentina=1		5.269	1.519	5.768	3.789	4.272	4.552	3.644	1.634	3.320	4.816	2.267	1.985	2.045	3.226	3.967	1.545	5.037	5.430	4.195	1.519
Australia=2	5.269		4.784	0.662	5.991	1.056	0.813	6.504	6.525	2.116	0.637	3.891	4.361	3.567	3.160	1.952	4.451	0.660	1.158	1.883	0.660
Brazil=3	1.519	4.784		5.306	3.424	3.742	4.176	2.973	2.620	2.735	4.270	2.026	1.869	1.889	2.559	3.794	1.445	4.465	4.990	3.554	1.445
Canada=4	5.768	0.662	5.306		6.311	1.575	1.272	6.918	6.950	2.610	1.140	4.236	4.733	4.051	3.461	2.142	4.867	0.928	1.314	2.228	0.662
China=5	3.789	5.991	3.424	6.311		5.131	5.358	1.553	3.590	4.463	5.452	3.535	3.432	3.989	4.143	4.841	3.506	5.641	5.715	4.156	1.553
France=6	4.272	1.056	3.742	1.575	5.131		0.627	5.562	5.526	1.077	0.640	2.895	3.361	2.592	2.218	1.364	3.422	0.825	1.615	1.240	0.627
Germany=7	4.552	0.813	4.176	1.272	5.358	0.627		5.917	5.767	1.577	0.574	3.242	3.717	2.940	2.660	1.334	3.790	0.911	1.346	1.410	0.574
India=8	3.644	6.504	2.973	6.918	1.553	5.562	5.917		3.529	4.744	5.945	3.841	3.610	4.110	4.413	5.511	3.553	6.133	6.334	4.737	1.553
Indonesia=9	1.634	6.525	2.620	6.950	3.590	5.526	5.767	3.529		4.599	6.037	3.057	2.753	3.401	4.116	4.990	2.452	6.245	6.648	5.240	1.634
Italy=10	3.320	2.116	2.735	2.610	4.463	1.077	1.577	4.744	4.599		1.689	1.965	2.367	1.604	1.505	1.471	2.398	1.768	2.442	1.480	1.077
Japan=11	4.816	0.637	4.270	1.140	5.452	0.640	0.574	5.945	6.037	1.689		3.455	3.948	3.205	2.703	1.730	4.007	0.684	1.384	1.337	0.574
Mexico=12	2.267	3.891	2.026	4.236	3.535	2.895	3.242	3.841	3.057	1.965	3.455		0.678	1.413	1.281	2.314	0.844	3.460	4.090	2.782	0.678
Russia=13	1.985	4.361	1.869	4.733	3.432	3.361	3.717	3.610	2.753	2.367	3.948	0.678		1.335	1.873	2.809	0.553	3.937	4.458	3.242	0.533
Suadi Arabia=14	2.045	3.567	1.889	4.051	3.989	2.592	2.940	4.110	3.401	1.604	3.205	1.413	1.335		2.059	2.381	1.315	3.269	3.640	2.734	1.315
South Africa=15	3.226	3.160	2.559	3.461	4.143	2.218	2.660	4.413	4.116	1.505	2.703	1.281	1.873	2.059		1.982	1.925	2.660	3.605	2.231	1.281
Rep. of Korea=16	3.967	1.952	3.794	2.142	4.841	1.364	1.334	5.511	4.990	1.471	1.730	2.314	2.809	2.381	1.982		2.988	1.662	2.200	1.738	1.334
Turkey=17	1.545	4.451	1.445	4.867	3.506	3.422	3.790	3.553	2.452	2.398	4.007	0.844	0.553	1.315	1.925	2.988		4.067	4.632	3.340	0.553
United Kingdom=18	5.037	0.660	4.465	0.928	5.641	0.825	0.911	6.133	6.245	1.768	0.684	3.460	3.937	3.269	2.660	1.662	4.067		1.333	1.612	0.660
United States=19	5.430	1.158	4.990	1.314	5.715	1.615	1.346	6.334	6.648	2.442	1.384	4.090	4.458	3.640	3.605	2.200	4.632	1.333		1.908	1.158
European Union=20	4.195	1.883	3.554	2.228	4.156	1.240	1.410	4.737	5.240	1.480	1.337	2.782	3.242	2.734	2.231	1.738	3.340	1.612	1.908		1.240

Source: Authors' work based on GII data

Table 51 Compound distance matrix for G20 economies in 2015 ("D" matrix)

2015	Argentina	Australia	Brazil	Canada	China	France	Germany	India	Indonesia	Italy	Japan	Mexico	Russia	South Africa	Rep. of Korea	Turkey	United Kingdom	United States	European Union	Shortest distance
		5.323	1.544	5.633	3.655	4.267	4.789	3.695	1.400	3.385	4.908	2.420	2.270	3.068	3.931	1.423	5.165	5.329	4.253	1.400
	5.323		4.822	0.426	5.756	1.113	0.690	6.442	6.230	2.131	0.813	4.040	4.083	3.407	1.982	4.495	0.652	1.069	1.789	0.426
	1.544	4.822		5.120	3.237	3.750	4.410	2.983	2.412	2.845	4.313	2.121	2.232	2.317	3.720	1.345	4.575	4.866	3.635	1.345
	5.633	0.426	5.120		5.944	1.434	0.971	6.667	6.487	2.439	0.936	4.255	4.340	3.582	2.145	4.775	0.741	1.282	1.977	0.426
	3.655	5.756	3.237	5.944		4.866	5.299	1.479	3.385	4.253	5.224	3.404	3.735	3.824	4.571	3.360	5.467	5.384	3.987	1.480
	4.267	1.113	3.750	1.434	4.866		0.842	5.476	5.184	1.026	0.956	2.986	3.021	2.426	1.257	3.393	0.950	1.397	1.170	0.841
	4.789	0.690	4.410	0.971	5.299	0.842		6.047	5.669	1.798	0.799	3.652	3.681	3.138	1.566	4.047	0.993	1.111	1.452	0.689
	3.695	6.442	2.983	6.667	1.479	5.476	6.047		3.496	4.730	5.890	3.745	4.048	4.105	5.343	3.487	6.115	6.142	4.741	1.480
	1.400	6.230	2.412	6.487	3.385	5.184	5.669	3.496		4.319	5.761	2.844	2.868	3.654	4.613	2.145	6.016	6.204	4.980	1.400
	3.385	2.131	2.845	2.439	4.253	1.026	1.798	4.730	4.319		1.866	2.069	2.066	1.662	1.272	2.408	1.850	2.221	1.471	1.026
	4.908	0.813	4.313	0.936	5.224	0.956	0.799	5.890	5.761	1.866		3.664	3.818	2.930	1.847	4.104	0.852	1.496	1.356	0.799
	2.420	4.040	2.121	4.255	3.404	2.986	3.652	3.745	2.844	2.069	3.664		0.704	1.168	2.359	1.068	3.639	4.071	2.943	0.704
	2.270	4.083	2.232	4.340	3.735	3.021	3.681	4.048	2.868	2.066	3.818	0.704		1.653	2.403	0.988	3.733	4.052	3.130	0.704
	3.068	3.407	2.317	3.582	3.824	2.426	3.138	4.105	3.654	1.662	2.930	1.168	1.653		2.114	1.836	2.957	3.654	2.470	1.169
	3.931	1.982	3.720	2.145	4.571	1.257	1.566	5.343	4.613	1.272	1.847	2.359	2.403	2.114		2.972	1.710	2.112	1.608	1.257
	1.423	4.495	1.345	4.775	3.360	3.393	4.047	3.487	2.145	2.408	4.104	1.068	0.988	1.836	2.972		4.200	4.501	3.391	0.988
	5.165	0.652	4.575	0.741	5.467	0.950	0.993	6.115	6.016	1.850	0.852	3.639	3.733	2.957	1.710	4.200		1.241	1.572	0.652
	5.329	1.069	4.866	1.282	5.384	1.397	1.111	6.142	6.204	2.221	1.496	4.071	4.052	3.654	2.112	4.501	1.241		1.595	1.069
	4.253	1.789	3.635	1.977	3.987	1.170	1.452	4.741	4.980	1.471	1.356	2.943	3.130	2.470	1.608	3.391	1.572	1.595		1.171

Source: Authors' work based on GII data

Table 52 Compound distance matrix for G20 economies in 2016 ("D" matrix)

2016	Argentina	Australia	Brazil	Canada	China	France	Germany	India	Indonesia	Italy	Japan	Mexico	Russia	South Africa	Rep. of Korea	Turkey	United Kingdom	United States	European Union	Shortest distance
Argentina=1		5.123	1.392	5.470	3.682	4.286	4.716	3.676	1.716	3.266	4.926	2.146	2.295	2.696	3.855	1.168	5.149	5.323	4.210	1.168
Australia=2	5.123		4.928	0.501	5.604	0.906	0.583	6.198	5.955	2.012	0.748	3.982	4.066	3.460	1.903	4.681	0.508	0.990	1.694	0.501
Brazil=3	1.392	4.928		5.270	3.311	4.066	4.626	2.927	2.466	3.009	4.667	1.974	2.312	2.152	3.875	1.136	4.867	5.132	3.894	1.136
Canada=4	5.470	0.501	5.270		5.831	1.296	0.881	6.454	6.258	2.407	0.718	4.308	4.437	3.735	2.189	5.051	0.599	1.220	1.907	0.501
China=5	3.682	5.604	3.311	5.831		4.871	5.224	1.457	3.352	4.205	5.216	3.323	3.462	3.687	4.500	3.434	5.470	5.378	3.942	1.457
France=6	4.286	0.906	4.066	1.296	4.871		0.727	5.424	5.096	1.120	0.928	3.087	3.189	2.601	1.237	3.789	0.906	1.383	1.181	0.727
Germany=7	4.716	0.584	4.626	0.881	5.224	0.727		5.888	5.502	1.747	0.811	3.647	3.718	3.228	1.523	4.333	0.856	1.041	1.411	0.584
India=8	3.676	6.198	2.927	6.454	1.457	5.424	5.888		3.605	4.628	5.804	3.636	3.869	3.857	5.226	3.434	6.049	6.068	4.617	1.457
Indonesia=9	1.715	5.955	2.466	6.258	3.352	5.096	5.502	3.605		4.124	5.688	2.355	2.435	3.216	4.322	1.907	5.902	6.097	4.840	1.715
Italy=10	3.266	2.012	3.009	2.407	4.205	1.120	1.747	4.628	4.124		1.927	2.082	2.196	1.709	1.242	2.686	1.980	2.308	1.496	1.120
Japan=11	4.926	0.748	4.667	0.718	5.216	0.928	0.811	5.804	5.688	1.927		3.742	3.945	3.119	1.835	4.498	0.556	1.415	1.371	0.556
Mexico=12	2.146	3.982	1.974	4.308	3.323	3.087	3.647	3.636	2.355	2.082	3.742		0.741	1.097	2.415	1.217	3.847	4.215	2.998	0.741
Russia=13	2.295	4.066	2.312	4.437	3.462	3.189	3.718	3.869	2.435	2.196	3.945	0.741		1.710	2.428	1.350	3.983	4.185	3.139	0.741
South Africa=14	2.696	3.460	2.152	3.735	3.687	2.601	3.228	3.857	3.216	1.709	3.119	1.097	1.710		2.264	1.896	3.251	3.857	2.600	1.097
Rep. of Korea=15	3.855	1.903	3.875	2.189	4.500	1.238	1.523	5.226	4.322	1.242	1.835	2.415	2.428	2.264		3.305	1.837	2.182	1.599	1.238
Turkey=16	1.167	4.681	1.136	5.051	3.434	3.789	4.333	3.434	1.907	2.686	4.498	1.217	1.350	1.896	3.305		4.633	4.875	3.728	1.136
United Kingdom=17	5.149	0.508	4.867	0.599	5.470	0.906	0.856	6.049	5.902	1.980	0.555	3.847	3.983	3.251	1.837	4.633		1.240	1.579	0.508
United States=18	5.323	0.990	5.132	1.220	5.378	1.383	1.041	6.068	6.097	2.308	1.415	4.215	4.185	3.857	2.182	4.875	1.240		1.609	0.990
European Union=19	4.210	1.694	3.894	1.907	3.942	1.181	1.411	4.617	4.840	1.496	1.371	2.998	3.139	2.600	1.599	3.728	1.579	1.609		1.180

Source: Authors' work based on GII data

Table 53 Compound distance matrix for G20 economies in 2017 ("D" matrix)

2017	Argentina	Australia	Brazil	Canada	China	France	Germany	India	Italy	Japan	Mexico	Russia	South Africa	Rep. of Korea	Turkey	United Kingdom	United States	European Union	Shortest distance
Argentina=1		5.144	1.289	5.435	3.527	4.112	4.746	3.471	3.366	5.066	1.981	1.809	1.985	3.901	1.282	4.886	5.458	3.816	1.282
Australia=2	5.144		5.155	0.460	5.718	1.107	0.635	6.223	2.078	0.654	4.188	4.499	3.988	1.955	5.318	0.498	1.068	1.918	0.498
Brazil=3	1.289	5.155		5.463	3.278	4.094	4.872	2.821	3.327	5.088	1.994	1.868	1.535	4.074	1.200	4.825	5.423	3.736	1.200
Canada=4	5.435	0.460	5.463		5.919	1.461	0.870	6.448	2.412	0.518	4.464	4.827	4.244	2.173	5.672	0.730	1.280	2.167	0.460
China=5	3.527	5.718	3.278	5.919		4.832	5.332	1.460	4.253	5.463	3.253	3.288	3.566	4.561	3.600	5.404	5.553	3.824	1.460
France=6	4.112	1.107	4.094	1.461	4.832		0.928	5.291	0.995	1.211	3.109	3.405	2.953	1.221	4.234	0.840	1.555	1.195	0.840
Germany=7	4.746	0.635	4.872	0.870	5.332	0.928		5.923	1.821	0.765	3.845	4.138	3.762	1.575	4.983	0.801	1.172	1.598	0.636
India=8	3.471	6.223	2.821	6.448	1.460	5.291	5.923		4.691	6.000	3.564	3.570	3.445	5.237	3.448	5.867	6.177	4.370	1.460
Italy=9	3.366	2.078	3.327	2.412	4.253	0.995	1.821	4.691		2.108	2.161	2.447	2.210	1.013	3.373	1.766	2.339	1.374	0.995
Japan=10	5.066	0.654	5.088	0.518	5.463	1.211	0.765	6.000	2.108		4.072	4.478	3.851	1.865	5.343	0.591	1.397	1.784	0.591
Mexico=11	1.981	4.188	1.994	4.464	3.253	3.109	3.845	3.564	2.161	4.072		0.822	1.372	2.572	1.923	3.843	4.403	2.923	0.823
Russia=12	1.809	4.499	1.868	4.827	3.288	3.405	4.138	3.570	2.447	4.478	0.822		1.822	2.943	1.353	4.201	4.606	3.190	0.823
South Africa=13	1.985	3.988	1.535	4.244	3.566	2.953	3.762	3.445	2.210	3.851	1.372	1.822		2.906	2.168	3.601	4.400	2.809	1.372
Rep. of Korea=14	3.901	1.955	4.074	2.173	4.561	1.221	1.575	5.237	1.013	1.865	2.572	2.943	2.906		4.043	1.730	2.190	1.664	1.013
Turkey=15	1.282	5.318	1.200	5.672	3.600	4.234	4.983	3.448	3.373	5.343	1.923	1.353	2.168	4.043		5.043	5.481	3.980	1.200
United Kingdom=16	4.886	0.498	4.825	0.730	5.404	0.840	0.801	5.867	1.766	0.591	3.843	4.201	3.601	1.730	5.043		1.256	1.666	0.498
United States=17	5.458	1.068	5.423	1.280	5.553	1.555	1.172	6.177	2.339	1.397	4.403	4.606	4.400	2.190	5.481	1.256		1.916	1.068
European Union=18	3.816	1.918	3.736	2.167	3.824	1.195	1.598	4.370	1.374	1.784	2.923	3.190	2.809	1.664	3.980	1.666	1.916		1.194

Source: Authors' work based on GII data

Table 54 Compound distance matrix for G20 economies in 2018 ("D" matrix)

2018	Argentina	Australia	Brazil	Canada	France	Germany	Italy	Japan	Mexico	Russia	South Africa	Rep. of Korea	Turkey	United Kingdom	Shortest distance
Argentina=1		5.388	3.448	5.725	4.429	5.104	3.480	5.534	1.921	2.570	1.758	4.057	1.000	5.023	1.000
Australia=2	5.388		6.357	0.624	1.254	1.293	2.322	2.130	4.493	5.014	4.545	1.889	5.105	1.034	0.624
Brazil=3	3.448	6.357		6.516	5.123	5.584	4.356	5.342	4.164	2.054	3.200	5.062	2.789	5.524	2.054
Canada=4	5.725	0.624	6.516		1.471	1.295	2.672	1.864	4.845	5.266	4.804	2.110	5.445	1.099	0.624
France=5	4.429	1.254	5.123	1.471		0.879	1.373	1.593	3.699	3.828	3.577	1.157	4.041	0.712	0.712
Germany=6	5.104	1.293	5.584	1.295	0.879		2.117	1.246	4.438	4.306	4.363	1.577	4.661	0.990	0.878
Italy=7	3.480	2.322	4.356	2.672	1.373	2.117		2.576	2.513	2.835	2.635	1.191	3.049	1.788	1.190
Japan=8	5.534	2.130	5.342	1.864	1.593	1.246	2.576		4.868	4.380	4.527	2.229	5.034	1.348	1.246
Mexico=9	1.921	4.493	4.164	4.845	3.699	4.438	2.513	4.868		2.671	1.750	3.045	2.067	4.162	1.750
Russia=10	2.570	5.014	2.054	5.266	3.828	4.306	2.835	4.380	2.671		2.515	3.465	1.701	4.314	1.700
South Africa=11	1.758	4.545	3.200	4.804	3.577	4.363	2.635	4.527	1.750	2.515		3.387	1.845	4.007	1.750
Rep. of Korea=12	4.057	1.889	5.062	2.110	1.157	1.577	1.191	2.229	3.045	3.465	3.387		3.723	1.586	1.157
Turkey=13	1.000	5.105	2.789	5.445	4.041	4.661	3.049	5.034	2.067	1.701	1.845	3.723		4.635	1.000
United Kingdom=14	5.023	1.034	5.524	1.099	0.712	0.990	1.788	1.348	4.162	4.314	4.007	1.586	4.635		0.712

Source: Authors' work based on GII data

3.6 Step 6: Results (Ranking of Economies in Terms of Institutional Development)

Following step 5, if in each of the three groups, namely, the European Union economies, once with and then without the United Kingdom, and also the G20 economies, homogeneity is not achieved within the first stage of homogenization, then the new data matrices should be formed by eliminating the economies, which do not fall in the range of d(−) and d(+), and then computing the standard matrices and reiterating the process, until economies are settled in homogeneous groups.

The homogenization processes for each group (i.e., the European Union economies, once with and then without the United Kingdom, and the G20 economies) are depicted in Figs. 2, 3, and 4 showing economies eliminated in various stages of homogenization.

It is recalled, for instance, that 28 economies correspond to the European Union economies in the years 2010–2018 (except in 2010 where the GII did not report any data for Malta; hence, in this year, the European Union was considered with 27

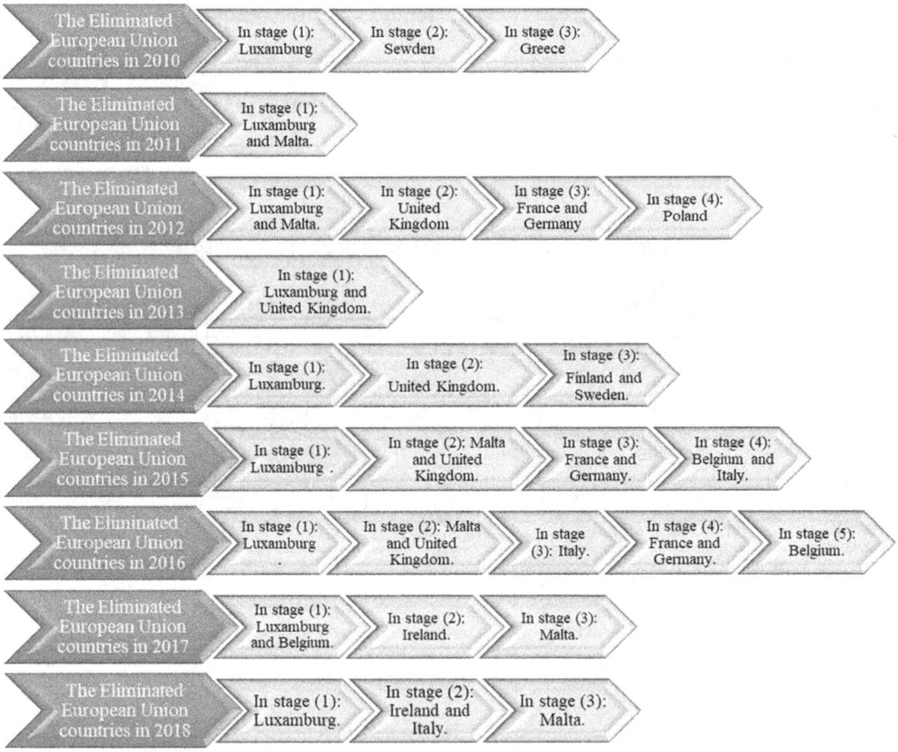

Fig. 2 Economies eliminated in various stages of homogenization processes for the European Union economies in the years 2010–2018. (Source: Authors' work based on Taxonomic computation)

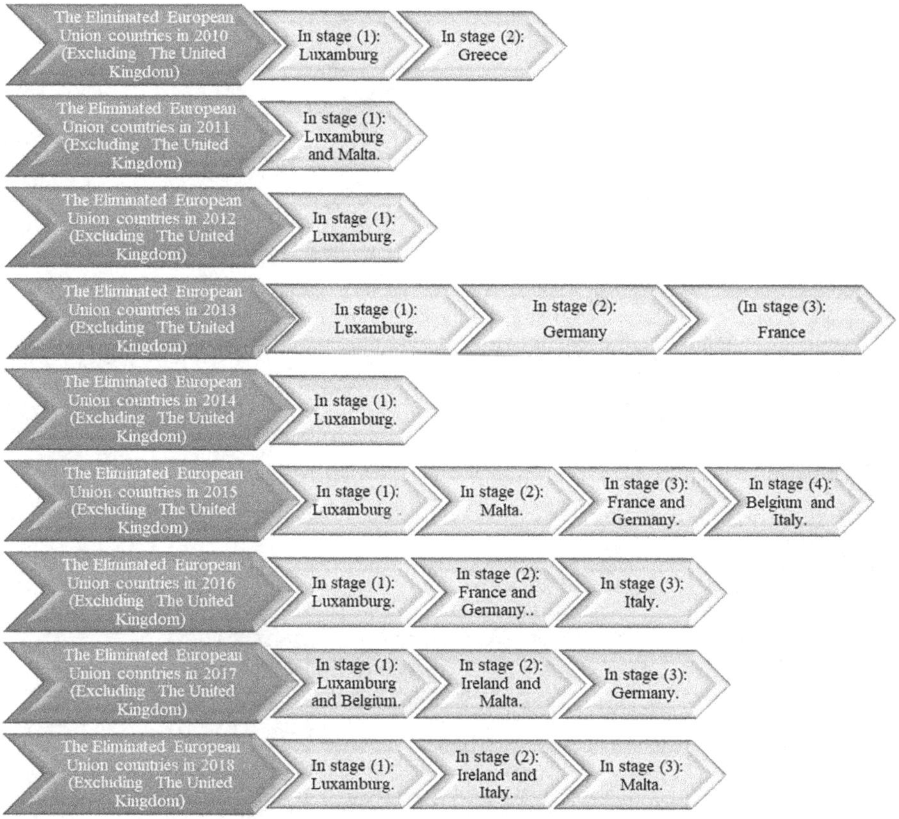

Fig. 3 Economies eliminated in various stages of homogenization processes for the European Union economies (excluding the United Kingdom) in the years 2010–2018. (Source: Authors' work based on Taxonomy's calculation)

members). As below, some descriptions are also given for several economies that are settled together for comparison with each other at the end of the homogenization processes.

For the European Union Economies (with 28 Economies)

- In 2010, after the third stage, Luxemburg, Sweden, and Greece were eliminated, and 24 economies were obtained in the group homogenization.
- In 2011, after the first stage, Luxemburg and Malta were eliminated, and 26 economies were obtained in the group homogenization.
- In 2012, after the fourth stage, Luxemburg, Malta, the United Kingdom, France, Germany, and Poland were eliminated, and 23 economies were obtained in the group homogenization.
- In 2013, after the first stage, Luxemburg and Malta were eliminated, and 26 economies were obtained in the group homogenization.

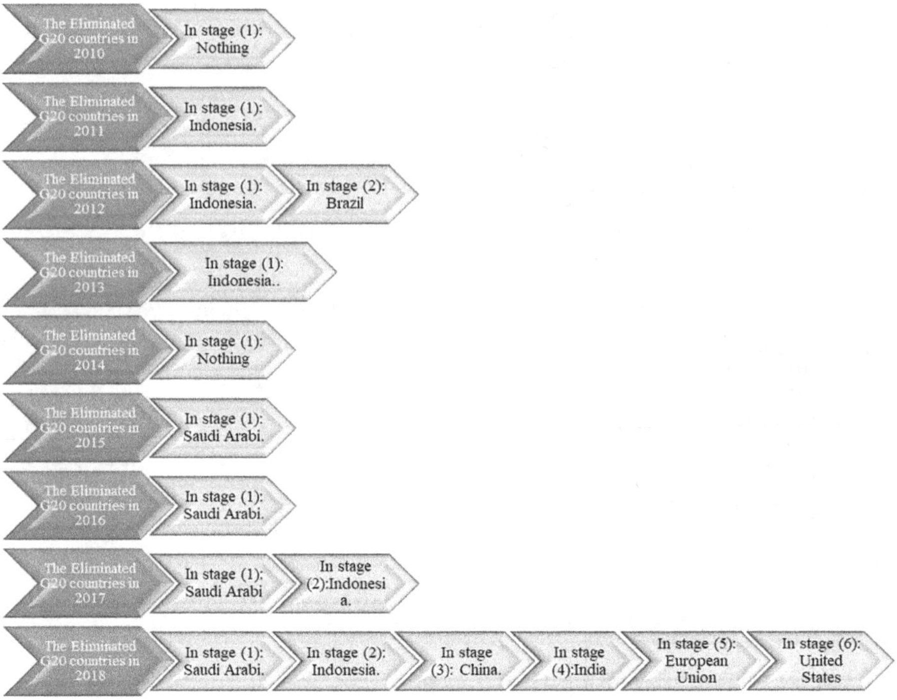

Fig. 4 Economies eliminated in various stages of homogenization process for the Group of Twenty (G20) in the years 2010–2018. (Source: Authors' work based on Taxonomy's calculation)

- In 2014, after the third stage, Luxemburg, Malta, the United Kingdom, Finland, and Sweden were eliminated, and 21 economies were obtained in the group homogenization.
- In 2015, after the fourth stage, Luxemburg, the United Kingdom, France, Germany, Belgium, and Italy were eliminated, and 24 economies were obtained in the group homogenization.
- In 2016, after the fifth process, Luxemburg, Malta, the United Kingdom, Italy, France, Germany, and Belgium were eliminated, and 21 economies were obtained in the group homogenization.
- In 2017, after the third stage, Bulgaria, Luxemburg, Ireland, and Malta were eliminated and 24 economies were obtained in the group homogenization.
- In 2018, after the third stage, Luxemburg, Ireland, Italy, and Malta were eliminated and 24 economies were obtained in the group homogenization.

For the European Union Economies Without the United Kingdom (with 27 Economies)

- In 2010, after the second stage, Luxemburg and Greece were eliminated, and 24 economies were obtained in the group homogenization.

- In 2011, after the first stage, Luxemburg and Malta were eliminated, and 25 economies were obtained in the group homogenization.
- In 2012, after the first stage, Luxemburg was eliminated, and 26 economies were obtained in the group homogenization.
- In 2013, after the third stage, Luxemburg, Germany, and France were eliminated, and 24 economies were obtained in the group homogenization.
- In 2014, after the third stage, Luxemburg was eliminated, and 26 economies were obtained in the group homogenization.
- In 2015, after the fourth stage, Luxemburg, Malta, France, Germany, Belgium, and Italy were eliminated, and 22 economies were obtained in the group homogenization.
- In 2016, after the third process, Luxemburg, France, Germany, and Italy were eliminated, and 23 economies were obtained in the group homogenization.
- In 2017, after the third stage, Bulgaria, Luxemburg, Ireland, Malta, and Germany were eliminated, and 22 economies were obtained in the group homogenization.
- In 2018, after the third stage, Luxemburg, Ireland, Italy, and Malta were eliminated, and 23 economies were obtained in the group homogenization.

For the Group of Twenty (G20) Economies (with 20 Economies)

- In 2010, after the first stage, 20 economies were obtained in the group homogenization.
- In 2011, after the first stage, Indonesia was eliminated, and 19 economies were obtained in the group homogenization.
- In 2012, after the second stage, Indonesia and Brazil were eliminated, and 18 economies were obtained in the group homogenization.
- In 2013, after the first stage, Indonesia was eliminated, and 19 economies were obtained in the group homogenization.
- In 2014, after the first stage, 20 economies were obtained in the group homogenization.
- In 2015, after the first stage, Saudi Arabia was eliminated, and 19 economies were obtained in the group homogenization.
- In 2016, after the first stage, Saudi Arabia was eliminated, and 19 economies were obtained in the group homogenization.
- In 2017, after the second stage, Saudi Arabia and Indonesia were eliminated, and then 18 economies were obtained in the group homogenization.
- In 2018, after the sixth stage, Saudi Arabia, Indonesia, China, India, the European Union (as a member), and the United States were eliminated, and 14 economies were obtained in the group homogenization.

3.7 Step 7: More Results (Computation of the "Institutional Development Degrees")

The "institutional development degree" (*fi*), for each member within the economic groups, can be computed by measuring *Co*, i.e., the upper limit of the development pattern, and then substituting in Eq. (7):

$$fi = \left(Cio / Co\right) \tag{7}$$

In Eq. (7), *Cio* is a development pattern over the upper limit of the development pattern, and *Co* is obtained from Eq. (8):

$$Co = \overline{Cio} + 2Sio \tag{8}$$

where $\overline{Cio}$ and *Sio* are the average and standard deviation of the development pattern corresponding to *fi* (Le Quesne 1969; Phillips 1983; Faghih and Sazegar 2019).

The institutional development degree is between "0" and "1," that is, with "*fi*" values approaching "0," the institutions are more developed as compared to "*fi*" values increasing to "1"; in other words, an economy corresponding to the latter case is less successful in institutional development. Consequently, by measuring *Cio* and *fi* for every economy in each group (i.e., the European Union economies, once with and then without the United Kingdom, and the G20 economies), the economies were ranked based on the institutional development degrees.

In this step, results obtained for the three groups under study lead to the globalization development degrees (*fi*) for each of the member states, as demonstrated in Tables 55, 56, 57, 58, 59, 60, 61, 62, 63, 64, 65, 66, 67, 68, 69, 70, 71, 72, 73, 74, 75, 76, 77, 78, 79, 80, and 81.

(a) *For the European Union:*
(b) *For the European Union without the United Kingdom*:

Germany for years of 2010 and 2012 and 2018 and the Netherlands for 2013, 2014, 2015, and 2017, and especially France for 2011 and Austria for 2016 were in the top development ranking as shown in Tables 64, 65, 66, 67, 68, 69, 70, 71, and 72 during 2010–2018.

(c) *For the Group of Twenty (G20):*

The United States for the years 2010, 2011, 2012, 2013, 2014, and 2017, the United Kingdom for the year 2016, and Japan for the year 2018 have had the highest development ranking.

Table 55 Development degrees for the European Union in 2010

Development Ranking *'fi'*		2010 year	*fi=*
United Kingdom	0.348	Austria	0.562
Germany	0.393	Belgium	0.516
Denmark	0.411	Bulgaria	0.884
Netherlands	0.427	Croatia	0.879
Ireland	0.430	Cyprus	0.607
Finland	0.477	Czech Republic	0.615
Belgium	0.516	Denmark	0.411
Austria	0.562	Estonia	0.696
France	0.580	Finland	0.477
Cyprus	0.607	France	0.580
Czech Republic	0.615	Germany	0.393
Portugal	0.649	Hungary	0.705
Slovenia	0.681	Ireland	0.430
Slovakia	0.696	Italy	0.800
Estonia	0.696	Latvia	0.822
Hungary	0.705	Lithuania	0.770
Poland	0.734	Netherlands	0.427
Lithuania	0.770	Poland	0.734
Italy	0.800	Portugal	0.649
Latvia	0.822	Romania	0.966
Croatia	0.879	Slovakia	0.696
Bulgaria	0.884	Slovenia	0.681
Spain	0.923	Spain	0.923
Romania	0.966	United Kingdom	0.348

Source: Authors' work based on Taxonomic computation

4 Dynamics of Institutional Change Within the Studied Groups

Based on the concepts and theories of complex adaptive systems, a perfect realization of the individual elements, parts, or members does not necessarily lead to a perfect realization of the whole system's behavior. The whole (the ensemble) can be more complicated, complex, and meaningful than its elements, parts, members, and their aggregates. Moreover, the study of such nonlinear dynamical systems and the behavior of the ensemble is highly interdisciplinary and can develop insights and system-level models that allow for phase transition, heterogeneous agents, and emergent properties and behaviors, not necessarily depending on the constituent parts but on their dynamic networks of interactions and interrelationships that are not mere aggregations of the individual components or entities (Miller and Page 2007; Holland 1998; Lansing 2003; Durlauf and Young 2001; Weidlich 1997; Backstrom et al. 2006). Thus, the dynamics of institutional change within a group of economies can also be impacted by the behavior of the group, the interactions

Table 56 Development degrees for the European Union in 2011

Development Ranking '*fi*'		2011 year	*fi*=
United Kingdom	0.259	Austria	0.531
France	0.356	Belgium	0.455
Netherlands	0.398	Bulgaria	0.885
Denmark	0.416	Croatia	0.820
Sweden	0.428	Cyprus	0.537
Finland	0.430	Czech Republic	0.768
Ireland	0.445	Denmark	0.416
Germany	0.449	Estonia	0.643
Belgium	0.455	Finland	0.430
Austria	0.531	France	0.356
Cyprus	0.537	Germany	0.449
Slovenia	0.629	Greece	0.911
Italy	0.636	Hungary	0.733
Estonia	0.643	Ireland	0.445
Spain	0.679	Italy	0.636
Hungary	0.733	Latvia	0.780
Poland	0.739	Lithuania	0.804
Czech Republic	0.768	Netherlands	0.398
Slovakia	0.771	Poland	0.739
Latvia	0.780	Portugal	0.783
Portugal	0.783	Romania	0.933
Lithuania	0.804	Slovakia	0.771
Croatia	0.820	Slovenia	0.629
Bulgaria	0.885	Spain	0.679
Greece	0.911	Sweden	0.428
Romania	0.933	United Kingdom	0.259

Source: Authors' work based on Taxonomic computation

and interrelationships of group members, the group-level behaviors, changes over time, the role of feedbacks, and occasionally, non-equilibrium behavior. This is especially the case for the groups formed in order to achieve common goals through structuring the economic and political relationships, conducting harmonious dynamics of institutional change, and shaping interrelationships and interactions to construct the evolvement route of member states through time and also determined by social, economic, and political institutions, as well as technology.

As already stated, the institutional indicators (institutions, political environment, regulatory environment, and business environment) reported by the Global Innovation Index (GII) were used in the taxonomic analysis of this chapter. Thus, the analysis was based on six sets of preliminary data, namely, the latter four indicators plus population and GDP. The taxonomic analysis was performed in three groups of countries, including major advanced and emerging economies, organized to achieve their goals through targeted planning, aligning their laws and regulations, and conducting harmonious dynamics of institutional change.

Table 57 Development degrees for the European Union in 2012

Development Ranking '*fi*'		2012 year	*fi*=
Netherlands	0.396	Austria	0.502
Sweden	0.475	Belgium	0.482
Belgium	0.482	Bulgaria	0.927
Denmark	0.483	Croatia	0.894
Finland	0.487	Cyprus	0.634
Austria	0.502	Czech Republic	0.708
Ireland	0.508	Denmark	0.483
Spain	0.519	Estonia	0.753
Italy	0.593	Finland	0.487
Cyprus	0.634	Greece	0.861
Slovenia	0.700	Hungary	0.784
Czech Republic	0.708	Ireland	0.508
Slovakia	0.718	Italy	0.593
Malta	0.734	Latvia	0.772
Estonia	0.753	Lithuania	0.851
Latvia	0.772	Malta	0.734
Hungary	0.784	Netherlands	0.396
Portugal	0.808	Portugal	0.808
Lithuania	0.851	Romania	0.924
Greece	0.861	Slovakia	0.718
Croatia	0.894	Slovenia	0.700
Romania	0.924	Spain	0.519
Bulgaria	0.927	Sweden	0.475

Source: Authors' work based on Taxonomic computation

During the years 2010–2018, in addition to the Group of Twenty (G20) economies, the other two groups (of the abovementioned three groups) included the European Union economies, once with and then without the United Kingdom, i.e., before the occurrence of Brexit, as a hypothetical study to explore some reflections of Brexit on the dynamics of institutional change.

Thus, the institutional development degrees for the abovementioned three groups were computed. As a result, for instance, in the European Union, Luxemburg was constantly eliminated in every homogenization process from 2010 to 2018 irrespective of the presence or absence of the United Kingdom. In other words, from the institutional development point of view, Luxemburg could not be comparable to the other economies of the European Union.

Moreover, the United Kingdom exhibited an unstable behavior in institutional development and alignment within the European Union. That is, in the years 2012, 2014, 2015, and 2016, the United Kingdom did not settle in a homogenous group, but maintained the top-ranking status for the years 2010, 2011, and 2017. This partly reflects an incompatibility between the United Kingdom and the European Union in institutional development policies and practices.

Table 58 Development degrees for the European Union in 2013

Development Ranking '*fi*'		2013 year	*fi*=
Netherlands	0.367	Austria	0.461
Denmark	0.433	Belgium	0.452
Finland	0.434	Bulgaria	0.934
Sweden	0.435	Croatia	0.890
Germany	0.446	Cyprus	0.609
Belgium	0.452	Czech Republic	0.702
Austria	0.461	Denmark	0.433
Ireland	0.463	Estonia	0.706
France	0.494	Finland	0.434
Cyprus	0.609	France	0.494
Spain	0.624	Germany	0.446
Italy	0.646	Greece	0.915
Slovenia	0.669	Hungary	0.814
Poland	0.691	Ireland	0.463
Malta	0.697	Italy	0.646
Czech Republic	0.702	Latvia	0.757
Estonia	0.706	Lithuania	0.801
Portugal	0.709	Malta	0.697
Latvia	0.757	Netherlands	0.367
Slovakia	0.764	Poland	0.691
Lithuania	0.801	Portugal	0.709
Hungary	0.814	Romania	0.972
Croatia	0.890	Slovakia	0.764
Greece	0.915	Slovenia	0.669
Bulgaria	0.934	Spain	0.624
Romania	0.972	Sweden	0.435

Source: Authors' work based on Taxonomic computation

Tables 55, 56, and 62, for instance, show that the United Kingdom had the highest values of institutional development degrees fi, in the years 2010, 2011, and 2017 (0.348, 0.259, and 0.230, respectively). Similarly, from Tables 64, 65, 66, 67, 68, 69, 70, 71, 72, 73, 74, 75, 76, 77, 78, 79, 80, and 81, for the three groups of economies under study in the years 2010 to 2018, the results for the leading and the following economies can be summarized in Table 82, which shows the top-ranking economies in institutional development (based on the GII data). Table 82 exhibits the leading economies marked in blue and the following economies underlined.

As depicted in Table 82, for the top-ranking economies in institutional development (based on the GII data), within the three studied groups, from 2010 to 2018 (the leading and the following economies):

- In the year 2010, within the European Union, the United Kingdom followed by Germany led in institutional development, and in the (hypothetical) absence of the United Kingdom, Germany followed by the Netherlands led in institutional

Table 59 Development degrees for the European Union in 2014

Development Ranking *'fi'*		2014 year	*fi*=
Netherlands	0.325	Austria	0.434
Germany	0.346	Belgium	0.498
Denmark	0.381	Bulgaria	0.916
France	0.394	Croatia	0.868
Ireland	0.429	Cyprus	0.665
Austria	0.434	Czech Republic	0.699
Belgium	0.498	Denmark	0.381
Portugal	0.615	Estonia	0.627
Spain	0.621	France	0.394
Estonia	0.627	Germany	0.346
Slovenia	0.630	Greece	0.901
Italy	0.656	Hungary	0.815
Cyprus	0.665	Ireland	0.429
Poland	0.693	Italy	0.656
Malta	0.698	Latvia	0.707
Czech Republic	0.699	Lithuania	0.809
Latvia	0.707	Malta	0.698
Slovakia	0.757	Netherlands	0.325
Lithuania	0.809	Poland	0.693
Hungary	0.815	Portugal	0.615
Croatia	0.868	Romania	0.899
Romania	0.899	Slovakia	0.757
Greece	0.901	Slovenia	0.630
Bulgaria	0.916	Spain	0.621

Source: Authors' work based on Taxonomic computation

development. In the same year, within the Group of Twenty (G20), the United States followed by the European Union (including the United Kingdom) led in institutional development.

- In the year 2011, within the European Union, the United Kingdom followed by France led in institutional development, and in the (hypothetical) absence of the United Kingdom, France followed by the Netherlands led in institutional development. In the same year, within the Group of Twenty (G20), the United States followed by the European Union (including the United Kingdom) led in institutional development.
- In the year 2012, within the European Union, the Netherlands followed by Sweden led in institutional development, and in the (hypothetical) absence of the United Kingdom, Germany followed by the Netherlands led in institutional development. In the same year, within the Group of Twenty (G20), the United States followed by the European Union (including the United Kingdom) led in institutional development.

Table 60 Development degrees for the European Union in 2015

Development Ranking '*fi*'		2015 year	*fi*=
Netherlands	0.332	Austria	0.490
Sweden	0.430	Bulgaria	0.933
Denmark	0.443	Croatia	0.881
Finland	0.453	Cyprus	0.640
Ireland	0.462	Czech Republic	0.704
Austria	0.490	Denmark	0.443
Spain	0.576	Estonia	0.672
Poland	0.635	Finland	0.453
Cyprus	0.640	Greece	0.892
Portugal	0.644	Hungary	0.837
Slovenia	0.649	Ireland	0.462
Estonia	0.672	Latvia	0.737
Czech Republic	0.704	Lithuania	0.816
Latvia	0.737	Netherlands	0.332
Slovakia	0.755	Poland	0.635
Lithuania	0.816	Portugal	0.644
Hungary	0.837	Romania	0.845
Romania	0.845	Slovakia	0.755
Croatia	0.881	Slovenia	0.649
Greece	0.892	Spain	0.576
Bulgaria	0.933	Sweden	0.430

Source: Authors' work based on Taxonomic computation

- In the year 2013, within the European Union, the Netherlands followed by Denmark led in institutional development, and in the (hypothetical) absence of the United Kingdom, the Netherlands followed by the Sweden led in institutional development. In the same year, within the Group of Twenty (G20), the United States followed by the European Union (including the United Kingdom) led in institutional development.
- In the year 2014, within the European Union, the Netherlands followed by Germany led in institutional development, and in the (hypothetical) absence of the United Kingdom, again the Netherlands followed by Germany led in institutional development. In the same year, within the Group of Twenty (G20), the United States followed by the European Union (including the United Kingdom) led in institutional development.
- In the year 2015, within the European Union, the Netherlands followed by Sweden led in institutional development, and in the (hypothetical) absence of the United Kingdom, again the Netherlands followed by Sweden led in institutional development. In the same year, within the Group of Twenty (G20), the United States followed by the European Union (including the United Kingdom) led in institutional development.

Table 61 Development degrees for the European Union in 2016

Development Ranking *'fi'*		2016 year	*fi*=
Netherlands	0.348	Austria	0.469
Sweden	0.422	Bulgaria	0.944
Denmark	0.446	Croatia	0.904
Ireland	0.460	Cyprus	0.634
Finland	0.463	Czech Republic	0.650
Austria	0.469	Denmark	0.446
Spain	0.535	Estonia	0.661
Poland	0.606	Finland	0.463
Portugal	0.610	Greece	0.924
Cyprus	0.634	Hungary	0.840
Slovenia	0.642	Ireland	0.460
Czech Republic	0.650	Latvia	0.726
Estonia	0.661	Lithuania	0.797
Latvia	0.726	Netherlands	0.348
Slovakia	0.753	Poland	0.606
Lithuania	0.797	Portugal	0.610
Romania	0.835	Romania	0.835
Hungary	0.840	Slovakia	0.753
Croatia	0.904	Slovenia	0.642
Greece	0.924	Spain	0.535
Bulgaria	0.944	Sweden	0.422

Source: Authors' work based on Taxonomic computation

- In the year 2016, within the European Union, the Netherlands followed by Sweden led in institutional development, and in the (hypothetical) absence of the United Kingdom, Austria followed by Denmark led in institutional development. In the same year, within the Group of Twenty (G20), the United Kingdom followed by the United States led in institutional development.
- In the year 2017, within the European Union, the United Kingdom followed by Germany lad in institutional development, and in the (hypothetical) absence of the United Kingdom, the Netherlands followed by France led in institutional development. In the same year, within the Group of Twenty (G20), the United States followed by the European Union (including the United Kingdom) led in institutional development.
- In the year 2018, within the European Union, Germany followed by the United Kingdom led in institutional development, and in the (hypothetical) absence of the United Kingdom, Germany followed by France led in institutional development. In the same year, within the Group of Twenty (G20), Japan followed by Germany led in institutional development.

Table 62 Development degrees for the European Union in 2017

Development Ranking '*fi*'		2017 year	*fi*=
United Kingdom	0.230	Austria	0.468
Germany	0.246	Belgium	0.494
Netherlands	0.343	Croatia	0.921
France	0.386	Cyprus	0.596
Sweden	0.387	Czech Republic	0.628
Denmark	0.396	Denmark	0.396
Finland	0.404	Estonia	0.622
Austria	0.468	Finland	0.404
Belgium	0.494	France	0.386
Spain	0.526	Germany	0.246
Slovenia	0.577	Greece	0.961
Italy	0.585	Hungary	0.852
Cyprus	0.596	Italy	0.585
Portugal	0.606	Latvia	0.738
Estonia	0.622	Lithuania	0.807
Czech Republic	0.628	Netherlands	0.343
Poland	0.692	Poland	0.692
Latvia	0.738	Portugal	0.606
Slovakia	0.756	Romania	0.903
Lithuania	0.807	Slovakia	0.756
Hungary	0.852	Slovenia	0.577
Romania	0.903	Spain	0.526
Croatia	0.921	Sweden	0.387
Greece	0.961	United Kingdom	0.230

Source: Authors' work based on Taxonomic computation

5 Conclusion

The research reported in this chapter presents a computational method for assessing institutional development through taxonomic study. Numerical taxonomic analysis is applied to the Global Innovation Index (GII) data on institutions.

The quantitative results of the research reported in this chapter were obtained through a series of advanced computations and a large amount of input data. The computational method assessed institutional development degrees for the European Union and the Group of Twenty (G20) economies. The European Union economies were considered, once with and then without the United Kingdom, i.e., before the occurrence of Brexit, as a hypothetical study to explore some reflections of Brexit on the dynamics of institutional change. Within the three groups under study, the economies corresponding data were examined for homogeneity through taxonomic analysis to assess their institutional development degrees. In certain years, a few economies were eliminated from the homogenous groups, while in other years they were ranked highest in institutional development.

Table 63 Development degrees for the European Union in 2018

Development Ranking '*fi*'		2018 year	*fi*=
Germany	0.237	Austria	0.463
United Kingdom	0.246	Belgium	0.514
France	0.339	Bulgaria	0.912
Netherlands	0.351	Croatia	0.897
Sweden	0.397	Cyprus	0.598
Denmark	0.407	Czech Republic	0.618
Finland	0.417	Denmark	0.407
Austria	0.463	Estonia	0.614
Belgium	0.514	Finland	0.417
Spain	0.522	France	0.339
Slovenia	0.586	Germany	0.237
Portugal	0.597	Greece	0.902
Cyprus	0.598	Hungary	0.799
Estonia	0.614	Latvia	0.709
Czech Republic	0.618	Lithuania	0.730
Poland	0.688	Netherlands	0.351
Latvia	0.709	Poland	0.688
Lithuania	0.730	Portugal	0.597
Slovakia	0.766	Romania	0.896
Hungary	0.799	Slovakia	0.766
Romania	0.896	Slovenia	0.586
Croatia	0.897	Spain	0.522
Greece	0.902	Sweden	0.397
Bulgaria	0.912	United Kingdom	0.246

Source: Authors' work based on Taxonomic computation

Input indicators of highest ranked economies can be utilized for better comprehension of their dynamics of institutional change and performance accomplishment in this regard. GDP is also a crucial determinant of input data impacting the homogenization process and elimination of an economy within the cycles of these operations. For instance, the United Kingdom often allocated the highest degree of institutional development. With a profound scanning over the input indicators – i.e., GDP, institution, and regulatory environment indices – for each European Union economy, all of the United Kingdom's numerical values are among the highest in comparison with many other economies not only within European Union but also within the G20 economies.

Regulatory environment includes three sub-indices that are regulatory quality, rule of law, and cost of redundancy dismissal and salary weeks (regulatory quality and rule of law are obtained by survey questions of GII). Regulatory qualities certainly play a role in sustaining an organization's growth and development. Furthermore, with the principles of the rule of law based in any institution, an increased innovative improvement can be observed in organizations with institutional rule.

Table 64 Development degrees for the European Union without the United Kingdom in 2010

Development Ranking '*fi*'		2010 year	*fi*=
Germany	0.383	Austria	0.594
Netherlands	0.446	Belgium	0.540
Denmark	0.454	Bulgaria	0.897
Ireland	0.468	Croatia	0.896
Finland	0.506	Cyprus	0.630
Sweden	0.520	Czech Republic	0.639
Belgium	0.540	Denmark	0.454
France	0.575	Estonia	0.719
Austria	0.594	Finland	0.506
Cyprus	0.630	France	0.575
Czech Republic	0.639	Germany	0.383
Portugal	0.665	Hungary	0.723
Slovenia	0.700	Ireland	0.468
Slovakia	0.716	Italy	0.801
Estonia	0.719	Latvia	0.840
Hungary	0.723	Lithuania	0.790
Poland	0.742	Netherlands	0.446
Lithuania	0.790	Poland	0.742
Italy	0.801	Portugal	0.665
Latvia	0.840	Romania	0.975
Croatia	0.896	Slovakia	0.716
Bulgaria	0.897	Slovenia	0.700
Spain	0.932	Spain	0.932
Romania	0.975	Sweden	0.520

Source: Authors' work based on Taxonomic computation

In the European Union, the Netherlands exhibits a situation similar to the United Kingdom (as it is shown in Table 80); that is, in the institutional development analysis of the European Union in this research, the United Kingdom and the Netherlands were mostly the top-ranking economies of the European Union, while Luxemburg was constantly eliminated in every homogenization process from 2010 to 2018 irrespective of the presence or absence of the United Kingdom.

Moreover, examining the European Union without the United Kingdom, i.e., before the occurrence of Brexit, as a hypothetical study to explore some reflections of Brexit on the dynamics of institutional change in this Union, Table 82 shows that the Netherlands and Germany would alternate as the leading and following economies in institutional development.

The United States has maintained its top-ranking position of institutional development within the Group of Twenty (G20) from 2010 to 2015, and the year 2017. It is noticeable that the United States has the highest value of the GDP among the rest of the G20 countries and also in other indices of institutions (as shown in Tables 19, 20, 21, 22, 23, 24, 25, 26, and 27, in the Appendix). This is a substantial evidence to

Table 65 Development degrees for the European Union without the United Kingdom in 2011

Development Ranking *'fi'*		2011 year	*fi*=
France	0.433	Austria	0.667
Netherlands	0.502	Belgium	0.571
Denmark	0.527	Bulgaria	1.079
Sweden	0.541	Croatia	1.005
Finland	0.545	Cyprus	0.669
Germany	0.552	Czech Republic	0.950
Ireland	0.560	Denmark	0.527
Belgium	0.571	Estonia	0.797
Austria	0.667	Finland	0.545
Cyprus	0.669	France	0.433
Italy	0.773	Germany	0.552
Slovenia	0.779	Greece	1. 115
Estonia	0.797	Hungary	0.901
Spain	0.829	Ireland	0.560
Hungary	0.901	Italy	0.773
Poland	0.907	Latvia	0.956
Czech Republic	0.950	Lithuania	0.988
Slovakia	0.951	Netherlands	0.502
Latvia	0.956	Poland	0.907
Portugal	0.961	Portugal	0.961
Lithuania	0.988	Romania	1.137
Croatia	1.005	Slovakia	0.951
Bulgaria	1.079	Slovenia	0.779
Greece	1.115	Spain	0.829
Romania	1.137	Sweden	0.541

Source: Authors' work based on Taxonomic computation

deduce that the United States is advanced more than its peers, especially in institutional development and innovation. Indeed, Saudi Arabia has a high GDP, but institutional-wise, by no means comparable to the United States; Saudi Arabia has lower values of institution indices than the other G20 economies, particularly relative to the United States. Consequently, Saudi Arabia has been eliminated from the cycle of the homogenous group of G20 economies from 2015 to 2018 (as shown in Fig. 4). Even the United States was eliminated from the homogenous group of G20 economies in 2018, due to its high GDP dominating and preventing formation of a homogenous group. However, it is observed from Table 82 that the United States, the European Union, the United Kingdom, Germany, the Netherlands, and sometimes France and Japan, are leading in institutional development.

Acknowledgement The authorization granted to use the data and material originally provided by WIPO (the World Intellectual Property Organization) is appreciatively acknowledged. The secretariat of WIPO supposes no responsibility or liability with regard to the transformation of this data.

Table 66 Development degrees for the European Union without the United Kingdom in 2012

Development Ranking '*fi*'		2012 year	*fi*=
Germany	0.187	Austria	0.238
Netherlands	0.193	Belgium	0.232
Denmark	0.221	Bulgaria	0.474
Finland	0.222	Croatia	0.452
Sweden	0.225	Cyprus	0.301
Belgium	0.232	Czech Republic	0.358
Ireland	0.234	Denmark	0.221
Austria	0.238	Estonia	0.369
France	0.246	Finland	0.222
Spain	0.285	France	0.246
Cyprus	0.301	Germany	0.187
Italy	0.320	Greece	0.443
Slovenia	0.341	Hungary	0.398
Poland	0.350	Ireland	0.234
Slovakia	0.356	Italy	0.320
Czech Republic	0.358	Latvia	0.381
Malta	0.358	Lithuania	0.427
Estonia	0.369	Malta	0.358
Latvia	0.381	Netherlands	0.193
Hungary	0.398	Poland	0.350
Portugal	0.413	Portugal	0.413
Lithuania	0.427	Romania	0.484
Greece	0.443	Slovakia	0.356
Croatia	0.452	Slovenia	0.341
Bulgaria	0.474	Spain	0.285
Romania	0.484	Sweden	0.225

Source: Authors' work based on Taxonomic computation

Table 67 Development degrees for the European Union without the United Kingdom in 2013

Development Ranking *'fi'*		2013 year	*fi=*
Netherlands	0.367	Austria	0.478
Sweden	0.451	Belgium	0.462
Denmark	0.461	Bulgaria	0.928
Belgium	0.462	Croatia	0.891
Finland	0.462	Cyprus	0.634
Austria	0.478	Czech Republic	0.700
Ireland	0.491	Denmark	0.461
Spain	0.590	Estonia	0.723
Italy	0.620	Finland	0.462
Cyprus	0.634	Greece	0.903
Poland	0.658	Hungary	0.809
Slovenia	0.687	Ireland	0.491
Czech Republic	0.700	Italy	0.620
Portugal	0.707	Latvia	0.770
Malta	0.717	Lithuania	0.808
Estonia	0.723	Malta	0.717
Slovakia	0.768	Netherlands	0.367
Latvia	0.770	Poland	0.658
Lithuania	0.808	Portugal	0.707
Hungary	0.809	Romania	0.949
Croatia	0.891	Slovakia	0.768
Greece	0.903	Slovenia	0.687
Bulgaria	0.928	Spain	0.590
Romania	0.949	Sweden	0.451

Source: Authors' work based on Taxonomic computation

Table 68 Development degrees for the European Union without the United Kingdom in 2014

Development Ranking '*fi*'		2014 year	*fi*=
Netherlands	0.374	Austria	0.487
Germany	0.379	Belgium	0.540
Finland	0.423	Bulgaria	0.925
Denmark	0.426	Croatia	0.884
Sweden	0.435	Cyprus	0.707
France	0.438	Czech Republic	0.728
Ireland	0.486	Denmark	0.426
Austria	0.487	Estonia	0.672
Belgium	0.540	Finland	0.423
Spain	0.643	France	0.438
Portugal	0.646	Germany	0.379
Estonia	0.672	Greece	0.909
Slovenia	0.673	Hungary	0.836
Italy	0.674	Ireland	0.486
Cyprus	0.707	Italy	0.674
Poland	0.709	Latvia	0.741
Czech Republic	0.728	Lithuania	0.829
Malta	0.737	Malta	0.737
Latvia	0.741	Netherlands	0.374
Slovakia	0.781	Poland	0.709
Lithuania	0.829	Portugal	0.646
Hungary	0.836	Romania	0.902
Croatia	0.884	Slovakia	0.781
Romania	0.902	Slovenia	0.673
Greece	0.909	Spain	0.643
Bulgaria	0.925	Sweden	0.435

Source: Authors' work based on Taxonomic computation

Table 69 Development degrees for the European Union without the United Kingdom in 2015

Development Ranking '*fi*'		2015 year	*fi*=
Netherlands	0.394	Austria	0.583
Sweden	0.511	Bulgaria	1.109
Denmark	0.527	Croatia	1.047
Finland	0.538	Cyprus	0.761
Ireland	0.549	Czech Republic	0.837
Austria	0.583	Denmark	0.527
Spain	0.684	Estonia	0.799
Poland	0.754	Finland	0.538
Cyprus	0.761	Greece	1.061
Portugal	0.765	Hungary	0.995
Slovenia	0.772	Ireland	0.549
Estonia	0.799	Latvia	0.876
Czech Republic	0.837	Lithuania	0.970
Latvia	0.876	Netherlands	0.394
Slovakia	0.897	Poland	0.754
Lithuania	0.970	Portugal	0.765
Hungary	0.995	Romania	1.005
Romania	1.005	Slovakia	0.897
Croatia	1.047	Slovenia	0.772
Greece	1.061	Spain	0.684
Bulgaria	1.109	Sweden	0.511

Source: Authors' work based on Taxonomic computation

Table 70 Development degrees for the European Union without the United Kingdom in 2016

Development Ranking '*fi*'		2016 year	*fi*=
Austria	0.481	Austria	0.481
Denmark	0.492	Belgium	0.547
Netherlands	0.500	Bulgaria	0.892
Finland	0.526	Croatia	0.862
Belgium	0.547	Cyprus	0.623
Ireland	0.578	Czech Republic	0.637
Cyprus	0.623	Denmark	0.492
Sweden	0.631	Estonia	0.662
Czech Republic	0.637	Finland	0.526
Poland	0.641	Greece	0.953
Portugal	0.658	Hungary	0.855
Estonia	0.662	Ireland	0.578
Spain	0.666	Latvia	0.740
Latvia	0.740	Lithuania	0.839
Slovenia	0.743	Malta	0.823
Malta	0.823	Netherlands	0.500
Slovakia	0.825	Poland	0.641
Lithuania	0.839	Portugal	0.658
Romania	0.853	Romania	0.853
Hungary	0.855	Slovakia	0.825
Croatia	0.862	Slovenia	0.743
Bulgaria	0.892	Spain	0.666
Greece	0.953	Sweden	0.631

Source: Authors' work based on Taxonomic computation

Table 71 Development degrees for the European Union without the United Kingdom in 2017

Development Ranking '*fi*'		2017 year	*fi*=
Netherlands	0.399	Austria	0.561
France	0.451	Belgium	0.590
Sweden	0.463	Croatia	1.112
Denmark	0.482	Cyprus	0.727
Finland	0.492	Czech Republic	0.754
Austria	0.561	Denmark	0.482
Belgium	0.590	Estonia	0.758
Spain	0.613	Finland	0.492
Italy	0.691	France	0.451
Slovenia	0.705	Greece	1.154
Cyprus	0.727	Hungary	1.023
Portugal	0.729	Italy	0.691
Czech Republic	0.754	Latvia	0.896
Estonia	0.758	Lithuania	0.975
Poland	0.818	Netherlands	0.399
Latvia	0.896	Poland	0.818
Slovakia	0.912	Portugal	0.729
Lithuania	0.975	Romania	1.079
Hungary	1.023	Slovakia	0.912
Romania	1.079	Slovenia	0.705
Croatia	1.112	Spain	0.613
Greece	1.154	Sweden	0.463

Source: Authors' work based on Taxonomic computation

Table 72 Development degrees for the European Union without the United Kingdom in 2018

Development Ranking '*fi*'		2018 year	*fi*=
Germany	0.273	Austria	0.561
France	0.389	Belgium	0.615
Netherlands	0.434	Bulgaria	1.055
Sweden	0.490	Croatia	1.042
Denmark	0.504	Cyprus	0.712
Finland	0.514	Czech Republic	0.729
Austria	0.561	Denmark	0.504
Spain	0.604	Estonia	0.729
Belgium	0.615	Finland	0.514
Slovenia	0.700	France	0.389
Portugal	0.706	Germany	0.273
Cyprus	0.712	Greece	1.045
Estonia	0.729	Hungary	0.930
Czech Republic	0.729	Latvia	0.833
Poland	0.793	Lithuania	0.856
Latvia	0.833	Netherlands	0.434
Lithuania	0.856	Poland	0.793
Slovakia	0.897	Portugal	0.706
Hungary	0.930	Romania	1.029
Romania	1.029	Slovakia	0.897
Croatia	1.042	Slovenia	0.700
Greece	1.045	Spain	0.604
Bulgaria	1.055	Sweden	0.490

Source: Authors' work based on Taxonomic computation

Table 73 Development degrees for the Group of Twenty (G20) in 2010

Development Ranking *'fi'*		2010 year	*fi=*
United States	0.395	Argentina	0.918
European Union	0.414	Australia	0.479
Canada	0.468	Brazil	0.909
Australia	0.479	Canada	0.468
United Kingdom	0.485	China	0.795
Germany	0.500	France	0.550
Japan	0.501	Germany	0.500
France	0.550	India	0.820
Rep. of Korea	0.569	Indonesia	0.877
Italy	0.618	Italy	0.618
South Africa	0.698	Japan	0.501
Saudi Arabia	0.706	Mexico	0.793
Turkey	0.764	Russia	0.855
Mexico	0.793	Saudi Arabia	0.706
China	0.795	South Africa	0.698
India	0.820	Rep. of Korea	0.569
Russia	0.855	Turkey	0.764
Indonesia	0.877	United Kingdom	0.485
Brazil	0.909	United States	0.395
Argentina	0.918	European Union	0.414

Source: Authors' work based on Taxonomic computation

Table 74 Development degrees for the Group of Twenty (G20) in 2011

Development Ranking *'fi'*		2011 year	*fi=*
United States	0.393	Argentina	0.835
European Union	0.430	Australia	0.478
Canada	0.468	Brazil	0.841
United Kingdom	0.475	Canada	0.468
Australia	0.478	China	0.891
France	0.504	France	0.504
Japan	0.517	Germany	0.538
Germany	0.538	India	0.920
Rep. of Korea	0.588	Italy	0.602
Italy	0.602	Japan	0.517
South Africa	0.696	Mexico	0.796
Saudi Arabia	0.717	Russia	0.844
Mexico	0.796	Saudi Arabia	0.717
Argentina	0.835	South Africa	0.696
Brazil	0.841	Rep. of Korea	0.588
Russia	0.844	Turkey	0.856
Turkey	0.856	United Kingdom	0.475
China	0.891	United States	0.393
India	0.920	European Union	0.430

Source: Authors' work based on Taxonomic computation

Table 75 Development degrees for the Group of Twenty (G20) in 2012

Development Ranking '*fi*'		2012 year	*fi*=
United States	0.374	Argentina	0.932
European Union	0.421	Australia	0.457
Canada	0.446	Canada	0.446
Australia	0.457	China	0.874
United Kingdom	0.460	France	0.539
Japan	0.466	Germany	0.485
Germany	0.485	India	0.873
France	0.539	Italy	0.594
Rep. of Korea	0.560	Japan	0.466
Italy	0.594	Mexico	0.763
South Africa	0.712	Russia	0.820
Mexico	0.763	Saudi Arabia	0.782
Saudi Arabia	0.782	South Africa	0.712
Russia	0.820	Rep. of Korea	0.560
Turkey	0.847	Turkey	0.847
India	0.873	United Kingdom	0.460
China	0.874	United States	0.374
Argentina	0.932	European Union	0.421

Source: Authors' work based on Taxonomic computation

Table 76 Development degrees for the Group of Twenty (G20) in 2013

Development Ranking '*fi*'		2013 year	*fi*=
United States	0.376	Argentina	0.925
European Union	0.428	Australia	0.471
Canada	0.460	Brazil	0.880
Australia	0.471	Canada	0.460
Japan	0.473	China	0.847
United Kingdom	0.475	France	0.538
Germany	0.488	Germany	0.488
France	0.538	India	0.851
Rep. of Korea	0.573	Italy	0.595
Italy	0.595	Japan	0.473
South Africa	0.712	Mexico	0.762
Saudi Arabia	0.742	Russia	0.810
Mexico	0.762	Saudi Arabia	0.742
Russia	0.810	South Africa	0.712
China	0.847	Rep. of Korea	0.573
Turkey	0.847	Turkey	0.847
India	0.851	United Kingdom	0.475
Brazil	0.880	United States	0.376
Argentina	0.925	European Union	0.428

Source: Authors' work based on Taxonomic computation

Table 77 Development degrees for the Group of Twenty (G20) in 2014

Development Ranking *'fi'*		2014 year	*fi*=
United States	0.401	Argentina	0.958
European Union	0.446	Australia	0.511
Canada	0.498	Brazil	0.882
Japan	0.503	Canada	0.498
Australia	0.511	China	0.762
United Kingdom	0.515	France	0.548
Germany	0.518	Germany	0.518
France	0.548	India	0.887
Rep. of Korea	0.590	Indonesia	1.073
Italy	0.627	Italy	0.627
South Africa	0.727	Japan	0.503
China	0.762	Mexico	0.779
Saudi Arabia	0.762	Russia	0.825
Mexico	0.779	Saudi Arabia	0.762
Russia	0.825	South Africa	0.727
Turkey	0.856	Rep. of Korea	0.590
Brazil	0.882	Turkey	0.856
India	0.887	United Kingdom	0.515
Argentina	0.958	United States	0.401
Indonesia	1.073	European Union	0.446

Source: Authors' work based on Taxonomic computation

Table 78 Development degrees for the Group of Twenty (G20) in 2015

Development Ranking *'fi'*		2015 year	*fi*=
United States	0.374	Argentina	0.909
European Union	0.396	Australia	0.470
Canada	0.466	Brazil	0.830
Japan	0.467	Canada	0.466
Germany	0.468	China	0.701
Australia	0.470	France	0.504
United Kingdom	0.475	Germany	0.468
France	0.504	India	0.830
Rep. of Korea	0.559	Indonesia	0.983
Italy	0.579	Italy	0.579
China	0.701	Japan	0.467
South Africa	0.707	Mexico	0.752
Mexico	0.752	Russia	0.774
Russia	0.774	South Africa	0.707
Turkey	0.812	Rep. of Korea	0.559
Brazil	0.830	Turkey	0.812
India	0.830	United Kingdom	0.475
Argentina	0.909	United States	0.374
Indonesia	0.983	European Union	0.396

Source: Authors' work based on Taxonomic computation

Table 79 Development degrees for the Group of Twenty (G20) in 2016

Development Ranking *'fi'*		2016 year	*fi=*
United Kingdom	0.369	Argentina	0.949
United States	0.402	Australia	0.470
European Union	0.402	Brazil	0.883
Italy	0.462	Canada	0.463
Canada	0.463	China	0.739
Germany	0.468	France	0.501
Australia	0.470	Germany	0.468
Turkey	0.470	India	0.841
France	0.501	Indonesia	0.589
South Africa	0.580	Italy	0.462
Indonesia	0.589	Japan	0.794
China	0.739	Mexico	0.798
Russia	0.744	Russia	0.744
Japan	0.794	South Africa	0.580
Mexico	0.798	Rep. of Korea	0.885
India	0.841	Turkey	0.470
Brazil	0.883	United Kingdom	0.369
Rep. of Korea	0.885	United States	0.402
Argentina	0.949	European Union	0.402

Source: Authors' work based on Taxonomic computation

Table 80 Development degrees for the Group of Twenty (G20) in 2017

Development Ranking '*fi*'		2017 year	*fi*=
United States	0.370	Argentina	0.903
European Union	0.422	Australia	0.468
Japan	0.450	Brazil	0.885
Germany	0.460	Canada	0.462
Canada	0.462	China	0.714
Australia	0.468	France	0.506
United Kingdom	0.473	Germany	0.460
France	0.506	India	0.821
Rep. of Korea	0.556	Italy	0.579
Italy	0.579	Japan	0.450
China	0.714	Mexico	0.777
Mexico	0.777	Russia	0.806
South Africa	0.781	South Africa	0.781
Russia	0.806	Rep. of Korea	0.556
India	0.821	Turkey	0.916
Brazil	0.885	United Kingdom	0.473
Argentina	0.903	United States	0.370
Turkey	0.916	European Union	0.422

Source: Authors' work based on Taxonomic computation

Table 81 Development degrees for the Group of Twenty (G20) in 2018

Development Ranking '*fi*'		2018 year	*fi*=
Japan	0.247	Argentina	0.915
Germany	0.370	Australia	0.509
United Kingdom	0.415	Brazil	0.773
France	0.440	Canada	0.471
Canada	0.471	France	0.440
Australia	0.509	Germany	0.370
Rep. of Korea	0.524	Italy	0.553
Italy	0.553	Japan	0.247
Russia	0.695	Mexico	0.860
Brazil	0.773	Russia	0.695
South Africa	0.791	South Africa	0.791
Turkey	0.824	Rep. of Korea	0.524
Mexico	0.860	Turkey	0.824
Argentina	0.915	United Kingdom	0.415

Source: Authors' work based on Taxonomic computation

Table 82 Top-ranking economies in institutional development from 2010 to 2018

Year	Top-ranking economies of the European Union (including the United Kingdom)	Top-ranking economies of the European Union (excluding the United Kingdom)	The Group of Twenty (G20)
2010	The United Kingdom: "*fi*" = 0.348 Germany: "*fi*" = 0.393	Germany: "*fi*" = 0.383 The Netherlands: "*fi*" = 0.446	The United States: "*fi*" = 0.395 The European Union: "*fi*" = 0.414
2011	The United Kingdom: "*fi*" = 0.259 France: "*fi*" = 0.356	France: "*fi*" = 0.433 The Netherlands: "*fi*" = 0.502	The United States: "*fi*" = 0.393 The European Union: "*fi*" = 0.43
2012	The Netherlands: "*fi*" = 0.396 Sweden: "*fi*" = 0.475	Germany: "*fi*" = 0.187 The Netherlands: "*fi*" = 0.193	The United States: "*fi*" = 0.374 The European Union: "*fi*" = 0.421
2013	The Netherlands: "*fi*" = 0.367 Denmark: "*fi*" = 0.433	The Netherlands: "*fi*" = 0.367 Sweden: "*fi*" = 0.451	The United States: "*fi*" = 0.376 The European Union: "*fi*" = 0.428
2014	The Netherlands: "*fi*" = 0.325 Germany: "*fi*" = 0.346	The Netherlands: "*fi*" = 0.374 Germany: "*fi*" = 0.379	The United States: "*fi*" = 0.4 The European Union: "*fi*" = 0.446
2015	The Netherlands: "*fi*" = 0.332 Sweden: "*fi*" = 0.43	The Netherlands: "*fi*" = 0.394 Sweden: "*fi*" = 0.511	The United States: "*fi*" = 0.379 The European Union: "*fi*" = 0.396
2016	The Netherlands: "*fi*" = 0.348 Sweden: "*fi*" = 0.422	Austria: "*fi*" = 0.481 Demark: "*fi*" = 0.492	The United Kingdom: "*fi*" = 0.369 The United States: "*fi*" = 0.422
2017	The United Kingdom: "*fi*" = 0.23 Germany: "*fi*" = 0.246	The Netherlands: "*fi*" = 0.399 France: "*fi*" = 0.451	The United States: "*fi*" = 0.37 The European Union: "*fi*" = 0.422
2018	Germany: "*fi*" = 0.237 The United Kingdom: "*fi*" = 0.246	Germany: "*fi*" = 0.273 France: "*fi*" = 0.389	Japan: "*fi*" = 0.247 Germany: "*fi*" = 0.37

Source: Authors' results obtained by numerical taxonomy

References

Aghion, P., & Howitt, P. W. (1992). A model of growth through creative destruction. *Econometrica, 60*(2), 323–351.

Arnold, R. D., & Wade, J. P. (2015). A definition of systems thinking: A systems approach. *Procedia Computer Science, 44*, 669–678. https://doi.org/10.1016/j.procs.2015.03.050.

Backstrom, L., Huttenlocher, D., Kleinberg, J., & Lan, X. (2006). *Group formation in large social networks*. Proceedings of the 12th ACM SIGKDD international conference on Knowledge discovery and data mining – KDD '06. p. 44. https://doi.org/10.1145/1150402.1150412

Barro, R. J. (1991). Economic growth in a cross section of countries. *Quarterly Journal of Economics, 106*(2), 407–443.

Bruce, G. C. (2012, December). *Institutional dynamics: When is change "real change"?* Sociology, Northwestern University.

Chan, C. M. (2008). Which country matters? Institutional development and foreign affiliate performance. *Strategic Management Journal, 29*, 1179–1205., published online in Wiley Inter Science (www.interscience.wiley.com). https://doi.org/10.1002/smj.705.

Cornell University, INSEAD, and WIPO. (2013). *The Global Innovation Index 2013: The local dynamics of innovation* (S. Dutta & B. Lanvin, editors, 6th Ed.). Geneva/Ithaca/Fontainebleau.

Durlauf, S., & Young, P. (2001). *Social dynamics*. Cambridge, MA: MIT Press.

Faghih, N., & Sazegar, M. (2019). Globalization development within the Group of Twenty (G20) as indicated by globalization and innovation indices. In N. Faghih (Ed.), *Globalization and development. Contributions to Economics*. Cham: Springer.

GII, Global Innovation Index. (2017). *Innovation feeding the world*. Ithaca/Fontainebleau/Geneva: Cornell University, INSEAD, and WIPO. https://www.globalinnovationindex.org/about-gii#reports. Accessed 16 Dec. 2017.

Grossman, G. M., & Helpman, E. (1990). Trade, innovation, and growth. *The American Economic Review*, 86–91.

Grossman, G. M., & Helpman, E. (2001). *Innovation and growth in the global economy*. Cambridge, MA:

Hall, R. E., & Jones, C. I. (1999). Why do some countries produce so much more output per worker than others? *Quarterly Journal of Economics, 114*(1), 83–116.

Holland, J. H. (1998). *Emergence: From chaos to order*. Reading: Helix Books.

Jones, C. I. (1995). R&D-based models of economic growth. *Journal of Political Economy, 103*(4), 759–784.

Khan, Z. U., et al. (2017, Winter). Institutions and innovation: Evidence from countries at different stages of development. *Pakistan Development Review, 56*(4), 297–317.

Khanna, T., & Rivkin, J. W. (2001). Estimating the performance effects of business groups in emerging markets. *Strategic Management Journal, 22*(1), 45–74.

Knack, S., & Keefer, P. (1997). Does social capital have an economic payoff? A cross-country investigation. *Quarterly Journal of Economics, 112*(4), 1251–1288.

Krueger, A. B., & Lindahl, M. (2001). Education for growth: Why and for whom? *Journal of Economic Literature, 34*, 1101–1136.

Lansing, J. S. (2003). Complex adaptive systems. *Annual Review of Anthropology, 32*(1), 183–204. https://doi.org/10.1146/annurev.anthro.32.061002.093440.

La Porta, R., Lopez-de-Silanes, F., Shleifer, A., & Vishny, R. (1997). Trust in large organizations. *American Economic Review, 87*(2), 333–338.

Le Quesne, W. J. (1969). A method of selection of characters in numerical taxonomy. *Systematic Biology, 18*(2), 201–205. https://doi.org/10.2307/2412604.

Lipset, S. M. (1960). *Political man: The social basis of modern politics*. New York: Doubleday.

Miller, J. H., & Page, S. E. (2007). *Complex adaptive systems: An introduction to computational models of social life*. Princeton University Press.

Mokyr, J. (1992). *The lever of riches: Technological creativity and economic progress*. New York: Oxford University Press.

Nambisan, S., & Sawhney, M. (2007). The innovation Bazaar. *Harvard Business Review*, June. https://hbr.org/2007/06/a-buyers-guide-to-the-innovation-bazaar. Accessed 20 Jan 2018.

North, D. C. (1990). *Institutions, institutional change and economic performance*. Cambridge, MA: Cambridge University Press.

Olson, M. (1996). Big bills left on the sidewalk: Why some nations are rich, and others poor. *Journal of Economic Perspectives, 10*(2), 3–24.

Phillips, R. B. (1983). Shape characters in numerical taxonomy and problems with ratios. *Taxon, 32*(4), 535–544.

Romer, P. (1990). Endogenous technological change. *Journal of Political Economy, 98*, S71–S102.

Sattar, A., & Mahmood, T. (2011). Intellectual property rights and economic growth: Evidences from high, middle- and low-income countries. *Pakistan Economic and Social Review*, 163–186.

Scott, W. R. (1995). *Institutions and organizations (foundations for organizational science)* (1st ed.). Sage: Thousand Oaks.

Solow, R. M. (1956). A contribution to the theory of economic growth. *The Quarterly Journal of Economics*, 65–94.

Solow, R. M. (1957). Technical change and the aggregate production function. *Review of Economics and Statistics, 39*(3), 312–320.

Tebaldi, E. (2013). Does institutional quality impact innovation? Evidence from cross country patent granted data. *Applied Economics, 45*(7), 18.

Tebaldi, E., & Elmslie, B. (2008). Institutions, innovation and economic growth. *Economica, 5*(2), 20.

The Global Innovation Index. (2018). *Creating healthy lives—The future of medical innovation*. Ithaca/Fontainebleau/Geneva: Cornell University/INSEAD/WIPO.

Weidlich, W. (1997). Sociodynamics applied to the evolution of urban and regional structures. *Discrete Dynamics in Nature and Society, 1*, 85–98.

Williamson, O. E. (1985). *The economic institutions of capitalism*. New York: Free Press.

Overview of Institutional Change Contexts and Dynamics

Adeleke O. Banwo, Uchechi Onokala, and Paul Kojo Ametepe

1 Introduction

This chapter highlights complexities related to institutional change by providing an overview of major perspectives and theories related to this construct. We delineate the general areas related to these constructs through the perspective of context and human behavior dynamics.

Institutional change is a constant phenomenon, a multidisciplinary research area that affects economies. A recent review of extant literature confirms the focus on institutional entrepreneurs and the multiple processes involved in institutional change (Micelotta et al. 2017).

Institutional change belongs to the domain of institutional economics and is premised on some fundamental features: "formal and informal group action of all economic agents, conformity-restraint mechanism, cost-benefit dyad within the sphere of economic reciprocity, economics, legal system, and ethics" (Commons 1936). Informal institution variables such as customs, cultures, and social and business norms often require a longer time to experience some forms of modification and adaptations rather than a total change (Lauth 2015; Tsai 2006). These features are essential in understanding the process of institutional change in any context and represent a broad subset of the macroeconomic system. For example, there are sharp differences in the effectiveness of the legal systems of developed and developing countries as well as the ethical values and norms even across different cities in a country. In ensuring conformity to the collective values, sanctions are used as punitive measures to deter and realign the actors.

A. O. Banwo (✉)
Consulate General of the Federal Republic of Nigeria, Shanghai, China

U. Onokala · P. K. Ametepe
Department of Business Administration, University of Lagos, Lagos, Nigeria

N. Faghih, A. H. Samadi (eds.), *Dynamics of Institutional Change in Emerging Market Economies*, Contributions to Economics,
https://doi.org/10.1007/978-3-030-61342-6_3

Though institutions are common in every economic system, the form of institutional change varies across different strata of society. These changes are influenced by the interplay of endogenous and exogenous factors within the micro and macroeconomy (Abdelnour et al. 2017).

Institutions have many meanings and there is no concession as to which definition is the best for the construct. It has different terminologies, and as such, there are different perspectives. Institutional change emerges from the combination of the two words, institution and change. In simple terms, institutional change entails the shift from one state to another in the ways things are done in an institution. That is the shift in the rule of the game in the society, organization, individual, or state of mind. Changes occur within an organization as well as in the larger society. It can be spontaneous, occurring in a matter of minutes, or delayed, taking place over a long period.

Institutional change is reshaping different facets of institutions. Similarly, the rate of institutional change in most developing economies is dependent on its adaptive capacity in response to external disturbances, decision-making processes, experience, and the economic system (Miner 2015). Also, several empirical studies assert that some developing economies have weak institutions and the volatile business environment increases the frequency of institutional changes in some segments of the economy, while other segments experience less institutional changes (Barasa et al. 2017; Diop et al. 2010; Fosu 2015). For example, the process of institutional change in the judiciary and legal system might be slower compared to institutional changes in education and other sectors.

It is therefore pertinent to emphasize that context plays a critical role in having positive or negative influences on institutional change. Institutions are exposed to different levels of context and boundary-spanning roles that might be environmental, regulatory, cultural, structural, and socio-political. Several studies have investigated different dimensions of institutional change in different economies; the prevailing context of such studies seems to be a major factor in determining the outcomes and nature of changes that arise over some time (Bakir and Jarvis 2017; Campos 2000). Contexts are not static and subject to changes that are described as evolutionary, proactive, reactive, and extinct. The non-static nature of institutions in any context is hinged primarily on its stage of life cycle and multiple forces of change models (Abbott et al. 2016). The apparent complexity and non-uniformity in the change models confirm that these changes might take varied forms. Some of the change processes are described as either gradual or destabilizing depending on the myriad of dynamics in different sectors (Streeck and Thelen 2009). When the process of institutional change is gradual, the economic actors and agents involved can adapt their behavior and process to reduce the level of uncertainty, disruption, and shocks. On the contrary, sometimes disruptive changes are not anticipated and the effect is usually negative for institutions that did not foresee the change and lack the resources to adapt. It is plausible to assert that the continuum of gradual-disruptive institutional changes is interlinked and evolutionary (Lockwood 2016).

Institutions evolve through the conscious actions and decisions of economic agents. It also evolves through unconscious and unplanned behaviors and decisions that are accepted as culture and norm that shapes the group behavior. Understanding the group dynamics that influence the organizational culture and behavior is fundamental since it gives insights to the behaviors of actors and the possible effects of the individual and corporate decisions (Forsyth 2018; Lucas and Kline 2008). This reinforces the fact that underlying behavior motivations, ethical values, norms, organizational structures, and institutional goals are dependent on rational and irrational decisions made by human beings which might result in favorable and unfavorable outcomes (Oliver 1991).

This chapter provides an overview of perspectives in studying institutional change dynamics and is divided into three sections: the first section focuses on institutional change perspectives, using different theories. The second section focuses on the institutional change behavioral framework, and the third section summarizes the major findings from the study.

2 Institutional Change Theory Perspectives

Thompson (2017) asserts that human behavior is subject to multiple influences and variables, and therefore it is necessary to understand the dynamics and dyad of the individual actors, the opportunities and threats, and mediating role of cognition and culture. Arising from this is the system interaction involving institutions and its multiple internal and external individual stakeholders to determine the change dynamics (Peters 2000). The validity of these assertions transverses both informal and formal institutional changes providing insight on some of the reasons for the ever-changing nature of some facet of institutionalization. The multiple influences of stakeholders and economic agents have impacts on institutions depending on the dynamics of control and participation in the economy (Hardy and Maguire 2008; Mahoney and Thelen 2009; Wieland et al. 2016). For example, though the government might not have a direct stake in all institutions, its administrative and regulatory agencies exert different forms of pressure and are not immune to changes. Similarly, internal organizational stakeholders such as employees, investors, and management do not operate in a vacuum, and thus to survive the vagaries of the local and international environment, they try to continuously adapt over a period. The institutional change theories are investigated using different perspectives, some of which are presented as follows.

2.1 Deinstitutionalization

Deinstitutionalization is the view that beliefs and norms of an institution weaken and disappear over time (Scott 2013). Tina Dacin et al. (2002) noted: "It is useful to place studies of deinstitutionalization in a broader context of institutional change since the weakening and disappearance of one set of beliefs and practices is likely to be associated with the arrival of new beliefs and practices."

From the foregoing, deinstitutionalization can arise from problems associated with performance level or problems associated with institutionalized practices (Clemente and Roulet 2015; Oliver 1997). There are pressures associated with environmental changes, such as competition for resources and pressure from a shift in power distribution and legitimized institutional arrangement. These are seen in the area of performance crises, changes in the environment, and such other factors that bring about changes in the legitimacy of a given practice. Aside from this, institutional change and deinstitutionalization are also affected by social pressure (Chaudhry and Rubery 2019). These are pressure associated with differentiation of groups, e.g., diversity in the workforce, heterogeneous beliefs, and changes in laws associated with the social group. In a nutshell, the pressures associated with deinstitutionalization are functional pressures, political pressures, and social pressures (Berger 2019).

2.2 Hierarchies of Rules Theory

This institutional change covers specified sets of rules by a collective political entity like the community, the state, as well as individuals and organizations that engage in collective action, conflict, and bargaining in trying to make changes to these rules to their advantage. Therefore, this explains the origins of "property rights" seen as rules which govern the day-to-day interaction in an institution (Libecap 1993). As such, property rights entail different distributional consequences; hence, individuals and groups engage in lobbying and bargaining as well as in a political action to alter the rules for their advantage. They see the rule-changing activity as "contracting," depicting a game governed by a higher level of political rules, which shape the direction of institutional change of the lower-level (property rights) rules.

Libecap (1993) posits that exogenous institutions are factors leading to institutional change. The distribution of benefits depends on a change in the parameter, which can lead to a change in property rights rule. Ostrom (2005) differentiates between "operational rules," which govern everyday interactions, and "collective-choice rules" and recognizes causes of institutional change as endogenous and exogenous. Examples of endogenous and exogenous causes are seen in the depletion of a resource over time and technological changes.

2.3 Evolutionary Theories of Institutional Change

The evolutionary theory refers to the processes, which follow the principles of Charles Darwin, the biology evolutionist (a source of mutations), the survival of the fittest (selection), and the replication of successful traits (reproduction). Note that this does not rule out the rational action of actors in different institutions. Indeed, in most of the evolutionary institutional change explanations, the impetus for institutional change arises from deliberate human actions (Brousseau et al. 2011).

Institutions and governments ensure the survival of core institutional systems with several forces dictating the pace of changes. In the process of institutional change, new rules emerge from the uncoordinated choices of many individuals rather than a single, collective-choice, or political process. Transaction cost is considered, and according to Williamson (2000), it arises because of the rationality and opportunism of the transacting parties. Transaction cost theory assumes that the most efficient institution develops to achieve an optimal match with another transaction. Therefore, in this theory, competitive pressure displaces the weak or inefficient forms of institutions (Kingston and Caballero 2009). An efficient institution achieves positive returns. For instance, if a change in a particular process renders the existing process inefficient, then the new and more efficient process will emerge to replace them. Hayek (1973) describes evolutionary theory from the aspect of a social group where rules evolve because of the group practicing such rules and displacing other existing rules. Also, group selection is a process which generates rules to achieve optimal configuration based on consistent general principles. Young (1996) in his view argues that institutional change arises due to the historical accident that follows "punctuated equilibrium" process. Overall, evolutionary theory considers institutional change as a resultant of exogenous parameters.

2.4 *The "Equilibrium View" of Institutions*

D North (1990) explains the equilibrium view of institutional change by relating it to the relationship between formal and informal rules. In his 1990 book, he proposed, "we need to know much more about informal rules and how they interact with formal rules." In equilibrium view, each of the agents is constrained by exogenous constraints and by endogenous institutional rules of the game. Examples of exogenous constraints are laws of physics, resource endowments, technology, capital stock, and so on. Institutional change is not about changing rules but about changing expectations. Aoki (1996) submits that a new rule that cannot modify people's expectations in the right direction will not affect their behavior. Ostrom (2005) views it as a "rule-in-form" but not a "rule-in-use." In the equilibrium view, enforcement of rules is different from their contents and considered as endogenous. Change in technology, which is exogenous, for instance, can disrupt an equilibrium, and this can lead to change in formal rules in an institution in order to achieve a coordinated shift of many players' beliefs about each other's strategies.

3 Institutional Change Behavioral Framework

The complexity and framework for studying institutional change will continue to vary across disciplines and economic settings. Douglass North propositions provide a major behavioral framework using key variables that are needed to understand major reasons for differences in the dynamics of institutional change (North 1993) (see Fig. 1). The primary premise of the proposition is the definition of institutions as the soft and intangible constraints (constitutions, cultural values, regulations, social and business norms) placed on human interactions and decisions within the formal and informal organizations. Though the nomenclatures of the organizations might be similar globally, the actions and objectives of the individuals in the different organizations determine the opportunities and threats in the business environment. For instance, trade unions, political parties, and institutions alongside other economic organizations shape social organizations. Besides, they directly, indirectly adapt and influence the soft institutions' effect on their continued survival.

Thy dyadic relationship in Fig. 1 illustrates a simplified typology of the basic variables that shape institutional change from the micro- and macro-perspectives. Institutions' forces consist of local and external intangibles that are powerful enough to cause a process of the gradual or disruptive change process in organizations within their domestic business environment and beyond (Meyer et al. 2009; Papandreou 1998).

For example, the rippling effect of the UK Brexit issue and US-China trade wars has either a positive or a negative effect on different organizations globally depending on the ability of the individual players to maximize some of the dynamics. Organizations might face different types of competition depending on the market system in the economy, size, and objectives and positioning. Thus, the ability of the

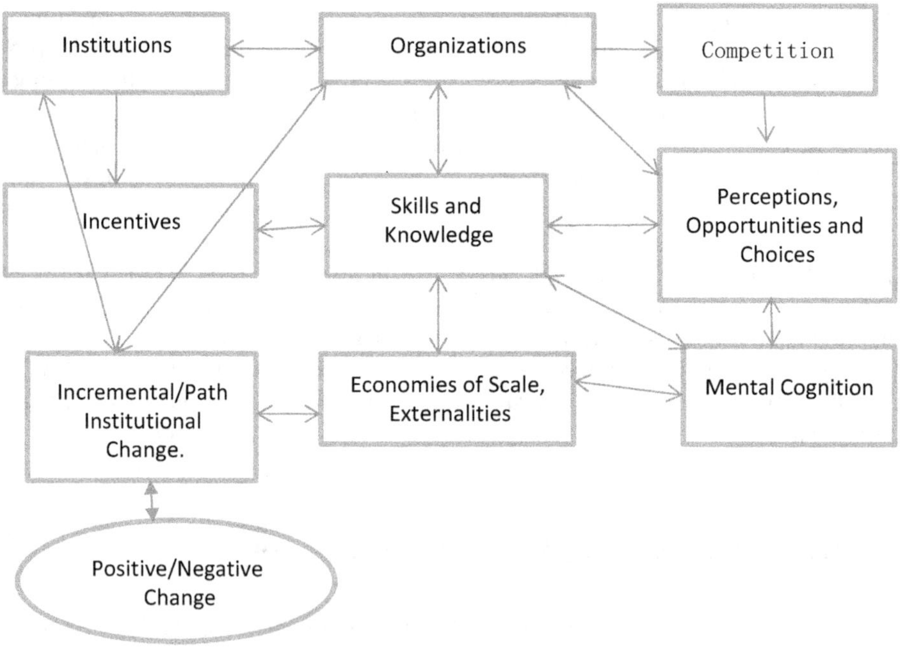

Fig. 1 Institutional change framework. (Source: Adapted from David North Propositions on Institutional Change)

internal stakeholders to sustain the competitive advantage and react depends on their perceptions of inherent opportunities or threats and available choices they can make, taking resource constraint and other factors into consideration. The uneven distribution of resources and the insatiable needs of individuals are some basic tenets that make competition common in every society. In trying to ensure fair playing ground and protect the core sectors of the economy and economic growth and development, various governments enforce institutional frameworks in the economy's interest (Mahoney and Thelen 2009; North 1994).

It is essential to note that variations would always occur in perceptions, opportunities, and choices due to the mental cognition and goals of major actors in each organization. Major factors responsible for these include the quality of skills and knowledge within a local context and in similar contexts in other economies (Harmon et al. 2015; Knight 1997). This could explain the underlying differences like institutional change in developed and developing economies in similar organizations and exposed to similar institutions. Depending on the organizations, information needs and acquisition of soft skills and knowledge are paramount for adapting to the change process (Ramezan 2011). Interestingly, the focus is also on the availability of perceived incentives to the organizations. Motivations and organizational structures could determine the adaptive strategy to adopt. The increasing presence of learning organizations suggests that environmental scanning, lobbying, pressure groups, and objectives are covertly influencing several incremental institutional changes over some time in favor of the dominant stakeholders and interest groups (Caldwell 2012; Thomsen and Hoest 2001). Conversely, other economic agents suffer negatively from the incremental change and decisions of the stronger or more influential interest groups in most societies and might cease to exist if they are unable to survive the change process (Berry and Wilcox 2018).

3.1 Public Policy and Institutional Change Uncertainty

Change, competition, class struggle, and conflicting interests are salient concepts in institutional change research (Kufuor 2017; Rahim 2017). These concepts influence the policies of formal and informal institutions through various channels depending on the economic and governance structures. We advance the need to incorporate the dynamics of existing local, public, and private policy dynamics at the macro- and micro-levels of each society as critical to understanding the uncertainties surrounding institutional change. Using the Williamson concept, the institutional hierarchical analogy of the elements comprises of inter-related subsets (see Fig. 2) that continuously cause institutional uncertainty. However, in reality, it does not follow a stratified process as advanced (Bylund and McCaffrey 2017; Williamson 1985). The Schumpeter's creative destruction is also synonymous with the process and problems that arise over the different time horizons in the course of interactions and stresses the relative importance of having a holistic view of a change given the context and nature of competition (Schumpeter 1942).

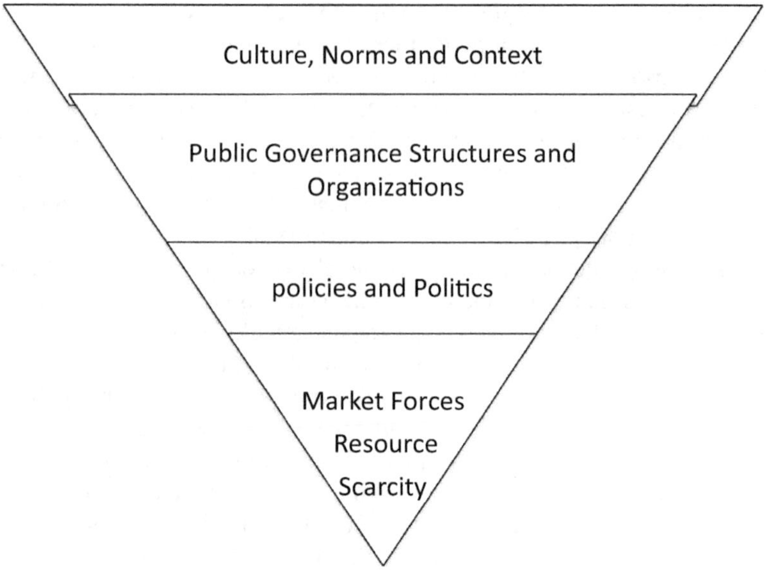

Fig. 2 Public policy, entrepreneurship, and uncertainty framework. (Source: Adapted from A theory of entrepreneurship and institutional uncertainty (Bylund and McCaffrey 2017))

All economic systems and institutions evolve and experience different levels of changes and scholars have described these responses as organic and a primary driver of competition among interest groups with rational and irrational conflicting interests (Aiken and Hage 1971; Freeman 2015; Hage 2017). In general, there are clear shreds of evidence that changes in social structures and groups predate modern civilization and have led to the rise and extinction of empires through incremental and disruptive mechanisms hinged on behaviors of interest groups. In mitigating some of the changes that occurred in primordial times, groups of individuals established restraints through the adoption of cultures, values, and social and business norms given their context (see Fig. 2) (Weinberg 2007).

These restraints provide a framework for different organizations and subgroups to adopt variants that might suit their objectives and interests. However, this creates a scenario where conflict and class struggles create negative impacts that sometimes are detrimental to the common good of society. In ensuring that the institutional framework is subservient, formal and informal organizational structures are created through political actors empowered to govern and enact public policies and regulatory processes that should protect the common interest of all economic agents and mitigate against disruptive institutional change at all levels (Dunn 2015).

Similarly, it is assumed that formal institutions cannot change within a short time frame compared to informal institutions due to their nature. Formal institutions are typified by local and international laws, edicts, and regulations that govern a group of people or enforceable in a given geographical area, while the informal institutions comprise of religions, values, culture, and norms (North 1991). The regular interactions of the stakeholders and economic agents in the institution-organization continuum might necessitate different changes which might be short-lived or long-lasting (Schiavo-Campo 1994). Arising from this, the cost-benefit analysis is skewed to some interest groups due to constraints of time and barriers that hinder making a rational decision. This often leads to conflicts and situations that need to be managed through information channels and media to mitigate the effect of the losses.

It follows that the process of implementing changes is complex and with a variety of hybrid models such as process model, group model, elite model, incremental model, and rational and public choice models could exert intervening influences in different contexts (Dye 2013).

Governments and economies have established institutions to serve as restraints on even the government with organizational frameworks that act as checks and balances (see Fig. 2). For instance, the strength and efficacy of institutions can be sustained over the long-term frame. However, the continued sustenance of these institutions is related to threshold effect dynamics (Islam 2018). Once the threshold point of economic agents to maintain status quo is reached or interests are collectively threatened, a change process can arise to alter the economic benefits or loss framework. Recent civil disturbances in developed and developing countries confirm the ability of disequilibrium in the threshold effect to initiate a disruptive change process that challenges the existing institutional frameworks. Forces of endogenous and exogenous influences are some of the major factors causing changes (see Fig. 3).

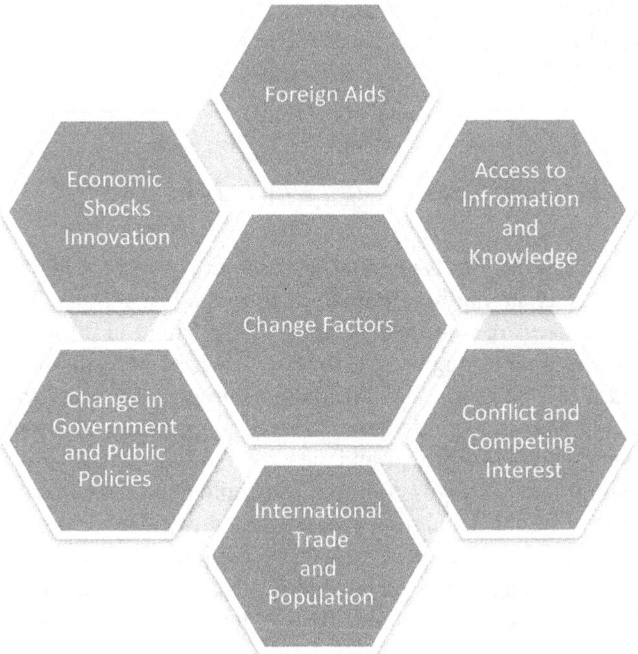

Fig. 3 Institutional change factors. (Source: Authors)

3.2 Foreign Aids

Some developing and developed countries often secure foreign aids and loans from international agencies such as the World Bank, International Finance Corporation, and African Development Bank to tackle specific problems and execute projects. Usually, before this aid is secured, both parties consent to specific terms and conditions that serve as a legal binding contract. Several schools of thought and researchers have found that foreign aids could bring about gradual and disruptive changes to major institutions in the receiving countries (Storm 2015; Swiss 2016). For instance, the process of implementing the conditions of the donors, in the end, could either distort market forces, not fit for the context, or have a positive impact on the economic institutions. There are several motives and interests in the foreign aid deliberation process; usually, foreign aid agencies protect their interests and are governed by their institutional values, while the beneficiaries most of the time have to make reforms in their institutional frameworks (Asongu and Nwachukwu 2016; Devarajan et al. 2002; Martens et al. 2002). Implementing reforms sometimes always lead to institutional changes in some of the government agencies that might be general or specific to an area of the economy. The effect of foreign-induced institutional reforms in some developing economies is fraught with contextual problems that make the implementation process difficult with resultant negative effect (Briggs 2017; Jones and Tarp 2016; Tavares 2003). Several endogenous problems also arise in economies with weak institutional frameworks and policies that often result in corruption, economic depression, economic losses, and the extinction of existing institutions. Nevertheless, research also confirms that foreign aid and grants have some positive effects in economies by providing relief and support in needed areas (Arndt et al. 2015; Asongu and Nwachukwu 2017).

3.3 Access to Information and Knowledge

Individuals and organizations have more access to information with increasing frontiers of knowledge changing more rapidly than in the last century. Technology and public media agencies are continually reshaping the nature of information available to different generations through social media platforms and communication channels (Birkland 2017; McCombs 2005), thus resulting in the decline of traditional information and knowledge platforms and the rise of variants of online mobile platforms. For example, interest groups and the media influence the agenda-setting process for institutional changes through customization and dissemination of information for different demography at the speed of light through mobile social media platforms (Dye 2013). These influences and information are sometimes subtle and available by a single click on the internet irrespective of the location. Beyond the role of the media, increasing innovations in technology platforms have become a veritable tool to initiate and promote cohesive actions and process that can disrupt the organizations and institutions. In some economies, governments and other institutions strive to provide this information to promote transparency, awareness, and inclusiveness (Lollar 2006). Sometimes, this noble intention and provision of uncensored access to information and knowledge might become distorted and result in misrepresentation by various interest groups. For example, knowledge of a relaxed tax system in some countries has resulted in multinational agencies, individuals, and organizations incorporating their business in such countries (Deng et al. 2019; Zucman 2015). Similarly, the diffusion of information and knowledge across geographical boundaries has benefited many countries through solving of many domestic problems and adaptation of successful institutional models from other contexts (Wang 2018). For example, many countries along the Belt and Road corridors have modified their institutions, and China's "one city one product model" is replicated in other countries in Asia and Africa. Universities, research scholars, think-tank, and data banks provide reliable knowledge repository and avenues to nurture initiatives, ideas, research findings, and innovations essential for changes.

3.4 Conflicts and Competing Interests

Von Bertalanffy (1968) systems theory posits that systems comprise of inter-related units with a common purpose. Inherent features of this theory also include a macro- and micro-system, group dynamics, and interests. Since economic systems cannot exist in isolation or vacuum individuals at different levels of the organization interface in groups within and outside the system with competing interests, the interaction dynamics and motives in each group include formal and informal processes and in-group and out-group dynamics effect (Litwin and Eaton 2018; Pratt 2001). How these invisible dynamics manifest is related to the economic, political, and social environment and resources.

It is plausible to assert that the whole world is a general system comprising of different micro-systems that vary in size, influence, orientation, public policy interests, and resource endowments. Historical evidence shows the culture of stronger economies taking over weaker economies through colonization, treaties, and other economic alliances usually against their free will and interests (Englebert 2000). This process created many conflicts in forms of physical wars, battles, and unrest over the centuries with the implementation of foreign institutional frameworks in the host countries. In this century, international politics, foreign interests, and multiple conflicting interests have resulted in wars in stable countries through the collective influences of countries (Carpenter 2013; Öniş and Kutlay 2013). No country and economy are immune to changes arising from internal and external conflicts, motivated by power struggle and economic resources distribution.

3.5 International Trade

Johnson Jr. (1995) posited the resource dependency theory of organizations' behavior as open systems with resource limitations and constantly interacting with the external environment in an exchange and acquisition of resources. Also, Barney's resource-based view main premise asserts that organizations seek competitive advantage due to the uneven distribution of resource endowments (Barney 2001). Both theories underpin the dynamics of international trade flows and exchanges among countries in goods and services. These flows between countries provide various avenues for institutional changes to protect or diversify the interests of multiple stakeholders. International trade flows are strong and countries are often confronted with the need to protect their national interests as well as liberalization of economic activities. Business interests and national interests have conflicting goals with covert pressures from local and external organizations to influence institutions. The protection of national sovereignty is a basic duty of every government – more so international trade agreements and flows from other countries with diverse cultures and economic interests require legislation of institutions and legislation aimed at regulating and providing institutional frameworks that govern flows in their countries (Méon and Sekkat 2008). Despite this presumed responsibility of governments, international trade flows and exchanges between most economies remain unbalanced and skewed to favor the stronger party in the exchanges in a given time horizon. Business and multinational organizations are driven by business profit and maximization of resources at their disposal in the host country. However, when aspects of the diplomatic and political relationships with another country are strained, disruptive institutional changes would usually arise to limit the flows (Bolen 2019; Jerger et al. 2019).

3.6 Population

Institutions and organizations experience changes as the population increases and decreases. An increasing rate of population growth puts much pressure on existing institutions, and sometimes governments enact policies to manage population growth. For example, in China, the one-child policy was institutionalized to manage the population explosion and then the two-child policy was implemented to increase the percentage of the younger population. Such changes might be tied to institutional frameworks, economic growth, availability of resources, epidemic, and war with resultant changes in the population demography (Tucker et al. 1992). Contextually, the population demography data and trend are used as a tool for influencing changes at different levels of society. For example, countries with a high level of aged populations adjust their institutional frameworks to address the diverse problems peculiar to this group.

Population figures also represent a political tool used by the government in resource allocations, power-sharing, and provision of infrastructural facilities and benefits. Policymakers, politicians, lobbyists, and multinational companies are constantly struggling to protect their interests using different segments of the populations. Politicians know the importance of population clusters in winning elections, and based on the peculiar demographics, interests in each cluster promote institutional values that benefit the majority of the political class and the dominant population group. For example, in most developed countries, aging is a major problem and politicians are easily disposed to appeasing the aged populations by supporting institutional policies related to Medicare, accommodation, pension, and other ancillary needs. Conversely, in most developing countries where the young population is much higher, issues related to unemployment are common and institutional frameworks are introduced to alleviate the problems of unemployment.

Similarly, countries with small populations regardless of the demography might experience minimal institutional changes depending on the available resources. However, over a given period, several societal problems, economic and social needs, and resource deficiency are likely to necessitate changes in response to population growth. Failure to address population-related issues can result in serious negative consequences for countries and breakdown of law and order.

Issues related to population are influenced by endogenous factors that are often enshrined in the institutional values of the country and exogenous influences that arise from immigration, refugee crises, and migration. Increasing global migration has led to an increase in immigrant populations in several developed countries due to the enactment of new institutional policies. The resultant effect of this is a continuous global supply of human labor at a lower cost in developed countries and brain drain.

Increasing mobility and migration dynamics has either been voluntary or forced depending on several factors such as war, economic opportunities, and search for a better life (Tichenor 2009). The effects of this migration issue put lots of pressure on organizational and institutional frameworks with resultant changes to address the human flows (Hampshire 2016).

3.7 Change in Government and Public Policies

Economic systems and organizations consist of formal and informal leadership and governance structures. The process of choosing these leaders is always political due to competing interests of group members, power dynamics, and external influences. Several variations in government structures are supported by institutions, which sometimes might experience disruptive changes to favor and sustain the current political group. Politics and governance comprise of political actors with ideologies that influence their public policy orientation more than the interests of other political groups (Bylund and McCaffrey 2017). Changes in political structures sometimes arise from social unrest, general discontent with the current government, transitions, and coups driven by internal and external forces. Several governments and countries have gone through transformation periods which might have resulted in positive changes in economic and social institutional frameworks or negative changes (Bayat 2017). For example, countries practicing democracy are likely to experience more disruptive changes compared to countries practicing communism. Global interest groups and countries have used institutional mechanisms such as embargoes to reduce changes driven by military take-overs and coups in most developing economies (Crawford and Kacarska 2019). Public policies are also a major subset of government and many governments have used these policies to bring rapid economic growth and development to their country and other regions (Cao 2012). A typical example is China's economic transformation and institutional changes since its opening up in 1949 and the United States of America's public policies and institutional changes in maintaining global security. In the past two decades, many changes in government have arisen from the social uprising that has radically changed the institutional frameworks. For example, the success of the Tunisian and Egyptian revolution influenced the rise of the social uprising in other countries. Even in the absence of social uprising, countries undergo social evolution and change over different time horizons.

3.8 Economic Shocks and Innovation

All countries experience some forms of economic shock that might be localized or induced globally. Since the majority of these shocks are unpredictable and sudden, the intensity of changes that arise could either be positive or negative (Tiwari and Zaman 2010). For instance, the global financial-economic meltdown caused multiple negative effects and economic recession in most countries. Several institutional changes and adaptations were necessary to revive most economies and prevent total economic collapse. Recently, more countries experience diverse forms of economic shocks and disruptive changes either through public policy decisions and actions of other countries (Kierzenkowski et al. 2016). Recent Brexit issues in the United Kingdom and the European Union could trigger an economic shock in both contexts and other countries. On the other hand, positive economic shock could also arise from innovations and discoveries. Major economies experiencing technological and scientific innovations experience creative destruction and constantly remodel institutions to adapt to the changes that are likely to occur (Bergeaud et al. 2016; Wan et al. 2015).

The domain of innovation varies across different organizations, countries, and contexts. Institutional frameworks, environment, and availability of problems are some of the latent factors responsible for variations in cognitive capacity development vis-à-vis innovation. Facets of innovations vary in most contexts, and though some of the discovery might be accidental and research finding and problem-solving based, it might necessitate changes to develop and protect them (Bergek et al. 2015). For instance, patents are an effective way to protect innovation discoveries and creations. When this is done, the process of diffusion to other organizations and economies sometimes requires some institutional changes to use and enjoy the benefits of the innovation (Redmond 2003). For example, Huawei 5G technology deployment to other countries has necessitated institutional changes to address security concerns and protect local technologies. Depending on the interests and institutional frameworks, some innovations are a threat to local organizations, and pressure groups might initiate changes to resist its adoption and control its usage. A typical example is the drone technology, which has multiple uses that vary across disciplines. Similarly, the innovation in hailing transportation services like Uber and Taxify (bolt) in the Nigerian economy resulted in a simple technological method of using an android phone or IOS devices to order for transportation services. The shift from the traditional method of hailing for taxi and the new method (Uber) of ordering for transportation services brought about a change in the consumption of the services by the populace.

Using a basic classification, the group dynamics of the actors comprise of social and political interest groups exerting pressures from the elite to the masses and the other group exerting pressures from the masses to the elite. The two groups consist of actors commonly referred to as institutional (policy) entrepreneurs with distinct and vested interests (Capoccia 2016). Bakir and Gunduz (2017) describe these groups as having multiple identities that include ideational, academician, framer, and meditator. These heterogeneous affiliations of the agents result in a complex process of decisions and actions aimed at influencing the process of institutional changes in concerned domains.

Using the agency and context framework, the effectiveness of the agency at the micro-level (individual) and macro-level (groups and organization) is usually a function of the social governance system, social class, skills, and stages involved in the change process (Levchenko 2016). Therefore, the dominant agent group is usually able to influence and control the process to determine the effectiveness of the institutions, power, and resource allocation.

4 Conclusion

Institutional change has played a significant role in the development of new institutions. These new institutions may be formal or informal, thereby reshaping different facets of the institution. Institutional change theory refers to the theories used in explaining institutional change processes. A few of the theories, such as deinstitutionalization, and hierarchy of rules, evolutionary theories, and equilibrium theory, were examined. Institutional change is the reason behind such changes in trade unions, political parties, and social organizations as well as the change in the society as a whole. At the organizational level, there are formal and informal settings that shape the organization and ultimately affect the employees and the processes.

In all, institutional change has different perspectives. It has both positive and negative effects on the formal and informal settings of the micro- and macroeconomies. The positive changes should be implemented, while the negative changes are challenges that should be investigated to aid more development in the different institutions.

References

Abbott, K. W., Green, J. F., & Keohane, R. O. (2016). Organizational ecology and institutional change in global governance. *International Organization, 70*(2), 247–277.

Abdelnour, S., Hasselbladh, H., & Kallinikos, J. J. (2017). Agency and institutions in organization studies. *Organization Studies, 38*(12), 1775–1792.

Aiken, M., & Hage, J. J. (1971). The organic organization and innovation. *Sociology, 5*(1), 63–82.

Aoki, M. (1996). Towards a comparative institutional analysis: Motivations and some tentative theorizing. *The Japanese Economic Review, 47*(1), 1–19.

Arndt, C., Jones, S., & Tarp, F. J. (2015). Assessing foreign aid's long-run contribution to growth and development. *World Development, 69*, 6–18.

Asongu, S. A., & Nwachukwu, J. C. (2016). Foreign aid and governance in Africa. *International Review of Applied, 30*(1), 69–88.

Asongu, S. A., & Nwachukwu, J. C. (2017). Foreign aid and inclusive development: Updated evidence from Africa, 2005–2012. *Social Science Quarterly, 98*(1), 282–298.

Bakir, C., & Gunduz, K. A. (2017). When, why and how institutional change takes place: A systematic review and a future research agenda on the importance of policy entrepreneurship in macroeconomic bureaucracies. *Policy and Society, 36*(4), 479–503.

Bakir, C., & Jarvis, D. S. (2017). *Contextualizing the context in policy entrepreneurship and institutional change*. Taylor & Francis.

Barasa, L., Knoben, J., Vermeulen, P., Kimuyu, P., & Kinyanjui, B. (2017). Institutions, resources, and innovation in East Africa: A firm-level approach. *Research Policy, 46*(1), 280–291.

Barney, J. B. (2001). Resource-based theories of competitive advantage: A ten-year retrospective on the resource-based view. *Journal of Management, 27*(6), 643–650.

Bayat, A. (2017). *Revolution without revolutionaries: Making sense of the Arab spring*. Stanford University Press.

Bergeaud, A., Cette, G., & Lecat, R. (2016). Productivity trends in advanced countries between 1890 and 2012. *Review of Income and Wealth, 62*(3), 420–444.

Bergek, A., Hekkert, M., Jacobsson, S., Markard, J., Sandén, B., & Truffer, B. (2015). Technological innovation systems in contexts: Conceptualizing contextual structures and interaction dynamics. *Environmental Innovation and Societal Transitions, 16*, 51–64.

Berger, L. (2019). *Deinstitutionalization of a management practice-the the abandonment of value-based management.* In Paper presented at the Academy of Management Proceedings.

Berry, J. M., & Wilcox, C. (2018). *The interest group society*. Routledge.

Birkland, T. A. (2017). Agenda setting in public policy. In *Handbook of public policy analysis* (pp. 89–104). Routledge.

Bolen, J. B. (2019). The dynamic properties of institutional reform: An analysis of US states. *Journal of Institutional Economics, 15*(3), 539–551.

Briggs, R. C. (2017). Does foreign aid target the poorest? *International Organization, 71*(1), 187–206.

Brousseau, E., Garrouste, P., & Raynaud, E. (2011). Institutional changes: Alternative theories and consequences for institutional design. *Journal of Economic Behavior and Organization, 79*(1–2), 3–19.

Bylund, P. L., & McCaffrey, M. (2017). A theory of entrepreneurship and institutional uncertainty. *Journal of Business Venturing, 32*(5), 461–475.

Caldwell, R. (2012). Systems thinking, organizational change and agency: A practice theory critique of Senge's learning organization. *Journal of Change Management, 12*(2), 145–164.

Campos, N. F. (2000). *Context is everything: Measuring institutional change in transition economies*. The World Bank.

Cao, S. (2012). Why China's approach to institutional change has begun to succeed. *Economic Modelling, 29*(3), 679–683.

Capoccia, G. (2016). When do institutions "bite"? Historical institutionalism and the politics of institutional change. *Comparative Political Studies, 49*(8), 1095–1127.

Carpenter, T. G. (2013). Tangled web: The Syrian civil war and its implications. *Mediterranean Quarterly, 24*(1), 1–11.

Chaudhry, S., & Rubery, J. (2019). Why do established practices deinstitutionalize? An actor-centred approach. *British Journal of Management, 30*(3), 538–557.

Clemente, M., & Roulet, T. J. (2015). Public opinion as a source of deinstitutionalization: A "spiral of silence" approach. *Academy of Management Review, 40*(1), 96–114.

Commons, J. R. (1936). Institutional economics. *American Economic Review, 26*(1), 237–249.

Crawford, G., & Kacarska, S. (2019). Aid sanctions and political conditionality: Continuity and change. *Journal of International Relations and Development, 22*(1), 184–214.

Deng, Z., Yan, J., & Sun, P. (2019). Political status and tax haven investment of emerging market firms: Evidence from China. *Journal of Business Ethics*, 1–20.

Devarajan, S., Dollar, D. R., & Holmgren, T. (2002). *Aid and reform in Africa*. The World Bank.

Diop, A., Dufrénot, G., & Sanon, G. (2010). Is per capita growth in Africa hampered by poor governance and weak institutions? An empirical study on the ECOWAS countries. *African Development Review, 22*(2), 265–275.

Dunn, W. N. (2015). *Public policy analysis*. Routledge.

Dye, T. R. (2013). *Understanding public policy: Pearson new international edition*. Pearson Higher Ed.

Englebert, P. J. (2000). Pre-colonial institutions, post-colonial states, and economic development in tropical Africa. *Political Research Quarterly, 53*(1), 7–36.

Forsyth, D. R. (2018). *Group dynamics*. Cengage Learning.

Fosu, A. K. (2015). Growth and institutions in African development. In *Growth and institutions in African development* (pp. 23–40). Routledge.

Freeman, J. J. W. E. o. M. (2015). *Contingency theory*. 1–1.

Hage, J. J. T. W. B. E. o. S. T. (2017). *Organization Theory*. 1–10.

Hampshire, J. (2016). European migration governance since the Lisbon treaty: Introduction to the special issue. *Journal of Ethnic and Migration Studies, 42*(4), 537–553.

Hardy, C., & Maguire, S. (2008). Institutional entrepreneurship. *The Sage Handbook of Organizational Institutionalism, 1*, 198–217.

Harmon, D. J., Green, S. E., Jr., & Goodnight, G. T. (2015). A model of rhetorical legitimation: The structure of communication and cognition underlying institutional maintenance and change. *Academy of Management Review, 40*(1), 76–95.

Hayek, F. A. (1973). *Economic freedom and representative government*. London: Wincott Foundation.

Islam, R. (2018). *One more time: What are institutions and how do they change?* The World Bank. 8422.

Jerger, J., Mullineux, A., & Welfens, P. J. (2019). *Institutional changes and economic dynamics of international capital markets in the context of BREXIT*. Springer.

Johnson, B. L., Jr. (1995). *Resource dependence theory: A political economy model of organizations*.

Jones, S., & Tarp, F. (2016). Does foreign aid harm political institutions? *Journal of Development Economics, 118*, 266–281.

Kierzenkowski, R., Pain, N., Rusticelli, E., & Zwart, S. (2016). *The economic consequences of Brexit*.

Kingston, C., & Caballero, G. (2009). Comparing theories of institutional change. *Journal of Institutional Economics, 5*(2), 151–180.
Knight, J. (1997). Social institutions and human cognition: Thinking about old questions in new ways. *Journal of Institutional and Theoretical Economics (JITE)/Zeitschrift für die gesamte Staatswissenschaft, 153*(4), 693–699.
Kufuor, K. O. (2017). *The Institutional Transformation of the Economic Community of West African States*. Routledge.
Lauth, H.-J. (2015). Formal and informal institutions. In *Routledge handbook of comparative political institutions* (pp. 70–83). Routledge.
Levchenko, A. A. (2016). *The impact of trade openness on institutions*. World Bank.
Libecap, G. D. (1993). *Contracting for property rights*. Cambridge University Press.
Litwin, A. S., & Eaton, A. E. (2018). Complementary or conflictual? Formal participation, informal participation, and organizational performance. *Human Resource Management, 57*(1), 307–325.
Lockwood, M. (2016). Creating protective space for innovation in electricity distribution networks in Great Britain: The politics of institutional change. *Environmental Innovation and Societal Transitions, 18*, 111–127.
Lollar, X. L. (2006). Assessing China's E-Government: Information, service, transparency and citizen outreach of government websites. *Journal of Contemporary China, 15*(46), 31–41.
Lucas, C., & Kline, T. (2008). Understanding the influence of organizational culture and group dynamics on organizational change and learning. *The Learning Organization, 15*(3), 277–287.
Mahoney, J., & Thelen, K. (2009). *Explaining institutional change: Ambiguity, agency, and power*. Cambridge University Press.
Martens, B., Mummert, U., Murrell, P., & Seabright, P. (2002). *The institutional economics of foreign aid*. Cambridge University Press.
McCombs, M. (2005). A look at agenda-setting: Past, present, and future. *Journalism Studies, 6*(4), 543–557.
Méon, P. G., & Sekkat, K. (2008). Institutional quality and trade: Which institutions? Which trade? *Economic Inquiry, 46*(2), 227–240.
Meyer, K. E., Estrin, S., Bhaumik, S. K., & Peng, M. W. (2009). Institutions, resources, and entry strategies in emerging economies. *Strategic Management Journal, 30*(1), 61–80.
Micelotta, E., Lounsbury, M., & Greenwood, R. (2017). Pathways of institutional change: An integrative review and research agenda. *Journal of Management, 43*(6), 1885–1910.
Miner, J. B. (2015). Behavioral theory of the firm. In R. Cyert & J. March (Eds.), *Organizational behavior* (Vol. 2, pp. 78–95). Routledge.
North, D. (1990). *Institutions, institutional change and economic performance*. Cambridge/New York.
North, D. (1991). Institutions. *Journal of Economic Perspectives, 5*(1), 97–112.
North, D. (1993). *Five propositions about institutional change*.
North, D. C. (1994). *Institutional change: A framework of analysis* (pp. 189–201).
Oliver, C. (1991). Strategic responses to institutional processes. *Academy of Management Review, 16*(1), 145–179.
Oliver, C. (1997). Sustainable competitive advantage: Combining institutional and resource-based views. *Strategic Management Journal, 18*(9), 697–713.
Öniş, Z., & Kutlay, M. (2013). Rising powers in a changing global order: The political economy of Turkey in the age of BRICs. *Third World Quarterly, 34*(8), 1409–1426.
Ostrom, E. (2005). *Understanding institutional diversity* (pp. 393–432). Princeton University Press.
Papandreou, A. A. (1998). *Externality and institutions*. Oxford University Press.
Peters, B. G. (2000). *Institutional theory: Problems and prospects*.
Pratt, M. G. (2001). Social identity dynamics in modern organizations: An organizational psychology. In *Social Identity Processes in Organizational Contexts* (p. 13).
Rahim, M. A. (2017). *Managing conflict in organizations*. Routledge.

Ramezan, M. (2011). Intellectual capital and organizational organic structure in knowledge society: How are these concepts related? *International Journal of Information Management, 31*(1), 88–95.
Redmond, W. H. (2003). Innovation, diffusion, and institutional change. *Journal of Economic Issues, 37*(3), 665–679.
Schiavo-Campo, S. (1994). *Institutional change and the public sector in transitional economies* (Vol. 241). World Bank.
Schumpeter, J. (1942). Creative destruction. In *Capitalism, socialism democracy* (Vol. 825, pp. 82–85).
Scott, W. R. (2013). *Institutions and organizations: Ideas, interests, and identities*. Sage Publications.
Storm, S. (2015). Structural change. *Development and Change, 46*(4), 666–699.
Streeck, W., & Thelen, K. (2009). Institutional change in advanced political economies. In *Debating Varieties of Capitalism: A Reader* (pp. 95–131).
Swiss, L. (2016). A sociology of foreign aid and the world society. *Sociology Compass, 10*(1), 65–73.
Tavares, J. (2003). Does foreign aid corrupt? *Economics Letters, 79*(1), 99–106.
Thompson, J. D. (2017). *Organizations in action: Social science bases of administrative theory*. Routledge.
Thomsen, H. K., & Hoest, V. (2001). Employees' perception of the learning organization. *Management Learning, 32*(4), 469–491.
Tichenor, D. J. (2009). *Dividing lines: The politics of immigration control in America* (Vol. 104). Princeton University Press.
Tina Dacin, M., Goodstein, J., & Richard Scott, W. (2002). Institutional theory and institutional change: Introduction to the special research forum. *Academy of Management Journal, 45*(1), 45–56.
Tiwari, S., & Zaman, H. (2010). *The impact of economic shocks on global undernourishment*. The World Bank.
Tsai, K. S. (2006). Adaptive informal institutions and endogenous institutional change in China. *World Pol, 59*(1), 116–141.
Tucker, D. J., Baum, J. A., & Singh, J. V. (1992). The institutional ecology. In *Human Services as Complex Organizations* (p. 47).
Von Bertalanffy, L. (1968). General system theory. *General Systems, 41973*, 40.
Wan, F., Williamson, P. J., & Yin, E. (2015). Antecedents and implications of disruptive innovation: Evidence from China. *Technovation, 39*, 94–104.
Wang, C. (2018). Changing international system structures and the belt and road initiative. In *Rethinking the silk road* (pp. 269–279). Springer.
Weinberg, H. (2007). So what is this social unconscious anyway? *Group Analysis, 40*(3), 307–322.
Wieland, H., Koskela-Huotari, K., & Vargo, S. L. (2016). Extending actor participation in value creation: An institutional view. *Journal of Strategic Marketing, 24*(3–4), 210–226.
Williamson, O. (1985). *The economic institutions of capitalism* (Vol. 36, pp. 453–486). New York: The Free Press.
Williamson, O. E. (2000). The new institutional economics: Taking stock, looking ahead. *Journal of Economic Literature, 38*(3), 595–613.
Young, O. R. (1996). Institutional linkages in international society: Polar perspectives. *Global Governance, 2*, 1.
Zucman, G. (2015). *The hidden wealth of nations: The scourge of tax havens*. University of Chicago Press.

Institutions and Institutional Change: Concepts and Theories

Ali Hussein Samadi and Masoumeh Alipourian

1 Introduction

Although the importance of institutions, as one of the main drivers of development, dates back to the time of Adam Smith (1776), the attention to institutions in the classical economy is most clearly reflected in the concept of property rights security (Stam and Nooteboom 2011). In the last few decades, the diverse performance of various developing countries and transition economies from socialism to capitalism has drawn renewed attention to Adam Smith's views on a range of economic issues. The revival of Adam Smith's ideas has received increasing attention and growing support from institutional economists (North 1990; Williamson 1975, 1985). To better understand the relevance of Adam Smith's ideas regarding institutions, it is necessary to understand how the interaction between rapidly and slowly changing institutions is possible. Reforms in a given country must be tailored to the local and native conditions of that country. In other words, countries with cultures and historical paths must find the roots of change in their institutions and introduce those changes at a fast pace, given how slowly institutions change (Roland 2004).

Rodrik et al. (2004) cited three factors, i.e., geography, trade, and institutions, as the main potential contributors to differences in access to innovation and capital accumulation, concluding that institutions, particularly property rights and the rule of law, were the most important factors because they accounted for the differences between different countries in terms of development. This idea was supported by the World Bank (2006) report, stating that "the dominant forms of wealth in the world are human capital and the quality of formal and informal institutions." Acemoglu et al. (2004) regarded the improvement of political and economic institutions as the

A. H. Samadi (✉) · M. Alipourian
Department of Economics, Shiraz University, Shiraz, Iran
e-mail: asamadi@rose.shirazu.ac.ir

N. Faghih, A. H. Samadi (eds.), *Dynamics of Institutional Change in Emerging Market Economies*, Contributions to Economics,
https://doi.org/10.1007/978-3-030-61342-6_4

empowerment of those individuals and political groups who were conversant with their desired institutions and sought to create similar institutions. Improving political and economic institutions also leads to the improvement of factors affecting per capita income.

Economic history shows that in countries with effective institutional structures, changes in institutions have resulted in developmental gains. Thus, it is important to understand what kinds of institutional changes are necessary to drive development and what conditions should be provided so that such changes will be effective in policymaking. However, there are some questions that need to be addressed first: What is an institution? How do institutional changes occur? This chapter seeks to address these and some other relevant questions. In this regard, the rest of this chapter is organized as follows. In Sect. 2, the concept of institution, different types of institutions, and institutional environment are discussed. Section 3 briefly introduces feasibility and describes some concepts related to institutional change and different types of institutional changes. In Sect. 4, the theories of institutional change are explained. The last section offers some conclusions.

2 Institution

To understand institutions, it is necessary to first define what institutions and different types of institutions are. Since the institutional environment of any country has an impact on the formation of its institutions and their functions, we also have to define the institutional environment as well.

2.1 The Concept of Institution

One of the most important questions that institutional economists seek to answer is the following: What is an institution?

There are many definitions for institutions. A summary of the most important definitions offered by some of the institutional economists is presented in Table 1. As it can be observed in Table 1, there are myriads of definitions for an institution. In this section, the definition suggested by North (1991) is presented. Finally, a summary of attributes reflected in different definitions of the institution is provided below.

According to North (1991), institutions are the limitations imposed by humans on the formation of economic, social, and political interactions. These restrictions include *informal restrictions*, such as prohibitions, customs, traditions, norms of conduct, etc., and *formal constraints*, such as the constitution, laws, etc. From the North's perspective, formal and informal constraints, together with economic constraints, determine choices, the cost of production, the cost of transactions, and thus the profitability and feasibility of doing business.

Table 1 Different definitions of the concept of institution

Row	Institutionalists	Definition
1	Veblen (1909)	Institutions are habits created in the mind of the public and between them in common
2	Mitchell (1910)	Institutions are nothing but thought habits, as the guiding norms of conduct within an occupation
3	Commons (1931)	An institution is a collective action to control, liberate, or expand individual actions
4	Hamilton (1932)	An institution is a way of thinking or acting that is rooted in the habits or customs of a group of people and is somewhat common and durable
5	Foster (1981)	Institutions are patterns of order defined and regulated by correlated behaviors
6	Ruttan and Hayami (1984)	Institutions are the rules of society or organizations that lead to harmony among people. They facilitate coordination by helping people form rational expectations when interacting with other people
7	Williamson (1985)	Institutions are mechanisms, which govern exchanges, and arrangements, which lower the costs of transactions. These arrangements have evolved and will be changed by changing the nature of transaction expenses
8	North (1990)	Institutions are rules of the game in society or constraints that are imposed by people to regulate interactions. Institutions exist due to the structured incentives in human transactions (economic, social, and political)
9	Dopfer (1991)	Economic institutions are the centerpieces of the work of agents, who are introduced through their own organizations or boards. Institutions are created under identical circumstances, which occur repeatedly
10	Knight (1992)	An institution is a set of rules that give structure to social interrelations in a particular manner
11	Burki and Perry (1998)	Institutions are formal and informal rules and enforcement mechanisms that shape the behavior of individuals and organizations in a society
12	Nelson and Sampat (2001)	Institutions are social technologies in the utilization of productive economic activities through which human interaction is patterned, yet they are not intended to bring about social engineering
13	Acemoglu et al. (2003)	An institution is the cluster of social arrangements, including social and constitutional limits on the power of politicians and political elites, the rule of law, implementation of property rights, a minimum amount of equal opportunity, access to education, etc.
14	Rodrik et al. (2004)	Institutions are rules of the game and are created as a result of desirable economic behavior, especially, that of property rights and the rule of law
15	Chong and Zanforlin (2004)	Institutions are implicit and explicit rules which help the members of a community influence each other, shape the behavior of economic agents, and help us explain the economic performance of countries
16	Searle (2005)	An institution is any system with a number of rules that enable us to create institutional realities.

(continued)

Table 1 (continued)

Row	Institutionalists	Definition
17	Brown (2005)	The concept of institution refers to a set of organizations, such as families, churches, schools, companies, stock market, business organizations, and trade unions, that try to have independent behavioral patterns
18	Hodgson (2006)	Institutions are durable systems of established social norms that give structure to social interactions
19	Greif (2006)	Institutions are a set of social factors, rules, beliefs, values, and organizations that motivate regularity in individual and social behavior
20	Aoki (2007)	Institutions are sustainable patterns of social interaction that give rise to common knowledge among the players, which, in turn, can lead to a particular equilibrium condition in the game
21	Rutherford (2007)	Institutions shape the preference and values of individuals in society

Source: Personal elaboration of authors

Institutions may be created or formed slowly and gradually over time. Institutional restrictions include cases where individuals are prohibited from doing something, as in the case of taboos or where certain individuals are permitted to perform certain activities, as in the case of customs, traditions, and norms of conduct. Institutions are the frameworks within which human interaction is realized.

Institutions are quite similar to the rules of a competitive team sport. That is, they include both formal written laws and informal rules and principles underlying and supplementing formal laws (North 1990).

North regarded institutions as rules and norms that were different from organizations. From the perspective of North (2005), organizations, as a group of individuals, are motivated by goals that help them compete to win the race within the existing institutional structure as well as making changes in the institutional structure. That which organizations emerge and evolve over time is influenced by the rules, norms, and "institutions" within different societies (Hollingsworth 2000).

Hodgson (2006) stated that in the North's perspective, people were perceived as a type of organization and not a type of institution. In this regard and to avoid terminological ambiguity, Lin and Nugent (1995) suggested that there should be a distinction between "*institutional arrangements*" and "*institutional structure*" (Samadi 2008). From their point of view, *institutional arrangements* were a set of structural rules that influenced the behavior of individuals in a certain domain. However, the *institutional structure* encompassed the institutional arrangements, as a whole, in the economy and included organizations, rules, customs, and ideologies.

According to Lin (1989), formal institutional arrangements refer to a type of arrangement whereby a change or modification in the existing rules requires the formal approval of a group of individuals, whose behavior is governed by institutional arrangements. In contrast, informal institutional arrangements refer to a type of arrangement whereby individuals modify or change rules without the need for taking collective action. Informal arrangements are values, ethical norms, habits, customs, and ideologies.

According to Lin and Nugent (1995), what economists mean by the word "institution" is generally related to *institutional arrangements* (e.g., independence of the Central Bank, budgetary transparency, degree of openness, etc.). In addition, whenever the term institutional change is used, it generally refers to changes in one of the institutional arrangements and not in all arrangements.

Some of the attributes reflected in the definition of the institution are presented below:

- Most definitions offered by scholars so far are focused on "human interaction' (Samadi 2008);
- For North (1990), institutions were exogenous constraints on behaviors. For others, including Aoki (2001) and Greif (1993, 1994), however, institutions were endogenous equilibrium rules of a repetitive game.
- Some definitions have highlighted the role of institutions in reducing uncertainty (Samadi 2008).
- Some scholars have argued that in any economic analysis, the individual should not be taken for granted. In their perspective, people interact with each other and the outcome of their interaction is the formation of institutions. However, their goals and preferences are shaped by the socio-economic conditions surrounding them. The individual is both the creator and the product of conditions (Hodgson 1998).
- Some scholars have focused on the exchanges between economic agents whereas others have focused on the authority and control between economic agents. Also, some have emphasized the importance of reaching an agreement and harmony for which there is some collective interest (Samadi 2008).
- Some scholars have referred to transaction costs as the origin of institutions. For example, in his article entitled "Nature of the Firm," Coase (1937) emphasized that the main reason that a firm was cost-effective was that the use of price mechanisms had some costs. Williamson (2000) argued that we could create some opportunities to reduce transaction costs by pushing the boundaries of informal and formal rules introduced.
- Some scholars have used the term institution to refer to "behavioral patterns which are in line with the law ". Others have used the term to refer to the factors and forces that support "traditional and ordinary behavior patterns" or limit them (e.g., norms and systems of ideas, game rules, or governance structures) (Samadi 2008);
- Some scholars have defined institutions based on factors related to specific behavioral patterns while others have defined it in terms of the broader social and cultural context (Samadi 2008).

2.2 Types of Institutions

Different categories have been proposed for classifying institutions (Table 2). In a general classification, the institutions can be categorized into three general groups: *Economic institutions*, *social institutions*, and *political institutions*. One of the main objectives of economics is to provide a mechanism to allocate resources among individuals and over time. One of the responsibilities and functions of **economic institutions** is to meet this goal. For this purpose, the market, price mechanisms, and the structure of property rights can be considered as instances of economic institutions. One of the main goals of the markets is to facilitate economic activities through the efficient allocation of resources. Price mechanisms, through the market, also transfer information to producers, consumers, and policymakers. Systems and structures of property rights are arrangements that control the use of resources. The system of property rights determines the type of markets, their structure and performance, and the body of stimuli and opportunities that each individual agent is provided with (Acemoglu and Robinson 2005; Veeman and Politylo 2003; Kaufman 2003).

With regard to values, beliefs, cultural experiences, and specific situations, social institutions, or norms, are identified by sociologists as informal institutions that manage and guide human behavior and attitude in different social settings (Parsons 1951) and allow for group socialization (Ritchie 2016). Social norms usually refer to "situations" where there is a conflict between individual and collective interests (Biccheri 2010).

Kandori (1992) showed that societies played an important role in norm development and implementation. Once a norm is firmly established in a given situation, it becomes socially acceptable, is recognized as part of local culture, and will be more difficult to change.

Social institutions are important social organizations the primary duty of which is to provide the most basic needs of human beings. Five primary social institutions, namely, family and kinship institutions, legal institutions, religious institutions, educational institutions, and economic institutions, have been created in society to

Table 2 Types of institutions

Row	Types of institutions	Scholars
1	Economic, social, and political	Acemoglu and Robinson (2005), Veeman and Politylo (2003), Kaufman (2003) and Samadi (2008)
2	Formal rules and informal restrictions	North (1990)
3	Durable and non-durable	Roland (2004)
4	Agent-sensitive and agent-insensitive	Hodgson (2006)
5	Predator-friendly and development-oriented	Evans (1989), Acemoglu and Robinson (2006) and Shleifer and Vishny (1994)

Source: Personal elaboration of authors

meet these needs. **Political institutions** include various types of governance (e.g., democratic, dictatorship, monarchy, republic, aristocratic, timocratic, and oligarchic), the limits imposed on politicians and political elites, etc. (Samadi 2008).

North (1990) divided institutions into two categories: "formal rules," such as formal laws and constitutions, and "informal constraints," such as norms and customs. The word "formal" is often used to refer to the rules formulated and implemented by the government. Another interpretation is that formal rules are implemented by individuals with defined roles (individual action), but informal codes of conduct are enforced collectively by members of a group (collective action). Informal constraints are also community-approved behavioral norms that expand, generalize, modify, and transform formal rules and enforce behavioral standards endogenously (North 1990).

Formal rules are the basis for informal constraints (North 1990). Formal rules can complement the constraints imposed by informal rules and improve them. These laws can reduce the costs of information acquisition, monitoring, and enforcement, thereby allowing the utilization of formal constraints as a solution to more complex transactions (Milgrom et al. 1990).

Roland (2004) classified institutions into two categories of durable and non-durable. In his view, the institutions which were usually slow to change, such as social norms and values, were developmental and sustainable institutions. On the contrary, he added that fast-changing institutions, such as political institutions, were enduring institutions with non-continuous changes at multiple stages. Political institutions can potentially change at different stages during big decision-making steps. Therefore, political institutions can change rapidly, sometimes changing overnight as during revolution and political upheaval. In contrast, social norms and values are examples of slow-changing institutions. For instance, because the norms are rooted in religions, ethical rules have remained unchanged for centuries and even thousands of years.

According to Hodgson (2006), institutions can be divided into two groups of agent-sensitive and agent-insensitive. An agent-sensitive institution is an institution in which any change in the agents' preferences or desires through possible sets of personality types can significantly change the governing equilibrium or custom. Conversely, agent-insensitive institutions are not sensitive to changes occurring in agents. Regular market behavior may be due to institutional constraints, so there are models that focus on institutions and structures. Such models provide regular and predictable behavior resulting from institutional constraints place the burden of explanation on the structure of the system rather than on preferences or psychological analyses. In such cases, the institutions are said to be insensitive to the agents because the consequences are relatively insensitive to the behavior or personality of the agents. Therefore, regular and predictable behaviors, as supported in agent-insensitive institutions, can be explained by the structure of the system rather than the preferences or the behavior of individuals.

Evans (1989), Acemoglu (2006), and Shleifer and Vishny (1994) divided institutions into two categories of predator-friendly (or rent-seeker-friendly) and development-oriented institutions. Rent-seeker-friendly institutions are institutions that allow a minority group to exercise its power to both compromise and control economic agents by reducing investment and production incentives. In contrast, development-oriented institutions are those that encourage development and growth. This is achieved by providing private agents with propitious conditions, encouraging investment, and providing individuals with public goods, such as education, infrastructure, etc.

2.3 *Institutional Environment*

People do their business in an institutional environment, which includes all formal and informal rules and affects individuals' behavior in economic transactions. Due to the institutional differences in different parts of the world, every society, on a local or national scale, has its own institutional environment. It involves a hierarchy of different types of institutions, including values, norms, customs, and rules (formal and informal) (Williamson 2000; North 1990). According to institutional economists, values, norms, customs, and laws should be seen as the consequences of an ongoing dialogue between groups within a society. Institutions are part of a process of continuous change. People do not always adhere to one belief, and if things change, they reconsider their goals. As a result, institutions will change, too.

Values, norms, and laws are the result of social and political processes. These processes are never independent of values and always represent the thoughts and interests of groups and individuals. Institutions are systems of hierarchical rules that shape social behavior and interactions. They comprise old, durable, and stable rules and incorporate social values as well as norms and rules derived from specific principles (Groenewegen et al. 2010). Institutional arrangements and capacities are determined by the spatial, socio-cultural, and historical characteristics (Stam and Nooteboom 2011). In other words, the institutional environment varies from country to country, and successful companies and organizations are the ones that can best adapt their activities to the institutional environment in which they are located (Hollingsworth 2000). Figure 1 summarizes the components of a typical institutional environment.

3 Institutional Change

3.1 *Is Institutional Change Possible?*

Institutionalists have provided different answers to this question. A summary of their views is provided in Table 3. Some of them have argued that the economic behavior of individuals is interdependent, unified, and harmonious (Groenewegen et al. 1995). Some others have asserted that while individuals' goals or preferences

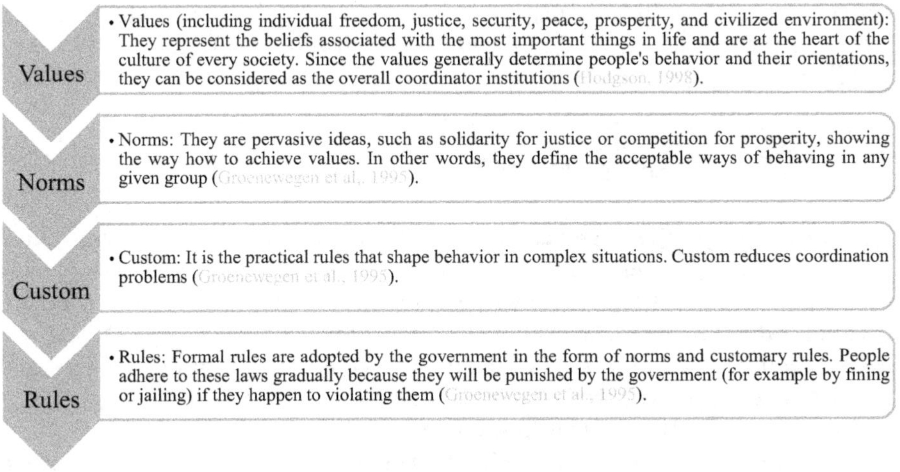

Fig. 1 Institutional environment. (Source: Personal elaboration of authors)

Table 3 Institutionalists' views on institutional change

Institutionalists	Whether or not institutional change is possible?
Rational choice institutionalists	Institutional change is difficult
Historical institutionalists	Change due to path dependence is non-attractive
Sociological institutionalists	Institutions hardly change

Source: Personal elaboration of authors

are shaped by socio-economic conditions, they interact with one another, resulting in the formation or transformation of institutions. The individual both changes the conditions and is changed by conditions (Hodgson 1998).

From the perspective of *rational choice institutionalists*, institutional change is difficult because the institutions provide the related agents with some benefits. However, institutional reform can happen as a result of some intentional changes in institutions. This situation occurs when the structure of preferences is changed. From their point of view, cultural change in society causes institutions to change so as to maintain their legitimacy (Hall and Taylor 1996). For *historical institutionalists*, existing institutions usually have good stability, and any change due to path dependency is unattractive (Gorges 2001). In their view, institutions change due to the inconsistent responses that should be given to external events, such as new technology, the economic crisis, and so on. From the perspective of *sociological institutionalists*, institutions are difficult to change because they form a structure in which the actors first evaluate institutions and then think about changing them. They see any change in institutions and organizations as a result of culture change at the community level and believe that the criteria used by individuals to evaluate and reform institutions are established by institutions themselves (Torfing 2001).

3.2 Some Concepts Related to Institutional Change

The ***phenomenon of change*** has been one of the mental concerns of humankind over the centuries and one of the most challenging subjects among scholars of various sciences. The challenges include the time of change, the problem of failure (Medlin 1963), and the adaptability to or inconsistency of change (Mortensen 2008). ***Change*** typically involves adapting to a composite set of laws, norms, and practices that consolidate the institutional framework (North 1990).

Dacin et al. (2002) stated that "institutions can shape the ***nature of change*** across different levels and contexts as well as changing their character, behavior, and potency over time and space." David (1994, 2007) defined ***institutional change*** as the processes involved in path dependency, i.e., the observed institutions at any point in time can be part of the function of the current technology and institutions that have an established record. Coccia (2018, 2019) considered ***institutions*** as rules and expectations that governed human interactions and ***institutional change*** as ***paths of development*** in society. Chang (2005) highlighted three important functions of institutions in promoting more balanced economic development as follows: learning and innovation, income redistribution, and social cohesion. However, more importantly, ***institutional change*** may stimulate and reinforce new cultural values, attitudes, and practices (Hodgson 2002), which can have broad implications for democratic and inclusive development (Ritchie 2016).

The major role of institutions in society is to reduce uncertainty by establishing a stable, but not necessarily efficient, structure for human interactions. The stability of institutions does not mean, in any way, that institutions are not changing. Customs, principles, and rules of conduct, norms of behavior, complex legislation, customary law, and individual contracts gradually change and so do the choices available (North 1990). Informal institutions are the foundation for institutional continuity and stability, because they are embedded in individuals' norms, beliefs, and shared understanding, and provide a framework for organizational activities and social constraints (Swidler 1986). Formal and informal methods used to solve problems in the past are also used in the present; thus, past institutions are an important source of continuity for change in the long run (North 1990). Past institutions are elements of society that can evolve in the face of organizational and technological innovations (Greif 2003). Institutions do not disappear in the face of changing situations but provide the basis for the upcoming changes. Accordingly, "path dependency" means that past institutions do not determine change but influence the direction of change. As pursuing their evolutionary path through time, past institutions impose limits on people's future choices (Levi 1990). Long-standing institutions implicitly coordinate behavior by establishing mechanisms that can facilitate the collection and exchange of information. If institutions change, these mechanisms must also be rebuilt. This, nevertheless, devalues the knowledge gained in the past and makes the reproduction of knowledge through learning processes a must (Greif 2003).

Fundamental changes in relative prices are the most important ***origin*** of changes in institutions. Changes in relative prices alter the motivations of individuals in their interactions with others. The only other source that can trigger this type of change is individuals' tastes (North 1990).

The agent of institutional change can be an entrepreneur. Schumpeter (1934) introduced an entrepreneur as an agent of change who aims to disrupt the existing equilibrium by using new technologies, knowledge, and values. In his view, the entrepreneur was the one who could make a connection between innovation and development, change environmental information, break symmetries, and make great strides in diversifying the economy.

In North's (1990) view, ***the process of institutional change*** was a very gradual process. Because large-scale changes are damaging to existing organizations, they strongly react to or, in some cases, resist such changes. Within the framework proposed by Ostrom (2005), during the process of institutional change, each individual weighs up the costs and benefits that could result from the institutional change. If there is minimal agreement on accepting a change, the change will be legal. Kantor (1998) argues that political processes, as the arena of competition for the interest groups who are seeking to formulate formal rules in their own favor, are also important in the process of institutional change. Consequently, institutional change is dependent on the status of interest groups and the political structure of a society.

Motivation and determination for institutional change arise when some groups or individuals come to understand that an opportunity has arisen to change the rules in their favor. This is materialized through an exogenous change in the main parameters. Change can also be endogenous, and this happens when people's choices fall under a set of rules, gradually leading to changes in the value of parameters (Kingston 2018). Because individuals create institutions, institutions have to constantly adapt to the internal and external environment (Jones 2001; Powell and DiMaggio 1991).

3.3 Types of Institutional Changes

Institutional change can be categorized into different types depending on how it is defined. These types are listed in Table 4.

Roland (2004) categorized institutions according to how rapidly or slowly they were able to change and whether or not these changes were continuous. In his view, *fast-changing institutions* do not change by necessity but change very quickly and overnight. Political institutions are fast-changing institutions that change overnight during the revolution and political upheavals. In contrast, social norms and values are examples of *slow-changing institutions* because norms are rooted in religions and ethics and religious and ethical values have remained unchanged for centuries and even thousands of years. Slow-changing institutions are constantly changing

Table 4 Types of institutional changes

Row	Scholars	The basis for an attitude toward institutional change	Types
1	Roland (2004)	Changes in the institutional system	Rapid change
			Slow changes
2	Lin (1989)	Changes in institutional arrangements and institutional structure	Induced change
			Imposed change
3	North (1990)	Changes in the structure of human interactions	Change in formal rules
			Change in informal restrictions
4	Florensa (2004)	Change at different levels of institutional structure	Bottom-up changes
			Top-down changes
5	Mahoney and Thelen (2010)	Gradual change in formal and informal rules	Replacement
			Layering and sorting
			Subject to change
			Becoming

Source: Personal elaboration of authors

but they change slowly, and by impacting fast-changing institutions, they are harbingers of more rapid change. Earthquakes can best represent the interaction between fast- and slow-changing institutions; pressure is built up along fault lines continuously over time but slowly; then, this pressure leads to a sudden earthquake that changes the map of a given area. Slow-change institutions are like fault lines which change slowly over time, but fast-changing institutions are similar to sudden earthquakes with extremely rapid changes.

According to Lin (1989), there are two types of institutional change: Induced and imposed. *Induced institutional change* refers to the modification or replacement of existing institutional arrangements or the emergence of new institutional arrangements that are voluntarily established, organized, and implemented by individuals or groups of individuals in response to lucrative opportunities. *Imposed institutional change* refers to the transformation or modification of institutional arrangements with the aim of income redistribution among the main and different groups of voters. For induced institutional change to occur, there must be some lucrative opportunities resulting from institutional imbalances, such as changes in institutional choices, changes in technology, long-term changes in the relative prices of factors and products, and changes in other institutional arrangements. When imbalances occur, the process of institutional change starts from one institutional arrangements and gradually spreads to others. Thus, the processes that have been operative throughout history determine the new institutional structure and make it meaningful with reference to the existing institutional structure. As a result, some institutional arrangements that may be desirable are not sustainable and durable because of their incompatibility with other institutional arrangements. Imposed institutional change occurs when the continuity of supply cannot be maintained with the existing institutional arrangements and, thus, the government decides to intervene and compensate for the insufficient supply.

From North's (1990) perspective, there were two types of institutional change: *Changes in formal rules* and *changes in informal constraints*. *Changes in formal rules* are the main sources of change and can be the result of changes made by either the legislature, such as the adoption of a new law, or the judiciary, including court decisions that change the standard law, changes in regulatory rules adopted by regulators, and changes in regulations. The process of change is an evolutionary process and the change may be due to some changes in the legal or religious principles. *Informal constraints* may also change, as in the gradual abolition of socially accepted norms and customs or the gradual adoption of new rules. Formal rules may change regularly, but informal constraints do not.

Informal institutions change at a slower rate than do formal institutions. Thus, the persistence of informal constraints in the face of a change in formal rules (political, economic environment) is likely to result in a discrepancy between the new formal rules and the existing informal constraints. One solution to such tension is to rebuild the entire constraints, in both formal and informal institutions, to adjust the level of compatibility between them and strike a new balance between formal and informal constraints (Florensa 2004).

For Florensa (2004), institutional change had a multidimensional nature. According to her, changes may occur at different levels of the institutional structure. Therefore, a change in one level can lead to changes in the deeper levels of the institutional structure or vice versa. As a result, a distinction can be made between the "*bottom-up*" and "*top-down*" *patterns*. In *bottom-up patterns*, change processes at the executive level can trigger deeper changes. This happens when a large number of members of a group (or an organization) support it, or when there is sufficient pressure for change by agents and circumstances prone to change. If participants find that the rules at the deeper levels are the cause of problems at the executive level, they will consider the possibility of a change in the set of assumptions regarding the rules of practice. In this case, their action will be based on the process of change at the level of collective choice. In *top-down patterns*, it is assumed that changes at the constitutional level can lead to changes at the lower levels of the configuration of rules (collective choice and functional levels). Constitutional changes, which are difficult and costly, increase the stability of mutual expectations among agents (Ostrom et al. 1994).

Mahoney and Thelen (2010) examined how small endogenous changes could lead to fundamental institutional changes and categorized them into four types of gradual changes: (1) *replacement*, new rules substitute existing ones; (2) *layering* and *sorting*, new rules are added to the old rules and both will exist together; (3) *subject to change*, rules remain the same but change due to environmental changes; and (4) *becoming*, rules remain the same but are interpreted or adopted differently, or applied to new purposes. Their analysis is expanded by distinguishing between formal and informal rules. For example, adding informal rules to the pre-existing formal rules is an instance of "layering and sorting" from the bottom, by which new hidden elements are added to the old explicit elements.

4 Theories of Institutional Change

Since the process of institutional change is complex and its evolution is not easily predictable (Hall and Taylor 1996), we need to use tools that can determine key variables and the relationships between them in situations that individuals deal with. These variables are influenced by physical and social factors and the institutional environment (Ostrom et al. 1994).

North (2001) argued that the economic and institutional conditions that led to the best performance were well recognized, but what we did not know was how to create those conditions. In other words, North (2001) was trying to suggest that we know a lot about institutions and their economic performance, but we do not know how institutions change. He contended that we needed a theory to explore the process of economic, political, and social changes. Once such a theory is available, we can make further progress in resolving development problems.

There are several theories in the literature of institutional economics that can help us better understand the mechanisms underlying institutional changes. From an "*agent of change perspective*," theories of institutional change can be grouped into the following theories: *Efficient Institutions View or Political Coase Theorem (PCT), Ideology or the Generalized PCT, the Incidental Institutions View, the Social Conflict View, Transaction Cost Theory of Institutional Change, Entrepreneurial View of Institutional Change, and Globalization View of Institutional Change* (Samadi 2019). The first four theories are explained by Acemoglu et al. (2003); the entrepreneurial view of institutional change and the globalization view of institutional change are expounded in Samadi (2018, 2019), respectively.

However, from a "*source of change perspective*," these theories can be classified into four types: *Institutional design theory, evolutionary theory, equilibrium theory, and deinstitutionalization*. The first three theories discuss the emergence of new beliefs and practices while the last theory discusses the weakening and disappearance of beliefs and practices (Dacin et al. 2002). In what follows, these theories are briefly explained.

4.1 Institutional Design Theory

Over the past two decades, there has been a great deal of research in designing institutions that can provide economic agents with more desirable options and effective nudges. A good example in this regard is the development of a strong auction system against the Sakura system and the discovery of an effective nudge to encourage energy and money saving. Collecting and analyzing data on the actual behavior of economic agents and sharing information are necessary for the institutional design and discovery of an effective nudge. This issue can be investigated using natural data, but, today, laboratory experiments, field experiments, and web surveys are conducted regularly. These new methods have some advantages and disadvantages, and although none of them are totally comprehensive, each is necessary to examine the behavior of economic agents (Ogawa 2019).

Many scholars regard institutional change as a process of collective choice, which is authorized by a collective political institution, such as society or government. Individuals and organizations which are involved in collective action strive and negotiate to change the rules through "collective choice" or political processes in their favor (Kingston and Caballero 2009).

In Bromley's (1991) terms, institutions are relationships that are intentionally and consciously created. In other words, institutions are created through institutional design. Alexander (2002) defined *institutional design* as the invention and understanding of the rules, methods, and institutional structures that were capable of restricting the behaviors and actions of individuals to maintain harmony with the established values, making easier the achievement of intended goals, and facilitating the performance of certain tasks. Therefore, it can be concluded that institutional change is the process of "path dependency"; that is, institutions may be a function of current technology or previous institutions and technologies (Libecap 1989).

The process of institutional change means that each individual will assess the expected costs and benefits of an institutional change, and if there is a "minimum coalition" to make such a change, this change will happen. According to Ostrom (2005), if winners of institutional change cannot compensate for the losses of the losers, powerful groups can impede an institutional change or impose an ineffective change. How seriously these powerful groups will impede an effective institutional change depends on the degree of rationality of the players. Some players have false beliefs about the possible effects of the proposed institutional change(s). Thus, an institutional change pivots on higher-level rules[1] and the decision-makers' understanding of the possible effects of a change in rules. According to Alston (1996), institutional change is the result of ongoing interaction and bargaining between demand and supply. Demanders can be conceived as voters and suppliers as the government. In Kantor's (1998) conceptual framework, voters try to change the official rules by lobbying politicians, and politicians have an incentive to respond to their voters' demands. However, because politicians have their own interests and often face political and constitutional restrictions in changing rules, their response to the voters' demand may be slow and discouraging.

In Commons' view, if existing rules, as a limiting factor, are found to be inappropriate, individuals or groups will attempt to change them through the courts or the legislature. Thus, courts play an important role in orienting institutional change (Kingston and Caballero 2009).

Libecap (1989) considered the shift in the exogenous parameter as the driving factor behind institutional change. Whether or not parameter shifts lead to changes

[1] Ostrom (2005) distinguished between "operational rules" (rules governing day to day interactions), "collective choice rules" (rules for choosing operational rules), "constitutional rules" (rules for choosing collective choice rules), and "meta constitutional rules" (rules for choosing constitutional rules).

in property rights rules depends on, first, how the benefits are distributed under the existing system and how they will be distributed under the proposed new systems and, secondly, whether the loser groups have the ability to prevent changes under the rules framing political competition. Sources of institutional change can be both exogenous, such as technology, and endogenous, such as depleting resources over time (Ostrom 2005).

Theories that regard institutional change as a process of deliberate collective choice face many unanswered questions. These theories cannot explain why formal rules fail to produce their intended outcomes. They can hardly explain why some specific institutions, and not others, in a particular time and place are selected. These theories cannot either provide an explanation of why some institutions continue to survive in the long run and remain stable. One reason that the collective choice approach cannot provide convincing answers to such questions is that it has a weak mechanism for dealing with some types of "informal rules." As described below, there are three types of informal rules:

First, the term "informal" is sometimes used to refer to unwritten rules or rules not implemented by the government. If it is possible to change informal rules, they can be categorized in the context of collective choice. **Secondly**, informal rules are sometimes used to refer to the codes of ethics or moral norms, which directly reflect the preferences of the players. These types of codes and norms influence institutional change by affecting the selection processes through which the informal rules will ultimately emerge. However, there is an important **third** set of informal rules which include social norms and conventions. This category of rules usually evolves in a decentralized and spontaneous way, so they cannot be easily incorporated into the theory of collective choice. This is one of the weaknesses of this theory because it does not account for the development of informal rules, which are widely seen as an important topic in institutional change (Kingston and Caballero 2009).

4.2 Evolutionary Theory

Many scholars see institutional change as a gradual "evolutionary" process. In this view, institutions grow organically and are selected based on their efficiency. Such a view of institutional change can be attributed to Hayek and evolutionary economists. The basis of this theory is that individuals pursue their preferences in the market rationally. The market is self-sufficient in driving change and making effective choices (Webster and Lai 2003). The efficiency perspective has led to the development of a new approach in economics called "*Transaction Cost Economics*" (Demsetz 1967; Williamson 1985). Transaction cost economics assumes that the most efficient institutional forms, which can minimize transaction costs, have already been created; that is, institutions are developed in such a way that they can produce the most beneficial outcomes in a transaction. However, the transaction cost economics approach can hardly explain why countries with similar technologies choose different institutions to manage similar transactions, why inefficient institutions are often sustainable, and why less developed countries often fail to adopt the institutional structure of more-developed countries (Kingston and Caballero 2009).

Hayek (1973) expanded the evolutionary theory of institutional change based on the choices at the social-group level. In his view, humans' thoughts and actions are guided and governed by the rules that evolve in the process of choice in society and are therefore the product of the experience of generations. Some of the rules are formalized and may be used to design new rules; Hayek considered these rules to be deliberately designed. He also argued that organizations, including the government, were formed through a spontaneous process. In Hayek's perspective, the configuration of rules would evolve to an optimal configuration based on consistent rules and through group selection.

Hayek, instead of rules, considered shared expectations to be the main source of order in society: "matching of the intentions and expectations that determine the actions of different individuals is the form in which order manifests itself in social life" (Hayek 1973). Similar to Hayek's argument, transaction cost economists maintain that evolutionary pressure will destroy inefficient institutions and thereby optimize institutional gains.

In evolutionary theory, new rules or altered behaviors may arise through deliberate human actions, including learning, imitation, and experience, or they may develop spontaneously through the non-coordinated choices of many people. Ethical norms, customs, and social norms sometimes change over time, but they do not easily fit into the theory of collective choice because they, rather than being deliberately designed and implemented, have evolved in a spontaneous and decentralized manner. In addition, informal rules can be considered as voluntary patterns of behavior that are developed within society and may be formalized later (Milgrom et al. 1990; Kingston 2007). Evolutionary processes often represent *multiple equilibria*. According to North (1990), the process of institutional change is a path-dependent process because people learn, organizations develop, and ideologies are formed based on a particular set of formal and informal rules. Organizations try to change formal rules based on their interests. Over time, this will affect the informal rules and result in *multiple equilibria*. In Knight's (1995) view, different sets of rules had different distributive results, so different actors tended to create different rules. Therefore, in a new situation, before the rules that are supposed to govern and guide interactions are created, people start to bargain about which rules are beneficial to the interactions between individuals. If some people have more bargaining power, this will systematically affect the kind of rules that will eventually be used by the general public.

Stable multiple evolutionary equilibria have two important implications. First, existing institutions are not necessarily efficient. An efficient institution is an institution designed to minimize transaction costs and increase economic efficiency. Secondly, a change may point to a path dependence effect, meaning that previous socio-economic conditions and historical events can have lasting effects on the existing institutions. For example, an optimized institutional structure at the present may have initially been optimized due to the changing environmental conditions, but without a coordinating tool, such as a legislator or a political entrepreneur, to guide the change of rules, this institution may fall into a sub-optimal balance and remain so for the near future (Kingston 2018).

Young (1996) argued in an evolutionary framework that historical phenomena could lead to the selection of particular conventions and that in the long run, the pattern of institutional change would follow a punctuated equilibrium process, based on which fast switching between conventions would be limited and conventions would have long-term stability.

A wide range of issues have been discussed within the institutional economics literature. One of the issues which have been given special attention is the role of institutional change in economic thinking with regard to the role of "habits" (Ritchie 2016). In his evolutionary theory, Veblen (1899) focused on the concept of thinking habits and proposed that durable thinking habits tended to be adjusted in different ways. In this regard, Hodgson (2000) had an interpretation of the influence of habits in Veblen's evolutionary theory. In his view, just as individuals create and shape institutions, so too the institutions shape and influence individuals' motivations and preferences (Hodgson 2000). Current thinking habits, both individual and collective, are rooted in the past, influenced by the present, and attributed to influence the future direction of institutional change (Brette 2003).

Both evolutionary and design theory consider a change in the exogenous parameters, such as technology and population, as the primary source of institutional change. From the perspective of Veblen (1899), considering that the current institutions and thinking habits are inherited from the past and cannot meet today's needs, a change in technology and population can possibly initiate and guide institutional change. Therefore, institutions and habits evolve continuously. According to Nelson (2005), the physical change of technology, as an agent of institutional change, is more desirable than the social change of technology.

The main difference between evolutionary theory and the theory of collective choice is the decentralized selection processes, which determine which rule(s) will ultimately be widely followed. While theories proposing that institutional change results from a centralized collective choice process have difficulty explaining the changes in informal constraints, such as social norms, which evolve in a decentralized manner, evolutionary theories tend to ignore the role of collective action and political processes. As North (1990) suggested, some institutions evolve spontaneously and others are created deliberately. Formal rules change through political processes as a result of deliberate actions by organizational and individual entrepreneurs whereas informal rules evolve in parallel and along with the formal rules. Informal rules play an important role in institutional change because they grow slowly and cannot be changed in a pre-planned and deliberate manner. Consequently, as formal rules change, informal rules, which gradually evolve in parallel with the existing formal rules, undergo some changes, resulting in the reconstruction of all constraints and formation of a new equilibrium (North 1991). Thus, formal rules basically play the role of the driver in institutional change and informal constraints act as a brake on institutional change.

Roland (2004) distinguished between (political) fast-moving (formal rules) and (cultural) slow-moving (informal rules) institutions. In his view, political institutions can change rapidly through centralized political processes whereas cultural institutions change slowly following continuous, evolutionary, and decentralized changes. He likened fault lines formed over time to slow institutional changes (informal rules) and sudden earthquakes to rapid institutional changes (formal rules). In contrast to North (1991), Roland (2004) held that changes in informal rules, rather than formal rules, were the drivers of institutional changes.

4.3 Equilibrium Theory

Equilibrium theory seeks to provide a unified framework for formal and informal rules by focusing on self-enforcing, rather than monitoring, rules. For Calvert (1995), an institution was a name that represented certain types of equilibria. Institutions are equilibrium patterns of behavior rather than behavioral stimuli. Aoki (2001) viewed the institution as a stable system of beliefs about the expected behavior of members of a society in various situations. According to Greif (2006), an institution is a system of rules, beliefs, norms, and organizations, which together regulate social behavior. The common feature of all these definitions is that an institution is defined as behavioral patterns rather than rules controlling behavior. In equilibrium, each factor is constrained by both the physical exogenous constraints and the endogenous institutional rules, which reflect the strategies of other players of the game (Kingston and Caballero 2009).

In equilibrium theory, institutional change does not mean the change of rules, but the change of expectations. These expectations may be in the form of formal or informal rules. The main purpose of introducing and presenting new rules is to help players have common beliefs about each other's behavior during the course of the game, thereby helping them to reach equilibrium through multiple equilibria. However, in equilibrium, it is ultimately behavioral expectations, rather than prescribed rules, that are accepted and adhered to. For various reasons, attempts to introduce new rules to change these expectations and equilibrium patterns of behavior may fail or may change them in unpredictable ways (Kingston 2018).

Greif and Laitin (2004) emphasized the importance of endogenous institutional change and introduced the term "quasi-parameters," which refer to some parameters, such as income distribution and information available to players, that are exogenous in the short-run but gradually change as a result of the game. Changes in quasi-parameters occur when the behavioral pattern is in equilibrium or there are some institutional imbalances and provide an incentive for institutional change. Thus, institutional change follows a "punctuated equilibrium" process, i.e., gradual changes in quasi-parameters lead to institutional change when it becomes clear that existing behavioral patterns are the source of an unstable equilibrium.

It is important to note that both collective choice (or institutional design) theory and evolutionary theory are consistent with the equilibrium theory. Changes in exogenous parameters, such as changes in technology or preferences, can disrupt the equilibrium and cause individuals or organizations to attempt to change formal rules to achieve some kind of harmony between players about each other's strategies during the game. Previous institutions are the focal points that can influence the equilibrium point in the new situation (Sugden 1989). Alternatively, gradual changes in parameters will gradually adjust expectations and behaviors. Because formal rules remain unchanged in this scenario, this type of institutional change can be interpreted as a change in the informal rules. Basically, what is changed is the pattern of equilibrium behavior (Kingston 2018).

4.4 Deinstitutionalization

Some of the scholars who have studied the theory of institutional change have focused on the sources of institutional change and referred to the *deinstitutionalization* of existing norms and practices as one of the prime sources of institutional change.

Oliver (1992) pointed to three important sources of pressure for institutional change: *functional, political*, and *social*. *Functional pressures* arise from an understanding that there are some problems either at the performance level or with the utility associated with institutionalized practices. These pressures may be related to widespread environmental changes, including intensified competition for resources. *Political pressures* are primarily due to the changes in the distribution of power or the interests of power groups, which support and legitimize existing institutional arrangements. Such changes may occur in response to performance crises, environmental changes, and other factors that cause organizations to question the legitimacy of a particular action. Institutional change and *deinstitutionalization* may also be associated with *social pressures***,** resulted from group diversity (e.g., increased workforce diversity), heterogeneous or incompatible beliefs and practices as a result of, say, integration, and changes in laws or social expectations which may hinder the continuation of an action (Oliver 1992; Scott 2001). "New members with backgrounds and experiences that differ from existing members bring different interpretive frameworks and social definitions of behavior to the organization that act to diminish consensus and unquestioning adherence to taken-for-granted practices" (Oliver 1992).

Scott (2001) emphasized the importance of *deinstitutionalization* and stated: "it is useful to place studies of deinstitutionalization in a broader context of institutional change since the weakening and disappearance of one set of beliefs and practices is likely to be associated with the arrival of new beliefs and practices." In brief, *Deinstitutionalization* refers to the weakening and erosion of organizational practices and activities due to the loss of organizational consensus on them and can eventually lead to their abandonment and disappearance (Oliver 1992; Scott 2001). Entrenched practices are not interrupted because better options are available, but because political, social, and functional pressures from within and outside the organization have robbed them of their legitimacy and meaning (Maguire and Hardy 2009; Oliver 1992).

A *deinstitutionalization process* relies on discourse struggles between actors who want to leave a practice and those who try to maintain it (Greenwood et al. 2002). Discourse struggles over institutions usually occur simultaneously at the discourse level (Oliver 1992) and outside at the community level (Hauser 1998), with one discourse affecting the other. *Outsider-driven deinstitutionalization*, such as public opinion, affects the dynamics of discourse within a field. Public opinion is a form of social control (Noelle-Neumann 1993) and pressures individuals to conform to the dominant view(s) (McLeod and Hertog 1992) to gain social approval in the public eye. *Insider-driven deinstitutionalization*, such as field opinion, is key in deinstitutionalizing a practice because it can ultimately affect individuals' decisions whether to participate in a practice (Clemente and Roulet 2015). Field opinion represents the dominant view of insiders in the context of a particular practice. A practice must be socially approved to be institutionalized (Maguire and Hardy 2009).

5 Concluding Remarks

This chapter sought to address the following questions: what is an institution? and how do institutional changes occur?

Scholars in the field have suggested different definitions for institutions and have classified them into different categories. In this regard, in Sect. 2, some of the key definitions of institution were presented in Tables 1 and 2, and the institutional environment was explained. The types of institutional change and some theories of institutional change were presented and discussed in Sects. 3 and 4, respectively.

The theories of institutional change analyze how institutions change over time. Several theories have been proposed to explain institutional change. In this chapter, four of these theories were examined; these theories included *Institutional design theory, Evolutionary theory, Equilibrium theory*, and *Deinstitutionalization*. The first three of these four theories discuss the arrival of beliefs and practices whereas the last one discusses the weakening and disappearance of beliefs and practices.

Although the first three theories seek to explain the source(s) of institutional change, they have some limitations. *Institutional design theory* may not be able to explain why formal rules fail to produce their intended outcomes. *Evolutionary theories* do not consider a central mechanism (e.g., legislation) that can cause a coordinated shift in how rules are perceived by players. Institutional design and Evolutionary theories consider exogenous parameters, such as technology, as the prime source of institutional change. *The Equilibrium approach* endeavors to treat formal and informal rules within a unified framework by shifting the focus from the rules which prescribe behavior to the rules which describe behavior. In institutional design theory and evolutionary theory, the enforcement of rules is considered different from their content, but in the equilibrium theory, enforcement is endogenous.

Scott (2001) defined deinstitutionalization as the weakening and disappearance of beliefs and practices. He stated, "it is useful to place studies of *deinstitutionalization* in a broader context of institutional change since the weakening and disappearance of one set of beliefs and practices is likely to be associated with the arrival of new beliefs and practices."

Given the importance of institutional change in transition countries, the theories discussed in this chapter can be of particular interest to the decision-makers and government officials in these countries because these four theories can explain why some countries have succeeded in introducing and implementing institutional changes and others have failed to.

References

Acemoglu, D., & Robinson, J. (2005). The rise of Europe: Atlantic trade, institutional change, and economic growth. *American Economic Review, 95*(3), 546–579.

Acemoglu, D., & Robinson, J. (2006). Economic backwardness in political perspective. *American Political Science Review, 100*(1), 115–131.

Acemoglu, D., Johnson, S., Robinson, J., & Thaicharoen, Y. (2003). Institutional causes, macroeconomic symptoms: Volatility, crises and growth. *Journal of Monetary Economics, 50*, 49–123.

Acemoglu, D., Johnson, S., & Robinson, J. (2004). *Institutions as the fundamental cause of long-run growth*. NBER Working Paper, No 10481.

Acemoglu, D. (2006). A simple model of inefficient institutions. Scandinavian *Journal of Economics 108*(4), 515–546.

Alexander, E. R. (2002). *Acting together: From planning to institutional design*. Paper presented at XIVAESOP conference, Volos, School of Architecture and Urban Planning, University of Wisconsin-Milwaukee, Milwaukee, WI, USA.

Alston, L. (1996). Empirical work in institutional economics: An overview. In L. Alston, T. Eggertsson, & D. North (Eds.), *Empirical studies in institutional change* (pp. 25–30). Cambridge: Cambridge University Press.

Aoki, M. (2001). *Toward a comparative institutional analysis*. Cambridge: MIT Press.

Aoki, M. (2007). Endogenizing institutions and institutional changes. *Journal of Institutional Economics, 3*(1), 1–31.

Biccheri, C. (2010). Norms, preferences and conditional behavior. *Politics, Philosophy and Economics, 9*(3), 297–313.

Brette, O. (2003). Thorstein Veblen's theory of institutional change: Beyond technological determinism. *European Journal of Economic Thought, 10*(3), 455–477.

Bromley, D. W. (1991). *Environment and economy: Property rights and public policy*. Oxford: Blackwell.

Brown, C. (2005). Is there an institutional theory of distribution? *Journal of Economic Issues, 39*(4), 515–931.

Burki, S. J., & Perry, G. (1998). *Beyond the Washington consensus: Institutions matter*. Washington, DC: The International Bank for Reconstruction and Development/The World Bank.

Calvert, R. (1995). Rational actors, equilibrium and social institutions. In J. Knight & I. Sened (Eds.), *Explaining social institutions* (pp. 57–94). Ann Arbor: University of Michigan Press.

Chang, H. J. (2005). *Understanding the relationship between institutions and economic development: Some key theoretical issue*. Paper presented at the WIDER Jubilee conference, Helsinki, 17–18 June.

Chong, A., & Zanforlin, L. (2004). Inward-looking policies, institutions autocrats, and economic growth in Latin American: An empirical exploration. *Public Choice, 121*, 335–361.
Clemente, M., & Roulet, T. J. (2015). Public opinion as a source of deinstitutionalization: A "spiral of silence" approach. *Academy of Management Review, 40*, 96–114.
Coase, R. H. (1937). The nature of the firm. *Economica, 4*(16), 386–405.
Coccia, B. (2018). An introduction to the theories of institutional change. *Journal of Economics Library, 5*(4), 337–344.
Coccia, M. (2019). Comparative institutional changes. In A. Farazmand (Ed.), *Global encyclopedia of public administration, public policy, and governance*. Cham: Springer. isbn: 978-3-319-20927-2.
Commons, J. R. (1931). Institutional economics. *American Economic Review, 21*(4), 648–657.
Dacin, M. T., Goodstein, J., & Scott, W. R. (2002). Institutional theory and institutional change: Introduction to the special research forum. *Academy of Management Journal, 45*(1), 45–57.
David, P. A. (1994). Why are institutions the 'carriers of history'. *Structural Change & Economic Dynamics, 5*(2), 205–220.
David, P. A. (2007). Path dependence, its critics and the quest for 'historical economics'. In G. M. Hodgson (Ed.), *The evolution of economic institutions: A critical reader* (pp. 120–142). Cheltenham: Edward Elgar.
Demsetz, H. (1967). Toward a theory of property rights. *The American Economic Review*, Papers and proceedings of the seventy-ninth annual meeting of the American Economic Association, *57*(2), 347–359.
Dopfer, K. (1991). Toward a theory of economic institutions: Synergy and path dependency. *Journal of Economic Issues, 25*(2), 535–555.
Evans, P. (1989). Predatory, developmental and other apparatuses: A comparative political economy perspective on the third world state. *Sociological Forum, 4*(4), 561–587.
Florensa, C. (2004). *Institutional stability and change: A logic sequence for studying institutional dynamics*. Tenth biennial conference of the International Association for the Study of Common Property (IASCP), Oaxaca, México, pp. 9–13.
Foster, J. F. (1981). The theory of institutional adjustment. *Journal of Economic Issues, 15*(4), 923–928.
Gorges, M. J. (2001). New institutionalism explanations for institutional change: A note of caution. *Politics, 21*(2), 137–145.
Greenwood, R., Suddaby, R., & Hinings, C. R. (2002). Theorizing change: The role of professional associations in the transformation of institutionalized fields. *Academy of Management Journal, 45*(1), 58–80.
Greif, A. (1993). Contract enforceability and economic institutions in early trade: The Maghreb trader's coalition. *American Economic Review, 83*(3), 525–548.
Greif, A. (1994). Cultural beliefs and the organization of society: A historical and theoretical reflection on collectivist and individualist societies. *Journal of Political Economy, 102*(5), 912–950.
Greif, A. (2003). *Institutions: Theory and history*. Cambridge: Cambridge University Press, Chapters 1, 5 and 9.
Greif, A. (2006). *Institutions and the path to modern economy. Lessons from medieval trade*. Cambridge: Cambridge University Press.
Greif, A., & Laitin, D. (2004). A theory of endogenous institutional change. *American Political Science Review, 98*(4), 633–652.
Groenewegen, J., Kerstholt, F., & Nagelkerke, A. (1995). On integrating new and old institutionalism: Douglass North building bridges. *Journal of Economic Issues, 29*(2), 467–475.
Groenewegen, J., Spithoven, A., & Van den Berg, A. (2010). *Institutional economics: An introduction*. London: Palgrave Macmillan.
Hall, P., & Taylor, R. C. R. (1996). Three new institutionalisms. *Political Studies, XLIV*, 936–957.
Hamilton, W. (1932). Institution. In *Encyclopedia of the social science* (Vol. 8, pp. 84–89). New York: Macmillan.

Hauser, G. A. (1998). Vernacular dialogue and the rhetorically of public opinion. *Communications Monographs, 65*(2), 83–107.
Hayek, F. A. (1973). *Law, legislation and liberty, vol. 1: Rules and order*. Chicago: University of Chicago Press.
Hodgson, G. M. (1998). The approach of institutional economics. *Journal of Economic Literature, 36*(1), 166–192.
Hodgson, G. M. (2000). What is the essence of institutional economics? *Journal of Economic Issues, 34*(2), 317–329.
Hodgson, G. M. (2002). Reconstitutive downward causation: Social structure and the development of institutional agency. In E. Fullbrook (Ed.), *Intersubjectivity in economics: Agents and structure*. London: Routledge.
Hodgson, G. M. (2006). What are institutions? *Journal of Economic Issues, 40*(1), 1–25.
Hollingsworth, J. R. (2000). Doing institutional analysis: Implications for the study of innovations. *Review of International Political Economy, 7*(4), 595–644.
Jones, B. D. (2001). *Politics and the architecture of choice. Bounded rationality and governance*. Chicago: Chicago University Press.
Kandori, M. (1992). Social norms and community enforcement. *The Review Economic Studies, 59*, 63–80.
Kantor, S. E. (1998). *Politics and property rights: The closing of the open range in the postbellum south*. Chicago: University of Chicago Press.
Kaufman, B. E. (2003). The organization of economic activity: Insights from the institutional theory of John R Commons. *Journal of Economic Behavior & Organization, 52*, 71–96.
Kingston, C. (2007). Marine insurance in Britain and America, 1720–1844: A comparative institutional analysis. *Journal of Economic History, 67*(2), 379–409.
Kingston, C. (2018). *Institutional change*. Berlin: Springer.
Kingston, C., & Caballero, G. (2009). Comparing theories of institutional change. *Journal of Institutional Economics, 5*(2), 151–180.
Knight, J. (1992). *Institutions and social conflict*. Cambridge: Cambridge University Press.
Knight, J. (1995). Models, interpretations and theories: Constructing explanations of institutional emergence and change. In J. Knight & I. Sened (Eds.), *Explaining social institutions* (pp. 95–120). Ann Arbor: University of Michigan press.
Levi, M. (1990). A logic of institutional change. In K. S. Cook & M. Levi (Eds.), *The limits of rationality* (pp. 402–419). Chicago: Chicago University Press.
Libecap, G. D. (1989). *Contracting for property rights*. Cambridge: Cambridge University Press.
Lin, J. Y. (1989). An economic theory of institutional change: Induced & imposed change. *Cato Journal, 9*(1), 1–33.
Lin, J. Y., & Nugent, J. B. (1995). Institutions and economic development. In *Handbook of development economics* (Vol. 3, Chapter 38, pp. 2301–2370). Amsterdam: North Holland.
Maguire, S., & Hardy, C. (2009). Discourse and deinstitutionalization: The decline of DDT. *Academy of Management Journal, 52*(1), 148–178.
Mahoney, J., & Thelen, K. (2010). A theory of gradual institutional change. In J. Mahoney & K. Thelen (Eds.), *Explaining institutional change: Ambiguity, agency, and power*. Cambridge: Cambridge University Press.
McLeod, D. M., & Hertog, J. K. (1992). The manufacture of public opinion by reporters: Informal cues for public perceptions of protest groups. *Discourse & Society, 3*(3), 259–275.
Medlin, B. (1963). The origin of motion. *Mind, 72*, 155–175.
Milgrom, P., North, D., & Weingast, B. (1990). The role of institutions in the revival of trade: The law merchant, private judges, and the champagne fairs. *Economics and Politics, 2*, 1–23.
Mitchell, W. C. (1910). The rationality of economic activity. *Journal of Political Economy, 18*(3), 197–216.
Mortensen, C. (2008). *Change*, Stanford Encyclopedia of Philosophy, Edward N. Zalta (Ed.).
Nelson, R. R. (2005). *Technology, institutions, and economic growth*. Cambridge: Harvard University Press.

Nelson, R. R., & Sampat, B. N. (2001). Making sense of institutions as a factor shaping economic performance. *Journal of Economic Behavior & Organization, 44*, 31–54.
Noelle-Neumann, E. (1993). *The spiral of silence: Public opinion – Our social skin* (2nd ed.). Chicago: University of Chicago Press.
North, D. C. (1990). *Institutions, institutional change and economic performance*. Cambridge: Cambridge University Press.
North, D. C. (1991). Institutions. *The Journal of Economic Perspectives, 5*(1), 97–112.
North, D. C. (2001). Needed: A theory of change. In G. M. Meier & J. E. Stiglitz (Eds.), *Frontiers of development economics; the future in perspective*. Oxford: Oxford University Press.
North, D. C. (2005). *Understanding the process of economic change*. Princeton: Princeton University Press.
Ogawa, K. (2019). Special feature: Institutional design and experimental economics. *Evolutionary and Institutional Economics Review, 16*, 327–328.
Oliver, C. (1992). The antecedent s of deinstitutionalization. *Organization Studies, 13*(4), 563–588.
Ostrom, E. (2005). *Understanding institutional diversity*. Princeton: Princeton University Press.
Ostrom, E., Gardner, R., & Walker, J. (1994). *Rules, games and common-pool resources*. Ann Arbor: University of Michigan Press.
Parsons, T. (1951). *The social system*. New York: Free Press.
Powell, W. W., & DiMaggio, P. J. (1991). *The new institutionalism in organisational analysis*. Chicago: The University of Chicago Press.
Ritchie, H. A. (2016). Unwrapping Institutional Change in Fragile Settings. World *Development, 83*, 39–53. https://doi.org/10.1016/j.worlddev.2016.03.007.
Rodrik, D., Subramanian, A., & Trebbi, F. (2004). Institutions rule: The primacy of institutions over geography and integration in economic development. *Journal of Economic Growth, 9*(2), 131–165.
Roland, G. (2004). Understanding institutional change: Fast moving and slow-moving institutions. *Studies in Comparative International Development, 38*(4), 109–131.
Rutherford, M. (2007). American institutional economics in the interwar period. In W. J. Samuels, J. E. Biddle, & J. B. Davis (Eds.), *A companion to the history of economic thought*. Malden: Blackwell.
Ruttan, V., & Hayami, Y. (1984). Toward a theory of induced institutional innovation. *Journal of Development Studies, 20*(4), 203–223.
Samadi, A. H. (2008). *Property rights and economic growth: An endogenous growth model*. Unpublished PhD dissertation, University of Isfahan, Faculty of Administrative Science and Economics Department of Economics.
Samadi, A. H. (2018). Institutions and entrepreneurship in MENA countries. In N. Faghih & M. R. Zali (Eds.), *Entrepreneurship ecosystem in the Middle East and North Africa (MENA), contributions to management science*. Cham: Springer.
Samadi, A. H. (2019). Institutional quality and globalization in developing countries. In N. Faghih (Ed.), *Globalization and development – Economic and socio-cultural perspectives from emerging markets*. Cham: Springer.
Schumpeter, J. A. (1934). *The theory of economic development*. Cambridge, MA: Harvard University Press.
Scott, W. R. (2001). *Institutions and organizations* (2nd ed.). Thousand Oaks: Sage.
Searle, J. R. (2005). What is an institution? *Journal of Institutional Economics, 1*(1), 1–22.
Shleifer, A., & Vishny, R. (1994). Politicians and firms. *The Quarterly Journal of Economics, 109*(4), 995–1025.
Smith, A. (1776). An inquiry into the nature and causes of the wealth of nations. Edwin Cannan.
Stam, E., & Nooteboom, B. (2011). Entrepreneurship, innovation and institutions. In *Handbook of research on innovation and entrepreneurship* (pp. 421–438). Cheltenham: Edward Elgar.
Sugden, R. (1989). Spontaneous order. *Journal of Economic Perspective, 3*(4), 85–97.
Swidler, A. (1986). Culture in action: Symbols and strategies. *American Sociological Review, 51*, 273–286.

Torfing, J. (2001). Path-dependent Danish welfare reforms: The contribution of new institutionalism to understanding evolutionary change. *Scandinavian Political Studies, 24*(4), 277–309.
Veblen, T. (1899). *The theory of the leisure class: An economic study of institutions*. New York: Macmillan.
Veblen, T. (1909). The limitation of marginal utility. *Journal of Political Economy, 17*(9), 620–636.
Veeman, T. S., & Politylo, J. (2003). The role of institutions and policy in enhancing sustainable development and conserving natural capital. *Environment, Development and Sustainability, 5*(3/4), 317–332.
Webster, C. J., & Lai, L. W. C. (2003). *Property rights, planning and markets: Managing spontaneous cities*. Cheltenham: Edward Elgar.
Williamson, O. E., (1975). Markets and Hierarchies: Analysis and Antitrust Implications: A Study in the Economics of Internal Organization, University of Illinois at Urbana-Champaign's Academy for Entrepreneurial Leadership Historical Research Reference in Entrepreneurship, Available at SSRN: https://ssrn.com/abstract=1496220.
Williamson, O. E. (1985). *The economic institutions of capitalism: Firms, markets, relational contracting*. New York: Free Press.
Williamson, O. E. (2000). The new institutional economics: Taking stock, looking ahead. *Journal of Economic Literature, 38*(3), 595–613.
World Bank. (2005). Where is the Wealth of Nations? Measuring Capital for the 21st Century. Washington, DC. © World Bank. https://openknowledge.worldbank.org/handle/10986/7505 License: CC BY 3.0 IGO.
World Bank. (2006). *Where is the wealth of nations? Measuring capital for the 21st century*. Washington, DC: The International Bank for Reconstruction and Development/The World Bank. isbn-10: 0-8213-6354-9.
Young, H. P. (1996). The economics of convention. *Journal of Economic Perspective, 10*(2), 105–122.

Understanding Institutions and Revisiting the Theories of Institutional Change

Kirti and Vineet Kumar

1 Introduction

The "Theory of Institution" is that domain of study, which explicates the actions of an organisation as well as the unit of an organisation viz. an individual. There are various significant themes which revolve around the theory of institutions; one of them is "Institutional Change," the institutions have the potency to steer change across multiple levels of the individual. The society and the Institution itself can bring transformation in the primary feature, behaviour, and structure of these units over some time. This chapter is an attempt to conceptualise the foundation of institutions and institutional change. In brief, we can refer to institutions as that "set of established cognitive inclinations towards specific relationships along with the scrupulous individual and community activities" (Veblen 1899a).

On one hand, it has been described as "the set of rules of the society which governs each action, and more precisely, they are the ethically designed standards and restrains that guide and mould every interaction, leaving fewer chances of mistakes and ambiguities" (North 1990). Whereas on the other hand, they are also referred to as just "they are the basis of the expectance mutually shared among the member rather being the guiding principles" (Hayek 1973a). Institutions are the results of objective-based, consistent solution-seeking efforts for managing the issues, which surround human existence and to find as well as fill the gaps lying between the facts regarding other entities co-habiting the same volatile environment. The institutional change is indeed a cycle it brings about a difference in the entities of the

Kirti (✉)
Chanakya National Law University, Patna, India
e-mail: kirti@cnlu.ac.in

V. Kumar
St. Xavier's College of Management and Technology, Patna, India

N. Faghih, A. H. Samadi (eds.), *Dynamics of Institutional Change in Emerging Market Economies*, Contributions to Economics,
https://doi.org/10.1007/978-3-030-61342-6_5

environment and over a while due to that very change again the institutions get affected. It is a process which has steps involved and follows a pattern. The Institution can be understood as a system, as it binds the entities of the environment in an interdependent loop and binds them for the attainment of common objectives that is survival, growth, and success. Human interactions are deliberate and complex and so are the institutions; they are not separate from each other instead; and they are the wheels on which the world runs, dynamics take place, and advancements happen. This chapter is thus an effort towards deciphering the notions surrounding the institutions and institutional change; the covered topics are given below in the chapter outline.

Chapter Outline

I. The Institution: A brief discussion.
II. Causes of Institutional Change.
III. Analysis of significant theories of Institutional Change.
IV. Conclusion

2 The Institution: A Brief Discussion

The term Institution has enormous usage across the social sciences such as economics, politics, sociology, philosophy, and even geography over the past many years. The term was used by the infamous Italian political philosopher in his book titled "La Scienceza Nuova" (The New Science), in 1725. One such approach was given by Douglas North. North was an American economist who won the Nobel Memorial Prize together with Robert William Fogel, who was claimed by the Nobel Committee as the re-newer of the Economic History, bringing quantitative techniques in the field of Economic Research. Douglas North was the one who raised the question of why don't the other economies learn and adopt what the best institutions of the better-doing economies have achieved. North (1990) claimed that "institutions are the rules of the society, involving humanly formal and informal rules, in such a manner that they are the by-products of the human interactions, their features, implementation of rules and norms which govern reiterated individual relations" (North 1990); in this definition, it can be figured out that institutions are not just the organisations or firms, but they are the guiding principles of humanity, along with the manners in which they are implemented. Human beings are the creators of these guidelines, and another noteworthy implication of this definition can be that organisations, firms, communities, and governments all formulate the society and are ruled by the institutions, the common factor which exists among all these entities is interdependency and interactions. North's approach was a strong dimension to the theories of Institution. Still, it got lots of criticism as well on several grounds as it did not differentiate organisations and institutions, failed to explain the role of social rule, and lacked micro-level perspective.

Another economist M. Aoki (2007) referred Institution as "long-lasting as well as a shared set of ideologies relating to the collective actions of the society and its members in varying situations" (Aoki 2007). Institutions are not just the set of guiding rules rather the set of beliefs and value system that channelises the endeavours of the members of the society. Moreover, Aoki emphasises that these set are stable ones which have been shared by various agents of the Institution. Defining the term broadly, one can say that "institutions are the systems of guidelines, standards, values and organisations which mutually produce stability of collective actions" (Greif 2006).

Human beings are social creature; being so, they have several needs and doled out means to achieve them. An institution is a predominant and permanent, cognitive method or activity, which is instilled in the routine actions and beliefs of the individuals. It can be said that Institutions are the means to an end, and that end is the wants and needs of the individual, organisations, and society. They are the practices, principles, and the systems that guide the actions and behaviour of individual and group towards the attainment of a common objective. If taken from a sociological perspective "a social institution is that framework which leads to the fulfilment of needs of the individuals with the help of deep-rooted methods" (Bogardus 1922).

3 The Effects of the Institution on Growth and Development

The Institution has an overwhelming effect on the procedure of economic growth, as they decide the dispositions, inspirations, and conditions for improvement of the nation. An overall economic development can be achieved if the institutions have enough changeability, urge individuals to take advantage of the economic growth and further to lead a better quality of living and invite them to get on with it, failing which will hamper and make the economy down. So, Institutions set the right tone for the overall economic development of the nation. Institutions have great significance across different disciplines. In simple words, intuitions are those human-designed rules which guide the human deeds and cognitive processes. In economics, they are considered as a relevant essence for economic performance and growth; in sociology, almost every concept or pillar of the society (be it marriage, family, organisation, custom) has been referred as an Institution; this term has been in the core of almost every social science discipline, but the usage and implication are somewhat different. The origin of Institution is latent in human behaviour and interactions, which are sometimes intended and sometimes unintended. Humans are part of an economic environment having limited resources and characterised as social, economic, and rational beings. They are driven by their economic actions as believed by the traditional economics; they are the centre of Institution and understanding of Institution. It is the interaction and interdependency of individuals and groups that give rise to an institution, further developing, nurturing, and moulding, and channelising the human behaviour, decisions, and attainment of desired objectives.

Geoffrey and Hodgson in their work "How Economics Forgot History" suggested that "fundamentally, institutions are long-lasting structures of deep-rooted and entrenched societal rules and standards that mould human interactions" (Hodgson 2001). In the words of Schotter (1981), "the unanimous uniformity in societal behaviours that stipulate behaviour in a particular type of recurrent circumstances; self-devised rules or devised by an outside authority is a Social Institution" (Schotter 1981).

4 Causes of Institutional Change

There are two types of arguments revolving the theme of institutional change (i.e. strong ones and weak ones) regarding "path dependence." Path dependence suggests how history matters, our past decides our future, when analysed the weak argument carefully tends to indicate a full potentiality of augmented change along these rigid paths. The arguments put forward a particular aspect to view the institutional change, which are as follows:

- functionalism and technicality,
- diffusion,
- conflict and power.

The previous studies in the field of political economy on institutional change rose from the concept of *functional* view. In one of the research of Alfred Chandler (1977), "the emergence of the United States contemporary co-operation, it was argued that the executives of those corporations had a shift from the single divisional to the multi-divisional organisational framework. It was due to the enhancements in the interactions, transportation, and technology leading to the growth of a country's internal as well as global exchanges for goods and services" (Chandler 1977).

It was the multi-divisional organisations which proved to enjoy the economies of scale and successfully survive in the emerging markets. This argument of Chandler (1977) was supported by Powell (1990), as well as according to him "the institutional change is a response to new and efficient ways of communication, transportation, technology, logistics; creating a whole dynamic market scenario which brings out a functional retort in organisation's structure" (Powell 1990).

On the contrary to the above-discussed functionalism and technological efficiency induced institutional change, another group of institutional theorists argue that neither it is the technical efficiency nor the functionality. Still, it is "the *diffusion* of organisations that desire more legitimate relations with the realm of a connected organisation operating in the same industry" (Thomas et al. 1987).

This group of theorist was from Stanford University led by John Meyer, who came with this fresh idea of "diffusion" in the institutions and institutional change study. As per March and Olsen (1989), "organisations work as per the logic of appropriateness rather of instrumentality" (March and Olsen 1989).

But, the question still unanswered was that which type of diffusion created most of the institutional change; the argument was somewhat addressed by DiMaggio and Powell (1983); in their study claimed that "it either the normative process of the mimetic process which leads to institutional change; former gives rise to convergent results by which organisations discover the best practices and then tend to inculcate them in the system, whereas the latter helps the organisation to monitor its environment, find out the best performing organisations and learn from them their practices to excel in their endeavours" (DiMaggio and Powell 1983).

The third approach to institutional change is *conflict and power struggle*; this approach suggests that "institutional change is largely the outcome of the conflict and power struggle to gain the control over valuable and scarce resources, to position oneself as a market leader and have a powerful existence in the global economy" (Amable 2003).

"Those who attain this position obtain the Institution they desire and are mould them to serve them as they demand" (Campbell 2004). Most of the studies of this approach emphasised the linkage between the economy and the state. One such study says that "the political ground within which the organisation exists is determined and governs them" (Campbell and Lindberg 1991).

5 Analysis of Significant Theories of Institutional Change

The significant theories that explain institutional change discussed in this chapter are as follows:

(a) Designed-based approach.
(b) Evolutionary approach.
(c) Equilibrium perspective.

First set of Theories are categorised as *Designed-based theories* of Institutional Change; this theory emphasises on the accomplishment of collective endeavours, conflict resolution, and collective bargaining by the cooperative political agencies for decision-making and taking the matters in a centralised manner. One of the prominent economists Libecap (1989) was of the view that Institutional Change is a process based on old rules, as technology advancement has led to the current institutional change but that is also dependent upon previous technological developments; further, he insisted that Institutional change was more of extrinsic alterations of criticisms, for instance, a change in the rules regarding "property rights" will mould the dimensions of profit distributions. Libecap (1989) explored "the foundations of property rights which are the 'rules'; and then takes these rule-modifying actions as constricting game administered by an upper-rank political policy, and these upper-rank rules combined with the deeds along with views of agents of these parties" (Libecap 1989).

Another Economist named Ostrom (2005), in his work titled as "Understanding Institutional Diversity," emphasised on both extrinsic and intrinsic factors of institutional change; doing so, he differentiated between the rules. So, he classified those rules that preside over routine interactions as Operational Rules; rules which helped in selecting the various operational rules were referred to as Collective Decision-Making Rules. Then he classified those rules that let the making of the Collective Decision-Making Rules and thus termed them as the Constitutional Rules. Further, there are rules which as per his claims aided in making of constitutional rules which he classified as the Meta Rules.

According to him, "institutional change is a process, in which every single party to it evaluates the cost to be incurred and the gain they can make out of it, then if a process of institutional change is that: each individual calculates their expected costs and benefits from an institutional change, and if the least alliance strong enough to create an influence will lead to an institutional change" (Ostrom 2005).

In this aspect, the least alliance is decided by the upper-rank rules, for instance within a democracy, it is the majority that makes up a victorious alliance. However, it must be noted that these theories fail to describe the reason for the failure of designed rules to provide the desired results as these rules are formed out of deliberations and rational collective decision-making processes.

The second set of theories can be categorised as "*Evolutionary Theories*," of Institutional Change. But, one must first decipher the term "evolution." The term has been used very casually across various study fields such as economics, pure sciences, political science, and sociology, etc., to put simply bring into play the idea of change. The literal connotation of the term implies an interrelated set of historical episodes. The sociologist Campbell J. defines evolution as "an avant-garde long run accretion of diminutive and augmented change" (Campbell 2005).

The definition of Campbell implies that there should be a somewhat repetitive series of interrelated historical events occurring one after the other. Evolution theorists claim that factors that cause Institutional change are individual and organisations deeds and cognitive processes. What differentiates the two categories, i.e. designed and evolutionary, is the role which decision-making process plays in the determination of emerging and adaptable rules in the socio-economic environment. As per the study of Kingston and Caballero (2009), "several researchers explored the field of institutional change with an evolutionary approach" (Kingston and Caballero 2009).

As per this approach, it is not the centralised system which creates a synchronised alteration in the regulations as viewed by the deed or values of critical agents of the Institution but it is caused by the decentralisation of the selection procedure of the rules which as a result leads to the successful change, adaptation, and growth of the Institution. Thus, nutshell it can be laid down that it is the discord in the decision-making regarding the rules selection, which leads to institutional change and not the coordinated choice. Another Evolutionary theorist Veblen (1899) also has strong viewpoints regarding Institutional Change. His ideas suggested that "it is the cognitive tendencies, which are characterised as long-lasting, enduring, and adaptable dispositions to comprehend and behave in a certain manner; it is the Darwinism which gives rise to evolving institutions" (Veblen 1899b). He further advocates that "technological and population dynamism channelises the institutional change, by assuring that the past inherited institution and cognitive tendencies never fit in with the current environment demands" (Ibid).

So, it can be said that both cognitive tendencies and institutions are persistently coevolving. The fruition of society is notably a procedure of an individual's psychological adjustment influenced by the pressure of situations, which apparently won't be enough to put up with cognitive tendencies formulated during the varying past conditions.

Institutional change can be triggered by the exogenous technical advancements, as Ayres (1944) claimed that "institutions tend to resist change as it intimidates ongoing power, capital and status, on the contrary, technological advancement demands change as it also changes the materialistic setting where it exists" (Ayres 1944).

Another development that evolutionary theory saw was based upon "the choices at the social group hierarchy; it is the place at which the rules of the behaviour grew as the hierarchical level which applied and followed them used to be more thriving and expatriated others" (Hayek 1973b).

On the other hand, Levi (1990) succeeded in explaining that "few groups can avail power through the formal rules while the other groups which are the losing end can drive a change in the institution through taking back their assent from the ongoing institutional system; this, in turn, can even bring into play the collective action which will again happen by the action decentralisation of several entities" (Levi 1990); in this way, he accentuated the benefits of the formal rule.

Yet another argument by Knight (1995) is that "varying set of rules create varying distributional outcomes, in a manner that various agents of the institution might support the rise of various rules; but the power in the bargaining these agents have can again vary to a certain degree, and it can have an influence the kind of rule which will become conventional for society at large" (Knight 1995).

Young (1996) suggested that "events of impact in history, in the long run, might direct to the selection of a specific rule and natural selection procedure, in which swift exchange amid rules are scattered with durability" (Young 1996).

The *third* set of a theory is "*Equilibrium approach*." The work of North (1990) proposed a challenge for the other economists; it was to fathom informal rules more profoundly and how it relates to the formal rules; the Equilibrium approach is an answer to this proposed challenge; and it integrates both the formal and informal practices into a unified structure. The essence of this approach lies in the paradigm shift from the rules guiding behaviour to human behaviour itself. The renowned works in this approach are credited to Calvert (1995), Aoki (2001), Greif and Latin (2004), Greif (2006).

In the words of Calvert (1995), "there isn't a separate organism which can be referred to as an institution; it is only the logical and expectations governed behaviour, and others react to it that exists; the bits of some type of equilibrium is termed as an institution" (Calvert 1995). Equilibrium can be understood as a condition in which there is a state of nature; there is no concept of rules that govern behaviour;

all these behaviours are equally important; and the only limitation for these behaviours is the short-run extrinsic factors for instance laws of gravity, motion, resource limitations, etc. The human behaviour, the Institution, and the results of their interaction are affected by the limitations of the technology. The approach lays equal significance to both the formal and informal rules in the process of channelising the players, i.e. the agents or units of the institutions towards their fulfilment of a shared set of values regarding another's behaviour regardless of the play path. On the other hand, Aoki (2001) explains that "institutions are durable, deeply embedded set of values concerning the desired behaviour of society members in varying situations" (Aoki 2001).

Expanding the idea of Aoki (2001), Greif (2006) claims that "institution can be referred to a structure of rules, values, beliefs, societal norms, and organisations which combined give uniformity in the societal behaviour" (Greif 2006). The idea of Aoki (2001) and Greif (2006) suggests Institution is recognised along with the equilibrium patterns of deeds than the rules which influence these deeds and actions. To be precise, the thoughts of both scholars are different than the other thinkers of equilibrium theory.

6 Conclusion

In the past decades, it has been observed that managing the dynamism of emerging economies is a tough task, and this chapter has brought together the various previous researches into the light for understanding the concept of Institution and Institutional change along with the forces and its theories. The theme plays a significant role in today's scenario as it helps us to gain insight into past situations and plan for a better institutional framework. There exist a vast number of studies in this field. Still, there is need of more to anticipate the future challenges and their possible answers, the change is the phenomenon which has a wide range of direction to it, and the concept of Institution remains in the centre of social science discipline. Understanding the Institution helps in creating, maintaining, and again changing it as per the contingencies. One must keep it in mind that institutions are an integral part of society and economy, and they will remain to be so till humanity exists. As change is the only constant, it is the only way we can fight for survival and growth in the long run. Institutions can steer change across various levels of the individual and the society, and its better understanding will lead to sustainable growth and development of the different stakeholders. The limitation of the study is that the research studies revolving this theme are mostly conducted before the year 2010. Hence, more new theories have to be developed as per the changes in today's scenario. Further, it is concluded that more studies in this regard are conducted to develop new theories and model based on primary as well as secondary data.

References

Amable, B. (2003). *The diversity of modern capitalism*. New York: Oxford University Press.

Aoki, M. (2001). *Towards a comparative institutional analysis*. Cambridge, MA: MIT Press.

Aoki, M. (2007). Endogenizing institutions and institutional changes. *Journal of Institutional Economics, 3*(1), 1–31.

Ayres, C. E. (1944). *The theory of economic progress*. Chapel Hill: University of North Carolina Press.

Bogardus, E. S. (1922). Psycho-sociological thought (continued). In *A history of social thought* (pp. 389–422). Los Angeles: University of Southern California.

Calvert, R. (1995). Rational actors, equilibrium and social institutions. In J. Knight & I. Sened (Eds.), *Explaining social institutions*. Ann Arbor: University of Michigan Press.

Campbell, J. L. (2004). *Institutional change and globalization*. Princeton: Princeton University Press.

Campbell, J. L. (2005). *Institutional change and globalization* (p. 264). Princeton: Princeton University Press.

Campbell, J. L., & Lindberg, L. N. (1991). The evolution of governance regimes. In J. L. Campbell, J. R. Hollingsworth, & L. N. Lindberg (Eds.), *Governance of the American economy* (pp. 319–355). New York: Cambridge University Press.

Chandler, A. D., Jr. (1977). *The visible hand: The managerial revolution in American business*. Cambridge: Harvard University Press.

DiMaggio, P. J., & Powell, W. W. (1983). The iron cage revisited: Institutional isomorphism and collective rationality in organizational fields. *American Sociological Review, 48*, 147–160.

Greif, A. (2006). *Institutions and the Path to the Modern Economy: Lessons from Medieval Trade* (Political Economy of Institutions and Decisions). Cambridge: Cambridge University Press.

GREIF, A., & LAITIN, D. (2004). A Theory of Endogenous Institutional Change. *American Political Science Review, 98*(4), 633–652. https://doi.org/10.1017/S0003055404041395

Hayek, F. A. (1973a). *Law, legislation and liberty, Vol. 1: Rules and order*. Chicago: University of Chicago Press.

Hayek, F. A. (1973b). *Law, legislation and liberty*. London: Routledge and Kegan Paul.

Hodgson, G. M. (2001). *How economics forgot history*. London: Routledge.

Kingston, C., & Caballero, G. (2009). Comparing theories of institutional change. *Journal of Institutional Economics, 5*(02), 151–180.

Knight, J. (1995). Models, interpretations and theories: Constructing explanations of institutional emergence and change. In J. Knight & I. Sened (Eds.), *Explaining social institutions* (pp. 95–120). Ann Arbor: University of Michigan press.

Levi, M. (1990). A logic of institutional change. In K. Schweers & M. Levi (Eds.), *The limits of rationality*. Chicago: University of Chicago Press.

Libecap, G. D. (1989). *Contracting for property rights*. Cambridge: Cambridge University Press.

March, J. G., & Olsen, J. P. (1989). *Rediscovering institutions: The organizational basis of politics*. New York: Free Press.

North, D. (1990). *Institutions, institutional change and economic performance*. Cambridge: Cambridge University Press.

Ostrom, E. (2005). *Understanding institutional diversity*. Princeton: Princeton University Press.

Powell, W. (1990). Neither market nor hierarchy: Network forms of organization. *Research in Organizational Behavior, 12*, 295–336.

Schotter, A. (1981). *The economic theory of social institutions*. Cambridge: Cambridge University Press.

Thomas, G. M., Meyer, J. W., Ramirez, F. O., & Boli, J. (Eds.). (1987). *Institutional structure: Constituting state, society, and the individual*. Newbury Park: Sage.

Veblen, T. (1899a). *The theory of the leisure class: An economic study of institutions*. New York: Macmillan.

Veblen, T. (1899b). *Theory of the leisure class*. The Floating Press.

Young, H. P. (1996). The economics of convention. *Journal ofEconomic Perspectives, 10*(2), 105–122.

Measuring Institutional Quality: A Review

Ali Hussein Samadi and Masoumeh Alipourian

1 Introduction

From Veblen's point of view, economics is the theory of processes and habits, and institutions shape these processes. In his view, institutions influence the behavior of economic agents and therefore their economic performance through multiple channels. Institutions affect the structure of the economic incentives of people in a society. Institutional economists believe that institutions determine people's choices and guide their interactions. Thus, creating a stable structure for human interactions can reduce uncertainty. In other words, the main role of institutions is to organize groups, facilitate interaction and coordination between them, reduce uncertainty in economic activities, and encourage economic development (Samadi 2008). Institutions can play an important role in improving economic performance by using the resources most efficiently, encouraging factor accumulation, and stimulating innovation (North 1990). However, the impact of institutions on economic performance depends on the quality of institutions. Now, the question arises as to what institutional quality is and how it can be evaluated? These and other relevant questions will be addressed in the later sections of this chapter.

Institutional quality has received much attention in the institutional economics literature. Institutional quality and institutional change are two different aspects of institutions. Existing indicators only reflect the status quo of institutions and reveal little about the institutional change. Assessing the quality of institutions does not necessarily translate into adjustments to institutions (Voigt 2013). North (2001) argued that a lot was known about institutions and their economic performance, but little was known about how institutions changed. Accordingly, understanding

A. H. Samadi (✉) · M. Alipourian
Department of Economics, Shiraz University, Shiraz, Iran
e-mail: asamadi@rose.shirazu.ac.ir

N. Faghih, A. H. Samadi (eds.), *Dynamics of Institutional Change in Emerging Market Economies*, Contributions to Economics,
https://doi.org/10.1007/978-3-030-61342-6_6

institutional quality is the first step in understanding institutional change. If institutions in a country are not in good quality, the theories of institutional change can be applied.

Institutions have different dimensions and each dimension is measured by an index or a number of indices. Nevertheless, there is no consensus among scholars on which proxies to use to measure the quality of institutions. Therefore, an important issue when investigating the effects of institutions and institutional quality on economic performance in empirical studies is to choose an appropriate index. Recently, individuals and international organizations have suggested numerous indicators. In this regard, the main purpose of this chapter is to address the following fundamental question: Can any indicator be used as a proxy for measuring institutional quality? Some of the most commonly used indicators are introduced below using a descriptive-analytic method.

This chapter is organized in five sections. In Sect. 2, many of the most commonly used indicators of institutional quality are introduced and some complementary points are mentioned about them. It is hoped that this section will provide readers with a comprehensive list of the most commonly used indicators used to measure the quality of institutions. Also, it is shown that each of the indicators introduced can represent only one dimension of institutional quality. This highlights the importance of selecting an appropriate index or a number of indices. Accordingly, a number of general suggestion is offered about the use of these indices.

In Sects. 3 and 4, the concepts of Rule of Law (RoL) and Property Rights (PR), along with the indicators used to measure them, are described, respectively. The status of institutional quality in transition countries is worse than that in developed countries. Improving the status of property rights and the rule of law can contribute more to the economic performance of these countries than can other aspects of institutional quality. Therefore, in Sects. 3 and 4, the definitions of these concepts and indicators used to measure them are discussed in detail. The final section summarizes the chapter.

2 Measurement of Institutional Quality

2.1 The Concept of Institutional Quality

Indicators are statistical metrics used to transform complex data into comprehensible and simple numbers for policymakers and the public (Merry 2011) and reflect changes in social phenomena over time (Wang et al. 2019, p. 276). It is inevitable to resort to indicators or benchmarks when evaluating the status of an economic and social phenomenon. In social sciences, in general, and especially in the context of institutional quality assessment, in particular, indicators are evaluated by three criteria, namely, ***validity, reliability,*** and ***bias***. *Validity* is an attempt to explore whether these indicators measure the same concept, i.e., institutional quality, *reliability* is the extent to which the repeated measures of the same phenomenon produce consistent results, and *bias* shows how far the indicators are from actual values. These are the criteria which should be heeded when choosing indicators to assess institutional quality (Ginsburg 2018, p. 53).

First, however, we need to define institutional quality. Different definitions have been proposed for institutional quality. To encapsulate, institutional quality measures the *power, consistency*, and *robustness* of institutions in each country. Institutional robustness refers to the *sovereignty*, *influence*, and the *real power* of institutions. The institutional quality of any country does not depend on its political structure. For example, the institutions of a country can be very traditional and undemocratic, but they may have internal strength and power. The institutional quality of any country is a function of the *institutional structure* and *institutional system* in that country. The institutional structure can be producer-friendly, rent-seeker friendly, or predator-friendly (Renani and Moayedfar 2012). In fact, the institutional structure frame motivations and seeks to shape social behaviors (Alonso and Garciamartin 2009, p. 7).

Institutional quality can be assessed based on the following four criteria: *Static efficiency*, *dynamic efficiency (adaptability)*, *credibility (legitimacy)*, and *security (predictability)*. These four criteria are intended to meet the two basic economic tasks of institutions, namely, reducing transaction costs and facilitating coordination among economic actors.

Institutional quality can also be assessed using the three factors of "*institutional performance*," "*compatibility and adaptability*," and "*stability*." *Institutional performance* is the "capacity and ability of the state" to manage administrative, legislative, and judicial tasks, manage the economy, provide social services, use natural resources to an acceptable extent, support human, economic, social, political, and civil rights, and provide people with all kinds of security. *Compatibility and adaptability* is the ability to adapt to the conditions ahead and creativity and innovation to meet future needs. *Stability* measure the ability of an entity to reduce its functional weakness (UNDP 2010).

2.2 *Institutional Quality Indicators*

Various criteria have been proposed for measuring institutional quality. These criteria are extracted from surveys and objective data. Accordingly, indicators used to evaluate institutional quality can be categorized into objective (or quantitative) and subjective (or qualitative) indicators.

Qualitative criteria are derived from expert opinion while quantitative criteria are extracted from quantitative data. Indicators such as the status of democracy and the quality of governance are qualitative variables. However, *Contract Intensive Money* (CIM) is a quantitative variable that can be calculated based on aggregate monetary variables (Voigt 2013, p. 2; Ginsburg 2018, p. 53). Table 1 presents the most commonly used indicators for a variety of legal-economic, social, and political

Table 1 Indexes for measuring institutional quality

Economic-legal institutions
Anti-Director Rights Index (ADRI) (La Porta et al. 1998)
Capital controls-EFW index (Fraser Institute)
Contracting Institutions-International Country Risk Guide (ICRG) repudiation of contracts, enforcement of contracts
CBR datasets: Centre for Business Research in Cambridge (legal rules)
Domestic business environment (the cost of doing business, the security to property rights, contract enforcement, dispute resolution, the extent of internet diffusion, and the strength of legal rights)
Economic freedom index, which includes the following factors:
1. Size of government: expenditures, taxes, and enterprises;
2. Legal structure and protection of property rights;
3. Access to sound money: inflation rate and the possibility to own foreign currency bank accounts;
4. Freedom to trade internationally: taxes on international trade, regulatory trade barriers, capital market controls, the difference between official exchange rate and black market rate, etc.; and
5. Regulation of credit, labor, and business.
Economic Governance (including sub-indices of regulatory quality and government effectiveness)-WB WGI
Financial Freedom Index of economic freedom (Heritage Foundation and WSJ)
Foreign ownership/investment restrictions-EFW index (Fraser Institute)
Freedom of the press: legal environment (Freedom House)
Freedom of the press: economic environment (Freedom House)
Freedom to own foreign currency bank accounts-EFW index (Fraser Institute)
Global Competitiveness Index (GCI)
Government efficiency
Government effectiveness-WB WGI
Regulatory quality-WB WGI
Functioning of government (EIU)
Indicator of quality of government (IRCG)
Investment profile-ICRG
Impartial courts: EFW index (Fraser Institute)
International Property Right Index, which includes the following factor:
Physical property rights
Intellectual property rights
Legal and political environment (including judicial independence, rule of law, political instability, and control of corruption)
Labor protection index
Judicial independence indicators
EFW index (Fraser Institute)
The power and reach of the judicial system-La Porta et al. (2004)
A de jure (comprising twelve variables) and de facto (comprising eight factors) judiciary independence Index-Feld and Voight (2003)

(continued)

Table 1 (continued)

Measures of dispute resolution in courts: the legal origin and legal formalism index-Djankov et al. (2003)
Rule of law-WB WGI
Labor market institutions, which include the following factors:
Unemployment insurance system (the replacement rate, benefit length, and a measure of active labor policy),
Employment protection (the tax wedge),
Collective bargaining (union contract coverage, union density, and union-employer coordination of bargaining),
Labor market regulation (employment laws, collective relation laws, and social security laws),
Labor market freedom indicator, employment protection or minimum wage legislation-Fraser Institute,
Labor market regulations of the Economic Freedom of the World (EFW)-Fraser Institute[a]
Law and order-ICRG
Legal datasets (La Porta et al. 1998, 2008)
Legal formalism index
Legal regulation (de jure and de facto)
Legal system Quality-Economic Freedom index, Fraser Institute
Procedural formalism
Property rights (PR) indices, such as EFW index (Fraser Institute)
Property rights institutions: ICRG expropriation risk, degree of legal protection that producers enjoy
Quality of contract enforcement
Quality of the court system or judicial quality
Religion in politics-ICRG
Regulation of credit, labor, and business: credit market regulations-EFW index (Fraser Institute)
Regulation of credit, labor, and business: labor market regulations-EFW index (Fraser Institute)
Regulation of credit, labor, and business: business regulations-EFW index (Fraser Institute)
Regulatory quality-WB WGI
Rent-seeking
Rule of law-WB WGI
Shareholder protection index with 60 variables in it (SPI-60) or Lele-Siems index (Lele and Siems 2007)
Supreme Court justices
The tax and fee burden
The quality of legal protection
Social institutions
Corruption
Objective measures of corruption (such as comparing the quality of the physical infrastructure with the money that was invested in it, control of corruption-WB WGI)
Subjective measures of corruption (such as Corruption Perception Index-Transparency international)
Domestic and transnational terrorism
Ethnic fragmentation

(continued)

Table 1 (continued)

Institutional governance (including sub-indices of the rule of law and control of corruption)-WB WGI
Social capital indices
Trade barriers (such as longer distances, lack of contiguity, and cultural differences)
Political institutions
Bureaucratic quality-ICRG
Checks and balances measure-WB DPI
Civil Liberties-Freedom in the world: Civil liberties (Freedom House)
Colonial Origin
Corruption in Government-ICRG
Database of Political Institutions (DPI)-Development Research Group of the World Bank
Democracy and dictatorship dataset
Democratic accountability-ICRG
Freedom in the World (a composite indicator depicting both political rights and civil liberties)
Freedom of the press: Political environment-(Freedom House)
Quality of Government or Predatory behavior (including bureaucratic quality and corruption in government)
Index of federalism
Institutionalized democracy-institutionalized autocracy index (Polity IV)
Internal conflict-ICRG
Military in politics-ICRG
Political constraints index
Political freedoms
Political governance (including sub-indices of voice, accountability, and political stability)-WB WGI
Political instability indicators, which include the following factors:
Cross-Polity Time-Series Data-(Banks 1971): measuring civil protest (general strikes, riots, and antigovernment demonstrations), politically motivated aggression (guerrilla warfare, assassinations, and purges), and political regime instability (coups d'état and revolutions),
International Country Risk Guide (ICRG)-government instability, internal conflicts, external conflict, military in politics, religious tensions, and ethnic tension,
The database of political institutions-Beck et al. (2001).
Political party fractionalization index,
Political rights-freedom in the world (Freedom House)
Political terror scale (political terror scale)
The Polity IV democracy scores
The CIRI Human Data Rights Project
Voice and accountability
Overall (all dimensions of institutional quality)
Doing business indicators-World Bank
General governance (including economic, political, and institutional governance)-WB WGI-created based on the principal component analysis (PCA) technique
Economic Freedom index: The Heritage Foundation
Economic Freedom index: The Freedom House

(continued)

Table 1 (continued)

EFW (Economic Freedom of the World) index-Fraser Institute
Institutional Efficiency-Business International Institute (BI index)
Kunčič's (2014) Index-legal, political, and economic World Institutional Quality Ranking (WIQR)-created based on the factor analysis,
Objective governance indicators (OGI)
The KOF Index of Globalization-Khalid (2016)

Source: Kunčič (2014), Samadi (2019); further elaboration is added by the authors
This index consists of six sub-indices that measure the influence of hiring regulations and minimum wages, hiring and firing regulations, centralized collective bargaining, hours regulation, mandated cost of worker dismissal, and conscription

institutions as well as some indicators used to measure all aspects of institutional quality.

Numerous indicators have been introduced for evaluating formal and informal institutions. Although informal institutions play a key role in the process of economic development, they are difficult to measure and few scholars have attempted to introduce an index to measure them. Voigt (2013) examined these challenges and reviewed several indicators, such as social capital and trust, used in empirical studies. The purpose of this section is to present these indicators briefly.

The measurement of formal and informal institutions is usually described as "hard" and "soft," respectively. Indicators used to measure "hard" institutions are mainly based on verifiable written documents and are not subject to interpretation. The indices measuring "soft" institutions are influenced by the scholars' or participants' opinions (Woodruff 2010). For example, the "limitation on the executive branch," which measures the legislature and judiciary degree of independence from the executive branch, is also influenced by the opinions of the scholar although it is a hard measure based on constitutional differences. This index is subject to change even without the differences between official constitutions. Therefore, the "constraints on executive power" index should be considered as a composite index which can be applied to both formal and informal institutions (Glaeser et al. 2004). The "World Bank's Doing Business" is another hard-soft indicator used to evaluate institutional quality. On the other hand, some indicators measure a combination of formal institutional factors and the informal institutional environment. For example, the "risk of expropriation" index is among such indices.

2.3 *Some Important Insights*

The purpose of this section is to provide some insights into the limitations of the proposed indicators in empirical studies. In what follows, some points regarding the limitations and selection of indicators are briefly mentioned:

1. Institutional quality and institutional change are two different aspects of institutions. Existing indicators only reflect the status quo of institutions and reveal little of the institutional change. The measurement of the current quality of institutions may not necessarily lead to adjustments to institutions (Voigt 2013).
2. Institutions have specific functions. Proposed indicators may not necessarily evaluate all the functions of institutions (Alonso and Garciamartin 2009, p. 8).
3. Limiting the behavior of individuals and preserving stability are the chief characteristics of institutions. Not all the indicators proposed above do necessarily include these two characteristics. Some of the abovementioned indicators, such as ICRG and WB WGI, are actually a measure of policy choice (Voigt 2013, pp. 3–4). However, some institutions, such as political institutions, are not stable, at least in the long run (Ibid., p. 9).
4. Most indicators available for measuring institutional quality have limited reliability. Therefore, it is necessary to exercise caution in interpreting the results of experimental studies (Alonso and Garciamartin 2009, p. 8).
5. Reliability and bias are more of a concern in subjective indicators than other indicators (Ginsburg 2018, p. 53).
6. Some scholars have attempted to examine the importance and role of institutions in the economy. However, many indicators do not provide sufficient evidence to either confirm or reject this hypothesis. Therefore, more data should be collected before making any conclusions (Voigt 2013, p. 22).
7. Each of the indicators introduced above has its own characteristics. Thus, the researcher(s) must first decide about which definition of institution is relevant and then select an appropriate index which corresponds to that definition (Alonso and Garciamartin 2009, p. 8).
8. A certain period must pass before institutions can exert influence on economic variables. This should be taken into consideration when selecting an index to assess the quality of institutions (Voigt 2013). If it takes more than 1 year for the effect of the institution to emerge, a lag structure should be used that matches the indicator selected.
9. The nature of a study plays a key role in selecting the type of indicator(s). Cross-country, country, state, and provincial nature of studies influence the type of indicator(s) to be selected (Voigt 2013).
10. In measuring the quality of institutions, assumptions about their potential impact on economic variables should always be considered (Voigt 2013, p. 8).
11. Some indices have sub-indices. For example, the WB WGI Index has ten sub-indices. In such cases, some researchers calculated the overall index based on, for instance, a simple or weighted average. However, it is advisable to use Factor Analysis (FA) to extract the overall index when dealing with such indices (Voigt 2013).
12. Some indices, such as democracy and the rule of law, include different institutions. Another example is the "Freedom in the World Index" of Freedom House. It represents political rights and civil liberties (simultaneously) and is a composite index. When a specific institution is concerned, these indices are not good proxy variables (Voigt 2013, p. 2).

As it is clear from Table 1, there are many indices available to assess the quality of institutions. It is not possible to describe and review all the indicators in this chapter. Countries in transition face a multitude of problems, but the rule of law and property rights, two indicators representing legal-economic institutions, are particularly underdeveloped in these countries. Accordingly, in what follows, special attention is paid to these two indicators, i.e., the rule of law and property rights.

3 Rule of Law

Understanding the "RoL" requires an understanding of the "law." Law can be defined as the rules that govern the behavior of individuals in a society. These rules promote discipline in society by providing conflict resolution mechanisms. Official, religious, natural, international, and customary laws are laws that exist in every country. These laws consistently and dynamically shape people's relationships. These rules sometimes complement each other and sometimes negate each other. In some cases, the scope of these rules is completely different. Individuals in society should feel that laws are enacted and enforced through legal institutions. They must feel assured that all people, especially those who are in power, are responsible and accountable to the law. In this context, the term "Rule" in the phrase "RoL" is of great significance (McKay 2015).

Two relevant questions deserving more attention are as follows: What does the word "RoL" mean? How can RoL quality be measured across countries, regions, and states? These two crucial questions are addressed in the following two sub-sections.

3.1 The Concept of Rule of Law

"RoL" is as old as "law" itself. About 4000 years ago, Hammurabi introduced a legal code that incorporated the core elements of modern RoL theory. The term was first used by Daisy in 1885. Radically, the term "RoL" refers to a system in which "law" can impose significant restrictions on the state and its rulers (Peerenboom 2002).

Overall, RoL is one of the eight principles of good governance and one of its most important pillars. Although several definitions have been suggested for RoL in the literature, it is a complex concept and there is no consensus on how to define it. Table 2 presents the definition of RoL from the perspective of some scholars and organizations.

RoL is meant to measure the level of peace of mind and mental security created in society. This means that litigants are convinced that there is always a clear and reassuring solution to resolve legal conflicts. The RoL, as a prerequisite for good governance, is the foundation based on which the relationship between the

Table 2 Definitions of rule of law

Definition	Author/organization
The rule of law means that all individuals, institutions and organizations, the public and private sectors, including the state, are equal, independent in the face of publicly held law and in accordance with international human rights norms and standards, and responsible to laws legislated	United Nations Security Council (UNSC) (2004)
The rule of law is to promote law and order, equality and justice, and peace and to control and manage conflicts	United Nations Development Program (UNDP) (2005)
It shows people's willingness to observe laws and the degree of confidence in the judicial system of a country	World Bank (2005)
The rule of law guarantees the rights of individuals in a fair trial, reduces the uncertainty, increases the predictability of interactions with the government and other members of society, and restricts the behavior of government officials	Tamanaha (2007)
The "rule" in the phrase "rule of law" reflects an interactive relationship and cooperation between one who governs and who follows the rule. It refers to a system that creates laws and regulations to address the needs of the members of the society and uphold their fundamental rights	Wade (2010)
It is the perceptions of the extent to which agents have confidence in and abide by the rules of society, in general, and the quality of contract enforcement, property rights, the police, and the courts, as well as the likelihood of crime and violence, in particular	Kaufmann et al. (2010)
The rule of law is to provide conditions to deal with internal and external threats	World Bank (2011)
The rule of law is the legal framework for promoting economic efficiency within the market mechanism	Karimi (1995)
Rule of law means transparent and secured property rights, community-wide access to PR, and predictable rules for resolving PR-related disputes	Karimi (1995)
The rule of law means ensuring that the PR is impartial and predictable	Karimi (1995)
All persons and authorities within the state, whether public or private, should be bound by and entitled to the benefits of laws which are (1) made publicly, (2) will take effect (generally) in the future, and (3) are publicly administered in the courts	Bingham (2010)
The rule of law means the government of law, not men. In fact, the rule of law refers to a system in which the rules are based on neutral and universal rules	Gomes (2017)
The rule of law is "the subordination of all citizens and all representatives of the state to well-defined and established laws"	Gutmann and Voigt (2018)
Effective rule of law will reduce corruption, eradicate poverty and disease, and protect the public against any small or large injustice	World Justice Project (2019)

Note: Further elaboration is added by the authors

government and the citizens is established. It is informed by any discussion about democracy and democratic institutions.

RoL has both "process elements" and "real and content elements." Process elements, such as the legislative process, should be transparent. Laws must be accessible, be enforced vigorously, promote equality and fairness, and reassure citizens that justice is achieved through an independent process of decision-making. Real and content elements, such as laws, must be made in accordance with international human rights norms and standards and be transparent, accurate, and predictable, i.e., people can predict the legal outcome of their actions (UNDP 2005).

There are two interpretations of RoL (May and Winchester 2018), namely, *thin (narrow, formal)* and *thick (broad, substantive)* interpretations. In fact, the *thick* interpretation embodies the *thin* interpretation as well as other topics such as democracy and fundamental rights (Gutmann and Voigt 2018, p. 68) and has a multidimensional nature (Moller 2018, p. 22).[1]

3.2 Rule of Law Indicators

Many indicators have been proposed to evaluate RoL quality. There are over 70 indicators to assess the quality of RoL in the literature (Nardulli et al. 2013, p. 153). Table 3 lists 25 of these indicators which have been widely used in experimental studies.

In what follows, some of these indicators introduced recently are presented and compared.

The Global Justice Project (WJP) was implemented by the American Bar Association in 2007. As part of this project, the association proposed a new quantitative measure to measure the quality of RoL across countries, known as the WJP-RoL index. This index is based on the *thick* conception of RoL. The index is composed of nine main factors, including Constraints on Government Powers, Absence of Corruption, Order and Security, Fundamental Rights, Open Government, Regulatory Enforcement, Civil Justice, Effective Criminal Justice, and Informal Justice, and 52 sub-factors.[2] These factors are based on the following four notions related to the relationship between government and civil society: The control and balance of government power, the efficiency of the government in its primary functions, and partnership and cooperation between government and citizens, and the absence of abuse of power by rulers.

Some key points must be noted with regard to this index:

1. Some subsets of these nine factors are common between different government and non-government actors and institutions. For example, the freedom of the press is both a constitutional element and one of the non-state elements used to check government power. Similarly, the criminal justice system is concerned

[1] For more on these two interpretations and the advantages of thin interpretation of RoL, see Moller (2018) and Bender (2018).

[2] See Versteeg and Ginsburg (2017) or https://worldjusticeproject.org ›our-work› wjp-rule-law-index for further details.

Table 3 The rule of law indices

Row	Indicator	Sub-indicator	Author/organization
1	Bertelsmann Transformation Index	Rule of Law (BTI)/Property Rights	Bertelsmann Foundation
2	Freedom in the World	Rule of Law (FW)	Freedom House
3	Countries at the Crossroads	Rule of Law (CC)	Freedom House
4	Nations in Transition	Judicial Framework and Independence (NT)	Freedom House
5	Global Integrity Index	Rule of Law and Access to Justice (GI)	Global Integrity
6	International Country Risk Guide (ICRG)	Law and Order (PRS)	The Political Risk Services Group
7	Worldwide Governance Indicators (WGI)	Rule of Law	Kaufmann et al. (2010)
8	WJP Index	Rule of Law Index	American Bar Association
9	Economic Freedom Index	Rule of Law	Heritage Foundation
10	Nardulli, Peyton, and Bajjalieh's Index	$LEGAL_{ORDER}$/ $LEGAL_{INFRA}$	Nardulli et al. (2013)
11	Economic Freedom Index	Legal Structure/Security of Property Rights	Fraser Institute
12	Economic Freedom Index	Legal Effectiveness/Rule of Law	World Economic Forum
13	Henisz's Index	Judicial Independence	Henisz (2000)
14	Cingranelli and Richards's Index	Judicial Independence/Human Rights	Cingranelli and Richards (2010)
15	Howard and Carey's Index	Judicial Independence	Howard and Carey (2004)
16	Apodaca and Keith's Index	Judicial Independence	Apodaca (2004)
17	Feld and Vogt's Index	De Jure Judicial Independence	Feld and Voight (2003)
18	Feld and Voigt's Index	De Facto Judicial Independence	Feld and Voight (2003)
19	Clague et al.'s Index	Contract Intensive Money (CIM)	Clague et al. (1999)
20	La Porta et al.'s Index	Judicial Checks and Balances	La Porta et al. (2004)
21	Heritage Foundation/Wall Street Journal	Property Rights	Heritage Foundation/ Wall Street Journal
22	Wood and Gibney's Index	Political Terror	Wood and Gibney (2010)
23	Voigt's Index		Voigt (2012)
24	Gutmann and Voigt's Index	De Facto Rule of law	Gutmann and Voigt (2018)
25	Wang et al.'s Index	Rule of law Index (for Land and Resources Management)	Wang et al. (2019)

Source: Skaaning (2010), Nardulli et al. (2013); further elaboration is added by the authors

with both the legal process and the fundamental rights of the accused because an efficient criminal system does not punish the innocent.

2. Because of the importance of justice in the informal justice system (Factor 9), the WJP collected data from countries where the formal justice system is weak,

ineffective, and out of reach. However, for a meaningful cross-sectional comparison between countries, this index is not a reliable indicator because the overall scoring and ranking of countries are not taken into account in it.
3. In WJP-RoL, countries are ranked and scored based on 500 variables extracted from the opinions of over 120,000 households and 3800 experts in 126 countries and jurisdictions.

Based on the theoretical findings of Voigt (2012), Gutmann and Voigt (2018) introduced a new index which had the following features: (1) It emphasizes the *thin* conception of RoL; (2) It is based on the de facto criterion; (3) It is a modified version of the WJP-RoL index. Gutmann and Voigt (2018) factored out some of the questions used in the WJP, including those related to law and order, corruption in the medical sector, environmental protection, free media, judicial efficiency, political rights, workers' rights, etc. The rest of the questions were arranged in 11 components, representing 11 dimensions of RoL. Gutmann and Voigt used factor analysis (FA) and converted the scale of questions into 11 zero-and-one components. The index was calculated for 99 countries. The 11 dimensions in the index proposed by Gutmann and Voigt (2018) for RoL are as follows: Universalizability, checks on the executive power, judicial independence, judicial accountability, prosecutorial independence, procedurally fair trials, procedures for imprisonment, basic human rights, corruption-free judiciary, corruption-free law enforcement, and the discrimination-free judiciary.

The advantage of this index is that the substance of the law and its enforcement are reflected in it (Gutmann and Voigt 2018, p. 76).

Some scholars have developed a composite index with all its components. Butkiewicz and Yanikkaya (2006), for example, developed a composite index based on the five major criteria of bureaucracy quality, political corruption, the likelihood of government default, the risk of expropriation by the government, and the overall maintenance of RoL. They also defined some individual components for each of these criteria.

Voigt (2012) proposed a more pragmatic indicator for assessing the quality of RoL by taking into account the most important aspects of the RoL concept. His proposed indicator represents eight different dimensions of RoL, including separation of powers, judicial review, constitutional review, judicial independence, judicial accountability, prosecutorial independence, procedurally fair trials, and basic human rights.[3] Using weak partial correlation coefficients between these eight components, he concluded that each of these dimensions represented different aspects of RoL and should not be conflated into one index. Rather, he added, each of them should be represented by an individual index (Voigt 2012, p. 276).

Nardulli et al. (2013) also examined 18 indices used to evaluate the RoL quality (rows 1–2, 6–7, and 11–22 in Table 3). By comparing these 18 indices against

[3] The detail of calculation and further explanation of this index are given in Voigt (2012, pp. 270–276).

theoretical and methodological considerations, they proposed two new indices, namely, $LEGAL_{ORDER}$ and $LEGAL_{INFRA}$.[4]

The indicators introduced so far in this chapter are used to assess the quality of RoL within the legal and judicial system of a particular country. However, there have been few attempts to evaluate the RoL quality at the regional level. For example, in one study, Yohang and Zhejiang evaluated the RoL quality in some Chinese provinces. Dutta and Kar (2018) also used different indices to measure the RoL at the state level. Indicators used by them included murder, dacoit (burglary), riots, arson, civil police, and armed police.

Recently, there have been few attempts to assess the quality of RoL in specific topics, such as resource and land management, rather than at the national or regional level. Using a Delphi and AHP method, Wang et al. (2019) developed a quantitative index to examine the quality of RoL with regard to resource and land management.[5] Theoretically, the index was based on public administration theories and land and resources laws. They also tested the empirical validity of the index using data related to Zhejiang Province, China.

The increasing prevalence of indicators and their fundamental defections in evaluating RoL quality in cross-country studies led many scholars to review and compare indicators and highlight their limitations. Voigt (2012), for example, cited a list of these limitations in his study. Also, Skanning (2010) reviewed and compared 7 indices (rows 1–7 in Table 3), Nardulli et al. (2013) 18 indices (rows 1–2, 6–7, and 11–22 in Table 3), and Versteeg and Ginsburg (2017) 4 indices (rows 2 and 7–9 in Table 3) related to the assessment of RoL quality. Based on their findings, a number of points must be emphasized here:

1. All the indicators presented differ in scope, conceptualization, measurement, and level of aggregation (Skaaning 2010, p. 449).
2. Nardulli et al. (2013) investigated and compared a large number of indicators based on theoretical (Table 1, pp. 154–157) and methodological (Table 2, pp. 158–160) considerations.
3. In most of the proposed indicators, the conceptualization of RoL is not based on the framework of a particular theory; therefore, these indicators should be used with caution (Skaaning 2010, p. 449). In other words, it is important to consider what field of study is the proposed indicator suitable for and what definition of RoL the indicator is established on.
4. Skaaning (2010) also showed that the seven indicators underlying the level of RoL differed in both form and degree of suitability with regard to different fields of study or subject matters. Thus, it is perfectly possible that using each of them renders different results (Skaaning 2010, p. 449). Indicators also differ in their scope (Ibid., p. 450). In general, it is safe to state that none of these seven indicators are preferred over the other (Ibid., p. 458).

---

[4]The detail of calculation and further explanation of this index can be found in Nardulli et al. (2013, pp. 165–175).

[5]For further detail on the calculation of this index, see Wang et al. (2019, pp. 277–278).

5. Versteeg and Ginsburg (2017) showed that the four indicators employed in their study were different in terms of conceptions and measurement, but they observed that there was a strong correlation between them (Versteeg and Ginsburg 2017, p. 100).
6. WGI-RoL index is the most widely used index in the literature (Gutmann and Voigt 2018, p. 69). Generally, this index assesses the security status of individuals and their property and crime (Haggard and Tiede 2011, p. 676; Nardulli et al. 2013, p. 140). The index has also received the most criticism. The major criticism is that it is survey-based and not based on a "thoughtfully systematized" concept (Gutmann and Voigt 2018, p. 69).
7. The index proposed by Gutmann and Voigt does not have many conceptual flaws among the previous indices and is based on "a rather minimal conception" of RoL (Gutmann and Voigt 2018, p. 68).

3.3 *Some Insights*

Below, some final points to consider when studying the concept of RoL are touched upon:

1. The RoL index does not measure the efficiency or inefficiency of laws or the legal system. Rather, it refers to the extent that laws and the legal system are utilized in organizing a particular society (Wang et al. 2019, p. 277). It, therefore, is necessary to distinguish between the quality of laws and the extent to which these RoL are followed (Voigt 2012, p. 277).
2. Some indicators of RoL, such as the Heritage Foundation and Freedom House, are based on expert opinion and, accordingly, are classified as qualitative and subjective indicators. Other indicators, such as the CIM Index, are quantified by numbers and, thus, are referred to as objective indicators. The difference between these objective and subjective indices has been a subject of considerable debate among scholars (Haggard and Tiede 2011, p. 676).
3. Several indicators have been proposed to evaluate RoL based on the *thin* and *thick* or *de jure* and de facto interpretations of the RoL. Given that the *thick* interpretation encompasses a wide range of RoL and is subject to aggregation bias, Gutmann and Voigt (2018) argued that the *thin* interpretation may lead to more valid results.
4. The *de jure* interpretation does not provide much information about the real world. Therefore, the de facto interpretation appears to be more appropriate (Voigt 2012, p. 276).
5. It is important to distinguish between *ideal* and *more practical* indicators (Voigt 2012, p. 263). There is a huge cost involved in preparing the data. Ideal indicators seem to disregard these costs. However, the challenges and financial constraints facing researchers in collecting data have led them to look for more practical indicators for measuring the quality of RoL. An ideal indicator includes both the quality of the rules and the quality of the organizations implementing those rules (Voigt 2012, pp. 269–270).

4 Property Rights

4.1 The Concept of Property Rights

Classical economists were not blind to the issue of private PR and assumed it given. Smith wrote relatively little about PR in the "Wealth of Nations." Malthus also mentioned PR as one of the most important factors affecting the wealth of nations. However, Ricardo and Mill paid little attention to PR. Say also wrote about PR. Since the mid-1800s, there has been certain skepticism about private ownership. Marx and Engels argued for the abolition of private property. In Keynes's theory, private ownership and the incentives it could create were completely unattended. However, since the mid-1960s, some economists have discussed PR in detail and have in effect revived the role of PR in the economic development process of countries. Arguably, the gradual revival and evolution of PR can be attributed to the Coase, Demsetz, Alchian, Williamson, and North (CDAWN) School. As a concept, PR was founded by Coase (1960), Alchian (1977), Demsetz (1967), North (1973), and Williamson (2000). The intellectual work of these economists falls largely within the framework of the new institutionalism school (Samadi 2008, 2010). The question begging an answer is what PR are.

Ownership, PR, and PR enforcement have different meanings. Ownership means the attribution of an asset or ability to a natural or legal person in a given period of time (Renani 2005, p. 287). Ownership and possession are two different concepts. According to Demsetz (1967), new institutional economists have not been able to distinguish correctly between these two terms. PR enforcement also includes facilitating private contracts and limiting coercion, threats, and expropriation by the government. The PR is a concept that has been of interest to both economists and lawyers. These two groups have different and, sometimes, conflicting and divergent definitions of PR (Cole and Grossman 2001). In this chapter, only the definitions offered by the institutional economists are considered. In a simple and non-technical language, PR can be defined as the right to use, the right not to use, and the right to abuse. However, different scholars in the fields of law and economics have offered numerous definitions of PR. Some of these definitions are presented in Table 4. It is clear from these definitions that PR are rights attached to real property, such as land ownership, personal property, such as physical possessions, and intellectual property, such as industrial PR and copyrights.

4.2 Indicators of Property Rights Measurement

Both individuals and the government may violate an individual's PR and contracts. The government can violate the individuals' and citizens' PR in a number of ways, including expropriation of assets, debt default, money debasing, the prohibition of

Table 4 The definition of PR

Definition	Author
Property rights are rights related to scarcity. It includes all activities that individuals or society are free to do or not do and to own a free asset	Commons (1950)
It is a means of protection against other people who tend to use resources in spite of individual use	Alchian (1965)
It is the right to benefit or harm oneself or others	Demsetz (1967)
There are prescribed behavioral relationships among those who derived products and their use. These relationships and behavioral norms related to goods stipulate that each person should be able to deal with them in their daily interactions with other people or pay for their own inaction	Furuboton and Pejovich (1974)
It is a social institution that determines the range of privileges and special rights granted to persons of a particular asset	Libecap (1989)
It means the right of using the benefits derived from an asset	Bromley and Cernea (1989)
These are the rights, or the ability, to consume properties, earn money from them, and be able to transfer them. Making profits and transferring resources require transactions and transactions should be based on the exchange (transfer) of mutual rights	Barzel (1989)
It is the rights of individuals to benefit from the interests of what they own or from the goods and services of interest they have seized	North (1990)
It is the people's right to use the resources. There are two distinct concepts, one is economic PR (EPR) and the other is legal PR (LPR). EPR is the ability to consume goods, services, and assets or use them indirectly through their exchange. However, LPR rights are granted by the government and support the economic benefit of PR	Eggertsson (1990)
It is the protection of individuals against the government trying to confiscate their assets or reduce the value of their assets	Clague et al. (1997)
It is the most effective means of ensuring civil rights and civil liberties, which are under the authority of the citizens	Pipes (1999)
Ownership is based on the freedom of trade and authority in practice. It is the right to ownership and possession of property. Also, it is the right to transfer property, perform transactions, and deal with it in whatever ways one wishes to	Bovard (2000)
It can be defined through its seven components, namely, the right to possess, the right to use, the right to manage, the right to invest, the right to transfer, the right to protect properties, and liability to execution	Fedderke et al. (2001)
PR are of two kinds: Possessory rights and rights to transfers. Tenure allows people to use things and prevent other people to use them. However, the transfer right allows individuals to transfer of the things they possess to others	Shavell (2003)

Source: Samadi (2008); further elaboration is added by the authors

any transactions except for official transactions, and failure to provide legal infrastructure for impartial execution of contracts or adjudication of PR disputes. There is no single indicator that can encompass all these aspects of PR and contracts (Clague et al. 1996, p. 254). Therefore, in the literature on PR, several indices have been proposed with different considerations behind them.

Some key points regarding these indicators are listed below:

1. Among the descriptive indicators, some are meant to be utilized when evaluating the "*attributes of institutions*" while others are meant to be used to assess the "*performance of institutions.*" For example, the ICRG composite index measures the performance of an institution.
2. Some indicators are related to the "*protective rights*" while others deal with the "*intrusive rights.*" Protective rights protect the ownership and property of individuals against voluntary seizure by the government or other groups whereas intrusive rights allow the distribution of resources among members of a community.
3. The distinction between "*Contract Institutions*" and "*PR Institutions*" must be made clear. Contract Institutions strengthen personal contracts between citizens while PR Institutions protect citizens from property expropriation by the government and other powerful elected officials.
4. Some indicators of PR are subjective and some others are objective. (Samadi 2008, p. 35).

In most studies, subjective indicators have been used. These indicators are based on expert opinion about the status of PR in a particular country or a particular region (Chong and Zanforlin 2004, pp. 339–340). The *ICRG, Business Environment Risk Intelligence (BERI), Business International (BI), Economic Freedom Index (from Freedom House, Fraser Institute, and Heritage Foundation), International PR Index (IPRI), Doing Business (DB) indices,* and the indexes suggested by Haji Ibrahim (1996), Fedderke et al. (2001), Johnson et al. (2002), among others, are all examples of subjective indicators.

These indicators, which are general indicators, are used to assess the "institutional quality" of countries, but some of their sub-components can be used to assess the status of PR in different countries. The following indices and sub-indices belong to this category: *Repudiation of contracts, risk of expropriation, rule of law, and the general and composite index of PR from the ICRG index; the contract enforceability from the Doing Business and BERI indices; all the three sub-indices of the IPRI index; the sub-index of bureaucratic efficiency from the BI index; RoL, individual autonomy, and individual rights from the Freedom House economic freedom index; PR from the Heritage Foundation economic freedom index; and legal security of private PR, the possibility of establishing contracts, and RoL from the Fraser Institute economic freedom index.* A summary of these indicators is provided in Table 5. In addition, Fedderke et al. (2001), Johnson et al. (2002), and Haji Ibrahim (1996) introduced their own subjective indicators (Table 5).

The sub-index of "*repudiation of contracts*" measures the risk of government adjusting or changing contracts in the form of contract cancellation, postponement, or reduction due to changes in government policies.

The sub-index of "*risk of expropriation*" measures the risk of expropriation, i.e., to predate on private property, and indeed the risk of outright confiscation, also referred to as forced nationalization, of private ownership by the government.

Table 5 The property rights indices

Scale	Sub-indicators or components	Types of indicators	Index
Rank: 0–10 Lower scores mean a higher risk of the repudiation of contracts	Repudiation of contracts	International Country Risk Guide (ICRG)	Subjective indicators
Rank: 0–10 Higher scores mean less risk of confiscation and expropriation (Dincer 2007)	Risk of expropriation		
Rank: 0–6 Lower scores show the dependence of physical force or unlawful means to settle claims (Norton 2003; Dincer 2007; Clague et al. 1996; Keefer and Knack 2002)	Rule of law		
To construct such a measure, first, the ranks between 0 and 6 should be multiplied by 6/10 so that some equal ranks emerge. After homogenization, the ranks are tied together and the composite index is achieved between zero to 50 (Clague et al. 1996; Keefer and Knack 2002)	ICRG general and composite index of PR		
Rank: 0–4 Higher values mean less risk to forced nationalization and lower risk of unilateral adjustment to contracts	Contract enforceability	Business Environment Risk Intelligence (BERI)	
Rank: 0–100 Values close to 100 mean better contract performance	Contract enforceability	Doing Business	
Rank: 0–10 Values closer to 10 mean more legal protection	Legal and political environment (LP)	International PR Index (IPRI)	
This scale of this index ranges from 1 (very difficult access to loans) to 7 (very easy access to loans)	Physical PR (PPR)		

(continued)

Table 5 (continued)

Scale	Sub-indicators or components	Types of indicators	Index
This index comprises the protection of intellectual PR (on a scale of 1 = not any support to 7 = the broad support), protection of patents (on a scale of 0 (lowest) to 5 (highest)), plagiarism and copyright (on a scale of 0% (best) to 100% (worst))	Intellectual PR (IPR)		
Rank: 1–10 The lower is the rating, the less protection of private property exists	Bureaucratic efficiency	BI Index	
Rank: 0–4 This scale ranges from zero (lowest) to (highest)	Rule of law (four questions), individual autonomy, and individual rights (four questions)	Economic Freedom Index (Freedom House)	
Rank: 1–5 The higher the rating reflects the weak protection of PR by law	PR	Economic Freedom Index (Heritage Foundation)	
Rank: 1–10 Higher scores indicate greater protection of PR and support from the legal system	Legal security of private PR	Economic Freedom Index (Fraser Institute)	
	The possibility of establishing contracts		
	Rule of law		
Rank: 1–100 Values less than 100 mean less protection of property rights	The seven components reflected in the definition of PR	Fedderke et al. (2001) Index	
Rank: 0–3 Zero means the lack of this type of payment and thus no protection of PR; 3 means that all three types of payment are common and thus a high level of PR protection	A combination of three sub-indices: extralegal payments for licenses, extralegal payments for services, and payments for protection	Johnson et al. (2002) Index	
The occurrence of these events means less protection of PR	Revolutions, coups, and political assassinations	Political Instability Indicators	

(continued)

Table 5 (continued)

Scale	Sub-indicators or components	Types of indicators	Index
Explanation is provided in the text	Index 1: PRS=PR + ED + GP + EL PR: a measure of political rights; ES: a measure of the economic system; GP: a measure of government policy; EL: a measure of economic freedom. Index 2 and Index 3 are based on the estimation of the following equation: PRSi = a + Xib + ei; Based on the Probit and linear models. Xi is a vector of institutional variables	Haji Ibrahim (1996) Indicators	
The higher values in this indicator mean that the enforcement of contracts and PR is more favorable	CIM = (M2−C)/M2 M2 is a broad definition of money; C is money held outside banks and therefore M2−C is non-currency money	Contract Intensive Money (CIM)	Objective indicators
A high inflation rate may indicate the incompetence of the government and the expropriation of private assets (Haji Ibrahim 1996)	Inflation	Other quantitative indicators	
Explanation is provided in the text	Money debasing = [Inflation rate/(Inflation rate+100)]		
Explanation is provided in the text	Levels and changes of taxation, degree of state ownership and private sector credits, and Renani's proposed indices		
Higher values in this index mean that the control over the exchange rate and import restrictions are severe	Black market benefits from foreign exchange rate and currency controls		

Source: Samadi (2008); further elaboration is added by the authors

RoL means that PR should not only be defined but also be enforced. RoL with regard to PR means whether there is a peaceful and secure mechanism for disputing both the process and outcome of adjudication if necessary.

The "*contract enforceability*" component from the Doing Business and BERI indices and the "*repudiation of contracts*" risk component from the ICRG index are measures used to evaluate how contracts are executed. The IPRI index has three core components and ten sub-components. The three core components, namely, legal and political environment group, *physical PR*, and *intellectual PR*, along with their sub-components, directly address the issue of the protection of PR. The sub-index of "*bureaucratic efficiency*" from the BI index comprises three indicators, i.e., legal system efficiency, reduced red tape, and lack of corruption. The efficiency of the judiciary system measures the efficiency and impartiality of the legal environment affecting business activities.

The RoL, individual autonomy, and individual rights from the section related to the Freedom House index of economic freedom are specifically relevant to the protection of PR. The PR component from the Heritage Foundation index of economic freedom includes the following indicators: (1) Judicial independence from government influence, (2) Commercial code-defining contracts, (3) Permission of foreign arbitration on contract disputes, (4) Risk of government expropriation of property, (5) Corruption within the judicial system, (6) Delays in judicial delivery of decisions, and (7) Free accumulation and protection of private property. The Fraser Institute index of economic freedom includes three components as follows: *Legal security of private PR* (i.e., the risk of expropriation and seizure of property by the government), *the possibility of establishing contracts* (i.e., the risk of cancellation by the government), and the *rule of law* (i.e., the presence of legal mechanisms, such as having access to the judicial system, which support the enforcement of the law).

The index proposed by Fedderke et al. (2001) for PR included all the seven components present in a comprehensive definition of PR. These seven components, which together are referred to as the ideal set of PR, included the right to possess, the right to use, the right to manage, the right to invest, the right to protect capital, of the right to transfer, and liability to execution. Johnson et al. (2002), pp. 1339–1340) also created an index called "*Insecure PR*," which was intended to measure the extent to which property rights were protected. This index consisted of three sub-indicators: (1) Payments for licenses, (2) Extralegal Payments for services, and (3) Payments for protection. Indicators such as political instability and its sub-indices, such as the occurrence of revolutions, coups, and political assassinations, can also be used to investigate whether PR are protected in a particular society or country. However, when such events occur, different institutional mechanisms founded to protect PR will be undermined and the entrepreneurs will be exposed to expropriation and possible abuses. As a result, the protection of PR is compromised.

The first index proposed (Index 1) by Haji Ibrahim (1996) was a simple set of institutional indicators, which included a measure of political rights, a measure of the type of economic system, a measure of government policy, and a measure of economic freedom. Each of these components, except for the government policy, can be used separately to measure the protection of the PR index. Haji Ibrahim (1996) introduced Index 2 and Index 3 to provide an objective approximation of the protection of the PR index. According to these two indices, first, the nationalization risk, BERI bureaucratic contracts, and bailouts sub-indices should be summarized; then, the PRS of the country must be determined. When PRS = 1, the country PR system is in the worst situation, and when PRS = 0, it has the best protection of

PR. Since it is assumed that the PRS variable is the sum of the three indices mentioned above for the BERI index and that it has a linear statistical model, the lower the PRS means, the worse the status of the country is based on the BERI index.

Contrary to the subjective indicators introduced and described above, the objective indicators can be calculated based on official data released by the governments. For example, the index which was introduced by Clague et al. (1996, 1999) and referred to as "Contract Intensive Money (CIM)" is an objective index. Other quantitative indices include inflation rates, money debasing, black market rewards, currency controls, tax levels and reforms, state ownership, private sector credits, and Renani's proposed indices. Renani's proposed indices, for instance, comprised the following: The share of public spending in the government budget, the share of public spendings in GDP, the ratio of public spending to government spending, the ratio of public spending to the total expenditure of economic, social, and public affairs, the ratio of public spending in public affairs to that in defense affairs, the ratio of population to the number of transactions registered, the ratio of population to the number judicial authorities, the ratio of population to the number of pending cases, the number of lawsuits reviewed for unpaid checks, the ratio of population to the ratio of checks, and the ratio of transactions registered to the unpaid checks.

The Clague et al.'s (1996, 1999) index, "CIM," is an objective measure of contract enforceability and protection of PR. This index is generally used to measure the quality of governance, institutions, and protection of PR and contracts. A higher ratio in this index means that the enforcement of contracts and PR institutions are more favorable. Inflation and debt default by the government can also be considered as a direct measure of expropriation.

5 Concluding Remarks

The indices introduced above can be used to measure and compare the institutional quality across different countries. These indices can highlight deficiencies, inequalities, human rights abuses, and other problems which need to be tackled in different societies. Institutions have different dimensions. Therefore, there is no consensus among scholars on a single index for measuring the quality of institutions. Some indicators focus on only one dimension while some others are developed to target several dimensions of a phenomenon. Accordingly, various scholars have tried to introduce different indicators that can evaluate these dimensions more precisely, leading to a great number of indicators proposed by different researchers. Nonetheless, this area of study is still an active research field.

Due to the importance associated with the assessment of the growth and development of countries and also the increasing attention paid by the global scientific associations to the impact of institutions on individuals and countries across the world, this chapter was aimed to offer some insights into the measurement of institutional quality. First, in the second section, some indicators that could be employed to measure the quality of legal-economic, social, and political institutions were listed. Then, the most widely used indicators were specified. It is hoped that this chapter contributes to the literature by paying attention to all types of institutions, i.e., economic-legal, social, and political, and introducing the indicators most widely used in empirical studies (Table 1).

It is not possible to describe all the indicators which are used to measure institutional quality in one chapter. The available data indicate that the institutional quality in transition countries is economically-legally, socially, and politically inappropriate. Therefore, to achieve economic growth and development, it is necessary to pay more attention to certain institutions and their quality. These countries are characterized by economic, political, and social uncertainties.

One of the main institutional obstacles to economic growth and development in these countries is the high level of transaction costs. RoL and strong protection of PR against individuals and the government are prerequisites for reducing transaction costs. Promoting the RoL and securing PR will lead to economic, social, and political development. Accordingly, in the third and fourth sections of this chapter, the concepts of RoL and PR, as two legal-economic institutions, were defined and several indicators used to assess them were presented and explained (Tables 2, 3, 4 and 5). This could be considered as another contribution of this chapter. These tables and the explanation following them clearly manifest the complexity of these two concepts, namely RoL and PR. Finally, the authors would like to offer a number of key recommendations on the use of these indicators in experimental studies. To the best of our knowledge, this has not been done in any previous study.

Based on the review of the available literature and the issues discussed throughout this chapter, some important insights about the use of institutional quality indicators, in general, are offered below:

1. These indicators only allow us to have an understanding of the current status of an institutional quality; they do not reveal anything about the institutional change (Institutional change, related theories, and the mechanism for institutional change are discussed in detail in the other chapters of this book).
2. Not all indicators have a common feature. In fact, for each specific institution, several indicators have been proposed. The reason for this variety is that institutions have various dimensions.
3. Some indicators deal with only one dimension whereas some other indicators focus on several dimensions of a phenomenon.
4. Each indicator can be evaluated by three criteria: Validity, reliability, and bias. The issue of reliability and bias is more serious in subjective indicators than in objective indicators. Therefore, it is recommended that the researchers rely more on objective indicators than subjective indicators when trying to measure institutional quality. If that is not possible, they can at least use some objective indicators in addition to the subjective indicators.
5. An appropriate index is an indicator that (a) can be used to evaluate all the functions of institutions, (b) pays attention to the stability of institutions and that institutions are aimed to limit people's behavior to maintain that stability, (c) are more valid and reliable but less biased, and (d) only focus on one particular

aspect of the institutions. None of the indicators described above met all of these criteria. Thus, future researchers are encouraged to develop an index or indices that meet these criteria.
6. It is possible that an index (e.g., WGI index) includes sub-indicators. However, if a researcher looks for a more general indicator, he/she is recommended to use the PCA technique rather than the geometric or arithmetic/simple mean.

The aforementioned points were general in nature and should be borne in mind when using any of the indicators introduced in this chapter.

More specifically, two indicators, namely, RoL and PR, were also discussed in detail in this chapter. When using the RoL index, it is necessary to pay attention to the following points:

1. The RoL index is not a measure of the efficiency or inefficiency of laws and the legal system, it essentially informs us of the use or non-use of laws and the legal system;
2. The proposed indicators are based on de jure and de facto criteria, also thin and thick interpretations of RoL. Studies have shown that it is better to use the proposed indicators based on a de facto interpretation but a thin definition of RoL;
3. Suggested indicators (Table 3) differ in terms of conceptualization, scope, measurement, and aggregation;
4. In general, no indicator is superior to another. The reason is that the scope of the described indicators is different. Therefore, in experimental research, the scope of the study should be specified and then an appropriate indicator which corresponds to that scope should be selected;
5. Although most criticisms have been leveled at the WGI-RoL index, it is still the most widely used indicator.

Also, PR indicators were discussed in this chapter. PR indicators measure the extent to which property rights are protected or violated by the government and citizens. Violations of property rights by the government and others are committed in a number of ways. Accordingly, several indicators have been proposed to measure the quality of this concept in different countries (Table 5). These indicators measure each of the various aspects of the violation of property rights. The following points should be considered when using PR indicators:

1. These indicators can be either subjective or objective;
2. In some indicators, attention is paid to the violation of property rights (contract institutions) whereas in some other indicators, the emphasis is put on the violation of contracts and the expropriation of property by the government (PR institutions).
3. Some indicators describe the attributes of PR while others describe the performance of the PR.

With this explanation, it is clear that even several indicators may not be enough to accurately measure the quality of the protection of PR. In experimental studies, it is necessary to select an appropriate index or indices based on the points raised above. The accurate measurement of institutional quality, in general, and the RoL and protection of PR (in particular) are among the important applications of institutional quality indicators.

Care must be taken in interpreting the results of applied studies. This caveat is particularly important for two reasons: (1) the existence of various definitions and measurement indicators for each concept due to the complexity and multidimensionality of concepts in this area of research and (2) the subjective nature of indicators derived from the survey data.

References

Alchian, A. A. 1977 [1965], "Some Economics of property rights", Il Politico, 30:816–829, reprinted in Alchian, A. A., Economic Forces at work, Indianapolis: Liberty fund.

Alonso, J. A., & Garciamartin, C. (2009). The determinants of institutional quality: More on the debate. Últimos Títulos Publicados, WP03/09.

Apodaca, C. (2004). The rule of law and human rights. *Judicature, 87*(6), 292–299.

Banks, A. S. (1971). *Cross-polity time-series data*. Cambridge: MIT Press.

Barzel, Y. (1989). *Economic analysis of property rights (political economy of institutions and decisions)*. Cambridge: Cambridge University Press.

Beck, T., Clarke, G., Groff, A., Keefer, P., & Walsh, P. (2001). New tools in comparative political economy: The database of political institutions. *World Bank Economic Review, 15*(1), 165–176.

Bender, A. (2018). The promise of a thick view, In Handbook on the Rule of Law, Christopher May and Adam Winchester (Editors), Edward Elgar Publishing, Inc.

Bingham, T. (2010, November). The rule of law. *The British Journal of Criminology, 50*(6), 1202–1205.

Bovard, J. (2000). Property and liberty. Foundation for Economic Education. Articles (Justice) September 1.

Bromley, D. W., & Cernea, M. M. (1989). *The management of common property natural resources: Some conceptual and operational fallacies*. Washington, DC: World Bank.

Butkiewicz, J. L., & Yanikkaya, H. (2006). Institutional quality and economic growth: Maintenance of the rule of law or democratic institutions, or both? *Economic Modelling 23*, 648–661.

Chong, A., & Zanforlin, L. (2004). Inward-looking policies, institutions autocrats, and economic growth in Latin American: An empirical exploration. *Public Choice, 121*, 335–361.

Cingranelli, D. L., & Richards, D. L. (2010). The Cingranelli and Richards (CIRI) human rights data project. *Human Rights Quarterly, 32*(2), 401–424. https://doi.org/10.1353/hrq.0.0141.

Clague, C., Keefer, P., Knack, S., & Olson, M. (1996). Property and contract rights in autocracies and democracies. *Journal of Economic Growth, 1*, 243–276.

Clague, C., et al. (1997). Democracy, autocracy, and the institutions supportive of economic growth. In C. Clague (Ed.), *Institutions and economic development*. Baltimore: John Hopkins University Press.

Clague, C., Keefer, P., Knack, S., & Olson, M. (1999). Contract-intensive money: Contract enforcement property rights, and economic performance. *Journal of Economic Growth, 4*, 185–211.

Cole, D. H., &, Grossman, P. Z. (2001). *The meaning of property rights: Law vs. economics?* ww.google.com

Commons, J. R. (1950). *The economic of collective action*. Madison: University of Wisconsin Press.

Coase, R. (1960). The problem of social cost. *The Journal Of Law & Economics, 3*, 1–44.

Demsetz, H. (1967). Toward a theory of property rights. *The American Economic Review, 57*(2). Papers and proceedings of the seventy-ninth annual meeting of the American Economic Association, May 1967, pp. 347–359.

Dincer, O. C. (2007). The effects of property rights on economic performance. *Applied Economics, 39*(7), 825–839.

Djankov, S., La Porta, R., Lopez-de-Silanes, F., & Shleifer, A. (2003). Courts. *Quarterly Journal of Economics, 118*(2), 453–517.

Dutta, N., & Kar, S. (2018). Relating rule of law and budgetary allocation for tourism: Does per capita income growth make a difference for Indian states? *Economic Modelling, 71*, 263–271.

Eggertsson, T. (1990). *Economic behavior and institutions*. Cambridge: Cambridge University Press, pp. xv+385, $17.95.

Fedderke, J. W., de Kadt, R. H. J., & Luiz, J. M. (2001). Indicators of political liberty, property rights and political instability in South Africa: 1935–97. *International Review of Law and Economic, 21*, 103–139.

Feld, L., & Voight, S. (2003). Economic growth and judicial Independence: Cross-country evidence using a new set of indicators. *European Journal of Political Economy, 19*(2), 497–527.

Furuboton, E. G., & Pejovich, S. (Eds.). (1974). *The economics of property rights*. New York: Ballinger Publishing Company.

Ginsburg, T. (2018). Difficulties with measuring the rule of law. In C. May & A. Winchester (Eds.), *Handbook on the rule of law*. Northampton: Edward Elgar.

Glaeser, E. L., et al. (2004). Do institutions cause growth? *Journal of Economic Growth, 9*, 271–303.

Gomes, T. M. R. C. (2017). Promoting the rule of law in Serbia. What is hindering the reforms in the justice sector? *Communist and Post-Communist Studies, 50*, 331–337. https://doi.org/10.1016/j.postcomstud.2017.10.004.

Gutmann, J., & Voigt, S. (2018). The rule of law: Measurement and deep roots . European Journal of Political Economy, 54, 68–82. https://doi.org/10.1016/j.ejpoleco.2018.04.001.

Haggard, S., & Tiede, L. (2011). The rule of law and economic growth: Where are we? *World Development, 39*(5), 673–685.

Haji Ibrahim, M. (1996). Property rights security and savings behavior in developing countries. Unpublished PhD dissertation, Washington University.

Henisz, W. J. (2000). The institutional environment for economic growth. *Economics and Politics, 12*(1), 1–31.

Howard, R. M., & Carey, H. F. (2004). Is an independent judiciary necessary for democracy? *Judicature, 87*(6), 284–290.

Johnson, S., McMillan, J., & Woodruff, C. (2002). Property rights and finance. *The American Economic Review, 92*(5), 1335–1356.

Karimi, Z. (1995). *Several articles on the institutional barriers to economic development*. Tehran: Majlis Research Center.

Kaufmann, D., Kraay, A., & Mastruzzi, M. (2010). The worldwide governance indicators: Methodology and analytical issues. World Bank Policy Research Working Paper No. 5430.

Keefer, P., & Knack, S. (2002). Polarization, politics and property rights and growth. *Public Choice, 111*, 127–154.

Khalid, U. (2016), Catch-up in institutional quality: An empirical assessment, CREDIT Research Paper, No. 16/04, The University of Nottingham, Centre for Research in Economic Development and International Trade (CREDIT), Nottingham

Kunčič, A. (2014). Institutional quality dataset. *Journal of Institutional Economics, 10*(1), 135–161. https://doi.org/10.1017/S1744137413000192.

La Porta, R., Lopez-de-Silanes, F., Shleifer, A., & Vishny, R. (1998). Law and finance. *Journal of Political Economy, 106*(6), 1113–1155.

La Porta, R., Lopez-de-Silanes, F., Pop-Eleches, C., & Shleifer, A. (2004). Judicial checks and balances. *Journal of Political Economy, 112*(2), 445–470.

La Porta, R., Lopez-de-Silanes, F., & Shleifer, A. (2008). The economic consequences of legal origins. *Journal of Economic Literature, 46*(2), 285–332.

Lele, P., & Siems, M. (2007). Shareholder protection: A Leximetric approach. *Journal of Corporate Law Studies, 7*(1), 17–50.

Libecap, G. D. (1989). Distributional issues in contracting for property rights. *Journal of Institutional and Theoretical Economics, 145*, 6–24.

May, C., & Winchester, A. (Eds.). (2018). *Handbook on the rule of law*. Northampton: Edward Elgar.

McKay, L. (2015). *Toward a rule of law culture, exploring effective responses to justice and security challenges*. Washington, DC: United States Institute of Peace (USIP).

Merry, S. E. (2011). Measuring the world: Indicators, human rights, and global governance: With CA comment by John M. Conley. *Current Anthropology, 52*(S3). *Corporate lives: New perspectives on the social life of the corporate form.* Edited by D. J. Partridge, M. Welker, & R. Hardin (Supplement to April 2011), pp. S83–S95.

Moller, J. (2018). The advantages of a thin view. In C. May & A. Winchester (Eds.), *Handbook on the rule of law*. Northampton: Edward Elgar.

Nardulli, P. F., Peyton, B., & Bajjalieh, J. (2013). Conceptualizing and measuring rule of law constructs. *Journal of Law and Courts, 1*(Spring), 139–192.

North, D., & Thomas, R. (1973), The Rise of the Western World: A New Economic History, Cambridge University Press.

North, D. C. (1990). *Institutions, institutional change and economic performance*. Cambridge, MA: Cambridge University press.

North, D. C. (2001). Needed: A theory of change. In G. M. Meier & J. E. Stiglitz (Eds.), *Frontiers of development economics; the future in perspective*. New York: Oxford University Press.

Norton, S. W. (2003). Economic institutions and human well-being: A cross-national analysis. *Eastern Economic Journal, 29*(1), 23–44.

Peerenboom, R. (2002). *China's long march toward rule of law*. New York: Cambridge University Press.

Pipes, R. (1999). *Property and freedom*. New York/Knopf and London: Alfred A./The Harvill Press.

Renani, M. (2005). Market or nonmarket? A study of market failure in Iranian economy. Plan and budgeting organization publication. isbn: 964-425-011-7.

Renani, M., & Moayedfar, R. (2012). *The decline cycles of morals and economy: The social capital and development in Iran*. Tehran: Tarh-E-No Press.

Samadi, A. H. (2008). Property rights and economic growth: An endogenous growth model. Unpublished PhD Thesis, Faculty of Administrative Science and Economics, Department of Economics, University of Isfahan.

Samadi, A. H. (2010). The position of property rights in economic thoughts and schools with emphasis on new Institutionalist views. *Law Quarterly (Journal of the Faculty of Law and Political Science-Tehran University), 40*(3), 229–246.

Samadi, A. H. (2019). Institutional quality and globalization in developing countries. In N. Faghih (Ed.), *Globalization and development – Economic and socio-cultural perspectives from emerging markets*. Cham: Springer International Publishing. ISBN 978-3-030-14370-1 (eBook). https://doi.org/10.1007/978-3-030-14370-1.

Shavell, S. (2003). Economic analysis of property law. NBER working paper series. http://www.nber.org/papers/w9695

Skanning, S. (2010). Measuring the Rule of Law. *Political Research Quarterly, 63*(2), 449–460. Retrieved from http://www.jstor.org/stable/20721503.

Tamanaha, B. Z. (2007). A concise guide to the rule of law. Florence workshop on the rule of law, Neil Walker, Gianluigi Palombella, eds., Hart Publishing Company, St. John's Legal Studies Research Paper No. 07-0082. Available at SSRN: https://ssrn.com/abstract=1012051.

United Nations Development Programme. (2005). *A practitioner's guide to a human rights-based approach to access to justice* (p. 178). Bangkok: UNDP.

United Nations Development Programme. (2010). *8 governance principles, institutional capacity and quality*. New York: UNDP Bureau for Development Policy One.

United Nations Security Council. (2004). The rule of law and transitional justice in conflict and post-conflict societies: report of the secretary general. Para. 6, S/2004/616.

Versteeg, M., & Ginsburg, T. (2017). Measuring the rule of law: A Comparison of indicators. *Law & Social Inquiry, 42*(1), 100–137. https://doi.org/10.1111/lsi.12175.

Voigt, S. (2012). How to measure the rule of law. *Kyklos, 65*(2), 262–284.

Voigt, S. (2013). How (not) to measure institutions. *Journal of Institutional Economics, 9*(1), 1–26. https://doi.org/10.1017/S1744137412000148.

Wade, C. (2010). Grammar lessons learned: Dependent clauses, false cognates, and other problems in rule of law programming. *University of Pittsburgh Law Review, 72*(2010), 174.

Wang, H., Wang, Z., Chen, J., Chen, J., Guan, N., & Li, G. (2019). Development of rule of law index for state land and resources in China. *Land Use Policy, 81*, 276–290. https://doi.org/10.1016/j.landusepol.2018.10.053.

Williamson, O. E. (2000). The New Institutional Economics: Taking Stock, Looking Ahead. *Journal of Economic Literature, 38*, 595–613.

Wood, R. M., & Gibney, M. A. (2010). The political terror scale (PTS): A re-introduction and a comparison to CIRI. *Human Rights Quarterly, 32*(2), 367–400. https://doi.org/10.1353/hrq.0.0152.

Woodruff, C (2006). Measuring Institutions, In: Susan Rose-Ackerman (ed.), International Handbook on the Economics of Corruption. chapter 3, *Edward Elgar Publishing*, 105–125.

Woodruff, C. (2010, forthcoming). Measuring Institutions. In S. Rose-Ackerman (Eds.), *Handbook on corruption.*

World Bank (2005). Where is the Wealth of Nations? Measuring Capital for the 21st Century. Washington, DC. © World Bank. https://openknowledge.worldbank.org/handle/10986/7505 License: CC BY 3.0 IGO

World Bank (2011). Worldwide governance indicators (WGI) project.

World Justice Project. (2019). *Rule of law index*. Washington, DC/Seattle: WJP.

Part II
Mechanisms of Institutional Change

Institutional Change: Evidence from Some Emerging Market Economies

Masoumeh Alipourian and Ali Hussein Samadi

1 Introduction

In recent decades, many researchers have analyzed the causes of differences in the economic performance of countries. Several reasons have been cited in the literature for this discrepancy. Some scholars have referred to the geographical conditions and the abundance of natural resources, some have pointed to the historical and cultural factors, and others have highlighted the political conditions and modes of governance as potential reasons which can explain the differences between the countries with regard to their economic development. In fact, these scholars consider the differences in the performance of institutions in different countries as an important factor affecting different aspects of development.

Due to the existence of inefficient institutions and a variety of other contributing factors, including corruption, insecure property rights, poor taxation system, limited participation of the legislative branch in decision-making, lack of oversight over the executive branch, and inefficient judicial system, in developing countries, there is a high risk of investment in these countries; therefore, potential investors do not feel confident and secure to invest in these countries (Luiz 2009). Inefficient institutions cause instability and thus increase business costs and have a negative impact on the economic performance. In developing countries, the lack of strong institutions, the unbalanced representation of different ethnicities and races, the weak development of political rights, and the failure to set and implement successful policies have led to racial and ethnic conflicts and damage to the economic structure of these countries (Fosu et al. 2006).

M. Alipourian · A. H. Samadi (✉)
Department of Economics, Shiraz University, Shiraz, Iran
e-mail: asamadi@rose.shirazu.ac.ir

N. Faghih, A. H. Samadi (eds.), *Dynamics of Institutional Change in Emerging Market Economies*, Contributions to Economics,
https://doi.org/10.1007/978-3-030-61342-6_7

The ultimate cause of the differences in the economic growth of countries is the difference in the quality of their institutions. If the rules of the game and the economic incentive system in a society are organized in such a way as to encourage innovations, increased savings, capital accumulation, etc., high per capita income will be achievable (North and Thomas 1973). Different ideologies create different institutions and these institutions will have different effects on growth and development (Acemoglu 2009). For example, North Korean leaders have adopted destructive institutions, such as the nationalization of capital and expansion of public ownership, and anti-market policies, fueled by ideological beliefs, which have stifled the private sector and disrupted market mechanisms in this country. However, South Korea has achieved sustainable development by taking advantage of growth-enhancing institutions, such as protection of private property rights, financial discipline, and market-friendly mechanisms. The importance of property rights and the rule of law in a society depend to a great extent on the historical, geographical, political, economic, and other basic aspects of that society (Rodrik et al. 2004).

The main purpose of this chapter is to review the experience of institutional change in some emerging market economies. Accordingly, this chapter is arranged into four sections. The second section outlines some of the factors influencing institutional change and the barriers to institutional change in some emerging market economies. The dynamics of institutional change in emerging market economies, including East Asian countries, ASEAN region, Latin America, MENA countries, and transition countries, are presented in Sect. 7.3. The final section provides a summary of the findings and conclusions.

The key conclusion of this chapter is that East Asian and Southeast Asian countries have been able to experience significant economic development by implementing economic, cultural, and political institutional changes. However, other emerging market economies have not achieved the same economic development because they suffer from poor institutional quality and their governments are reluctant to bring about radical changes.

2 Factors and Barriers to Institutional Change in Emerging Market Economies

2.1 Factors Influencing Institutional Change

Factors influencing institutional change in different countries can be categorized into economic, social, cultural, and political factors. Table 1 lists some of these factors and their channels of influence.

Institutional change is at the heart of economic change. The institutional environment, in turn, is influenced by economic factors, such as the level of community welfare, level of urbanization, citizens' level of education, and the abundance or lack of natural resources. If the benefits of institutional change outweigh its costs,

Table 1 Factors influencing institutional change

Factors	Channels
Economic	Level of community welfare, level of urbanization, citizens' level of education, abundance or lack of natural resources
Social and cultural	Diversity of language, race, creed, and religion
Political	Political authorities' ability and willingness to implement reforms, interaction with international organizations, and membership in international organizations

Note: Elaboration by the authors

institutions will welcome change (North and Thomas 1973). Economic factors also influence political freedoms. A certain level of welfare is a precondition for democracy. Politically underdeveloped societies tend to follow populist policies, making it difficult for democracy to survive. A successful transition to democracy is typically associated with increased levels of well-being in society (Lipset 1959). Urbanization is considered as an indicator of economic development since countries with lower income levels have more villages in average (De Melo et al. 2001). Education can cause structural change in human capital and prepare individuals to accept the consequences of changes in a changing economic system (Diez and Zvirgzde 2013).

Countries rich in natural resources usually have weak institutions (Sachs and Warner 2001). The abundance of natural resources in these countries is the cause of rent-seeking activities, which can lead to political instability, violence, and even war (Rus 2014). In such countries, the government is dominated by interest groups and corruption is rampant (Beck and Laeven 2006).

Economic performance is influenced by ethical practices, behaviors, and norms. The history of economic development shows that cultural differences are the main causes of differences between countries (Landes 2000). Cultural changes occur slowly and bring about rapid change to formal institutions (Roland 2004). Diversity of language, race, and creed, among the cultural factors, can have a long-term impact on the political and economic institutions in transition countries. The greater the diversity of language and race is, the weaker the socialization and the longer the political divisions would be. Racial discrimination, along with ethnic and racial prejudices, lead to political violence, delayed democratization, and economic instability (Pop-Eleches 2007). The presence of a variety of creeds and rituals in society improves people's tolerance of others' opinions, beliefs, and ideas (Landes 1998) and enhances the efficiency and effectiveness of the government (La Porta et al. 1997).

Institutions are formed by individuals in power (North 1981). The ability and determination of political authorities to introduce reforms is a key factor in bringing about institutional change (Petrovic 2008). Membership in international organizations can be effective in accelerating the necessary economic and political reforms because these organizations oblige their members to abide by the standards of democracy, support civil liberties, and promote a market economy (Di Tommaso et al. 2007). Therefore, the membership of a country in international organizations and the way in which its government interacts with international organizations can influence the institutions in that country and lead to changes in some of those institutions.

2.2 *Barriers to Institutional Change*

Barriers to institutional change in some less developed countries can be categorized into internal and external barriers. Some of the internal barriers include lack of public trust, incompatibility between formal and informal rules, slight benefits of institutional change, defective legal structure, entrenched habits and patterns of behavior, asymmetry in power, and corruption. Globalization and imported institutions are among the external barriers to institutional change (Table 2).

Lack of public trust will limit opportunities for economic growth and innovation (Fellner 2008). High-trust communities experience more investment and thus faster growth. Trust among members of a community reduces transaction costs. Protecting and properly defining property rights can also reduce transaction costs by reducing uncertainty and ensuring efficient allocation of resources (Furubotn and Pejovich 1972).

The interaction between formal and informal institutions can have a significant effect on institutional change. If the changes introduced to the formal institutions are compatible with the informal institutions, the interaction between formal and informal rules will result in lower costs during the transition period.

The incompatibility between formal and informal rules increases the transaction costs and limits the size of the production (Pejovich 1999). The discrepancy between formal and informal rules can lead to the slow implementation of formal rules, increase uncertainty, and impede the whole process of transformation (Tridico 2011). Old habits, past patterns of behavior, ethnic customs and practices, and the existence of old lobbies prevent the emergence and strengthening of new official institutions (Tridico 2011). When a particular formal institutional structure has

Table 2 Barriers to institutional change

Barriers	Dimensions
Lack of public trust	Internal (economic, social, political, and legal)
Incompatibility between formal and informal rules	
Slight benefits of institutional change	
Defective legal structure	
Undesirable habits and patterns of behavior	
Asymmetry in power	
Corruption	
Globalization	External
Imported institutions	

Source: Elaboration by the authors

lower net benefits for the society than an alternative institutional structure, that institutional structure will have negative effects on economic performance, lead to a lower level of welfare in society (Khan 1995), and act as a barrier to institutional change. A defective legal structure reflects lack of government commitment to strengthen and uphold the rule of law, pervasive corruption, and low quality of legislation. Such an ineffective legal structure can lead to political instability and uncertainty (Badawi 2019) and slow the process of institutional change.

Institutions have different stakeholders and any attempt to change institutions will inevitably lead to a group of winners and a group of losers. If losers are strong enough, they will hinder successful institutional reforms (Knight 1992). Powerful political groups seeking to preserve their power have a strong incentive to prevent institutional change, which, in turn, will deprive the society of the potential benefits that could be offered by those changes (Acemoglu and Robinson 2000). Power holders modify institutional arrangements to protect their interests rather than the interests of the society (North and Weingast 1989).

Corruption is one of the causes of institutional failure (Kaufman et al. 2006) because it halts productive activities, hampers the optimal allocation of resources, undermines incentives for innovative activities, and reduces investment and, as a result, economic growth. Powerful stakeholder groups in transition countries manage political processes. The sway of these power groups over decision-making processes, on the one hand, and an increasing sense of insecurity and a lack of economic stability, on the other hand, will ultimately lead to the emergence of different political pressure groups. These groups will try to influence the rules of the game. In addition, the feeling of uncertainty reinforces the position of populist parties. These parties advocate the active role of government in the economy and the adoption of precautionary policies (Pejovich 1999).

Being acutely aware of the pros and cons of globalization, East Asian nations, instead of ignoring it, have made dynamic changes in tandem with the global economy to manage the uncertainty of globalization. In this regard, these countries have upgraded institutional capacity, built effective legal institutions, and accelerated the process of globalization to reap the benefit of it.

Another obstacle to institutional change is the incompatibility of imported institutions with the domestic ones. Imported institutions may not be effective or even worse than the domestic institutions and can cause social outrage and political turmoil. Therefore, in order to make successful institutional changes, imported institutions need to be adapted to the specific needs and conditions of local and informal institutions; alternatively, attempts should be made to adapt the informal institutions to these imported institutions. Establishing effective new institutions by modifying imported institutions or changing domestic institutions to be adapted to the imported institutions is a slow evolutionary process (North 1990).

3 Institutional Changes in Some Emerging Market Economies

Although the institutional framework in developed countries has changed very slowly and gradually, the process of institutional change has not been the same between developing and transition countries (Lin and Nugent 1995).

In this section, the process of institutional change in some emerging market economies, including East Asian countries[1] (China, Japan, and South Korea), the Association of Southeast Asian Nations (ASEAN)[2] (Singapore and Malaysia), some Latin American countries, some Middle East countries, and some countries from the North Africa (MENA), was reviewed and compared with that of some transition countries.

3.1 Institutional Change in East Asian Countries and ASEAN

3.1.1 East Asian Countries

The rapid growth in East Asia has challenged growth elsewhere. The East Asian economy outperforms other regions for many reasons. One of the most primary reasons is the establishment of a high-quality institutional framework in these countries, which has led to better economic performance in these countries and changed them to an economic hub in the world. Compared to other developing countries and emerging market economies, East Asian countries have been more successful in "creating a strong legal environment," capable of protecting property rights and the rule of law. Moreover, the governments in East Asia countries focused on "working with local business activists" that were effective in building trust and confidence in the government. This has played a crucial role in the long-term development of these countries.

From the government's perspective, business activists were important policy elements. As such, economic activists advocated the supportive role of government in establishing and maintaining effective market competition. Encouraging strong relationships in the workplace was also effective in establishing a trusting and supportive relationship between institutions and the economy. The governments of Japan, Korea, Taiwan, Singapore, and China restructured the business environment by eliminating trade-based labor unions and establishing enterprise-based labor unions, which meant that the companies had the opportunity to be directly involved

---

[1] The region includes China, Mongolia, Korea (North and South), Taiwan, Japan, Hong Kong, and Macao Autonomous Regions.

[2] The ASEAN was established on August 8, 1967, and includes ten countries. Founder countries included Indonesia, Malaysia, the Philippines, Singapore, and Thailand. Later, five countries joined the association including Brunei (1984), Vietnam (1995), Laos (1997), Myanmar (1997), and Cambodia (1999).

in the process of decision- and policy-making (World Bank 1993). This increased confidence instilled in companies by the government was one of the key factors in building an effective institutional environment in these countries.

East Asian governments fulfilled their supportive and facilitating role in two stages. In the first stage, to enhance the functioning of domestic businesses, they provided a financial incentive for business development, protection of intellectual and physical properties, and enforcement of regulatory laws and policies. Secondly, they attracted foreign direct investment (FDI) to effectively import the knowledge and technology needed by the domestic firms. Obviously, the prerequisite for attracting FDI is to create a legal and secure environment to protect property rights. East Asian countries have done so successfully (Rodrik et al. 2004). As such, the newly developed institutional framework became a system of concepts and criteria which determined the course of development for business activities.

Initially, East Asian countries focused on small- and medium-sized enterprises (SMEs), but later on, they also sought to increase institutional quality in both domestic and foreign-owned firms. Japan, Korea, Taiwan, and China were successful in extending financial support to SMEs. As of 1989, these firms, i.e., SMEs, accounted for about 52% of the value added and sales of industry sectors. In Korea, about 52% of all employment was in these firms in 1988. In China and Taiwan, due to the government support, SMEs accounted for about 90% of firms in both public and private sectors (World Bank 1993). Thus, one of the factors which led to successful institutional change in East Asian countries during the transition period was the special attention paid to the institutional growth of small- and medium-sized businesses, both domestic and foreign businesses. This facilitated the transfer of knowledge and technology.

Government intervention in East Asia to support market was not meant to give rise to a self-regulating market. Rather, the government played a complementary role to the market without undermining market discipline. The goal was to develop the industry so that it could compete internationally. To this end, East Asian countries needed strong leaders and governments. The Japanese government, by establishing heavy industries in the 1950s, and the South Korean government, by establishing the telecommunications industry, facilitated the transfer of technology into their countries and increased the competitiveness of their industrial enterprises.

Another successful initiative in East Asian countries was the establishment of export-based firms. From 2008 to 2014, among the top 15 exporting countries in the world, five were from Asia, including China, Japan, South Korea, Hong Kong, and Singapore. The largest share of exports from all over the world in 2014 belonged to China.

The following is a review of the successful experience of some East Asian countries in bringing about institutional change.

The Case of China

China is the most populous country in the world that was a developing, poor, rural, backward country until the 1970s. During three decades, by providing a favorable business environment, China increased the share of the private sector from less than 20% at the end of the 1970s to more than 70% in 2004. Although it had to follow a centralized planning system, China was able to achieve rapid growth by transforming its economy into a market economy. Economic change in China took place in two phases: during the first phase, innovative institutions were created, and, during the second phase, the first steps were taken to establish a market system, which could work best with international institutions. In the first phase, and given the fact that existing institutions were weak at the time, the government played an active role by being directly involved in corporate governance through corporate control and ownership. In the second phase, the government focused on the creation of market-oriented institutions, reduction of its tenure through privatization, corporate divestiture, and job security (Stiglitz and Yusuf 2001). Indeed, without privatization and simply by removing barriers to the private sector and creating a friendly business environment, China could transform its state economy into a nonstate economy and consequently save more than 500 million Chinese from absolute poverty. In the 1980s and 1990s, China was able to change the role of academic and scientific institutions, including universities, to promote academic research and encourage R&D collaboration between these institutions and the business sector.

University managers in China were told that they would be responsive for their decisions and actions, and they soon recognized that deviating from investment goals would further delay achieving the desired goals set by the government (Zhou 2012; Rhoads et al. 2014). China's gross domestic expenditure on R&D (GERD) has grown rapidly over the past two decades due to enhanced international cooperation. This was due to increased business enterprise expenditure on R&D (BERD) and the focus on industrial research. This strategy improved industrial efficiency (Zheng and Tong 2014) and promoted industrial innovation (McKinsey Global Institute 2015).

Anti-corruption efforts in China also restricted predatory practices in business (Wedeman 2012). During this period, the private sector became more vibrant and productive and the official statistics indicated that the private sector took a larger share of the Chinese economy (Lardy 2014). This impressive record of achievement in China could be attributed to the cooperation between the government officials and members of the academic and business community (Jonkers 2010). In addition, university-industry collaboration in China resulted in creative solutions, offered by universities, to the problems which the industry had to deal with (Block 2011). The Chinese government alone could not facilitate economic development in such a vast country. The continual collaboration between government reformers, successful entrepreneurs, and domestic and foreign investors helped China to meet the challenge of reform (Zweig 2002; Howell 1993; Pei 1994). These efforts led to widespread institutional change in China and fostered its increasing economic development.

The Case of Japan

Japan has changed steadily over the past 150 years. During two long periods, i.e., 1895–1914 and 1919–1932, the average per capita growth rate in Japan was less than 0.6%. However, in the wake of these two periods of recession, and in spite of the war, Japan achieved strong economic growth (Weinstein 2001). From 1953 to 1973, the annual economic growth rate in Japan averaged 8.2%. Such a development was only made possible within a specific institutional framework, based on which the male workforce in industrial and service enterprises were provided with a lifelong employment, corporate governance institutions were reformed, government control over the capital flows was tightened to ensure the allocation of funds to projects related to infrastructure and industries prioritized by the state, technology policymaking was framed in a way that could ensure the distribution of technologies among Japanese industries, and a close cooperation was established between the trade unions and industry without the constraints imposed by the state bureaucracy (La Croix and Kawaura 2005). The labor unrest of the 1950s led to the creation of new labor market institutions, such as lifelong employment. The system of lifelong employment was originated from a balanced relationship between the managers, the workers, and the government. It was reinforced through complementary institutions, such as government welfare policies, labor law, corporate governance, social norms, family values, and the education system. Since then, the employment system has managed to survive both supply-side and demand-side shocks in the labor market although in the economic crisis of the 1990s, this system was seriously threatened (Ono and Moriguchi 2004).

Another important challenge facing the Japanese labor market was how to deal with the trade unions. The emergence of "bargaining on the basis of productivity" at the enterprise level, the institutionalization of the Shantou bargaining system for wages, and job security paved the way for the creation of trade unions. This was done through the lifelong employment system and the adjustment made to the workforce institutions. The initial shift in the Japanese labor market was the result of a prolonged economic crisis in Japan during the 1990s and increased pressure of international competition. Subsequent changes in this era happened as a result of the efforts made by the organized labor force to transform the Japanese view from a collective communal system into a reassuring individual welfare system through more direct government interventions (Carlile 2004).

The efforts made by the Japanese government to engage in structural reform during the decades following World War II is an important feature of the Japanese post-World War II economy. These reforms ranged from the initial privatization of coal, silk, and flax, processed foods and toys during the 1970s and the 1980s to automobiles, electronics, steel, and semiconductors. The subsequent changes in Japan took place in the area of finance, insurance, computer software, and telecommunications (Weinstein 2001).

Following the resumption of growth in the early 1980s, the Japanese government implemented numerous privatization, decentralization, and deregulation programs to achieve balanced budgeting and slow liquidity growth to reduce and control inflation. In the mid-1980s, a wave of privatization occurred in Japan, including the privatization of Japanese National Railway (JNR) in 1987, shipping lines in 1985, and telephone lines in 1985. During the 1990s, major decentralization occurred in the freight, airline, taxi, telecommunications, and electricity industries. In 1997, the Japanese government abolished the law on large-scale retail stores and delegated the power to local governments to regulate these stores (La Croix and Kawaura 2005). Financial reforms took place between 1998 and 2001, with decentralization in the financial and banking sectors (Hoshi and Kashyap 2001).

In April 2001, the Japanese government reformed its investment and lending program. Since 2002, the Japanese government has been working hard to settle outstanding debts in the banking system. Loans were consolidated with the commercial banks in Japan. In 2004, the post office acquired legal personality and its privatization was discussed in 2005. In Japan, the amendments to the laws on "corporate legal personality," "the principle of complementarity between corporate legal personality and other entities," and "the relationship between corporate legal personality and corporate governance" were introduced in the early 1990s. Thus, the Japanese corporate law became more consistent and responsive to the demand-side incentives, but introducing changes in the corporate governance was more challenging because that required more changes in the shareholder distribution, capital markets, and management incentive structures (Milhaurpt 2004). The Japanese government also facilitated the export of high-tech industrial goods to other businesses around the world through trade liberalization and free trade agreements.

The Case of South Korea

After the Korean independence from Japan in 1945, Korea was divided into two parts, the North and the South. Prior to the separation of the two parts, South Korea and North Korea were similar in terms of history, geography, climate, culture, access to world markets, and shipping costs, but North Korea was far richer in natural resources than South Korea. Given the common features between the two countries, the only reason that can be cited for the differences in their levels of economic performance and development is the presence of very different institutions in these two countries. In fact, the two countries chose two completely different sets of institutions and styles of governance. North Korea abolished property rights under the Soviet Union and China and disregarded the role of market in economic decisions. In contrast, South Korea sought to prosper economically by maintaining a system of private ownership and strengthening market-friendly mechanisms. Reforms in South Korea largely took place in the 1980s and the 1990s in both the financial and industrial sectors when the government interventions were eliminated. In the early 1990s, the South Korean government deregulated the market in order to increase economic efficiency and promote competition in the financial market (Lee 2005).

The president of South Korea stated that the Korean economy was based on an open and pure market economy, not a government-driven growth model. Some critics attribute the failure of post-crisis reform to the early abandonment of the state-driven growth model, which, by the way, was not the ultimate goal in establishing a free market economy (Crotty and Lee 2001).

South Korea fully recovered from the financial crisis of 1997 and its economy has grown rapidly since 1999. As Jwa (2003) pointed out, the most effective and beneficial factor in leading Korea to prosperity was market competition and not formal enforcement of government rules. However, one of the limitations of these processes was that the newly established institutions were public goods and therefore could not rely solely on market forces. An open market required some specific regulations that allowed completion in the market and were applicable only to the market forces (Toye 1995). Accordingly, the challenge of institutional reform was to find a framework that could foster economic growth but may not necessarily be in line with the institutional framework of other countries.

3.1.2 The Case of ASEAN Members

The ASEAN is the only successful post-EU regional cooperation union which was established in 1967 with the membership of five countries, including Indonesia, Malaysia, the Philippines, Singapore, and Thailand, and another ten members joining the union in the following years. The main goal of the union was to improve regional stability through economic and practical cooperation. Over the decades since the establishment of ASEAN, this union has had its ups and downs. At the end of the 1990s, ASEAN faced numerous development challenges. Regionally, with the financial crisis coupled with the political turmoil in Indonesia, the debate over the credibility of ASEAN and its ability to overcome looming crises intensified. The financial crisis showed that ASEAN countries could rely on foreign assistance, especially from the IMF, to solve their financial woes (Hernandez 2002). The inclusion of new ASEAN members, which included all South Asian countries, presented ASEAN with new challenges, especially in relation to the development gap between its new and old members. ASEAN members realized that the pressure of globalization was eroding their competitiveness in the global market and that the solution to overcome that problem was greater economic convergence. At the same time, ASEAN lost its competitiveness to China, which had quickly become an economic power. Finally, the changes started to occur when the political change took place in Indonesia and it headed ASEAN in 2003. Indonesia proposed an action plan for change that transformed ASEAN. According to the proposed plan, the first step was to transform ASEAN into the ASEAN Security Community (ASC). Indonesia offered political and security cooperation, based on democracy, human rights, peace, and reconciliation, which required ASEAN members to change their views of government and its role in the society and establish a new institutional structure. Indonesia's efforts to introduce meaningful reforms during its presidency of ASEAN paved the way for major changes and institutionalization in ASEAN. Eventually ASEAN members agreed to establish the ASEAN 2020 community based on the following three pillars: the ASEAN Economic Community (AEC), the ASEAN Political-Security Community (APSC), and the ASEAN Socio-Cultural Community

(ASCC). Based on new goals and within the framework of partnership, ASEAN soon realized that it needed to rebuild or change existing institutions in its member states. The most significant of these changes was the announcement of the ASEAN Charter in December 2007, reflecting ASEAN's will to strengthen the institutional structure in its member states by adhering to the principles of simultaneous sovereignty and integration despite regional differences (Sukma 2014). Interventions by the governments of Thailand, Malaysia, and Indonesia played an important role in the successful development of industries and agriculture in these countries (Stiglitz and Yusuf 2001).

The process of institutional change in some of the ASEAN countries is described and discussed below.

The Case of Singapore

Singapore was a British colony since 1819, playing the role of shipping fleet between Britain, India, and China. During this period, it was able to attract large numbers of immigrants from China and India. After independence from the United Kingdom in 1959 and Malaysia in 1965, Singapore had no assets except the deep harbor. It was a small and poor country of tropical lands with scarce natural resources, poor drinking water, rapid population growth, substandard housing, and conflict between different racial, ethnic, and religious groups. There was no compulsory education and there were few high school and college graduates and skilled labor. It had no economy, no army, and no water or energy. Singapore seemed unable to become a country with an advanced economy and trained human resources. The political and economic risk of working with such a country was high for more advanced countries. However, Singapore was one of the Southeast Asian countries that could transform itself from a less developed country into a modern industrialized country and a global hub for trade, investment, and tourism. It is one of the third-world countries which transformed into a first-world country, symbolizing the successful transformation of East Asian and Southeast Asian countries (Yew 2000).

How could Singapore undergo such a sea change? The first prime minister of Singapore, Lee Kuan Yew, pursued two objectives: building a modern economy and shoring up the image of Singapore among other nations. To achieve the first goal, he attempted to stimulate economic growth and higher employment. In the 1960s, the emphasis was on attracting foreign labor-oriented industries which needed less-skilled labor force to increase employment among less-skilled labor. In the 1970s and the 1980s, the emphasis was on attracting foreign labor-oriented industries which required more-skilled labor force. Since the mid-1990s, Singapore has played an important role in the global knowledge economy by encouraging industries that are based on R&D and innovation (OECD 2010). By adopting a strategy of export-oriented industrialization, using political legitimacy, and increasing institutional capacity, the Singapore government has been able to accelerate its process of globalization and capitalize on its benefits.

The development-oriented government of Singapore has always regarded political credibility and stability as the prerequisite for attracting global capital and sought to reduce economic uncertainty caused by globalization. In both labor and capital markets, the government has had the best governance and consistently considered flexibility and domestic interests to attract global capital. As globalization has made capital more mobile, Singapore rushed to seize the opportunity and addressed the problems posed by globalization through the establishment of domestic legal institutions (Wai-Chung Yeung 2005).

Recent government strategies have included efforts to increase job support by reforming the Central Provident Fund (CPF), hand over power slowly to second-generation political officials, and reform government policies related to economic activities through privatization and cooperation between government, law firms, and the Chamber of Commerce. Due to the economic policies adopted by the government, this country has witnessed rapid and surprising growth and transformed into a developed economy with high per capita income.

Singapore has a free market and a friendly business environment. The Singapore government is effective, flexible, and accurate in implementing reform programs. An important feature of Singapore economic and political development is "imagination, design, and presentation."

The small size of Singapore and its political stability have made it a large and stable global city. Singapore with its small and narrow domestic market needs to be integrated into the global economy, but to cope with the global crises and uncertainty caused by the global economy, innovation must continue.

Singapore education system has evolved over the past 40 years to fit the changing economy. Its education system has gained the highest ratings in the last few decades. One of the competitive advantages of Singapore education system has been its ability to match the demand for training with the skills needed.

Singapore has ethnic, racial, linguistic, and religious diversity, but with the mixed settlement of these different groups in government-built buildings, the government has prevented separation and encouraged them to coexist. Loyalty, striving for betterment, teamwork, discipline, integrity, philanthropy, social courtesy, and an emphasis on the public good are the characteristics of Singapore society and government (OECD 2010).

The Case of Malaysia

Malaysia is currently one of the most developed Southeast Asian countries with a high cultural diversity, which before the 1980s affected the cultivation of mussel, pineapple, and cabbage fields, and countryside rural areas and villages. The per capita income in Malaysia was less than 100 dollars, and the country was extremely unsafe due to the internecine religious conflicts between the 18 races in this country. In 1981, Mahathir Mohamad became prime minister of Malaysia and, by mapping out the future of Malaysia up to 2020, succeeded in transforming Malaysia into a developed country. He prioritized public education and scientific research, earmarked the largest amount of capital to public education and technical skills, eradicated illiteracy, and, most importantly, promoted English language training and learning. He converted military barracks, which were made by Japanese in Malaysia during World War II, to tourism attractions, paving the way for Malaysia to reap huge revenues over ten years from tourism.

In the 1980s and the 1990s, Malaysia managed to transform its economy from an economy which was dependent on agriculture into an industrial economy stimulated by production. In 1996, with a growth rate of 0.46% in electricity and electronic products, it could become one of the exporters of such products in the world.

By introducing and implementing the necessary institutional changes, Mahathir Mohamad opened the economy to foreign investment, and the giant Petronas Twin Towers Kuala Lumpur City Center has turned over million dollars of transactions each day since its establishment. He was able to establish the new federal administrative capital in Putrajaya, a city with two million people near the commercial capital of Kuala Lumpur. Furthermore, due to his efforts in creating the right infrastructure to attract investment from home and abroad and investing in heavy industry and export development, the Malaysia GDP grew quickly and averaged 7% in the 1980s and the 1990s.

In recent years, Malaysia has been under pressure to make changes to its political, economic, and social institutions, and the agents of change have come to realize that reforms are not possible without institutional change and higher institutional quality. In the 2018 election, the majority of voters voted for the Pakatan Harapan coalition (PH), a defeat and blow to the Barisan Nasional (BN) coalition which had ruled since independence in 1957. Some of the PH coalition plans, which reflect the expectations of most voters, included limiting the prime minister's power, improving the performance of the financial management systems run by the government, and enhancing the transparency of the financial system(s) to combat corruption and fairer allocation of resources. Some of the strategies introduced to achieve these goals included ensuring the independence of the legislature, enhancing the role of parliament and improving the quality of the law-making processes, reforming the judiciary to eliminate the influence of politicians in selecting judges and their decision-making, and empowering the judiciary to monitor the government its decisions (Lee 2018).

Table 3 lists some of the important institutional reforms in East and Southeast Asia countries.

3.2 *The Case of Latin American Countries*

In Latin America, institutional change is occurring rapidly. In these countries, the rules are very volatile and change before they are implemented. In fact, due to the low cost of change for powerful actors in these countries, there is no sustainable model for institutional change in them. In some countries, such as Argentina, Bolivia, and Peru, the governments have undertaken rapid institutional reforms,

Table 3 Some important institutional reforms in East Asian and Southeast Asian countries

Reforms	Effects
Development of human capital and its accumulation through implementation of appropriate training programs	Upgrading technology, enhancing the capacity of businesses, and achieving successful growth
Changing the role of academic sciences and universities to promote research and encourage R&D efforts	Increasing efficient industrial capabilities and increasing innovation
Change the incentive structure	Stimulating economic growth
Making the economy competitive and not imposing formal rules by the government	Boosting economic growth
Collaboration between government, universities, and industry	Increasing the share of the private sector, more productive and vibrant private sector
The complementary role of governments for the market	Development of industry and agriculture, and to compete on the international stage
The fight against corruption	Limiting the predatory-friendly activities
Financial support to SMEs and increase institutional quality in both domestic and foreign-owned firms	Development of small- and medium-sized businesses, increase the added value of the industrial sector, transfer of knowledge and technology
Creating a legal and security environment for property rights	Protection of property rights, enhance the performance of domestic firms, and attracting foreign direct investment
The elimination of trade-based trade unions and the creation of enterprise-based trade unions	Build the institutional environment needed to rise and grow
Government collaboration with local business activists	Build confidence and faith in the government and create effective competition in the market
The role of government support and facilitate the implementation of a program of financial incentives for business development, protection of intellectual and physical property, enforcement of regulatory laws and policies	Enhancing the performance of domestic enterprises, attracting foreign direct investment and thus transferring the knowledge and technology required of domestic enterprises
Establishing heavy industries and telecommunications	Transfer of technology into the country and increase the capacity of industrial enterprises
Building legal internal institutions and enhancing institutional capacity, enhancing political credibility and political stability, and reducing economic uncertainty	Exploit the benefits and opportunities created by globalization

Source: Elaboration by the authors

including large-scale privatization, sweeping financial regulatory reforms, and the reconstruction of foreign trade and investment regimes belonging to the previous dictatorial regimes. Reforms are introduced and implemented hastily in Latin America; consequently, these reforms fail to bring about the same desired results achieved in advanced industrial countries following institutional reforms. In addition, the new market institutions established in some countries are immediately replaced with some other institutions. In Venezuela, Argentina, Bolivia, and some other countries, various market-oriented institutions were established during the 1980s and 1990s, but they were either dissolved or replaced in the 2000s (Levitsky and Murillo 2012).

Argentina's labor law is the most durable institution compared to other institutions in this country; however, the financial system, the payment system, trade and investment rules, and other economic and social institutions have changed more than once during the 1990s and 2000s (Murillo 2005). Similarly, in Peru, civil service law and other bureaucratic rules were enforced through the Central Bank and the Ministry of Finance, but other laws were not enforced (Dargent 2012). In fact, well-designed institutions that can bring about great change are threatened by powerful stakeholder actors, whereas those institutions that are not well-designed and do not interfere with the interests of the interest groups have been durable. The Chilean constitution, for example, is an institution with limited social rights, so it is both enforceable and durable. Nevertheless, Argentine Constitution of 1949, in which the rights of workers and the elderly, as well as the right to family life, education, and property, were guaranteed was short-lived due to the reasons touched upon above (Levitsky and Murillo 2012).

In Latin America, the interest of institutions that are expected to stimulate economic growth and development is generally at odds with those of citizens, leading to poor public service delivery. In these countries, limited contract enforcement, economic uncertainty, manipulation of the judicial system, corruption, bribery, tax evasion, poor property rights, and weak institutions, as instances of ineffective institutional arrangements, have made these countries unattractive to investors due to high investment risks (Charnock 2009; Fosu et al. 2006). In these countries, due to the fact that economic freedom is limited, labor market rules and regulations are inefficient, and foreign investment is woefully low, little attention is paid to technological innovation. The prevalence of corruption has slowed down their economic growth and resulted in poor performance. In addition, a largely unskilled and uneducated labor force and the lack of institutional arrangements, such as laws and regulations, have created an informal economy in these countries (Dell'Anno 2010). Developing countries in Latin America have a low level of public trust, which has made it difficult to promote entrepreneurship and create opportunities for economic growth and innovation (Fellner 2008).

Another barrier to institutional change in Latin American countries is the changes made in the electoral system. For example, Venezuela experienced 13 different electoral laws during the years 1958 to 1998 (Remmer 2008). Argentina experienced 34 electoral system reforms in its 24 provinces from 1983 to 2003 (Calvo and Micozzi 2005). Contrary to this, the electoral systems and rules in developed countries are stable (Lijphart 1994).

Studies on Colombia and Venezuela during the years 1995–1997 showed that democracy was severely weakened in both countries and that political corruption was a major problem in both of them (Fellner 2008). As a Latin American country,

Argentina also failed to achieve significant economic growth due to the political instability and turmoil beginning in the 1950s (Doğruel and Doğruel 2006). Among the Latin American countries, Chile and Brazil have been more successful than other Latin American countries in carrying out institutional reforms and changing their institutional structures, while Venezuela has had the weakest institutional structure.

3.3 *The Case of MENA Countries*

Empirical and theoretical studies have shown that poor institutional quality has a significant negative impact on the economic performance of the MENA countries and has led to uprising, overthrow of regimes, and political instability. Despite having abundant natural resources (62% of world gas reserves and 65% of world oil reserves), Middle East countries suffer from a lack of investment and slow economic growth. In these countries, political instability, which is deteriorated by terrorism, regional wars, and poor governance, has exacerbated economic uncertainty. In African countries, continuing political and economic uncertainty, inefficient judiciary, corruption, bribery, tax evasion, poor protection of property rights, and inefficient institutions have made these countries unattractive to investors.

In the Arab world, the overall picture is mixed. In other words, in some of these countries, institutional reforms have been done precipitously, followed by political and financial crises, while in some other countries the institutional reforms have been introduced gradually. In some cases, bottom-up and top-down approaches have been adopted to implement institutional reforms. In most of these countries, contrary to the Southeast countries, the private sector comprises a small number of large corporations and is not a key driver of economic growth. Due to the protectionist policies of the government in such countries, only a small number of firms have access to official capital and government support. The export activities of the private enterprises are limited because these countries primarily export oil and the companies allowed to export oil are state-owned.

The poor performance of institutions, instability, and selective enforcement of laws have resulted in reduced investment, poor business environment, and reduced productivity growth in MENA countries. Institutional uncertainty is also an impediment to business growth and consequently employment growth in the region (Sandri and Alshyab 2018).

The World Bank Doing Business Report (2020) indicates that most of the reforms implemented to facilitate doing business have been implemented in MENA countries, with 57 regulatory adjustments. The Ease of Doing Business Index in MENA countries has increased by an average of 1/8 points. According to the report, Middle East economies, notably those of Jordan, Bahrain, Saudi Arabia, and Kuwait, have had the most regulatory and trade facilitation reforms in the world in the past year (World Bank 2020).

Iran, as a member of OPEC and a member of MENA countries, holds about 16% of world gas reserves and 14% of world oil reserves but still accounts for less than 1% of world GDP. Some scholars have argued that the factors behind Iran's failure to achieve economic development and growth are endogenous and have to do with the institutional functions (Dadgar and Nazari 2018). One of the factors affecting domestic and foreign investment and consequently economic growth in any country is its legal system and institutions. Among these institutions is the business environment. The ambiguity in trade policies is one of the problems that prevail in Iran's business environment. According to the International Bank for Reconstruction and Development (IBRD), Iran ranked 127th, with 58.5 out of 100 possible points, among 190 countries. Iran ranked 152th in the world in terms of business ease in 2014; then, its rank improved to 130th and 117th in 2015 and 2016, respectively, but it declined to 128th in 2019 according to the 2019 Ease of Doing Business Report. In fact, for the first time since 2016, Iran has been able to reverse its downward trend in ease of doing business rankings in 2020. According to the 2020 World Bank Doing Business Reforms section, the cost of "ownership registration" increased as a result of a 0.4% increase in property tax rates. Despite a 0.4% increase in spending in 2020, Iran's rank in this index improved by 20 points. The creation of electronic databases, the systematization of processes in Iranian institutions and agencies, and, more importantly, the coordination between various government ministries and judicial system to exchange private business information are expected to improve Iran's position in ease of doing business ranking and other economic rankings in the coming years. Bankruptcy law reform and an increase in the number of small shareholders can also have a positive impact on Iran's economic reputation in the world business community.

3.4 The Case of Transition Countries

In the 1980s and 1990s, following the end of communist rule, the countries in Central and Southern Europe and the Soviet Union began to undergo a fundamental transformation by leaving behind the communist system, electing a form of representative government, and reorganizing the legitimacy of their governments (Judt 2005). The gap between the economies of these countries and the democratic market economies was very wide. Given that these countries inherited deeply entrenched systems of ineffective governments, their experience and understanding of democracy were limited. Thus, it has been suggested this group of countries had a "unique historical experience" of democracy (Kornai 2006).

Caliński and Harabasz (1974) divided these countries into four groups based on their fundamental differences in institutional quality. The first group, which is also the largest group, comprises countries from Central European and Baltic States (CEBS), such as Croatia; the countries in this group are similar to other post-communist countries with regard to their economies. The second group includes Albania, Bulgaria, Georgia, Moldova, Romania, and Ukraine, with even worse institutional quality than that of the previous group. The third group includes countries with low-quality institutions, such as Armenia, Azerbaijan, Kazakhstan, Russia, Georgia, and Tajikistan. The fourth group comprises three countries, including Belarus, Turkmenistan, and Uzbekistan; these countries have financially autocratic and repressed economies which impede the transition to a market economy.

When the Soviet Union collapsed, the Russian Soviet Federated Socialist Republic, with its planned economy and state sovereignty, instituted communist-type institutional infrastructure and structures for the independent states. These institutional infrastructures and structures were based on excessive bureaucracy, weak rule of law, and poor protection of property rights and resulted in rampant corruption and inefficient market institutions in most post-Soviet countries. The market institutions in these countries were not ready to implement the necessary changes after the collapse of the Soviet Union and, consequently, failed to build trust in the government. In the former Soviet Union, the state was considered above the law; thus, it could commit any crime, take bribes, and breach the law whatever it wanted (Nagy 2002).

The process of change in Central Asia, Eastern Europe, and the Caucasus, including Southern Russia, Georgia, Armenia, and Azerbaijan, varied considerably. In most of these countries, especially in Belarus and Russia, increased economic freedom was associated with and followed by less political freedom, whereas in countries from Central Europe and the Baltic States, and Southeast Europe, in most cases, political and economic freedoms were increased simultaneously in 1993–1994, indicating that political freedom and economic growth are inextricably linked.

From the perspective of Estrin et al. (2009), Central and Eastern Europe countries (CEEC), including the Baltic republics of Estonia, Latvia, and Lithuania, had a stronger institutional, cultural, and legal framework for a successful transition to market economies because they already had successful capitalist economies. During the nineteenth century, when these countries attempted to adopt EU institutions and codes, their economies underwent some fundamental reforms (Bevan and Estrin 2004). In contrast, the former Soviet Union (FSU) countries, which were founded in 1922, faced serious difficulties in transitioning to a market economy after the fall of the communist regime. When their attempts ended in market failure, they tried to replace something else with the market (Stiglitz 1996).

In many transition economies, not just FSU countries, governments have begun to intervene in corporate affairs in line with new privatization (Shleifer and Vishny 1999). The longer a county has been under the communist rule, the harder it will be to leave the cultural legacy and the negative impacts of the planned economy behind and, consequently, bring about the transition to a market economy. On the one hand, transition societies are hostile to the government, and, on the other hand, they have high expectations and demands of their government. Wilczyński and Ustrojowy (2005) referred to such a situation as a "hostile welfare state syndrome." Therefore, the legacy of planned economics does not allow the transition to a democratic market economy, in which economic initiative and entrepreneurship are important (Mickiewicz 2010). Although the legacy of the communist era was not easy to slough off in some countries, the transition period could create opportunities for entrepreneurship (Estrin et al. 2006). It is worth reminding ourselves that under the communist rule, individuals were not allowed to accumulate financial assets and all wealth was in state ownership, which was a major obstacle to entrepreneurship.

In some countries, there were no large financial markets early in the transition period; thus, the progress was slow. In addition, the banking sector lacked the experience of lending to the private sector, and lacked the organizational capacity to support entrepreneurial businesses (Pissarides 1999). Entrepreneurs were thus affected by corruption and ineffective laws and regulations and did not have bargaining power over the excessive bureaucracy (Estrin and Mickiewicz 2010).

Bureaucracy, corruption, and poor standards, which were all the legacies of planned economics in the former Soviet Union, led to what Stiglitz and Yusuf (2001) referred to as "corrupt government theory," which explains a situation in which a state's involvement in business activists leads to corruption. This led to the formation of informal institutions and increased economic uncertainty, which, in turn, negatively affected the development of business culture and attitudes toward formal institutions. The feeling of uncertainty reinforced the position of post-communist populist parties, which demanded a more central role for the state in the economy and adopted non-ethnically-based prudential policies (Pejovich 1999).

One of the reasons that prevented the post-Soviet countries from replicating the economic success of the East Asian countries was their historical background. Institutional change is substantially path-dependent, but this dependency can be broken through economic and political liberalization and external anchors (Di Tommaso et al. 2007). Depending on the degree of their integration into the world economy and their transactional relationships with multinational corporations, the countries in transition felt the need for privatization to reduce government ownership and abandon central planning. Thus, the process of the transfer of state-owned enterprises to the private sector, which ended the state monopoly and strengthened the private sector with different interest groups, marked a turning point because, before that, there was no effective institutional framework to facilitate the flow of investment and capital (Nagy 2002). Another reason that deterred transition countries from achieving the same desired results which the East Asian countries managed to achieve with regard to institutional change was their dependence on natural resources (Ben Yishay and Grosjean 2014).

4 Conclusion

This chapter sought to answer the following fundamental question: Why did some emerging market economies succeed and others fail to carry out institutional changes? In this regard, first, we reviewed some of the institutional facilitative factors and barriers to the process of institutional change in emerging market economies. Then, the process of institutional change in some emerging market economies was reviewed and discussed.

The experience of the East Asian and Southeast Asian countries shows that their leaders' determination to establish a high-quality institutional framework has turned them into economic hubs in the world. However, the experience of other emerging market economies shows that the lack of well-established institutions, on the one hand, and the lack of a political will among their leaders to introduce institutional reforms, on the other hand, have prevented these countries from achieving considerable and long-term economic growth and development. Governments in East and Southeast Asia used incentive mechanisms, reduced uncertainty, and created the right business environment, by establishing new institutions and/or changing the existing institutions, to motivate economic and political actors and entrepreneurs to utilize human and physical capital for oiling the wheels of the economy. These countries have also capitalized on the opportunities created by globalization through institutional change, which have resulted in more domestic and foreign investment and transfer of knowledge and technology.

However, the efforts made by the post-Soviet, Latin American, and North African governments to bring about change have not been successful due to the lack of attention to informal institutions and social capital. Furthermore, the social norms and patterns of behavior in the post-Soviet, Latin American, and North African countries were not highly conducive to a successful process of institutional change. In these countries, instead of supporting the economy, the governments have made the prospect of long-term economic growth and development impossible by imposing restrictions on business activities and causing imbalances between the economy and the institutional framework, which have contributed to the loss of public trust in government.

The economic growth of East Asian and Southeast Asian countries has proven that the institutional framework, through rules, regulations, and government support, has an enormous impact on the activity of economic agents and their orientation.

From the perspective of Stiglitz (1996), East Asian success can be repeated in other countries if:

1. There are favorable macroeconomic conditions and political stability.
2. There is a significant investment in education.
3. The government policies are adapted to environmental change and changing economic, social, and political conditions.
4. The government can create effective market institutions, such as development banks, capital markets, etc.
5. The government can cooperate closely with the economic actors and successfully address their needs.

Finally, it can be suggested that emerging market economies need to create institutions that can create opportunities for entrepreneurs to achieve strong economic performance, increase people's motivation to use their resources in production and/or innovation, make the economy competitive, encourage productive activities, and compensate for the lack of public trust and confidence through the rule of law and its effective implementation.

References

Acemoglu, D. (2009). *Introduction to modern economic, growth.* Princeton: Princeton University Press.

Acemoglu D., & Robinson (2000), *A theory of political transitions*, MIT Department of Economics Working Paper No. 99-26.

Badawi, A. (2019). Institutions and economic performance in the southern Mediterranean partner countries: A renewed policy agenda to tackle institutional failure. EMNES Policy Paper No 005

Beck, T., & Laeven, L. (2006). Institution building and growth in transition economies. *Journal of Economic Growth, 11*(2), 157–186.

Ben Yishay, A., & Grosjean, P. (2014). Initial endowments and economic reform in 27 post-socialist countries. *Journal of Comparative Economics, 42*(4), 892–906.

Bevan, A., & Estrin, S. (2004). The determinants of foreign direct investment into European transition economies. *Journal of Comparative Economics, 32*(4), 775–787.

Block, F. (2011). Innovation and the invisible hand of government. In F. Block & M. R. Keller (Eds.), *State of innovation: The U.S. Government's role in technology development* (pp. 1–26). Boulder/London: Paradigm Publishers.

Caliński, T., & Harabasz, J. (1974). A dendrite method for cluster analysis. *Communications in Statistics, 3*(1), 1–27.

Calvo, E., & Micozzi, J. P. (2005). The Governor's backyard: A seat-vote model of electoral reform for subnational multiparty races. *Journal of Politics, 67.*

Carlile, L. (2004). *The Japanese labor movement and institutional reform* (Working Paper No. 200). European Institute for Japanese Studies, Stockholm School of Economics.

Charnock, G. (2009). Why do institutions matter? Global competitiveness and the politics of Policies in Latin Amerika. *Capital ve Class, 33*(2), 67–99.

Crotty, J., & Lee, K.-K. (2001, Summer). Economic performance in post-crisis Korea: A critical perspective on neoliberal restructuring. *Seoul Journal of Economics, 14*(2), 183–242.

Dadgar, Y., & Nazari, R. (2018, January). The institutional impact on economic development in Iran: A multidisciplinary approach. Macmillan, Palgrave. https://doi.org/10.1007/978-3-319-98494-0_6, a book chapter.

Dargent, E. (2012). *Determinants of agency capacity in the Latin American state: Lessons from Colombia and Peru.* Paper presented at the XXX meeting of the Latin American Studies Association, May 23–25, 2012, San Francisco, CA.

De Melo, M., Denizer, C., Gelb, A., & Tenev, S. (2001). Circumstance and choice: The role of initial conditions and Policies in transition economies. *World Bank Economic Review, 15*(1), 1–31.

Dell'Anno, R. (2010). Institutions and human development in the Latin American informal economy. *Const Polit Econ, 21*, 207–230.

Di Tommaso, M. L., Raiser, M., & Weeks, M. (2007). Home-grown or imported? Initial conditions, external anchors and the determinants of institutional reform in the transition economies. *Economic Journal, 117*(520), 858–881.

Diez, R. S. Zvirgzde (2013), Similarities and differences of institutional change in ENP and other catch-up countries, WP5/14 Search Working Paper.

Doğruel, F., & Doğruel, S. (2006). *Bıçak Sırtında Büyüme ve İstikrar Arjantin, Brezilya, Meksika, İsrail, Türkiye*. İstanbul: İstanbul Bilgi University Publishings.

Estrin and Mickiewicz (2010), Entrepreneurship in transition economies: The role of institutions and generational change, IZA Discussion Paper No. 4805.

Estrin, S., Meyer, K., & Bytchkova, M. (2006). Entrepreneurship in transition economies. In M. Casson (Ed.), *The Oxford handbook of entrepreneurship* (pp. 693–723). Oxford: Oxford University Press.

Estrin, et al. (2009). Privatisation in Central and Eastern Europe. *Journal of Economic Literature, 47*(3), 699–728.

Fellner, A. (2008). *Role of culture in economic development: Case study of China and Latin America.* Theses and dissertations. Paper 236. University of South Florida.

Fosu, A., Bates, R., & Hoeffler, A. (2006). Institutions, governance and economic development in Africa: An overview. *Journal of Afrıcan Economies, 15*(1), 1–9.
Furubotn, E. G., & Pejovich, S. (1972). Property rights and economic theory: A survey of recent literature. *Journal of Economic Literature, 10*(4), 1137–1162.
Hernandez, C. (2002). Institution building through an ASEAN charter. *Panorama, 1*, 13.
Hoshi, T., & Kashyap, A. K. (2001). *Corporate financing and governance in Japan: The road to the future*. Cambridge: MIT Press.
Howell, J. (1993). *China opens its doors: The politics of economic transition*. Boulder: Lynne Reiner.
Jonkers, K. (2010). *Mobility, migration and the Chinese scientific research*. London: Routledge, System.
Judt, T. (2005). *Postwar: A history of Europe since 1945*. New York: Penguin Press.
Jwa, S.-H. (2003). In search of 'global standards': The fallacy of Korea's corporate policy. *Harvard Asia Quarterly*, 45–52.
Kaufman, D., Kraay, A., & Mastruzzi, M. (2006). *Governance matters V: Governance indicators for 1996–2005*. Washington, DC: World Bank.
Khan, M. (1995). State failure in weak states: A critique of new institutionalist explanations. In J. Harris, J. Hunter, & C. Lewis (Eds.), *The new institutional economics and third world development*. London/New York: Routledge.
Knight, J. (1992). *Institutions and social conflict*. Cambridge: Cambridge University Press.
Kornai, J. (2006). The great transformation of Central Eastern Europe: Success and disappointment. *Economic Transition, 14*(2), 207–244.
La Croix, Sumner, and Akihiko Kawaura (2005), Institutional change in Japan: Theory, evidence, and reflections. Working Paper No. 82, Economic Series, East-West Center.
La Porta, R., Lopez-de-Silanes, F., Shleifer, A., & Vishny, R. (1997). Trust in large organizations. *American Economic Review, 87*(2), 333–338.
Landes, D. (1998). *The wealth and poverty of nations*. New York: W. W. Norton.
Landes, D. (2000). Culture makes almost all the difference. In L. E. Harrison & S. P. Huntington (Eds.), *Culture matters: How values shape human progress* (pp. 2–13). Basic Books.
Lardy, N. R. (2014). *Markets over Mao: The rise of private business in China*. Washington, DC: The Peterson Institute for International Economics.
Lee, C. (2005). The political economy of institutional reform in Korea. *The Journal of the Asia Pacific Economy, 10*(3), 257–277.
Lee, C. (2018). *Making Sense of Malaysia's institutional Reforms*, Researchers At Iseas – Yusof Ishak Institute analyse Current events, issue: 2018 No. 79.
Levitsky, S. and M. Murillo (2012), Building institutions on weak foundations: Lessons from Latin America, forthcoming in Daniel Brinks, Marcelo Leiras, and Scott Mainwaring, eds. Reflections on uneven democracies: The legacy of Guillermo O'Donnell Baltimore Johns Hopkins University Press).
Lijphart, A. (1994). *Electoral systems and party systems: A study of twenty-seven democracies, 1945–1990*. Oxford: Oxford University Press.
Lin, J., & Nugent, J. (1995). Institutions and economic development. In T. N. Srinivasan & J. Behrman (Eds.), *Handbook of development economics* (Vol. 3A). Amsterdam: North-Holland.
Lipset, S. M. (1959). Some social requisites of democracy: Economic development and political legitimacy. *American Political Science Review, 53*(1), 69–105.
Luiz, J. M. (2009). Instıtutıons and economic performance: Implıcatıons for Afrıcan development. *Journal of International Development, 21*.
McKinsey Global Institute (2015) *The China effect on global innovation*.
Mickiewicz, T. (2010. *Economics of institutional change: Central and Eastern Europe*, rev. 2nd ed. (first published as: Economic Transition in Central Europe and the Commonwealth of Independent States). London: Palgrave Macmillan.

Milhaurpt, C. (2004). *A lost decade for corporate governance: What's changed, what hasn't and why* (Working Paper No. 202). European Institute for Japanese Studies, Stockholm School of Economics.

Murillo, M. V. (2005). Partisanship amidst convergence: Labor market reforms in Latin America. *Comparative Politics, 37*(4), 441–458.

Nagy, A. (2002). Evolving institutions and catching up by the candidate countries of the EU. International Institute for Applied Systems Analysis. Interim Report.

North, D. C. (1981). *Structure and change in economic history*. New York/London: W. W. Norton Company.

North, D. (1990). *Institutions, institutional change and economic performance*. Cambridge: Cambridge University Press.

North, D. C., & Thomas, R. P. (1973). *The rise of the western world: A new economic history*. Cambridge: Cambridge University Press.

North, D. C., & Weingast, B. (1989). Constitutions and commitment: The evolutions of institutions governing public choice in seventeenth-century England. *Journal of Economic History, 49*(4), 803–832.

OECD. (2010). *Total unemployment rates as percentage of total labor force*. OECD Publishing.

Ono, H., & Moriguchi, C. (2004). *Japan's lifetime employment: A century's perspective* (Working Paper No. 205). European Institute for Japanese Studies. Stockholm School of Economics.

Pei, M. (1994). *From reform to revolution: The demise of communism in China and the Soviet Union*. Cambridge, MA: Harvard University Press.

Pejovich, S. (1999). The effects of the interaction of formal and informal institutions on social stability and economic development. *Journal of Markets & Morality, 2*(2), 164–181.

Petrovic, M. (2008). The role of geography and history in determining the slower progress of post-communist transition in the Balkans. *Communist and Post-Communist, 41*(2), 123–145.

Pissarides, F. (1999). Is the lack of funds the Main obstacle to growth? EBRD's experience with small and medium-sized businesses in central and Eastern Europe. *Journal of Business Venturing, 14*, 519–539.

Pop-Eleches, G. (2007). Between historical legacies and the promise of Western integration: Democratic conditionality after communism. *East European Politics and Societies, 21*(1), 142–161.

Remmer, K. L. (2008). The politics of institutional change: Electoral reform in Latin America, 1978–2002. *Party Politics 14, 1*(January), 5–30.

Rhoads, R. A., Wang, K., Shi, X., & Chang, Y. (2014). *China's rising research universities: A new era of ambition*. Baltimore: Johns Hopkins University Press.

Rodrik, D., Subramanian, A., & Trebbi, F. (2004). Institutions rule: The primacy of institutions over geography and integration in economic development. *Journal of Economic Growth*, 131–165.

Roland, G. (2004). Understanding institutional change: Fast-moving and slow-moving institutions. *Studies in Comparative International Development, 38*(4), 109–131.

Rus, H. A. (2014). Corruption, conflict and the Management of Natural Resources. *Economics of Governance, 15*(4), 355–386.

Sachs, J. D., & Warner, A. D. (2001). The curse of natural resources. *European Economic Review, 45*(4), 827–838.

Sandri, S., & Alshyab, N. (2018). *The impact of institutional uncertainty on employment generation perspectives of firms in Jordan* (EMNES Working Paper No. 18, September 2018).

Shleifer, A., & Vishny, R. (1999). *The grabbing hand: Government pathologies and their cures*. Cambridge, MA: Harvard University Press.

Stiglitz, J. E. (1996). *Some lessons from the east-Asian miracle*. Washington, DC: The World Bank Researcher.

Stiglitz, J. E., & Yusuf, S. (2001). *Rethinking the east-Asian miracle*. Washington, DC: World Bank/Oxford University Press.

Sukma, R. (2014). ASEAN beyond 2015: The imperatives for further institutional changes, Centre for Strategic and International Studies, ERIA Discussion Paper Series, ERIA-DP-2014-01.

Toye, J. (1995). The new institutional economics and its implications for development theory. In J. Harris, J. Hunter, & C. M. Lewis (Eds.), *The new institutional economics and third world development*. London: Routledge.
Tridico, P. (2011). *Institutions, human development and economic growth in transition economies*. Palgrave Macmillan.
Wai-Chung Yeung, H. (2005). *Institutional capacity and Singapore's developmental state managing economic (in)security in the global economy* (pp. 85–106). London: Routledge.
Wedeman, A. (2012). *Double paradox: Rapid growth and rising corruption in China*. Ithaca/London: Cornell University Press.
Weinstein, D. E. (2001). Historical, structural, and macroeconomic perspectives on the Japanese economic crisis. In M. Blomström, B. Gangnes, & S. La Croix (Eds.), *Japan's new economy: Continuity and change in the twenty-first century*. New York: Oxford University Press.
Wilczyński, W., & Polski przełom ustrojowy. (2005). *Ekonomia epoki transformacji* [The Polish political breakthrough 1989–2005. Economics of transformation]. Poznań: Wydawnictwo WSB.
World Bank (1993), The east-Asian miracle. Economic growth and public policy. A World Bank Policy Research Report.
World Bank, (2020), Doing business: Comparing business regulation in 190 economies.
Yew, L. K. (2000). *From third world to first*. New York: harper Collins.
Zheng, Y., & Tong, S. Y. (2014). Introduction. In Y. Zheng & S. Y. Tong (Eds.), *China's evolving industrial policies and economic restructuring* (pp. 1–14). London: Routledge.
Zhou, C. (2012). From a university-run enterprise to a leading group of regional IT industrial clusters: In a perspective of an academia government industry triple helix. In C. Petti (Ed.), *Technological entrepreneurship in China: How does it work?* (pp. 66–85). Northampton: Edward Elgar.
Zweig, D. (2002). *Internationalizing China*. New York: Cornell University Press.

Social Media: Harbinger of Institutional Change and Its Impact on Branding

Vineet Kumar and Kirti

1 Introduction

Institution and institutional change is a broad discipline, and its theories can be used to explain the behaviour of both the individuals and organisations. One of the significant areas of research revolving the 'theory of institutions' theme is the assessment of the process and manner in which the institutional change takes place in the course of time. A class of scholars like Tina Dacin et al. (2002), Williams (2000) and DiMaggio and Powell (1991) proposed in their research work that institutions are the catalyst of change at various levels and contexts. They were also of the view that in due course of time and space, institutions also change or evolve in capabilities, character and behaviour as well. According to them are taken into consideration, social interactions are one of the focal points of institutional theory, and they not only have evolved in the past two decades but also brought the world together, giving rise to the concepts like glocalisation and global village. This 'social interaction' shapes the way the society functions and transforms, and this potency or capability has come from the technological advancement and rise of the internet.

Internet along with the rise of SNSs (social networking sites) has proved to be a very cost-effective medium for communication and carries out economic activities amongst the society members and players of institutions and institutional change. Despite its usage there is less work to support this notion that social networking sites are also acting as a medium of institutional change. Hence, the effectiveness of social media as a harbinger of institutional change can be understood with the perspective of integrated marketing communication. For this purpose in the present

V. Kumar (✉)
St. Xavier's College of Management and Technology, Digha, Patna, India

Kirti
Chanakya National Law University, Mithapur, Patna, India

N. Faghih, A. H. Samadi (eds.), *Dynamics of Institutional Change in Emerging Market Economies*, Contributions to Economics,
https://doi.org/10.1007/978-3-030-61342-6_8

chapter, institutional change which has been taken into context is 'branding' activity taken by the marketers, and the shift in this activity is due to the impact of social media. The chapter is a theoretical perspective to the theme with examples of selected companies and their successful campaigns and opens the dimension for future empirical research. The basic outline of the chapter is given below:

Chapter Outline:

I. Social Media
II. Social Media Marketing
III. Brands and Branding
IV. Social Media and Branding (SMB)
V. Examples of Select Companies with Social Media Branding Success Stories
VI. Conclusions

2 Social Media

The term Web 2.0 has widely spread and was first introduced in the year 2004 by Tim O'Reilly; this user-friendly interface lets the user use the website and services with much convenience and ease, leading to the emergence of social media, which has quite a number of sites in its basket to hook the internet users to their phones and electronic devices. Social media is a wagon that carries the various campaigns of companies, targeting the prospective customer's attention, as well as ensures strong brand loyalty amongst the existing ones. Kim and Ko (2012) admit that 'due to its escalating usage not only companies and existing social networks but Government and Non-Government agencies are also utilizing it to attract the citizens for different causes' (Kim and Ko 2012). The 'capabilities of brand and branding' through social media tools (SMTs) are the most significant medium of gaining competitive edge over the competitors for the company, enhancing the revenue and profitability. According to Lu-Anderson and Pitts (2012), traditional marketing mix has been challenged by the social media; they provide an excellent and economical way to connect with the desired audience. Utilisation of social media needs an in-depth knowledge of the trends and taste of the target customers.

Due to the explosive rate at which internet users are increasing, standing out with the help of SMTs has become a tough task. The usage of SMTs dates back to the year 2002 when the first platform came to surface, named as 'Friendster'. It was developed by Jonathan Abraham, a British programmer; the site was quite a success in the Asian region, but the success was short-lived and lasted only till the year 2004. The year 2004 saw the rise of the SM giant Facebook, introduced by Mark Zuckerberg and a few of his friends, and again was followed by micro-blogging site (MBS), Twitter. Jack Dorsey who is from United States introduced Twitter. As per the reports, Twitter had higher revenue than Facebook in the year 2008. It was not long after that the virtual population welcomed Instagram, pioneered by Kevin

Systrom, wholeheartedly in the year 2010 and gained a hell lot of popularity till the year 2013.

Social media has proved to be a boon for the companies which are mostly older and have existed for quite a few years; even for the start -ups. India has one of the largest populations present virtually on the SNSs after China, and it is the result of the widespread usage of smartphones, affordable telecommunication charges and falling data services. Even the rural population is now connected with the internet in some way or the other due to the changing scenario. We can without much of a stretch contend with validity and conviction that for a large portion of the early web clients, social media truly is the entire internet that they know of. The world has witnessed the expeditious expansion of social media, which has given the marketing communication strategies a whole new dimension. This expansion is leading the companies to interact and engage with the target audience in the best possible manner and create brand awareness. There are enough evidences to show that the 'Integrated Marketing Communications through the use of SMTs has proved to be helpful in STP (Segmenting-Targeting-Positioning) of the Brands' (Kartikasari 2014).

The social media presence has brought about a drastic change in the connection between a brand and purchaser because of its effect. Social networking sites have endowed the customers a great deal of supremacy and control that neither the brand nor the company can claim it; they have realised that gone are the days when there was only one-way communication. The social media has created such an impact on the branding process that customers' opinion and reviews can make or break the entire branding game of the company, compelling them to create and maintain an impressive and recognisable presence in all the popular SNSs such as Facebook, Twitter, Instagram, etc. On the other hand, SMTs also serve as the medium for continuous and rigorous marketing research tool and a source of information to decipher the psych of the customers.

It can be said that social media has become an indispensable element of our lives and has transformed the way we have interacted throughout the centuries within just two decades; it is ever-evolving and as dynamic as it could be and has turned out to be a global phenomenon. It has proved to be the most economical channel (both in terms of monetary and time consumption) for people across the globe to connect and interact with others, be it another individual, community, cause they care about or a brand. Brands are not left untouched by the sprouting effect of social media and its tools, the conventional medium now has been entirely taken over by modern tech-based paradigm. It should be noted that it is not only the positive effect that SMTs have on the Branding, there are costs to be paid as well, which calls for the aggressive recognition of target audience psych and well-planned strategies.

During the past two decades, social media has become the holy grail for brands; it has not only given a new IMC (integrated marketing communication) channel but also has facilitated them to contact existing as well as prospect customers, disperse their message and establish, maintain and monitor their brands. DellaPosta et al. (2017) in his research claimed that 'companies are furiously taking the advantage of Social Media Marketing Tools (SMTs) and cashing out from the virtual presence of its target audiences; the strategy of 'attract-link-create awareness' adopted by companies has led to the achievement of desired marketing communication goals'. According to Kaplan and Haenlein (2010), 'social media is an assortment of applications and websites that lets the user create and spread their content, which are present on the internet, established on the logic and technique of Web 2.0' (Kaplan and Haenlein 2010). Web 2.0 is that version of the internet which has allowed the generation of sharable user content, which again can be modified. Built upon Web 2.0, SMTs or SNSs, it is the technological advancement which enables an individual to create and share their desired content termed as 'post' on the SNSs, which can be viewed and reviewed/responded (i.e. liked, loved, etc.) and can be shared further by another mutually connected SNS' member.

Social media has also been referred to as 'the set of virtual WOM platforms, which enlist vlogs, blogs, SNSs, channels, and forums' (Mangold and Faulds 2009). Social media tools are the extremely interactive sites based on the internet and smartphone technological advancement, attempting to bring about a sense of belongingness and close communities where people share mutual values and culture. The SNSs are a 'bundle of applications and platforms which vary in their utility and meeting the distinguished needs of the virtual citizens coming from each level of the society. To name a few Facebook helps the general mass, whereas LinkedIn caters to the demand of professional interactions, YouTube provides creation of own channel and let the creator share their own videos, Instagram lets the user post their pictures and make stories with short videos' (Kietzmann et al. 2011).

Social media tools have enabled the marketers to build up an interactive and direct connection with their target customers; it has additionally helped both the parties to create and share their own content on SNSs, and it further aimed at active, real-time and economical discussions. The interaction process is immensely simplified, as on one side marketers share their campaign and messages targeting a massive base of potential and existing customers, and on the other side the target customers are independently able to respond to these messages/campaigns in both positive and negative manner as per their choice and experience.

As per the study of Nwokah and Gladson-Nwokah (2015) 'making Social Media Tools the core part of Marketing Communication Strategy' is not a just piece of cake, and as mentioned in the previous section it can make or break a brand, mostly the firms are utilising the SMTs in a constraint manner by just using it as a source of collecting the marketing research data and a supplementary to the other marketing communication mix tools instead of relying on SMTs solely' (Nwokah and Gladson-Nwokah 2015).

3 Social Media Marketing

Social media and social media marketing are two words which are often used interchangeably, but one must understand the fundamental concepts to distinguish both. Every single virtual citizen irrespective of region, religion, culture and nationality is well aware of these two terminologies, as these two have touched the lives of individuals in every stratum. Social media is 'the medium for disseminating self-generated information, serving as the basis for establishing brand awareness'(Blackshaw and Nazzaro 2004), whereas 'social media marketing is the link between a brand and its audience, offering an individual channel for customer-centric networking and interaction' (Chi 2011). Expansion provided for SNSs the purpose of 'segmenting-targeting-position' (STP) of an offering and establishing it as a brand is termed as 'social media marketing is the retractions of the marketing conceptions; when fused with social media, catering the target audience' (Chan and Guillet 2011).

The studies reveal that social media marketing influences brand value, sales volume and WOM (word of mouth); moreover, social media influencers utilise and share data and reviews about the brands. The marketer has to keep in mind that the content must vary from product to product and it serves well, as each brand whether it's a product or service carries different set of attributes and meaning for the consumers. The better customised and uniformed is the message/content on social networking site, the more it will gain the brand popularity, and this is what the social media marketing strives for, along with the calling action from the target audience and triggering campaigns aimed at enhanced customer attitude for the brand.

Social media marketing is way beyond the traditional or conventional marketing; it gives a two-way communication channel that binds the marketer and the customers effectively. 'It brings congruency between the two, providing them a platform for real-time interaction, helping marketers in Branding, as well as creating and maintaining Brand Loyalty' (Erdoğmuş and Çiçek 2012). One significant phenomenon on SNs is E-word of mouth (E-WOM), which has an overwhelming effect on the virtually present consumers' buying decision process and purchase behaviour, and marketers are taking it as an opportunity. As claimed by Ler (2014), 'it is the customers who are continuously exploring brands options, reviews of such brands' (Ler 2014).

4 Brands and Branding

A brand is referred to as a 'name, sign, symbol, term or a combination of all these, that identifies the maker or seller of the product and services offered by a company and distinct them to that of their competitors' (Kotler and Armstrong 2006). Brands assist customers to recognise and select a product, which they perceive as superior when compared to the product's alternatives. 'Brands were first used on livestock as an ownership marker, but their usage has continued in the same way to the modern-day as they play a significant role to be a 'guide to choice' for the customers'(Clifton et al. 2003). While this remains the core concept of a brand, now the notion of brand comprehensibly envelopes it as much more than merely being a symbol or name of a tangible product. Brand has been defined as the sum of all links, belief, approach and discernment which an individual has in relation to the physical and intangible features of a firm or firm's offering.

A brand can be viewed as a composite image of everything people associate it with. Brand can be referred to as a fixed intangible asset, which helps in creating an identity and distinguished feature, steers consumer for making a product's choice and binds the consumer to the product, resulting to various benefits to the company, society and most importantly the product. 'When it comes to customers, brand is an indicator of quality' (Kapferer 2008a); 'for a company it is the link to create and enhance brand loyalty, profitability as well as increased sales volumes'(Kotler and Pfoertsch 2006); and 'on the other hand indirectly it helps in societal development by empowering both company and customer' (Keller 2001). In this era of cut-throat competition, to gain a competitive edge over its competitors, a company needs a sharp brand image.

Brands now stand for emotions, values and lifestyle. They are, in fact, an 'intangible, but a key component of what a company stands for' (Davis and Bojalil Réora 2002). With positive brand equity, brands might fix a premium price of their products and services and even can achieve increased sales; it helps creating an emotional bond with customers to a different level. Likewise, the paradigm of advertisement has also shifted from describing the manufacturer's offerings to positioning it as a brand, beseeching emotions in consumers and presenting an offering as combination of value and worth and not just merely being a product or service. Kotler and Keller (2012) remarked that 'it is this reason that many companies seek to build favourable, positive and strong brands' (Kotler and Keller 2012).

Weilbacher (1999) mentioned in his work that 'the success of a brand relies upon the experience from an offering that a customer garners, a brand succeeds if the customer perceives the product to be superior when compared to the competitor's offerings' (Weilbacher 1999). In the social media marketing era, it is more prevalent when the entire marketing strategies revolve around the consumer.

Heidi Cohen, Chief Content Officer, Heidi Cohen's Actionable Marketing Guide, a marketing management content writer, social media consultant, trainer and speaker, explains brands as 'a shorthand marketing message which invokes emotional connections with customers'. She further adds that 'Brands are a combination of intangible components correlated to a brand's explicit promise, positioning, personality, and tangible and identifiable elements such as logos, colour, sound, and graphics. A brand offers some strong values for its consumers through its identity, which makes it distinguishable from the similar available products' (https://heidicohen.com/30-branding-definitions/).

The concept of branding has seen an enormous shift over a period of time; there was a time when it was a mere tool to represent the entire herd with just one sheep, and now each and every company's offering is tried to be presented as a brand; meaning, branding is an age-old technique to 'stand out', to get identified and to create a long-lasting impact. 'One major ingredient in branding is creating a relationship or a bond which creates emotional link and loyalty towards product' (Kapferer 2008b). It is the activity to improve the brand equity.

5 Social Media and Branding (SMB)

'Many brands have gained customer's attention and engagement through the use of social media' (Graves 2016); interaction with target customers and enhancing sales volume are the primary focus of social media branding. The fundamental utility of social media for brands is 'branding-attainment/motivation-retention', and it is all due to the exponentially booming rate of the time that consumers are spending on the use of social media. The popularity and versatility of smartphones have made social media even more itinerant and ubiquitous, which is indeed an opportunity for the marketers; they take advantage of content creation, reviews and sharing activities by the customers on these SNSs. The biggest advantage that a marketer has due to the use of social media is its cost-effectiveness, which the traditional media lacks, and this is the reason why social media is not just a tool for branding but also for market research, managing customer relationships and creating communities of like-minded consumers.

Anyhow, one must not ignore the importance of conventional media, and it is the mixture of both conventional and contemporary media that can assure the achievement of integrated marketing communication goals of the firm along with the maintenance of the uniformity, consistency and appeal.

Now the moot question arises: 'How can firms be in an advantageous position?' The answer to that question is that social media presence involves either low cost or no cost, apart from demanding very few resources, which makes it even more vital for firms of all scales and types. Additionally, 'social media lets the marketer to engage its target customers indirect interactions and activities like survey, polls, etc.; leading the brand to achieve the desired awareness and loyalty' (Montero Torres 2015).

In reality, we have the term WOM (word of mouth), but virtually this term is referred to as E-WOM (electronic word of mouth); the implication is not that different except from the fact that in E-WOM, the users' opinion and reviews spread quickly and proliferate in much more intensity. Furthermore, it also means that it will not only carry forward the positive attitude but also the negative ones. 'The social media lets the marketer strategise its message targeting its audience in demographics as well as geographic way' (Turban et al. 2008). 'Facebook helps the marketers to target their audiences or do their segmenting activity with much ease and accuracy' (Facebook 2015), based upon biographical factors like age and gender and geographical factors like country or region, and psychologically, i.e. addressing the culture, values, norms and beliefs. SNSs, for example, also serve as a medium to categorise a group of people, as well as the formulation of sub-groups, breaking them into small target units. The fundamental element of Facebook is its ability to develop over the years to let marketer categorise its target audiences and keep a measurement of the relevant data, which is again an advantage. These data are used by marketers to gain deep insights regarding the attitude of the consumers towards the brand and to formulate more specific marketing communication strategies.

Another edge that SNSs provide to the marketers is information in real time, which further enhances the chance for marketer to achieve the desired advertising goals by analysing these real-time data and formulating target and segment-based in-depth marketing campaigns. Due to the reach of SNSs, they are now considered to be more potent for creating brand awareness as they have an excellent reach capability and that too in a very lesser time when compared to conventional media of advertising. On the other hand, the conventional media lacks this targeting, segmenting and the quality of measurability and even so it reaches to those consumers as well who are not the target of the firms. As the marketers always focus that triumphant of the brand awareness focused campaigns can be only achieved once it reaches the right audiences. In order to reap the benefits of strength, in the SMTs, the marketer must realise that there should be a consistency, clarity and conformity in the campaigning strategy; this will lead to a positive brand image creation, making it more powerful. The strategy should be provoking enough to generate attention from the audience, and once it happens, the marketers should create an acquisition strategy to engage the customers in SM activities such as discussions, polls, quizzes and formation of social cause communities relevant to the brand image creation. The content, quality and a robust social or emotional message are the bases to every branding campaign. SNSs not only will let a strong brand image, but it also helps in CRM (i.e. customer relationship management) with the existing consumers, hereby creating powerful brand loyalty and maintaining it in the long run. Further benefit that SNSs provide is customer service, by identifying the issues and after-sales services that the products/services demand after the sales, as the customers can directly contact the marketer through SNSs as Facebook, Twitter, Instagram, etc.

The most crucial factor to be kept in consideration while branding through social media should be consistency and synchronisation throughout the various SNSs in every aspect, i.e. text, text type and colour, visual effects and pictures, etc. so that the message becomes more and more potent in the mind of the customer over a period of time and helps in maintaining familiarity. To put it differently, we can say that this clarity, consistency and conformity will lead to brand awareness and recognition, and even the critical visual content will boost customer engagement, and if they are thought-provoking, the users have a tendency to like and share the content which will again fetch user attention further. Thus, the strategy must be a 'visual-branding strategy' to help the brand achieve its desired success.

6 Examples of Select Companies with Social Media Branding Success Stories

In the year 2018, experts and researchers alleged that SM is losing its lustre as a marketing communication tool, and it seemed accurate to an extent that in the month of June due to several political and privacy concerns Facebook suffered a downhill in its MAU (monthly active users). Even Twitter had to deactivate its almost nine million fake ids from June to September in the year 2018. Even after this fall, speculations are rising day by day, as in the year 2019, the number of added users, as well as the money spent on branding activities by the marketers, has increased exponentially.

The year 2018 cleared the point that the marketers need a cutting-edge social media branding strategy; they need diversification of their existence on SNSs, but uniformity in their message and content. The current section is an attempt to explore such impacts that social media has created on brands using the data from SNSs such as Facebook, Twitter, Instagram, LinkedIn, etc. for the food-serving firms which are the examples of one of the fastest-growing sectors.

Social media has proved to be a boon for the companies which are mostly older and have existed for quite a few years but also not so for the start-ups. It is worth mentioning that the year 2019 has been the best year by far, for the branding perspective, as not only the old brands have gained much success but start-ups like Ola, Uber, Airbnb, Oyo, Trivago, Zomato, Swiggy, etc. are not far behind, though some of these companies have also gone for IPOs (initial public offerings) despite their short-lived existence.

The major element of this success is the well-strategised social media branding, keeping in mind the right type of content, right time of the release of the campaign and the 3 Rs, i.e. right target, which if followed consciously by the marketers will yield colossal success in terms of brand awareness, brand values, new customers and ease in the maintenance of existing customers. It was the year 2008 which hit the economy adversely, but after that, the foodservice sector has seen an immense and steady success. The sector recovered over the past decade and is speculated to have a long way to go, and the credit goes to the technological advancement; now technology dictates the food we eat, the way eat, where we do eat and the way we let other connected individuals on SNSs know about our dining-out activities.

The first example is McDonald's, one of the most powerful food brands on SNSs, having 86 million followers on Facebook, Twitter, Instagram and LinkedIn when compared to other sites even after combining the followers of Amazon and Apple Inc. It has set an example for the other similar brands, which have lost much business due to its increasing popularity, and they are trying to cope with it, which is now rather a difficult task for them. McDonald's has achieved its customer engagement by listening to its customers' views, and they have an active resolution team of consumer complaints, which not only answers the queries but also works on the entire menu for its customers based on social media reviews. It has also launched the mobile app for attaining deep market reach and getting orders from all possible locations, which has led McDonald's back in the race of being one of the top fast foodservice brands.

The second excellent example is Subway, another foodservice brand; when it comes to footfalls it is even massive than McDonald's, and it is the giant of all fast-food serving chains with almost 40,000+ locations. This success couldn't have been of this scale if the SNSs hadn't been utilised. Subway offers fresh, healthy and customised menu and also highlights this feature across every SNSs, one of which was the #SubYAY Campaign on Instagram. During the campaign, the followers were asked to post their stories with the this hashtag and show their love for music, as they created 'The Subway Baked, Green Rooms' across the 5 musical fests in the United States, which indeed resulted in increased followers: from 63,000 to 38.6 million. The user engagement was recorded to be around 176,000 and an enhanced brand awareness of up to 13% and a rise in potent viewers to approximately to 39 million. Currently, Subway has 29 million followers, and they have recruited a new marketing team for managing their social media interactions recently.

The third best example is the American fast-food serving brand, Domino's Pizza, which is an American king of pizza chains, for many years. Domino's was overshadowed by its competitor Pizza Hut, but it fought and came above it with its efficient social branding techniques. It involves the use of social media to order through Facebook Messenger as well as a hashtag or an emoticon on Twitter; moreover, it lets their followers review the quality on social media and has launched a mobile app as well to enhance their reach.

7 Conclusions

It is the need of the hour to recognise the importance of active social media presence, and at the same time, it must be noticed that the content created by the marketers can be controlled by them but the content created by the users/followers is out of their control; so the consistency, clarity and conformity must be followed with the right quality products and services. Thus, branding through social media is cost-effective, but it demands precision and promptness, as an effective strategy can lead to triumph but if it has gone wrong will break the brand image which will take years to be built again. It is apparent from the various studies that social media provides an opportunity to have excellent E-WOM publicity, taking the brand to the next level and influencing its brand equity both in terms of quality and quantity. The study can be validated with empirical analysis in future as there are various aspects and dimension to the impact of social media on branding which needs to be explored and this will pave a way for more research in this field.

References

Aoki, M. (2007). Endogenizing institutions and institutional changes. *Journal of Institutional Economics, 3*(1), 1–31. https://doi.org/10.1017/S1744137406000531.

Blackshaw, P., & Nazzaro, M. (2004), _consumer-Generated (CGM) 101: Word of mouth in the age of the web fortified consumer.

Chan, N. L., & Guillet, B. D. (2011). Investigation of social media marketing: How does the hotel industry in Hong Kong perform in marketing on social media websites? *Journal of Travel & Tourism Marketing, 28*, 345–368.

Chi, H.-H. (2011). Interactive digital advertising VS. virtual brand community: Exploratory study of user motivation and social media marketing responses in Taiwan. *Journal of Interactive Advertising, 12*, 44–61.

Clifton, R., Simmons, J., & Ahmad, S. (2003). *Brands and branding*. London: Profile Books.
Davis, S., & Bojalil Réora, M. (2002). *La marca: Máximo valor de su empresa*. Méico: Pearson Educació.
DiMaggio, P. J., & Powell, W. W. (1991). The new institutionalism in organisational analysis.
Erdoğmuş, İ. E., & Çiçek, M. (2012). The impact of social media marketing on brand loyalty. *Procedia – Social and Behavioral Sciences, 58*, 1353–1360. https://doi.org/10.1016/j.sbspro.2012.09.1119.
Facebook. (2015). [Web page]. Facebook for business. [Ref. 03. October 2015].
Graves, J. (2016). What can social media intelligence do for your brand. [Web page] American marketing association [Ref. 28 Jan. 2016].
https://heidicohen.com/30-branding-definitions/
Kapferer, J. (2008a). *The new strategic brand management: Creating and sustaining brand equity long term* (4th ed.). London.
Kapferer, J.-N. (2008b). *The new strategic brand management – Creating and sustaining brand equity long term*. London/Philadelphia: Kogan Page.
Kaplan, A. M., & Haenlein, M. (2010). Users of the world, unite! The challenges and opportunities of social media. *Business Horizons, 53*, 59–68.
Kartikasari, N. P. (2014). Pengaruh komunikasi pemasaran terpadu terhadap ekuitas merek. *INTERAKSI: Jurnal Ilmu Komunikasi, 3*(2), 162–167.
Keller, K. L. (2001). *Building customer-based brand equity: A blueprint for creating strong brands*. Cambridge, MA: Marketing Science Institute.
Kietzmann, J. H., Hermkens, K., McCarthy, I. P., & Silvestre, B. S. (2011). Social media? Get serious! Understanding the functional building blocks of social media. *Business Horizons, 54*(3), 241–251.
Kim, A. J., & Ko, E. (2012). Do social media marketing activities enhance customer equity? An empirical study of luxury fashion brand. *Journal of Business Research, 65*, 1480–1486.
Kotler, P., & Armstrong, G. (2006). *Principles of marketing* (11th ed.). Upper Saddle River: Prentice Hall.
Kotler, P., & Keller, K. L. (2012). *Marketing management* (Global edition 14e ed.). London: Pearson Education Limited.
Kotler, P., & Pfoertsch, W. (2006). *B2B Brand Management*. Berlin: Springer.
Ler, S. (2014). *The attitudes of consumers towards viral marketing in Malaysia*. Doctoral dissertation, Universiti Tunku Abdul Rahman, Sg Long, Malaysia.
Lu-Anderson, D., & Pitts, L. (2012). Theory into practice: Social media's new "Communication relationship marketing" (CoRM) model - applications in the sport business industry. Paper presented at the North American Society for Sport Management, Seattle.
Mangold, W. G., & Faulds, D. J. (2009). Social media: The new hybrid element of the promotion mix. *Business Horizons, 52*, 357–365.
Montero Torres, R. (2015). *Las Redes Sociales en la Empresa*. Vigo: IT Campus Academy.
Nwokah, N. G., & Gladson-Nwokah, J. (2015). Impact of social network on customer acquisition in the banking industry in Nigeria. *Information and Knowledge Management, 5*, 150–163.
Tina Dacin, M., Goodstein, J., & Richard Scott, W. (2002) Institutional theory and institutional change: Introduction to the special research forum. *Academy of Management Journal, 45*(1), 45–56.
Turban, E., King, D., Mckay, J., Marshall, P., Lee, J., & Viehland, D. (2008). *Electronic commerce 2008 a managerial perspective*. London: Pearson Education.
Weilbacher, W. (1999). *El marketing de la marca*. Barcelona: Granica.
Williamson, O. (2000). The new institutional economics: Taking stock, looking ahead. *Journal of Economic Literature, 38*(3), 595–613. Retrieved December 5, 2020, from http://www.jstor.org/stable/2565421

Does Economic Globalization Have a Similar Effect on Governance for All Countries in the World?

Ali Hussein Samadi and Sakine Owjimehr

1 Introduction

Douglass North says: "We know a lot about institutions and their economic impact, but what we don't know is how to change institutions and institutional conditions." This is still an open question that has been given special attention in the literature of institutional economics. There are several theories in the literature of institutional economics to explain the reasons for the changes in the quality of institutions. Some of these theories include *efficient institutions view* or *political coase theorem* (PCT), *ideology* or the *generalized PCT*, the *incidental institutions view*, the *social conflict view*, *transaction cost theory of institutional change*, *entrepreneurial view of institutional change*, and *globalization view of institutional change* (Samadi 2019).[1]The globalization view of institutional change generally seeks to answer how (economic, social, political, and overall) globalization underlies the changes (improvement or decline) in the (economic, legal, social, cultural, and political) institutions. In other words, in the globalization view of institutional change, the effective channels of economic, social, political, and overall globalization on the improvement or deterioration of the institutions are examined. Trade openness can affect the quality of institutions through many channels, such as *institutional structure*, *change of rents, technology transfer, foreign competition and political power* (Samadi 2019), *the type of political system* (Segura-cayuela 2006; Stefanadis 2010), *the level of economic*

[1]The first four theories are explained in Acemoglu et al. (2003), entrepreneurial view of institutional change in Samadi (2018), and globalization view of institutional change in Samadi (2019) and other references cited herein.

A. H. Samadi (✉) · S. Owjimehr
Department of Economics, Shiraz University, Shiraz, Iran
e-mail: asamadi@rose.shirazu.ac.ir; s.ojimehr@shirazu.ac.ir

N. Faghih, A. H. Samadi (eds.), *Dynamics of Institutional Change in Emerging Market Economies*, Contributions to Economics,
https://doi.org/10.1007/978-3-030-61342-6_9

development and the presence or absence of natural resources (Bergh et al. 2014), *the induction of specialization in sectors requiring good institutions* (Jacobs and Van Der Ploeg 2019; Do and Levchenko 2009; Potrafke 2013), *the type of institutionally intensive goods exported* (Levchenko 2013), and *the existence of constituencies responsible for social infrastructure reform* (Hall and Jones 1999).

There are several definitions for governance (e.g., Dixit 2009; Gisselquist 2012) (as a proxy variable for measuring institutional quality[2]). One definition is that: "traditions and institutions by which authority in a country is exercised" (Kaufmann et al. 2009). This definition is operationalized in *Worldwide Governance Indicators (WGI)*. WGI have six sub-indices. The components of the WGI governance indicator are regulatory quality, voice and accountability, rule of law, government effectiveness, control of corruption, and political stability. These components can be categorized in different ways based on different aspects (Asongu 2017): *economic governance* (including sub-indices of regulatory quality and government effectiveness), *political governance* (including sub-indices of voice and accountability and political stability), *institutional governance* (including sub-indices of the rule of law and control of corruption), and *overall governance*[3] (including all dimensions of governance: economic, political, and institutional governance).

In some empirical studies, as in Long et al. (2015) and Challe et al. (2019), only the rule of law sub-index is used as a proxy for governance. Some other studies (e.g., Bergh et al. 2014) used all the components of governance. Some studies, including Nadeem et al. (2014), have used the combined index ICRG. Furthermore, a few other studies (e.g., Amavilah et al. 2017; Asongu 2017) created a combined index for overall governance using the PCA technique. It is possible that the separate use of each of the different dimensions of governance (economic, political, and institutional) in empirical work will lead to different results.

An examination of the channels and mechanisms which affect all aspects of globalization and its impact on all components of governance is beyond the scope of this chapter. Therefore, the purpose of this chapter was to examine the impact of *economic globalization* (trade openness) on the quality of *overall governance* in countries with varying degrees of governance quality.

Although there are relatively good theoretical and empirical studies done on the impact of globalization on the institutional quality, there are few studies (e.g., Long et al. 2015; Challe et al. 2019; Bergh et al. 2014; Nadeem et al. 2014; Asongu and Biekpe 2017; Amavilah et al. 2017; Asongu et al. 2018) which have attempted to evaluate the impact of globalization on governance quality. It should be noted that very different results have been obtained. In some studies, economic globalization has been reported to have positive effects, while in others it has been shown to have negative effects. Selecting different indices and sub-indices for globalization and governance and selecting different groups of countries (with different levels of

[2] As can be seen in the table in the Appendix, *governance* used as a proxy variable for measuring *institutional quality* by Nadeem et al. (2014), Asongu (2017), Amavilah et al. (2017), Asongu et al. (2018), Challe et al. (2019), and Samadi (2019). See Samadi (2019) for more information.

[3] Which concerned the status of all dimensions of governance, and called *overall governance*.

development) can be the reasons for this discrepancy manifested in findings. Based on the findings of these studies, it can be deduced that the level of economic development of countries is a key factor in deciding whether, and to what extent, globalization can improve their governance. Most developed countries benefit from globalization and improve their governance because of good institutional infrastructure, but the initial state of governance quality seems to be important in benefiting from globalization.

Countries with good governance can expand trade, reduce rent, increase competition, and ultimately improve governance by strengthening the existing institutions, eliminating bad institutions (or deinstitutionalization), and building good institutions. This is something that has not been addressed in thc empirical literature and is one of the contributions of this chapter.

The rest of the chapter is organized as follows: The theoretical and empirical literature on the impact of globalization on the quality of institutions and, in particular, the quality of governance is presented in Sect. 2. Model specification, estimation method, and description and classification of data are presented in Sect. 3. Section 4 is dedicated to the empirical results and a discussion of them; and the last section is devoted to conclusions.

2 Theoretical Background and Literature Review

Economic globalization, in particular trade openness, affects the quality of governance directly and indirectly. This direct effect of economic globalization can be explained at least through the following three channels and is currently an open research area: *rent-seeking channel*, *competition-reducing channel*, and *the cost of monitoring public officials channel. The rent-seeking channel* was first proposed by Krueger (1974) and later expanded by Bhagwati (1982) and Bhagwati and Srinivasan (1982). *The competition-reducing channel* was introduced by Ades and Tella (1999) along with the rent-seeking channel; and *the monitoring channel* was introduced by Wei (2000).

Krueger's (1974) main argument has been that the imposition of legal restrictions on imports will lead to the emergence of economic rents for individuals and influential merchants. In this case, economic agents will try to engage in unproductive activities, such as rent-seeking, smuggling, engaging in the black market, and doing corruptive activities in general. These activities will lead to a suboptimal threshold level in some economic activities and impose new welfare costs; thus, the quality of governance will get worse. The overall argument is that trade openness can eliminate these negative effects.

The main argument of the *competition-reducing channel* is that the level of rent created by applying legal restrictions on imports and the degree of rent-seeking in markets can reduce competition and thus encourage bribery. This will weaken the governance through the spread of corruption. The kernel of this channel is that trade openness can lead to the elimination of corrupt activities and strengthen governance by reducing rent-seeking and encouraging competition.

As regards the *monitoring channel*, the main focus is on open economies, compared to isolated and autarky economies. It is believed that with the expansion of trade openness, the government is likely to spend more resources to improve institutional quality as well as building good institutions. In this way, they will achieve lower costs and more benefits (Bonaglia and Macedo 2002; Nadeem et al. 2014; Asongu and Biekpe 2017; Amavilah et al. 2017; Asongu et al. 2018; Challe et al. 2019).

It, however, should be noted that how greatly a country benefits from globalization depends on the structure and quality of institutions. If the institutional structure of a country is producer-friendly, globalization can improve the quality of governance of that country. Nevertheless, if the institutional structure of the country is rent-seeker-friendly, globalization will even worsen the institutional quality (Samadi 2019).

Although there are relatively good empirical and theoretical studies on the impact of globalization on institutional quality, there are few empirical studies on the impact of economic globalization on the quality of overall governance. A summarized account of some of these studies could be found in the Appendix. In what follows, some studies are reviewed to answer the following questions: Which indices are used as a proxy for globalization and governance quality? What is the overall impact of globalization on the quality of governance in countries?

There are various indices of globalization used in the literature, including *financial openness*, *trade openness*, and *trade liberalization*, *KOF index of economic globalization*, *KOF index of overall globalization*, and *KOF index of economic, social, political, and overall globalization*. However, in studies related to the governance quality, only a few indices have been used, including *financial openness*, *trade openness*, and *KOF index of globalization*.[4]

Numerous indices have also been used to assess the quality of governance. In the studies related to governance quality, there is no consensus on the choice of indices. *The rule of law* sub-index in some studies (e.g., Long et al. 2015; Challe et al. 2019), all six sub-indices of governance separately in some other studies (e.g., Bergh et al. 2014), and general indices such as ICRG in other studies (e.g., Nadeem et al. 2014) have been used to evaluate governance quality. In just a few studies (e.g., Asongu and Biekpe 2017; Amavilah et al. 2017; Asongu et al. 2018), the six sub-indices of governance are categorized into economic, political, and institutional governance, and a general index is created.

In many studies, globalization is reported to have a positive impact on the quality of institutions, whereas in some other studies it has been shown to have a negative effect. As noted before, some studies have indicated a mixed picture, reporting simultaneously both positive and negative impacts for globalization,[5] Ju and Wei (2010) categorized countries based on their financial system and property rights status and observed a positive relationship between a good financial system and good protec-

[4] See Appendix.

[5] See Appendix.

tion of property rights and a negative relationship between a weak financial system and weak protection of property rights. Moreover, they observed an ambiguous relationship when some countries with a weak financial system had adequate protection of property rights. This latter finding has also been echoed in some other studies (e.g., Potrafke 2009; Dreher et al. 2012; Scruggs and Lange 2002) which have tried to evaluate the very mixed and contradictory relationship between these two variables. In addition, some studies (e.g., Kant 2016;[6] Potrafke 2013; Potrafke 2010) have highlighted that globalization does not affect the quality of institutions.

The literature on governance is also marked with mixed and even conflicting results. Long et al. (2015) pointed to the positive impact of financial openness on the rule of law for China (at the firm level), but Challe et al. (2019) reported a negative for four groups of countries (see Appendix). Nadeem et al. (2014) also evaluated the negative impact of overall KOF on the ICRG index in a panel of 91 countries. Only two studies, including Amavilah et al. (2017), and Asongu et al. (2018), have used economic, political, institutional, and overall governance. Asongu (2017) and Asongu et al. (2018) examined the impact of economic, social, political, and overall KOF on economic, political, institutional, and overall governance in 51 African countries. Asongu (2017) found a positive relationship between the two variables; Asongu et al.'s (2018) study showed that overall globalization had a positive effect on the overall governance indices, while the results for the rest of the sub-indices were mixed.

An overview of studies shows that:

- In general, the impact of globalization on the quality of institutions is positive. This means that globalization has improved the quality of institutions.
- The level of the economic development of countries plays a pivotal role in how globalization impacts the quality of their institutions.
- The results of a few studies, for instance, Kant (2016), Potrafke (2013), and Potrafke (2010), showed that globalization did not impact the quality of institutions, but, generally, the effect, positive or negative, of globalization on institutional quality has been confirmed in almost all studies.
- In some studies (e.g., Kant 2016; Li and Reuveny 2003; Bergh et al. 2014), countries are categorized by their level of economic development, or a particular homogeneous group with specific features with regard to their economic development has been chosen. Only in two studies (Challe et al. 2019; Ju and Wei 2010) that certain categories, such as the rule of law status and protection of property rights, respectively, have been considered with regard to the institutional quality status of countries.

This chapter differs from the existing studies in two respects, and it is hoped that it fills such a gap:

1. The classification of countries is based on both their level of economic development (high per capita income, low per capita income) and the status of their

[6] Just for developed countries.

quality of overall governance (high and low). Here, high and low are applied in comparison with the world average of these variables.

2. A larger sample size and more comprehensive indices have been used for economic globalization.

3 Model and Data

3.1 Model Specification and Estimation Method

Econometric models have been one of the tools used to examine the impact of globalization on the institutional quality of countries, in general, and the quality of governance, in particular. The general form of panel data econometric models used to investigate the globalization-institutional quality nexus can be written as Eq. (1):

$$\text{Inst}_{it} = \alpha_0 + \alpha_1 \text{Glob}_{it} + \alpha_2 \text{Control}_{it} + \varepsilon_{it} \tag{1}$$

where Inst_{it} is a proxy for institutional quality, Glob_{it} is a proxy for globalization, and Control_{it} represents control variables. α_j are the coefficients of variables and ε_{it} is error term. i and t represent country and time, respectively.

There are various proxies for $Inst_{it}$ and Glob_{it}, some of them are presented in a table in the Appendix.[7] However, the fundamental difference between the models used in the studies of globalization-institutional quality nexus is in the control variables. Each study used a series of control variables that met the objectives and scope of that study.[8] Notwithstanding that, some variables, including per capita income and population growth rates, have been used in most of the studies. Since the purpose of the present study was to examine the impact of economic globalization on overall governance, the specified econometric model chosen was as shown in Eq. (2):

$$\text{Gov}_{it} = \alpha_0 + \alpha_1 \text{Glob}_{it} + \alpha_0 \text{Gov}_{it-1} + \alpha_2 \text{GDPg}_{it} + \alpha_3 \text{Pop}_{it} + \varepsilon_{it} \tag{2}$$

where Gov_{it} is the overall governance index, Glob_{it} is globalization index, and control variables include Gdpg_{it} (per capita income), Pop_{it} (population growth rate), and Gov_{it-1} (general governance with one lag).

In Samadi (2019), unidirectional causality was confirmed from globalization to the rule of law in developing countries, but there may be bidirectional causality between globalization and overall governance. Therefore, the globalization index can be endogenous and may correlate with disturbance terms. Also, the existence of governance with one lag as an independent variable in the model increases the

[7] Samadi (2019) also referred to some of them.

[8] See Appendix.

probability of correlation with disturbance terms. As a result, in this chapter, the system-generalized method of moments (SYS-GMM) estimation procedure was used to estimate Eq. (2).

SYS-GMM method proposed by Arellano and Bover (1995) and difference GMM (DIFF-GMM) proposed by Arellano and Bond (1991) are two methods to estimate a dynamic panel data. SYS-GMM estimates the system of the level and first-difference equations using the lagged levels and the lagged difference of the series as instruments, but DIFF-GMM estimates the first-difference equation using the lagged levels of the series as instruments. Blundell and Bond (1998) showed that for small T, the result of SYS-GMM was more efficient than DIFF-GMM (as in our case). Therefore, we used SYS-GMM to estimate Eq. (2).

3.2 Data Description

The data used in this study included overall governance index, globalization index, per capita income, and population growth rates of 182 countries for 2002–2016. The reason for using this period was due to data limitations.[9] This data are collected from the global economy website.[10]

One of the problems in most studies is how to select the appropriate proxy for governance quality and globalization. In line with the purpose of the present study, which concerned with the status of overall governance, the PCA technique was preferred and a combined index of six governance components was created. The results are presented in Table 1.

The results (Table 1) showed that only the eigenvalues of the first principal component (first PC) were greater than 1. Therefore, the index of overall governance must be computed on the basis of the first principal component. Kaiser-Meyer-Olkin (KMO) criterion and Bartlett test were used to validate the variables used in factor analysis. KMO criteria always fluctuate between 0 and 1. If the value of this index is greater than 0.7, the correlations between the data would be appropriate enough for performing factor analysis. The KMO value was 0.895 in this study. Bartlett's test is another method used to identify the appropriateness of data. For a useful and meaningful factor analysis model, variables need to be correlated. The null hypothesis of Bartlett's test is that the data are not correlated; therefore, it is desirable to reject the null hypothesis. In this research, the null hypothesis was rejected. Thus, the data were suitable for factor analysis.

Many variables are used as a proxy for the globalization index. Some of these indices are listed in the Appendix and Samadi (2019). In this chapter, to emphasize the economic globalization, three indices of the KOF index of globalization (eco-

[9] Data before 2002 are incomplete for many countries.

[10] https://www.theglobaleconomy.com/indicators_list.php

Table 1 Principal component analysis (PCA) for overall governance

Principal components	Component matrix (loadings)						Eigenvalue
	RQ	VA	RL	GE	CC	PS	
First PC	0.939	0.871	0.979	0.960	0.957	0.809	5.09
Second PC	−0.224	−0.055	−0.032	−0.150	−0.039	0.581	0.416
KMO test				Bartlett's test			
0.895				2.724E4(0.00)			

Source: Personal elaboration of authors
Note: *PC* principal component, *RQ* regulatory quality, *VA* voice and accountability, *RL* rule of law, *GE* government effectiveness, *CC* control of corruption, *PS* political stability, *KMO* Kaiser-Meyer-Olkin and for Bartlett's test, Significance shows in parenthesis

nomic and overall) and trade openness (ratio of total exports plus imports to GDP) are used.

3.2.1 Data Categorization

One of the issues considered in the majority of studies is whether to choose a single country or a number of countries to be investigated. As it can be seen from the Appendix, time-series data have been used in a few studies, including Long et al. (2015) for China and Walter (2010) for Switzerland. Most studies have used (balanced/unbalanced) panel data, but the classification varies. The panel data studies used the following categories: *OECD countries* (Potrafke 2009, 2010), *some industrial democracies* (Scruggs and Lange 2002), *African countries* (Amavilah et al. 2017; Asongu and Biekpe 2017), *developing countries* (Kant 2018; Rudra 2005), *some developing and developed countries in one sample* (Potrafke 2013; Bhattacharyya 2012; Young and Sheehan 2014; Martin and Steiner 2016; Dreher et al. 2012), and some *specific categorizations* (Kant 2016; Challe et al. 2019; Li and Reuveny 2003; Ju and Wei 2010; Bergh et al. 2014; Rudra 2005).

Kant (2016) divided the 169 studied countries into 3 groups: developing countries, developed countries, and all countries. Bergh et al. (2014) classified 101 studied countries into 3 groups: overall, subsample of low-income countries, and subsample of high-income countries. Li and Reuveny (2003) classified 127 studied countries into 3 categories, including all countries, LDCs, and non-OECD. Challe et al. (2019) classified 95 open economies into 4 categories, i.e., full sample, excluding 9 oil-dependent countries, excluding 18 countries at the bottom, and excluding 18 countries at the top of the rule of law distribution. Rudra (2005) divided 59 studied developing countries into 3 groups, including 20 upper-middle- and high-income (non-OECD) LDCs, 21 lower-middle-income LDCs, and 18 low-income LDCs. The only study that used a different category was Ju and Wei (2010). They catego-

Table 2 Countries categorized by average per capita income and quality of overall governance compared to their global average

	High income	*Low income*
High overall governance quality	*A*	*D*
Low overall governance quality	*B*	*C*

Source: Personal elaboration of authors

rized the 97 studied countries into 3 groups according to the countries' financial system status and protection of property rights.

In this chapter, quite different from the existing studies, countries were categorized into four groups, namely A, B, C, and D (Table 2), based on the average value of overall governance quality and countries' per capita income levels compared to the global average. The purpose of this classification was to investigate whether the level of economic development of countries and the level of quality of their overall governance were important in how greatly they benefit from the changes that the globalization of the economy has bought about in institutions.

According to Table 2, each group is defined as follows:

Group A: Countries whose average per capita income and quality of overall governance are higher than the global average

Group B: Countries whose average per capita incomes is higher but their levels of overall governance are lower than the global average

Group C: Countries whose average per capita income and quality of overall governance are below the global average

Group D: Countries whose average per capita income is less but the quality of their overall governance is higher than the global average

The list of these 182 countries and their global map are demonstrated in Fig. 1.

The average quality of governance was 0.022891 and the average per capita income was 11750.49. For example, Italy and the United States, with an average of overall governance and per capita income above the global average, belonged to Group A. In Fig. 1, the countries belonging to each of the groups A, B, C, and D are specified. It must be noted that the only country in Group B is Saudi Arabia that has been excluded from the analysis due to the small sample size.

The disadvantage of this type of classification is that the data dynamics is not considered. In other words, the changes in the quality of overall governance and per capita income of the studied countries may make a country fall into all three groups while we assumed that each country could only belong to a specific group. For example, Brazil was put in Group D, but when its data were analyzed, it was found that in 2011, it belonged to Group A; in 2002–2003, 2009, 2010, and 2012–2013, it belonged to Group D; and in 2004–2008 and 2014–2016, it belonged to Group C. Actually, Brazil was the only country that could be put in all three groups at dif-

Fig. 1 Selected countries
Source: Personal elaboration of authors
Note:
Group A: 47 countries (including Andorra, Antigua and Barbuda, Australia, Austria, Bahamas, Bahrain, Barbados, Belgium, Brunei, Canada, Cyprus, Czech Republic, Denmark, Estonia, Finland, France, Germany, Greece, Hong Kong, Iceland, Ireland, Israel, Italy, Japan, Kuwait, Luxembourg, Liechtenstein, Macao, Malta, Netherlands, New Zealand, Norway, Oman, Portugal, Puerto Rico, Qatar, Singapore, Slovakia, Slovenia, South Korea, Spain, Sweden, Switzerland, Trinidad and Tobago, United Arab Emirates, United Kingdom, United States)
Group B: 1 country (Saudi Arabia)
Group C: 101 countries (including Afghanistan, Albania, Algeria, Angola, Azerbaijan, Argentina, Armenia, Belarus, Benin, Bosnia and Herzegovina, Bolivia, Burkina Faso, Burma (Myanmar), Burundi, Cambodia, Cameroon, Central African Republic, Chad, China, Colombia, Comoros, Cuba, Congo Dem. Rep., Dominican Rep., Djibouti, Ecuador, Egypt, El Salvador, Equatorial Guinea, Ethiopia, Fiji, Gabon, Gambia, Georgia, Guatemala, Guinea, Guinea-Bissau, Guyana, Haiti, India, Indonesia, Iran, Iraq, Jordan, Ivory Coast, Kazakhstan, Kenya, Kyrgyzstan, Liberia, Laos, Libya, Lebanon, Lesotho, Madagascar, Malawi, Mali, Macedonia, Maldives, Mauritania, Mozambique, Mexico, Moldova, Mongolia, Morocco, Nepal, Nicaragua, Niger, Nigeria, Pakistan, Palestine, Papua New Guinea, Paraguay, Peru, Philippines, Russia, Rwanda, Senegal, Sierra Leone, Serbia, Sao Tome and Principe, Sri Lanka, Sudan, Switzerland, Tanzania, Tajikistan, Thailand, Togo, Tunisia, Turkey, Turkmenistan, Uganda, Ukraine, Uzbekistan, Vietnam, Yemen, Zambia, Zimbabwe)
Group D: 34 countries (including Belize, Bhutan, Botswana, Brazil, Bulgaria, Chile, Costa Rica, Croatia, Dominica, Ghana, Grenada, Hungary, Jamaica, Kiribati, Lithuania, Latvia, Malaysia, Mauritius, Micronesia, Namibia, Panama, Poland, Romania, Saint Lucia, Saint Vincent and the Grenadines, Samoa, Seychelles, South Africa, Suriname, Tonga, Tuvalu, Uruguay, Vanuatu)

ferent times. Other countries belonged to one or two groups. A closer look at the data revealed that 77% of the selected countries, from 2002 to 2016, always belonged to one group and their status did not change. Accordingly, the authors believed that they could rely on this type of classification to achieve study objectives.

4 Empirical Results and Discussion

Equation (2) is estimated using data from the three groups studied, namely, A, C, and D.[11] Before estimating the models, cross-sectional dependency (CD) tests, some unit root tests, and Pesaran and Yamagata (2008) (PY) test's slope homogeneity test were performed.

The results of the Pesaran's CD test showed that there was a cross-sectional dependency for all series in all groups, except for the overall governance quality (in group C) and population growth rate (in groups C and D). Based on these results, the PP-Fisher unit root test was used to test the stationarity of the overall governance quality of group C and population growth rate of groups C and D. The results indicated that these variables were I(0).

For the other variables, we had to use the unit root tests that were valid with cross-sectional dependency including cross-sectionally augmented Im, Pesaran, and Shin (CIPS) and Hadri and Rao (2008) tests. The results of Hadri and Rao's test showed that all variables were stationary at the significant level of 5%.[12] Thus, overall, all the variables in the model were stationary. The results of the PY test for each of the groups A, D, and C (Table 3) based on delta (Δ) and adjusted delta (Δ_{adj}) statistics showed that all models had homogeneous slope coefficients.

After ensuring that the slope coefficients were homogeneous, the models were estimated by the SYS-GMM method. The results are reported in Table 4. The results of Hansen or Sargan tests (J-Statistic), Diff-in-Hansen test, and Arellano-Bond autocorrelation test in all models confirmed the exogeneity of instrumental variables (instrumental variable validity) and the lack of autocorrelation.

The results of the estimation of the nine models showed that the quality of overall governance with one lag had a positive and significant effect on itself. However, the impact of per capita income and population growth rate varied depending on the globalization index.

The results presented in Table 4 are summarized in Table 5 for a better comparison of how economic globalization could affect overall governance quality. The results (Table 5) showed that:

- In Group A, countries with high levels of income and quality of overall governance, the overall globalization and trade openness had a significant and positive impact on the quality of overall governance, while economic globalization did

[11] However, there was another classification in that all data, regardless of any country, were classified into groups A, B, C, and D based on the average quality of overall governance and per capita income. Estimates of models for each group were also based on this type of classification. Still, due to the lack of a specific time sequence, it was not possible to perform pre-estimation tests (cross-sectional dependency test, unit root tests, and homogeneity test). The results of this classification were not desirable. These results are available to the authors.

[12] The distinctive feature which distinguishes the Hadri and Rao (2008) test from CIPS is the consideration of the structural break in the data along with the cross-sectional dependency. Since the period used in this study was relatively long (15 years), the Hadri and Rao (2008) test was used to consider the probability of a structural break in the data.

Table 3 Pesaran and Yamagata (2008) slope homogeneity test

	Homogeneity test statistics	Explanatory variable: OGLO	Explanatory variable: EGLO	Explanatory variable: OPENNESS
Group A	Δstatistics	0.98)−2.23)	0.89)−1.21)	0.66)−0.43)
	Δ_{adj} statistics	0.99)−2.69)	0.93)−1.46)	0.69)−0.51
Group C	Δstatistics	0.55)−0.14)	0.97)−1.92)	0.26)−0.63)
	Δ_{adj} statistics	0.57)−0.17)	0.99)−2.32)	0.22)−0.76)
Group D	Δ statistics	0.96)−1.77)	0.94)−1.56)	0.99)−2.52)
	Δ_{adj} statistics	0.98)−2.14)	0.97)−1.87)	0.99)−3.03)

Source: Personal elaboration of authors

Table 4 Model estimation results using SYS-GMM

	Variables	Group A	Group C	Group D
Explanatory variable: OGLO	GOV(−1)	0.93(0.00)	1.04(0.00)	0.92(0.00)
	GDPG	2.2e-06(0.00)	2.88e-06(0.14)	1.99e-06(0.14)
	OGLO	**0.002(0.03)**	**−0.0008(0.08)**	**0.0017(0.03)**
	POPG	−0.006(0.1)	0.037(0.00)	0.0004(0.7)
	J-statistic	38.59(1.00)	96.50(0.49)	25.8(1.00)
	Diff-in-Hansen test	38.22(1.00)	8.45(0.81)	16.28(1.00)
	AR(1)	−3.42(0.00)	−7.20(0.00)	−3.47(0.00)
	AR(2)	0.56(0.6)	−0.68(0.49)	−0.11(0.91)
Explanatory variable: EGLO	GOV (−1)	1.006(0.00)	0.99(0.00)	1.07(0.00)
	GDPG	5.44e-07(0.00)	−5.6e-06(0.00)	−4.8e-07(0.7)
	EGLO	**0.003(0.46)**	**0.0006(0.03)**	**0.0026(0.08)**
	POPG	−0.0003(0.8)	−0.0009(0.8)	0.002(0.2)
	J-statistic	32.56(1.00)	79. 9(0.86)	17.83(1.00)
	Diff-in-Hansen test	8.45(0.29)	2.54(0.99)	10.07(1.00)
	AR(1)	−5.06(0.00)	−6.43(0.00)	−3.42(0.00)
	AR(2)	0.44(0.6)	−0.56(0.57)	0.28(0.7)-
Explanatory variable: OPENNESS	GOV (−1)	0.96(0.00)	1.02(0.00)	0.97(0.00)
	GDPG	2.13e-07(0.29)	7.89e-06(0.00)	2.96e-06(0.44)
	OPENNESS	**0.0004(0.03)**	**0.0008(0.00)-**	**−0.0007(0.2)**
	POPG	−0.003(0.04)	0.023(0.00)	0.003(0.3)
	J-statistic	39.45(1.00)	90.57(0.66)	26.22(1.00)
	Diff-in-Hansen test	36.32(1.00)	3.36(0.99)	16.19(1.00)
	AR(1)	−3.74(0.00)	−6.8(0.00)	−3.41(0.00)
	AR(2)	0.71(0.48)	0.91(0.36)-	0.36(0.71)-

Source: Personal elaboration of authors
Note: The numbers in parentheses indicate the p-value

Table 5 Summary of research results

Dependent variable: Overall governance			
	Explanatory variable: OGLO	Explanatory variable: EGLO	Explanatory variable: OPENNESS
Group A	Positive and significant at 95%	Insignificant	Positive and significant 95%
Group C	Negative and significant at 90%	Positive and significant at 95%	Negative and significant at 95%
Group D	Positive and significant at 95%	Positive and significant at 90%	Insignificant

Source: Personal elaboration of authors

not show a statistically significant effect on the quality of overall governance. This result has also been reported in some other studies (e.g., Bergh et al. 2014) for developed countries.

- In Group C, countries with low quality of overall governance and low per capita income, the overall globalization and trade openness had a negative impact on the overall governance quality, but economic globalization had a positive and significant effect on the quality of overall governance. This result has also been echoed in a number of other studies (e.g., Bergh et al. 2014) for developing countries.
- In Group D, countries with high overall governance quality but low per capita income level, the overall globalization index and economic globalization had a positive effect on the overall governance quality, whereas trade openness did not have a statistically significant effect on the quality of overall governance.

By comparing the results for groups A, C, and D, it can be clearly seen that in groups A and D, i.e., countries with high overall governance quality though with different incomes, globalization had more often a positive effect on the overall governance quality, while in Group C, countries with poor overall governance quality and low-income levels, globalization had a negative effect on overall governance quality. The overall result is that in countries with high levels of overall governance, above world average, the overall globalization (OGLO) could have a positive and significant effect on their overall governance quality, yet for low levels of overall governance, below world average, the overall globalization may have had an adverse effect on the quality of overall governance, thereby weakening it.

However, the impact of economic globalization (EGLO) depends on the level of per capita income. In countries with higher per capita income levels than the global average (group A), economic globalization did not seem to have affected the overall governance quality, but in countries with low per capita income levels (groups C and D), economic globalization had a positive effect on the quality of overall governance. Nevertheless, the interesting conclusion is that when the definition of the index of economic globalization becomes narrower (i.e., trade openness), both the levels of overall governance quality and per capita income will carry more weight. Thus, in countries with high quality of overall governance and high per capita income (group A), trade openness can have a positive impact on the overall governance quality, but in countries with high quality of overall governance and low per capita income (group C), trade openness may have a negative impact on the overall governance quality. No significant effect was observed with regard to other countries (group D).

In general, according to the results, economic globalization can lead to improved overall governance in low-income countries with any level of overall governance. To explain further, we first refer to the definition of economic globalization. EGLO has two dimensions: *actual flows* and *international trade and investment restrictions*. Actual flows sub-index includes trade openness, FDI, and portfolio investment to GDP. International trade and investment restrictions sub-index includes hidden import barriers, mean tariff rates, taxes on international trade (as a share of current revenue), and an index of capital controls (Dreher et al. 2012).

It can be seen that economic globalization encompasses a wide range of international economic concepts. If low-income countries, along with the development of trade in goods and services (trade openness), strengthen foreign investment flows and reduce trade barriers, such free trade flows will not only increase the welfare of society but also raise people's expectations. On the other hand, the government will automatically improve many governance sub-indices by committing to international trade laws. Therefore, the overall governance in these countries will improve.

The results of the present study are in accordance with the theories of the impact of economic globalization on governance in literatures (e.g., *rent-seeking channel*, *competition-reducing channel*, and *the cost of monitoring public officials channel*). However, if only trade openness is taken into account, in countries with low overall governance levels and low incomes, it can lead to further weakening of overall governance. This is because in low-income countries with low level of overall governance, exports are mainly in the form of raw materials. Therefore, it provides the conditions for rent-seeking and corruption. As a result, the level of overall governance is further weakened.

5 Concluding Remarks

In this chapter, the effect of globalization on the quality of overall governance in different groups of countries was investigated. These countries were categorized according to their levels of per capita income and quality of overall governance. In fact, the key question was whether economic globalization had improved the status of overall governance at every level of development and governance.

In the present study, the overall governance quality index was calculated by combining six sub-indices of WGI index using the PCA technique. We used the three indices of overall globalization, economic globalization, and trade openness. In other words, overall globalization was used at first. Then, the scope of the definition was narrowed down and only the index of economic globalization was allowed to enter the model. Then, the definition of the index was narrowed further and only the index of trade openness was considered. Accordingly, the purpose of this chapter was to compare the impact of globalization on overall governance quality by considering three different indices of globalization, namely, overall globalization, economic globalization, and trade openness. The most important findings of this chapter can be summarized as follows:

1. The results are sensitive to the choice of globalization index, level of per capita income, and the quality of overall governance.
2. The decisive variable in how the overall globalization affects overall governance was the level of overall governance in each country. The impacts of overall globalization on overall governance in countries with high and low levels of governance were positive and negative, respectively.
3. The decisive variable in how economic globalization could affect overall governance was the level of per capita income in each country. The impacts of economic globalization on overall governance in countries with high and low per capita income were insignificant and positive, respectively.
4. The main determinants of how trade openness could affect overall governance were the governance level and per capita income (both). The impact of trade openness on overall governance was positive for countries with high levels of overall governance and high per capita income and negative in countries with low levels of overall governance and low per capita income.

The most important finding of the present study is that, although trade openness may not have a positive effect in low-income countries and with weak overall governance, economic globalization has a positive effect by considering different trade dimensions and removing barriers to trade. This finding could be a lesson for countries in transition. In most countries in transition, incomes are low and overall governance is poor. So, the suggestion for policymakers in emerging countries is to focus on economic globalization rather than trade openness, to improve the quality of overall governance.

Finally, it should be noted that an examination of the channels and mechanisms which affect all aspects of globalization and its impact on all components of governance is beyond the scope of this chapter. But it can be done in a separate research in line with the current research.

Appendix

Table A Regression model used in literature for testing the effects of globalization on institutional quality

Num.	Author(s)	Country and sample	Proxy variables for Institutional Quality (Dependent Variable)	Proxy variables for Globalization (Independent Variable)	Control variables	Estimation methods	Main results: The globalization changes the quality of Institutions
1	Scruggs and Lange (2002)	Sixteen industrial democracies	Economic institutional arrangements (union membership trends – density)	-Financial openness -Total direct investment -Trade openness	-Cabinet center of gravity -Unemployment rate -% of civilian labor force in service sector -Other control variables (inflation rate, share of government employment (first difference), and the change in the log of dependent labor force (not lagged))	OLS with panel-corrected standard errors (PCSE) procedure	**Yes** (very mixed, at times contradictory)
2	Bonaglia and Macedo (2002)	A larger sample of countries	Corruption	Openness (ratio of imports on GDP)	Gross domestic output per capita, political rights, economic policy variables (such as the degree of trade liberalization or more general state intervention in the economy), exports' sectoral concentration, trade remoteness, country size and additional "cultural" traits	OLS, instrumented variables (IV)	**Yes** (positively)

3	Li and Reuveny (2003)	127 countries (all countries, LDCs, non-OECD countries)	Democracy	-FDI -Trade - Economic globalization	Economic growth, economic development, inflation, diffusion, portfolio, prior democracy, Gini coefficient, education	OLS regression analysis	**Yes** (both positively and negatively)
4	Rudra (2005)	59 developing countries (including 20 upper-middle and high-income (non-OECD) LDCs, 21 lower middle-income LDCs, and 18 low-income LDCs)	-Democracy - Political and civil liberties - Elite disunity	-Trade as percent of GDP - Capital flows as percent of GDP	-- Potential labor power - Economic development (GDP per capita logged and growth) - Urbanization - Inflation - Regional democracy - World democracy - * Social spending (% of gov. expenditure)	Unbalanced panel data and the fixed effects method	**Yes** (positively)
5	Potrafke (2009)	OECD countries	Growth rate of social expenditures (as a share of GDP)	KOF index of globalization	- Ideological orientation of the respective government - The growth rate of real GDP per capita -The growth rate of the unemployment rate -The growth rate of the dependency ratio - Lagged dependent variable	-Panel-corrected standard errors (PCSE) -Dynamic panel fixed effects model - Random effect	**Yes** (mixed, at times contradictory)

(continued)

Num.	Author(s)	Country and sample	Proxy variables for Institutional Quality (Dependent Variable)	Proxy variables for Globalization (Independent Variable)	Control variables	Estimation methods	Main results: The globalization changes the quality of Institutions
6	Ju and Wei (2010)	1–32 economies with both a good financial system and adequate property rights protection 2–33 economies with an inadequate financial system but still pass able property rights protection 3–32 economies with both a poor financial system and poor property rights protection	- Quality of financial system -Strength of property rights protection	- Per capita net financial capital outflows - Per capita net FDI outflows	–	panel OLS	**Yes** (both positively and negatively)
7	Walter (2010)	Switzerland (survey data)	- Feelings of job security	- Trade exposure -FDI exposure - Job offshore ability	- Individual skill levels, the interaction term between variables, the sectoral unemployment rate, education, income –Gender, age, labor union membership, whether the person works in the public sector, respondents' level of risk aversion	Binary logit Ordered logit	**Yes** (positively)

8	Potrafke (2010)	20 OECD countries	Labor market deregulation (employment protection, active labor market expenditures, replacement rate, benefit duration, tax wedge, union density)	- KOF index of globalization (economic, social, political, and overall)	- Ideology (left-wing) - Lagged dependent variable - Working-age population - Unemployment rate	Dynamic bias-corrected estimator	**No**
9	Dreher et al. (2012)	106 countries	Human rights (physical integrity rights and empowerment rights)	- KOF index of globalization (economic, social, political, and overall) - Economic liberalization - FDI	- A proxy for democracy (polity IV), population size, GDP per capita, a set of dummy variables controlling for legal origin, a dummy variable indicating the presence of a civil and/or international war, lagged dependent variable, legal origin, war	Unbalanced panel data regression (ordered probit)	**Yes** (positive and mixed)
10	Bhattacharyya (2012)	103 countries	ICRG expropriation Risk ICRG repudiation of contracts	Trade liberalization (measured by Sachs and Warner openness index)	- A country dummy variable controlling for country fixed effects - A year dummy variable controlling for time-varying common shocks - Log income per capita, rainfall, export partner growth, tariff, export growth rate	Limited information maximum likelihood (LIML) fuller estimation method (panel data)	**Yes** (positively)

(continued)

Num.	Author(s)	Country and sample	Proxy variables for Institutional Quality (Dependent Variable)	Proxy variables for Globalization (Independent Variable)	Control variables	Estimation methods	Main results: The globalization changes the quality of Institutions
11	Potrafke (2013)	137 countries	Labor market deregulation (labor market freedom)	KOF index of globalization (economic, social, political, and overall)	Labor market deregulation (−1), population, government expenditures	Dynamic panel (system GMM panel estimator)	**No** (the results do not show that globalization induced labor market deregulation)
12	Young and Sheehan (2014)	116 countries	- Polity IV democracy ranking - Economic freedom of the world index - Index for number of checks and balances	Foreign aid flows	Oil production as a share of GDP, population growth rate (over 5-year periods), urban population share expressed as a percentage, primary school enrollment rate expressed as a percentage, secondary school enrollment rate expressed as a percentage, real per capita GDP, 2005 US$, life expectancy at birth, agricultural share of GDP expressed as a percentage, lagged value of dependent variable	OLS period fixed effects 2SLS period fixed effects	**Yes** (negatively)
13	Nadeem et al. (2014)	91 countries	Governance (ICRG index)	- KOF index of globalization	- Freedom of press, labor force participation rate, per capita income, presidential system, regime type, size of largest party, property rights	Panel fixed effects model and GMM	**Yes** (negatively)

14	Bergh et al. (2014)	101 countries (overall, subsample of low-income countries, subsample of high-income countries)	Six aggregate indicators of governance (government effectiveness, control of corruption, regulatory quality, political stability, rule of law, and voice and accountability)	- KOF index of globalization (economic and social) - Lagged globalization	- GDP per capita (PPP adjusted, in constant USD) -Total population -Share of total rent from natural resources in GDP	Panel fixed effects model	**Yes** (positively in rich countries, negatively in poor countries)
15	Long et al. (2015)	China (host regions)	Tax rate, number of fee items, satisfaction with local courts, rule of law quality	Foreign direct investment (FDI)	Set of firm characteristics, city-level features	OLS, 2SLS	**Yes** (positively impact in firm level)
16	Kant (2016)	169 countries (including developing countries, developed countries, all 169 countries)	Ease of doing business	FDI to GDP ratio	Lender-borrower rights index	OLS, 2SLS	-**Yes** (positively impact in developing countries) - **No** (no statistically significant effect in developed countries)

(continued)

Num.	Author(s)	Country and sample	Proxy variables for Institutional Quality (Dependent Variable)	Proxy variables for Globalization (Independent Variable)	Control variables	Estimation methods	Main results: The globalization changes the quality of Institutions
17	Martin and Steiner (2016)	78 countries	-PR - Political institutions (changes to the voting rules)	Economic globalization (trade to GDP ratios (exports + imports/GDP), KOF economic integration	Tariff rate, population Gross national income (GNI), GNI per capita, GDP, GDP per capita, government consumption as a share of GDP	OLS with panel-corrected standard errors (PCSE) procedure -Random effects logit regression -Logistic regression with time dummies	**Yes** (positively)
18	Amavilah et al. (2017)	53 African countries (excluding South Sudan)	Governance (economic, institutional, and general governance)	Trade openness, FDI (financial openness)	GDP per capita growth, government expenditures, inflation	HAC panel fixed effects	**Yes** (both positively and negatively)
19	Asongu and Biekpe (2017)	51 African countries	Terrorism variable (domestic, transnational, unclear or total)	KOF index of globalization (economic, social, political, and overall)	Internet penetration, GDP growth, political stability, inclusive development, military expenditure	System GMM estimation procedure	**Yes** (both positively and negatively)

20	Asongu (2017)	51 African countries	-Economic governance (entailing regulation quality and government effectiveness) - Political governance (consisting of "voice and accountability" and political stability/ nonviolence) -Institutional governance (comprised of the rule of law and corruption control) - General governance	- KOF index of globalization (economic, social, political, and overall)	-Gross domestic product (GDP) growth -Foreign aid -Public investment -Inflation -Middle income -English common law	Instrumental variable quantile regressions	**Yes** (positively)
21	Kant (2018)	48 developing countries	- The average of "protecting investors" - Enforcing contracts through courts	Alternative portfolio variables (the ratio of net portfolio inflow to its GDP in current US dollars	-The strength of lender's and borrower's legal rights index -Growth rate in per capita income in PPP dollars	2SLS/IV estimation	**Yes** (positively)

(continued)

Num.	Author(s)	Country and sample	Proxy variables for Institutional Quality (Dependent Variable)	Proxy variables for Globalization (Independent Variable)	Control variables	Estimation methods	Main results: The globalization changes the quality of Institutions
22	Asongu et al. (2018)	51 African countries	Governance (political, economic, institutional, and general)	Globalization (economic, political, social, or overall)	GDP growth, foreign aid, public investment, and inflation	Generalized method of moments	**Yes** (positively) Global globalization and general governance Sub-indices: very mix
23	Challe et al. (2019)	95 open economies (1, full sample; 2, excluding 9 oil-dependent countries; 3, excluding 18 countries at the bottom; and 4 excluding 18 countries at the top quintile of the rule of law distribution)	Economic institutions (property rights, WGI rule of law, ICRG index)	- Lagged current account to GDP ratios (to measure cross-country capital inflows)	- GDP growth rate - GDP per capita - Initial value institutional quality - Initial GDP per capita	Dynamic GMM estimates (unbalanced panel data)	**Yes** (negatively)

References

Acemoglu, D., Johnson, S., Robinson, J., & Thaicharoen, Y. (2003). Institutional causes, macroeconomic symptoms: Volatility, crises and growth. *Journal of Monetary Economics, 50*, 49–123. https://doi.org/10.1016/S0304-3932(02)00208-8.

Ades, A., & Tella, R. D. (1999). Rents, competition, and corruption. *The American Economic Review, 89*(4), 982–993.

Amavilah, V., Asongu, S. A., & Andrés, A. R. (2017). Effects of globalization on peace and stability: Implications for governance and the knowledge economy of African countries. *Technological Forecasting and Social Change, 122*, 91–103. https://doi.org/10.1016/j.techfore.2017.04.013.

Arellano, M., & Bond, S. (1991). Some tests of specification for panel data: Monte Carlo evidence and an application to employment equations. *The Review of Economic Studies, 58*(2), 227–229.

Arellano, M., & Bover, O. (1995). Another look at the instrumental variable estimation of error-components models. *Journal of Econometrics, 68*(68), 29–51.

Asongu, S. (2017). Does globalization promote good governance in Africa? An empirical study across 51 countries. *World Affairs, 180*(2), 105–141. https://doi.org/10.1227/01.NEU.0000349921.14519.2A.

Asongu, S. A., & Biekpe, N. (2017). Globalization and terror in Africa. *International Economics*, (November), 1–12. https://doi.org/10.1016/j.inteco.2017.12.005.

Asongu, S. A., Efobi, U., & Tchamyou, V. S. (2018). Globalisation and governance in Africa: A critical contribution to the empirics. *International Journal of Development Issues, 17*(1), 2–27. https://doi.org/10.1108/IJDI-04-2017-0038.

Bergh, A., Mirkina, I., & Nilsson, T. (2014). Globalization and institutional quality — A panel data analysis globalization and institutional quality — A panel data analysis. *Oxford Development Studies, 42*(3), 365–394. https://doi.org/10.1080/13600818.2014.884555.

Bhagwati, J. N. (1982). Directly unproductive, profit-seeking (DUP) activities. *Journal of Political Economy, 90*(5), 988–1002. https://doi.org/10.1086/261104.

Bhagwati, J. N., & Srinivasan, T. N. (1982). Revenue seeking: A generalization of the theory of tariffs--a correction. *Journal of Political Economy, 90*(1), 188–190. https://doi.org/10.1086/261049.

Bhattacharyya, S. (2012). Trade liberalization and institutional development. *Journal of Policy Modeling, 34*, 253–269. https://doi.org/10.1016/j.jpolmod.2011.08.005.

Blundell, R., & Bond, S. (1998). Initial conditions and moment restrictions in dynamic panel data models. *Journal of Econometrics, 87*, 115–143.

Bonaglia, F., & Macedo, J. B. De. (2002). *How globalisation improves governance* (OECD Development Centre, Working Paper No. 181, (June 2001)).

Challe, E., Lopez, J. I., & Mengus, E. (2019). Institutional quality and capital inflows: Theory and evidence. *Journal of International Money and Finance, 96*, 168–191. https://doi.org/10.1016/j.jimonfin.2019.05.005.

Dixit, B. A. (2009). Governance institutions and economic activity. *American Economic Review, 99*(1), 5–24. https://doi.org/10.1257/aer.99.1.5.

Do, Q., & Levchenko, A. A. (2009). Trade, inequality, and the political economy of institutions. *Journal of Economic Theory, 144*, 1489–1520. https://doi.org/10.1016/j.jet.2008.11.007.

Dreher, A., Gassebner, M., & Siemers, L. R. (2012). Globalization, economic freedom, and human rights. *The Journal of Conflict Resolution, 56*(3), 516–546. https://doi.org/10.1177/0022002711420962.

Gisselquist, R. M. (2012). *Good governance as a concept, and why this matters for development Policy* (Working Paper, United Nations University (UNU) (No. No. 2012/30)).

Hadri, K., & Rao, Y. (2008). Panel stationarity test with structural breaks. *Oxford Bulletin of Economics and Statistics, 70*(2), 245–269. https://doi.org/10.1111/j.1468-0084.2008.00502.x.

Hall, R. E., & Jones, C. I. (1999). Why do some countries produce so much more output per worker than others ? *The Quarterly Journal of Economics, 114*(1), 83–116.

Jacobs, B., & Van Der Ploeg, F. (2019). Redistribution and pollution taxes with non-linear Engel. *Journal of Environmental Economics and Management, 95*, 198–226. https://doi.org/10.1016/j.jeem.2019.01.008.
Ju, J., & Wei, S. (2010). Domestic institutions and the bypass effect of financial globalization. *American Economic Journal: Economic Policy, 2*(4), 173–204.
Kant, C. (2016). Are institutions in developing countries malleable? *Journal of Policy Modeling, 38*(2), 272–289. https://doi.org/10.1016/j.jpolmod.2016.01.002.
Kant, C. (2018). Financial openness & institutions in developing countries. *Research in International Business and Finance, 46*(February), 240–250. https://doi.org/10.1016/j.ribaf.2018.03.001.
Krueger, A. O. (1974). The political economy of the rent-seeking society. *American Economic Review, 64*(3), 291–303. Retrieved from https://www.jstor.org/stable/1808883.
Levchenko, A. A. (2013). International trade and institutional change. *Journal of Law, Economics, and Organization, 29*(5), 1145–1181. https://doi.org/10.1093/jleo/ews008.
Li, Q., & Reuveny, R. (2003). Economic globalization and democracy : An empirical analysis. *British Journal of Political Science, 33*(1), 29–54. https://doi.org/10.1017/S000712340300002.
Long, C., Yang, J. I. N., & Zhang, J. (2015). Institutional impact of foreign direct Investment in China. *World Development, 66*(71273217), 31–48. https://doi.org/10.1016/j.worlddev.2014.08.001.
Martin, C. W., & Steiner, D. N. (2016). Economic globalization and the change of electoral rules. *Constitutional Political Economy, 27*(4), 355–376. https://doi.org/10.1007/s10602-015-9203-5.
Nadeem, M., Hayat, M. A., & Nazir, R. (2014). Exploring interlinks between globalization and governance a panel data evidence. *Pakistan Economic and Social Review, 52*(2), 187–208.
Pesaran, M. H., & Yamagata, T. (2008). Testing slope homogeneity in large panels. *Journal of Econometrics, 142*, 50–93. https://doi.org/10.1016/j.jeconom.2007.05.010.
Potrafke, N. (2009). Did globalization restrict partisan politics? An empirical evaluation of social expenditures in a panel of OECD countries. *Public Choice, 140*(1–2), 105–124.
Potrafke, N. (2010). Labor market deregulation and globalization : Empirical evidence from OECD countries. *Review of World Economics/Weltwirtschaftliches Archiv, 146*(3), 545–571. https://doi.org/10.1007/s10290-010-0056-8.
Potrafke, N. (2013). Globalization and labor market institutions : International empirical evidence. *Journal of Comparative Economics, 41*, 829–842. https://doi.org/10.1016/j.jce.2013.02.002.
Rudra, N. (2005). Globalization and the strengthening of democracy in the developing world. *American Journal of Political Science, 49*(4), 704–730.
Samadi, A. H. (2018). Institutions and entrepreneurship in MENA countries. In *Contributions to management science*. https://doi.org/10.1007/978-3-319-75913-5_3.
Samadi, A. H. (2019). Institutional quality and globalization in developing countries. In *Contributions to economics*. https://doi.org/10.1007/978-3-030-14370-1_6.
Scruggs, L., & Lange, P. (2002). Have all the members gone ? Globalization, institutions, and union density. *The Journal of Politics, 64*(1), 126–153.
Segura-cayuela, R. (2006). *Inefficient policies, inefficient institutions and trade* (Banco de España Working Paper 0633).
Stefanadis, C. (2010). Appropriation, property rights institutions, and international trade. *American Economic Journal: Economic Policy, 2*(4), 148–172.
Walter, S. (2010). Globalization and the welfare state: Testing the microfoundations of the compensation hypothesis. *International Studies Quarterly, 54*(2), 403–426.
Wei, S.-J. (2000). *Natural openness and good government* (NBER Working Paper 7765).
Young, A. T., & Sheehan, K. M. (2014). Foreign aid, institutional quality, and growth. *European Journal of Political Economy, 36*, 195–208. https://doi.org/10.1016/j.ejpoleco.2014.08.003.

Public Administration Reforms in the Emerging Markets' Era

Nazak Nobari

1 Introduction

Globalization, a dominant force in the twentieth century's last two decades, is shaping a new era of interaction among nations, economies, and people. The impact of globalization on nations and societies is mixed, with benefits accruing due to dynamic interaction and competition along with economic crisis, weakened state apparatus, resource constraints, propagation of market-oriented values, increasing international competition, new market requirements, and disturbing wealth concentration, increasing poverty level, changing citizens' expectations, social crises, environmental crisis with significant repercussions on the development process, and sustainability challenges.

Globalization has affected the nature and processes of administrative systems due to the impact of pressures generated on that by global institutions, information technology, international competitiveness, and increasing concern for efficiency and productivity. These pursuers have changed the state's role, public administration strategies, managerial orientation in governance, and market-driven approach to development. Countries' development paths have changed over time, and these are challenging times for governments around the world. In other words, emerging markets will remain the growth engine of the global economy over the next decades.

In fact, in an increasingly dynamic global economy, a significant challenge for governments is introducing a different set of opportunities to develop the economic country's strategies and change their development stage. Emerging markets can be considered as those opportunities.

According to International Financial Corporation, emerging markets are growing in size and completeness degree, as opposed to small markets – which are inactive

N. Nobari (✉)
Administrative and recruitment organization, Tehran, Iran

N. Faghih, A. H. Samadi (eds.), *Dynamics of Institutional Change in Emerging Market Economies*, Contributions to Economics,
https://doi.org/10.1007/978-3-030-61342-6_10

and do not seem to change. Emerging markets are seen now as a unique environment which needs a systematic approach to create new business models, governance model, and policies. In most nations, governments in emerging markets are under pressure to stimulate even faster growth and catch up with living standards.

This chapter aims to develop a viable framework for public managers and politicians to act in an increasingly complex global environment and benefit from emerging markets and their capacities to adapt to dynamic environment changes. In particular, the institution-based view is used for this purpose. Because under this view, public administration can consider dynamic interactions between institutions and organizations and examine reference choices as the outcome of those interactions. The institution-based view has emerged as a significant paradigm to understand organizational phenomena (system) and management activities in emerging economies. In other words, this chapter tries to highlight how public administrations, at various levels, encompass institutional changes and change over varying timescales from the processes of constant changes found in markets to fundamental changes occurring through environmental dynamics.

The institution-based view's key elements are formal institutions (laws and regulations) and informal institutions (norms, values, and beliefs), and changes in these institutions over time form business systems behavior in a society. The majority of definitions have two elements: the emerging economies include institutional contexts that are becoming more market-oriented and less market-supporting, and income or GDP is increasing, facilitating economic growth (Xu and Meyer 2013).

The remainder of this chapter is structured as follows: the first section focuses on the development and economic growth as a result of public administration activities. The second section includes institutional theory and its implications to public administration by reviewing main public administration reform theories and concept and role of institutions. The third section emphasizes on emerging markets and their dynamics. The focus is on systematic interactions between regulations, markets, and institutions to understand the appropriateness of the public administration framework. One of the findings of this study is developing a policy framework entitled institutional characteristics effect on the economy. After briefly outlining the methodology of the empirical study, this chapter focuses on analyzing collected various longitudinal and cross-sectional variables in the 26 nations from MSCI Emerging Markets Index, and they are compared based on various longitudinal and cross-sectional variables. Finally, the chapter concludes with a discussion of core findings.

2 Development and Economic Growth

Development is a broad concept, and it is almost as old as civilization. In general, development means an "event constituting a new stage in a changing situation."[1] In other words, it can be defined as a set of processes and policies which are seen to hold the potential for improving people's lives in certain parts of the world (Jones 2000).

Development is a multidimensional phenomenon and entails social, economic, political, and human development, and considerable changes have occurred in the world's socioeconomic and political setting since the "start" of the development era. Therefore, to increase the government's capacity to manage the development path, countries must promote human well-being in the end, with liberalized markets, economic growth, and distributive justice (United Nations 2004).

Five typical qualifications can be considered for its concept, referring to the development of specific dimensions, as below (Bellù 2011):

- Economic development
- Human development
- Territorial development
- Sustainable development
- Institutional development

As this study aims and each qualification means, economic development and institutional development are two qualifications that provide a comprehensive view to define the conceptual framework to improve a country's productivity performance. Economic development is one of those phenomena that involve a diverse range of actors, and it can be defined as a multidimensional process including significant changes in social structure, popular attitudes, and national institutions, as well as accelerating the economic growth and reducing poverty and inequality (Todaro and Smith 2009: 16). It is important to distinguish between three types of growth: physical growth, economic (GDP) growth, and human welfare growth (Ekins 2000).

Institutional development is the development of a set of rules, mechanisms, processes, and cultural norms contributing directly or indirectly to support development by guaranteeing government effectiveness, equal levels of freedom, secure property rights, and preventing risk of appropriation (Battaglia et al. 2011). Relying on institutional development, institutions play a central role in explaining growth (De Dios 2008) and public administration through public institutions. In general, the public sector has a crucial role in achieving economic development. Institutions form a system of rules, beliefs, norms, and organizations that generate a regularity of social behavior (Greif 2006, Chaps. 2 and 5). The regularity of behavior is the key to the success of market transactions.

[1] Oxford English Dictionary. http://oxforddictionaries.com

Furthermore, public administrative system and economics have always overlapped, and public administration has been strongly linked to economic development in terms of information market failure, spillovers, sunk investments, social impacts, and political pressures (Kane 2004). Economists have recently started to consider the role of institutions for economic growth (Acemoglu et al. 2001). According to Azfar, institutions with lower transaction costs and secure property rights are essential to bring changes in the private sphere (Azfar 2006).

Various theories try to conceptualize the administrative system framework. In this chapter, the institutional theory is chosen to interpret the public administration characteristics, to lead the country's development path, and to regard economic growth characterized by specialization of actors and division of labor. The institutional theory is useful in understanding changes in the economic environment. According to Scott, neo-institutionalism is better prepared than ever to inform research on institutions and other forms of temporary organization (Scott 2004: 460–484).

The drive for institutional reform and the creation of "effective" systems of governance are central to the current debate on developing public policy to improve government productivity. In most countries, governments in emerging markets are under pressure to stimulate even faster growth to meet dynamic environment requirements.

3 Institutional Theory and Its Implications to Public Administration

The quality of public administration is an essential driver of a country's competitiveness (World Economic Forum 2011), and today's economic environment surrounding all countries is globalizing, and any public administration reform cannot succeed without taking it into account. In reality, administrative reform is a complex and multifaceted issue, and reform will proceed only when a country's leaders are committed and in the driver's seat (World Bank 2000).

Although public administration reform is crucial, there is no unique model/program for all countries to adapt to their context and environment. Efficient and effective public administration means such an administrative system that acts as a productive, fair, accountable, and transparent manner to assure the citizens' effective delivery of public services. In this situation, relying on theories to find driving variables is conducive.

Public administration as an interdisciplinary field entails the convergence of organizational theory, social theory, political theory, and related studies in this era. Unlike most public administration theories, which are deeply rooted in political science, institutional theory is rooted in sociology and is now highly interdisciplinary. Institutionalism is not a theory in the formal sense; it is instead the framework, the language, and the set of assumptions that hold and guide empirical research and theory-building in much of public administration (Frederickson et al. 2012: 67), and institutionalism emphasizes on the relationship between institutions and individuals and considers it mainly at the organizational or societal level (Scott 2008). Traditionally, there are two main streams of institutional theory: old and new institutionalism.

Old institutionalism as a theoretical stream emerged in the early 1980s (Hall 1986) and labeled as such later (Thelen 1999). From the literature review, this old institutional study, as a theoretical paradigm, focused on how formal structures, such as law and form of government, affect political processes and outcomes.

The roots of emerging new institutionalism can be found in new institutional economics, positive theory of institutions, sociological approaches to institutions, and organization theory (Caravella 2011).

The new institutionalism in organizational theory tends to focus on institutions, their organizational structure, and processes at both national and international levels (DiMaggio and Powell 1991). New institutionalism includes a more dynamic conception of institutions, where informal elements, such as informal rules and conventions, are considered (Lowndes and Roberts 2013: 69). New institutional theory switches the focus to the interaction of institutions with others in the internal socio-economic and political environment or the external environment or the blend of interaction between both internal and external environments.

Approaches to studying institutions differ in how they understand and explain the nature of institutions; how institutions form, change, and improve; and how these processes impose and facilitate human and community behavior (Schmidt 2010; Peters 2012: 139–140; Lowndes and Roberts 2013: 74).

There are three broad approaches to institutional studies that emerged in new institutionalism. They are rational choice institutionalism, historical institutionalism, and sociological institutionalism (Hall and Taylor 1996). Schmidt extended these categories into four streams, including historical institutionalism, rational institutionalism, sociological institutionalism, and discursive institutionalism (Schmidt 2010).

Rational choice institutionalism views political life as the exchange of self-interested actors aiming to maximize their utility and act predictably. This approach uses rational choice theory to explain how institutions affect individual behavior and decisions. Institutions are understood as structures constraining individuals and provide incentives and opportunities for collective action; the actors can also change the rules and recalculate their strategies (Shepsle 2006: 31; Nilsson 2018).

Historical institutionalism is a path-dependency approach and seeks to explain the creation of institutions in the past contexts and explores the interactions between creators of the institutions and the contextual structure. This approach more focuses on how the historical ways of performing actions remain and how hard it is to change them (Sanders 2006: 40; Hall and Taylor 1996).

Sociological institutionalism emphasizes on the role of values and norms in understanding institutional phenomena. In this approach, actors lie in a dense institutional environment where institutions provide opportunities for action and reflect a shared understanding of the norms. Institutions affect individuals' behavior through shared beliefs and cognitions that individuals internalize and enact (March and Olsen 1989, 1998, 2006).

According to Schmidt (2008, 2010), discursive institutionalism is strongly focused on ideals and discourses that are at the forefront of dynamic organizational change. This approach emphasizes on how ideas and discourses overcome limitations and obstacles to steer the change. Through institutional theory, institutions and organizational arrangements are the most critical determinants of a nation's administrative capabilities because they affect the utilization of all resources.

The study of public administration has a tradition, and over the years, many theories and concepts have been developed to analyze how governments steer societal issues. Therefore, developing a better understanding of the public administrative system is essential for a range of policy fields, both conceptually and practically, especially about institutions that govern a country's economic and social interactions.

Public administration faces many changes and issues in societies, but it has two closely related meanings (United Nations Economic and Social Council 2006):

(a) The aggregate machinery (policies, rules, procedures, systems, organizational structures, and personnel) funded by the state budget and in charge of the management and direction of the affairs of the executive government, and its interaction with other stakeholders in the state, society, and external environment
(b) The management and implementation of the whole set of government activities dealing with the implementation of laws, regulations, and decisions of the government and the management related to the provision of public services

Public administration literature shows three influential schools of thought in this field: scientific management, new public management, and new public governance (Authors' conclusion).

According to Osborne, the first school of the public administration as the traditional public administration (PA) includes vital elements such as a dominance of the "rule of law," role of bureaucracy in policymaking and implementation, a duality of politics and administration inside the public organizations, commitment to incremental budgeting, and the hegemony of the professional in the public service system (Osborne 2006).

In the 1980s of the twentieth century, the movement of public change made the new public management (NPM) paradigm an outstanding contribution to government management and public administration science (Xu et al. 2015). Although the NPM model has several projections such as managerialism (Pollitt 1993:3), new public management (Hood 1991), market orientation public administration (Lan and Rosenbloom 1992; Hughes 1998), and entrepreneurial government (Osborne and Gaebler 1993), the basic premises are the same assuming that public sector organizations need to learn from the private sector (Hood 1991; Pollitt 1993: 52–58). Osborne argues even though PA is a historical model, many of its assumptions of vertical hierarchy and the system of policymaking, policy implementation, and value base of public sector ethos are still assumed to echo in the modern public service systems (Osborne 2006).

After the emergence of "the new public management," "the new public governance" was developed as a theoretical paradigm adapted to the contemporary government public administration. According to Osborne, new public governance is a theoretical model to complement new public management and public administration (Osborne 2006). This new paradigm was relative to the new public management and the new public service, and the "new" was reflected by how transition of the governance concept adapted to modern social public affairs (Xu et al. 2015). According to Hughes's discussion about differences between government and governance, governance refers to the institutions of the ruling power to govern, which is a much broader concept, including government forms (2003:76). Based on the context of local governance studies, complexity has been understood as a significant factor in governance activities (Haveri 2006) (Table 1).

Based on the literature review, administrative paradigms are approached from an ex-ante or an ex-post perspective (Dingwerth and Pattberg 2006), and administrative

Table 1 Elements of the NPG, in contrast to PA and the NPM

Paradigm/key elements	Traditional public administration	New public management	New public governance
Theoretical basis	Political science and public policy, bureaucratic system	Rational and public choice theories, management philosophy, transaction cost theories	Institutional theory, complex social system, organizational sociology, integrity theory and network theory
Research method	Institutionalism research method	Positivism research method	Collectivism research method
Nature of the state	Unitary	Disaggregated (organizational and administrative units)	Plural and pluralist, institutional system
Focus	The political system	Intra-organizational management	Inter-organizational governance
Emphasis	Policy creation, implementation	Management of organizational services, inputs and output, business tools	Service processes and outcomes
Relationship to external (non-public) organizational partners	Potential elements of the policy system	Independent contractors within a competitive marketplace	Preferred suppliers, and often inter-dependent agents within ongoing relationships
Governance mechanism	Hierarchy	Market and competition, classical or neo-classical contracts	Trust, networks, or relational contracts
Role of citizens	Leader	Customer	Participation in decision
Value base	Public sector ethos, regime and procedure	Efficacy of competition and the marketplace	Neo-corporatist, democracy, and efficiency

Source: Authors' own table

paradigms have been considered as one major source for institutional change in the public sector organizations. Inevitably, such a three-stage model is a simplification – elements of each stage can often coexist or overlap (Klijn 2002; Osborne 2006).

New Public Management (NPM) and New Public Governance (NPG) can be seen as the dominant (reform) paradigms of the last decades, both aiming to overcome the traditional public administration (Pollitt and Bouckaert 2011). According to Osborne (2010), the NPG model is based on institutional and network theories (such as open systems and neo-institutional theories). The summary of comparative review shows public administration and policy science theories and methodologies have been developed and provide the theoretical and normative underpinning of network governance. In summary, public administration schools consider public institutions through three different lenses: as pillars of political order, as outcomes of societal values, and as self-constructed social systems.

It also indicates that NPG provides different answers to the complexities faced by governments, such as emerging forms of trust-based, networked structures of collaboration and coordination, and policy tools to shape network structures and functions. The governance and steering activities such as policy processes, decision making, and management are made according to the institutional system logic (Kanniainen 2017), and administrative system is a socio-cybernetic system dynamic in its interrelations. It is focused on communication between the actors and the environment.

Osborne describes the complexity of political-administrative systems with the terms of plural state and pluralist state. Plural state refers to multiple interdependent actors contributing to the delivery of public services, and pluralist state to multiple processes informing the policymaking system (Osborne 2006). One of the core assumptions of new institutional theory is that specific institutions formulate rules that need to be followed by individuals if they seek to obtain legitimacy (Lowndes and Wilson 2003). Thus, institutions as agencies are the actors' possibilities to affect the practical reasoning and the institutional governance logics in the institutional system.

Institutions are the core object of institutionalism. Some researchers focus on the definition of institutions as the rules and norms for activities of organizations, firms, and industries (Peng et al. 2008; Greenwood et al. 2011). Some others define institutions as humanly made constraints that form political, economic, and social orders and relations (North 1991).

Among divergent views to recognize institutions, Peters introduces four shared elements to study institutions and their interactions under this new institutionalism approach (Peters 2012: 1–46):

1. Focus on a structural feature of society. It can be either formal (e.g., a legal framework) or informal (e.g., a set of shared norms).
2. Stability over time.
3. The existence of some shared values or ways of constructing the meaning of the members of an institution.
4. Ability to influence on the behavior of individuals.

Based on definitions of institutions, the role of the institutions becomes more decisive in the private sector of the economy, considering the proprietary rights protection, operations in capital markets, laws reducing uncertainties, and promotion of development (Banerjee et al. 2006). Over the last two decades, the economics literature has emphasized on the role of high-quality institutions and governance structures as important growth determinants beyond classical growth drivers (Knack and Keefer 1995; Mauro 1995; Olson et al. 2000; Acemoglu et al. 2001; St. Aubyn 2008; Pitlik et al. 2012: 1).

Institutions are affected by their social, economic, and political context, but they also affect that context powerfully. Therefore, the importance of institutions' design affecting their behavior and their political outcomes has been amply proved (Lijphart 1984: 4; Weaver and Rockman 1993).

Institutions perform several economic functions in a market system that affect efficiency and equity objectives (Subramanian 2007):

- First, institutions create markets.
- Second, institutions regulate and/or substitute for markets.
- Third, institutions, such as the central banks or fiscal, stabilize markets by ensuring low inflation and macroeconomic stability and helping to avoid financial crises.
- Fourth, institutions legitimize markets through mechanisms of social protection and insurance and, importantly, through mechanisms for redistribution and managing conflict.

Institutions and government policies determine the economic environment and stimulate economic growth through "market enhancing" and "market complementing" channels. Today's growth strategies in emerging markets related to government capacity building and government effectiveness are noticed as fundamental determinants of spread for emerging markets (Eichler 2014). To be effective, governments need to work with their partners to understand and address the broad range of environmental incentives and pressures (Authors' conclusion). Research shows that the rules which govern business transactions are also essential to foster the competitiveness of local enterprises and the attractiveness of a country for foreign investment (Pitlik et al. 2012: 2).

4 Emerging Markets

Many comparative capitalism and public policy scholars generally agree that the direction of institutional change during the last decades is toward the forms of governance through market dynamics. Contextually, the establishment of new market rules is a long-term public-political project through distinct political dynamics of different countries.

Emerging countries are those countries whose economies are increasing fast, respective in the transition phase to a market economy (Simon 1997: 913), and emerging markets, also known as emerging economies, have become major players in the global economy and a primary source of growth in the twenty-first century.

The term "emerging markets" was coined in 1981 by an economist at the International Finance Corporation, Antoine van Agtmael (Carrasco and Williams 2012). At first, it became popular among financial market analysts (1983; Harvey 1995) and has later been adopted by management scholars studying business organizations operating in these economies (Khanna and Palepu 1997; Hoskisson et al. 2000). The term emerging markets describes new developing stock markets (Aybar and Thirunavukkarasu 2005) and, in summary, and at best, it has tended to rely on single-factor theories of explanation, predominantly size and growth in the area of economics and demographics (Sharma 2014). Along with the changes in the global political economy, the term emerging markets evolved to encompass countries that were considered to be transitioning from developing to developed economies (Serban et al. 2012).

Every EM has its characteristics and is a unique one. Most common characteristics of EMs could be summarized in the following (Miller 1998: 17–37):

1. Physical characteristics, in terms of an inadequate commercial infrastructure as well as the inadequacy of all other aspects of physical infrastructure (communication, transport, power generation)
2. Sociopolitical characteristics, including political instability, inadequate legal framework, weak social discipline, and reduced technological levels, besides (unique) cultural characteristics
3. Economic characteristics in terms of limited personal income, centrally controlled currencies with an influential role of government in economic life expressed besides others, in managing the transition to the market economy

The term "emerging economies" is mostly used as a synonym for emerging markets (Wright et al. 2005; Xu and Meyer 2013); its advantage is that it indicates that these economies play a variety of different roles for businesses, for example, as production bases within global value chains or as home bases for emerging market multinational enterprises (EM MNEs) (Meyer and Grosse 2018: 6).

Different entities have different definitions. Thus, to better understand the concept of emerging markets, Table 2 shows the differences between the emerging markets and the developed markets.

In developing countries, the state assumes a crucial role in policymaking, and they are the most important actors in placing issues on the agenda for government action, assessing alternatives, and superintending implementation (Grindle and Thomas 1991: 43). Over the decades, governments in emerging economies have tried many different policy agendas to stimulate development, accelerate growth and productivity, alleviate poverty, and achieve other goals to mixed success (Madgavkar et al. 2019) because the tremendous responsibility of any government is to manage the nation's economy. Therefore, governments are required to provide the stable ground rules that make commerce work and care about financial markets that can be sources of power – or threats to them. For this reason, governments use many tools to intervene in the economy, such as planning priorities, tax collection,

Table 2 Market characteristics

	Developed markets	Emerging markets
Legal system as an institutional system	Stable, transparent	Evolving, vague
Growth	Varied growth opportunities and tend to be at different points in the business cycle	Higher potential growth and tend to grow much faster than
Asset structure	Employ a lower level of fixed assets	Employ a higher level of fixed assets
Diversification	Broader diversification	More diversification
Market infrastructure	Developed	Undeveloped (being built)
Governmental involvement	Not so high	Relatively high
Market institutions	Developed	Undeveloped (being built)
Business context	Relatively formal contractual relationship between businesses	Large number of informal business relationships between business to business and largest buyers are often government-owned enterprises
Price sensitivity	Relatively low	Relatively high
Access to the information	High information availability and reliability	Low information availability
Individual economic status	Small changes	Large change
Urbanization	High	Low
Population growth rates	Negative	High

Source: Authors' own table and adapted from Nationwide Fund 2017; Grewal and Lilien 2015; Sunje and Civi 2000

and regulation. Studies show that another common intervention is to improve the capabilities of the public sector by hiring better government clerks, inspectors, and regulators and seeking innovative ways to train them (Madgavkar et al. 2019). Besides, many governments in emerging markets control and influence banks and allocate financial resources based on strategic criteria rather than market rules and market forces (La Porta et al. 2002).

It should be noticed that every framework is unique for each nation, and within any government capacity limitations, government interference enables the expansion of production and unstainable corporate strategic development. In countries with emerging markets, the incentives, and the quality of government officials and regulators are critical determinants of corporate behavior (Zhao 2016). Among all frameworks and tools, the most suitable and effective regulatory framework will significantly depend on how formed and evolved the market, the legal and institutions, and the history and culture of a particular economy (Pistor 2000). According to Fig. 1, institutional factors that occur in a period affect the economic performance and affect the distribution of resources in the following period (Chang 2010).

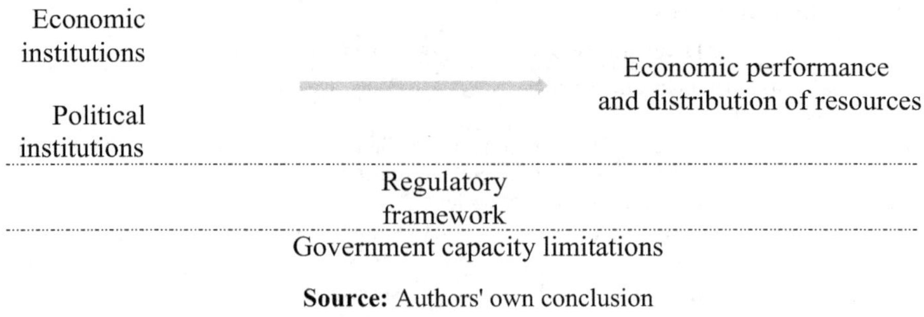

Fig. 1 Institutional characteristics' effect on economy. (*Source*: Authors' own conclusion)

In addition to economic differences, an administrative system includes numerous political, legal, sociocultural, and technological factors differentiating the business environment of emerging economies in the context of government capacity.

5 Data and Methodology

In this chapter, the World Bank's Governance Indicators[2] is used to explore administrative system characteristics of 26 countries introduced and ranked as emerging markets.[3] According to the World Economic Outlook (WEO), the main criteria used to classify the world into advanced economies and emerging market and developing economies are as follows:

1. Per capita income level
2. Export diversification (oil exporters that have high per capita GDP would not make the advanced classification because around 70% of their exports are oil)
3. Degree of integration into the global financial system

The MSCI Emerging Markets Index developing economies are including Argentina, Brazil, Chile, China, Colombia, Czech Republic, Egypt, Greece, Hungary, India, Indonesia, Korea, Malaysia, Mexico, Pakistan, Peru, Philippines, Poland, Qatar, Russia, Saudi Arabia, South Africa, Taiwan, Thailand, Turkey, and the United Arab Emirates.

Six dimensions of governance are included in the set of indicators: voice and accountability, political stability and absence of violence, government effectiveness, the rule of law, regulatory quality, and control of corruption. Here, the focus is on four indices: "rule of law," "regulatory quality," "control of corruption," and "government effectiveness." These are selected because they are more related to public administration reform activities. e-Government development index is another

[2] https://datacatalog.worldbank.org/dataset/worldwide-governance-indicators

[3] https://www.msci.com

related index.[4] In addition to recognizing the performance of the institutional economy of selected countries, the global competitiveness index[5] and 2 pillars of this index as institution and market efficiency (from its 12 pillars), doing business index[6] and GDP world contributions of each country are considered. The indicators provide data from 2014 to 2018.

6 Empirical Results

Comparative and correlation analyses were conducted for main variables to consider the relationship between public administration model/characteristics and the capacity of emerging economies. Therefore, multiple regression models were used to identify any patterns seen in the data. Multiple regression models were widely used in economic research and helped determine the effects of each independent variable on dependent variables. It was decided to use this method to produce comparable results.

The behavioral patterns were generated as crucial indicators of all 26 countries (emerging markets) over the selected time to fulfill the purpose of this study at the first level. At the second level, a set of multivariate regression models were employed, and the correlations between administrative system reform indicators and the performance of emerging markets were examined.

Behavioral patterns in all 26 countries are presented in Fig. 2 to summarize the findings and focus on the results of administration reform activities.

The comparative linear graphs represent relatively similar behavior patterns across selected countries as emerging economies. In most diagrams, the set of predictor variables and the set of dependent variables behave similarly over time.

It is generally seen that those affected by government performance behave the same as the market.

Observably, it seems that there is a relationship between institutions and global competitiveness with market efficiency, and theoretical market efficiency has had a significant effect on the economic growth of government performance.

It is concluded that e-government implementation does not affect market efficiency directly.

Patterns indicate the need to focus on public administration reform to develop emerging markets to improve the countries' economic performance.

Unlike the same patterns of variables among countries, the existence of the relationship between the administrative system model and the emerging markets' performance at each country is ambiguous.

[4] https://publicadministration.un.org/egovkb/en-us/Reports/UN-E-Government-Survey

[5] https://www.weforum.org/reports/the-global-competitveness-report

[6] https://www.doingbusiness.org/content/dam/doingBusiness/media/Annual-Reports

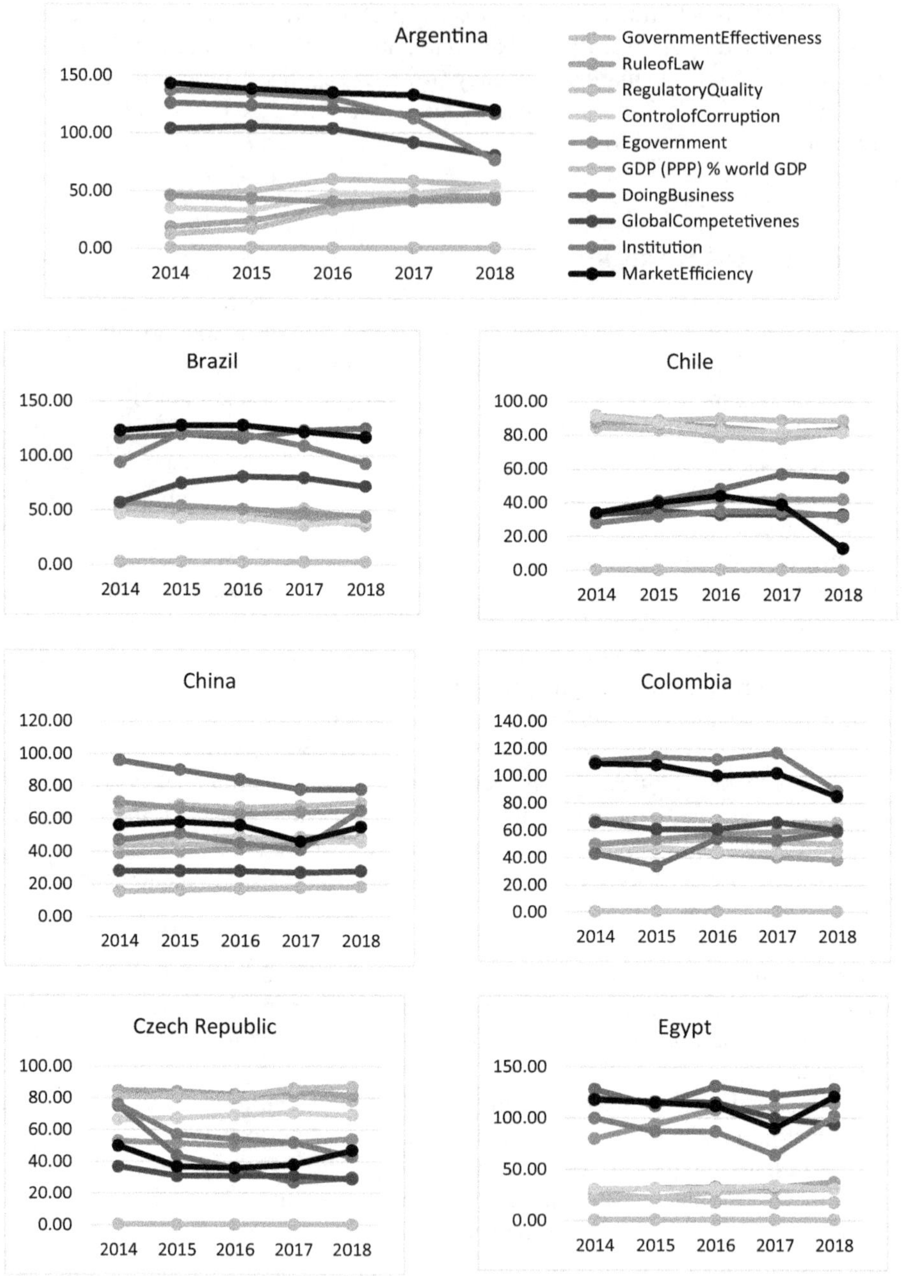

Fig. 2 Results of comparative analysis for 26 emerging economies. (*Source*: Authors' own figures)

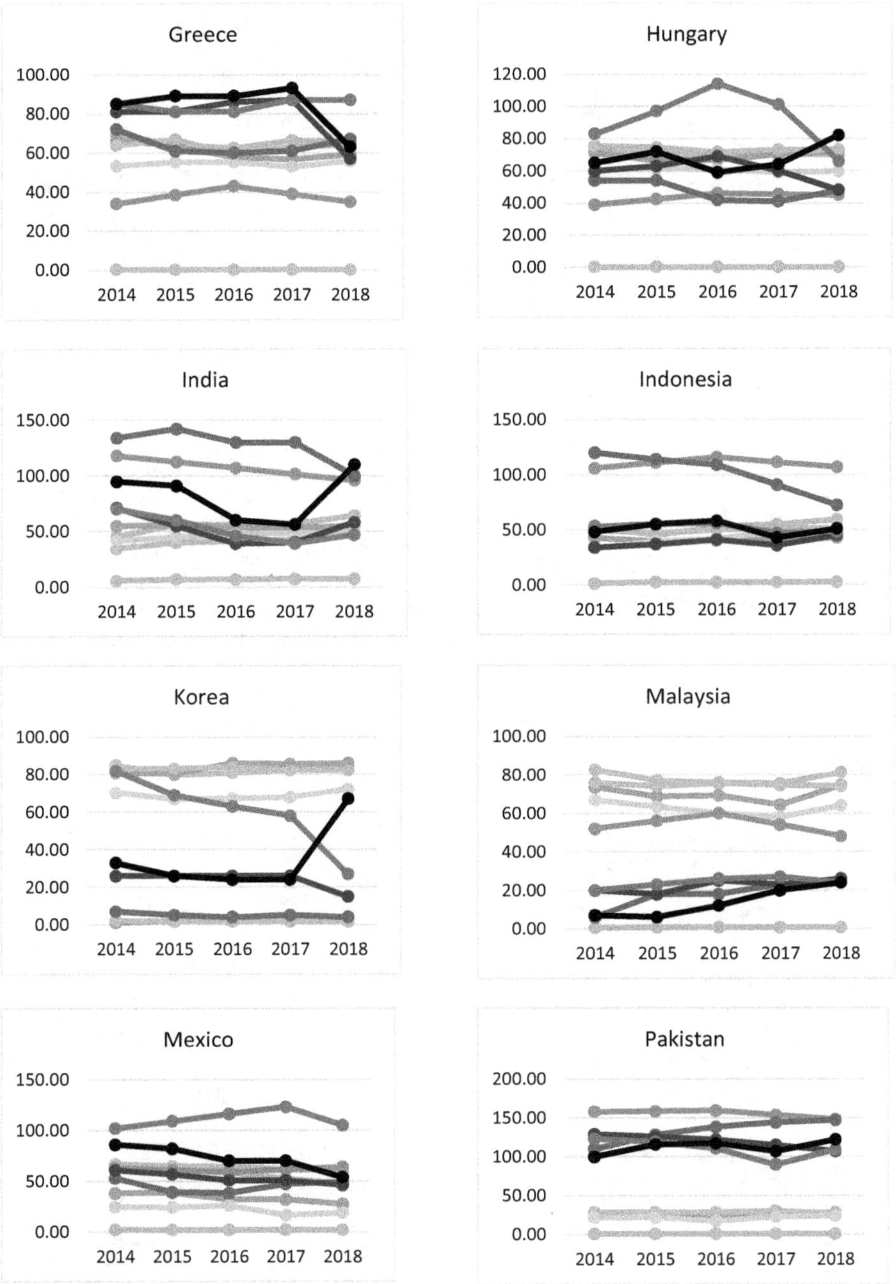

Fig. 2 (continued)

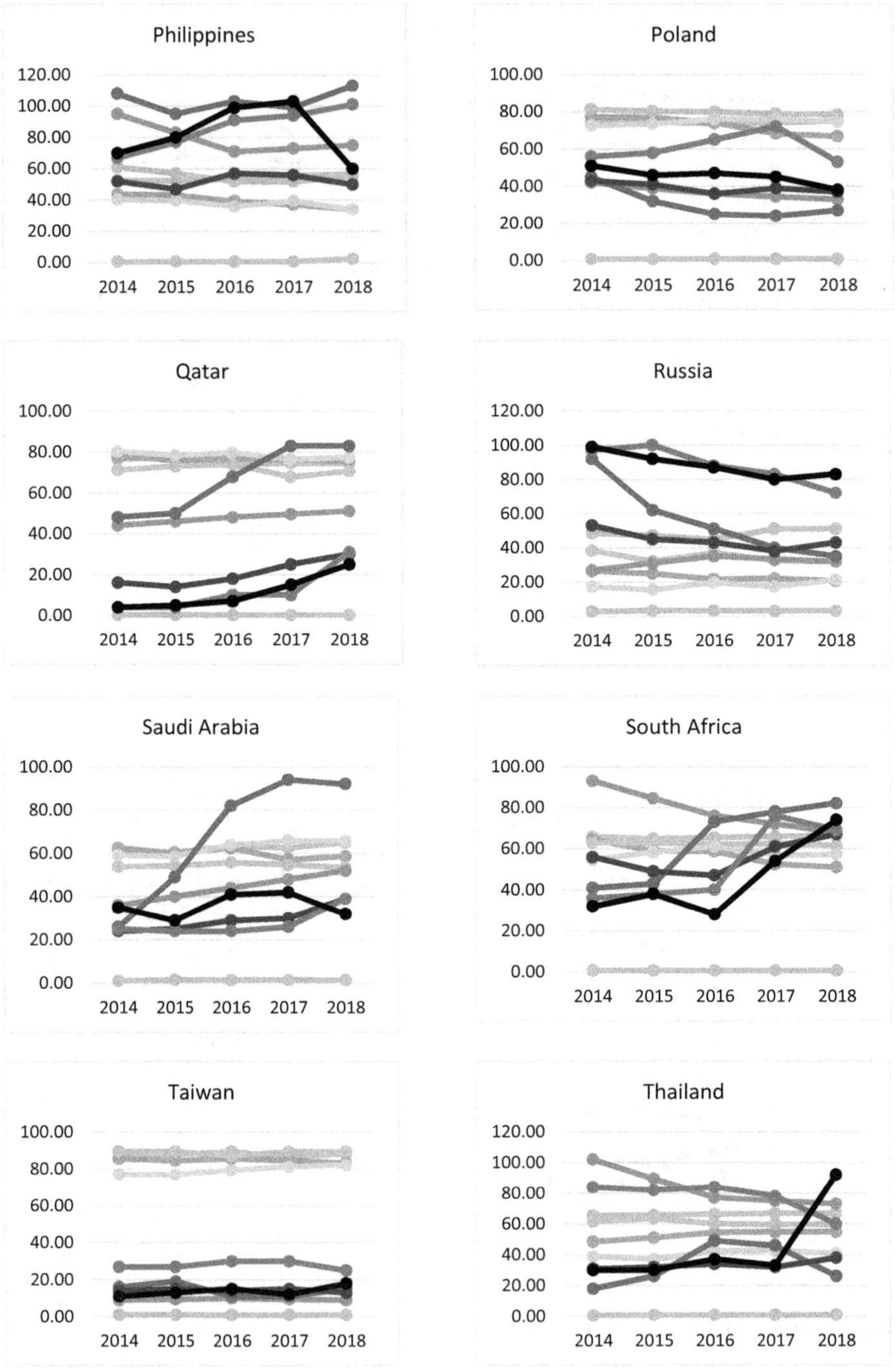

Fig. 2 (continued)

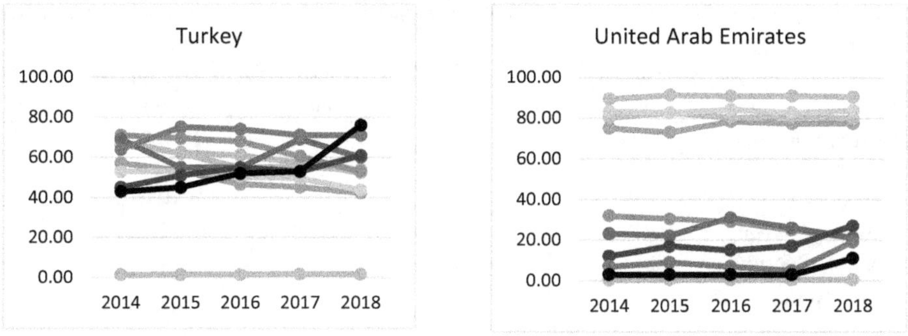

Source: Authors' own figures

Fig. 2 (continued)

In order to better understand those relationships, the impacts of the public administration model and government capacity on the functions of emerging markets were tested by employing multivariate regression models. Reviewing the literature on state-building and development determined government capacity and, in particular, administrative capacity as central factors. Capacity has been equated with state/government development and is used to explain the emergence of its autonomy.

As this study aims, the results from correlations and the proportion of the variance in the dependent variable that is predictable from the independent variables are presented.

Table 3 provides a correlation matrix that suggests strong relationships between public administration variables with correlation coefficients ranging from 0.76 to 0.93, suggesting that the control of corruption is strongly associated with the rule of law (R = 0.93), and control of corruption is also associated with regulation quality, though with a lower correlation (R = 0.76). These findings imply that government effectiveness is enhanced when the government plays its regulatory role as the best. These findings are not surprising but indicate that the measures perform as might be anticipated and give us some confidence to focus on capabilities of administrative reform programs.

As demonstrated below, all public administration variables affect emerging market performance positively (Table 4).

As illustrated in Table 5, public administration status has a positive and significant impact on nation global competitiveness with a correlation value of 92% and the R2 values of 0.84. The adjusted R2 of 80%, which explains variations in the dependent variables, indicates considerable aggregate explanatory power for the estimated impacts of public administration reforms on the status of emerging markets.

The same can be said for better performance of business indicators (R2 = 0.79, adjusted R2 = 74%; Table 6) and also for the quality and capacity of institutions (R2 = 0.85, adjusted R2 = 81%; Table 7).

Table 3 Correlation between the World Bank governance regulatory, effectiveness, and corruption indicators

Indicators	Government effectiveness	Rule of law	Regulation quality	Control of corruption
Government effectiveness	1.000	0.869	0.818	0.864
Rule of law	0.869	1.000	0.786	0.935
Regulation quality	0.818	0.786	1.000	0.761
Control of corruption	0.864	0.935	0.761	1.000

Source: Authors' own calculations

Table 4 Public administration and country's share of world GDP at purchasing power parity

Model summary				
Model	R	R square	Adjusted R square	Std. Error of the estimate
1	.606[a]	0.367	0.209	3.22500

[a]Predictors: (constant), e-Government, rule of law, regulatory quality, government effectiveness, control of corruption
Source: Authors' own calculations

Table 5 Public administration and the country's global competitiveness

Model summary				
Model	R	R square	Adjusted R square	Std. Error of the estimate
1	.918[a]	0.842	0.803	10.20960

Source: Authors' own calculations
[a]Predictors: (constant), e-Government, rule of law, regulatory quality, government effectiveness, control of corruption

Table 6 Public administration and the country doing business

Model summary				
Model	R	R square	Adjusted R square	Std. error of the estimate
1	.888[a]	0.789	0.736	19.94703

Source: Authors' own calculations
[a]Predictors: (constant), e-Government, rule of law, regulatory quality, government effectiveness, control of corruption

Table 7 Public administration and the country institutional capacity

Model summary				
Model	R	R square	Adjusted R square	Std. error of the estimate
1	.923[a]	0.851	0.814	12.15214

Source: Authors' own calculations
[a]Predictors: (constant), e-Government, rule of law, regulatory quality, government effectiveness, control of corruption

Table 8 Public administration and the country market efficiency

Model summary				
Model	R	R square	Adjusted R square	Std. error of the estimate
1	.813[a]	0.661	0.576	22.55786

Source: Authors' own calculations
[a]Predictors: (constant), e-Government, rule of law, regulatory quality, government effectiveness, control of corruption

Among all, the relationship between the administrative system and the efficiency of the goods market is different. Table 8 shows the positive impact of public administration situation on the goods market efficiency with a correlation value of 81%. The R2 = 0.66 and adjusted R2 = 0.57 are acceptable, but they indicate the total variation in the dependent variable that can be explained by the public administration model as the independent variable is not huge.

However, it is worth noticing that both R2 and the adjusted R2 for the country's share of world GDP at purchasing power parity are not significant and do not depict any considerable explanatory variable (Table 4).

7 Conclusion

This chapter suggests an approach that explains public administration attitudes toward the performance of the emerging markets by concentrating on the country's institutional economy and the government role. Therefore, the main task of planners is to inspect the relationships between the public administration variables to formulate the public administration reform model. The first step is to find if there are positive relationships between global competitiveness of the country's capacity, engaging in any financial transaction or pecuniary gain or profit in the country, and the country's share of world GDP at purchasing power parity.

The results show that five criteria of e-government, rule of law, regulation quality, government effectiveness, and control of corruption have a positive impact on the country's capacity to act as an emerging market. In this regard, the behavioral patterns of administrative system variables emphasize the integrity of the administrative system. Therefore, government interference could be used as a governance mechanism to develop the new public governance and create a proper environment for institution activities.

Another noteworthy finding is that the country's share of world GDP at purchasing power parity has poor direct relation with public administration attributes. Thus, governments should not expect to quickly increase their share of world GDP by implementing administrative reform programs. According to the findings, the rule of law has fundamental importance for all states. It has a strong positive impact on government effectiveness and creates political stability. The more the government properly acts to meet the goals and be more productive with the ideal use of resources in the stable and transparency era, the more productive would be the investment and faster would be the implementation of social and economic policies, leading to higher economic growth. It implies the benefits of broad and comprehensive reform methodologies.

The last finding is about an institutional capacity. It is more strongly correlated with public administration characteristics. According to the institution index definition, effective regulatory policy and institutions performance support each other, opening up pathways for innovation, enhanced consumer benefits, and entrepreneurship. They have dynamic interaction with firms and the other active, organized entities. Thus, they play as a driving factor in the market landscape. This finding remains valid within emerging markets.

Since developing economies and emerging markets are expected to continue growing relatively fast, their governments need to be more open to experiment new approaches on markets. Running pilot programs allow governments to test new ideas in different contexts, modify them, and then scale up the policies that work.

Based on the core practical implication of this chapter and from a broader perspective, the new and emerging roles of the governments as enablers and facilitators should be emphasized in public policy development. The findings empower public administration to act under globalization pressures by paying particular attention to the global economic interdependence and managing the effects of emerging markets' growth through the administrative system's model. In this respect, administrative reform programs help nations to adapt to institutional environment dynamics continuously.

References

Acemoglu, D., Robinson, J., & Johnson, S. (2001). The colonial origins of comparative development: An empirical investigation. *American Economic Review, 91*(5), 1369–1401.

Aybar, B., & Thirunavukkarasu, A. (2005). Emerging market multinationals: An analysis of performance and risk characteristics. *Journal of Asia Pacific Business, 6*(2), 5–39.

Azfar, O. (2006). The new institutional economic approach to economic development: A discussion of social, political, legal and economic institutions. *The Pakistan Development Review, 45*(4), 965–980.

Banerjee, A., Banerji, R., Duflo, E., Glennerster, R., & Khemani, S. (2006). *Can information campaigns spark Local participation and improves outcomes? A study of primary education in Uttar Pradesh, India* (The World Bank, policy research working paper, no. 3967). Washington, DC: World Bank.

Battaglia, L., Bellú, G. L., Dieng, C., & Tedesco, I. (2011). *Development paradigms and related policies*. Food and Agriculture Organization of the United Nations (pp. 1–162). Retrieved from http://www.fao.org/fileadmin/user_upload/tcas/projects/dev_paradigms_LiteratureReview2011.Pdf

Bellù, L. G. (2011). *Development and development paradigms: a (reasoned) review of prevailing paradigms*. Issue papers, EASYPol series 102. Food and Agriculture Organization of the United Nations - Rome. www.fao.org/docs/up/easypol/882/defining_development_paradigms_102EN.Pdf

Caravella, K. D. (2011). *Mimetic, coercive and normative influences in institutionalization of organizational practices: The case of distance learning in higher education*. Dissertation. Doctor of philosophy. The College for Design and Social Inquiry. Florida Atlantic University. Boca Raton, Florida.

Carrasco, E. R., & Williams, S. (2012). Emerging economies after the global financial crisis: The case of Brazil. *Northwestern Journal of International Law & Business, 33*(1), 81–119.

Chang, H. J. (2010). Institutions and economic development: Theory, policy and history. *Journal of Institutional Economics, 7*(4), 473–498.

De Dios, E. S. (2008). *Institutional constraint to Philippine growth*, UP School of economics. Discussion papers 200806, University of the Philippines School of economics.

DiMaggio, P. J., & Powell, J. J. (1991). Introduction. In W. W. Powel & P. J. DiMaggio (Eds.), *The new institutionalism in organizational analysis* (pp. 1–38). Chicago: University of Chicago Press.

Dingwerth, K., & Pattberg, P. (2006). Global governance as a perspective on world politics. *Global Governance, 12*(2), 185–203.

Eichler, S. (2014). The political determinants of sovereign bond yield spreads. *Journal of International Money and Finance, 46*, 82–103. https://doi.org/10.1016/j.jimonfin.2014.04.003.

Ekins, P. (2000). Economic growth and environmental sustainability. In *The prospects for green growth*. London: Routledge.

Frederickson, H. G., Smith, K. B., Larimer, C. W., & Licari, M. J. (2012). *The public administration theory primer* (2nd ed.). Boulder: Westview Press.

Greenwood, R., Raynard, M., Kodeih, F., Micelotta, E. R., & Lounsbury, M. (2011). Institutional complexity and organizational responses. *The Academy of Management Annals, 5*(1), 317–371.

Greif, A. (2006). *Institutions and the path to the modern economy: Lessons from medieval trade*. Cambridge: Cambridge University Press.

Grewal, R., & Lilien, G. (2015). Trends in business markets. Customer needs and solutions. *Springer Institute for Sustainable Innovation and Growth (iSIG), 2*(3), 191–192. https://doi.org/10.1007/s40547-015-0052-1.

Grindle, M. S., & Thomas, J. W. (1991). *Public choices and policy change: The political economy of reform in developing countries*. Baltimore/London: The Johns Hopkins University Press.

Hall, P. A. (1986). *Governing the economy: The politics of state intervention in Britain and France*. New York: Oxford University Press.

Hall, P. A., & Taylor, R. C. R. (1996). Political science and the three new institutionalisms. *Political Studies, 44*(5), 936–957. https://doi.org/10.1111/j.1467-9248.1996.tb00343.x.

Harvey, C. R. (1995). The risk exposure of emerging equity markets. *World Bank Economic Review, 9*(1), 19–50.

Haveri, A. (2006). Complexity in local government change. *Public Management Review, 8*(1), 31–46.

Hood, C. (1991). A public management for all seasons? *Public Administration, 69*(1), 3–19.

Hoskisson, R. E., Eden, L., Lau, C. M., & Wright, M. (2000). Strategy in emerging economies. *Academy of Management Journal, 43*, 249–267.

Hughes, O. E. (1998). *Public management and administration: An introduction* (2nd ed.). New York: Palgrave Macmillan.

Hughes, O. E. (2003). *Public management and administration: An introduction* (3rd ed.). New York: Palgrave Macmillan.

Jones, P. S. (2000). Why is it alright to do development over there but not here? Changing vocabularies and common strategies of inclusion across the first and third worlds. *Area, 32*(2), 237–241.

Kane, M. (2004). *Public-sector economic development: Concepts and approaches*. Washington, DC: Northeast-Midwest Institute.

Kanniainen, J. (2017). *New public governance and new public management in the funding and contractual steering of the Finnish higher education system*. Thesis seminar and pro gradu –thesis, 40 ECTS, Faculty of Management, administrative sciences, University of Tampere.

Khanna, T., & Palepu, K. (1997). Why focused strategies may be wrong for emerging markets. *Harvard Business Review, 75*(4), 41–48.

Klijn, E.-H. (2002). Governing networks in the hollow state: Contracting-out, process management or a combination of the two. *Public Management Review, 4*(2), 149–166.

Knack, S., & Keefer, P. (1995). Institutions and economic performance: Cross-country tests using alternative institutional measures. *Economics and Politics, 7*(3), 207–228.

La Porta, R., Lopez-De-Silanes, F., & Shleifer, A. (2002). Government ownership of banks. *The Journal of Finance, 57*(1), 265–301.

Lan, Z., & Rosenbloom, D. H. (1992). Public administration in transition*? Public Administration Review, 52*(6), 535–537.

Lijphart, A. (1984). *Democracies. Patterns of majoritarian and consensus government in 21 countries*. New Haven/London: Yale University Press.

Lowndes, V., & Roberts, M. (2013). *Why institutions matter: The new institutionalism in political science*. New York: Palgrave Macmillan.

Lowndes, V., & Wilson, D. (2003). Balancing revisability and robustness? A new institutionalist perspective on local government modernization. *Public Administration, 81*, 275–298.

Madgavkar, A., Seong, J., & Woetzel, J. (2019). *How governments in emerging economies can help boost and sustain growth*. Online article. McKinsey & Company. https://www.mckinsey.com/industries/public-sector/our-insights

March, J. G., & Olsen, J. P. (1989). *Rediscovering institutions. The organizational basis of politics*. New York: Free Press.

March, J. G., & Olsen, J. P. (1998). The institutional dynamics of international political orders. *International Organization, 52*, 943–969.

March, J. G., & Olsen, J. P. (2006). Elaborating the new institutionalism. In R. A. W. Rhodes, S. A. Binder, & B. A. Rockman (Eds.), *The Oxford Handbook of Political Institutions*. New York: Oxford University Press.

Mauro, P. (1995). Corruption and growth. *Quarterly Journal of Economics, 110*(3), 681–712.

Meyer, K. E., & Grosse, R. (2018). *The Oxford handbook of management in emerging markets*. Online publication (R. Grosse & K. E. Meyer (Eds.)). New York: Oxford University Press. https://doi.org/10.1093/Oxfordhb/9780190683948.013.1.

Miller, R. R. (1998). *Selling to newly emerging markets*. New York: Quorum Books.

Nationwide Funds. (2017). *Know the difference between developed and emerging markets*. Retrieved from https://nationwidefinancial.com/media/pdf/MFM-2599AO.pdf

Nilsson, L. (2018). *What logics drive the choices of public decision-makers?* Doctoral thesis. Luleå University of Technology Department of business administration, technology and social sciences division of social sciences. ISBN: 978-91-7790-020-7 (electronic).

North, D. C. (1991). Institutions. *Journal of Economic Perspectives, American Economic Association, 5*(1), 97–112.

Olson, M., Sarna, N., & Swamy, A. (2000). Governance and growth: A simple hypothesis explaining cross-country differences in productivity growth. *Public Choice, 102*(3–4), 341–364.

Osborne, S. P. (2006). The new public governance? *Public Management Review, 8*(3), 377–387. https://doi.org/10.1080/14719030600853022.

Osborne, S. P. (Ed.). (2010). *The new public governance: Emerging perspectives on the theory and practice of public governance*. Routledge.

Osborne, D., & Gaebler, T. (1993). *R reinventing government: how the entrepreneurial spirit is transforming the public sector*. New York: A Plume Book.

Peng, M. W., Wang, D. Y. L., & Jiang, Y. (2008). An institution-based view of international business strategy: A focus on emerging economies. *Journal of International Business Studies, 39*(5), 920–936.

Peters, B. G. (2012). *Institutional theory in political science: The new institutionalism*. London/New York: Continuum.
Pistor, K. (2000). The standardization of law and its effect on developing economies. *The American Journal of Comparative Law., 50*(1), 97–130.
Pitlik, H., Hölzl, W., Brandtner, C., Heinemann, F., Misch, F., Yeter, M., Steurs, G., Gagnage, S., & Mertens, K. (2012). *Excellence in public administration for competitiveness in EU member states*. European Commission Report, DG Enterprise and Industry.
Pollitt, C. (1993). *Managerialism and the public services: Cuts or cultural change in the 1990s?* (2nd ed.). Oxford: Blackwell Publishers.
Pollitt, C., & Bouckaert, G. (2011). *Public management reform. A comparative analysis: New public management, governance, and the Neo-Weberian State*. Oxford: Oxford University Press.
Sanders, E. (2006). Historical institutionalism. In R. A. W. Rhodes, S. A. Binder, & B. A. Rockman (Eds.), *The Oxford handbook of political institutions*. Oxford University Press.
Schmidt, V. A. (2008). A discursive institutionalism: The explanatory power of ideas and discourse. *Annual Review of Political Science, 11*(1), 303–326.
Schmidt, V. A. (2010). Taking ideas and discourse seriously: Explaining change through discursive institutionalism as the fourth new institutionalism. *European Political Science Review, 2*(1), 1–25.
Scott, W. R. (2004). *Institutional theory: Contributing to a theoretical research program*, (revised 2004). In K. J. Smith & M. A. Hitt (Eds.), *Great minds in management: The process of theory development*. Oxford: Oxford University Press.
Scott, W. R. (2008). Approaching adulthood: The maturing of institutional theory. *Theory and Society, 37*(5), 427–442.
Serban, E., Borisov, D., & Dobrea, R. C. (2012). Emerging markets: Concept evolution and business environment particularities. *Management Research and Practice, 4*(2), 5–19.
Sharma, R. (2014). The ever-emerging markets: Why economic forecasts fail. *Foreign Affairs, 93*(1), 52–56.
Shepsle, K. A. (2006). Rational choice institutionalism. In R. A. W. Rhodes, S. A. Binder, & B. A. Rockman (Eds.), *The Oxford handbook of political institutions*. Oxford University Press.
Simon, Y. (1997). *Encyclopedie des marches financiers*. Paris: Editura Economica.
St. Aubyn, M. (2008). Modernising public administration and economic growth. Paper presented at the *European Central Bank Public Finance Workshop: Challenges for government spending in the EU*, Frankfurt, 6 December 2007, Mimeo.
Subramanian, A. (2007). The evolution of institutions in India and its relationship with economic growth. *Oxford Review of Economic Policy, 23*(2), 196–220.
Sunje, A., & Civi, E. (2000). Emerging markets: a review of conceptual frameworks. *Proceedings of 1st International Joint Symposium on Business Administrator: Challenges for Business Administration in the millennium* (pp. 203–216).
Thelen, K. (1999). Historical institutionalism in comparative politics. *Annual Review of Political Science., 2*, 369–404.
Todaro, M. P., & Smith, S. C. (2009). *Economic development*. Harlow: Addison Wesley.
United Nations. (2004). *Globalization and the state: Challenges for economic growth and human development*. Department of economic and social affairs. Division for public administration and development management. ST/ESA/PAD/SER.E/80.
United Nations Economic and Social Council. (2006). *Definition of basic concepts and terminologies in governance and public administration*. Committee of experts on public administration. Agenda item 5, Compendium of basic terminology in governance and public administration, E/C.16/2006/4, 1-15.
Weaver, R. K., & Rockman, B. A. (1993). Institutional reform and constitutional design. In R. K. Weaver & B. A. Rockman (Eds.), *Do institutions matter? Government capabilities in the United States and abroad* (pp. 462–482). Washington, DC: The Brookings Institution.
World Bank. (2000). *Reforming public institutions and strengthening governance: A World Bank strategy, implementation update, parts 1 and 2*. Washington, DC: World Bank.

World Economic Forum. (2011). *Global competitiveness report 2011–2012*. Geneva: Centre for Global Competitiveness and Performance.

Wright, M., Filatotchev, I., Hoskisson, R. E., & Peng, M. W. (2005). Strategy research in emerging economies: Challenging the conventional wisdom. *Journal of Management Studies, 41*, 1), 1–1),33.

Xu, D., & Meyer, K. E. (2013). Linking theory and context: Strategy research in emerging economies. *Journal of Management Studies, 50*(7), 1322–1346.

Xu, R. Y., Sun, Q. G., & Si, W. (2015). The third wave of public administration: The new public governance. *Canadian Social Science, 11*(7), 11–21.

Zhao, J. (2016). Promoting a more efficient corporate governance model in emerging markets through corporate law. *Washington University Global Studies Law Review, 15*(3), 447–493.

Exploring the Emergence of Industrial Revolution 4.0: A Journey to Higher Education 4.0

Farzaneh Yarahmadi

1 Introduction

The main objective of this study is to explore the emergence of Higher Education 4.0 (HE4) in Oman and examine Oman's readiness and preparation in adopting Higher Education 4.0. This chapter provides a summary of the industrial revolution and the evolution of education from 1.0 to 4.0 and discusses the importance of this transition. The chapter also attempts to review new trends, techniques and teaching methods practised in Oman. The IR 4.0 affects not only the business, governance and the people, it also affects education as well; thus, the name Education 4.0 came to existence.

The advancements of technologies affect not only the business, governance and the people, it also affects education. Throughout history, it has been proved that advancements of technologies and science evolved industries and industrial evolution advanced education. Over the last few decades, there has been a rapid technological innovation which has driven the world into the Fourth Industrial Revolution. The Fourth Industrial Revolution (4IR) is considered as the global technological transition and revolution based on various modern technologies, which has brought a significant shift in the education field. In the context of the Fourth Industrial Revolution, education must be prepared to change with technology. Education 4.0 has been introduced with the emergence of the Fourth Industrial Revolution. Education 4.0 is a response to the digital penetration and aims to enhance the digital technological competencies in teaching and learning process. Therefore, there is a need for changing the process of using technological advancements in teaching and learning in education and higher education sectors. It is expected that the use of technological advancements in education 4.0 would play a significant role in higher

F. Yarahmadi (✉)
Oman Tourism College, Muscat, Oman

N. Faghih, A. H. Samadi (eds.), *Dynamics of Institutional Change in Emerging Market Economies*, Contributions to Economics,
https://doi.org/10.1007/978-3-030-61342-6_11

education institutions (Blaschke 2012). According to Vawn (2018), by integrating the new technology, teaching and learning practices can be more efficient. Technology has a significant influence on higher education worldwide as it brings new opportunities. For higher education institutions (HEIs) to produce successful graduates, they must prepare and train their students for a worldwide technological advancement where the artificial intelligence (AI) and cyber-physical systems are widespread across all industries.

In the next few decades, the future of higher education may change drastically as its systems are becoming incompatible with the increasing pace of technological advancement brought by the Industrial Revolution 4.0. This study aims to examine the evolution of higher education in a few emerging Asian countries as they encounter the need for sustainability and global competitiveness. In this context, higher education is one of the essential factors for sustainability and competitiveness of emerging market countries. The main objective of this study is to explore the emergence of Higher Education 4.0 (HE 4.0) and review new trends, techniques and teaching methods practised in few Asian emerging markets in adopting HE 4.0. The study also provides a summary of the industrial revolution and educational evolution from 1.0 to 4.0 and addresses the significance of this transition.

2 Literature Review

2.1 Emerging Markets

In the twenty-first century, emerging markets or emerging economies have become predominant players in the world economy. According to Medel (2019), countries with excessive per capita incomes are categorized as "developed". In contrast, those countries with medium, middle and upper-middle per capita incomes are classified as "developing", or "emerging" and nations with much lower per capita income levels are known as "frontier economies". Reynold and Thompson (2018) highlight that the distinction between "developing "and "emerging" is that emerging nations are overgrowing and turning more important or significant in world economics. These countries have made remarkable gains in industrial and economic growth and maybe suppliers of labor or resources to other more advanced nations. While developing nations are struggling and still look for support from trade partners around the world and depend in particular on agriculture and have a low income per capita.

According to Tsunekawa (2019), there are two primary reasons why emerging markets have attracted widespread attention in the contemporary world. First, that emerging market in "developing" countries earlier than the 1980s is now known as "emerging" because their speed of economic growth with the "advanced" industrial nations is very high, and second, their share in the global economy has expanded. They are regarded as the companions of "advanced" nations and as such must share unique obligations and responsibilities in the governance of various components of the world economic system. Tsunekawa (2019) stated that emerging countries had achieved solid economic performances by collaborating in and benefiting from economic globalization.

2.2 *Industrial Revolution and the Technology Revolution*

Throughout history, there have been two massive changes in human society which is called revolution. The first, Neolithic Revolution or First Agriculture Revolution, begins in 8000 BC, which affects the transition of human cultures from a mostly nomadic hunter gathered to a more settled lifestyle. The second, Industrial Revolution (IR) or First Industrial Revolution, is considered as the turning point in human history. It started in Europe and the United States of America in the eighteenth century. It was the transition from a pre-industrial to an industrial society, of modern economic growth. Industrialization is a constant process. The First Industrial Revolution began in Great Britain in the eighteenth century with the invention of the steam engine used in factories, and later it was revolutionized to water transportation by attaching a steam engine to peddle wheels in America to send steaming ships to the rivers in America. In history, this invention is considered the "atmospheric engine" (Sinclair 1907). According to Singh (2015), IR is technological advances through machines. There were various developments during the indusial revolution, such as development of the textile industry, development of iron and steel industries, development of chemical production, agricultural revolution, improvements of transportation and economic growth.

In the Second Industrial Revolution in the late nineteenth century, the United States was in the lead, with reforming communication and technological advancement in mobility and production. After the Civil War was over, Americans were looking for ways to grow and develop new industries. Many American pioneers invented new technologies that improved communication, transportation and industrial production like Alexander Graham Bell and Thomas Alva Edison.

In the third Industrial Revolution, the internet became an essential factor and succeeded in being a public service technology rather than a proprietary technology (Carr 2003). According to Jedaman et al. (2018), "There are three main factors of using technology to get the most out of it, which are: using the internet, creative thinking, and social interaction". The world economic landscape has been transformed by the internet, and this transformation is anticipated to continue with the internet of things (IoT). The rapid development of smart cities also opens the way for a more collaborative world (Kanter and Litow 2009). Recent years have witnessed a fast pace of new technological development which played a crucial role in the previous industrial revolutions.

The Fourth Industrial Revolution (Industry 4.0) came with the rise of new digital industrial technology and new ways of interacting with the world through evolving cyber-physical systems. Industry 4.0 is the latest revolution which has been a big issue discussed in the past few years. For a society to be prosperous in an emerging market, education plays a vital role. Still, for the industry to be thriving, there is a need for a highly qualified candidate to work in this new era of the industrial revolution. In the early twentieth century, the industrial revolution set a vital pattern in education. Industry 4.0 plays an essential role in a giant transition in the education sector. The main objective of this study is to outline the concept of the Fourth Industrial Revolution and its impact on transforming strategies and methods of teaching in higher education. The chapter is to explore the readiness for the adoption and transformation of the Fourth Industrial Revolution in higher education in emerging markets.

2.3 *Industrial Revolution and Educational Evolution*

Before industrialization, not everyone affords to go to school, but the First Industrial Revolution created the need for compulsory public education. After the First Industrial Revolution, knowledge transferred directly into the mind of the students from the instructor, and instructivism was the method taught in the classroom. The students were passive receivers of contents, and there was not much interaction. During this period, a vision for a new kind of curriculum began, but there was no formal curriculum system. The technology was forbidden in the classroom and rarely used in the learning process. Education 1.0 slowly evolved from the basis of informal education to the beginning of Higher Education 1.0 (Gavhane 2019).

Education 2.0 happened during the Second Industrial Revolution from 1860 to 1900. It was initiated by the improvement of Web 2.0 when the technologies used to enhance the traditional approach to education. In Education 2.0, instructors were still transferring knowledge into the mind of the students, but they were implementing some new strategies as communication and collaboration were beginning to grow. The educators started talking about learning and learning outcomes but still on paper. Due to the invasion of technology and social networking, the students learn to become passive to the active learner. There was new learning, and teaching methods called blended learning are generated by technology. Higher Education 2.0 appeared when printing press invention changed the nature of knowledge production and sharing mechanism of knowledge during the mid-fifteenth century (Gavhane 2019). In this period, universities were formed as the centre of higher education.

The instructors apply technology to the classroom but with the same structure. The students learn to communicate faster and smarter through electronic methods. During Education 2.0, progressivism was the method of teaching, and the students learned to use the internet in their learning activities; however, internet access was still limited. According to Makrides (2019), "The education systems implemented in most countries today are characterized by the definition of Education 2.0, while very few emerging countries are pushing for reforms defined by Education 3.0".

Nowadays, Education 3.0 has been practised more often in emerging markets. In Education 3.0, the method of education is more of a heutagogical approach known as self-determined learning which emphasizes the development of independence capability. The classical style classroom has been isolated and no longer exists, and in many ways, technology has changed education. The existence of online information and social media caused the third transition of the education system. In this period, social media spread into the education sector up to this date, including virtual learning (Jeschke and Heinze 2014). The education system in the new era of technological advancement, information technology and ICT can be viewed as the advent of modernization in higher education, which has expanded the availability of higher education to everyone. The institutions widely use a Massive Open Online Course (MOOC) and Flipped classroom method. MOOC has been a great initiative in Education 3.0.

In the past few years, Industry 4.0, which is the latest revolution in the industry field, has been a big debate. Since the Fourth Industrial Revolution remarkably influenced everything in human life, including education, the term Education 4.0 has become a global discussion. Industry 4.0 is the period of not only automating production but also automating of knowledge. The Fourth Industrial Revolution needs more transition in technology and teaching method from the current education system. Education 4.0 is the most recent term used among researchers and scholars, and it is the starting point to the education system for a transition. Industrial 4.0 has changed the landscape of education sectors as these sectors were responsible for training the students to be a qualified candidate for the industry.

Precisely speaking, the Fourth Industrial Revolution has changed the education sector significantly, as the industry needs highly skilled and trained applicants to work in this new age and communicate with digital interfaces. The Industrial Revolution 4.0 and advancement of technology affect the higher learning institutions to produce workers who can fit the needs of the industry. In line with the Fourth Industrial Revolution, in few Asian emerging markets, higher education has introduced an Education 4.0 programme. The Education 4.0 attempts to provide students with the skills and competencies needed by the digital industry. In the Fourth Industrial Revolution (HE 4.0), higher education is a complex and the incredible opportunity that can potentially transform society for the better.

2.4 *Industrial Revolution 4.0 (4IR)*

During the industrial revolution, there are significant economic, geopolitical and demographic changes that have taken place in many countries. This industrial revolution globally impacted almost every aspect of human life besides manufacturing, such as human development, health and life longevity, information and communication technology (ICT), workforce recruitment, business, education and many more. As mentioned above, the First Industrial Revolution introduced machine-driven production with the use of water and steam powers; the Second Industrial Revolution represents mass production with the use of electricity. Third Industrial Revolution introduced advanced mechanization production with the use of information technology. Finally, the Fourth Industrial Revolution which is known as Industry 4.0 or Digital Revolution introduced the utilization of the cyber-physical systems (CPS), which is a shift in industries.

According to the World Economic Forum, the Fourth Industrial Revolution (4IR) is considered the emergence of "cyber-physical technologies" involving completely new human and computer capabilities. The formation of the Fourth Industrial Revolution is supported since the start of the twenty-first century by Klaus Schwab and the World Economic Forum. The Fourth Industrial Revolution is characterized by a fusion of technologies that blurs the lines between the physical, digital and biological spheres (Schwab 2017). In other words, the Fourth Industrial Revolution is an outline of new methods interacting with the world through evolving cyber-physical systems. It is an innovative global change based on diverse modern technologies.

The Fourth Industrial Revolution represents the growing trend towards digital technologies in the manufacturing industry, including artificial intelligence, smart manufacture, the cyber-physical systems, internet of things and cloud computing. Digital, physical and biological technologies are the most important driving force of the Fourth Industrial Revolution in which digital technology plays an important role. Almost all the innovations and advances coming with the Fourth Industrial Revolution tide are made possible and enhanced through digital power (Schwab 2016). According to Baygin et al. (2016), devices, machines, sensors and people are planned to be able to communicate with each other by using the internet technology known as the internet of things. This process is known as a cyber-physical system where the whole elements in the system, machines-to-machines and machines-to-humans, could communicate with each other from the production to consumption process (Baheti and Gill 2011).

The primary purpose of Industry 4.0 is to achieve improvements in terms of automation and operational efficiency, as well as effectiveness (Schwab 2016). The rise of the Industrial Revolution 4.0 has brought abundant opportunities for economic development in emerging markets. Still, it has also made many industries face difficulties as they are not highly skilled in technologies that surround the Industry 4.0. The required skillsets and future job market would be different from now due to the job replacements and displacements generated by artificial intelligence (Siau 2017; Rainie and Anderson 2017).

3 The Need of Transition in Higher Education

The new age of Education 4.0 and Higher Education 4.0 will be the next mechanism happening in the globe; therefore, it is essential for emerging markets to prepare on this occasion and cope with the expected situation towards this transition. There will be a continuous evolution of information and technologies through transformation processes. Education 4.0 and Higher Education 4.0 are a response to the needs of the Fourth Industrial Revolution, where human and technology integrate to support new scenarios of education. According to Marwala (2007), "we gradually find ourselves in the Fourth Industrial Revolution, which is driven by artificial intelligence (AI) and cyber-physical systems (CPS)". It is essential to acknowledge the dimension of the inevitable transformation of higher education. In preparing the higher education ecosystem for the 4IR, there is a need for the transition that is suited for the automation economy which refers to the process of producing goods and services automatically by using robots, control systems and other appliances with the minimal direct human operation.

Learning within the bounds of the Education 4.0 and the Fourth Industrial Revolution appears to be complicated, as the preferences of learning among the Gen Z are different from the previous generation as they are more energetic and involved in the learning process. According to Kozinski (2017), Gen Z students engage in their learning process. They enjoy group discussions and a highly interactive learning environment. Generation Z can learn anywhere and anytime and have unlimited access to new information. They enjoy an active learning process and learning at places other than their classroom. They prefer the use of digital tools and their integration with their learning process.

Generation Z newly emerging or entering the workforce will face significant challenges as the Fourth Industrial Revolution needs highly skilled workers. They should be able to efficiently work with disruptive technologies such as cyber-physical systems and artificial intelligence. Nowadays, the goal of most recognized HEIs is to develop the capacity for academic accomplishment and retention of knowledge among graduates to prepare for lifelong learners.

4 Approaches Towards Educational Transition

The rapid technological transition affects almost every field of the emerging markets in economy, environment, culture and education. In the context of the Fourth Industrial Revolution, education must be prepared to change with this technological transition. Higher education institutions also need to remain competitive; therefore, they need to incorporate digital transformation. Reforming Higher Education for Industry 4.0 is an essential initiative that discusses education strategies in an automated world. As a result of Education 4.0, the higher education structure has changed partially.

Many emerging markets have taken several approaches towards Education 4.0 to sustain the higher education ecosystem. Concerning the Fourth Industrial Revolution, the Ministry of Higher Education (MoHE) in Malaysia has developed the Education Blueprint 2015–2025 known as MEB in 2013, which aims to achieve Malaysia's education system in line with global trends (MoHE 2015). This programme aims to improve the education system in Malaysia that is compatible with the increasing pace of technological and social changes brought by the Industrial Revolution 4.0. It is also to provide guidelines and strategies for higher education stakeholders (MoHE 2015).

In line with the Fourth Industrial Revolution, Malaysian Higher Education has implemented an Education 4.0 programme. There are specific programmes and technologies involved in reforming the higher education system, which are CEO@ Faculty, 2u2i, MOOC, APEL, Gap Year, MEA and My E-Profile (Maria et al. 2018). CEO@Faculty is specifically designed to provide valuable guidance and information to university students and staff by inviting local and international CEOs to hold seminars and workshops for students, lecturers and institutions. 2u2i is a study programme based on vocational training in which the students are exposed to industrial training. The programme provides 2 years of study plus 2 years of industrial training to learn and gain real-life learning experience. MOOC and e-learning became the latest learning process in many countries that makes learning and educational practice centred on students, providing new, more flexible learning methods (Shopova 2011).

Another initiative was the launch of the "Roadmap" by President Joko Widodo in 2018 in Indonesia. According to the Global Education Census by the Cambridge Assessment International Education in 2018, Indonesian students are among the highest educational users of technology. The government is intending to get easy access to technology and provide education through initiatives like online courses. The intention is to prepare the country for 4IR and improve in education by inspiring investment in innovation and technology of the next decade, such as artificial intelligence and robotics. However, still, Indonesia is lagging behind other ASEAN countries.

India's emerging digital learning landscape reviews significant initiatives undertaken by Indian authorities to facilitate lifelong learning for teachers, students and those in work. Nowadays in India, Amity and other higher education institutions are digitizing study material for the portable delivery of knowledge to every part of the world. Makoni (2019), stated that "India has 462 million internet users with a penetration rate of 35% of the total population, and it has the second-largest national group enrolled in MOOCs after the United States, which the Government of India is striving hard to leverage". According to Pushpanadham UNESCO report (2019), for many students in India, MOOCs supplement traditional higher education, where nearly 40% of Indian MOOC students are also enrolled in a traditional undergraduate or graduate degree. The report noted that government funding through the National Skill Development Corporation, set up in 2009, has resulted in an increase in vocational training programmes in an effort to meet the training target of 500 million people by 2022.

5 Latest Trends in Educational Technology

Learning can be supported on an individual basis by using technology as an intelligent tool. Most learning contents these days can be digitized and shared across learning platforms accessible on any smart devices around the globe. The most recent step in the human/computer interaction is known as AI. The Fourth Industrial

Revolution, which is powered by AI, changes the way we work, the way we learn and the way we live. AI refers to the way of simulating the intelligence capabilities of the human brain (Badaró et al. 2013). Artificial intelligence is developing drastically, and this has impacted the services within higher education. Universities are now using IBM's first form of artificial intelligence, the Watson supercomputer. This approach offers student counselling for Deakin University in Australia through 365 days of the year at any time 24/7 (Deakin University 2014). The Siri iPhone is a typical example of artificial intelligence solutions that have become part of everyday experiences. Artificial intelligence is impacting four crucial areas in higher education, namely, student acquisition, learning and instruction, student affairs and institutional efficiency (Klutka et al. 2019).

Artificial intelligence has several strengths, such as speed, accuracy and consistency. However, on the other hand, it has its weaknesses in soft skills such as creativity, innovation, critical thinking, problem-solving, socializing, leadership, empathy, collaboration, communication and hard skills such as science, math and engineering. In many countries, some universities have started training students on the fundamentals of science and math, and at the same time, they provide opportunities and training for students to enhance their soft skills (Ma and Siau 2018). Some universities have already introduced AI and machine learning courses that are a sub-area of AI that requires the ability of the IT system to identify patterns in the database separately, do calculations and apply the newly discovered patterns to circumstances that were not included or protected by their initial design. The Education 4.0 programme aims to provide the capabilities and competencies required to the graduates.

6 Transition Readiness

Over the past 10 years, the higher education landscape has changed drastically. Technology is growing faster than ever, and the market for online education is still growing. Therefore, it is difficult for institutions of higher education to keep pace with the changes. The higher education system needs to change to suit the needs of the younger generation. With the fast pace of technological change, the educationalists need to adapt their skills to remain consistent with the transition. Blended learning is capable of improving educationalist's skills and creating an exciting learning experience, but educationalists are confronted continuously with difficulties in meeting student's demands. According to Abraham and Reginald (2016), there is a high degree of resistance to change among academic towards the use of classroom technologies. A Higher Education Commission research (2016) also stated that a shift in culture between both students and teachers is necessary to adopt to changes. Howard and Mozejko (2015) highlighted the three main factors that could inspire an educator's decision about technological integration in teaching: culture, confidence and beliefs.

7 Findings and Conclusion

In a world of change, there is an increasing demand across emerging markets economies to improve the quality of education. The Fourth Industrial Revolution is already influencing the education industry, which is one of the essential factors in sustainable development goals. In the new era of technology, there is a considerable shortage of skilled workers having data analytics and data science skills, and students are almost unaware of current science, technology and algorithms. With this fast pace of technological change, the students need to match their knowledge with changes to stay competitive. They need to have the opportunities to gain digital skills and abilities to respond to the current changes. It is also a challenging task for the instructors to keep up with the pace because technology advancement takes place every second.

Accordingly, there is a huge need to change educators' mindset towards the use of classroom technologies. To create a culture of change, institutions of higher education need to change and create values-based education. Education 4.0 is regarded to be a student learning centre in which self-learning, collaborative learning, flexibility and critical thinking and problem-solving need to be possessed by every student.

Nowadays, a Massive Open Online Course, which has been a great initiative in Education 3.0, is practised in many emerging markets. However, in the Fourth Industrial Revolution, the form of a university is different such as virtual classrooms, virtual instructors, virtual laboratories and virtual libraries which require vast resources. Emerging countries need to improve and develop the education system in order to stay competitive in the world.

In the new era of Education 4.0, higher education institutions need to prepare students to compete in the age of artificial intelligence. Higher education needs to invest in this transition and emphasize on the applicable changes to the education system. Due to the high technological cost and lack of technological 4.0 awareness, emerging markets are not still ready for the pace of Education 4.0, especially the implementation of artificial intelligence; therefore, higher education institutions need to boost the initial awareness of education 4.0 among students as well as instructors by providing conferences, workshops, seminars and training to enhance their professional development. The new graduate students must be trained for the innovative and entrepreneurial skills as they must deal with complexity. This is because they have to consider robots as their working colleagues apart from humans. The need for better communication and collaborative skills will be far more significant than ever. Graduates must acquire self-learning skills to remain relevant in the era of rapid changes.

References

Abraham, O., & Reginald, A. (2016). *E-education: Changing the Mindsets of resistant and saboteur teachers.*

Badaró, S., Ibañez, L., & Agüero, M. (2013). Sistemas expertos: fundamentos, metodologías y aplicaciones. *Ciencia y Tecnología, 13*, 349–364. https://doi.org/10.18682/cyt.v1i13.122.

Baheti, R., & Gill, H. (2011). Cyber-physical systems. *The Impact of Control Technology, 12*, 161–166.

Baygin, M. H., Karakose, Y. M., & Akin, E. (2016). An effect analysis of industry 4.0 to higher education. In *15th international conference on information technology based higher education and training.*

Blaschke, L. M. (2012). Heutagogy and lifelong learning: A review of heutagogical practice and self-determined learning. *International Review of Research in Open and Distance Learning, 13*(1), 56–71.

Carr, N. (2003). IT Doesn't matter. *Harvard Business Review, 81*(5), 41–49.

Deakin University. (2014). *IBM Watson now powering Deakin.* A new partnership aims to exceed students' needs. http://archive.li/kEnXm. Accessed 30 Oct 2016.

Gavhane, S. (2019). *Higher education: A journey from 1.0 to 4.0 (PART 2).*

Howard, A. K., & Mozejko, A. (2015). *Teachers: Technology, change and resistance.*

Jedaman, P., Buaraphan, K., Pimdee, P., Yuenyong, C., Sukkamart, A., & Suksup, C. (2018). Analysis of sustainable leadership for science learning management in the 21st Century under education THAILAND 4.0 framework. *AIP Conference Proceedings, 1923*(1), 030062.

Jeschke, S., & Heinze, U. (2014). *Higher education 4.0 – Trends and future perspectives for teaching and learning.*

Kanter, M. R., & Litow, S. (2009). *Informed and interconnected: A manifesto for smarter cities.* Harvard Business School Working Paper (pp. 09–141).

Klutka, J., Ackerly, N., & Magda, A. J. (2019). *Artificial intelligence in higher education, current users and future application.*

Kozinski, S. (2017). *How generation Z is shaping the change in education.* Retrieved from https://www.forbes.com/sites/sievakozinsky/2017/07/24/how-generation-z-isshaping-the-change-in-education/#304059746520

Ma, Y., & Siau, K. L. (2018). *Artificial intelligence impacts on higher education.* Berlin/Heidelberg: Springer.

Makoni, M. (2019). *Digital learning transforms spread of higher education.*

Makrides, G. A. (2019). *The evolution of education from Education 1.0 to Education 4.0: Is it an evolution or a revolution?* https://www.l-cloud.eu/wp-content/uploads/2019/03/Evolution_of_Education.pdf

Maria, M., Shahbodin, F., & Pee, N. (2018). Malaysian higher education system towards industry 4.0 – Current trends overview. *AIP Conference Proceedings, 2016*, 020081.

Marwala. (2007). *Computational intelligence for modelling complex systems.* Delhi: Research India Publications. ISBN 978-81-904362-1-2.

Medel, D. (2019). *Essay on emerging markets.* Thesis.

Ministry of Education Malaysia. (2015). *Malaysia education blueprint 2015–2025, (Higher Education).* Ministry of Education Malaysia.

Pushpanadham, K. (2019). *Massive open online courses: The emerging landscape of digital learning in India.* UNESCO report.

Rainie, L., & Anderson, J. (2017). The future of jobs and jobs training. Pew Research Center. Retrieve from http://www.pewinternet.org/2017/05/03/the-future-of-jobs-and-jobs-training

Reynold, J., & Thompson, J. (2018). *Differences between developing countries and emerging countries.*

Schwab, K. (2016). *The fourth industrial revolution* (pp. 25–38). Geneva: World Economic Forum.
Schwab, K. (2017). *The fourth industrial revolution*. New York: Crown Business.
Shopova, T. (2011). E-learning in a higher education environment. In *Proceedings of the international conference the future of education* (pp. 16–17).
Siau, K. (2017). Impact of artificial intelligence, robotics, and automation on higher education. In *Americas Conference on Information Systems* (AMCIS 2017), Boston, MA, August 10–12.
Sinclair, A. (1907). *Development of the locomotive engine*. New York: Angus Sinclair Publishing Company.
Singh, V. (2015). The technologies & machines that powered the industrial revolution. *Journal of Research in Humanities and Social Science, 3*(4), 27–29.
Tsunekawa, K. (2019). Globalization and the emerging state: Past advance and future challenges. In T. Shiraishi & T. Sonobe (Eds.), *The emerging states and economies: Their origins, drivers, and challenges ahead* (pp. 31–72). Singapore: Springer Nature Singapore Pte Ltd..
Vawn, H. (2018). *6 Pros & cons of technology in the classroom in 2018*. Retrieved from https://tophat.com/blog/6-pros-cons-technology-classroom/

Part III
Energy and Institutional Change

De Jure and De Facto Power of Oil and Institutional Change in Modern Iran: A Critical Historicism Analysis (1900–1979)

Amir Forouharfar

1 Introduction

At the turn of the nineteenth century, Iran, formerly known as Persia, began its modern history with prospecting for oil. The birth of the Iranian oil industry and modern Iran were coincided. Oil, a harbinger of historical vicissitudes, was going to foreshadow future fundamental transformations in Iranian economy, politics, society, culture and methods of state administration. *William Knox D'Arcy*, British oil explorer, in 1901 signed the *D'Arcy Concession* with *Mozzafar al-Din*, Shah of Persia. After seven years of continuous drilling at different southern regions of the country, he was near to bankruptcy and in full desperation, getting ready to give up, ordered *George Reynolds*, the chief engineer, to pack up and dismantle the equipment. Mere sense of fiasco before the first twilight of *Masjid Suleiman's* sun at 4:00 a.m. on May 26, 1908 with the natural gusher of the first Middle East oil well changed into cheering and shouting of happiness. The incident not only attracted more future rivalry among the superpowers, but more attention to the heart of the Middle East as a new fuel source for the industrialized West. The day radically changed the geopolitics of the region. One year ago, the *Anglo-Russian Convention of 1907* had been signed between Britain and Russia, separating Persia into northern and southern halves. The northern was Russia's share and the southern, Britain's zone of influence, and a central neutral zone in between. The politics of the country was never at ease from the Anglo-Russian influence, which was a heavy burden on the national identity shoulders. 28 days later after the gushing of the oil well, on 23 June 1908, bombardment of the *Majlis* (Iranian Parliament), a newly-established and shaky national institution and the emblem of national will for democratic governance took place in the reign of *Mohammad Ali Shah Qajar*, a new sovereign

A. Forouharfar (✉)
Department of Public Administration, University of Sistan and Baluchestan, Zahedan, Iran

N. Faghih, A. H. Samadi (eds.), *Dynamics of Institutional Change in Emerging Market Economies*, Contributions to Economics,
https://doi.org/10.1007/978-3-030-61342-6_12

succeeded to the throne. The bombardment and the constitutionalists' execution were led by *Vladimir Platonovitch Liakhov*, a Russian colonel who was the commander of *Cossack Brigade*. Although the shelling damaged the parliament building, the prevailing zeitgeist of the age was numerous ethnic groups passing the metamorphic stages of modern nation-building, burning in the relentless quest for sociopolitical freedom. The Iranian ethnic groups were in the epoch when Persia was shedding its old skin for the formation of a modern nation-state with its modern institutions. The preliminary steps for oil prospecting in Iran pursued in such an epochal context amid the endeavors of *Constitutional Revolution* (1905–1911). Persia was still a group of ethnic minorities consisting Persians, Kurds, Lurs, Balochs, Azerbaijanis, Arabs, Turkic tribes, etc. keeping a more than two thousand and four hundred year old territorial integrity. However, history was determining prominent roles for two of these ethnic groups, *Bakhtiaries* (a subgroup of the Lurs) and *Azerbaijanies* to save the revolution and give fresh impetus to the revolutionary spirit of the time. The pro-constitution forces mainly under the command of *Sardar Asa'ad Bakhtiari* in 1909 conquered Tehran, the capital, the king fled to Russia and for the first time in Iranian history a national institution, the *Majlis* abdicated the king and authorized the succession of his son as the heir to the throne. 13 July 1909 is one of the fundamental turning points in modern Iranian history, showing national power in opposition to absolutism. Although "Persian revolutionaries were pro-British and anti-Russian […]" the *Anglo-Russian Convention of 1907* "[…] aroused great bitterness among the Iranians …" (Kazemzadeh 2019, p. 68–70) and finally anti-British and anti-Russian sentiments dominated the age. The disgust from the two colonial powers in rivalry was intensified while their support for the puppet king was revealed by the aforementioned incidents. Accompanied with the Iranian memories in losing "Tbilisi and Baku to Russia in the 1813 *Treaty of Gulistan* and the khanates of Yerevan and Nakhichevan in the 1828 *Treaty of Turkmanchai* (Katouzian, 2009, p. 144);" Russia to the Iranians was an arch enemy of the country. The same partnership in the Second World War was Soviet-British invasion of Iran, without respecting the asserted neutrality of the country, institutionalized a strong sense of repugnance to the both powers. Ashraf (1992, p. 138) believes the incidents such as "[…] the *Anglo-Russian Convention of 1325/1907*, […]; the occupation of Persian territory by Great Britain, the Russians, and the Ottomans during World War I; the abortive *1337/1919 Anglo-Persian Agreement*, by which Persia was to become a kind of semiprotectorate; and the British-backed *Coup D'etat of 1299 Š./1921*, which led to the establishment of the Pahlavi dynasty, encouraged the development of conspiracy theories focused on foreign powers." The conspiracy sentiment was so strong which is fixated and has remained in the collective memory of even modern Iranians. As Jack Straw (2019), former British politician calls it "the English Job", countless historical documents have verified numerous interferences, oil monopoly and secret plots of Britain in Iran. Nevertheless, it is not negligible that the Ottoman, German and Russian propaganda in the late 19th and 20th against the British and their dissemination and amplification of its interference gossips played a crucial role in depicting Britain as foxy, cunning and professional in trickery (Ashraf 1992; Sepehr 1957; Mojtahedi 1974). Iranian oil discovery in the early days, its extraction and processing by Britain should be studied and contextualized within the mentioned historical context, which was a prelude to the epic institutional changes of future modern Iran. Therefore, the main purpose of the chapter is to historically depict the impact of oil on the main institutional changes of modern Iran between its two revolutions in the twentieth century. Hence, with the intention of setting the stage for later discussions, after a short review of the concepts of institution and institutional change and the author's subjective clarifying views on power ontology, its de jure and de facto emergences, historical studies, historical meaning, and his adopted critical historicism approach, the chapter mainly covers the interrelated Persia's leading historical turning points, the Persian oil and her twentieth century institutional changes. To easily follow the discussions, they were organized within the following decades and their subheadings' historical contexts:

1900s: The early days of the Persian oil
1910s: The First World War and the abortion of constitutional reforms
1920s: Stabilization of Persia
1930s: Institutional revolution and a modern state
1940s: Oil, Persian Corridor and the Second World War
1950s: Iranian oil nationalization
1960s: Oil and Shah's White Revolution
1970s: Oil curse and the collapse of the Pahlavi Dynasty.

2 Literature Review

To have clear vision of the concepts of institution and institutional change for the subsequent discussions through the chapter; first we should have a clear answer to what an institution is and what we mean by institutional change? In the following, the term institution is defined; and then an instance of a rentier institutional change theory is unfolded:

Accepting the possibility of institutional change in human social, political, cultural and economic lives is presuming a historical evolutionary drive over a time span in human existence. It is the institutional change, which has made societies what they are and us who we are; otherwise, we were still cave-dwelling Homo sapiens entrapped in a hunter society and its archaic institutions of polygamous marriage, bartering and other primitive manifestations of social life. But what is an institution? Institution is broadly "a significant practice, relationship, or organization in a society or culture" (Merriam-Webster's Collegiate Dictionary 2002, p. 606), but technically it is a multidimensional term that could have formal, tangible and collective manifestations such as governments, universities, schools, hospitals, public organizations, public laws or indicate informal, abstract and individual social entities such as marriage, religion, family, social class, etc. Although there is a consistency in comprehension of the term, there is not an all-embracing definition for it among social scholars. Hence, sociologists had been among the first scrutinizers of the concept. According to Giddens (1984, p. 24) "Institutions by definition are the more enduring features of social life." They are the social patterns constituting our social life. Huntington (1968, p. 12) defines these social patterns as "patterns of behavior" which are first "stable," second "valued" and third "recurring". Turner (1997, p. 6) also defines institutions as patterns, but "relatively stable patterns of human activity". The late *Douglass C. North* (1991, p. 97), a leading scholar of economic history and institutional change, defined institutions as, "the humanly devised constraints that structure political, economic and social interaction." Based on his definition we could consider institutions first as 'constraints'. These 'constraints' are 'humanly devised' which show they are fabricated by the human entity within society. Then, the 'constraints' (or institutions) have shaping capabilities, i.e. they shape or 'structure' human 'interaction'. Moreover, "They consist of both informal constraints (sanctions, taboos, customs, traditions, and codes of conduct), and formal rules (constitutions, laws, property rights)" (Ibid.). Hence, institutions have evolutionary existence, i.e. "They evolve incrementally, connecting the past with the present and the future; history in consequence is largely a story of institutional evolution in which the historical performance of economies can only be understood as a part of a sequential story" (Ibid.). Thus, the chapter's author defines institution not only as enduring and recurring patterns of human activity, but also as characterizing and determining social frameworks, which give social entities special character and guide them toward special evolutionary path. Coming back to North (1991), his economic institutional evolution is market-driven and trade-oriented. He believed, "The earliest economies are thought of as local exchange within a village (or even within a simple hunting and gathering society). Gradually, trade expands beyond the village: first to the region, perhaps as a bazaar-like economy; then to longer distances, through particular caravan or shipping routes; and eventually to much of the world. At each stage, the economy involves increasing specialization and division of labor and continuously more productive technology" (North 1991, pp. 98–99). In Persia, especially before the First World War, we could see an extremely dominant bazaar-like economy. Then during Reza Shah's reign and before the end of the Second World War we could witness the first economic indications in Iran for an industry-based economy. However, Iran has always been a strange and complicated state in respect to the institutional changes. For example, in case of economic development although the state underwent massive industrialization under the Pahlavies, it could not let go of her bazaar-like economy, even up to very modern era. This inexplicable and sometimes subtle aspect of the evolution in Iranian institutions always superimposed a constant bidirectional pulling-pushing forces to the progress and evolution of the country. Iran is an old state deeply-rooted in her 2500-year-old institutions that sometimes pulling her backward and simultaneously a state with mostly a young population that at least from the end of the *Qajar* dynasty she wanted to be modernized and stand shoulder to shoulder with the developed world. *Constitutional Revolution* at its time was an immense pushing force forward but it never reached its goals in a long run. Thus, the proposed institutional changes theories in the West sometimes could not explain and fall short within the Iranian context. Moreover, the bazaar-like economy of

Iran – as an old economically oriental institution –in the 70s beside her industrial and large class of workers – as a modern and economically occidental institutions – was one of the familiar exemplary gaps which have always existed in Iranian politics, economy, culture, society, and so forth. Additionally, some institutions are categorized as meta-institutions, i.e. "they are institutions (organizations) that organize other institutions (including systems of organizations)" (Miller 2019, p. 1). Bearing in mind the concept of meta-institution could contribute the chapter reader through the future discussions. For example, government is an example of a meta-institution, since it organizes numerous other institutions such as the police, universities, businesses, economy, etc. Although oil is merely a natural resource, while it has contextually tremendous social, political, cultural and economic effects and arouses recurring patterns of activity, privately in private lives, publically in collective lives of a nation, and officially in the administration of a state, then it should be considered as meta-institutions, especially in petro-rentier states, as the states which gain their substantial national revenues from renting petroleum to the foreign clients (Forouharfar 2020a). Oil in Iran has had such determining, organizing and institution-making functions. Moreover, *National Iranian Oil Company* (NIOC) has functioned as a meta-institution, which has had a long trans-generational enduring impact in modern Iran. On the other hand, institutional change is a context-related process (Brady 2001), i.e. it depends crucially on the cultural, economic, political, environmental and social contexts. Accordingly, institutional change is a contextual phenomenon, which could be varied from context to context and hence differs across the countries. Acemoglu et al.'s (2005) theory is an example of institutional change, among numerous proposed theories, that is fundamentally a politico-economic theory of long-run economic growth. The main constituents of the theory are (1) political institutions; (2) economic institutions; (3) distribution of resources; and (4) distribution of political power (Fig. 1).

In Fig. 1, "the subscript t refers to current period and t + 1 to the future" (Acemoglu et al. 2005, p. 390). Additionally, political institutions within a state determine de jure political power in the current period. De jure is a legal term and means "by right" (Merriam-Webster's Collegiate Dictionary 2002, p. 304) and hence "de jure political power refers to power that originates from the political institutions in society" (Acemoglu et al. 2005, p. 390), i.e. political power by law. Besides, distribution of resources in the current period leads to de facto political

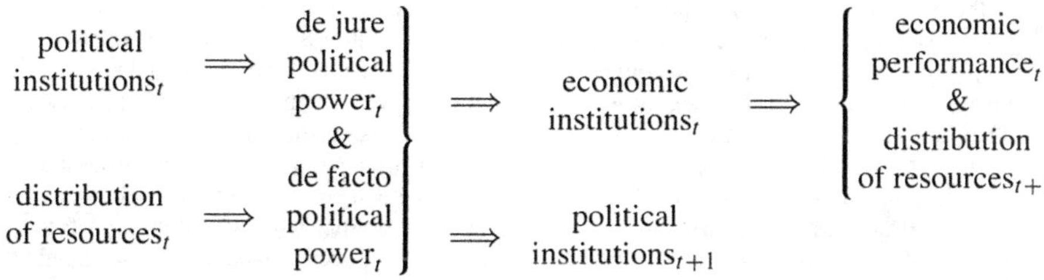

Fig. 1 Acemoglu et al.'s (2005) theory of institutional change. (Source: Acemoglu et al. 2005)

power in the current period. De facto is also a legal term, which means "in reality" and conveys the meaning "being such in effect though not formally recognized" (Merriam-Webster's Collegiate Dictionary 2002, p. 301). Thus, de facto political power is the power on the ground even though it was not recognized by the formal and legislated law of the state. Distribution of resources plays a crucial role in the determination of this political power. Next, by the presumptions that "different economic institutions lead to different distributions of resources" and "there will typically be a conflict of interest among various groups and individuals over the choice of economic institutions," Acemoglu et al. (2005, p. 390) assume "... political power will be the ultimate arbiter. Whichever group has more political power is likely to secure the set of economic institutions that it prefers" and the future (t + 1) distribution of resources. Moreover, the de facto political power in the current period determines the set of the future political institutions. In sum based on the abovementioned theory and the chapter's author interpretation political and economic institutions within a state have a reciprocal relationship. In other words, economy and politics are reinforcing and complementary wings of the power originated from state institutions. On the other hand, the rule of law and its efficient or inefficient degrees of implementation could fill or widen the gap between de jure (legally known) and de facto (in reality) political powers. Next section has clarified the ontological concept of the power in this chapter.

3 Methodology

In the methodology section first, the author clarifies his ontological view on the concept of power; then he clarifies his view on historical studies, and finally presents his own definition of critical historicism approach applied in the chapter.

3.1 Clarification of Author's Philosophical View on Power Ontology and Its de Jure and de Facto Emergences

According to Forouharfar (2020b):

> ...the ontological concept of power is built upon a triangular necessity that embraces the three fundamental constructing components of power: (1) interest, (2) need, (3) relationship. Initially, power shapes in a cognitive context. In other words, power is among animate creatures with the faculty of cognition, otherwise it is a force, which is a subject in physics. That is without the cognitive element (human) or its omission there is no such a power. Moreover, an isolated and separate entity does not form power. There must be at least a "relationship". Power is a structure-bound phenomenon, i.e. it emerges within specific relationship structures. These structures could be economic, political, social, cultural, professional, etc. The structurality of power is deeply rooted in the prerequisite of a fundamental constituting component of any power, which is relationship or interdependence. The relationships within any framing structure superimpose special characteristics on the essence of

> power. In other words, power metaphorically is a liquid in a structural container; it takes the shape of the structure (container). Moreover, relationship has a tendency toward directionality. What determines the dimensionality of this relationship is the existence of "need". Without "need" there will be no "interest". Furthermore, the two elements of "need" and "interest" do not show inferiority or superiority, i.e. "need" is not only in the inferior but also in the superior. For example, if an inferior finds his interest in subjectivity to fulfill his social needs such as welfare, security, etc., the superior finds his interest in supremacy on the subjects to fulfill his need for the expansion and maintenance of his power. (p. 9)

Figure 2 shows the ontological constituting entities for the emergence of power.

The dynamism of the three ontological components once legalized via the legislative branch or a legally accepted entity shapes de jure power (Fig. 3).

Finally, to acquire outward manifestation a fourth indispensable element must be added to the triple dynamism which could be even illegal in nature: enforcement. By enforcing, power changes into a tangible entity. Such a power is hence de facto, i.e. the power on the ground (Fig. 4).

Concerning the ontological elements of the power of oil in this chapter, the power originates from the industrial world's 'need' for oil to satisfy its 'interests' for politico-economic developments. In this context, the oil producing country (e.g. Iran) and the foreign technological country capable of exploiting oil (e.g. Britain, U.S.A) push into inevitable contexts of oil-based relationship which could be political or diplomatic, economic, colonial, technological, etc. Once the exploiting country exerts its power via oil concessions or the oil producing country's legislative branch, the power of oil is based on a de jure condition. On the other hand, in a condition when one of the engaged countries in the 'contextual' relationship exerts or shows up its power by reliance on one of the ontological factors (need, interest, relationship) to gain a better competitive position then the power of oil changes into a de facto condition. Hence, the relationship is 'contextual,' i.e. it shapes for example within military, political, economic, or technological contexts.

Furthermore, the dynamism of human history originates from powers. These powers, which could be political, military, economic, religious, informational, technological, etc., are always in constant flux, reaction, accumulation and confrontation. The power dynamism shapes the history of each age. The human to state and state to state 'will to interest' has seen as the core intention under the historical events discussed here.

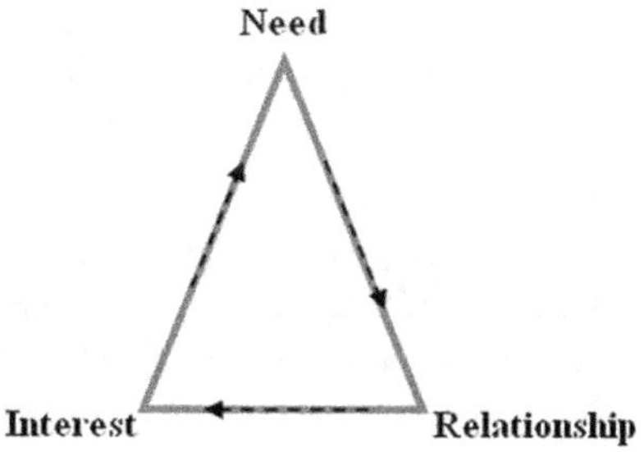

Fig. 2 Ontological elements of power. (Source: Forouharfar 2020b)

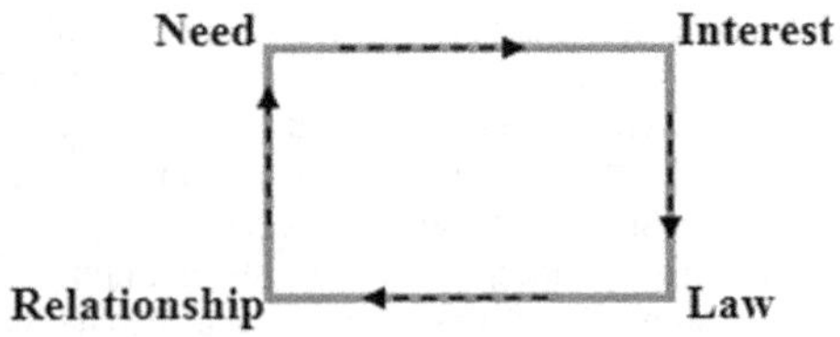

Fig. 3 Ontological elements of de jure power. (Source: Author's own work)

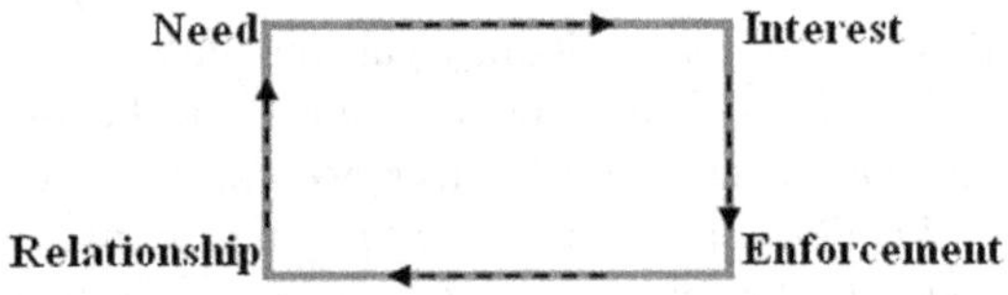

Fig. 4 Ontological elements of de facto power. (Source: Forouharfar 2020b)

3.2 Clarification of Author's View on Historical Studies and Historical Meaning

History is a cognitive phenomenon. It shapes within human cognition and because of his mental differentiation faculty of the past, the present and the future. Thus, history could not be discussed detached and separated from the living entity, human being, who creates it. This animate entity has collective memories and lived experiences. Here, the human entity of history inevitably uses his cognition, which is previously contaminated and foreshadowed with his individual, on one hand, and his collective memory, on the other. In other words, human interpretation of history could not be non-cognitive, non-interpretive and non-hermeneutical, since it deals with the perceived meaning of history. *Giambattista Vico* (1668–1744), the Italian political philosopher of the *Age of Enlightenment* who is one of the early philosophers refers to the philosophy of history believed, history's meaning is formed through human intensions since history is made by human beings (Werner 1879). Iggers (1995, p. 130) clarifying *Karl Werner's* idea on the *Giambattista Vico*'s notion of history mentions: "History is made by human beings and therefore reflects human intentions, that is, meaning. Nature, because it is not made by humans, reflects no meanings which can be understood in this way." Therefore, the meaning in history is shaped via a cognitive process under the shadow of human intensions; i.e. historical meaning is merely a manmade concept.

3.3 Clarification of Author's Critical Historicism Approach

First, there is no consensus on the meaning of historicism (Iggers 1995). The first registered usage of the term in English, according to Merriam-Webster's Collegiate Dictionary (2002), is in 1895. The dictionary has defined the term as, "A theory, doctrine, or style that emphasizes the importance of history: such as a theory in which history is seen as a standard of value or as a determinant of events"

(Merriam-Webster's Collegiate Dictionary 2002, p. 550). The term has originated from the German tradition of giving significance to historical interpretations. It was *Friedrich Schlegel* who coined the German term "Historismus" in 1797 to indicate this philosophical propensity (Leiter and Rosen 2007). However, the approach of some thinkers such as *Hegel*, *Marx*, *Gramsci*, etc. to their philosophical projects were described as a historicist approach. Furthermore, the modification of historicism with critical perspectives by the chapter's author partly indicates that type of historical orientations in social studies and philosophy that accentuates the critical recurring motifs of *Critical Theory*, which is also originated from the German tradition of *Frankfurt School*. As *Critical Theory* is the usage of critical views with liberating intentions to shed light on human societies' follies, inefficiencies, prejudices, exploitations, etc. the critical historicism approach of the chapter is using critical views to the historical oil events in Iran's modern history and its power dynamism to illuminate how the power of oil has catalyzed, formed or diverted institutional changes in Iran.

4 Discussions

According to Atabaki (2013b, p.154): "Iran has experienced…three major wars (1914–1918, 1941–1945, 1980–1988) …; two coup d'états (1921, 1953)…; and two revolutions (1905–1909, 1978–1982) …. But the event that, perhaps, has had the most significant impact on the history of twentieth-century Iran was the discovery of oil in 1908." Iran, a large and wealthy country in proximity to two world-renowned energy hubs, the Caspian Sea in the north, and the Persian Gulf in the south, owns one of the largest proven total oil and gas reservoirs in the world. Although it made Iran an exceptional and unique geopolitical producer of industrialized world current and future energy, modern Iran has acquired the reputation of a Petro-state in the global arena. Such overshadowing effect of fossil resources brought about a devil effect on the reputation of the state, which inadvertently manipulates the evaluation of less-acquainted observers for its long civilization history, culture, traditions, art, nature, etc. The question that could be raised is why most international observers neglect that Iran is among the top ten UNESCO-registered natural, archaeological and cultural heritage list (UNESCO 2019), and it is not merely the land of oil? The answer could be partially sought in de jure and de facto oil power in Iran's institutional change mechanism, its dynamism and metamorphic drive in shaping modern Iran. Studying the historical incidents of the following decades are pivotal for casting light on the power of oil in changing old Persia and shaping modern Iran and its institutions.

4.1 1900s: The Early Days of the Persian Oil

In 1908, oil was discovered under *D'Arcy Concession* amid a revolutionary atmosphere of *Iranian Constitutional Revolution* (1905–1911). The inefficient and shaky 112-year-old *Qajar* bureaucracy could not run a large state with mostly miserable population. The state affairs were under the hegemony of Britain and Russia and the dynasty with usually corrupt officials was pursuing its own benefit by granting concessions to the foreign powers without paying attention to the public needs and expectations. In the reign of the previous king, *Naṣer-al-Din Shah*, in 1872 there was a concession granted by the king to *Baron Julius de Reuter*. It "covered the entire territory of Persia, gave Reuter the exclusive rights and monopoly, for seventy years, to exploit all mineral resources including, but not limited to, coal, iron, copper, lead, and petroleum, and to construct and operate roads, railways, telegraph lines, water canals, irrigation systems, and customs services" (Mina 2004). Although this concession was cancelled later, the content of that concession and the future concession won by *Reuter*, *Bank-e-Shahi Concession* were revealing a monarchical establishment, which was treating the country as its inheritance and the dispersed peoples of Persia as its vassals. These concessions beside feudal revenues and exportations such as Persian carpets were preparing the financial resources for the system to be distributed among the *Qajar* aristocrats and their related families. The economic institutions of the era could be described as mostly feudal institutions. The economically feudal motives or as Hakimian (2011) describes it "the economic attractions of landholdings" were due to two main reasons (1) "the growing commercialization of agriculture," and (2) "increasing development of export crops". According to Lambton (1961) two major reasons were also catalyzed the thirst for the private ownership of the court's lands: (1) the diminishing political power of the dynasty; and (2) overwhelming fiscal crisis of the system. Therefore, the former "led increasingly to the *de facto* conversion of *toyūl*s into private property;" and the latter resulted "in the sales of the *ḵāleṣa* lands" (Lambton 1961, cited in Hakimian 2011). Thus, the economic and political power in the pre-oil era in Persia could be understood via the areas of land ownership and the de facto power in occupying more lands. Moreover, the cultivation of the lands needed the poor and illiterate working peasants who were not namely slaves but literally, there were no more than land slaves to the landowners. The powerful private landowners needed the peasant class to be subjugated excessively. Poverty was one of the means of class subjugation, which was mainly because of poor state administration of the age. One of the signs of corrupt bureaucracies is the fiscal policies that put the burden of inefficient administrative measures on the shoulders of the poorest classes. The peasant class was shouldering the increasing tax pressure (Bakhash 1978) and the inefficiency of the state administration had been resulted in myriad of decision-making islands within the state. By the discovery of oil in Persia, the first signs of economic institutional change could be seen in a limited domain. The *Bakhtiari* region in the west of Persia was one of these independent decision-making islands, which was being drilled by the British explorers and should be studied for the first signs of oil-driven institutional changes in Persia. Previously, technical reports such as "French reports in *Annales des Mines* (1892) on the availability of oil in the Qaṣr-e Šīrīn region" on the border of Persia and Iraq had been proved the availability of oil in the country and even *D'Arcy's First Exploitation Company*, in 1905 had discovered small quantities of oil (Kazemi 2012). Therefore, the search for oil in Persia was not a blind search. Moreover, the war machinery of Britain on the seas was in quest of oil, since the fuel system of the *British Royal Navy* was going to be changed from coal to oil fuel. In 1905 the antagonism, rivalry and diplomatic crises were rising in Europe (Stevenson 2014) and oil could give more speed and competitive advantage to the British naval warships. *Bakhtiari* chieftains or *Khans* were getting some shares of the exploited oil under British-created *Bakhtiari Oil Company* (1909–1924) to ensure the security of region for Britain's exploitation. These could be the first rents of oil in Iran's (at the time Persian) history and the first oil rent-seeking propensities in the Middle East. Therefore, Britain tried to increase the de facto, although not recognized de jure, autonomy of two tribal islands of decision-making in the west of Persia: the *Bakhtiari* region and later the Arab region or *Khuzestan*. These de facto autonomies were so powerful which persisted up to the final days of *Qajar* dynasty and the rise of *Reza Khan* as *Reza shah* the first monarch of *Pahlavi* dynasty. By the arrangement of the British government, the *D'Arcy Concession* and its company changed to the *Anglo-Persian Oil Company* (APOC) in 1909. *D'Arcy*, an ostensibly merchant, was at the backstage guiding the British government's scenario of questing for oil. According to Kazemi (2012):

> The company also acquired the rights and shares of the First Exploitation Company and later, of the British-created Bakhtiari Oil Company. D'Arcy became a director of the new conglomerate, a post which he held until his death in 1917. The British government foothold in Iranian affairs was solidified by a 1914 Act of Parliament which effectively gave the government control over APOC through ownership of fifty-three percent of the shares and the privilege of appointing two ex officio directors with veto powers over all acts of the company and its subsidiaries. A thirty-year contract between the Admiralty and the company ensured a steady supply of oil to the Royal Navy at substantially reduced prices.

On the other hand, change especially once it is in political, economic or social arenas raises tumultuous uproar in the ruling class. Although there were praiseworthy reformist endeavors by *Amir Kabir* – a prominent *Qajar* political figure and vizier in the reign of the previous monarch *Naṣer-al-Din Shah* – the corrupt dominant class was hampering any institutional change. Therefore, there were very suppressive and conservative measures to keep the status quo and block any economic and social institutional changes. The *Iranian Constitutional Revolution* was a de facto force, which was a reflection of long accumulated and now stupendous unsatisfied sociopolitical expectations behind the de jure dam of the state. Although its political power was accepted by *Mozzafar al-Din Shah* before his natural death and it was also changed into a de jure power by his signature, the heir to the throne, *Mohammad Ali Shah* who ascended the throne in 1907 did not accept the de jure results of the revolution and mainly because of his resistance against the pro-constitutionalists and his order for the bombardment of the newly-established political institution of *Majlis* he was deposed by the constitutionalists. Thus, his 11-year-old son, the last *Qajar* monarch, *Ahmad Shah* ascended the throne by the permission of *Majlis* in 1909.

The 1900s in Iran's history is a prominent era for the metamorphosis of the dominant political institution from a monarchical absolutism with secretive and inherently central decision-making; albeit myriad of decision-making domains around the country that was due to the diminishing de facto power of the *Qajar* monarchs, to a semi-consultative and parliamentary political institution under a constitution. Oil was still in its infancy in Persia's political and economic horizons and did not play a major role in this major institutional change but later the establishment of the *Anglo-Persian Oil Company* (APOC) in 1909 and its subsequent activities within the borders of Persia were interpreted by many Iranians as an insult on the national Iranian identity and gain a momentum in further politically institutional changes.

4.2 1910s: The First World War and the Abortion of Constitutional Reforms

The power of oil for fueling the British naval force, the First World War and the increasing usage of oil for industrial usages such as lubricating, which was known before, beside mass production of automobiles such as *Henry Ford's Model T* with the industrial usage of internal combustion engine more excessively were some of the reasons which led to the increasing importance of Oil for the industrial countries. Moreover, there was a fear that the oil production quantity of the United States as the major oil producer before 1910s was declining; thus, the quest for oil was changed into a worldwide tendency. Netherlands and Britain were two major winners of the quest: Netherlands long before in the *Dutch East Indies* (now Indonesia) in 1885 and Britain in 1908 in Persia. Oil prospecting and exploitation have usually demanded the most modern technology and techniques. Although the oil technology did not transfer to the Persian industry, the decade should be known as the advent of modern oil technology to the Persian soil. By the outbreak of the First World War, the de facto importance of the oil as a political commodity was increased and the oil-rich countries such as Persia were the focal point of politico-economic attentions. The weak, old and toothless Persian Lion under successive *Qajar* mismanagement and misadministration could not defend itself. The *Anglo-Russian Convention of 1907* – albeit it was not recognized by the Persian government – let Britain to accumulate more de jure political power in her south half zone of dominance in Persia. The convention let Britain gain de facto power by negotiating and mesmerizing the local tribes via sharing a small share of oil riches in order to defend its interests in the oil-rich regions of Persia. Seven years later, in the first year of the First World War in 1914, the last breathing *Ottoman Empire* forces – albeit, Persia's officially proclaimed neutrality – invaded Persia. The incident, which is known as *Persian Campaign/Invasion*, was to challenge Russia and Britain's powers. These rivalries, catalyzed by the importance of the oil in the war and the overall incidents of the First World War, which were threatening not only the territorial integrity of Persia but also its existence as an independent state, aborted the political institutional changes desired by the pro-constitution reformers.

Moreover, the modern Persian labor institution-making should be read from the same decade and from the opening of *Abadan Oil Refinery* in 1912. This is the core for the formation of industrial working class in Persia and the basis for the future seductions of communists for grabbing de jure political and economic powers in Iran. According to Atabaki (2013a, p.168) "The human migration to Masjid Suleiman, either to seek employment in the oil industry or to provide services to its employees, extended the frontiers of the newborn city. An oil field accommodating 523 employees in 1910 gradually developed into a company town with a population of 17,000 around 1920." With the establishment of *Abadan Oil Refinery* and the recruitment policy of the Labor Office in the refinery beside the demographic changes and new professional needs for the exploitation, administration, and compensation of the employees as well as manual works the first organizational labors and workers in Persia were emerged. Atabaki (2013a, p. 159) calls this institutional change of class, a change, "from *Amaleh* (Labor) to *Kargar* (Worker)." Furthermore, the First World War catalyzed the transformational class change and formation of workers' class (Atabaki 2013b, pp. 154–155):

> The demand for Iranian oil was heightened during the First World War, which resulted in a sharp increase in the number of workers in the oil industry. Throughout this early period, the Anglo-Persian Oil Company treated the oil-producing region of Iran like a colony, reaping eighty-eight percent of the industry's profits. Meanwhile, the migration of workers to the newly founded oil towns resulted in the formation of a new social class with a distinct class identity that intersected with elements of its members' preexisting communal and tribal identities.

In sum, the de facto power of oil in the decade was used by Britain for the expansion of its imperialist intentions and fueling its war machinery through the First World War. However, she tried to prepare de jure pretexts for justifying its exploitation of Persia's oil and its presence in the country via previously signed oil concessions.

4.3 1920s: Stabilization of Persia

The first strike in the Persian oil industry took place in the decade, in 1920 by the migrated Indian workers and it was also observed in the subsequent years in 1922 and 1929 by both the Persian and Indian workers. On the other hand, the historical stage before *Reza Khan's* 1921 military coup d'état is a chaotic Persia as a wandering ship in turmoil waves of history. There was no dominant de facto power to preserve the security and integrity of the state. Two major imperialists: Russia for the land-seeking intentions and Britain for the oil-seeking intentions were tearing the country apart:

In the north: From the middle of the 1910s to the following five years (1915–1920) *Jangali Movement* was emerged in resistance to the Tsarist Russian imperialist occupation of the north of Persia and with Bolshevik propensities after the *1917 Revolution* of Russia. "The political demands of the radical leaders of the Jangali movement eventually culminated in the establishment of the Soviet Republic of Gilān on 5 June 1920" (Dailami 2012). The north was going to be annexed to Russia.

In the west: Two months after the end of the state of war between the hostile parties of the First World War by the *Treaty of Versailles* on 28 June 1919, in August of the same year, the *Anglo-Persian Agreement of 1919* was signed between the government of Persia and the Great Britain. The *Anglo-Persian Oil Company* and its drilling rights were the main concerns of the agreement. In *Khuzestan, Sheikh Khazʿal*, an Arab chieftain, was running a *Moḥammara Shaikhdom*. He was under the direct protection of Britain and even received the title of *Knight Commander of the Indian Empire* and previously the *Royal Victoria Medal* from the same government (Shahnavaz 2013):

> In December 1902, December 1903, and December 1908 … Ḵazʿal received several written assurances from the British minister at Tehran, Arthur Hardinge, and the Resident in the Persian Gulf, Percy Cox, that Britain would see that his rights were respected by the Persian government.

Persia was a de facto colony within a colony. Not far from *Khazʿal*'s domain of control on the other side of the *Zagros Mountain* there were *Bakhtiari Khans*' estates and dominance as the guardians of the *Anglo-Persian Oil Company's* facilities and pipelines. Oil for Britain and cultivating and quality lands of Persia for Russia. Hence, the *Anglo-Persian Oil Company* was acting as a de facto colonial and imperialist institution within the departing territories of Persia. On the other hand, the puppet *Khans* were the de facto proxy powers of the foreigners. Moreover, Feudalism as fundamental institution of power was still strong in Persia and the beyond. E.g. in 1910 *Khazʿal* was "a large landowner both in Basrah and on the Turkish bank of the river" (Shahnavaz 2013). Additionally, the *Persian Famine of 1917–1919* exhausted the famished population of Persia and it made a stagnating condition for any institutional change via the constitutional reforms for the better. The successive reported droughts (Atabaki 2016) and the *British Occupation* (Majd 2003) were some of the reasons of the severity of the event. The situation was no better in the east and south of the country.

In the east: Britain had established numerous consulates in major cities. Especially *Kerman* and *Sistan* regions with mainly military consuls and she was pursuing the policy of enforcing a defending barrier against any threat to its India, its major colony in the east of Persia (Sehhat Manesh and Moradi Khalaj 2014).

In the south: The Persian Gulf was under the hegemony of British navy and the government of Persia had no clear strategy for its south waters. Even Britain had navy HQ in *Bushehr*, a major south port of Persia. In 1915 Britain occupied *Bushehr* and stamped the statement "BUSHIRE Under British Occupation" in bold black letters on the Persian official lion and sun postal stamps. However, the population of *Bushehr* was not reluctant to the occupation. On 12 March 1915, *Movaqre al-Dowleh* – the governor of *Bushehr* – telegraphed *Tehran*, the capital:

> …Public excitement is beyond imagination. There was never such a crowd in Bushehr … the gist of Olamas' [religious preachers] speech is: There are three years that Britain has made disruption and deployed troops, without any financial or life loss originated from the ports to Britain, and now they disrespected and did violate the government neutrality…(Mashayekhi 2011, p. 17).[1]

The summation of the abovementioned incidents in the four corners of Persia in the early 1920s, as well as Persian frustration from the stagnation of *Constitutional Revolution* in reaching its idealistic results that was encouraging self-sacrifice in advancing the democratic causes of the revolution in most social classes, besides the imperialist hegemonies of the Russian in the upper half and the British in the lower, which were added up with prevailing insecurity and diseases on one hand and diminishing power of the young and inexperienced *Qajar* monarch, *Ahmad Shah*, on the other, led to the *1921 Coup D'état* by a Cossack commander *Reza Khan*.

The four-year interval between the *1921 Coup D'état* up to the year 1925 – the accession of *Reza Shah Pahlavi* to the throne by the *Majlis* – was the period that Persian oil was under full monopoly of Britain. Britain had made its oil-protective power dynamism first on a tribal basis, which on one hand, involved *Bakhtiari* chieftains (*Khans*) and on the other the Arab chieftain, *Khazʿal*; second, she had built up a disciplined bureaucratic establishment within the *Anglo-Persian Oil Company*. Chaotic and disintegrated Persia was a perfect arena for the promotion of Britain's de facto oil policy as well as her imperialist motives in the Persian Gulf, besides her intention in barricading Persia as a shield against the Ottomans and safeguarding her interests in India.

Reza Shah's endeavor to establish a totally centralized government from the middle of the decade onward and its modernization policies under the supremacy of national identity over tribal identities were a threat to the backbone of Britain's policy of tribal supremacy and division for the promotion of its imperialist and oil exploitation intentions within Persia. It raised Britain's antagonistic sentiments toward him. According to Cronin (2012):

> During the reign of Reżā Shah (1925–1941) a profound transformation took place in both the character and the scope of British influence in Persia. Although Britain remained an imperial power, the British capacity to intervene directly in Persian politics, whether at central or provincial levels, underwent a general decline, with a shrinking of channels of patronage and a closing down of mechanisms of informal control.

The historical scene of Persia in the beginning of 1920s was so chaotic and turbulent that there is a wonder how the Persian state could continue its territorial integrity. Persia was on the verge of catastrophic implosion. The second half of the decade could be seen as the increasing rise of modern Iranian nationalism – a change in the institution of social identity: from a tribal to a national identity – to build a modern integrated polity. Furthermore, the shaping power of oil in changing the formally political or economic institutions of Persia or its bureaucracy was not conceivable

[1] Originally quoted in Persian, translated by the chapter's author.

and considerable yet. However, it had resulted in demographical and prevocational changes in the oil cities: *Abadan* and *Masjid Suleiman*.

4.4 1930s: Institutional Revolution and a Modern State

The decade is one of the most significant historical eras in studying modern institutional changes in Iran. It is described as a "big leap forward" (Agah 1958, p. 209; Floor 1984, p. 20, Hakimian 2012) and it embraces the establishment of a modern nation-state, state-induced definition of Iranian nationalism, bureaucratic centralization, population growth and urbanization, fast industrialization, empowerment of the national economy, formation of modern Iranian army and its military forces, establishment of new official institutions in the administrative and judiciary branches, foundation of modern educational institutes, such as *Tehran University*, etc. Therefore the chapter's author believes the 1930s should be studied as state-induced and -promoted *Institutional Revolution* in modern Iran. Furthermore, part of the state-induced institutional change process from a tribal society to an integrated polity was the change of the state's name from *Persia* to *Iran*. On 21 March 1935 with the advent of the first day of Iranian New Year – *Nowruz* – and suggestion of three Iranian scholars *Prof. Saeed Nafisi*, *Mohammad-ali Forouqi*, and *Seyed Hasssan Taqizadeh* the name of *Iran* was officially substituted for *Persia*. Iranians have called their land *Iran* from the antiquity several thousand years ago, and the name change was only in the foreign and international politics of the state. Therefore, in the chapter the name *Persia* is used for the time before the abovementioned date and *Iran* for the incidents after the date. Literally, *Iran* is an umbrella term, which embraces all the tribes and ethnic minorities of the polity but *Persia* and *Persian* refer to a small district in *Fars Province* and although they have positive connotations on foreigners mind, they bring to mind the antiquity. Thus, it was part of the modernization policy of the state to give a new façade to Persia.

Despite the small share of oil revenues in financing the major institutional changes of Iran at the time, consideration of the decade has a major importance in studying Iranian modernization and institutional changes. Additionally, the global atmosphere, when *Reza Shah* and his assisting Iranian elites promoted the "big leap forward," was the decade of *Great Depression* in the U.S. and the prevailing economic depression in the world major economies. However, one of the noteworthy oil-related incidents of the decade, which could be read as the first days of Iranian oil importance in the public and state administration, albeit its minor revenues at the time, was the cancellation of *D'Arcy Concession* in 1933 by the direct intervention of the monarch and renegotiation for a larger share by Iran. *Reza Shah* (1924, p. 152) shows his resentment from *D'Arcy Concession* and the oil politics of Britain in Iran in *Safarnameh-e-Khuzestan* [*Travelogue of Khuzestan*]:

> This concession is also one of the wonders of *Qajars*. There is no serious and well-pondered point in the concession to indicate Iranian courtiers' thoughtfulness; unless a ridiculous point. Shah and Iran's viziers after losing the beast thought about its saddle and have told

> the Company: Since the high-ranked government of Iran was benefiting 2000 Tomans per annum from the oil of *Qasre Shirin*, *Dalaki* and *Shoushtar* and has been deprived from the revenues after the concession, the Company must compensate the loss. Thus, Monsieur *D'Arcy* showed *Hatambakhshi* [super-overgenerosity] and shouldered the 2000 Tomans …![2]

The cancellation of the concession in 1933 was a reaction to the lion share of APOC from Iranian oil revenues, which was siphoning into Britain's Treasury. It was also originated from a major public resentment, which was accumulated for the next 18 years up to the nationalization of Iranian oil industry in 1951. Hakimian (2012) believes:

> Although the new agreement led to an increase in the oil revenues of the government per unit of production, it still did not bring about any significant changes in the extremely unequal shares of the oil proceeds … For instance, it is estimated that the profits of the AIOC during the 1919–30 period added up to approximately 200 million pounds, whereas the royalties paid to the Iranian government were no more than 10 million pounds.

Nevertheless, oil industry had generated considerable low-rank job opportunities for Iranian workers. According to Floor (1984), the number of employed workers by the APOC in 1910 was around 2460 although a quarter was foreign workers; however, in *Anglo-Iranian Oil Company* (AIOC) by 1939 the number was increased to 31,500. Therefore, due to two policies: the AIOC's human resources recruitment policies and Iran's government industrialization policies, workers' social class formed a social stratum which showed future de facto power manifestations in the political incidents of Iran; especially under the faddish communism and propensities of the subsequent decades.

4.5 1940s: Oil, Persian Corridor and the Second World War

On 25 August 1941 amid the Second World War, the *Anglo-Soviet Invasion of Iran* took place. Although the two imperialist forces fabricated the pretext of too much presence of Germans in Iran, oil and its dependency for the war machine of Britain and Russia as well as the geopolitics of Iran persuaded the *Anglo-Soviet Invasion*. Additionally, it was a preemptive measure to block Nazi accessing *Khuzestan* oil wells. Milani (2012) has clearly depicted the scene a few days before and after the invasion.

> The rapidly advancing Nazi forces inside the Soviet Union were moving toward the oil fields of Baku, and thus the Iranian border. The fact that eight Axis ships were also anchored off the Iranian port of Bandar Shapur made the Russo-British fears about a German threat more plausible. (p. 82)

Moreover, tactical gossiping and rumor dissemination could be possibly used by the British and Russian agents to aggravate the post-invasion chaos and increase the public fear:

[2] Originally written in Persian, translated by the chapter's author.

> Soon the city was abuzz with rumors of generals fleeing covered under women's veils. In the macho culture of the time, fleeing the scene of a fight, let alone doing so dressed as women, was as debilitating as any allegation. (Ibid. p. 89)

Besides, the propaganda machine of Britain was also at work to demonize the monarch to justify the invasion to Iranian territory:

> On the night after the invasion, the BBC began a series of programs attacking Reza Shah for his despotism, his breach of the constitution, and the millions and millions of dollars he had allegedly stashed away in banks, domestic and foreign. It was a "seven days weekly Persian Program" to expedite "the recommendations of the Embassy in Tehran," particularly in criticizing Reza Shah… In fact, during those months, directions for the programs critical of Reza Shah and suggestions on their content were sent from the embassy in Iran. (Ibid. p. 90–92)

Abadan Refinery and the newly-established railway system of Iran from the Persian Gulf in the south to the Caspian Sea in the north were also among the main matters in provoking Anglo-Soviet temptation for the intrusion. The former not only could partly quench their thirst for full monopoly over Iranian oil to fuel their increasing need to free and vast seas of oil during the Second World War, but also could block German's oil accession and the latter could easily and effectively enable their military logistics. The power of oil once again was applied by the foreign forces to violate Iran's integrity, national sovereignty and declared neutrality. The king was forced by Britain to resign and to go into exile. The occupation of Iran, which was freshening the *Anglo-Russian Convention of 1907* and Persia's invasion in the First World War through *Persian Campaign/Invasion* in the public mind led to the strengthening and metamorphosis of Iranian nationalism as the ever-growing social institution from mere chauvinist patriotism in the 1930s to a more mature and vigorous support for the integrity of country which culminated to the Iranian oil nationalization in the next decade.

Once power has a pyramidal dictatorial configuration any change at the pyramid peak could lead to the state chaos and paralyzation. The same incident took place in 1941. Power is a reciprocal phenomenon between the governing entity(s) and those who are governed. The need-interest relationship and its dynamism between the two sides configure the complicated power structure. Hence, Plato's view is applicable once he said, "This city is what it is because our citizens are what they are." The historical epoch in the 1940s is a traditional state between two World Wars with new public and state administration institutions, which were mostly established by the state full will and authority. It had recently got away with disintegration and implosion. Behind its borders were belligerent imperialist forces, which were planning for its fertile lands and oil wells. Moreover, the country had a male-dominant and patriarchal culture in villages with mostly strong tribal affinities who gave priority to security and calmness. Therefore, the political power configuration of the age should be studied in this reciprocal citizen-state context.

On the other hand the decade is a principal manifestation of the long-lasting institutional dichotomy of tradition versus modernity which is still present in the cultural and hence politics of Iran. The modernization policies of *Reza Shah* and his son *Mohammad Reza Shah* and the social, political, cultural, religious, etc. resistances in the subsequent decades should be read within this dichotomy.

The crown prince *Mohammad Reza* acceded the throne in 1941. He ruled the country for the next 37 years up to the *1979/ Islamic Revolution*. The major oil-related incidents from 1941 to 1949 is a fomentation period in Iran's history which culminated to the nationalization of Iranian oil industry in 1951. The eight years between 1941 to 1949 is a latent endeavor on the side of the government for acquiring more share from the Iranian oil. The government's resentment from the oil revenues, especially from the second half of the decade, was a prevailing atmosphere of the decade. According to Mina (2004):

> In the post-World War II period Iranian dissatisfaction with the level of oil revenues was greatly aggravated by the growing annoyance at the fact that the British government was extracting more income from APOC through taxation than the Iranian government was obtaining from the exploitation of Iran's national resources. For example, in the years 1945, 1946, and 1947, Iranian revenue (including royalties and taxes) amounted to 5.62, 7.13, and 7.10 million Pounds respectively, while British government taxation reached 15.63, 15.59, and 16.82 million Pound respectively for those three years.

Long before oil nationalization, the first signals for turning the status quo were originated from the *Majlis*. On 22 October 1947, a law passed the *Majlis* that called for the Iranian government to reconsider the *1933 Concession* with the AIOC. After successive years of negotiations between the Iranian government and AIOC president, on 17 July 1949 *Gass-Golshaian Agreement* was signed, although the agreement bill was withdrawn from the *Majlis* by *Razmara* in December 1950 and the ratification process did not complete. The unratified non-de jure agreement was a prelude to the de facto emergence of Iranian oil nationalization. The political arena of Iran at the end of the decade was a tripartite opposing atmosphere consisting the *National Front*, the *Tudeh Party* and the *Shah's* royalists.

4.6 1950s: Iranian Oil Nationalization

The 50s begun with the oil cause as a coalition-maker. Separate political parties were coalesced into a single coalition for the nationalization of the oil. Thus, Mina (2004) believes, "The one thing that united this coalition was vehement anti-British Sentiment, which found an outlet in the issue which dominated Iranian politics: the oil question." According to Victor Hugo, "all the forces in the world are not so powerful as an idea whose time has come." Oil nationalization was the dominant spirit of the public atmosphere. "Since the monopoly of Britain on [Iranian] oil, Iranian felt humiliated, as though there is a government within a government. Thus, the main point was not an increase in the revenues but on a more pivotal issue, which is the spirit of Iran's civilization and that, is non-submissiveness"[3]

[3] Originally written in Persian, translated by the chapter's author.

(Islami Nodoushan 2009, p. 13). The incidents of the decade were a metamorphic drive for the future institutional changes of Iran. Iran was not a previous state from the Iranian oil nationalization – in the year 1951– onward. At least, three institutions had been ripen which led to the nationalization. First the labor activism, which had been started from the early days of the establishment of the oil industry in Iran and the formation and maturity of a social class in Iranian society as an industrial working class or the worker's class. Six years before the oil nationalization, the Iranian oil industry had experienced numerous strikes that should be read as significant dissatisfaction among the Iranian oil industry employees and their increasing abilities in the organization of strikes. Kazemi (2012) depicts the 40s strikes as the following:

> On May Day, 1945, several thousand Iranian employees of the AIOC demonstrated for better working conditions, housing benefits, and higher wages. The British government responded by sending the first of a series of official missions to study existing conditions and make appropriate recommendations. In 1946, several major strikes, one of which turned into a riot, crippled the company's operations. With the active involvement of the Iranian government, company officials made partial accommodations to the workers' demands and offered them additional payments.

Second the propaganda and the utopian mottos of the *Soviet Communism* that were propagating the supremacy of the proletariat. Finally the evolution of Iranian modern nationalism detaching from chauvinist propensities in *Reza Shah's* era to a maturity which was defining nationalism as the fulfillment of national interests. Oil was at the center of the decade's definition of the national interest by the public. The man who led the public enthusiasm was the Prime Minister, *Dr. Mohammad Moṣaddeq*. He led the nationalization in de jure, or legal and de facto, or pragmatic national arenas. A Ph.D. in Law and a former member of the previous noble ruling class, the *Qajars*, he was familiar both with the judicial and political necessities for the Iranian oil nationalization. Always in politics, there are opposing powers. The main opposing de facto political power was the British imperialist hegemony not only in the state affairs but also over the region. The de jure political power for the oil nationalization was started from 28 April 1951 after his appointment as Iran's Prime Minister. In the same year, a law passed which legally claimed the dispossession of the AIOC and afterward, the *National Iranian Oil Company* (NIOC) found a de jure basis for its establishment in the year. The *Majlis* as a national institution played principal roles in the nationalization. The incident was impossible without the parliament, as the body, and democratically elected members, as its spirit.

From the Iranian oil nationalization on 28 April 1951 to *Moṣaddeq's* deposition via the *Coup D'état of 28 Mordad 1332* (19 August 1953) the state's affairs were in a checkmate condition. The British government first tried to refer the nationalization issue to the *International Court of Justice* and then to the UN's *Security Council.* However, both endeavors were unfruitful. The British countermeasure was blocking the Iranian oil production domestically by summoning the British employees and its international marketing via threats. The incident was the first historical attempts in sanctioning Iranian oil production and selling. The pro-*Moṣaddeq* forces, mostly the nationalists and the *Tudeh* members beside public demonstrations led a major threat to the monarchy, which forced the *Shah* to fled the country. Nevertheless, the superior de facto state power was possessed by the army, which had great economic and political interests in maintaining the political status quo. In historical turning points, the superior power, even if not to be publically popular will determine the future directions. The *1953 Coup D'état* by the army, as the most powerful state institution, ended *Dr. Moṣaddeq*'s sovereignty. Although might is determining historical direction, it could not control far-reaching consequences. State is an organic entity, once its natural evolution was blocked by aggressive measures such as the *1953 Coup D'état*, it culminates in unpredicted anomalies and deformed offspring.

The *Shah* was a constitutional monarch before the coup d'état, and an absolute monarch after. He returned and never forgot to control the prime minister's power. In 1954, an international consortium was arranged by the Iranian government to manage the oil company. The American companies had a 40 percent share of the consortium. Therefore, the interests of the U.S. in Iran, which were mostly blocking the Soviet expansion to the south and the Persian Gulf, accompanied with fuel interests, which lasted up to the final days of the *Pahlavi Dynasty*.

The nationalization of Iranian oil was changed to the *governmentalization* of the industry. From 1954 onward the government was the godfather of the company and has tried to fund its politico-economical projects and intentions via the oil revenues. The decade's incidents also added to the institutional supremacy of the army organization in staffing the top managerial positions of the country. Moreover, according to Pesaran (2011), "The fall of Moṣaddeq's government marked the beginning of a new era of 'oil and autocracy' in Persia's economic development."

4.7 1960s: Oil and Shah's White Revolution

Iran's 60s historical context started with the government stabilization program to tackle its financial crisis. Although the program had numerous financial benefits in running the state, according to Pesaran (2011) it made "…a deep recession developed in two politically sensitive sectors, namely, construction and domestic trade. … The recession, particularly affecting the migrant construction workers and the traditional merchants in the *bāzār*, rekindled the fire of social discontent, leading to political unrest throughout 1962–63 and, finally, mass demonstrations in June 1963. The Shah's response to the deteriorating socioeconomic conditions was a six-point reform program, known as the 'White Revolution' (Enqelāb-e safīd) and the suppression of opposition groups by force." The initial six points were later extended to nineteen points. The political stage emerged by the socioeconomic realities of the state necessitated the state's intention in preventing the escalation of social discontent via dramatic social, economic and agrarian reformations. The *White Revolution* embraced a large domain from land distribution among peasants to enfranchisement of women. It was the second wave of comprehensive modernization program of the state. The first wave was ardently pursued by the first *Pahlavi* Monarch, *Reza Shah*.

Under the second program literacy corps were sent to far corners of the state to teach the illiterate rudimentary of reading and writing, pastures, water resources and forests are nationalized, the profit of factories were also distributed among their workers, privatization of state industries was commenced, health corps were formed, educational reforms were started, policy of price stabilization was pursued, compulsory and free education for all the classes of the nation was promoted, free nutrition programs for poor mothers and infants– funded by the state budget – were set up, controlling land prices with the intention for public facilitation of home ownership, and the policy of fighting against bureaucratic corruption were followed. Oil revenues were mainly compensating the state budget for the industrialization section of the comprehensive program. The core institutional changes of the program were dramatic transformation of a feudal economy to an industrial economy, radical urbanization process, and ardent modernization policy from the above. The oil revenues also played a catalyzing role. It speeded up the industrialization, urbanization and modernization processes. The *White Revolution* was an initial deinstitutionalization and subsequent reinstitutionalization program. It tried to undo the traditional pluralistic feudal power structures and substitute them with a centralized state power. Bill (1970, p. 19) – writing on Iranian modernization – believed, "Modernization requires that a society possess the enduring capacity to generate and absorb persistent transformation." The Iranian society a religio-traditional community deep down could not absorb the modernization policies promoted and catalyzed by the petro-dollars. Four de facto sociopolitical powers were stimulated and resented by the comprehensive modernization policies: (1) feudal landowners who were mostly the tribal *Khans* (chieftains); (2) the *Bazaries* (Iranian traditional merchants mostly dwelling in down town oriental bazaars); (3) peasants; and (4) religious leaders. These four entities were constituting the traditional bedrock of Iranian society. Bill (1970) wrote his paper on modernization policies of Iran nine years before the *1979/Islamic Revolution* of Iran. He accentuated a significant point on the formation of new power structures via modernization policies. He pointed out, "Traditional power relations are torn and new patterns are introduced in a manner that builds a will and capacity to confront the challenge of change" (Bill 1970, p. 20). Institutional change once it is manipulated, encouraged or advocated by the state should be promoted in gradual and incremental steps. The degree of state's *traditionality* has a determining factor in adjusting the modernization speed. According to Pesaran (2011):

> The announcement of these reform programs, particularly those concerning land redistribution and female suffrage, aggravated the prevailing political and economic uncertainties instead of relieving social tensions and led to a revival of old alliances between the clergy, *bāzār* merchants, and intelligentsia in opposition to the Shah

The feudal *Khans* were dissident due to their dispossession of their lands that sometimes work out to large stupendous hectares of lands; embracing numerous villages. The *Bazaries* were dissatisfied because of the state manipulation and stabilization of the prices especially near the end of the *Pahlavi Dynasty*. The clergy were also discontent on the dispossession, segmentation and redistribution of the *Waqfi* (charitably endowed) large lands and finally the peasants who received their parcels of land for cultivation due to their financial background and inability to buy necessary tools of land cultivation or even seeds and mismanagement of borrowed loans from the state's banks – besides the reality that Iran is inherently a land with low precipitation – aggravated the situation. The mass immigration of unskilled and severely religio-traditional peasants to the large cities and their financial inability to rent or own decent accommodation day in day out added up to the megacities' suburbs and formed slums around the cities. The nonstop modernization policies funded by the oil revenues and the flamboyant urban life intensified their sense of perceived deprivation and induced their anger and dissatisfaction of the status quo. The size of the ring slums around the cities is analogous to the fat deposits around the waist and heart. If the state could not respond properly to the deposits that are usually accompanied with illiteracy, antisocial intentions, overpopulation, miserable living conditions, etc., the condition will end in the state's heart stroke. Although the social aspect of the *White Revolution* was an unprecedented increase in the rate of rural to urban immigrations and dissatisfaction of the four previously mentioned constituents of de facto traditional social powers that culminated in their coalition against the modernization policies, the economic aspect of the policies were successful. According to Pesaran (2011):

> The period between 1963 and the start of the revolutionary upheavals in 1978 undoubtedly represents the longest period of sustained growth in per capita real income the Persian economy has experienced... Persia's per capita income (in current prices) rose from $170 in 1963 to $2,060 in 1977... The production of cars, television sets, refrigerators, and other household durables increased manifold...Oil revenues, both as a percentage of government revenues and as a percentage of foreign exchange receipts, also rose substantially over the 1963–78 period. The share of oil revenues in the government budget was around 47 percent in 1963 and rose to 63 percent in 1978, after having fallen from its peak of 86 percent in 1974... Persia's rapid industrialization during the period under consideration was achieved primarily by government intervention and sustained by increased revenues from oil exports.

4.8 1970s: Oil Curse and the Collapse of the Pahlavi Dynasty

Iran entered 70s while a new class of deprived, underprivileged, unskilled, and mostly unemployed was wandering about the megacities of Iran. The economic trends of the country showed a prosperous state on the track of modernization and industrialization. The international increase in the oil price in 1973–1974 was a blessing for the system to pursue its *White Revolution* intentions. The oil revenues provided the lion share of the public budgeting and as Looney (1985, p. 61) believed the oil revenues "dominated government fiscal resources". One of the major state institutions which was absorbing a great quantities of the oil revenues was the Iranian army. Since the army was the backbone of the state and the threat of the Soviet Union as the neighboring northern country, beside Iran's role in providing the security of the Persian Gulf as a strategic international marine route and energy hub, as well as the *Cold War* atmosphere, great bulks of budget was dedicated to the army's power build-up, modernization and equipment. Hence, oil revenue was a major source of militarization of Iran (Gharehbaghian 1987). Additionally, one of the major incidents of the decade was the 1973 oil embargo of the OPEC on the exportation of oil to the U.S.A., the Netherlands and Denmark. The embargo reason was the assistance of the three mentioned states to Israel and the conflict between the Arab states and Israel because of its refusal in leaving the occupied Arab territories. The oil exporting Arab states took advantage of oil pricing as a tactical move against Israel and its allies. Moreover, "At OPEC's Tehran conference in December [1973], oil prices were raised another 130 percent, and a total oil embargo was imposed on the United States, the Netherlands, and Denmark. Eventually, the price of oil quadrupled, causing a major energy crisis in the United States and Europe that included price gouging, gas shortages, and rationing" (History Website 2019). Besides, the de facto power of "OPEC rose to international prominence during this decade [1970s], as its member countries took control of their domestic petroleum industries and acquired a major say in the pricing of crude oil on world markets." (OPEC official website 2019). These two incidents were dramatically threatened the energy security in the U.S.A. and Europe. The *Shah's* leading role in OPEC, his modernization ambitions, his frequent verbal attacks and humiliation of Western state administration routines, large army logistics, his large equipment and weapon purchases, the embargo and the high pricing tactics were enough to blame him as the major motivator of the situation and a future potential uncontrollable menace. Thus, according to *Los Angeles Times* (17 Oct. 2008):

> A new report based on previously classified documents suggests that the Nixon and Ford administrations created conditions that helped destabilize Iran in the late 1970s… "The shah is a tough, mean guy. But he is our real friend," Kissinger warned Ford, who was considering options to press the monarch into lowering oil prices, in an August 1974 conversation cited by the report. "We can't tackle him without breaking him."

Oil was not the single cause of the collapse of the Pahlavi dynasty but once a state relies excessively on the exportation of its resources to acquire predefined anticipated revenues of the budget then the state has leaned against a wrong and shaky wall since the oil price is liable to change rapidly. In economics, the overwhelming reliance of a state's budget and revenues on its resources could bring about 'resource curse' or paradoxical results, i.e. while a state produces and exports more resources, instead of prosperity it would move more paradoxically to the verge of economic collapse and unpredicted results such as lower economic development and downturn, political discontentment, and resource addiction for compensating the deficits in the budget. However, it will be very naive to think that the administrators of a state do not know it? The *Shah* of Iran in the 70s was relying so much on oil in order to reach the state to his programmed *Great Civilization*. He knew it. In 1971, in an interview with the *Echo* program on energy in response to the interviewer he acknowledged that the oil would not last forever. He said, "It is not eternal, eternal source of supply, 20 years, 30 years, 50 years, time to finish, in many cases this is the only source of wealth of some countries, it is not the same in mine, it's true, but actually it is the principal resource, and it is with money from oil that we are building our country " (Echo News Reel Number 88, 1971). This idea, as well as his lymphoma cancer that was kept hidden from the public and some researchers believed he was first diagnosed with the cancer in 1973, although "it is still unclear exactly when the Shah developed his first symptoms and when he was diagnosed with cancer" (Khoshnood and Khoshnood 2016, p. 207), beside his aspirations for the *Great Civilization* made him hasten to reach his goals. Oil was the panacea to fulfill his goals for Iran. This condition also pushed him toward more dictatorial decision-making. Nevertheless, once the oil in the 70s reached to an unprecedented rise, Iran entrapped in *Dutch Disease* (in economics broadly an increase in one economic sector that leads to decrease in another sector). According to Dadgar and Orooji (2020, pp. 138–139), "The groundwork of Dutch Disease and its related DRR [Dutch Disease, Rentier State, and Resource Curse] in Iran goes bank to 1970s when the price of petroleum raised rapidly and the Iranian government increased the annual budget accordingly. Iranian imports rose in the period of 1970–1978 and the domestic products diminished accordingly. Due to converting new dollars into domestic currency, liquidity went up and led to a higher inflation rate." The inflation was the last ingredient to the recipe of turmoil. The curse was in full potential and the amalgamation made collapse inevitable.

To sum up the discussion section, from the First World War to the last days of *Pahlavi Dynasty*, Iran always played the role of a triple functioning state: a buffer state, a stabilizing state, and an oil-producing state. Its function as a buffering state, i.e. a state that is usually trying to stay neutral and reduce the possibility of conflict among hostile and belligerent states, was mostly due to its geopolitics, broad and vast unprotected shores from the east to the west of the Persian Gulf, and its large territory and long borders. The state remained neutral in both World Wars, I and II. Through the *Cold War* period she tried not to fall far from its buffering tendencies among the two superpowers of the time: the U.S.A. and the former U.S.S.R. However, it was long the desire of the nation to modernize their state and implement democratic measures in the state's policymaking and administration. The *Constitutional Revolution* and the establishment of the *Majlis* – parliament – as a national decision making institution were rarely predictable incidents by an old nation that was not shouldering anymore the monarchical absolutism and desired modern political, social, and economic institutions to run its country and soothe its long accumulated but unanswered historical needs and necessities. Nevertheless, the exploitation of oil and its importance for the industrial West, the World Wars and monopoly of APOC and later, after its name change AIOC, over Iranian oil resources up to the nationalization of Iranian oil, and the ever-increasing conflicts of interests between Iran and Britain over the oil, proved more to the state decision makers and the public mind that oil was a political commodity which could not be free from the plotting and thirst of the industrial world. Iranians in one of the most conflicted regions of the world, the Middle East, the rivalry of the superpowers, and the frequent undeclared invasions of the imperialist forces in both World Wars, which violated their national integrity and manipulated the power structure, have tried to pursue transformative institutional changes from a traditional state to a modern polity. Oil in some incidents of the Iranian history was a curse and so many others a blessing.

Table 1 Major institution-making revolutions in modern Iran

Historical Period	Iranian De Jure and De Facto Revolutions	Major Domain of Institutional Changes
1905–1911	Constitutional Revolution	Political institutions
1925–1941	Institutional Revolution	State administrative institutions, bureaucratization, political centralism, educational institutions, military institutions, cultural institutions, judiciary institutions, nationalism, etc.
1963–1979	White Revolution	Transformative institutional changes from feudalism to industrialism
1979–1980	1979/Islamic Revolution	Islamic institutions

Source: Author's own work

Since the beginning of the twentieth century as the country approached the modern era, oil has played a fundamental role in providing the state budget and has always played a compensatory role for compensating the governments' budget deficits and mismanagements. Without oil and its power in making modern institutions, Iranians could not live more affluent than the inhabitants of their neighboring countries in the 60s and 70s. However, the institutional change in Iran was not only the result of oil but oil has had a catalytic and interest-conflicting major role in the course of the nation's modern history. The Iranian oil-induced institutional changes should be also studied by considering the impact of four revolutions: (1) the *Constitutional Revolution*; (2) the *Institutional Revolution*[4]; (3) the *White Revolution*; and (4) the *1979/Islamic Revolution*. These are major institution-making revolutions in modern Iran (Table 1).

Moreover, the metamorphosis of the Iranian oil company from *Bakhtiari Oil Company* to the current *National Iranian Oil Company* (NIOC) as the meta-institution which has had a great impact on the overall institutional changes of the state and its sponsoring role for the modernization, urbanization, industrialization and militarization of the state deserves focal attention in the study of Iran's history of class formation (the workers and the middle class), public budgeting, financing the state policies and programs, etc. (Table 2).

5 Conclusion

Oil is a politico-economic commodity, which has had great impact on the course of historical incidents in Iran and had been a major drive behind most state-sponsored development programs such as the top-down modernization, industrialization,

[4] *Institutional Revolution* was coined by the chapter's author to refer to the first stupendous reformist modernization policies, established modern institutions, and institutional reforms in the *Reza Shah* reign (1925–1941).

Table 2 The metamorphosis of *Iranian oil company* and its major institutional effects

Historical Period	Oil Company Name	Major Institutional Effects
1909–1924	Bakhtiari Oil Company (BOC)	Empowering of the *Bakhtiri Khans* and adding up to their autonomy and self interests in opposing to the general interests of the state
1909–1935	Anglo-Persian Oil Company (APOC)	Emergence of Iranian working class, fomentation of Anglo-Persian conflicts of interests between the two governments
1935–1954	Anglo-Iranian Oil Company (AIOC)	State modernization, intensification of interest conflict between the governments of Iran and Britain
1948-up to date	National Iranian Oil Company (NIOC)	Modernization, militarization, urbanization, bureaucratization, industrialization, socio-demographical frustration, massive immigration
From 1954	British Petroleum (BP)	Extra-state oil institution generation (BP as the Iranian oil company spinoff)

Source: Author's own work

urbanization and militarization policies of the state. Some but not all the effects of the implicit or de jure and explicit or de facto power of oil in the institutional changes of Iran could be summarized in (1) formation of the Iranian working class, (2) locally demographical and ethnic changes of the oil-raising regions of the country and the oil-induced nationwide demographical effects, (3) provision of the financial resources of the top-down modernization policies, (4) overwhelming ability of the governmental sector in staffing and recruiting superfluous public personnel, and (5) intensification of the bureaucratization of the state. As Iran proceeded to the modern era, no product or technically economic rent was so powerful in forming its power structure inside and outside. The intrastate hegemony through the government bureaucracy could not be possible without the oil revenues and the state sense of autonomy from the legitimization originates from the nation. Formation of international bodies such as OPEC – which Iran played a crucial role in its foundation and empowerment in the *Pahlavi* era – and its significant roles in oil pricing in the 70s, were an explicit and de facto extra-state power of oil in the global arena. However, the volatility of the oil price, the plotting of the industrial world for its acquisition, its politicalness, state dependency over its petro-dollars, besides the geopolitics of Iran, etc. have shown that any developmental plan based on it should be studied systemically and from different and especially sociopolitical and socio-economic inside, and globo-political and globo-economic dimensions outside. A comprehensive plan for the intrastate development could potentially threaten the implicit and undeclared interests of some foreign powers and affects the interstate relations of Iran. The experience of the *White Revolution* and its oil-based modernization and industrialization policies and the reaction of the world powers in respect to the oil pricing is a case in point. Furthermore, the institutional changes in modern Iran had always been an above-dictated project by the governments that induced public resistance. Iran's history has revealed once the institutional changes call for the deinstitutionalization of the former and usually traditional institutions, e.g.

culture, lifestyle, political behaviors, etc., and the reinstitutionalization of new and mostly state-favored institutions, it potentially raises public anger, resentment and in some cases fierce opposition. Speedy and hasty institutionalization programs, even if in the long run bring prosperity and affluence for the nations, could aggravate public resistance. The *1979 /Islamic Revolution* was an unexpected blow to such swift-advancing transformative measures of the state toward its project, *Great Civilization*. The golden lesson for the Iranian policymakers is the axiom that state-induced institutional changes should not exceed the national capacity for their absorptions.

References

Acemoglu, D., Johnson, S., & Robinson, J. A. (2005). Institutions as a fundamental cause of long-run growth. In P. Aghion & S. N. Durlauf (Eds.), *Handbook of economic growth* (Vol. 1A, pp. 385–472). Amsterdam: Elsevier. https://doi.org/10.1016/S1574-0684(05)01006-3.

Agah, M. (1958). *Some aspects of economic development of modern Iran*, Ph.D. dissertation, Oxford University.

Ashraf, A. (1992). Conspiracy theories. In E. Yarshater (Ed.), *Encyclopaedia Iranica* (Vol. 6, pp. 138–147). London: Routledge & Kegan Paul. at: http://www.iranicaonline.org/articles/conspiracy-theories.

Atabaki, T. (2013a). From 'Amaleh (labor) to Kargar (worker): Recruitment, work discipline and making of the working class in the Persian/Iranian oil industry. *International Labor and Working-Class History, 84*, 159–175.

Atabaki, T. (2013b). Writing the social history of labor in the Iranian oil industry. *International Labor and Working-Class History, 84*, 154–158.

Atabaki, T. (2016). Persia/Iran, in: 1914–1918-online. In U. Daniel, P. Gatrell, O. Janz, H. Jones, J. Keene, A. Kramer, & B. Nasson (Eds.), *International encyclopedia of the first world war*. Berlin. 2016-05-02: Freie Universität Berlin. https://doi.org/10.15463/ie1418.10899.

Bakhash, S. (1978). *Iran: Monarchy, bureaucracy and reform under the Qajars. 1858–1896*. London: Ithaca Press.

Bill, J. A. (1970). Modernization and reform from above: The case of Iran. *The Journal of Politics, 32*(1), 19–40.

Brady, D. W. (2001). Institutionalization. In N. J. Smelser & P. B. Baltes (Eds.), *International encyclopedia of the Social & Behavioral Sciences* (pp. 7558–7561). Amsterdam: Pergamon.

Cronin, S. (2012). Great Britain v. British influence during the Reżā Shah period, 1921–41. In E. Yarshater (Ed.), *Encyclopædia Iranica* (vol. XI, Fasc. 3, pp. 231–234). at: http://www.iranicaonline.org/articles/great-britain-v

Dadgar, Y., & Orooji, Z. (2020). Dutch disease, rentier state, and resource curse: A characteristic triangle and ultra challenge in the Iranian economy. *Iranian Economic Review, 24*(1), 129–157.

Dailami, P.(2012). Jangali Movement. In E. Yarshater (Ed.), *Encyclopædia Iranica* (vol. XIV, Fasc. 5, pp. 534–544). at: http://www.iranicaonline.org/articles/jangali-movement

Echo News Reel Number 88. (1971). *National Archives*, https://archive.org/details/gov.archives.arc.650286

Floor, W. (1984). *Industrialization in Iran: 1900–1941*, University of Durham, Centre for Middle Eastern and Islamic Studies, Occasional Paper, no. 23.

Forouharfar, A. (2020a). A contextualized study of entrepreneurship in the Arab states prior to the Arab spring: Reviewing the impact of entrepreneurship on political stability. In P. Sinha, J. Gibb, M. Akoorie, & J. M. Scott (Eds.), *Research handbook on entrepreneurship in emerging economies: A contextualized approach* (pp. 44–63). Northampton: Edward Elgar Publishing.

Forouharfar, A. (2020b). The anatomy and ontology of organizational power as a fractal metaphor: A philosophical approach. *Cogent Business & Management, 7*(1), 1728072. https://doi.org/10.1080/23311975.2020.1728072.

Gharehbaghian, M. (1987). Oil revenue and the militarisation of Iran: 1960–1978. *Social Scientist, 15*(4/5), 87–100.

Giddens, A. (1984). *The constitution of society: Outline of the theory of structuration*. Cambridge: Polity Press.

Hakimian, H. (2011). Economy in the Qajar period. In E. Yarshater (Ed.), *Encyclopædia Iranica* (vol. VIII, Fasc. 2, pp. 138–143) at: http://www.iranicaonline.org/articles/economy-viii-in-the-qajar-period

Hakimian, H. (2012). Industrialization: The Reza Shah period and its aftermath, 1925–53. In E. Yarshater (Ed.), *Encyclopaedia Iranica* (XIII/1, pp. 105–110) at http://www.iranicaonline.org/articles/industrialization-i

History Website. (2019). OPEC enacts oil embargo. *A&E Television Networks* at: https://www.history.com/this-day-in-history/opec-enacts-oil-embargo

Huntington, S. P. (1968). *Political order in changing societies*. New Haven: Yale University Press.

Iggers, G. G. (1995). Historicism: The history and meaning of the term. *Journal of the History of Ideas, 56*(1), 129–152.

Islami Nodoushan, M. (2009). Oil and Iran, In Mohammad-Ali Islami Nodoushan *Dirooz, Emrouz, Farda [Yesterday, today, tomorrow: selected essays]* (In Persian) pp. 11–15: Iran, Tehran: Sherkat-e-Sahami-e-Enteshar.

Kazemi, F. (2012). Anglo-Persian Oil Company. In E. Yarshater (Ed.), *Encyclopaedia Iranica* (II/1, pp. 61–65). at: http://www.iranicaonline.org/articles/anglo-persian-oil-company

Kazemzadeh, F. (2019). Anglo-Russian Convention of 1907. In E. Yarshater (Ed.), *Encyclopædia Iranica* (vol. II/1, pp. 68–70). at: http://www.iranicaonline.org/articles/anglo-russian-convention-of-1907-an-agreement-relating-to-persia-afghanistan-and-tibet

Khoshnood, A., & Khoshnood, A. (2016). The death of an emperor–Mohammad Reza Shah Pahlavi and his political cancer. *Alexandria Journal of Medicine, 52*(3), 201–208.

Lambton, K. S. (1961). Persian society under the Qajars. *Journal of the Royal Central Asian Society, 48*(April), 123–139.

Leiter, B., & Rosen, M. (Eds.). (2007). *The Oxford handbook of continental philosophy*. Oxford: Oxford University Press.

Looney, R. E. (1985). The impact of oil revenues on the pre-revolutionary Iranian economy. *Middle Eastern Studies, 21*(1), 61–71.

Los Angeles Times. (2008, October 17). U.S. may have had role in shah's fall, by Borzou Daragahi. at: https://www.latimes.com/archives/la-xpm-2008-oct-17-fg-shah17-story.html

Majd, M. G. (2003). *The great famine and genocide in Persia, 1917–1919*. Lanham: University Press of America. ISBN 978-0761826330.

Mashayekhi, A. (2011). The violation of Persia's neutrality in the First World War and the occupation of Bushehr by Britain (8 August 1915) [In Persian]. *Historical Studies*, 32(1) at: http://mtq.ir/?page=magazine&id=32

Merriam-Webster's Collegiate Dictionary. (2002). U.S.A.: Springfield, Massachusetts.

Milani, A. (2012). *The Shah*. New York: Palgrave Macmillan.

Miller, S. (2019). Social Institutions. In E. N. Zalta (Ed.), *The Stanford Encyclopedia of Philosophy*. at: https://plato.stanford.edu/archives/sum2019/entries/social-institutions/

Mina, P. (2004). Oil agreements in Iran (1901–1978): Their history and evolution. In E. Yarshater (Ed.), *Encyclopædia Iranica* at: http://www.iranicaonline.org/articles/oil-agreements-in-iran

Mojtahedi, M. (1974). *Īrān wa Engelīs [Iran and Britain]* [In Persian], Tehran, 1326 Š./1947.

North, D. C. (1991). Institutions. *The Journal of Economic Perspectives, 5*(1), 97–112.

OPEC. (2019). *Brief History* at: https://www.opec.org/opec_web/en/about_us/24.htm

Pesaran, M. H. (2011). Economy in the Pahlavi Period. In E. Yarshater (Ed.), *Encyclopædia Iranica* (Vol. VIII, Fasc. 2, pp, 143–156) at: http://www.iranicaonline.org/articles/economy-ix

Reza Shah (1924) *Safarnameh-e-Khuzestan [Travelogue of Khuzestan]* [In Persian].

Sehhat Manesh, R., & Moradi Khalaj, M.(2014) Objectives and functions of the Britain consulates in Kerman and Sistan (1894–1914) [In Persian], *Iran History*, 74/5, Summer-Autumn, pp. 55–87 at: http://irhj.sbu.ac.ir/article/view/9272/4704

Sepehr, M. (1957). *Īrān dar jang-e bozorg [Iran in the World War]* [In Persian], *1914–1918*, Tehran, 1336 Š./1957.

Shahnavaz, S. (2013). Ḵazʿal Khan. In E. Yarshater (Ed.), *Encyclopædia Iranica* (vol. XVI, Fasc. 2, pp. 188–197) at: http://www.iranicaonline.org/articles/kazal-khan

Stevenson, D. (2014). Europe before 1914, *British Library website* at: https://www.bl.uk/world-war-one/articles/europe-before-1914

Straw, J. (2019). *The English job: Understanding Iran and why it distrusts Britain*. London: Biteback Publishing.

Turner, J. (1997). *The institutional order*. New York: Longman.

UNESCO. (2019). *World heritage list statistics,* at: https://whc.unesco.org/en/list/stat

Werner, K. (1879). *Giambattista Vico als Philosoph und gelehrter forscher* (No. 25). New York: Burt Franklin.

Examining Institutional Barriers to Transition from a Natural State in Iran During 1941–1979

Mohsen Renani, Salman Gharakhani, and Mitra Mousavand

1 Introduction

Like many societies, Iran has failed on its path to development. The problem of Iran's lagging behind is rooted in a variety of factors that have been inherited throughout the history. As a turning point in the contemporary history of Iran, the 1941–1979 period was a golden opportunity to transcend these conditions, but despite the short-term economic growth provided under the shadow of high oil revenues and foreign aid, Iran could not use its historical crises contrary to expectations. The issue of Iran's lagging behind has occupied the minds of many scholars. Iranian scholars have dealt with the failure factors of Iran's economic development trend within the framework of various theories. Some scholars such as Zibakalam (2011), with an emphasis on the significance of geography, considered the problem of arid climate by focusing on its effect on the formation of political institutions.

Emphasizing the issue of culture, Alamdari (2005) investigated the integration of religion and state, the formation of the state religion and then the religious state, and consequently its effects on Iran's development path. Azimi-Arani (2014) raised the issue of human resources training in relation to the origins of underdeveloped circuits in the Iranian economy. Katouzian (2004) emphasized the concept of short-term society and identified the factors of Iran's failures in the development trends as legitimacy and succession, invalidity of property and lifestyle in Iran. Some scholars, such as Ashraf (1980), saw the problems of traditional state ownership as obstacles to economic development; some citations also consider colonialism and the formation of a dependent state as the most important causes of Iran's lagging behind. Despite emphasizing the role of oil in facilitating the import of goods; knowledge;

M. Renani (✉) · S. Gharakhani · M. Mousavand
Faculty of Administrative Sciences and Economics, Department of Economics, University of Isfahan, Isfahan, Iran

N. Faghih, A. H. Samadi (eds.), *Dynamics of Institutional Change in Emerging Market Economies*, Contributions to Economics,
https://doi.org/10.1007/978-3-030-61342-6_13

and technology, Esfahani and Pesaran (2009) pointed to the detrimental effects of oil revenues on the learning process in technological developments.

North's theory as a realistic approach can be used to explain the obstacles to Iran's economic development. Douglass North, an institutional economist and Nobel laureate of economics, has defined the development process as the way of transition from LAO (most people have limited access to political and economic markets) towards an OAO (people's access to political and economic markets is permitted). He believes that one of the important issues in the process of transition from a NS is the control of violence (North et al. 2009). This research will explain the reasons for the sustainability of LAO conditions and the creation of VC's during this era, as a way to examine North's approach to a NS. Historical evidence shows that after the reign of Reza Shah, Iran experienced conditions of LAO, and steadily progressed across the fragile and basic spectrum. In this era, Iran underwent massive changes; superordinates and citizens sought to withdraw from NS and to move towards an OAO; but the main problem was that Iran not only did not move toward an OAO, but after experiencing an era of social BLAO, it moved toward a FLAO and eventually the chaos. In line with this, this study seeks to answer the question of what factors prevented the transition from NS in Iran during this period; therefore, the role of each of the superordinates (members of the ruling coalition) in transition from the limited-access order is examined with an emphasis on the issue of violence here. During this period, the transition from NS has been influenced by issues such as the status of the semi-colony, ancient and religious culture, the unearned state revenues and the process of industrialization. In this study, it is attempted to address the four elements of formal political institutions, formal economic institutions, major domestic superordinate groups and rent sources by considering the aforementioned beside the framework of the limited access order and to investigate the institutional barriers to transition from NS as the main question of this research by providing an analytical narration of the situation in Iran.

To answer the research question, considering two situations of LAO and OAO and determining the quantitative and qualitative indices according to each condition using three fragile, basic and mature states are necessary. A history extracted from documents within the framework of North's theory will answer the question, providing a historical analytical account of the situation in Iran during this period. In this research, after explaining North's view on the development concept, the era studied is divided into two periods of FLAO and BLAO, and ultimately, the reasons for the sustainability of NS and failure in the transition from these conditions are discussed.

2 Theoretical Foundations

North has defined the development process as the way of transition from LAO towards an OAO. He believes that one of the important issues in the process of transition from a NS is the control of violence (North et al. 2006). NS is a type of political arrangement where the political system, by exploiting a LAO, limits the economic entry to create economic rent; then, it uses the generated rents to stabilize the political system and control violence. Powerful groups are entitled to valuable privileges such as monopoly rights to trade, monopolies in the production of cement or telecommunications, the exclusive right to create markets in specific areas, or monopoly on the importation of high-value goods (North et al. 2006). In the context of NS, the dominant coalition manages the issue of violence by imposing limitations on access to valuable resources, including land, labor, and capital, or by controlling valuable activities such as commerce, worship, education and threats, and access to such activities in favor of superordinate groups. In fact, the creation of standard rents by limiting access in NS is not merely a way to fill the pockets of the dominant coalition, it is also a fundamental tool for controlling violence (North et al. 2013).

In the transition from NS, North divided societies into three categories of fragile, basic, and mature LAO. He argued that in the process of development, societies must move from FLAO to MLAO. The criterion for distinguishing the fragile LAO from the mature LAO is the preservation of security and avoidance of chaos and violence.

FLAOs are systems where each faction of the dominant coalition has direct access to violence, and the capacity for violence is the main determining factor in the distribution of rents and resources. In such a situation, the existing order is fragile, because if the allocation of these rent flows does not coincide with the balance of power (considering that each group has the ability to commit violence), groups will be asking for more shares or contributing to war.

In BLAO, the official state, or more simply, a set of state organizations, is often the most durable organization. Although within the framework of a dominant coalition there are often non-state organizations, BLAO organizations do not support organizations outside the coalition circuit.

In mature limited access order (MLAO, the dominant coalition is supporting a wide variety of organizations outside and within the state), but it also limits access to private organizations approved and supported by the state. The dominant coalition uses this method to limit competition and it creates a rent to maintain itself (North et al. 2009).

The social order in the OAO is continued through competition, not the creation of rents. The free access to and entrance in economic and political organizations result in the continuation of economic and political competitions. Inclusive institutions are developing and therefore sustain this situation. These institutions provide economic opportunities for all society sectors through guaranteed property rights, law, public services, and the freedom to conclude contracts. Inclusive economic institutions are institutions that provide the opportunity for participation by the masses of people in economic activities and make the best use of their talents and skills, allowing them to make choices according to their desires. To spread economic institutions, there must be security for private property. In other words, there needs to be a neutral legal system and the provision of public services must be equal for everyone, and the opportunity and context for all people to participate in the exchange of goods and services and concluding contracts must be the same. The possibility of entering new businesses and choosing a career for the people should also be the same everywhere (North et al. 2013).

The traditional framework of development poses the question of the transition from NS to the OAO as the first development issue. But as a new institutionalist, North knows the transition of societies from LAO to those with OAO is the second development problem, believing that the first issue is to improve the conditions of NS, so that societies with LAO should move towards forms of social organizations which promote greater economic returns, less violence, stable political outcomes, and greater individual well-being. This is because OAO comes out of the LAO (North et al. 2009).

In the short run, NS can pave the way for economic growth and development in the society, but in the long run, it can result in the creation and perpetuation of extractive institutions which only serve the interests of a particular group. Dissemination and promotion of this type of institutions may lead to the creation of vicious cycles (VCs) in such societies. The existence of VCs in different societies prevents any reform because it will disrupt the distribution of rent and cause violence in these communities (Acemoglu and Robinson 2012; North et al. 2006). The prospect of LAO emphasizes that the stability of the ruling coalition is always threatened by violence arising from external or internal challengers. The economic performance depends on how these threats are ended. The solutions formulated by the ruling coalition to prevent violence are usually not optimal from the viewpoint of the organization of economic activity, but without these suboptimal arrangements there would be no economic accumulation. Therefore, LAOs are stable arrangements which inhibit violence through the distribution of rent (physical collision or threat of physical collision), but are only the second best in terms of productivity and growth. Consequently, various societies should seek to transition from it to OAO along with the improvement in the conditions of NS (North et al. 2009).

North et al. (2006) believe that in the transition from LAOs, personal coalitions must first be transformed into impersonal coalitions, and with the formation of stable organizations with long-term goals, the ground for replacing unlimited rent should be provided. The distribution of productive rent led to the movement of society towards a OAO. Consequently, inclusive political institutions and the opportunity for their participation were provided, and the inclusive economic institutions provided grounds for the creative destruction and then the economic development (Fig. 1).

North's model proposes three types of order (primitive order (PO), LAO, and OAO). In PO societies, informal institutions are sufficient to sustain expectations and discipline; because personal relations are dominant among members of these communities; with the complexity of the relations, however, the need for a third party, that is a state, is required. For the formation of a NS, there must be a coalition between groups with violence potential; if any of these groups think that they will obtain more benefits in the new structure, they will advance the society towards chaos by disturbing the order and creating conflict. The ruling coalition members must come to the conclusion that their interests in a coalition state are more than a

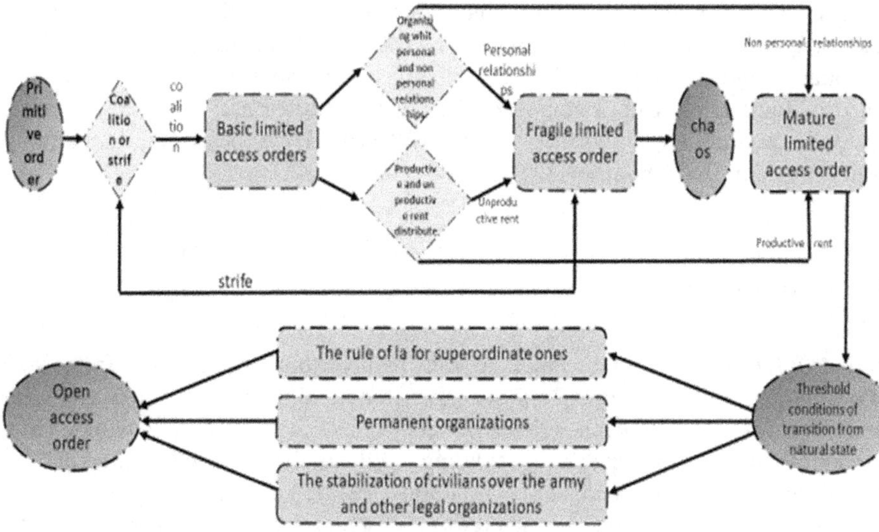

Fig. 1 Conceptual Model. (Source: authors' own figure)

state of conflict, so a NS can be formed. After the formation of a NS, personal relations should be replaced by impersonal relations, and decisions made by organizations should replace individual decisions so that the society moves to a BLAO; If relations remain at a personal level, the distribution of rents will be counterproductive, which will drive the society towards fragility and chaos. If impersonal relations dominate political and economic affairs; then, with the productive distribution of rents, society moves to a MLAO and organizations outside the ruling coalition, along with organizations within the ruling coalition, will have the right to live permanently, and conditions for moving to OAO will be available. Consisted of the institutionalization of the rule of law for superordinate ones, the permanent livelihoods of organizations in the public and private domains and the stabilization of civilians over the army and other legal organizations, the entry threshold has a capacity for violence. The OAOs are created during the institutionalization of the three threshold conditions of entry, only as a peak or the product of a long, completely inevitable historical process.

Extensive studies have been carried out on the transition from different LAOs. For example, You (2014) views South Korea's success in transition from NS as an issue of territorial reform and the disappearance of superordinate landlords from the power bloc, which resulted in the distribution of wealth and upgrading the level of individuals' education. In explaining the development trend in Bangladesh, Khan (2013) analyzed its economic growth under a vulnerable LAO. Bangladesh, despite experiencing a crisis of democracy and a one-party system under the shadow of an authoritarian populist regime, US restrictions on the apparel market, and foreign capital flows to the country as a historic turning point lead to its growth under the rule of a LAO. Roy (2013) explored India's development path within the framework of social order. In 1947, India had many of the features of BLAO and gradually found the features of a MLAO. India's LAO was at the same time emerging aspects of maturity and fragility, which is described as vulnerable maturity. Curbing violence in India dealt with a complex network of political and economic compromises. How rents were allocated to powerful groups was shared by institutions, policies, and political relations within each state.

3 Methodology

In line with neo-institutionalist methodology and North's institutionalist framework of analysis, a developmental and descriptive-analytical method is employed in this study. The research approach is deductive socio-historical in the framework of analytical institutionalism. That is, considering the deductive research method and the North's analytical framework and using library research techniques, historical facts and institutional developments related to the research subject which can be evaluated within the context of North's theory, are carefully described at the historical point in question. Then, in the context of North's theory of social order, we interpret and analyze the institutions' evolutions, and examine historical realities in the field of economic development. The resources of research data are primarily historical documents from which historical facts are extracted. The analytical instrument is the framework of the new institutionalist methodology to describe, analyze and interpret the facts within the framework of the North's theory and with a historical approach in timescale, during 1941–1979. The present study attempted to consider four elements of formal political institutions, formal economic institutions, superordinate internal groups, and rent resources alongside informal institutions by considering the framework of the LAOs and an analytical narrative of the situation of Iran.

To answer the research question, considering situations of both the LAOs and the OAOs and determining the quantitative and qualitative indices according to each condition using the three fragile, basic and mature orders are necessary. A history extracted from documents within the framework of North's theory will answer the questions, providing a historical analytical account of the situation in Iran during this period.

4 Iran in the Natural State

4.1 *First Era: FLAO (from 1941 to 1953)*

During this period, Iran suffered a lot of instability, so that it experienced chaos from 1941 to 1946, and from 1946 to 1953, it was dominated by a FLAO. During this period, each of the dominant coalition factions (especially foreign forces) had direct access to violence, and the capacity for violence was considered as the main determinant in the distribution of rents and resources. In the era of chaos resulting from the outbreak of World War II and the retirement of Reza Shah from power, the allies and profiteer groups in the country were heavily exploited by sources of wealth through the distribution of wealth that brings as many people as possible to poverty (Furan 2009).

The fall of Reza Shah in 1941 freed the merchants and the national bourgeoisie of Iran from the total control of the state. The weakness of the state between 1941–1951 resulted in the rapid growth of the national bourgeoisie and the merchants. The pseudo-democratic political system imposed by the Allies on the power bloc prevented the state from directly controlling political and economic institutions. The action taken by the state was to change the status quo and postpone economic growth based on the first seven-year plan (1948–1955) and the emergence of the Plan and Budget Organization (PBO) (Amjad 1989). The plan to form the PBO was one of the factors influencing the production and dissemination of economic institutions during this era. It was there that a small nucleus of several Iranian economists and a consulting group funded by the Ford Foundation tried to implement long-term economic policy and planning in Iran. In this way, they wanted to institutionalize economic planning in Iran and put it away from viewpoints of a group (Milani 2000).

A prominent aspect of the emergence of the PBO was the increasing role of the United States in Iran (Lotz 1950); consequently, American capital and corporations played a decisive role in the shaping of this organization. As one American researcher points out: "The World Bank and the US Embassy in Tehran, two American consulting companies, and Max Thornberg played a decisive role in establishing the PBO" (Baldwin 1967).

However, Max Thornberg, president of the Transatlantic Consulting Company, had the most influence on the structure and duties of the PBO (Elwell-Sutton 1955). The goal of the state in setting up the PBO was to drive oil revenues for economic development.

The first seven-year plan emphasized building infrastructures. The same goal was pursued by the Second Plan (1955–1962), where most of the budget was spent on building dams and major roads. The third (1962–1968), the fourth (1968–1973), and the fifth (1973–1978) plans were directed mostly toward a rapid industrialization. Despite the state's efforts, the PBO was not able to provide the needed change in the society for a true economic growth.

After the chaotic period, due to the dismissal of Reza Shah and World War II, the power groups did not attempt to form a coalition because they thought they were in a situation where they could use the fragile order, the conservative forces sought to regain their lost power, and the newly arrived Shah had no solid political and social status. On the political market, the young king was just one of several political actors, and a set of journalists, political parties and newly established labor unions organized political scenes. These were all in the atmosphere where Iran was occupied by the allies. Soviet troops were in the north, and British forces were in the south, and American advisers served in the state in Tehran, and Iran was the Soviet

Union's logistics line (Furan 2009 and Digard et al. 2007). During this period, the power of Mohammad Reza Shah was primarily dependent on the army and subsequently on the conservative and monarchist factions and the press (Furan 2009), and the Shah sought refuge in conservative forces, especially the clergy, for he was fearful of communism and the first powerful activists in the first period, such as Qawam and Mossadegh (Milani 2011). With the widening of the ruling coalition and the growing influence of the allies in the country, the ruling coalition, and in particular the court, had no ability to expand and stabilize its power, and at any moment it was possible for it to leave the country for external or internal reasons, but the Shah, while paying attention to this situation, was busy fixing his power and influence not only on the court but on the country (IBID). The Shah's triple policy was to consolidate his power, spread money in charitable institutions, attempting to crack down on the press and compromise with the clergy. All of this was done through the wealth left by Reza Shah (IBID). The members of the ruling coalition could not have a credible commitment to the laws and constitution because the balance of the coalition was constantly changing; however, they were not deprived of the potential benefits of domestic institutional structures.

In this era, personal relations could limit the possibility of expanding the power and creating large networks; the king could not enforce his orders, and he was faced problems with the realization of good or bad intentions. Conservative landlords and politicians formed the most powerful and influential social group with the unofficial alliance with the religious system. The new king relied heavily on the mentioned alliance, although he was pursuing his own personal strength improving through the army and foreign support (Katouzian 1981). Struggle over power is a major feature of FLAOs. Given the fact that the ministry election was held by the parliament during this period, the power struggle led to the formation of 19 cabinets by twelve prime ministers during 1941–1953, with almost none of them working. It was a manifestation of the political instability of the society. The Cabinets' instability dramatically reduced the efficiency of the state and allowed foreign powers to penetrate more and more in different parts of the society (Azghandi 2006).

In this period, due to the fragile situation and the dominance of personal relations on affairs, most organizations were often identified with their leaders. As he was enthroned, the new king tried to consolidate his position as much as possible, which made Mohammad Reza Shah not to change the structure to satisfy his supporters in the early days of his state. Therefore, in the first 12 years of Mohammad Reza Shah's rule, no change in the economic structure or social stratification was observed (Milani 2018). The shah made the slightest changes in the structure in order to satisfy the interests of his supporters and, on the other hand, he did not have the ability to deal with them, because the exclusion of each of these groups from the ruling coalition would lead to the emergence of uncontrolled violence by them. This has made personal relations between supporters shadow over the economic and political structures and prevented the creation of permanent organizations which were the opposite of personal relations.

At that time, Iran gained little revenue from economic growth, because in FLAO societies, obtaining a high income is a coincidence. In this era, the major economic affairs were under the control of the power struggle between individuals, and hence the decision of the private sector was at high risk. The country was incapable of generating wealth due to instability and the threats faced by members of the coalition by those outside the dominant coalition; because the creation of wealth and a better economic life depended on personal capacities or the capacity of the ruling coalition. The creation of an uncertainty atmosphere led to risk in the economic system, which caused the economic inefficiency of the ruling power. Although the ruling coalition factions understood the potential benefits of better institutional structures, the inability to maintain a coalition for long periods of time caused widespread uncertainty on the ultimate outcome of this change, and in many possible circumstances, it would have been desirable that short-term goals would be preferred over long-term ones. For example, implementing the first plan was faced with difficulties as a result of the mischief of superordinate landowners and businessmen who considered it as a threat to their economic and political domination, as well as the advice of clerics saying that industrialization and modernity were a threat to the traditional Islamic model of life of the Iranian people (Bostock et al. 2014).

One of the characteristics of FLAOs is that if the allocation of rental flows is not aligned with the balance of power, the factions may want more shares or fight for it. In such a situation, one or more self-powerful groups can overwhelm the existing order with struggling for power, or some power-makers make a coalition between themselves and resort to violence for the purpose of distributing power and rents. One of the manifestations of violence in this period was the formation of an autonomous state in Tabriz and Kurdistan, the assassinations of Fadaiian-e Eslam group and the nationalization of the oil industry. There was a possibility of violence by a number of militaries. There were elements in the army (in particular, Lieutenant-general Ali Razm Ara), whose goal was to create a modern military dictatorship and possibly without the presence of the king. Called for a radical approach to the implementation of Islamic law in the country, the Fadaiian-e Eslam group was also among the violent groups during this period, who wanted to carry out their goals by the assassination of people.

In this era, in line with the power of each of the coalition factions, they were able to reach the rental sources; especially the Allies and profiteers' groups who have been completely exploited by the conditions of chaos in the country. The plundering of the resources of the country led to the fact that the surviving forces from the rental sources who felt they should have a greater share of these resources seek to achieve their goals by creating a national flow, along with a nationalist spirit. In 1949, Jebhe-ye Melli, a coalition of nationalist parties led by Mossadegh, was set up to plan nationalization of the oil industry.

The Tudeh Party, blindly supporting the issue of oil for the sake of the Soviet Union, ruined their credibility against nationalist demands, which led the colonial leadership to be formed by Mossadegh as the leader of the Jebhe-ye Melli (IBID); Indeed, the National Movement was seen as a widespread, multi-class, and urban popular coalition against the ruling coalition and foreign forces, and faced defeats following the initial brilliant victories by the split of domestic leaders and foreign intervention and failed (Furan 2009).

Mossadegh's era (1951–1953) was a very important stage in the formation of economic institutions in Iran. The nationalization of the oil industry, prohibition of the royal family from interfering in economic and political affairs and land reforms were among fundamental principles to Mossadegh's policies (Mazdak 1982: 286); an alternative import sector was created to reduce dependence on European manufactured productions (Bharier 1971: 184). During Mossadegh era, the bazaaries and the national bourgeoisie grew, and as a result, offered him their support. As the national bourgeoisie and the bazaaries were becoming stronger, the power bloc-composed of the dependent bourgeoisie, the masters, the commanders of the army and the court- suffered a major setback (Ashraf 1971).

The growth of bazaaries and the national bourgeoisie reached its peak during Mossadegh's era (1951–1953). Mossadegh's policy was to reduce the Shah's power, strengthen bazaaries and the national bourgeoisie, and end Iran's dependence on foreign capital (Mazdak 1982). Mossadegh's policies resolved the court, the dependent bourgeoisie, the influential lords and clergy, while benefiting the national bourgeoisie and bazaaries. Not surprisingly, the latter supported him by heart, while the power bloc opposed him. Supported by Britain and the United States, the power block eventually toppled Mossadegh whose fall was a major blow to the national bourgeoisie and bazaaries, but the dependent bourgeoisie and the owners became more powerful followed by the coup d'etat. Mossadegh's fall reversed the situation. The power block appeared stronger than the past, and the national bourgeoisie and bazaaries were in trouble (Amjad 1989).

4.2 Second Era: BLAO (from 1953 to 1979)

After the power struggle of August 19, 1953; the king ruled an authoritarian regime with the support of internal forces (landowners, the army, bazaaries and the religious system) and foreign forces (The United States). After the collapse of the Jebhe-ye Melli coalition, the Shah, who returned to power with US support left the conservative forces out of power and sought to create a new coalition of bureaucrats and craftsmen. While the ruling coalition was seeking to create a stable political atmosphere, the country faced a financial crisis of balance of payments. The financial crisis forced the Shah to engage with the Jebhe-ye Melli leaders in order to establish a coalition state, but this effort did not come to an end.

During this period, the socio-economic logic of the state's policy on the political economy was that it sought to create a middle class as the social base of the regime. The real goal was the satisfaction of an educated and semi-educated urban community to prevent the emergence of a serious political opposition and, to create another power base against the great power of the owners; because they were economically more independent and politically more powerful than the Shah could bear, despite being Shah's allies (Katouzian 1981).

A coalition consisting of the court, landowners, some first-class clerics, prosperous merchants, armed forces and the United States, who had previously been able to overthrow Mossaddegh, broke up during the land reform plan of Shah. The collapse of the mentioned coalition marked the beginning of the tripartite coalition of the Iranian state, the middle and native class of the industrial sector and foreign investors, especially American investors (Milani 2018). The four pillars, the court, the bureaucratic system, the military forces, and the one-party system were the main pillars of the Shah's power during this period, replacing the relation between the Shah and the conservative forces (Azghandi 2006).

The White Revolution was the beginning of a new era in Iranian history. The formulation of the economy before Iranian capitalism was severely broken and the policy of industrialization was implemented rapidly. The old class structure of Iran collapsed and the masters disappeared from the economic and political scenes. Through the state-owned bank, local cooperatives and mechanized agriculture, capitalism penetrated the countryside. The old class union consisting of the court, the owners and the dependent bourgeoisie was broken up and was replaced by a new power bloc consisting of the court, the dependent bourgeoisie and the rural bourgeoisie. The state also made the former owners to be added to the new power block by selling state-owned factories to them. The modern Iranian bourgeoisie was the creation of the state. The only part of the modern bourgeoisie with a market background was the one that became dependent on the state. The modern bourgeoisie was also composed of former owners who sold their lands to the state and purchased state-owned factories after the white revolution. In this regard, when the bureaucratic landlord transitioned to the bureaucratic capitalist order, the former owners and affiliated bazaaries became the forerunners of the establishment of a new socio-economic formation; in addition, oil revenues prepared the state to invest directly in industrial planning and to help the "private sector" using the Realized assets (Amjad 1989). The Shah's reforms followed by the collapse of the distribution of rents separated from him scholars and upper-class landowners, who were regarded as the traditional middle class and were a traditional base of support for the Shah (IBID).

The scholars opposed the state following the reforms of Shah and the death of Ayatollah Boroujerdi. With the support of the lower classes and the conservative Shi'a scholars, the Shah sought to maintain the control of the new middle class who was supportive of socialism and nationalism, and was considered as the most serious threat to the stability of the country; however, the Shah's system was unable to effectively distribute or rebuild the power structure so that it could bring the hearts and minds of the lower classes together. As the hostility of the Shah had fueled hostility between him and the clergy, he was not able to attract full support of conservative scholars. More importantly, the Shah, with the suppression of the new middle class, deprived himself of a major source that was able to formulate an ideological backbone for his modernization, as well as a deterrent to leftist extremism and right-hand's bias (IBID); In fact, the withdrawal of conservative forces from the ruling coalition, the lack of support from the middle class, and their staying away from the rental, along with the use of repression, reduced the popularity of the ruling coalition on a daily basis.

By focusing its security and information acts on the suppression of the new middle classes, the Shah's regime made itself vulnerable to fundamentalist scholars.

With the separation of more groups from the regime, the state became increasingly isolated, and inevitably pushed for repression and foreign aid, in particular by the United States, to maintain its survival; hence, the state was on the one side and all other groups, except the ruling superordinates, were on the other side (IBID). Although the Shah was firmly opposed to intellectuals and workers, he carefully sought to avoid policies that led to the unification of large families of owners and middle-class bazaaries (Abrahamian 1982).

Leaving conservative groups out of the power caused their dissatisfaction, revealing their discontent as a violent incident on June 5, 1963; but the traditionally conservative and radical opposition failed; the economic foundations of the owners disappeared and the uprising of the people, organized and led by the religious community, was suppressed. Subsequently, the presidency of the endowment fell to the hands of the state; at the same time, oil revenues increased dramatically (Katouzian 1981).

The fifth June bloodshed made the possibility of reconciling the Shah even with his mediocre opponents more difficult. From the core of the Jebhe-ye Melli and other opposition forces, the Mojahedin-e Khalq Organization and Fadaie People's Guerrillas were formed which where both based on armed struggle (Milani 2011).

Followed by the reforms of the regime and the consolidation of its power, the Shah sought to use foreign-educated technocrats abroad. Mansour set up a Moteraghi club with the support of young technocrats. The Moteraghi club had come to the fore as an alternative to the Jebhe-ye Melli. It was supposed to attract the middle class and moderate political forces of Iran and to uphold the values of democracy and provide conditions in which the moderate forces could find a place in the politics of Iran. In this period, with the advent of the Iran-e Novin Party, it tried to turn powerful people to powerful organizations; the powerful people formed political, educational, religious, and economic organizations to advance their interests. The young technocrats, as bureaucrats, tried to increase their power through their relations in the Iran-e Novin party. Although the party was under the supervision of the Shah, most of the bureaucrats came to power based on the structure of this party, which made it possible to at least reduce personal relations at the intermediate levels of management, although at higher levels of management, and sometimes at the lowest levels, the Shah's opinion was applied.

In this period, given the country being at the base of the LAO communities, the country was not static and experienced some time of progress because it added to the rents, but due to the inexpediency of the power superordinates, the country lost power and moved toward FLAO instead of MLAO. In line with this, the economic renewal started from the upstream with the rise in oil prices. During this process, the state expanded its incumbency over the economy as an important lever to consolidate its personal foundations. The state controlled investment in oil and gas, infrastructure and heavy industries. In 1963 and 1977, Iran experienced a minor industrial revolution. The share of production in GDP reached from 11% to 17% and the annual industrial growth reached from 5% to 20%. In addition, the number of small factories with 10 to 49 workers increased from 1502 to 7000 units, the medium factories with 50 to 500 workers increased from 295 to 830 units and the number of large factories with over 500 workers increased from 105 to 159 units. These included new textile and steel factories, refineries, petrochemical complexes, machineries, aluminum smelting and fertilizer plants, and automobile, tractor and truck assembly facilities (Abrahamian 1982).

Regarding the country's economic growth trajectory during this period, Alikhani said, "The increase in oil revenues resulting from rising prices, although not as dramatic as it was before, has led to the growth of industrial production to be ignored. Non-oil exports were overshadowed by rising oil revenues, which prevented diversification of the economy. Oil's share in the budget was not decreased and the country's revenue became oil-dependent (cited from Dehbashi 2014: 183).

During this period, oil revenues not only did make the state independent from domestic production and social classes, but also in many cases made these very classes dependent on the state; these might include direct aid and various privileges, Loans for investment, access to booming domestic markets for obtaining high profits in manufacturing, trade, exchanging stocks, and public welfare plans. Therefore, state expenses which were the source of political and economic power, and tended to maintain and expand themselves, influenced the fate of different social classes (Katouzian 1981). The rise in oil revenues was formed under the shadow of thinking of moving quickly toward industrialization, Regardless of what the infrastructure would be and under the shadow of rent relations. Citing Dariush Homayun, Dehbashi says: Because of increased oil revenues and the fact that the private and part of the public sector was keen to make more profits, huge volumes of commodities were ordered as raw materials or in forms of industries which had nothing basically to do with the needs of the Iranian community and domestic transportation capacity in terms of ports and roads. Most of these goods were in ports and on the ways to their destinations because they were not imported based on planning but based on the order and recommendation of those who had influence (Cited from Dehbashi 2014: 270).

Just in the era when Iran witnessed this rapid economic growth, the Shah also invaded more and more in politics each day. Not only were all the forces of the Left and moderate parties eliminated or actually did abandon the possibility of their action, but even in the ranks of the regime's advocates, the Shah couldn't tolerate even small criticisms (Milani 2011). With the formation of a rental economy and an increase in oil revenues, economic modernization and changes in the administrative, educational and cultural systems began in the 1980s.

With the land reform, the state sought to create new state-dependent classes (the new middle class and payrolls and employees, and the release of long-standing dependency on landlords). The new middle-class members, as the new class base, were more educated in the West and were from the sons of the landlords, especially the children of senior staff and state officials. The Pahlavi state needed the administrative and technical, and especially political support of this class to support its state. It should be noted that a significant number of members of the new middle class were from the children of the landowners. Although the members of this class lost their political power as landlords in the politics and the state, after the White Revolution and land reforms, they became new capitalists by purchasing factories, then through kinship, intrusive and political mechanisms, they achieved a variety of economic, customs and banking privileges (Sardarniya 2007).

The increase in oil revenues made Shah not to need to create a coalition, and he himself took the total control of the political market, made all the groups depended on him, and suppressed the groups left out of power and sometimes even created violence. The rise in oil prices not only did cause the financial crisis of the 70's, but also made it possible for the power coalition supporters to no longer support the Shah. The Shah was introduced as an iniquitous factor of the economic problems of the West and was targeted from widespread international attacks. On the other hand, the Shah added insult to injury of people and futility provoked them by giving hollow promises, leading to more and more contradictions between the nation and the state, so that he lost the highest privilege to achieve open access conditions. By turning to the Jebhe-ye Melli leaders, the Shah chose Shapur Bakhtiar to form a national reconciliation state to prevent his overthrow; but the FLAO after the Dutch disease seemed to have come to an end, and the society was again chaotic, and eventually came to an end with a popular revolution that was the result of the violence accumulated during this period by the opposition, both domestic and foreign. In 1976, a series of factors such as economic downturn, inflation, excessive increase in urban population, state policies that severely damaged the bazaary class, a significant difference in income levels and the consumerism of the privileged community toward the Western community and, finally, the lack of freedom and political participation led to the fact that many state forecasts that the great civilization could easily be achieved in the perspective turned to be a big lie which facilitated the emergence of violence (Keddie and Richard 2006).

The market benefited from increased trade as a result of the sudden rise in the oil price and it was still regarded as a powerful economic institution by the late Pahlavi era, but the bazaaries benefited from a system with no loyalty to it. During the years of economic prosperity, the group gained a lot of power, but gradually the market moved out of the power bloc in line with the state policies and it came to the forefront of the ruling coalition despite the benefits it gained from the economic growth. When the modern bourgeoisie enjoyed easy state credits, low interest rates and supportive policies, the bazaaries were excluded from this atmosphere. The growth of the banks also undermined the functions of bazaaries in lending money. The state sought to weaken the bazaaries (because of their traditional independence from the state) and to replace them with the modern bourgeoisie. The struggle against the 1975–1976 price gouging also contributed to weaken the bazaaries. The establishment of banks and new shopping malls, expansion of supermarkets and large chain stores of Cyrus were other causes of bazaaries dissatisfaction with the state. With the massive migration of villagers to cities, many joined the shopkeepers' syndicate as competitors (Motallebi 2007).

The growth and development of modern financial organizations outside the marketplace has led to the loss of the independent bazaar power. Such organizations were run by a new generation of merchants who were way far from the bazaaries ideologically and in their lifestyle. However, the market continued to maintain its financial strength and its access to a fast mobilization network. The network was located within the syndicates' Organization. In the 1960s, more than 135 syndicates were members of the Supreme Syndicate Council under the influence of the regime. In 1971 the Majlis gave the state the authority to assign the Syndicates' Organization manager. Such an interference was perceived by the state as an unjustified act for market domination (Milani 2018). During this period, more than forty thousand shops were closed and 80,000 bazaaries were imprisoned or deported; hence, it is not surprising that bazaaries participated in the 1979 Revolution sincerely (Amjad 1989; Milani 2000).

A fourfold increase in oil revenues has forced the Shah to dream of Iran becoming the fifth industrialized country of the world in less than twenty years. The result of this policy was a rapid industrial growth, the impairment of the rural order and the migration of millions of farmers to cities. This royal craving, namely the industrialization of Iran, regardless of the low production amount, the lack of skilled personnel, the lack of port equipment and other economic bottlenecks, eventually became a nightmare. In 1975, the economy went out of control. The fall of international demand for Iranian oil was the main reason for this new situation. The fall of the monarchy brought to power a new power bloc consisting of the liberal bourgeoisie (i.e. the remnants of the national bourgeoisie), the bazaar bourgeoisie and the traditional petty bourgeoisie (i.e. the shopkeepers). In the power struggle, the liberal bourgeoisie lost the traditional bourgeoisie and petty bourgeoisie (Amjad 1989).

Regarding the existence of the conditions of NS in the country, it was expected that after the decline in oil revenues and the creation of critical conditions in the country, the dynamics of the dominate coalition would focus on old or new rents that continue cooperation and restrict violence, as well as create new rents for this purpose, but in this period, hopelessness about the country's future by the ruling coalition prevented the creation of a new rent. The state's severe budget deficit did not allow the dominate coalition to distribute oil resources. The king thought he would survive the crisis with the help of foreign agents. Many bazaaries and craftsmen were also from religious minorities, and maintaining the existing space for them was of high-risk because of the lack of social security, and they preferred to get their wealth out of the country. The middle class, and at the top of them, the courtiers also tried to take advantage of these rental sources in a more open political environment and felt that after the financial crisis the Shah would return to his former routine. In the light of their conditions, the clerics found themselves in favor of overthrowing the Pahlavi regime, and, despite the ideological differences between them, they eventually ended up in a queue. Also, the Marxist slogans among the workers did not allow any interactions between them. The lack of rental sources did not allow the king to keep his supporters in the ruling coalition, and eventually he remained alone against the popular protests, and even parts of the ruling coalition also joined the ranks of the protests, so that they can take advantage of more rental sources in the formation of the new regime. Eventually, with the decline in oil revenues giving the king a surprising power, he was left alone against the middle class and conservative forces, and there was no coalition except the king himself to support the Pahlavi dynasty. He even has driven his American friends as a result of his ambitious policies.

5 Iran under the Shadow of Violence

The main focus of this section is on responding to the reasons for the sustainability of the conditions of Iran's NS at the time of Pahlavi II; for this reason, the causes of the establishment of extractive institutions and the link between the inclusive and extractive economic and political institutions in this era are discussed. In this era, the unions between extractive economic and political institutions created a VC, and extractive institutions were created.

In this era, the political interests of coalition members did not match their economic contribution-seeking in the existing order, and as a result, the dual balance collapsed and the ruling coalition could not establish order. Among the issues prevented the production and dissemination of inclusive political and economic institutions in the country, and with the inconsistency of political and economic institutions caused the country been violently trapped, the following can be mentioned:

5.1 Lack of Rule of Law for Superordinates

The realization of the issue of the rule of law for the superordinates depends on the functioning of the judiciary, parties, and the press. Many factors prevented the realization of the rule of law for the superordinates in society, including: The existence of corruption, the involvement of information agencies such as SAVAK in judicial affairs, the existence of military tribunals, the domination of personal relations on all affairs and affiliation of the judiciary to the king, the involvement of political issues in judicial procedures, the influence of personal tastes on the affairs of the judiciary, the existence of demonstrative and ritual arrangements, the absence of parties and the press self-censorship.

5.2 Dominance of Personal Relations on all Affairs

The king, who, for various reasons -including increasing oil revenues- became a tyrant king, interfered in all matters and caused the increase in personal relations and the dependence of the affaires on him. Usually, in LAO societies, the ruling coalition is trying to increase its strength by increasing its economic growth; but in Iran, the ruling coalition did not need to do so, because the oil resources were well responsive to the needs of a devotee-king network in the country. Because of his nationalist thoughts, the Shah placed economic growth on top; therefore, he tried to open up the economic space. But since he considered himself as the only one who could handle this economic growth, he did not allow to open the political space. Under the influence of his socialist thoughts and his entourage, he launched large and ambitious projects. This confirms that, in addition to the political market, the

Shah extended his domination to the economic market, and although this kind of economic growth was in line with the benevolent goals of the Shah, but by breaking the balance of interests of stakeholders and benefiting of some rent-seekers from existing conditions, and due to his inefficiency, the political system was moving toward collapse.

In this power structure, sovereignty was manifested in practice in the king himself and the state was considered to be the same as the king. The shah was at the top of the pyramid of the absolute state and enjoyed the highest political power. The accumulation and concentration of power in the king and the court prevented them from any responsibility, criticism, and accountability in the areas of economic and political corruption.

In this era, periods of political gangs and kinship relations were the main focus of economic and political corruption surrounding Ashraf, Alam, Hoveyda, Iqbal, Hushang Ansari, and others. In this period, gaining power through these gangs and imposing political influence was an important precondition for wealth and seeking rents. These gangs tried to influence the decisions and views of the Shah of Iran through communication channels and to under-effect the public interests to their personal and gang interests. The Shah, as a "supporter", endorsed his state by giving privileges, rents and thousands of state facilities to the gangs as "followers". In these relations, there were corrupt support and rivalry within the political and social body for proximity to the king and the court, which enhanced the spread of economic corruption (cited from Dehbashi 2014 and Sardarniya 2007).

Another characteristic of the new father-king and the absolute structure of Pahlavi's power was the informality of politics and decision-making campaigns, which was a direct result of the personal power of the Shah. Closed and unclear policies and decision makings were an important platform for economic corruption. Political institutions such as the Majlis, which in practice consisted of representatives of the king, court and foreign powers, lacked the proper practical work of legislation and supervision in various fields, including economic corruption (Sardarniya 2007).

5.3 Lack of Formation of Permanent Organizations

"Permanent organizations"means organizations that their life-time is longer than the founders'. In the early days of Mohammad Reza Shah's rule, due to the chaotic situation of fragile order and the struggle for power, the conditions for the creation of organizations with a permanent life were not provided, and even political organizations could not survive because of participation in the National Oil Movement and the 1963 June incident. In this era, the formation of organizations and their survival were entirely dependent on personal relations. The king, who, with the help of oil resources and foreign aid, dominated on all affairs, interfered with the activities of all the organizations personally and the life of these organizations depended on the Shah. The rise of the oil shock caused the Shah, along with his nationalist thoughts, advance his pseudo-socialist thoughts in the shadow of his despotism, so that all successes were attributed to him. The reliance of the ruling coalition on oil resources did not allow them to open up a political space and pursue personal interests, as all the forces, whether directly or indirectly, were fed from these resources, and they did not need to create a permanent organization. Some of the issues which prevented the creation of permanent organizations in the country were: The limited life of the states, the domination of personal relations on all affairs, the promotion of socialist thinking among the country's executives, the emergence of oil shock and the state versatility, power struggles, short-term contradictions of stakeholders with the long-term goals of organizations, the rapid entry of technology and high-speed creative destruction, foreign affairs involvement, the presence of foreign investors, the lack of belief in the permanent life of organizations, the lack of hope for the future of the country, the ineffectiveness of formal institutions and the existence of a high exchange cost, the conflict in the management in high levels and lack of support from middle managers, the removal of good managers, flattering instead of expertise, lack of cooperation between managers, dependence of employees on the state, systematic corruption, the prevention of the independent management of organizations, the consideration of the Large projects, price volatility, instability, SAVAK intervention in organizations and other factors.

5.4 Military Dominance over Economic and Political Affairs

For the integrated control of the military, the separation of close ties between economics, politics and military forces in the natural state is necessary, but this has not happened in the history of Iran. During the past hundred years, the military has never performed its main role in defending the borders of the country against the foreign enemy. When soldiers can't play their main role for any reason, they have to play other roles in continuing their lives, whether they are military roles or not. These roles, in addition to the role of preserving the regime, included cultural, judicial, law enforcement, economic and financial affairs. The implementation of various roles resulted in the military's penetration into civilian areas and increased their magnitude and power, and most importantly, the military's participation in the cultural and economic affairs of the society led to militarization of civilian and the entire society, and for this reason, the military intervened in the economic and political affairs (Azghandi 2006).

5.5 Imbalance between Political and Economic Development

In this era, with the industrialization policy, other groups entered into power and needed political support in order to provide their own interests that were in line with economic development. These groups must either have entered the ruling coalition and thereby assumed all types of rents and legal protections, or concluded through a rental relation with the courtiers; but given that it was costly for them to be on the political market; therefore, they preferred to use these types of resources by sharing the companies' stock with the ruling coalition members, which would produce and spread extractive institutions on the economy market.

At the heart of the capitalist class and the modern industrialist bourgeoisie dependent on Shah, which was created and expanded as a result of modernization, were 300 families, of which 70 accounted for more than 17% of modern industries, and a considerable part of them were relatives and family members of Mohammad Reza. In order to accelerate their wealth accumulation and obtain facilities, the great capitalists began to partner with the Pahlavi family in parts of their own corporate stocks and economic units. The king and the court family also benefited from rent resources by interfering with the business affairs. The Pahlavi family was Iran's richest trader family in the early 1970s; the partnership of each family member was obvious in machinery factories, automobile-making complexes, construction products, mining companies and textile factories. Most of the assets were also managed and handled by the Pahlavi Foundation. It is estimated that the royal family had invested 5% of the total fixed gross domestic capital in the Fifth Plan as a domestic private sector (Sardarniya 2007).

Regarding the political market, the Shah believed that the interest of the state was in individual ruling and, by single-party political space, prevented the creation of any inclusive political institutions. The economic market was developed in spite of extractive economic institutions, while the existence of extractive institutions in the political market was seen as a barrier to political development. The craftsmen did not consider the existence of extractive institutions to develop an economy market and did not stand against these institutions; because their interests depended on the import of goods or assembly, which required the use of political and economic rents. Utilizing these rental resources which were based on the devotee-king network at that time, would cause economic development in the short term depending on the existence of extractive institutions on the political and economic markets. The convergence of extractive political and economic institutions as a VC did not allow the entry of new individuals and organizations into the political and economic market and prevented any creative destruction on the market. During the financial crisis, with the state intervening in pricing and determining workers' wages and policies such as sharing the profits of the factories with workers, a dual balance collapsed, and the state faced difficulty in creating order. On the other hand, the sustainability of economic development required the creation of inclusive institutions that allowed the entry of new individuals and organizations into the economic market; but further state intervention on the economic market prevented the realization of these types of institutions, and the dual balance collapsed with the collapse of the share of craftsmen.

5.6 Counterproductive Distribution of Rent

As the community moves towards the fragile end of the continuum, creating a durable business rent will gradually replace itself with a more personal, less sustainable rent. During this period, the oil shock caused the shah's power to be astonished, and he took over all the affairs. In such a situation, the distribution of rents instead of organized and impersonal distributions moved towards the personal distribution of rents and led society to move towards a FLAO instead of moving toward a MLAO.

The Rent Economy and the Land Reform Program under the guidance of the state in the 1960s and 1970s provided significant new resources and opportunities for gaining economic benefits, wealth, dignity and power for the nouveau rich ones. The Shah, on the one hand, made the construction of political power heavily monopolized and focused and, on the other hand, by pursuing and implementing economic programs, expanded groups and social and economic interests. In the process of industrialization, the state expanded its tenure on the economy as an important lever to consolidate its own foundations. It has controlled the investment in heavy, infrastructure, and oil and gas industries. In the construction of a rental economy, mainly a state one, economic modernization created a state-owned private sector. Modernization brought new sources of power, wealth, rent, and increased facilities, which became a major source of economic corruption and wealth accumulation (Sardarniya 2007; Katouzian 1999).

At the end of the second Pahlavi regime, the lack of rental resources made the Shah no longer keep his supporters in the ruling coalition, and eventually he remained alone against popular protests, and even parts of the ruling coalition joined the protest queues so that they can take advantage of more rental sources in the formation of the new regime.

5.7 Emergence of Oil Resources

Oil revenues as the largest source of rent during this period led to changes in the ruling coalition members and also to the closure of the political atmosphere by means of repression. The acquisition of this enormous resource also led to the production and dissemination of extractive institutions during this period. With the entry of oil revenues into the country's sources of power, the ruling coalition no longer needed to supply resources through the market. Also, by increasing the power of the ruling coalition through these sources, it was not necessary to obtain legitimacy through informal institutions, and this promoted the establishment of extractive political institutions in the country. The surplus oil revenues led the state to no longer pay particular attention to tax revenues and, given that the progress of the tax system is dependent on the transparency of economic activities, this kind of transparency did not take place due to the lack of tax revenues which led to the production and diffusion of extractive institutions in this era. Ultimately, the decline in oil revenues and the conflict of interest between the economic and political market in seeking shares of the economy led to a move toward FLAO and eventually the anarchy.

5.8 Withdrawal of Conservative Forces from the Ruling Coalition

After the power struggle on August 19th, conservative forces, including bazaaries and proprietors left the ruling coalition and their political power fell sharply. They no longer had the ability to pursue their economic interests through political power; therefore, bazaaries, with the help of clerics, sought to maintain their economic interests through informal institutions. The preservation of this relation between bazaaries and clerics needed this kind of relation to be monopolized because informal institutions did not have the ability to deal with official institutions that relied on oil resources; therefore, they could not embrace a vast array of markets. Owners also pursued their own interests through their children, who were young technocrats and were on the political market, and moved towards the bourgeoisie with reference to the direction of the institutional matrix in the country. The landowners who entered the market of economic and investment in the industrial sector were subject to aggravated violence due to land reforms; but the ruling coalition's interference in pricing due to extractive institutions and the VC during this period, has prevented them from waiting for imbalances in the share of economic benefits and causing instability in the country.

5.9 Existence of Hereditary Extractive Institutions

Owners who were themselves members of the bourgeoisie and their children who were now active in the legislature and law enforcement in the parliament and the state (due to their institutional dependence) were the heirs of extractive institutions of the past and this prompted the promotion of extractive institutions on the political and economic markets.

5.10 Entry of Young Technocrats into the Political Market

Young and educated technocrats in the West, especially in France, were influenced by socialist thoughts and attempted to develop their own thinking by gaining power. The further involvement of the state in economic affairs has led to the emergence of extractive institutions on the economic market under the influence of extractive political institutions on the political market. With the execution of Shah's orders without any controversy, they also increased the royal power of the Shah and strengthened the foundations of the creation of VCs in the country.

In addition, the technocrats, as educated intellectuals in the West, resisted the informal institutions, and, as a counterweight to the tradition, created the cause of violence in the country, causing inconsistencies between formal and informal institutions.

5.11 Uncertainty about the Future of the Country among the Political and Economic Superordinates

Given that most investors were disappointed about the country's future, they simply tried to profit indirectly through the import and assembly of oil resources, and to withdraw their profits from the country. Many of these investors were religious minorities (in particular Baha'is) who had been able to use rents through their court penetration; therefore, they did not pay attention to the extractive political institutions, and even tried to maintain these institutions, because the maintenance of the existing conditions was creating security for them. As a result, uncertainty about the country's future and the risk in the social atmosphere of the country and the threat of informal institutions prevented the establishment of a link between economic and political institutions because investors were only thinking about short-term profits and exiting the country.

5.12 Overcoming Political Objectives in Economic Activities

Political goals led the ruling coalition to move towards strategic industries (such as nuclear power plants). This caused the state to intervene more and more in the market, and it was possible for political reasons to endanger the economic interests and, given the importance of political issues, economic interests were often considered less, and this contributed to the conflict between political and economic institutions. Also, due to the fast-paced modernization, the state considered the interests of citizens more than villagers for political reasons. When Alikhani and Hoveyda were discussing an economic issue together, Hoveyda replied to Alikhani who asked whether we are the state for the Iranian townsmen or for all the people of Iran? "No! I am first the state-man of the Iranian urban population; because disturbance occurs in cities. In other words, Hoveida had a political intuition that I did not have. This was due to the fact that the state tried to buy at a lower rate than the global price from producers. Farmers were paying fines for the urban people become a little happier." (cited from Dehbashi 2014: 204).

These policies which benefited the citizens and harmed the villagers, led to the migration of villagers to cities and created a violent upheaval in the city.

5.13 Tremendous Share of Foreign Investors in the Process of Industrialization

Foreign investors sought security and exploiting the sources of rental resources which were possible under the shadow of Shah's autocracy. In connection with foreign investors, they could withdraw their interests from the country, and except for the oil industry, foreign investment was not significant; but foreign product sales and foreign personnel were much more important (Keddie and Richard 2006). Some foreign investors did not engage in the political system because they had the ability to withdraw their capital from the country; therefore, there was not a very deep link between the political and economic markets and this made it impossible to exert pressure through the economic market in order to widen the political institutions (Amjad 1989).

5.14 Preventing Creative Destruction on the Political and Economic Markets

The experience of Shah from the Mossadegh state and his tendency to flattering people, along with the United States' insistence on the assignment of certain individuals to important political positions, have led to the fact that there would not be a creative destruction on the political market. The king placed his friends only in important positions, although he did not trust them, and this did not allow for the creation of new thoughts on the political market. If people like Alinaghi Alikhani entered the political market, they would have left it because of the same VC.

The economic market also did not allow for creative destruction. Easy technology transfer and cheap labor force have made old technologies still profitable and no attempt was made to upgrade technology. One of the reasons for replacing rental relations with productive relations was the import of technology inside the country, for which no hassle was drawn, and as the former technology was still profitable, the society went to maintain that very technology. The cheap labor force, along with ease of importing technology, have led to no creative destruction process in the country. Promoting the level of technology abroad did not provide any competitive ability inside the country as well, and they merely attempted to import technology. In fact, creative destruction from abroad did not allow Iranians' entry into the process of creative destruction.

Bazaaries also sought to maintain the existing conditions and to maintain their traditional market, resisting against large and chain stores and they did not attempt to enter the creative destruction process in the distribution of goods. Their efforts were through informal institutions and creating violence in society, which led the Shah to stand against them, and instead of helping bazaaries, he continued to harm their interests. Bazaaries and clerics wanted economic institutions to be extractive, so as not to harm their interests, but economic institutions to be inclusive so that they can regain their lost power (Matlabi 2007).

5.15 Experience of the Financial Crisis in 1959

This issue, which was influenced by inclusive institutions in the country, led to the fact that because of the fear of the crisis, the ruling coalition leaders were reluctant to use this type of institution in the country; so that the Shah went hardly under the burden of the proposed reforms by the United States.

5.16 Existence of Unofficial Institutions in Forms of Religion and Ideology

The existence of an old texture of unofficial institutions that manifests itself in the form of tradition, religion, and ideology leads to the formation of such groups in that community, entering which is not possible for everyone. Typically, these groups enter the political and economic market in the form of devotee-king networks, promoting extractive institutions, and often showing strain at the time of conflict between formal and informal institutions. These groups will make the institutional structure to depend more and more on the VC. During this period, due to the hegemony of the Shah, different groups gradually left the ruling coalition and it was made possible for these groups to create Irregularities in the country in the form of various ideologies.

5.17 Conflict between Expectations of People and the State's Performance

The conflict between the demands of the people and the interests of the country, in the opinion of the political superordinates, led to the closure of the political and economic space of the country and in the late Pahlavi era, this conflict caused by the share-seeking of social groups led to a move towards a fragile order and eventually chaos (Majidi 2002: 48–49).

Faced with this conflict and the existence of conflicting ideology with modernization in the country, the Shah sought to bring the Rastakhiz Party as a single-party system to eliminate all the conflicts of interest and beliefs, which would increase his power more and more with the philosophy of reconciling the interests and beliefs; but this failed for a variety of reasons, such as the financial crisis and the inappropriate functioning of the party.

5.18 High Time Preference Rate

The high-time preference rate of the superordinates and social groups prevented long-term goals from being taken into consideration, and ultimately the society, following the pathological slogans, went toward fragility and chaos.

6 Conclusion

In this study, the reasons for the sustainability of LAO conditions and the creation of VCs in Iran during the second Pahlavi era were investigated. At that era, the synergies between extractive economic and political institutions created a VC, and extractive institutions were created; the existence of such institutions led to the maintenance of these institutions and the situation was even worsened. Competition and struggles in this era were merely to gain interest confined in the hands of one group. The power was the first thing, and no one monitored the distribution of wealth. With the uneven distribution of wealth and the confinement of wealth in the hands of a certain group, activities were formed which led to the closure of the political atmosphere so that this wealth would not be left out of the hands of this particular group. Disturbances in this period were in order to achieve rents trapped by other groups. Under such conditions, it was not possible to create long-term balance between political and economic institutions.

During this period, the ruling coalition had to monopolize its power through the establishment of the rule of law, especially for superordinates. The lack of rule of law prevented the legitimization of the power of the ruling coalition by social groups, and this lack of legitimacy led to the overthrow of the ruling coalition. Instead of focusing more on the distribution of rents, a NS should in general seek to legitimize its power through creating a balance between political and economic institutions along with the rule of law; hence, by the formation of permanent organizations, the life of the ruling coalition will also be continuous and durable. During this era, with the formation of a rental economy and an increase in oil revenues and the concentration of these revenues with the Shah and the state, the dual balance between political and economic systems was collapsed and contrary to the fact that wealth leads to power, the important preconditions of wealth were the political power, political influence and group relations. With an increasing state ownership of the oil economy and the economy in general, opportunities were provided for accumulation and preservation of wealth for the king, officials, and key actors in the social sphere. The political interests of the coalition members were not balanced by their economic share-seeking in the existing order, and as a result, the dual balance collapsed, and the ruling coalition was not effective in creating order. Some factors led to the continuation of a NS and ultimately the movement towards a FLAO, including the lack of rule of law for the superordinates, the domination of personal relations and the non-establishment of permanent institutions, the dominance of the military on political and economic affairs, the unproductive distribution of rents, the imbalance between political and economic development, the emergence of oil resources, the withdrawal of conservative forces from the ruling coalition, the existence of hereditary extractive institutions, the entry of young technocrats into the political market, the domination of the Shah over all affairs, uncertainty about the country's future, the overcoming of political goals on economic activities, the big share of the foreign investment, experiencing the financial crisis of 1959, the conflict between the expectations of the people and the state's performance, and the high-time preference rate between superordinates and social groups.

References

Abrahamian, E. (1982). *Iran between the two revolutions*. Princeton: Princeton University Press.

Acemoglu, D., & Robinson, J. A. (2012). *Why nations fail: The origins of power, prosperity, and poverty*. New York: Crown Books.

Alamdari, K. (2005). *Why Iran lagged behind & the west moved forward*. Tehran: Nashr-e Towse'a (Persian Edition).

Amjad, M. (1989). *Iran: From Royal Dictatorship to theocracy* (Vol. 242). New York: Greenwood Pub Group.

Ashraf. (1971). *Iran, Imperialism, class and modernization from above*. Ph.D. dissertation, New School for Social Research.

Ashraf. (1980). *Historical obstacles to the development of capitalism in Iran*. Tehran: Payam Press.

Azghandi, A. R. (2006). *The ineffectiveness of the Iranian political elite between the two revolutions*. Tehran: Ghomes Publisher.

Azimi-Arani, H. (2014). *Underdeveloped circuits in the Iranian economy*. Tehran: Nashr e Ney. (Persian Edition).

Baldwin, G. (1967). *Planning and development in Iran*. Baltimore: The Johns Hopkins University Press.

Bharier, J. (1971). Economic Development in Iran: 1900-1970. London and New York: Oxford University Press.

Bostock, F., & Jones, G. (2014). *Planning and power in Iran: Ebtehaj and economic development under the Shah*. London: Routledge.

Dehbashi, H. (2014). *Economics and security: Oral history, life and works of Alinaghi Alikhani*. Tehran: National Library and Archives of the Islamic Republic of Iran.

Digard, J. P., Richard, Y., & Hourcade, B. (2007). *L'Iran au XXe siècle: Entre nationalisme, islam et mondialisation*. Paris: Fayard.

Elwell-Sutton, E. A. (1955). *Persian Oil*. London: Lawrence and Wishart.

Esfahani, H. S., & Pesaran, M. H. (2009). The Iranian economy in the twentieth century: A global perspective. *Iranian Studies, 42*(2), 177–211.

Furan, J. (2009). *Fragile resistance: Social transformation in Iran from 1500 to the revolution*. London: Routledge.

Katouzian, H. (1981). *The political economy of modern Iran: Despotism and pseudo-modernism, 1926–1979*. Berlin: Springer.
Katouzian, H. (1999). *Musaddiq and the struggle for power in Iran*. London: IB Tauris.
Katouzian, H. (2004). The short-term society: A study in the problems of long-term political and economic development in Iran. *Middle-Eastern Studies, 40*(1), 1–22.
Keddie, N. R., & Richard, Y. (2006). *Modern Iran: Roots and results of revolution*. New Haven: Yale University Press.
Khan, M. H. (2013). The political settlement, growth and technical Progress in Bangladesh DIIS Working Paper 2013:01,33.
Lotz, J. (January 1950). Problems and proposal for the first seven-year plan. *The Middle-East Journal, 4*(1), 102–105.
Majidi, A. M. (2002). *Memoirs of Abdolmajid Majidi, minister of consultation and head of planning and budget organization (1972–1977)*. Tehran: Gam-e No Publishing.
Motallebi, M. (2007). Examining the reasons for the opposition of Bazaaries to the Pahlavi state. *Zamaneh Magazine, 57*, 70–61.
Mazdak. (1982). *The profiles of Mossadegh and the Tudeh party*. Florence.
Milani, A. (2000). *The Persian Sphinx: Amir Abbas Hoveyda and the riddle of the Iranian revolution: A biography*, I.B. Tauris, 2000 – Iran.
Milani, A. (2011). *The Shah*. New York: Palgrave Macmillan.
Milani, M. M. (2018). *The making of Iran's Islamic revolution: From monarchy to Islamic Republic*. New York: Routledge.
North, D. C., Wallis, J. J., & Weingast, B. R. (2006). *A conceptual framework for interpreting recorded human history* (No. w12795). Cambridge, MA: National Bureau of Economic Research.
North, D. C., Wallis, J. J., & Weingast, B. R. (2009). *Violence and social orders: A conceptual framework for interpreting recorded human history*. Cambridge: Cambridge University Press.
North, D. C., Wallis, J. J., Webb, S. B., & Weingast, B. R. (Eds.). (2013). *In the shadow of violence: Politics, economics, and the problems of development*. Cambridge: Cambridge University Press.
Roy, P. (2013). *The political economy of growth under Clientelism: An analysis of Gujarat, Tamil Nadu and Pakistan*. PhD thesis. SOAS, University of London.
Sardarniya, K. (2007). Explaining the political-economic structuralism of economic corruption in Iran-Pahlavi II, 1953–79. *Political Science Journal, 6*(26), 58–33.
You, J.-S. (2014). Land reform, inequality, and corruption: A comparative historical study of Korea, Taiwan, and the Philippines. *The Korean Journal of International Studies, 12*(1), 191–224.
Zibakalam, S. (2011). *How did we become what we are?* Tehran: Rozaneh Publishing. [In Persian].

Does Energy Security Affect Institutional Quality? Empirical Evidence from Emerging Economies

Nguyen Phuc Canh, Su Dinh Thanh, Dang Thi Bach Van, and Nguyen Quang Binh

1 Introduction

The recent emergence of institutional economics has received extensive attention from scholars (Nguyen et al. 2017, 2018c; Phuc Canh 2018). Institutions are considered as residuals of the production function that are important for explaining the differences in economic growth (North 1993). Institutional quality has been documented not only for important roles in socio-economic development (e.g., Young and Sheehan (2014), Canh et al. (2018), Huynh et al. (2019)) but also for environmental issues (Nguyen et al. 2018a; Phuc Nguyen et al. 2019). Some studies have explored the determinants of changes in institutional quality. For instance, Alonso and Garcimartín (2013) found that income inequality had a negative impact on institutional quality, while education had a positive impact. However, understanding of the dynamics of institutional quality, especially in emerging economies with their rapid economic growth in recent years, is still limited.

Energy is viewed as an economy's backbone; consequently, energy security has become one of the most critical goals of sustainable development (Le and Nguyen 2019). Changes in energy security may influence the stability and institutional

N. P. Canh (✉)
School of Banking, University of Economics Ho Chi Minh City, Ho Chi Minh City, Vietnam
e-mail: canhnguyen@ueh.edu.vn

S. D. Thanh · D. T. Bach Van
School of Public Finance, University of Economics Ho Chi Minh City, Ho Chi Minh City, Vietnam
e-mail: dinhthanh@ueh.edu.vn; bachvan@ueh.edu.vn

N. Q. Binh
University of Economics Ho Chi Minh City, Ho Chi Minh City, Vietnam
e-mail: binhnq@ueh.edu.vn

N. Faghih, A. H. Samadi (eds.), *Dynamics of Institutional Change in Emerging Market Economies*, Contributions to Economics,
https://doi.org/10.1007/978-3-030-61342-6_14

framework of a country. For instance, energy insecurity will lead to political risks, which are particularly relevant for energy-exporting countries, who usually employ energy delivery as a political weapon (Kocaslan 2014). Alternatively, rising energy consumption, which is a cause of environmental degradation, such as air and water pollution and climate change, could adversely and disproportionately influence human health, livelihoods, and social well-being. In particular, recognition justice in the energy justice field has gained increasing awareness from the public and other relevant factors (Graff et al. 2019), and has become a strong trend among younger environmental activists.[1] Thus, there has been significant demand for more actions to be taken by leaders against climate change.

Therefore, this study attempts to examine the influence of energy security on institutional quality. Specifically, this study follows Le and Nguyen (2019) work by employing eight indicators of energy security, including energy gap, energy supply capability, energy structure, energy efficiency, energy developability in terms of consumption, energy developability in terms of CO_2 emissions, and energy developability in terms of CO_2 emissions per unit of energy consumption and energy acceptability (renewable energy consumption), in the empirical analysis. Regarding institutional quality, the simple average of six institutional indicators, i.e., corruption control, government effectiveness, political stability, rule of law, regulatory quality, and voice and accountability, obtained from the worldwide governance indicators (WGIs), were calculated as a proxy for overall institutional quality. Overall institutional quality was employed to avoid complications in the empirical analyses of the different dimensions of energy security. Moreover, each of the six institutional indicators were estimated to check for robustness. The panel corrected standard errors (PCSE) models with time effects were utilized as the main estimators to manage cross-sectional dependence and fixed effects. The feasible generalized least squares (FGLS), pooled ordinary least squares (OLS), pooled OLS with time effects, and robust- pooled OLS methods were employed as robustness checks. The autoregressive distributed lag (ARDL) model was utilized for the long-run analysis. The pooled mean group (PMG) estimator was applied for ARDL estimation to manage endogeneity and heteroscedasticity.

The empirical analysis was conducted for a sample of 43 emerging economies for the period 2002–2017 based on the availability of WGI data. Emerging economies are an ideal sample for studying energy security for the following reasons. First, emerging economies have undergone rapid economic growth in the past two decades (Nguyen et al. 2018c) and are associated with high energy consumption (Cowan et al. 2014; Destek and Aslan 2017). The high energy demand for economic development makes these economies sensitive to energy insecurity. In the sample, primary energy consumption increased across the period of study (see Fig. 1). Additionally, economic development, along with socio-economic transitions, induced changes in institutional quality in these economies (Herrera-Echeverri et al.

---

[1] Many environmental activists from the younger generations, especially Greta Thunberg and other activists, have aggressively undertaken many actions to inspire climate change around the world (see https://www.bbc.co.uk/newsround/49676291).

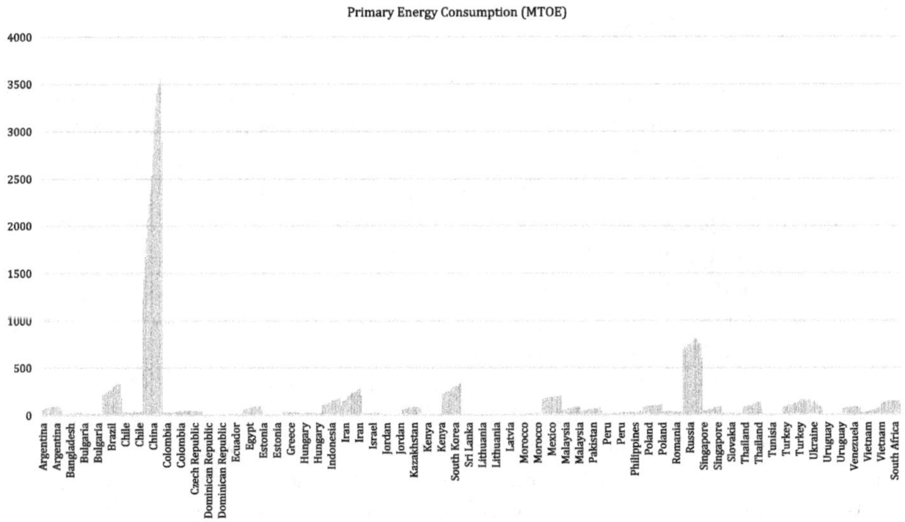

Fig. 1 Primary energy consumption. (Source: The International Energy Agency (IEA – US))

2014). Therefore, evaluating the impact of energy security on institutional quality would make a contribution to both literature and practice.

The empirical results show that energy production in comparison with energy consumption, energy production per capita, fossil energy consumption, energy intensity, energy consumption per capita, and CO_2 emissions per unit of gross domestic product (GDP) have significant negative impacts on overall institutional quality. In contrast to these results, the CO_2 emissions per unit of nonrenewable and renewable energy consumption have a significant positive impact on overall institutional quality. The long-run estimations show that the effects of energy security indicators on overall institutional quality are positive but insignificant in the short run, while seven of the eight energy security indicators have significantly negative impacts on overall institutional quality in the long run. Interestingly, renewable energy consumption was found to have a significant positive impact on overall institutional quality in the long run. Moreover, the effects of the energy security indicators on the six institutional dimensions were very consistent. These results likely present convincing evidence regarding the positive contribution of renewable energy consumption to institutional quality, whereas fossil consumption and emissions are likely to have a negative impact on institutions.

The remainder of this study is organized as follows. Section 2 presents the literature review while Sect. 3 describes the methodology and data. The results are presented and discussed in Sect. 4. Finally, Sect. 5 provides the conclusions.

2 Literature Review

Literature regarding institutional quality and energy security has recently attracted substantial attention due to their crucial importance for long-term sustainable development (Canh et al. 2019; Le and Nguyen 2019; Nguyen et al. 2017, 2018b, c). While there is a growing amount literature that have attempted to analyze the effects of institutional quality on energy security along various dimensions (Empinotti et al. 2019; Salman et al. 2019; Sun et al. 2019), the current paper seems to make a compelling contribution to literature regarding the influence of energy security on institutional quality. Table 1 summarizes the review of recent literature regarding institutional quality and energy security.

In recent years, several studies have investigated the determinants of institutional quality; however, the results have been mixed. From a broad perspective, institutional quality can be defined as an intertemporal contract in which a set of "social factors, rules, beliefs, values, and organizations" shapes individual and social behaviors (Alonso and Garcimartín 2013; Nguyen and Canh 2019; Nguyen et al. 2018b). Therefore, identifying the factors that significantly influence institutional quality might still be a potential topic for further research (Su et al. 2019; Thanh and Canh 2019). While political institutions govern the extent to which citizens can participate in the political process, economic institutions govern the level of economic freedom required to support entrepreneurial activities (Kotschy and Sunde 2017). Thus, the level of economic development is likely to affect institutional quality both on the supply and demand sides. Due to unsustainable development, income distribution may affect the predictable and legitimate aspect of institutional quality (Alonso and Garcimartín 2013). Income inequality can exacerbate social conflicts, which, in turn, can lead to socio-political instability and insecurity. This may be the primary reason for corruption and an incumbent's rent-seeking (Alonso and Garcimartín 2013; Easterly et al. 2006). Additionally, a well-structured tax system is positively correlated with institutional quality under an implicit fiscal contract (Alonso and Garcimartín 2013). Higher economic development can increase both public expenditure and the tax base. Similarly, high institutional quality can enhance tax administration capabilities, boost tax revenue, and thus improve the level of voluntary tax compliance.

Globalization can create a demanding environment that absorbs competition from international stakeholders, which could encourage institutional quality due to its dynamic efficiency (Islam et al. 2002). A competitive environment greatly facilitates the learning process and has helped many countries to improve their institutional quality by imitating other countries' achievements (Alonso and Garcimartín 2013). Increasing openness can enhance the efficiency of institutional reforms for sustained growth (Kar et al. 2019). Beside this exogenous factor, human capital accumulation through training and education is positively associated with institutional quality (Alonso and Garcimartín 2013) and is also directly correlated with national intelligence, which serves as important evidence of institutional quality (Kanyama 2014).

Table 1 Some recent literature review (2015–2019)

No	Authors	Countries	Data period (frequency)	Methodology	Main variables	Other variables	Main findings/implications
1.	Kucharski and Unesaki (2015)	Theoretical analysis		The energy system adopts a complex adaptive systems (CAS) approach	Energy security	Governance system, Infrastructure systems, Financial markets, Information and telecommunications systems, Global energy markets, International institutions	General framework for the assessment of energy security
2.	Kisel et al. (2016)			Energy security matrix	Energy security Operational Resilience		Energy security should be analyzed in Technical-Economic-Political terms
3.	Adamus and Florkowski (2016)	Poland	2016	Multicriteria analysis	Energy security (gas security)	Political, economic, environmental, and social criteria	Economic factors are most important drivers Political factors are in the second
4.	Filipović et al. (2018)	EU-28 member states	2006–2015	A new method measuring energy security	Energy security index Macroeconomic stability	Categories of political risk, economic risk, structural risk	GDP per capita, country risk, carbon intensity, energy intensity, final energy consumption per capita, and electricity prices → Energy security Macroeconomic stability → energy security (+)

(continued)

Table 1 (continued)

No	Authors	Countries	Data period (frequency)	Methodology	Main variables	Other variables	Main findings/implications
5.	Sarkodie and Adams (2018)	South Africa	1971–2017	CUSUM, OLS, ARDL	CO_2 emission	Urban population	Political institutional quality → social, governance, and economic readiness
					Energy use	Renewable energy	Social, governance and economic readiness → Environmental quality
					Political institutional quality	Fossil fuel energy	
						GDP per capita	
						Nuclear Electricity Net Generation	
6.	Sun et al. (2019)	71 developed and developing countries	1990–2014	Parametric stochastic frontier approach	Green technology, five sub-categories of institutional efficiency, capital stock, labor, energy use	GDP, carbon emission, trade openness, Human capital index, Urban population	Green innovation → energy efficiency (+) Institutional quality → energy efficiency (+) Trade openness and urbanization → energy efficiency (+)
				True Fixed Effects model			
				Pairwise Difference Estimator (PDE)			
7.	Empinotti et al. (2019)	São Paulo, Brazil in the context of water crisis	2013–2015	Case study	Water security governance		Good governance → water security (+)

No	Authors	Countries	Data period (frequency)	Methodology	Main variables	Other variables	Main findings/implications
8.	Israel and Jehling (2019)	Peru	2016/2017	21 semi-structured interviews	Solar energy use	Local population's awareness	local factors → decision-making process and legal-regulatory framework adjustments
					Public promotion program	Regulation	
						Alternative technologies	
9.	Opeyemi et al. (2019)	42 sub-Sahara African countries	2004–2016	System GMM	Trade outcome	Corruption control	Corruption control, regulatory framework → renewable energy usage (+)
					Total final energy consumption	Regulatory quality	
						Access to finance	
10.	Emenalo and Gagliardi (2019)	46 African former European colonies	2004–2013	OLS	Institutional quality	GDP per capita	Legal origins → institutional quality
					Legal origins	Ethnic fractionalization index	
					Disease endowment	Population density	
						Political stability	

Note: +, − are positive and negative impacts, respectively
Source: Authors' own table

Emenalo and Gagliardi (2019) found that legal origin has a remarkable effect on institutional quality, while endowment had a mixed impact on a sample of 46 African countries. Some scholars argued that former colonies, geographical conditions, and democracy can be potential determinants of institutional quality (Alonso and Garcimartín 2013; Kanyama 2014; Klasing 2013; Kotschy and Sunde 2017). Colonialism and colonization captures a country's legal system. For instance, the British-based colony system was considered to provide high economic freedom because it controlled government intervention in economic activities. In contrast, the French-based system hinders the state's ability to regulate social and economic activities, which can lead to weaker institutional quality (Alonso and Garcimartín 2013; La Porta et al. 1999). Thus, colonization had a mixed effect on institutional quality (Acemoglu et al. 2001; Emenalo and Gagliardi 2019; Treisman 2000). Additionally, some studies emphasized the role of culture in establishing institutional quality (Klasing 2013; Schwartz 1994). Improving the level of trust and religious culture can significantly enhance a nation's institutional quality. Exploring the cultural dimension, Klasing (2013) identified a robust link between culture, collective values, and institutional quality. Klasing concluded that individualism and power distance have a robust effect on institutional quality. Kanyama (2014) stated that intelligence is an official channel through which institutional quality might affect economic growth. Utilizing the two-stage least squares method and cross-sectional data regarding 164 countries for the period 2006–2010, Kanyama found evidence of the significant positive impact of average national intelligence on the quality of national institutions.

Further, some studies argued that geographical conditions and natural resources could affect institutional quality (Easterly and Levine 2003; Gallup et al. 1999). Resource-rich countries were found to have a positive effect on institutional quality. However, abundant natural resources can generate rent-seeking activities, which can lead to an inefficient institutional framework (Amiri et al. 2019).

The present study differs from existing research regarding institutional quality in the following critical aspects. Energy is viewed as the backbone of the economy; therefore, energy security has become one of the most critical goals of sustainable development (Le and Nguyen 2019). There has also been a recent trend of studies focusing on how the long-term (or short-term) transformation of the energy system affects energy security and efficiency (Gillessen et al. 2019; Mangla et al. 2019; Sun et al. 2019). Moreover, the relationship between energy security and institutional quality was indicated in discussions regarding the methods for assessing the short- and long-term effects of energy security indicators (Kisel et al. 2016). In the sustainable development context, the role of energy security has been documented in several research studies (Gillessen et al. 2019; Le and Nguyen 2019; Sun et al. 2019). Unfortunately, the question of whether energy security significantly affects institutional quality has not yet been investigated thoroughly. On one hand, energy security is now one of the most critical and intriguing concern for governments and citizens (Le and Nguyen 2019). On the other hand, better energy security would significantly contribute to economic growth (Le and Nguyen 2019). Thus, better energy security could have an important impact on institutional quality, leading to the following hypothesis:

H1: Energy security has an impact on institutional quality.

In existing literature, there seems to be no consensus regarding the measurement of energy security and institutional quality. Energy security has been described as a multidimensional concept that can be measured using different indicators and can be defined as "the ability of an economy to guarantee the availability of the supply of energy resources in a sustainable and timely manner with the energy price being at a level that will not adversely affect the economic performance of the economy" (APERC 2007). Recently, Le and Nguyen (2019) identified eight indicators: energy gap, energy supply capability, energy structure, energy efficiency, energy developability in terms of consumption, energy developability in terms of CO_2 emissions, energy developability in terms of CO_2 emissions per unit of energy consumption, and energy acceptability (renewable energy consumption) to proxy for the energy security variable. Similarly, institutional quality can be analyzed using an aggregate approach including governance, judgment specializing in the political and economic dimensions (Alonso and Garcimartín 2013), etc. The indicators extracted from the WGIs are well-established and well-supported in capturing institutional quality. This dataset introduces six main categories, including control of corruption, government effectiveness, political stability, rule of law, regulatory quality, and voice and accountability, that are used as proxies for overall institutional quality (Alonso and Garcimartín 2013; Kanyama 2014). In some studies, the indicators that served as proxies for institutional quality were obtained from the International Country Risk Guide (Klasing 2013) or other available datasets (Emenalo and Gagliardi 2019).

Following Le and Nguyen (2019), the five main aspects of energy security are availability, accessibility, acceptability, affordability, and developability.[2] Le and Nguyen (2019) found that energy security has positive impacts on economic growth, while energy insecurity (in the form of energy intensity and carbon intensity) has negative ones. In other words, energy security is expected to boost economic development and institutional quality, while energy insecurity, especially energy intensity and carbon intensity, might have the opposite effect. However, several studies in resource economics have highlighted the natural resource curse (Cockx and Francken 2016; Parcero and Papyrakis 2016), which may lead to the degradation of institutional quality. Thus, energy security may have a negative or positive impact on institutional quality:

[2] These aspects are defined in Le and Nguyen (2019) as follows: (i) Availability is the physical availability of oil (and other fossil fuels) and nuclear energy; (ii) Affordability refers to securing energy sources at affordable and competitive prices; (iii) Acceptability refers to the environmental issues that deal with the impact of energy production and utilization on the economy; (iv) Accessibility refers to the possibilities of energy supply in transport channels and geopolitical aspects; (v) Developability is "the sustainable development capacity of the energy system in a low-carbon, clean, optimized mode" (Fang et al. 2018).

H1a: Energy security has a negative/positive impact on institutional quality.
H1b: Energy intensity has a negative impact on institutional quality.
H1c: Carbon intensity has a negative impact on institutional quality.

As mentioned earlier, many ground-breaking studies have been conducted regarding the importance of institutional quality for sustainable development. This paper is unique, in that it is the first study to examine the influence of energy security on institutional quality.

3 Methodology and Data

To examine the influence of energy security on institutional quality, this study is based on the baseline model found in relevant literature (La Porta et al. 1999; Bertocchi and Canova 2002; Alonso and Garcimartín 2013).

In this model, the dynamics of institutional quality are a function of income level (*Income*), geographic location (*Lat*), and colonial history (*Col*). Additionally, there are other determinants of institutional quality from an economic perspective such as income inequality (*IIE*), human capital, and trade openness (*Trade*) (Alonso and Garcimartín 2013). Finally, energy security was employed as a supporting factor of institutional quality.

In classical economic literature, there has been difficulty in identifying the elements of institutional quality (Kostova 1997); thus previous literature is limited in this regard. In contemporary research, while a majority of current papers acknowledge institutional quality as an independent variable in a particular function, studies regarding institutional quality as a dependent variable are scarce. Innovative studies regarding institutional economics (e.g., see Kaufmann et al. 1999a, b, 2011) have been undertaken based on the WGIs, published by the World Bank (2019b). Despite debates regarding the reliability of this dataset (Voigt 2013), the WGIs are one of the most appropriate and extensively used indicators of institutional quality in economic analysis (Thomas 2010). Thus, the six WGIs have been used in several empirical studies (e.g., see Herrera-Echeverri et al. 2014; Zhang 2016; Nguyen et al. 2018a). This study employed the six WGIs, namely control of corruption (*Concor*), government effectiveness (*Goveff*), political stability and absence of violence (*Posta*), regulatory quality (*Requa*), rule of law (*Law*), and voice and accountability (*Voice*), and calculated the average of these indicators to proxy for overall institutional quality (*INST*). The higher value of the overall institutional quality or the six indicators imply improvements in the overall institutional quality or each dimension.

The study employed the control variables used by Alonso and Garcimartín (2013). The latitude of each country's capital was obtained from the Central Intelligence Agency (Bertocchi and Canova 2002) and divided by 90, to proxy for geographic location. Colonial history is a dummy variable based on Bertocchi and Canova (2002) work; *Col* equals 1 if a country was a former Spanish or Portuguese colony, and 0 otherwise.[3] The real GDP per capita (in log form) and trade (% GDP) were collected from the world development indicators (WDIs) and the World Bank (2019a) to proxy for income level and trade openness, respectively. The Gini index's after-tax and transfer (in log form) from the Standardized World Income Inequality Database (SWIID) (Solt 2019) was used to represent income inequality, while the human capital index (in log form) from the Penn World Table 9.1 (PWT 9.1) (Feenstra et al. 2015) was used as a proxy for human capital.

To proxy for energy security, we followed the standard procedures followed by Le and Nguyen (2019). There are eight indicators of energy security. First, we calculated the log of the ratio of total primary energy production to total primary energy consumption (*ES1*), which reflects the gap between energy supply and demand. Second, we calculated the log of the ratio of total primary energy production to total population (*ES2*), reflecting the national energy supply capacity and the equality of resources. Third, we calculated the ratio of nonfossil energy consumption to total energy consumption (*ES3*), reflecting the energy structure of a country (or energy acceptability) (Fang et al. 2018). Fourth, we calculated the log of the ratio of total primary energy consumption to GDP (*ES4*), reflecting the efficiency of energy consumption in producing a unit of output (or energy acceptability) (Fang et al. 2018). Five, we calculated the log ofthe primary energy consumption per capita (*ES5*), reflecting energy developability as the sustainable development capacity of the energy system (Fang et al. 2018). The remaining variables proxied for energy security comprised the log of CO_2 emissions per unit of GDP (*ES6*) and the log of CO_2 emissions per unit of primary energy consumption (*ES7*), respectively, reflecting the developability of energy security (Fang et al. 2018); and the ratio of renewable energy consumption to total energy consumption (*ES8*), reflecting energy acceptability. The data regarding primary energy production and consumption were collected from the International Energy Agency (IEA–US). The variables, definitions, sources, and data descriptions are presented in Table 2. The correlation matrix is depicted in Table 3.

As per the availability of annual data from the WGIs, the sample in this study includes 43 emerging economies over the period 2002–2017.[4] In the empirical analysis, variables of the regression equation were converted to natural logarithms (i) to evaluate the elasticity between variables; (ii) to reduce autocorrelation; and (iii) when the variables were measured in different units. Therefore, we utilized Eq. ((1) to estimate the impact of energy security on institutional quality as follows:

$$\begin{aligned} INST_{it} &= \beta_0 + \beta_1 Income_{it} + \beta_2 IIE_{it} + \beta_3 HC_{it} + \beta_4 Trade_{it} \\ &\quad + \beta_5 Lat_i + \beta_6 Col_{it} + \beta_7 ES_{it} + \delta_i + \rho_t + \varepsilon_{it} \end{aligned} \tag{1}$$

[3] In fact, there is a dummy variable for the colonial history of Great Britain (8 in 43 economies); however, our sample includes only a small number of economies with this history in comparison with those with a history of former Spanish or Portuguese colonization. Thus, we only used the dummy variable for former Spanish or Portuguese colony.

[4] See Table A1, Appendix, for the list of countries.

Table 2 Variables, definitions, calculations, sources, and data description

Variable	Definitions	Calculations	Sources	Obs	Mean	Std. Dev.	Min	Max
INST	Overall institutional quality	Average of six institutional indicators	WGIs	688	−0.014	0.676	−1.561	1.616
Concor	Control of corruption	Control of Corruption: Estimate	WGIs	688	−0.113	0.733	−1.497	2.326
Goveff	Government effectiveness	Government Effectiveness: Estimate	WGIs	688	0.160	0.684	−1.399	2.437
Posta	Political stability	Political Stability and Absence of Violence/ Terrorism: Estimate	WGIs	688	−0.278	0.879	−2.810	1.586
Requa	Regulatory quality	Regulatory Quality: Estimate	WGIs	688	0.180	0.786	−1.997	2.261
Law	Rule of Law	Rule of Law: Estimate	WGIs	688	−0.028	0.746	−2.255	1.825
Voice	Voice and Accountability	Voice and Accountability: Estimate	WGIs	688	−0.009	0.788	−1.749	1.293
Income	Income level	Log of GDP per capita (constant 2010 US$)	WDIs	685	8.793	0.941	6.283	10.919
IIE	Income inequality	Log of Gini index of inequality in equivalized (square- root scale) household disposable (post-tax, post-transfer)	SWIID	650	3.633	0.192	3.190	4.098
HC	Human capital	Log of Human capital index	PWT 9.1	688	0.992	0.192	0.465	1.380
Trade	Trade openness	Trade openness (% GDP)	WDIs	684	86.77	60.63	22.11	441.60
Lat	Latitude	Latitude of the capital of each country divides for 90 (if in North +, in South −)		688	0.251	0.297	−0.388	0.660
Col	Colonial history	If Former Colonies of Spain and Portugal are 1, otherwise 0		688	0.279	0.449	0.000	1.000

(continued)

Table 2 (continued)

Variable	Definitions	Calculations	Sources	Obs	Mean	Std. Dev.	Min	Max
ES1	Energy security 1 (the gap between energy supply and energy demand)	Log of Primary Energy Production/ Primary Energy Consumption	IEA	681	−0.810	1.377	−6.331	1.237
ES2	Energy security 2 (a national energy supply capacity and the equality of resources)	Log of Primary Energy Production/ Population (kg/ person)	IEA and WDIs	681	6.467	1.623	1.718	9.327
ES3	Energy security 3 (the energy structure – the acceptability)	Fossil Energy consumption to Total (%)	WDIs	568	77.15	18.73	13.00	99.57
ES4	Energy security 4 (the efficiency of energy consumption)	Log of Energy intensity level of primary energy (MJ/$2011 PPP GDP)	WDIs	602	1.586	0.409	0.690	3.040
ES5	Energy security 5 (the developability)	Log of Primary Energy Consumption/ Population (kg/ person)	IEA and WDIs	688	7.277	0.981	2.729	9.667
ES6	Energy security 6 (the developability)	Log of CO_2 emissions (kg per 2011 PPP $ of GDP)	WDIs	559	−1.291	0.539	−2.757	0.171
ES7	Energy security 7 (the developability)	Log of CO_2 emissions/Primary Energy Consumption (kg/ kg)	IEA and WDIs	559	0.864	0.348	−1.157	2.251
ES8	Energy security 8 (the acceptability)	Renewable energy consumption (% of total final energy consumption)	WDIs	602	20.35	17.71	0.469	83.18

Note: WGIs is Worldwide Governance Indicators, World Bank; SWIID is The Standardized World Income Inequality Database (Solt 2019); WDIs is World Development Indicators database, World Bank; PWT is Penn World Table version 9.0 (Feenstra et al. 2015); IEA is International Energy Agency, US; Latitude in value of each country's capital, divided by 90 from data of Central Intelligence Agency, Bertocchi and Canova (2002); Colonial Origin: Own elaboration based on Bertocchi and Canova (2002)
Source: Authors' own table

Table 3 Unconditional correlation matrix

Correlation	INST	Concor	Goveff	Posta	Requa	Law	Voice
ES1	−0.51***	−0.56***	−0.51***	−0.28***	−0.51***	−0.57***	−0.27***
	0.00	0.00	0.00	0.00	0.00	0.00	0.00
ES2	−0.12***	−0.19***	−0.11***	0.08**	−0.16***	−0.22***	−0.07*
	0.00	0.00	0.01	0.03	0.00	0.00	0.06
ES3	−0.04	0.01	0.07*	0.04	−0.08*	−0.01	−0.24***
	0.34	0.77	0.10	0.30	0.06	0.77	0.00
ES4	−0.07*	−0.18***	−0.05	0.12***	−0.07*	−0.12***	−0.11***
	0.08	0.00	0.18	0.00	0.08	0.00	0.01
ES5	0.51***	0.46***	0.53***	0.52***	0.45***	0.43***	0.26***
	0.00	0.00	0.00	0.00	0.00	0.00	0.00
ES6	−0.06	−0.14***	−0.04	0.15***	−0.07*	−0.09**	−0.14***
	0.19	0.00	0.40	0.00	0.08	0.03	0.00
ES7	−0.20***	−0.27***	−0.21***	−0.18***	−0.16***	−0.16***	−0.10**
	0.00	0.00	0.00	0.00	0.00	0.00	0.02
ES8	−0.20***	−0.18***	−0.27***	−0.29***	−0.16***	−0.19***	0.01
	0.00	0.00	0.00	0.00	0.00	0.00	0.77

Note: *, **, *** are significant levels at 10%, 5%, and 1%, respectively
Source: Authors' own table

where: i and t denote country i at time t, respectively; β is the coefficient; ε is the residual term; δ and ρ are country and time fixed effects, respectively.

Our panel dataset incorporated 43 economies for a 16-year period (2002–2017); therefore, to confront the problem of cross-sectional dependence (Pesaran 2004) and heteroscedasticity (Bertocchi and Canova 2002) in such a relatively large N and relative small T panel dataset, we focused mainly on econometric treatments. First, we recruited Pesaran's CD test (Pesaran (2004) to examine the existence of cross-sectional dependence).

The results in Table 4 show the existence of cross-sectional dependence in most of the variables (except for *Voice*, *ES3*, *ES7*, and *ES8*). Following Bailey and Katz (2011), we applied the PCSE model to estimate Eq. (1). When estimating the PCSE model, we included time effects to limit heteroscedasticity and unobserved errors. For the robustness check, we employed FGLS (Liao and Cao 2013; Reed and Ye 2011; Zhang and Nian 2013), pooled OLS, robust-pooled OLS, and pooled OLS with time effects.

In the next step, we aimed to examine this relationship in the long run. Panel unit-root tests, including the Pesaran panel unit-root test (Pesaran 2007), the Im-Pesaran-Shin unit-root test (Im et al. 2003), the Levin-Lin-Chu unit-root test (Levin et al. 2002), and the Harris-Tzavalis unit-root test (Harris and Tzavalis 1996) were employed to examine the stationarity of variables. These results (Table 4) show that the variables are likely to be stationary at different levels. The panel cointegration tests including the Kao cointegration test (Kao 1999), the Pedroni

Table 4 Cross-sectional dependence test and stationary tests

Variable	CD test	CIPS test (Pesaran Panel unit- root test)	IPS test (Im-Pesaran-Shin unit-root test)	LLC test (Levin-Lin-Chu unit-root test)	HT test (Harris-Tzavalis unit-root test)
Statistic		CIPS*	Z-t-tilde-bar	Adjusted t*	rho
INST	2.42**	−1.76	1.43	−1.50*	0.83
Concor	3.11***	−2.02	−1.60*	−1.70**	0.74***
Goveff	6.08***	−2.16**	−0.95	−3.01***	0.74***
Posta	3.85***	−1.85	−2.93***	−5.18***	0.78*
Requa	−0.49	−1.99	−0.59	−3.15***	0.78*
Law	7.03***	−1.88	0.16	−1.48*	0.83
Voice	0.01	−1.64	−1.07	−2.89***	0.83
Income	97.9***	n/a	−0.23	n/a	n/a
IIE	16.1***	n/a	3.20	n/a	n/a
HC	94.1***	−1.47	5.40	−1.22	1.00
Trade	16.5***	n/a	0.21	n/a	n/a
ES1	−1.35	n/a	4.49	n/a	n/a
ES2	20.4***	n/a	3.48	n/a	n/a
ES3	0.77	n/a	0.91	n/a	n/a
ES4	52.0***	−2.40***	1.63	−5.63***	0.85
ES5	37.8***	−1.67	1.78	2.45	0.59***
ES6	32.0***	−2.46***	0.76	−4.63***	0.69***
ES7	0.55	−2.23**	−2.44***	−5.86***	0.36***
ES8	−0.001	−1.28	3.20	−1.45*	0.87

Note: Under the null hypothesis of cross-section independence, CD ~ N(0,1), p-values close to zero indicate data are correlated across panel groups. In CIPS test: H0 (homogeneous nonstationary): bi = 0 for all i. In IPS test: Ho: All panels contain unit roots, Ha: Some panels are stationary. In LLC test: Ho: Panels contain unit roots, Ha: Panels are stationary. In HT test: Ho: Panels contain unit roots, Ha: Panels are stationary
Source: Authors' own table

cointegration test (Pedroni 1999), and the Westerlund cointegration test (Westerlund 2005) were then recruited to examine long-run cointegration.[5]

The results of the cointegration tests in Table 5 clearly show that there is a possible cointegration between variables in the long run. In such circumstances, with the existence of cointegration and stationarity at different levels in the variables, the ARDL model for panel data was proposed for empirical estimation (Abdullahi et al. 2015; Bildirici 2014; Odhiambo 2009). The ARDL model offers the advantage of identifying both the short-term and long-term effects regardless of whether the regressors are endogenous or exogenous (Pesaran and Shin 1998; Pesaran and Smith 1995), thus reducing endogeneity. Due to heteroscedasticity across economies, the PMG estimator (Pesaran et al. 1999) was recruited to estimate the ARDL model in this case.

[5] In long-run cointegration, the study excluded the variables of geographic location (*Lat*) and colonial history (*Col*), since they are not continuous variables.

Table 5 Cointegration tests

	Kao test	Pedroni test	Westerlund test
Model: f (INST, Income, IIE, HC, Trade, ES); Energy security=	Modified Dickey-Fuller t	Modified Phillips-Perron t	Variance ratio
ES1	0.75	6.14***	−2.98***
ES2	0.76	6.07***	−3.16***
ES3	1.56*	6.64***	−2.65***
ES4	0.32	7.15***	−2.23**
ES5	0.66	5.75***	−3.29***
ES6	0.89	7.52***	−2.08**
ES7	1.13	7.55***	−1.95**
ES8	0.26	6.99***	−2.11**

Note: In Kao test for cointegration: Ho: No cointegration, Ha: All panels are cointegrated. In Pedroni test for cointegration: Ho: No cointegration, Ha: All panels are cointegrated. In Westerlund cointegration test: Ho: No cointegration, Ha: Some panels are cointegrated. *, **, *** are significant levels at 10%, 5%, 1%, respectively. n/a means the test cannot be performed
Source: Authors' own table

4 Results and Discussion

Table 6 presents the impacts of energy security on overall institutional quality for 43 emerging economies over the period 2002–2017.

The results show that all six energy security indicators (ES1, ES2, ES3, ES4, ES5, ES6) had significant negative impacts on overall institutional quality, while ES7 and ES8 had significant positive impacts. The negative impact of *ES1* indicates that a 1% increase in ES1 had a negative effect on the institutional quality, which faced a corresponding reduction of 0.153%, suggesting that higher energy production, in comparison with energy demand, reduces institutional quality. *ES2*, representing the primary energy production per capita, also had a negative impact on institutional quality, wherein a 1% increase in energy production, compared to the population, reduced institutional quality by 0.132%. These results imply that countries with rich energy resources, i.e., oil and natural resources, in comparison with energy demand and population requirements, have a lower institutional quality. These results confirm our hypotheses regarding the negative impact of energy security on institutional quality (H1a) and are in-line with the natural resource-rent curse (Henri 2019; Manzano and Gutiérrez 2019). In other words, natural resources rents may cause many problems, including the degradation of institutional quality. For instance, Farzanegan et al. (2018) found that natural resource rents increased the risk of internal conflict in a sample of more than 90 countries over the period 1984–2004. Borge et al. (2015) observed that higher local government revenue from natural resources reduced the efficiency of providing public goods in Norway. Additionally, Bhattacharyya and Hodler (2010) found that resource rents fed corruption in a global sample of 124 countries over the period 1980–2004.

Table 6 Energy security and overall institutional quality

Dep. var.: INST	(1)	(2)	(3)	(4)	(5)	(6)	(7)	(8)
Income	0.334***	0.439***	0.485***	0.343***	0.725***	0.387***	0.394***	0.493***
	[0.008]	[0.005]	[0.008]	[0.009]	[0.009]	[0.009]	[0.008]	[0.010]
IIE	−0.439***	−0.504***	−0.315***	−0.344***	−0.479***	−0.259***	−0.391***	−0.294***
	[0.068]	[0.062]	[0.070]	[0.063]	[0.054]	[0.065]	[0.072]	[0.068]
HC	0.744***	0.785***	0.307***	0.969***	0.815***	0.840***	0.590***	0.540***
	[0.068]	[0.063]	[0.040]	[0.060]	[0.036]	[0.055]	[0.051]	[0.039]
Trade	0.002***	0.002***	0.003***	0.003***	0.004***	0.003***	0.003***	0.003***
	[0.000]	[0.000]	[0.000]	[0.000]	[0.000]	[0.000]	[0.000]	[0.000]
Lat	−0.697***	−0.695***	−0.516***	−0.620***	−0.628***	−0.495***	−0.760***	−0.322***
	[0.035]	[0.034]	[0.037]	[0.034]	[0.031]	[0.033]	[0.031]	[0.039]
Col	−0.186***	−0.216***	−0.245***	−0.391***	−0.363***	−0.343***	−0.286***	−0.198***
	[0.019]	[0.019]	[0.015]	[0.016]	[0.018]	[0.011]	[0.011]	[0.018]
ES1	−0.135***							
	[0.008]							
ES2		−0.132***						
		[0.007]						
ES3			−0.010***					
			[0.000]					
ES4				−0.363***				
				[0.018]				
ES5					−0.443***			
					[0.015]			
ES6						−0.270***		
						[0.015]		

(continued)

Table 6 (continued)

Dep. var.: INST	(1)	(2)	(3)	(4)	(5)	(6)	(7)	(8)
ES7							0.226***	
							[0.024]	
ES8								0.012***
								[0.000]
Constant	−1.943***	−1.693***	−2.546***	−1.873***	−2.009***	−3.408***	−2.660***	−3.989***
	[0.266]	[0.240]	[0.262]	[0.254]	[0.201]	[0.241]	[0.285]	[0.274]
Year-effects	Yes	Yes	Yes	Yes	Yes	Yes	Yes	Yes
Observations	643	643	568	599	648	559	559	599
R-squared	0.723	0.749	0.731	0.701	0.762	0.699	0.673	0.721
Number of country	43	43	43	43	43	43	43	43

Note: PCSE estimators; Standard errors are in []; *, **, *** are significant levels at 10%, 5%, and 1%, respectively
Source: Authors' own table

In terms of energy consumption, the effects of *ES4* (MJ/\$2011 PPP GDP), *ES5* (kg/person), and *ES6* (kg per 2011 PPP \$ of GDP) were negative. Specifically, a 1% increase in ES4, ES5, and ES6 led to a corresponding decrease in institutional quality of 0.363%, 0.443%, and 0.270%, respectively. This suggests that an increase in the energy intensity, energy consumption per capita, and emissions per unit of GDP impedes institutional quality. In other words, the higher the values of *ES4, ES5, ES6*, the lower the efficiency and technology of energy consumption (higher emissions), leading to reduced institutional quality. These results present empirical evidence that countries with higher energy intensity and emissions have reduced institutional quality. This raises the challenge of reducing the energy consumption and emissions in these countries to fight climate change and reduce the degradation of institutional quality. This is likely to be a common problem in emerging economies (Levin et al. 2012; Stavi and Lal 2013).

In terms of energy structure, the negative effects of *ES3* (fossil energy consumption, percentage of total final energy consumption) and positive effects of *ES8* (renewable energy consumption, percentage of total final energy consumption) suggest that increasing the use of renewable energy would improve institutional quality, while the use of fossil energy would impede it. These results show that if ES3 or ES8 rises by 1%, there will be likely be a 0.01% reduction and a 0.012% increase in institutional quality, respectively. This finding that the use of renewable energy could help to improve institutional quality is interesting and can be a good solution to the aforementioned dilemma.

All results were checked for robustness and sensitivity using various estimators (FGLS, pooled OLS, robust-pooled OLS, pooled OLS with year effects). All estimation results were quite consistent. The results from FGLS estimators are reported in Table A2 in the Appendix. Other results are available upon requests. The only issue was that *ES7* (log of ratio CO_2 emissions to primary energy consumption, kg/kg) was observed to have a positive impact on institutional quality, which means that higher CO_2 emissions per unit of energy consumption lead to higher institutional quality. This finding contradicts the impact of *ES6*. Therefore, this finding had to be re-checked for consistency and robustness in the long-run analysis. The long-run analysis based on the PMG ARDL model is presented in Table 7.

In the short run, the results show that the effects of all proxies of energy security on institutional quality were positive but insignificant. In other words, increased energy production (*ES1*, *ES2*), energy consumption (*ES3, ES5, ES8*), and energy intensity and emissions (*ES4, ES6, ES7*) may have had a positive impact on institutional quality in the short run. This may be due to the positive effect of energy use on economic growth (Wang et al. 2018; Wesseh and Lin 2018), especially in emerging economies that have fast growth and high energy demand (Shahbaz et al. 2018). Thus, economic development could improve institutional quality; however, this effect is not statistically significant and only occurs in the short run.

Regarding the long run, Table 7 shows that seven out of the eight proxies (*ES1, ES2, ES3, ES4, ES5, ES6, ES7*) had a significant negative impact on institutional quality, while only *ES8* had a significant positive impact. This significant finding implies that energy surplus (higher production than consumption) or energy inten-

Table 7 Energy security and overall institutional quality: short-run and long-run effects

Dep. var.: *INST*	(1)	(2)	(3)	(4)	(5)	(6)	(7)	(8)
Short-run effects								
EC term	−0.558***	−0.575***	−0.448***	−0.438***	−0.451***	−0.427***	−0.572***	−0.426***
	[0.080]	[0.082]	[0.104]	[0.082]	[0.072]	[0.082]	[0.085]	[0.100]
D.Income	0.405	0.488	0.602*	0.559*	0.366	0.290	0.414	0.421
	[0.334]	[0.353]	[0.317]	[0.337]	[0.285]	[0.248]	[0.298]	[0.268]
D.IIE	0.451	0.648	−0.727	0.465	0.425	−0.399	−0.152	−1.036
	[1.902]	[1.824]	[1.906]	[1.911]	[1.699]	[1.761]	[1.875]	[1.892]
D.HC	10.735	10.626	4.926	3.895	5.336	5.703	10.936	2.927
	[11.365]	[11.260]	[6.705]	[8.382]	[9.576]	[8.524]	[12.427]	[8.785]
D.Trade	0.000	−0.000	−0.000	−0.000	0.000	0.001	0.001	−0.001
	[0.001]	[0.001]	[0.001]	[0.001]	[0.001]	[0.001]	[0.001]	[0.001]
D.ES1	0.133*							
	[0.081]							
D.ES2		0.103						
		[0.074]						
D.ES3			0.012					
			[0.009]					
D.ES4				0.008				
				[0.105]				
D.ES5					0.005			
					[0.058]			
D.ES6						0.030		
						[0.086]		
D.ES7							0.082	
							[0.079]	

Dep. var.: *INST*	(1)	(2)	(3)	(4)	(5)	(6)	(7)	(8)
D.ES8								0.0003
								[0.014]
Cons.	−1.005***	−0.351	0.385***	−0.776***	−0.954***	−3.041***	−1.342***	−0.838***
	[0.257]	[0.216]	[0.131]	[0.203]	[0.217]	[0.572]	[0.316]	[0.263]
Long-run effects								
Income	0.443***	0.060***	0.604***	0.836***	0.826***	1.580***	−0.022	0.640***
	[0.060]	[0.017]	[0.071]	[0.094]	[0.109]	[0.088]	[0.019]	[0.076]
IIE	−0.607***	−0.224*	−1.388***	−1.241***	−1.154***	−0.953***	0.490***	−0.862***
	[0.143]	[0.123]	[0.155]	[0.216]	[0.223]	[0.197]	[0.113]	[0.147]
HC	−0.072	0.788***	−0.872***	−0.888***	−0.699***	−3.163***	0.738***	−0.587***
	[0.137]	[0.074]	[0.173]	[0.215]	[0.243]	[0.214]	[0.149]	[0.189]
Trade	−0.001**	0.001***	−0.001**	−0.001***	−0.001***	−0.002***	−0.000*	−0.001**
	[0.000]	[0.000]	[0.000]	[0.000]	[0.000]	[0.000]	[0.000]	[0.000]
ES1	−0.025***							
	[0.006]							
ES2		−0.028***						
		[0.004]						
ES3			−0.002***					
			[0.001]					
ES4				−0.077				
				[0.052]				
ES5					−0.043			
					[0.056]			
ES6						−0.195***		
						[0.039]		

(continued)

Table 7 (continued)

Dep. var.: *INST*	(1)	(2)	(3)	(4)	(5)	(6)	(7)	(8)
ES7							−0.186***	
							[0.035]	
ES8								0.004***
								[0.001]
Observations	600	600	525	556	605	516	516	556

Note: PMG ARDL estimators; Standard errors are in []; *, **, *** are significant levels at 10%, 5%, and 1%, respectively
Source: Authors' own table

Table 8 Energy security and institutional quality: six dimensions of institutions (summary)

Dep. var.:	Concor	Goveff	Posta	Requa	Law	Voice
Indep. Var:						
ES1	–[a]	–[a]	–[c]	–[a]	–[a]	–[a]
ES2	–[a]	–[a]	–[b]	–[a]	–[a]	–[a]
ES3	–[a]	–[a]	–[a]	–[a]	–[a]	–[a]
ES4	–[a]	–[a]	+	–[a]	–[a]	–[a]
ES5	–[a]	–[a]	–[b]	–[a]	–[a]	–[a]
ES6	–[a]	–[a]	+[b]	–[a]	–[a]	–[a]
ES7	+[a]	+[a]	+[a]	+[a]	+[a]	+[a]
ES8	+[a]	+[a]	+[a]	+[a]	+[a]	+[a]

Note: – is negative coefficient; + is positive coefficient; a, b, c are significant levels at 1%, 5%, and 10%, respectively. Detailed results are reported in Table A3, A4, A5, A6, A7 and A8, Appendix
Source: Authors' own table

sity or emissions negatively affect institutional quality. Only the use of renewable energy is a positive contributor to institutional quality. These results again revoke the dilemma in the nexus between energy, environment, and institutional quality, and only the solution to increase the use of renewable energy is a feasible one.

Finally, for the aggregate analysis, we estimated the effects of energy security on six institutional dimensions. The detailed results are reported in Tables A3, A4, A5, A6, A7 and A8 in the Appendix, and the summary is presented in Table 8. The results seem to be robust and consistent with the case of overall institutional quality. Six of the eight proxies of energy security (*ES1, ES2, ES3, ES4, ES5, ES6*) had a significant negative impact on control of corruption, government effectiveness, regulatory quality, rule of law, and voice and accountability, while *ES7* and *ES8* had significant positive impacts on these dimensions. Regarding political stability and the absence of violence, ES1, ES2, ES3, and ES5 had significant negative impacts, while ES4, ES6, ES7, and ES8 had significant positive impacts. This means that increasing primary energy production and consumption, especially fossil energy consumption, could lead to lower political stability, as expected from the natural resource curse theory. In contrast, increasing energy intensity, emissions, CO_2 emissions, and renewable energy consumption could lead to higher political stability, which may be explained through the positive impacts of these factors on economic development.[6]

[6]In fact, the term of office of a government may cause conditional changes in institutional quality. Thus, this study takes the additional step of using the 4-year average of the data for empirical analysis. The results are consistent, and can be provided upon request. The author(s) would like to thank the anonymous reviewer for his/her helpful comment.

5 Conclusion

Against the backdrop of climate change and energy insecurity, this study investigated the impact of energy security on institutional quality. Specifically, we examined the effects of eight different dimensions of energy security on overall institutional quality, and examined six institutional dimensions for 43 emerging economies that were among the highest energy-consuming countries for the period 2002–2017.

The study's contributions to literature are threefold. *First*, energy security, in terms of energy production (to energy consumption), energy supply capability, energy structure (fossil energy consumption), energy inefficiency (energy intensity), energy developability in terms of consumption, and energy developability in terms of CO_2 emissions, were found to have significant negative impacts on institutional quality. Interestingly, energy security in terms of CO_2 emissions per unit of nonrenewable and renewable energy consumption was found to have a positive impact on institutional quality. This means that energy surplus, renewable energy consumption, or nonrenewable energy consumption could reduce institutional quality. This raises the dilemma that the desire for high economic development leads to higher energy consumption and environmental degradation, which decreases institutional quality. Increasing the use of renewable energy may solve this problem. *Second*, the long-run analysis shows the short-run positive (but insignificant) effects of energy security indicators on institutional quality, suggesting that the positive impact of energy consumption on economic development can improve institutional quality. Notably, we found that seven of the eight energy security indicators had significant and negative long-run impacts on institutional quality, while renewable energy consumption had a positive impact on institutional quality. These results confirm the benefits of increasing the use of renewable energy to improve institutional quality. Finally, from the detailed analysis, we can conclude that energy security does indeed have an impact on the six dimensions of institutional quality, including control of corruption, government effectiveness, political stability, rule of law, regulatory quality, and voice and accountability.

Appendices

Table A1 List of countries (43 emerging economies)

Argentina	Ecuador	Kazakhstan	Pakistan	Tunisia
Bangladesh	Egypt	Kenya	Peru	Turkey
Bulgaria	Estonia	South Korea	Philippines	Ukraine
Brazil	Greece	Sri Lanka	Poland	Uruguay
Chile	Hungary	Lithuania	Romania	Venezuela
China	Indonesia	Latvia	Russia	Vietnam
Colombia	Iran	Morocco	Singapore	South Africa
Czech Republic	Israel	Mexico	Slovakia	
Dominican Republic	Jordan	Malaysia	Thailand	

Note: this study firstly chooses the countries in Emerging economies list from IMF classification in Global Outlook (2016). Due to the limited number of countries in this list, we have updated some others from "MSCI Emerging Markets Indexes" if MSCI (https://www.msci.com/index-solutions)

Source: IMF classification in Global Outlook (2016) and MSCI Emerging Markets Indexes

Table A2 Energy security and institutional quality (FGLS estimator)

Dep. var.: *INST*	(1)	(2)	(3)	(4)	(5)	(6)	(7)	(8)
Income	0.334***	0.439***	0.485***	0.343***	0.725***	0.387***	0.394***	0.493***
	[0.022]	[0.021]	[0.025]	[0.024]	[0.030]	[0.024]	[0.025]	[0.025]
IIE	−0.439***	−0.504***	−0.315**	−0.344***	−0.479***	−0.259*	−0.391***	−0.294**
	[0.119]	[0.114]	[0.127]	[0.130]	[0.111]	[0.135]	[0.145]	[0.125]
HC	0.744***	0.785***	0.307**	0.969***	0.815***	0.840***	0.590***	0.540***
	[0.117]	[0.112]	[0.126]	[0.130]	[0.110]	[0.130]	[0.135]	[0.122]
Trade	0.002***	0.002***	0.003***	0.003***	0.004***	0.003***	0.003***	0.003***
	[0.000]	[0.000]	[0.000]	[0.000]	[0.000]	[0.000]	[0.000]	[0.000]
Lat	−0.697***	−0.695***	−0.516***	−0.620***	−0.628***	−0.495***	−0.760***	−0.322***
	[0.078]	[0.074]	[0.084]	[0.085]	[0.072]	[0.090]	[0.099]	[0.087]
Col	−0.186***	−0.216***	−0.245***	−0.391***	−0.363***	−0.343***	−0.286***	−0.198***
	[0.044]	[0.041]	[0.046]	[0.049]	[0.041]	[0.049]	[0.051]	[0.046]
ES1	−0.135***							
	[0.012]							
ES2		−0.132***						
		[0.009]						
ES3			−0.010***					
			[0.001]					
ES4				−0.363***				
				[0.045]				
ES5					−0.443***			
					[0.028]			
ES6						−0.270***		
						[0.034]		

Dep. var.: *INST*	(1)	(2)	(3)	(4)	(5)	(6)	(7)	(8)
ES7							0.226***	
							[0.057]	
ES8								0.012***
								[0.001]
Constant	−1.943***	−1.693***	−2.546***	−1.873***	−2.009***	−3.408***	−2.660***	−3.989***
	[0.493]	[0.470]	[0.523]	[0.548]	[0.456]	[0.560]	[0.582]	[0.521]
Year-effects	Yes	Yes	Yes	Yes	Yes	Yes	Yes	Yes
Observations	643	643	568	599	648	559	559	599
Number of country	43	43	43	43	43	43	43	43

Note: Standard errors are in []; *, **, *** are significant levels at 10%, 5%, and 1%, respectively
Source: Authors' own table

Table A3 Energy security and Control of Corruption

Dep. var.: *Concor*	(1)	(2)	(3)	(4)	(5)	(6)	(7)	(8)
Income	0.439***	0.564***	0.582***	0.446***	0.823***	0.496***	0.503***	0.585***
	[0.009]	[0.006]	[0.010]	[0.010]	[0.012]	[0.010]	[0.009]	[0.012]
IIE	−0.288***	−0.340***	−0.025	−0.121*	−0.245***	0.009	−0.123*	−0.040
	[0.059]	[0.056]	[0.059]	[0.065]	[0.052]	[0.057]	[0.067]	[0.053]
HC	0.024	0.064	−0.332***	0.315***	0.081**	0.146***	−0.104***	−0.154***
	[0.055]	[0.049]	[0.045]	[0.040]	[0.037]	[0.035]	[0.035]	[0.037]
Trade	0.002***	0.003***	0.004***	0.004***	0.005***	0.004***	0.005***	0.005***
	[0.000]	[0.000]	[0.000]	[0.000]	[0.000]	[0.000]	[0.000]	[0.000]
Lat	−1.038***	−1.030***	−0.826***	−0.918***	−0.946***	−0.790***	−1.055***	−0.664***
	[0.038]	[0.038]	[0.040]	[0.039]	[0.038]	[0.036]	[0.037]	[0.035]
Col	−0.264***	−0.309***	−0.337***	−0.501***	−0.459***	−0.423***	−0.366***	−0.297***
	[0.018]	[0.018]	[0.016]	[0.015]	[0.016]	[0.011]	[0.012]	[0.017]
ES1	−0.171***							
	[0.009]							
ES2		−0.153***						
		[0.007]						
ES3			−0.008***					
			[0.000]					
ES4				−0.439***				
				[0.025]				
ES5					−0.420***			
					[0.015]			
ES6						−0.271***		
						[0.016]		

Dep. var.: *Concor*	(1)	(2)	(3)	(4)	(5)	(6)	(7)	(8)
ES7							0.226***	
							[0.026]	
ES8								0.010***
								[0.001]
Constant	−2.833***	−2.656***	−4.052***	−2.943***	−3.298***	−4.801***	−4.051***	−5.125***
	[0.257]	[0.246]	[0.271]	[0.339]	[0.255]	[0.259]	[0.311]	[0.261]
Year-effects	Yes	Yes	Yes	Yes	Yes	Yes	Yes	Yes
Observations	643	643	568	599	648	559	559	599
R-squared	0.739	0.755	0.703	0.703	0.735	0.693	0.671	0.695
Number of country	43	43	43	43	43	43	43	43

Note: PCSE estimator; Standard errors are in []; *, **, *** are significant levels at 10%, 5%, and 1%, respectively
Source: Authors' own table

Table A4 Energy security and Government effectiveness

Dep. var.: *Goveff*	(1)	(2)	(3)	(4)	(5)	(6)	(7)	(8)
Income	0.388***	0.464***	0.478***	0.394***	0.665***	0.421***	0.437***	0.483***
	[0.009]	[0.008]	[0.008]	[0.010]	[0.016]	[0.010]	[0.010]	[0.011]
IIE	0.070	0.024	0.174*	0.147*	0.036	0.203**	0.038	0.181**
	[0.083]	[0.079]	[0.090]	[0.080]	[0.075]	[0.087]	[0.094]	[0.087]
HC	0.239***	0.269***	−0.015	0.369***	0.282***	0.299***	0.088	0.107*
	[0.061]	[0.057]	[0.050]	[0.066]	[0.050]	[0.064]	[0.062]	[0.057]
Trade	0.004***	0.004***	0.005***	0.004***	0.005***	0.004***	0.005***	0.005***
	[0.000]	[0.000]	[0.000]	[0.000]	[0.000]	[0.000]	[0.000]	[0.000]
Lat	−0.516***	−0.514***	−0.418***	−0.462***	−0.477***	−0.394***	−0.645***	−0.289***
	[0.037]	[0.035]	[0.040]	[0.034]	[0.030]	[0.034]	[0.041]	[0.037]
Col	−0.295***	−0.317***	−0.344***	−0.429***	−0.423***	−0.406***	−0.366***	−0.312***
	[0.021]	[0.021]	[0.023]	[0.023]	[0.021]	[0.020]	[0.020]	[0.024]
ES1	−0.098***							
	[0.006]							
ES2		−0.096***						
		[0.005]						
ES3			−0.006***					
			[0.000]					
ES4				−0.228***				
				[0.020]				
ES5					−0.313***			
					[0.017]			
ES6						−0.174***		
						[0.014]		

Dep. var.: *Goveff*	(1)	(2)	(3)	(4)	(5)	(6)	(7)	(8)
ES7							0.278***	
							[0.025]	
ES8								0.007***
								[0.000]
Constant	−3.806***	−3.629***	−4.296***	−3.828***	−3.830***	−4.800***	−4.192***	−5.108***
	[0.343]	[0.326]	[0.353]	[0.322]	[0.289]	[0.337]	[0.371]	[0.335]
Year-effects	Yes	Yes	Yes	Yes	Yes	Yes	Yes	Yes
Observations	643	643	568	599	648	559	559	599
R-squared	0.722	0.735	0.708	0.702	0.744	0.697	0.696	0.707
Number of country	43	43	43	43	43	43	43	43

Note: PCSE estimator; Standard errors are in []; *, **, *** are significant levels at 10%, 5%, and 1%, respectively
Source: Authors' own table

Table A5 Energy security and Political stability and Absence of Violence

Dep. var.: *Posta*	(1)	(2)	(3)	(4)	(5)	(6)	(7)	(8)
Income	0.280***	0.298***	0.357***	0.297***	0.364***	0.294***	0.319***	0.351***
	[0.019]	[0.016]	[0.019]	[0.019]	[0.028]	[0.017]	[0.018]	[0.017]
IIE	−1.502***	−1.517***	−1.579***	−1.445***	−1.509***	−1.515***	−1.673***	−1.477***
	[0.125]	[0.121]	[0.120]	[0.109]	[0.114]	[0.124]	[0.126]	[0.120]
HC	0.773***	0.782***	0.486***	0.727***	0.797***	0.654***	0.601***	0.676***
	[0.168]	[0.168]	[0.167]	[0.184]	[0.160]	[0.178]	[0.165]	[0.156]
Trade	0.004***	0.004***	0.004***	0.004***	0.005***	0.004***	0.005***	0.005***
	[0.000]	[0.000]	[0.000]	[0.000]	[0.000]	[0.000]	[0.000]	[0.000]
Lat	−0.762***	−0.762***	−0.632***	−0.699***	−0.735***	−0.725***	−0.850***	−0.563***
	[0.053]	[0.054]	[0.053]	[0.048]	[0.050]	[0.051]	[0.047]	[0.067]
Col	−0.003	−0.008	−0.015	−0.035	−0.036	−0.036**	−0.045**	−0.003
	[0.039]	[0.036]	[0.027]	[0.023]	[0.031]	[0.017]	[0.020]	[0.029]
ES1	−0.022*							
	[0.013]							
ES2		−0.024**						
		[0.011]						
ES3			−0.006***					
			[0.001]					
ES4				0.016				
				[0.054]				
ES5					−0.099**			
					[0.041]			
ES6						0.074**		
						[0.038]		

Dep. var.: *Posta*	(1)	(2)	(3)	(4)	(5)	(6)	(7)	(8)
ES7							0.264***	
							[0.036]	
ES8								0.006***
								[0.001]
Constant	2.134***	2.195***	2.419***	1.788***	2.120***	2.253***	2.358***	1.349**
	[0.494]	[0.479]	[0.458]	[0.369]	[0.443]	[0.529]	[0.479]	[0.533]
Year-effects	Yes	Yes	Yes	Yes	Yes	Yes	Yes	Yes
Observations	643	643	568	599	648	559	559	599
R-squared	0.527	0.528	0.546	0.532	0.534	0.533	0.539	0.538
Number of country	43	43	43	43	43	43	43	43

Note: PCSE estimator; Standard errors are in []; *, **, *** are significant levels at 10%, 5%, and 1%, respectively
Source: Authors' own table

Table A6 Energy security and Regulatory quality

Dep. var.: *Requa*	(1)	(2)	(3)	(4)	(5)	(6)	(7)	(8)
Income	0.300***	0.420***	0.472***	0.300***	0.778***	0.353***	0.350***	0.501***
	[0.014]	[0.008]	[0.013]	[0.012]	[0.017]	[0.011]	[0.011]	[0.014]
IIE	0.451***	0.369***	0.607***	0.544***	0.374***	0.665***	0.577***	0.602***
	[0.098]	[0.089]	[0.092]	[0.086]	[0.078]	[0.088]	[0.097]	[0.093]
HC	1.230***	1.281***	0.726***	1.539***	1.322***	1.420***	1.126***	0.982***
	[0.076]	[0.070]	[0.052]	[0.079]	[0.049]	[0.067]	[0.064]	[0.048]
Trade	0.002***	0.002***	0.004***	0.003***	0.004***	0.003***	0.004***	0.004***
	[0.000]	[0.000]	[0.000]	[0.000]	[0.000]	[0.000]	[0.000]	[0.000]
Lat	−0.167***	−0.166***	0.039	−0.088**	−0.097**	0.087**	−0.189***	0.316***
	[0.052]	[0.050]	[0.049]	[0.041]	[0.039]	[0.042]	[0.043]	[0.051]
Col	−0.207***	−0.240***	−0.276***	−0.457***	−0.418***	−0.407***	−0.330***	−0.205***
	[0.023]	[0.024]	[0.021]	[0.023]	[0.024]	[0.019]	[0.020]	[0.026]
ES1	−0.153***							
	[0.012]							
ES2		−0.155***						
		[0.010]						
ES3			−0.012***					
			[0.000]					
ES4				−0.462***				
				[0.032]				
ES5					−0.547***			
					[0.024]			
ES6						−0.385***		
						[0.023]		

Dep. var.: *Requa*	(1)	(2)	(3)	(4)	(5)	(6)	(7)	(8)
ES7							0.156***	
							[0.028]	
ES8								0.016***
								[0.001]
Constant	−5.377***	−5.051***	−6.041***	−5.110***	−5.323***	−7.172***	−6.263***	−7.893***
	[0.399]	[0.363]	[0.356]	[0.357]	[0.308]	[0.344]	[0.391]	[0.375]
Year-effects	Yes	Yes	Yes	Yes	Yes	Yes	Yes	Yes
Observations	643	643	568	599	648	559	559	599
R-squared	0.636	0.666	0.658	0.625	0.695	0.633	0.582	0.659
Number of country	43	43	43	43	43	43	43	43

Note: PCSE estimator; Standard errors are in []; *, **, *** are significant levels at 10%, 5%, and 1%, respectively
Source: Authors' own table

Table A7 Energy security and Rule of Law

Dep. var.: *Law*	(1)	(2)	(3)	(4)	(5)	(6)	(7)	(8)
Income	0.343***	0.481***	0.498***	0.346***	0.823***	0.412***	0.420***	0.518***
	[0.009]	[0.009]	[0.007]	[0.009]	[0.013]	[0.008]	[0.007]	[0.010]
IIE	−0.324***	−0.400***	−0.128	−0.228***	−0.352***	−0.077	−0.243***	−0.117
	[0.082]	[0.074]	[0.083]	[0.077]	[0.065]	[0.076]	[0.092]	[0.081]
HC	0.557***	0.608***	0.128***	0.925***	0.632***	0.686***	0.352***	0.320***
	[0.062]	[0.056]	[0.035]	[0.041]	[0.030]	[0.041]	[0.039]	[0.034]
Trade	0.002***	0.002***	0.004***	0.003***	0.004***	0.003***	0.004***	0.004***
	[0.000]	[0.000]	[0.000]	[0.000]	[0.000]	[0.000]	[0.000]	[0.000]
Lat	−0.698***	−0.693***	−0.512***	−0.603***	−0.615***	−0.423***	−0.771***	−0.294***
	[0.040]	[0.038]	[0.045]	[0.035]	[0.031]	[0.033]	[0.040]	[0.042]
Col	−0.403***	−0.446***	−0.491***	−0.699***	−0.630***	−0.605***	−0.527***	−0.438***
	[0.015]	[0.016]	[0.013]	[0.018]	[0.015]	[0.010]	[0.006]	[0.015]
ES1	−0.182***							
	[0.009]							
ES2		−0.172***						
		[0.007]						
ES3			−0.009***					
			[0.000]					
ES4				−0.575***				
				[0.021]				
ES5					−0.537***			
					[0.015]			
ES6						−0.373***		
						[0.013]		

Dep. var.: *Law*	(1)	(2)	(3)	(4)	(5)	(6)	(7)	(8)
ES7							0.285***	
							[0.023]	
ES8								0.012***
								[0.001]
Constant	−2.311***	−2.028***	−3.271***	−1.917***	−2.502***	−4.295***	−3.289***	−4.693***
	[0.322]	[0.289]	[0.317]	[0.313]	[0.250]	[0.269]	[0.361]	[0.324]
Year-effects	Yes	Yes	Yes	Yes	Yes	Yes	Yes	Yes
Observations	643	643	568	599	648	559	559	599
R-squared	0.680	0.711	0.639	0.663	0.714	0.645	0.602	0.641
Number of country	43	43	43	43	43	43	43	43

Note: PCSE estimator; Standard errors are in []; *, **, *** are significant levels at 10%, 5%, and 1%, respectively
Source: Authors' own table

Table A8 Energy security and Voice and Accountability

Dep. var.: *Voice*	(1)	(2)	(3)	(4)	(5)	(6)	(7)	(8)
Income	0.256***	0.404***	0.523***	0.273***	0.896***	0.345***	0.337***	0.520***
	[0.012]	[0.010]	[0.012]	[0.014]	[0.013]	[0.014]	[0.012]	[0.013]
IIE	−1.043***	−1.158***	−0.940***	−0.960***	−1.178***	−0.837***	−0.920***	−0.914***
	[0.114]	[0.105]	[0.101]	[0.106]	[0.087]	[0.098]	[0.109]	[0.093]
HC	1.640***	1.709***	0.847***	1.939***	1.776***	1.837***	1.480***	1.311***
	[0.071]	[0.067]	[0.053]	[0.049]	[0.047]	[0.047]	[0.051]	[0.047]
Trade	−0.004***	−0.004***	−0.002***	−0.003***	−0.001***	−0.003***	−0.002***	−0.002***
	[0.000]	[0.000]	[0.000]	[0.000]	[0.000]	[0.000]	[0.000]	[0.000]
Lat	−1.001***	−1.003***	−0.749***	−0.948***	−0.902***	−0.728***	−1.050***	−0.437***
	[0.057]	[0.055]	[0.050]	[0.051]	[0.053]	[0.050]	[0.044]	[0.054]
Col	0.056**	0.021	−0.008	−0.224***	−0.211***	−0.180***	−0.082***	0.065***
	[0.023]	[0.025]	[0.018]	[0.021]	[0.024]	[0.017]	[0.016]	[0.021]
ES1	−0.182***							
	[0.013]							
ES2		−0.194***						
		[0.010]						
ES3			−0.018***					
			[0.001]					
ES4				−0.489***				
				[0.021]				
ES5					−0.742***			
					[0.024]			
ES6						−0.492***		
						[0.017]		

Dep. var.: *Voice*	(1)	(2)	(3)	(4)	(5)	(6)	(7)	(8)
ES7							0.149***	
							[0.034]	
ES8								0.020***
								[0.001]
Constant	0.536	1.009**	−0.032	0.775*	0.776**	−1.637***	−0.523	−2.468***
	[0.436]	[0.400]	[0.414]	[0.446]	[0.377]	[0.387]	[0.446]	[0.389]
Year-effects	Yes	Yes	Yes	Yes	Yes	Yes	Yes	Yes
Observations	643	643	568	599	648	559	559	599
R-squared	0.531	0.584	0.629	0.507	0.642	0.557	0.475	0.581
Number of country	43	43	43	43	43	43	43	43

Note: PCSE estimator; Standard errors are in []; *, **, *** are significant levels at 10%, 5%, and 1%, respectively

Source: Authors' own table

References

Abdullahi, M. M., Bakar, N. A. B. A., & Hassan, S. B. (2015). Determining the macroeconomic factors of external debt accumulation in Nigeria: An ARDL bound test approach. *Procedia – Social and Behavioral Sciences, 211*, 745–752. https://doi.org/10.1016/j.sbspro.2015.11.098.

Acemoglu, D., Johnson, S., & Robinson, J. A. (2001). The colonial origins of comparative development: An empirical investigation. *American Economic Review, 91*(5), 1369–1401.

Adamus, W., & Florkowski, W. J. (2016). The evolution of shale gas development and energy security in Poland: Presenting a hierarchical choice of priorities. *Energy Research & Social Science, 20*, 168–178.

Alonso, J. A., & Garcimartín, C. (2013). The determinants of institutional quality. More on the debate. *Journal of International Development, 25*(2), 206–226.

Amiri, H., Samadian, F., Yahoo, M., & Jamali, S. J. (2019). Natural resource abundance, institutional quality and manufacturing development: Evidence from resource-rich countries. *Resources Policy, 62*, 550–560.

APERC. (2007). *Quest for energy security in the 21st century: Resources and constraints*. Tokyo: Asia Pacific Energy Research Centre.

Bailey, D., & Katz, J. N. (2011). Implementing panel corrected standard errors in R: The pcse package. *Journal of Statistical Software, 42*(CS1), 1–11.

Bank, W. (2019a). In W. Bank (Ed.), *World development indicators*.

Bank, W. (2019b). In W. Bank (Ed.), *Worldwide governance indicators*.

Bertocchi, G., & Canova, F. (2002). Did colonization matter for growth?: An empirical exploration into the historical causes of Africa's underdevelopment. *European Economic Review, 46*(10), 1851–1871. https://doi.org/10.1016/S0014-2921(01)00195-7.

Bhattacharyya, S., & Hodler, R. (2010). Natural resources, democracy and corruption. *European Economic Review, 54*(4), 608–621. https://doi.org/10.1016/j.euroecorev.2009.10.004.

Bildirici, M. E. (2014). Relationship between biomass energy and economic growth in transition countries: Panel ARDL approach. *GCB Bioenergy, 6*(6), 717–726.

Borge, L.-E., Parmer, P., & Torvik, R. (2015). Local natural resource curse? *Journal of Public Economics, 131*, 101–114. https://doi.org/10.1016/j.jpubeco.2015.09.002.

Canh, N. P., Thai, N. V. H., & Schinckus, C. (2018). Stock-return co-movements and institutional quality: An empirical investigation of the European emerging markets. *Theoretical Economics Letters, 8*(05), 820–843.

Canh, N. P., Schinckus, C., & Thanh, S. D. (2019). Do economic openness and institutional quality influence patents? Evidence from GMM systems estimates. *International Economics, 157*, 134–169.

Cockx, L., & Francken, N. (2016). Natural resources: A curse on education spending? *Energy Policy, 92*, 394–408. https://doi.org/10.1016/j.enpol.2016.02.027.

Cowan, W. N., Chang, T., Inglesi-Lotz, R., & Gupta, R. (2014). The nexus of electricity consumption, economic growth and CO2 emissions in the BRICS countries. *Energy Policy, 66*, 359–368.

Destek, M. A., & Aslan, A. (2017). Renewable and non-renewable energy consumption and economic growth in emerging economies: Evidence from bootstrap panel causality. *Renewable Energy, 111*, 757–763.

Easterly, W., & Levine, R. (2003). Tropics, germs, and crops: How endowments influence economic development. *Journal of Monetary Economics, 50*(1), 3–39. https://doi.org/10.1016/S0304-3932(02)00200-3.

Easterly, W., Ritzen, J., & Woolcock, M. (2006). Social cohesion, institutions, and growth. *Economics and Politics, 18*(2), 103–120.

Emenalo, C. O., & Gagliardi, F. (2019). Is current institutional quality linked to legal origins and disease endowments? Evidence from Africa. *Research in International Business and Finance*, 101065.

Empinotti, V. L., Budds, J., & Aversa, M. (2019). Governance and water security: The role of the water institutional framework in the 2013–15 water crisis in São Paulo, Brazil. *Geoforum, 98*, 46–54.

Fang, D., Shi, S., & Yu, Q. (2018). Evaluation of sustainable energy security and an empirical analysis of china. *Sustainability, 10*(5), 1685.
Farzanegan, M. R., Lessmann, C., & Markwardt, G. (2018). Natural resource rents and internal conflicts: Can decentralization lift the curse? *Economic Systems, 42*(2), 186–205. https://doi.org/10.1016/j.ecosys.2017.05.009.
Feenstra, R. C., Inklaar, R., & Timmer, M. P. (2015). The next generation of the Penn World Table. *American Economic Review, 105*(10), 3150–3182.
Filipović, S., Radovanović, M., & Golušin, V. (2018). Macroeconomic and political aspects of energy security–Exploratory data analysis. *Renewable and Sustainable Energy Reviews, 97*, 428–435.
Gallup, J. L., Sachs, J. D., & Mellinger, A. D. (1999). Geography and economic development. *International Regional Science Review, 22*(2), 179–232.
Gillessen, B., Heinrichs, H., Hake, J.-F., & Allelein, H.-J. (2019). Energy security in context of transforming energy systems: A case study for natural gas transport in Germany. *Energy Procedia, 158*, 3339–3345.
Graff, M., Carley, S., & Pirog, M. (2019). A review of the environmental policy literature from 2014 to 2017 with a closer look at the energy justice field. *Policy Studies Journal, 47*, S17–S44.
Harris, R. D. F., & Tzavalis, E. (1996). *Inference for unit roots in dynamic panels*. Discussion Paper in Economics 96/04, University of Exeter.
Henri, P. A. O. (2019). Natural resources curse: A reality in Africa. *Resources Policy, 63*, 101406. https://doi.org/10.1016/j.resourpol.2019.101406.
Herrera-Echeverri, H., Haar, J., & Estévez-Bretón, J. B. (2014). Foreign direct investment, institutional quality, economic freedom and entrepreneurship in emerging markets. *Journal of Business Research, 67*(9), 1921–1932. https://doi.org/10.1016/j.jbusres.2013.11.020.
Huynh, C. M., Nguyen, V. H. T., Nguyen, H. B., & Nguyen, P. C. (2019). One-way effect or multiple-way causality: Foreign direct investment, institutional quality and shadow economy? *International Economics and Economic Policy, 17*, 1–21.
Im, K. S., Pesaran, M. H., & Shin, Y. (2003). Testing for unit roots in heterogeneous panels. *Journal of Econometrics, 115*(1), 53–74.
Islam, R., Montenegro, C. E., & Islam, R. (2002). *What determines the quality of institutions?* Washington, DC: The World Bank.
Israel, A., & Jehling, M. (2019). How modern are renewables? The misrecognition of traditional solar thermal energy in Peru's energy transition. *Energy Policy, 133*, 110905.
Kanyama, I. K. (2014). Quality of institutions: Does intelligence matter? *Intelligence, 42*, 44–52.
Kao, C. (1999). Spurious regression and residual-based tests for cointegration in panel data. *Journal of Econometrics, 90*(1), 1–44.
Kar, S., Roy, A., & Sen, K. (2019). The double trap: Institutions and economic development. *Economic Modelling, 76*, 243–259.
Kaufmann, D., Kraay, A., & Zoido-Lobatón, P. (1999a). *Aggregating governance indicators* (Vol. 2195). Washington, DC: World Bank Publications.
Kaufmann, D., Kraay, A., & Zoido, P. (1999b). *Governance matters*. World Bank Policy Research Working Paper (2196).
Kaufmann, D., Kraay, A., & Mastruzzi, M. (2011). The worldwide governance indicators: Methodology and analytical issues. *Hague Journal on the Rule of Law, 3*(02), 220–246.
Kisel, E., Hamburg, A., Härm, M., Leppiman, A., & Ots, M. (2016). Concept for energy security matrix. *Energy Policy, 95*, 1–9.
Klasing, M. J. (2013). Cultural dimensions, collective values and their importance for institutions. *Journal of Comparative Economics, 41*(2), 447–467.
Kocaslan, G. (2014). International energy security indicators and Turkey's energy security risk score. *International Journal of Energy Economics and Policy, 4*(4), 735–743.
Kostova, T. (1997). *Country institutional profiles: Concept and measurement.* In Paper presented at the academy of management proceedings.

Kotschy, R., & Sunde, U. (2017). Democracy, inequality, and institutional quality. *European Economic Review, 91*, 209–228.

Kucharski, J., & Unesaki, H. (2015). A policy-oriented approach to energy security. *Procedia Environmental Sciences, 28*, 27–36.

La Porta, R., Lopez-de-Silanes, F., Shleifer, A., & Vishny, R. (1999). The quality of government. *The Journal of Law, Economics, and Organization, 15*(1), 222–279.

Le, T.-H., & Nguyen, C. P. (2019). Is energy security a driver for economic growth? Evidence from a global sample. *Energy Policy, 129*, 436–451.

Levin, A., Lin, C.-F., & Chu, C.-S. J. (2002). Unit-root tests in panel data: Asymptotic and finite-sample properties. *Journal of Econometrics, 108*(1), 1–24.

Levin, K., Cashore, B., Bernstein, S., & Auld, G. (2012). Overcoming the tragedy of super wicked problems: Constraining our future selves to ameliorate global climate change. *Policy Sciences, 45*(2), 123–152.

Liao, H., & Cao, H.-S. (2013). How does carbon dioxide emission change with the economic development? Statistical experiences from 132 countries. *Global Environmental Change, 23*(5), 1073–1082.

Mangla, S. K., Luthra, S., Jakhar, S., Gandhi, S., Muduli, K., & Kumar, A. (2019). A step to clean energy-Sustainability in energy system management in an emerging economy context. *Journal of Cleaner Production*, 118462.

Manzano, O., & Gutiérrez, J. D. (2019). The subnational resource curse: Theory and evidence. *The Extractive Industries and Society, 6*(2), 261–266. https://doi.org/10.1016/j.exis.2019.03.010.

Nguyen, B., & Canh, N. P. (2019). The effects of regional governance, education, and in-migration on business performance. *Kyklos*.

Nguyen, C. P., Nguyen, T. V. H., & Nguyen, T. T. (2017, September). Institutional quality and fiscal policy: An empirical investigation in Asia Pacific countries. *Empirical Economics Letters, 16*(9).

Nguyen, C. P., Nguyen, N. A., Schinckus, C., & Su, T. D. (2018a). The ambivalent role of institutions in the CO2 emissions: The case of emerging countries. *International Journal of Energy Economics and Policy, 8*(5), 7–17.

Nguyen, C. P., Schinckus, C., Su, T. D., & Chong, F. (2018b). Institutions, inward foreign direct investment, trade openness and credit level in emerging market economies. *Review of Development Finance, 8*(2), 75–88.

Nguyen, C. P., Su, T. D., & Nguyen, T. V. H. (2018c). Institutional quality and economic growth: The case of emerging economies. *Theoretical Economics Letters, 8*(11), 1943.

North, D. C. (1993). The new institutional economics and development. *Economic History*, 9309002.

Odhiambo, N. M. (2009). Energy consumption and economic growth nexus in Tanzania: An ARDL bounds testing approach. *Energy Policy, 37*(2), 617–622.

Opeyemi, A., Uchenna, E., Simplice, A., & Evans, O. (2019). Renewable energy, trade performance and the conditional role of finance and institutional capacity in sub-Sahara African countries. *Energy Policy, 132*, 490–498.

Parcero, O. J., & Papyrakis, E. (2016). Income inequality and the oil-resource curse. *Resource and Energy Economics, 45*, 159–177. https://doi.org/10.1016/j.reseneeco.2016.06.001.

Pedroni, P. (1999). Critical values for cointegration tests in heterogeneous panels with multiple regressors. *Oxford Bulletin of Economics and Statistics, 61*(S1), 653–670.

Pesaran, M. H. (2004). *General diagnostic tests for cross-section dependence in panels*. Cambridge: University of Cambridge.

Pesaran, M. H. (2007). A simple panel unit-root test in the presence of cross-section dependence. *Journal of Applied Econometrics, 22*(2), 265–312.

Pesaran, M. H., & Shin, Y. (1998). An autoregressive distributed-lag modelling approach to cointegration analysis. *Econometric Society Monographs, 31*, 371–413.

Pesaran, M. H., & Smith, R. (1995). Estimating long-run relationships from dynamic heterogeneous panels. *Journal of Econometrics, 68*(1), 79–113.

Pesaran, M. H., Shin, Y., & Smith, R. P. (1999). Pooled mean group estimation of dynamic heterogeneous panels. *Journal of the American Statistical Association, 94*(446), 621–634.
Phuc Canh, N. (2018). The effectiveness of fiscal policy: Contributions from institutions and external debts. *Journal of Asian Business and Economic Studies, 25*(1), 50–66.
Phuc Nguyen, C., Schinckus, C., & Dinh Su, T. (2019). Economic integration and CO2 emissions: Evidence from emerging economies. *Climate and Development, 12*(4), 1–16.
Reed, W. R., & Ye, H. (2011). Which panel data estimator should I use? *Applied Economics, 43*(8), 985–1000.
Salman, M., Long, X., Dauda, L., & Mensah, C. N. (2019). The impact of institutional quality on economic growth and carbon emissions: Evidence from Indonesia, South Korea and Thailand. *Journal of Cleaner Production*, 118331.
Sarkodie, S. A., & Adams, S. (2018). Renewable energy, nuclear energy, and environmental pollution: Accounting for political institutional quality in South Africa. *Science of the Total Environment, 643*, 1590–1601. https://doi.org/10.1016/j.scitotenv.2018.06.320.
Schwartz, S. H. (1994). Beyond individualism/collectivism: New cultural dimensions of values. *Cross-Cultural Research and Methodology Series, 18*, 85.
Shahbaz, M., Zakaria, M., Shahzad, S. J. H., & Mahalik, M. K. (2018). The energy consumption and economic growth nexus in top ten energy-consuming countries: Fresh evidence from using the quantile-on-quantile approach. *Energy Economics, 71*, 282–301. https://doi.org/10.1016/j.eneco.2018.02.023.
Solt, F. (2019). *Measuring income inequality across countries and over time: The Standardized World Income Inequality Database*. In (SWIID Version 8.0, February 2019 ed.).
Stavi, I., & Lal, R. (2013). Agriculture and greenhouse gases, a common tragedy. A review. *Agronomy for Sustainable Development, 33*(2), 275–289.
Su, D. T., Nguyen, P. C., & Schinckus, C. (2019). Impact of foreign direct investment, trade openness and economic institutions on growth in emerging countries: The case of Vietnam. *Journal of International Studies, 12*(3), 243–264.
Sun, H., Edziah, B. K., Sun, C., & Kporsu, A. K. (2019). Institutional quality, green innovation and energy efficiency. *Energy Policy, 135*, 111002.
Thanh, S. D., & Canh, N. P. (2019). Fiscal decentralization and economic growth of Vietnamese provinces: The role of local public governance. Annals of Public and Cooperative Economics 91(1): 119-149.
Thomas, M. A. (2010). What do the worldwide governance indicators measure&quest. *European Journal of Development Research, 22*(1), 31–54.
Treisman, D. (2000). The causes of corruption: A cross-national study. *Journal of Public Economics, 76*(3), 399–457. https://doi.org/10.1016/S0047-2727(99)00092-4.
Voigt, S. (2013). How (Not) to measure institutions. *Journal of Institutional Economics, 9*(1), 1–26. https://doi.org/10.1017/S1744137412000148.
Wang, Z., Zhang, B., & Wang, B. (2018). Renewable energy consumption, economic growth and human development index in Pakistan: Evidence form simultaneous equation model. *Journal of Cleaner Production, 184*, 1081–1090. https://doi.org/10.1016/j.jclepro.2018.02.260.
Wesseh, P. K., & Lin, B. (2018). Energy consumption, fuel substitution, technical change, and economic growth: Implications for CO2 mitigation in Egypt. *Energy Policy, 117*, 340–347.
Westerlund, J. (2005). New simple tests for panel cointegration. *Econometric Reviews, 24*(3), 297–316.
Young, A. T., & Sheehan, K. M. (2014). Foreign aid, institutional quality, and growth. *European Journal of Political Economy, 36*(Supplement C), 195–208. https://doi.org/10.1016/j.ejpoleco.2014.08.003.
Zhang, S. (2016). Institutional arrangements and debt financing. *Research in International Business and Finance, 36*, 362–372. https://doi.org/10.1016/j.ribaf.2015.10.006.
Zhang, C., & Nian, J. (2013). Panel estimation for transport sector CO2 emissions and its affecting factors: A regional analysis in China. *Energy Policy, 63*, 918–926.

Index

N. Faghih, A. H. Samadi (eds.), *Dynamics of Institutional Change in Emerging Market Economies*, Contributions to Economics,
https://doi.org/10.1007/978-3-030-61342-6

CPSIA information can be obtained
at www.ICGtesting.com
Printed in the USA
LVHW081927130421
684382LV00002B/167

9 783030 613419